SIR RICHARD ROOS

SIR ROBERT AND SIR RICHARD ROOS AS BOYS.
FROM THE ST. WILLIAM WINDOW, YORK MINSTER

SIR RICHARD ROOS

c. 1410–1482

Lancastrian Poet

ETHEL SEATON

M.A. D.LITT. F.R.S.L.

HONORARY FELLOW OF ST HUGH'S COLLEGE OXFORD

RUPERT HART-DAVIS
SOHO SQUARE LONDON
1961

Made and Printed in Great Britain by Butler & Tanner Ltd., Frome and London

Contents

Contents

Illustrations

Preface

SOME twenty years ago I began work on Sir Richard Roos, starting from the solitary occurrence in literary documents of his name. I hoped to find enough material for a brief life with the ascription of a few poems—a study which could be kept in small compass and presented with some form and finish. But the material took control, and changed shape and size in Protean fashion. What has emerged is a hybrid of biography, history, 'chronique scandaleuse', cross-word puzzle, history of literature, and 'lecture expliquée', as untidily varied as a bad three-decker novel. Poetry, originally the chief concern, has tended to evaporate under the pressure of other interests, and especially of the people, groups, and individuals, for whom that poetry proves to have been written.

Pleasure at bringing to life a forgotten poet, and decorously assigning to him a few poems on literary evidence alone, governed the first and manageable draft of the study. Then the whole was metamorphosed by a discovery as disquieting as that of Bluebeard's wife: the acrostic anagrams and the uses to which they were put. The unexpected evidence slowly forced belief on my incredulous and reluctant mind; cumulatively it was overwhelming, and entailed total revision of the material, and complete rewriting, a matter of some five years. Some satisfaction came at first in the confirmation of purely literary conclusions. Thus I had already assigned to Roos (and Miss Dorothy Everett had accepted the evidence against Chaucer) *The Romaunt of the Rose*; the anagrams reinforced this at every point. But worse was to come. A chance query sent me to look for proof that later poets did not use the anagram, and I turned to Wyatt, with what result the reader will see in Chapter XII; the yardstick had turned to a serpent in my hands, and to my dismay had poisoned an honoured reputation. Like Dr. Faustus's incantations, 'Forward and backward anagrammatis'd', these innocent

9

diversions had raised a Mephistophilis of criticism as subversive as Goethe's:

> Mit Worten lässt sich trefflich streiten,
> Mit Worten ein System bereiten.

Roos rises like a Phoenix, but it gives little pleasure to 'pulle away the fethres bright' of other birds to deck him.

There will be inevitable dissentients from my conclusions, affronted by the seeming reduction of poetry to artifice, and scorning, like Ben Jonson, these 'hard trifles'. Like Camden, I foresee 'iudgements, preiudices, censures, reprehensions, obtrectations . . . in battaile array to environ me'. Yet the practice is known abundantly in French poetry, and it is in tune with the extreme complexity, notational and rhythmic, of music in the later Middle Ages, and also with the artist's impulse to betray and conceal in one symbol. It is a poetic anamorphosis, as M. Jurgis Baltrušaitis might say, like the skull in Holbein's 'Ambassadors'; the poem, if 'considered obliquely in a different perspective from direct vision', yields another meaning. As late as Caroline times, such were still judged to be a scholar-poet's preoccupations: 'all his songs and sonnets, | His anagrams, acrosticks, epigrams', not incompatible with 'deep and philosophical discourse'.

Another complicating result of the anagrams has been the overweighting of the historical balance. As Henry James knew, 'It takes a great deal of history to make a little literature', all the more so when the literary enquirer has plunged rashly into a century where the angelic historian still treads warily. The writer's lack of training in methods of historical research will be sadly obvious. But this only leaves much still for others to do, for example in manorial records, or in the lives of the many people whom Roos praised or pilloried. In the literary field, too, more may arise out of detailed work, such as the comparison of Duke Humphrey's books with Roos's poems (see on No. 37, *A Mumming*). More light on many matters is desirable.

Over this long period, I have received friendly help and furtherance from countless workers in the medieval field and in libraries, which I gratefully acknowledge. Most particularly am I indebted, beyond power of repayment, to Dr. Joan Evans and Miss E. A. Francis for their unfailing interest and expert aid; to Professor E. F. Jacob for his kind help in historical problems; to the late President of Queens' College, Cambridge, for information on Roos's connexion there; to Professor Norman Davis, for help connected with the Paston letters; to Dr. Anthony Wagner, Richmond Herald, for his aid in heraldry; to Miss

K. M. Lea, Professor K. Coburn, Miss Mary Giffin, and Miss P. Thomson for their practical aid and support; and last but by no means least to Professor R. M. Wilson for reading, and helpfully commenting on, the whole book, and for saving me from many errors; I hope for his further aid in the necessary edition of Roos's poetry. I am glad to remember that the late Miss Dorothy Everett read the book in its first form, and gave it her blessing.

I am glad to acknowledge with gratitude my indebtedness to the Marc Fitch Fund for the generous financial help given me towards publication; and also to St. Hugh's College for aiding my projects by electing me to a Research Fellowship for a considerable term of years.

I have had the misfortune to differ at points from Skeat, but never without a respectful sense of his massive scholarship, and of his acumen where the knowledge of his day was necessarily limited. Only by treading in his footsteps, and in those of the gifted Eleanor Hammond (whose papers Miss Margaret Rickert kindly gave me), is any progress possible in the track of English courtly poetry of the fifteenth century, a path

> that gretly had not used be,
> For it forgrowen was with gras and weede, . . .
> Thought I, this path som whider goth, parde,
> And so I folowèd, til it me brought
> To right a plesaunt herber.

ETHEL SEATON

Note on Texts Cited

F OR all fifteenth-century poems printed by Skeat in his *Works of Chaucer*, vol. VII, that edition is quoted. For other poems still ascribed to Chaucer, the text of Robinson (1933) is used. Poems printed by Miss Eleanor Hammond are quoted from her anthology, *From Chaucer To Surrey*, or from her work in various periodicals. Works hitherto ascribed to Lydgate are taken from MacCracken's *The Minor Poems of Lydgate* (E.E.T.S., Extra Series, No. 107, and Orig. Series, No. 192, 2 vols. with continuous paging). For lyrics Robbins's *Secular Lyrics of the XIVth and XVth Centuries* and Carleton Brown's *Religious Lyrics of the XVth Century* are used when possible, in preference to earlier editions such as Sidgwick and Chambers, *Early English Lyrics*, or to the older anthologies of Ritson, Halliwell Phillipps, etc. In Chapter XII, the editions cited are Kenneth Muir's *Wyatt*, Padelford's *Surrey*, and Hyder Rollins's edition of *Tottel's Miscellany* (2 vols.). I have at times ventured to lighten heavy editorial punctuation, which often seems to weigh down or obscure the lightness, speed and grace of this poetry.

Introduction

SIR RICHARD ROOS has hitherto been little more than a name in a fifteenth-century manuscript, where a contemporary hand ascribes to him the translation of Alain Chartier's poem *La Belle Dame sans Merci*.[1] It is the object of this book to round out this name into a flesh and blood person, into a poet whose writing was not confined to that one poem, and whose gifts in the sphere of courtly poetry deserve recognition.

Skeat, editing *La Belle Dame sans Merci* among doubtful poems in the supplementary seventh volume of his great edition of Chaucer's works, followed Tyrwhitt in accepting the manuscript attribution of the poem to Sir Richard Ros.[2] He took his information on the poet from Dr. H. Gröhler,[3] who had had the account sent him by Mr. Joseph Hall of Manchester, who had extracted it from Nichols's *Leicestershire*.[4] 'According to Nichols', says Skeat, 'the Sir Richard Ros who was presumably the poet, was the second son of Sir Thomas Ros; and Sir Thomas was the second son of Sir W. Ros, who married Margaret, daughter of Sir John Arundel. . . . Sir Richard was born in 1429, and is known to have been alive in 1450.' This house that Joseph built rests on sand, on a faulty reading of Nichols, who commits himself to no statement on the identity of the poet, and who appears indeed to be ignorant of the manuscript attribution. The derivative statement is inaccurate, misleading, and deplorable in its results: inaccurate, because the Richard Roos, second son of Thomas, eighth Lord Roos, and of Eleanor Beauchamp, who was born in 1428/9, was never knighted, but remained an esquire, even after the restoration of the family's fortunes under Henry VII; deplorable, because error upon error has by succeeding historians of literature been piled like a cairn on this faulty account which confuses the uncle and the nephew;

[1] British Museum, MS. Harleian 372, fol. 61.
[2] *Works of Chaucer*, ed. W. W. Skeat, VII, lii.
[3] *Englische Studien*, X, 206.　　　　[4] II, i, 37.

15

misleading, because it obscures the importance of the family connexion. The reader might excusably think the poet to be the son of simple country gentry. It is true that Skeat later refers to Belvoir in Leicestershire as the home of the family, but again without any indication of the significance of this setting. It is a background of some splendour. The Roos barony was the premier barony of England in the fifteenth century, and, after abeyance, is so still; the Roos family, though sorely depleted, played its part in every activity of camp and court; and its history mirrors in little the century's varied course of splendour and disorder, of magnificence and misery.

If Sir Richard Roos, the poet, is not Richard Roos, Esquire, who then is he? Fortunately he is not far to seek, for in all the branches of the wide Roos clan, there seems to have been only the one Sir Richard in the mid-fifteenth century, and he was in the main line of descent. He was the fifth and youngest son of William, sixth Lord Roos, and of Margaret Arundel, and therefore uncle to that Richard Roos, Esquire, with whom he has been confused. Fortunately again, the uncle has a more picturesque setting than the nephew; Richard Roos, Esquire, had his adventures in youth, as will be seen, but later he settled down into a worthy provincial gentleman of Norfolk. Sir Richard Roos's courtly connexions, his kinship with the royal and noble families of his time, his close contact with Humphrey, Duke of Gloucester, Edmund, Duke of Somerset, Henry VI, Queen Margaret of Anjou and possibly with Charles d'Orléans, all these make a fitting background for *La Belle Dame sans Merci*—and for much else.

The de Ros family, possibly originating in Normandy, were early influential at Hamlake (the modern Helmsley) in the North Riding of Yorkshire, acquired by marriage with a daughter of the Especs; branches of them still remained in the North, as at Ingmanthorpe and Kendal, long after Sir Robert de Ros (in the thirteenth century) had by his marriage with Isabel d'Aubigny acquired also the lordship and the broad lands of Belvoir, on the borders of Leicestershire and Lincolnshire. For the next two centuries the Lords de Ros of Hamlake and Belvoir remained great Yorkshire as well as Midland landowners, and were still very conscious of their patronal connexion with York and its Minster (to which the family gave the St. William window), and more especially with Rievaulx Abbey, which had adopted the de Ros arms, 'Gules, three water-bougets argent', themselves a variation of the Trusbut arms, reversing the colours. Throughout the thirteenth and fourteenth centuries, the de Ros family enlarged its already wide borders by judicious marriages with heiresses of such great or rising families as the Fauconbergs, the Vaux, the Badlesmeres, the Nevilles, the Staffords, and the Percies. In the fifteenth century they were among the most devoted of Lancastrian adherents, supporting the three Henry's with heart and mind and body, even at last to the death.

The family seems to have combined piety with activity. Margery, Lady de Ros (one of the well-known Badlesmere heiresses), was almost the only English person who was allowed to go on a pilgrimage to Rome in the Jubilee year, 1350. Her eldest son, William, third Lord de Ros, died in Palestine two years later on a pilgrimage; and his nephew John, fifth Lord de Ros, died at an early age in 1393 at Paphos in Cyprus, on the return journey from Jerusalem. He left no issue, and so his brother William, father of Sir Richard the poet, came early into the succession. Living over the turn of the century, from Richard II to Henry V, William begins the fifteenth-century history of his race, and carries his family into the Lancastrian camp.

CHAPTER I

The Roos Family in the Fifteenth Century

I. WILLIAM ROOS, SIXTH LORD ROOS

WILLIAM ROOS, sixth Lord Roos, is already familiar to readers of Shakespeare's *Richard II*. Disguised as Lord Ross, he and Lord Willoughby (his cousin), and the Earl of Northumberland, appear as representatives of the disaffected lords who, after the death of John of Gaunt, conspire to aid Bolingbroke. Again in Lord Willoughby's company, he comes 'Bloody with spurring, fiery-red with haste' to join Bolingbroke's forces in Gloucestershire.[1] Probably because of theatrical exigency, he does not appear in the deposition scene, at which in fact he was present; nor is he a character in *Henry IV*, though he was in reality active and honoured in that king's service.

William, sixth Lord Roos (c. 1369–1414),[2] was the second son of Sir Thomas de Ros, fourth Lord Ros (1336/7–84), who had fought in France under Edward III and later under the Black Prince. While preparing to go on pilgrimage, he had died on his estates at Uffington in Lincolnshire, and had been succeeded by his eldest son John. William's mother, the much-married Lady Beatrice, is a more living figure than her husband, and appears as something of a matriarch. Daughter of Ralph, first Earl of Stafford, she was the young widow of Maurice FitzMaurice, Earl of Desmond, when she married Thomas

---

[1] II, i, 225 ff.; II, iii, 57 ff.

[2] This account of the main line of the de Ros or (in the fifteenth century) Roos family is based on that in G.E.C., *Complete Peerage*, vol. XI (1949), pp. 100–7 (references are not given for statements from this source); on a few entries in *D.N.B.*; and on the account in Nichols, *Leicestershire*, vol. II, part i, pp. 34–41, supplemented from documentary and other sources as indicated below.

de Ros in 1358/9. In a little over a year after his death she married Sir Richard Burley, nephew of the ill-fated Sir Simon Burley whom the Lords Appellant were soon to force Richard II to yield to their fury. It was a brief union, for in May 1387 Sir Richard Burley died in Galicia. Lady Beatrice was again left a widow (a fate not uncommon among the Roos ladies of this period), and evidently retired then to Hamlake. She also survived her two eldest sons, John, fifth Lord Roos (and his wife, Maria Percy), and William, her 'precarissimum ac predilectum filium', to whom in her will she left a bed with coverlets worked with the arms of Roos and Stafford, and (ironically enough) with white roses, also a silver cup called Fawconberge, and a horse.[1] These gifts never reached him, since he predeceased her by seven months, dying in September 1414. Lady Beatrice had earlier (1408) secured a licence to found a chantry in St. Paul's for the souls of her last two husbands;[2] in her will she provided amply for masses for her dead relatives at Hamlake parish church, and throughout Yorkshire.

When in 1393, at the age of twenty-four and upwards, William Roos succeeded, presumably unexpectedly, to his elder brother John, his first act was to take to himself a wife. Within eight months of taking livery of seisin, he married Margaret Arundel. She was the daughter of that Sir John Arundel, son of Richard (FitzAlan), Earl of Arundel, who, after raiding the coast of Brittany, was wrecked and drowned in the Irish Sea in 1379, his astonishing wardrobe of fifty-two suits of clothes perishing with him.[3] Her mother Eleanor, Baroness Mautravers in her own right, had married again in 1384, Reginald Cobham, second Lord Cobham; and William's and Margaret's wedding took place at Stirborough Castle in Surrey. This Cobham connexion was later of importance to their son, Sir Richard the poet. Margaret Arundel had been lady in waiting to Queen Anne,[4] and she received from Richard II a handsome annuity (40 marks yearly till she married) for her services to his lately dead and beloved wife; this was followed by a still more handsome wedding-present (£200) to her as the king's kinswoman.[5]

William Roos was already a Privy Councillor and was regularly

---

[1] *Testamenta Eboracensia*, I, No. 270, p. 375. Isabella, Lady Fawconbergh, widow of Walter, Lord Fawconbergh, had in 1401 made Lady Roos responsible for the distribution of her household goods. In the thirteenth century, Isabel Roos had married a Fawconbergh.

[2] *Cal. Pat. Rolls, 1408–13*, p. 40.

[3] G.E.C., XI, 103; I, 260.

[4] William, Lord Roos, and Margaret Arundel were married by licence, Oct. 9, 1394; the queen had died on June 7.

[5] *Cal. Pat. Rolls, 1391–6*, p. 518; Devon, *Issues*, p. 259.

summoned to Parliament; in 1395 he was one of the signatories to a letter urging the king to return from Ireland and deal with the Scots. In 1396 he was in Calais for the king's politic marriage to the little Isabelle of France. What drove him over to Bolingbroke's side can only be conjectured: it may have been indeed what Shakespeare puts into his mouth, a sense of misgovernment through 'burdenous taxations' even to 'very wrack'; he would naturally be drawn into that 'group of able and influential men whose lands lay about the honour of Richmond, and who were connected by ties of marriage and common interest', the Nevilles, Dacres, Percies, Scropes, Welles and Latimers.[1]

Throughout the family's history, there had been little blind sub-servience to the reigning king, and William followed his family's tradition: the notable Robert ('Fursan') de Ros had opposed King John; another Sir Robert had sided with Simon de Montfort; Sir John, 'le bon compagnon', had landed with Queen Isabella from France,[2] and his brother, Sir William, had helped to depose Edward II.[3] As his forebears had done, so did the sixth Lord Roos; thus he was present at Richard's abdication in the Tower, and in the first parliament of the new reign he assented to Richard's fatal imprisonment. He and his cousin, Lord Willoughby, combined to furnish a ship with twenty men-at-arms, forty archers, and a sufficiency of sailors, and also agreed to be ready to support the king by land.[4] He was not a warmonger, however, for later he voted against resumption of war with France, in agreement with the Earl of Northumberland, and with his stepfather-in-law, Lord Cobham.[5]

With the reign of Henry IV, Lord Roos reaped the rewards of his support, and entered on a period of personal prosperity, and useful service of various kinds. He continued on the Council until two years before his death, and the town of Chingford in Essex was assigned to harbour his retinue during his stays in London. He was successively Treasurer of England for fourteen months (September 1403 to November 1404) and an auditor of the war accounts. As Treasurer, he and the Chancellor, Henry Beaufort, drew up in 1403 trade agree-ments with the Teutonic Knights of Prussia, with whom 'the bandes of unfained love and friendship have bin successively confirmed and kept inviolable in times past'.[6] He was made K.G. in 1404, the only

---

[1] M. V. Clarke, *Fourteenth Century Studies*, p. 37.
[2] Nichols, *Leicestershire*, II, i, 32.
[3] G.E.C., *Complete Peerage*, XI, pp. 93, 95, 98, 122.
[4] *Proceedings and Ordinances of the Privy Council*, I, p. 106 (ed. Sir Harris Nicolas, 1834).   [5] *Ib.*, p. 144.
[6] Hakluyt's *Voyages*, 1903, II, pp. 36, 40.

one of his name to bear this honour in the century. In December of
that year he went to Berwick to receive the bonds given by the Scottish
prisoners of Holmedon to the late Earl of Northumberland, and to
bring them to Henry IV at Pomfret, . . . 'those same noble Scots' whom
Shakespeare's Hotspur, 'wasp-stung and impatient', refused energetic-
ally to deliver up.[1] He was also one of the Commission that in 1405
tried and condemned Archbishop Scrope for treason.[2] His fidelity
and good repute are attested by a letter of May 1405 to the king at
Worcester from the Privy Council, which reports that they proposed
to send to the North to enquire into the Percy rising, Lord Chief
Justice Gascoigne and Lord Roos, as the two in whom the king
reposed especial trust—'come ceux desqueux vous portez especial
confiance'.[3] These dealings with his former allies and fellow con-
spirators (and connexions by marriage)[4] may well have been as difficult
and delicate for Lord Roos as for the king himself. All his tasks required
tact, moderation, and common sense.

Other difficult matters awaited him, loyal churchman that he was;
he was appointed chief commissioner of *oyer et determiner* as to rebellions
and treasons in three counties committed by the king's subjects,
commonly called Lollards. He was one of the Council that condemned
the Lollard, John Badby, in 1410 and it is possible that he was present
with the young king at the harrowing scene of the execution.[5] Whether
or not this and his many other duties affected his health and spirits, it
is impossible to say; he was continuously busy. As again Treasurer and
Keeper of the Privy Seal in 1412, drawing an annual salary of £100,
he had onerous dealings over the money for Thomas of Lancaster's
expedition to Guienne.[6]

His family life seems to have been uneventful, but from time to time
he had been mixed up in some tiresome matters. His brother-in-law,
Lord Grey de Ruthin, husband of his sister Margaret, had had trouble
with his Welsh neighbours, and the rebel Griffith ap Griffith had
promised him 'A rope, a ladder, and a ring, High on gallows for to hing,
And thus shall be your ending'.[7] Lord Grey was then unlucky enough
to be taken prisoner by Owen Glendower in 1402; Lord Roos recognized

---

[1] *1 Henry IV*, I, iii, 212 ff.   [2] Wylie, *Henry IV*, II, 232.
[3] *Proc. and Ord. of the Privy Council*, I, 262.
[4] His elder brother's wife, Maria, was a daughter of Henry Percy, Earl of
Northumberland, and of Joan, Lady Orreby, and so a (slightly younger) step-
aunt of Hotspur, whom in her will she called her beloved cousin.
[5] Wylie, *op. cit.*, III, 437.
[6] *Proc. and Ord. of the Privy Council*, II, 31.
[7] Ellis, *Orig. Letters*, 2nd ser., I, 3–7.

the claims of kinship by helping to ransom him. Later, in November 1411, Lord Roos was involved in a private difference with Sir Robert Tyrwhitt of Kettleby, judge of the King's Bench, a Lincolnshire neighbour who quarrelled with some Roos tenants at Wrawbey over rights of 'pasture and turbary and estovers'.[1] Lord Roos's old associate, Chief Justice Gascoigne, was the arbitrator, but on the love day appointed, whereas Lord Roos duly came 'in aisy wise' with two of his cousins, Henry, Lord Beaumont, and Thomas, Lord de la Warr, and few retainers, Tyrwhitt appeared with 500 men, 'armez et arrayez à faire la guerre', who drove off Roos's small band. Tyrwhitt had in the end to apologize publicly, to offer 500 marks (which Roos was to refuse), and by a pleasant touch to provide two fat oxen, twelve fat sheep, and two tuns of wine for a dinner to Roos's men at Melton Ross. A feast buried this quarrel but not all the unkindness between the Tyrwhitt and Roos families, since it flared up again at the same place two centuries later.[2]

Probably the death of Henry IV brought to Lord Roos a sense of discouragement and loss; for Henry V was under the influence of Henry Beaufort, Bishop of Ely, the bitter opponent of Archbishop Arundel, who was Margaret, Lady Roos's, uncle, and whom Lord William, as his will shows, had supported and admired. That will was made in February 1412/13, and in September 1414 he died at Belvoir and was buried there under the fine alabaster monument now in Bottesford church. He is represented in armour, with the collar of SS, and his helmet bears his crest, the peacock with trailing feathers. His family also put up to his memory the great St. William window in York Minster.

William Roos's intimate life we can only guess at from indications in his will.[3] It shows him as a good son of the church, remembering St. Thomas the Martyr as his patron saint,[4] and desiring if he died in London to be buried in Canterbury Cathedral near the chantry chapel of his most reverend father in God, Archbishop Arundel. Rievaulx Abbey, the traditional burial-place of his ancestors, rather than York Minster, was to receive his bones if he died in the York diocese, and there were money legacies to the abbot and to each monk, even down (proportionately) to each novice. He gave more to hermits and the

[1] Wylie, *Henry IV*, II, 189–90.
[2] Robt. Tyrwhitt, *Notices . . . of the Family of Tyrwhitt*, 1872, pp. 9–13.
[3] *The Register of Henry Chichele*, ed. E. F. Jacob, II. pp. 22–6.
[4] In 1408–9 he and his wife became members of the fraternity of the Trinity, and of SS. Fabian and Sebastian at St. Botolph's, Aldersgate (Brit. Mus., MS. Add. 37664, fol. 20).

poor than to his illegitimate daughter. Each church in his manors had a gift from his best herds. Belvoir Priory, together with a substantial donation for its fabric, had a new chantry foundation, a small college of eight chaplains (with two honest clerks to wait on them) to say mass on behalf of himself, his parents, his brothers and sisters, especially his elder brother Thomas, his benefactors and friends.

This chantry college was to serve also another purpose, the education of his younger sons, Thomas, Robert and Richard: 'I desire that my sons should be instructed and taught in discipline and grammar, so far as is fitting and seemly for them, by one of these chaplains well learned and knowledgeable in grammar'. One third of his possessions was to go to the governance, sustentation and subvention of these three boys, and they and their goods were to remain under his executors' control until they came to man's estate and were suitably married. His eldest son, John the heir, was to have an annuity of 40 marks, and also the knightly heirloom, all his father's armour and his golden sword.

William his second son, not yet of age, was enfeoffed with manors; and if he died childless the succession was to go from John to William, and then to Robert. This passed over Thomas, the third son, who was evidently intended for a clerkly career; fate, however, willed otherwise. To his most noble mother the testator gave a gilded cup and cover with a white knop; it is curious that a cup with an armorial 'bouget' (*bouse*) on the knop goes, not to one of the family, but to William Hoton, one of his executors. His wife, Margaret, had one third of his goods, but there is no distinguishing word of affection for her, nor any special gift. It is possible that Margaret Arundel, late waiting lady to Anne of Bohemia, did not always see eye to eye with her ardently Lancastrian husband; on the other hand, she alone of the Roos dowagers of this century did not remarry. She must have occupied herself with her little sons. It was she (dña Marguareta dña de Roos) who was appointed to accompany Queen Katherine to Rouen in 1422; her daughter-in-law is generally distinguished as Margery and the elder lady had had experience as a waiting-lady of Queen Anne.[1] Later she seems to have retired to remote Hamlake where she died in 1438 (July 3). It was evidently the family dower-house; Lady Beatrice's will shows her Yorkshire interests.[2]

---

[1] *Proc. and Ord. of the Privy Council*, II, 331.

[2] Both Eleanor Beaufort and Margery Wentworth, younger Roos dowagers who remarried, lived at Helmsley in the 1460s (*Yorks. Archæol. Journal*, XXIV, 332).

The will of Lord Roos, made some eighteen months before his death, reveals a man pious, careful, business-like, with a sense of his responsibilities as churchman, great landowner, son, husband, and above all father. His elder brother's sudden death had been spoken of as a great loss to all England.[1] One can but wonder if the death of this elder statesman, prudent, loyal, and moderate, was not an equal loss to England, and to the young king, Henry V.

On the breaking by Henry V of that long peace with France which stands originally to the credit of Richard II, the Roos sons began again a close connexion with service in Normandy, such as their grandfather had had under the Black Prince. And henceforward we shall learn almost as much of intimate interest about them from French records as from English.

II. JOHN ROOS, SEVENTH LORD ROOS

John, seventh Lord Roos, was seventeen at his father's death in 1414; his guardian was the Earl of Dorset, Sir Thomas Beaufort, later Duke of Exeter, the 'uncle Exeter' of Henry V in his French wars. John had been married in 1404 at a tender age to Margery, daughter and heir of Philip, Lord Despenser of Goushill, and of Elizabeth Tiptoft. There were no children of the union, and we know of him only as a fighting man. In 1415, as a knight-banneret of eighteen, he sailed for France with the king; presumably he witnessed at Southampton the exposure of the three conspirator lords. Of these, one was connected with him, the Earl of Cambridge, husband of his cousin Matilda Clifford, the daughter of his aunt Elizabeth Roos; in spite of her husband's execution, Lady Cambridge remained staunchly Lancastrian, in the tradition of her mother's family.[2]

Sir John Roos was among that 'happy few' who on October 25, 1415, 'bore their baners' at Agincourt, his arms the three silver water bougets on a crimson field, his crest the peacock. But his youth and inexperience keep the family name out of the roll-calls inherited by Elizabethan poets: 'Warwick and Talbot, Salisbury and Gloucester';

> Beaumont and Willoughby
> Bare them right doughtily,
> Ferrers and Fanhope.

In 1417 Lord Roos again crossed to France, and went through the siege

---

[1] *Annales Ricardi Secundi*, ed. Riley, Rolls ser., 28 (3), p. 165.
[2] *Testamenta Eboracensia*, II, No. 97, p. 118.

of Rouen, encamped before the walls between the forces of his guardian and his kinsman:[1]

> And fro Exsetre towards the kynge
> The Lorde Rose and Wylby was lyggynge,
> And also wyt hem the Lorde Fyhewe.

He must have taken part in Henry's entry in pomp into the captured city, when the king's display of the emblem of folly, the fox's brush, by way of streamer, 'afforded great matter of remark among the wiseheads'.[2] His services were rewarded by the grant of the castle and lordship of Bacqueville (April 1419), for a quitrent of a nosegay of red roses;[3] and by the end of the year he was captain of Château Gaillard, the massive rock-fortress that Richard Cœur de Lion had built at Les Andelys on an island in the loops of the Seine.[4] By the time that Lord Roos joined the Duke of Burgundy's forces at St. Quentin in February 1420/1, he was Marshal of England. He took part in the siege of Melun under the royal brothers, and at the turn of the next year he was Captain of Mantes, and had a command under the Duke of Clarence himself. His brother William, who had just been made Captain of Briqueville, was knighted by the Duke before Angers;[5] and so both brothers came in the Duke's army to the battle of Baugé, the only defeat suffered by Henry's arms, and the 'revanche' for Agincourt.

The most vivid account of Baugé, and of Roos's part in the battle, comes from Georges Chastellain,[6] who, as will be seen later, may have had particular knowledge of the family. The English, surprised, fought bravely:

> Sy fit le seigneur de Ros, mareschal d'Angleterre, qui en cestuy affaire rua maint dur et pesant coup de ses bras, et donna maintes mortelles playes celuy jour à ses ennemis.

When the Duke of Clarence was killed by one Bouteiller, Lord Roos fought to avenge him:

> Laquelle chose le seigneur de Ros voiant, plein de douleur et de desplaisir, que plus ne pouvoit sans errager, non désirant plus à vivre que jusques à tant qu'il eust vengé ce prince, s'en vint de randon férant sur le dit Bouteiller, et en dure et mortelle aigreur, tant le suivyt de près et si radde, que sans jamais partir de luy jusques à la mort de l'un d'eux, il lui fit sentir le mordant de son espée, si fellement que oncques ne se put

---

[1] Page's 'Sege of Roan', *Archaeologia*, XXI, p. 54.
[2] Monstrelet, transl. Johnes, II, lxxxv.
[3] Norman Rolls, *41st Report of the Dep. Keeper of . . . Records*, pp. 763, 808.
[4] P. Le Cacheux, *Actes de la Chancellerie d'Henry VI*, Rouen, 1907, I, 295.
[5] Holinshed, ed. R. S. Wallace, Oxf., 1923, p. 119.
[6] *Œuvres*, ed. Kervyn de Lettenhove, I, 225-6.

défendre que le dit Ros ne le prit par la bannière et le saisy au corpse et en luttant l'un contre l'autre lui bouta l'espée en la gorge, dont prestement il chéyt mort à terre; mais gaires ne demeura après que le payement ne lui fust rendu, tel comme il l'avoit baillé icy, et furent tués le seigneur de Ros, le comte de Quint [Kent] et toute la greigneur noblesse des Anglois.

Sir William Roos was killed also and was probably buried at Belfort near Baugé;[1] the elder brother was brought home to Belvoir Priory, only seven years after their father had been laid there.

Lord John Roos's wife, Margery Despenser, did not mourn her husband for long; it is true that she could have seen little of him. In less than a year from the day of Baugé, she married Roger Wentworth of Elmsall, armiger, 'dishonourably and without licence from the king'. It is possible that her undistinguished choice alienated her from her Roos connexions more than did her haste to remarry. She seems to have become entirely a Wentworth, devoted to her son Philip; at the same time, she retained her Roos name and title. Her will of 1478 has no mention of Roos though her youngest brother-in-law, Sir Richard, was still alive.[2] The only memorable thing about her is her patronage, in the wake of Margaret of Anjou and Elizabeth Wydville, of Queens' College, Cambridge. There she founded a Fellowship c. 1470, and in 1472 made gifts to the Chapel, where she wished to be buried. At her death in April 1478, she left to its President, Andrew Dokett, a covered goblet, 'cum Armis dni. de Roos' (P.C.C. Wills, Wattys 33). She and her first husband and her youngest brother-in-law are all remembered, together with many royal persons, in the 'Commemoration of Benefactors' of the College.[3]

III. THOMAS ROOS, EIGHTH LORD ROOS (1406–30)

William, Lord Roos, had made careful testamentary dispositions concerning his sons, that in the event of the death without heirs of John and William, Robert was to succeed. He must have presumed that by that far-off time Thomas the third son would be established in the Church or the Law. But in this sweeping away of the elder brothers,

---

[1] In MS. Harl. 4031, fol. 190, v., the genealogist says that William was buried 'at Bellvoire in france'; Clarence was besieging Belfort (Polidore Vergil ed. 1651, p. 582) and the writer has probably confused the two names.

[2] After Roger Wentworth's death in 1451 she married again, with John Hopton, according to Sir John Fastolfe and to Sir Thomas Howes (*Paston Letters*, ed. Gairdner, 1872, Nos. 154, 219).

[3] I am indebted for this information to the kindness of the late President of Queens' College. See also W. L. Rutton, *Three Branches of the Family of Wentworth*, 1891, pp. 2 ff.

seven years' interval had not sufficed to confirm Thomas in a clerkly life, nor even to bring him to full manhood; and Robert was still a boy of about thirteen. Thomas, then, succeeded as the eighth Lord Roos, in his fifteenth year; like Sir Robert Walpole he was probably 'saved from the Church by the death of his elder brother'.

The Acts of the Privy Council for 1423 show the many monetary arrangements that this minority entailed. His guardian, acting for the baby king Henry VI, was Humphrey, Duke of Gloucester, who took 1000 marks annually from Roos lands. His father's executor, William Hoton, received £40 annually 'for his sustentation', and also a yearly payment of 100 marks, and in 1423 arrears were paid up. Finally in December his lands were to be farmed on terms to be agreed with the Treasurer, then John Stafford; and he was to receive 1000 marks for his marriage with some lady 'of the king's allegiance'.[1]

Obviously his family was anxious for an heir to be provided as soon as possible; the choice of a wife fell, necessarily with Duke Humphrey's approval, on Eleanor Beauchamp, a year younger than her husband, second daughter of Richard Beauchamp, Earl of Warwick, and of his first wife, Elizabeth Berkeley. Although yet under age, Thomas was present in 1426 at the Parliament at Leicester, and took the oath of allegiance on March 4 (*Dominus de Roos, infra etatem*). On May 19 he was knighted by the little king, himself a new-made knight. Within six months he was obviously chafing at inaction. On December 8, 1426,[2] he petitioned the king for an allowance for his support out of his lands in the king's custody. Since his recent knighthood, he longs to serve the king in France, and to prove his chivalry; he has 'joefnesse dage resonable a travailer et dispocition de saintee', and he cannot, he feels, 'garder son honeur sanz luy emploier et faire son devoir a poursuir ce que lordre de chivalerie requiert', especially now, when the king aims at recovering his inheritance and his noble crown of France. Finally he recalls his family's past prowess, 'le service que ses auncestres ount fait a voz nobles progenitours a lour tresgrandes coustages et dispences'.

Lord Roos's plea was heard; he was granted £100, provided that he went forthwith into France in the retinue of John, Duke of Bedford.[3] Bedford had been forced to desert his proper sphere of authority in

---

[1] *Proc. and Ord. of the Privy Council*, III, 26, 88–9, 129–30.
[2] *Ib.*, III, 225.
[3] In his retinue went Philip Est, William Dayle, and Sir Hugh de Annesley of Rodyngton, Notts. (*48th Report*, etc., pp. 246–8), also Peter Horneby (who was a witness with Lord Roos to the marriage at Roche Abbey of Ralph, Earl of Westmoreland, and Elizabeth Percy, widow of John Clifford, in May 1426) (*Test. Ebor.*, III, 325).

France by the quarrels between Gloucester and his step-uncle, Cardinal Beaufort; he had patched up a ragged reconciliation between them at Leicester. Now, in 1427, he was returning to France to deal with the complications caused there by Gloucester's wanton and impolitic rejection of Jacqueline of Hainault, and soon to face the new threat of the influence of Joan of Arc. Nevertheless in 1427 there was not much fighting to prove Thomas Roos's chivalry.

Meanwhile Roos's personal affairs went well. In September, 1427, the much-desired heir was born at Conisbrough Castle (presumably Eleanor Roos had gone to stay with her husband's cousin, Matilda (Clifford), Countess of Cambridge); and in December of the same year the young father proved his age, and took livery of seisin. From that time his progress was steady—for three short years. Another son, Richard, and a daughter, Margaret, were born. In 1429, he was summoned to Parliament, made a Privy Councillor, and appointed one of the commissioners to treat of peace with Scotland.

Lord Roos also continued his service in France. In October 1428, he was in the army that came in force to lay siege to Orléans. Whether he was still there at its relief by Joan of Arc on May 18, 1429, there is no proof; possibly not, since he was in attendance at Windsor at the Feast of St. George.[1] In April 1430 he was among the many nobles who attended on the young king when he crossed to France for his coronation. But that ceremony Lord Roos did not live to see. In August 1430 he had been made governor of Paris; but he enjoyed this responsible honour for only two days. The minutes of the Privy Council record merely that he was killed in the king's wars in France,[2] and Chastellain simply that he was drowned in the Marne.[3] Fortunately the anonymous Bourgeois de Paris had more detailed information, and a more vivid pen; he tells first of Roos's entry with music into the city, evidently feeling that the Englishman, whom he thinks of as a mere 'chevalier', was making too much show:

le sire de Roz, ung chevalier angloys, vint à Paris le mercredi xvie jour d'aoust l'an mil iiii^cxxx, le plus pompeusement que on vit oncques chevalier, s'il n'estoit roy ou duc, ou conte; car il avoit devant lui iiii menesterelz jouans trompes, clerons, tous jouans de leurs instrumens.

But on the Friday, music was turned into mourning:

le vendredy ensuivant, . . . les Arminalx vindrent prendre la proie devers

---

[1] J. Anstis, *Register of the Order of the Garter*, II, 104.
[2] *Proc. and Ord. of the Privy Council*, IV, 88.
[3] *Œuvres*, ed. Kervyn de Lettenhove, II, 51.

la porte Sainct Anthoine, et prindrent beufs, vaches, brebis, et autre bestail, et s'en tournerent atout. Quant le sire de Roz le sceut, il alla à toutes ses gens après et poursuivy fort, et ung autre chevalier anglois qui estoit cappitaine du Boys de Vicennes, qui le suyvi de pres, et autres, et virent les Arminalx qui passoient Marne par dela Sainct-Mor; si les suyvirent, et aucuns se mirent en la riviere, qui bien virent le gué par où les Arminalx passerent, et allerent oultre. Le sire de Roz failly à trouver le gué et soy bouta en la riviere trop hardiement, et le cappitaine du Bois de Vicennes qui aussi faillyt, . . . et plusieurs autres qui tous furent noyez, et grant foison d'Arminalx aussi le furent; mais ceulx qui passerent besongnerent si bien qu'ilz rescouirent tous les prinsonniers et la proie, et avec ce prindrent le cappitaine . . . et plusieurs autres tuerent, et plusieurs d'eulx furent tuez.[1]

This picture of the hasty sortie after the Armagnac raiders, and of Lord Roos's impetuous plunge into the river, heedless of the safety of the ford, fits in with the impatience we have seen in him before, fretting to prove his chivalry in France. Those high hopes ended on August 18 in the waters of the Marne; presumably his body was never recovered, for there is no monument to him in Bottesford Church. As the Bourgeois says almost pityingly, 'fortune lui fut trop contraire'.

IV. THOMAS ROOS, NINTH LORD ROOS (1427–64)

Within seventeen years, three holders of the Roos barony had died in rapid succession, and again the heir was a minor, this time a child barely three years old, little Thomas, ninth Lord Roos. The two events which were to be most influential in his life were, first, the granting of his wardship and marriage to John, Lord Tiptoft, which resulted in his union with Philippa Tiptoft; and secondly, his mother's re-marriage between 1433 and 1438, with Edmund Beaufort, then Count of Mortain, later Earl of Dorset, later still Earl (by inheritance) and Duke (by royal proclamation) of Somerset.[2] For Somerset, although he was the ill-starred leader of the English armies in France, in that rapid *débâcle* which stripped England of almost all her remaining French possessions, was the most influential Lancastrian peer in England after the murder of William de la Pole, Duke of Suffolk.

The long minority of young Lord Roos was not allowed to run its full course. In consideration of his services (not specified) about the king's person, he was allowed livery of seisin early in 1445/6. Of his marriage there is little to say, except that his wife's kinship with

---

[1] *Journal d'un Bourgeois de Paris*, ed. Alexandre Tuetey, 1881, pp. 256–7 item 541.

[2] *Cal. Close Rolls, 1429–35*, p. 249; *Cal. Pat. Rolls, 1436–41*, p. 160.

the noted Yorkist Earl of Worcester probably stood the Roos family in good stead in the sixties. The heir, Edmund, was born at Stewkley in 1446, and this name, new in the Roos family tree, attests the good relations of the young Lord Roos with his stepfather. His fortunes as a soldier were closely bound up with Somerset's. He fought with him in the last campaign, and was one of the hostages given on the surrender of Rouen, together with other young nobles. His younger brother, Richard, as will be seen, was taken prisoner at the same siege, and remained for ten years in his captor's hands. The Duchess of Somerset seems to have had her young family with her in the walled towns which the English thought secure; she had a rude shock when a shot penetrated her nursery in the tower at Caen. Lively vignettes of her and her husband are given by the French chronicler, Thomas Basin, Bishop of Lisieux. He describes the Duke, then about fifty years old, as *specie decorus, . . . satis civilis et benignus atque humanus, communi patriae justitiae, satis affectus et intentus*. His two worst defects were avarice (in spite of the great wealth that he had inherited from his uncle, Cardinal Beaufort) and uncontrolled rages. Basin describes his fury at the news of the taking of Pont de l'Arche as vengeance for the English attack at Fougères.[1] The *Reductio Normanniae* gives an even more highly drawn picture of the despair of the Duchess, who rushed from her bed clad only in her shift, *matronalis pudore oblita*. She could be quick-witted on occasion, as is shown by her resourcefulness in saving a French doctor from her husband's unreasoning wrath; and the writer ends with a tribute to English women: *Anglia enim impios viros et malefidos, feminas vero pietate insignes et benefidas parit.*[2]

When Caen surrendered, and the English forces fell back, and finally retired across the Channel, leaving the Duke a prisoner in French hands, Lord Roos was free, and probably escorted home his mother and her young Somerset family. For a few years he was able to resume his private life and his civil duties. We even find him engaging in trade, licensed in 1453 to ship wool to the Continent, and again in 1457 together with his stepbrother, Henry, Duke of Somerset.[3] His heir, Edmund, his only son, was followed in 1449 by Eleanor, who after Edmund's death was to carry the name and the estates of Roos to the

---

[1] Thomas Basin, *Hist. de Charles VII*, etc., ed. Quicherat, I, 193.

[2] Robert Blondel, 'De Reductione Normanniae', in *Narratives of the Expulsion of the English*, etc., ed. J. Stevenson, Rolls ser., pp. 26–7.

[3] Dep. Keeper of the Public Records, *48th Report*, French Rolls, pp. 395, 421. Cf. Early Chanc. Proc., 28/286; and for ships owned by Lord Roos, *ib.*, 29/544, 546, 548; 25/200; these Chancery references I owe to the kindness of Mrs. W. Hodgkiss.

Manners family; and by Isabel, who married thirdly Sir Thomas Lovell of Ryhall, Treasurer of the Household to Henry VII. Lord Roos was summoned regularly to parliament, and later (1454–7) attended several Great Councils. He had been knighted before January 13, 1449/50.[1] His stepfather, ransomed at vast cost, and returned from France, became the head of the loyal party, and during 1452 maintained his position, despite his bitter unpopularity. As the Yorkist storm blew up, Lord Roos was given work to do; he had to guard the coasts of Norfolk and Suffolk, and had power to press crews for his ships. In July 1453, he was captain of the force ready to set out to sea to aid Talbot; but Talbot was already dead at Châtillon, and Gascony was soon to be lost irrecoverably. In the see-saw balancing of royal and Yorkist power during 1454, Roos, as a loyal Lancastrian, must have viewed with apprehension the illness of the king, and the consequent loss of influence and later the imprisonment of his stepfather Somerset. When the king recovered, and Somerset was released from the Tower in February 1454/5, Lord Roos was one of the four lords who offered 'mainprise, body for body', for his appearance before the Council.[2] Somerset's short triumph over his personal enemy, the Duke of York, ended with his death three months later at the first battle of St. Albans. He was not the only kinsman whom Roos lost then (the lords Northumberland and Clifford also lost their lives), but he was the most powerful. Roos himself survived the battle, and after the death of his kinsman, Lord Audley, at Blore Heath, he became, next to his stepbrother, Henry, Duke of Somerset, one of the leading Lancastrian lords. He accompanied young Somerset to Guisnes in the attempt to wrest Calais from the Yorkist trio in possession, Edward, Earl of March, Warwick, and Salisbury. He was not apparently involved in the defeat of the royal army at Northampton; but when the queen, having fled north, made York her centre and rallied the northern lords, Somerset and Roos (here in one of his spheres of influence) were with her. They took part in the sweeping victory of Wakefield on December 30, 1460, which by the Lancastrians' murders of York, Salisbury, and young Rutland, so deeply embittered the struggle. Roos's participation was given as the cause of his attainder: 'for being at the death of the Duke of York, at Wakefield'.[3] Again, Roos was at the queen's second victory of St. Albans, the fruits of which were thrown away by her tactical error in withdrawing again to the north, leaving London open to Edward's seizure, and proclamation of himself as king.

---

[1] *Cal. Pat. Rolls, 1446–52*, p. 437.   [2] *Cal. Close Rolls, 1454–61*, p. 44.
[3] Cotton, *Abridgement*, etc., p. 670, item 19.

When Edward's victory at Towton sent the royal family into flight towards Scotland, Lord Roos, who had been left to guard the king during the battle, fled with them; and when the queen was at Edinburgh in August 1461, three men of the Roos family were with her, Lord Roos, his son Edmund, and Sir Henry Roos.[1] This is the first notice we have of Edmund, then a lad of fifteen, possibly his father's page or squire, possibly taken north for safety. Sir Henry Roos was Lord Roos's first cousin, son and heir of Sir Robert Roos of More End; of both these more will be said later. Of the Lancastrians with them, two other names will later be of interest, Sir Thomas Fynderne and John Hawt.

Such display of Roos loyalty was not to be overlooked: Edward IV in his first proclamation included Lord Roos among those who were 'moved and stirred by the spirit of the Devil' to destroy England;[2] his estates had already been seized, and in August 1461 a receiver was appointed; in November he, his heir, and his cousin Sir Henry were attainted.

Lord Roos spent much of 1462, together with his stepbrother the Duke of Somerset, and Sir Ralph Percy, in defending Bamborough Castle against Edward's army. When the queen and the prince were again safely in Scotland, they surrendered on Christmas Eve, on condition that their lives should be spared. Somerset and Percy were won over to Edward IV, only to revert later; William of Wyrcester insinuates that Roos would have forsaken his allegiance if his lands had been restored to him. However that may be, he remained Lancastrian. There is no proof that he was with the little band of exiles that lived in great poverty with Margaret at St. Mihiel; his cousin Sir Henry was there. Lord Roos's whereabouts until the battle of Hedgeley Moor (April 25, 1464) are unknown; he escaped then, but not for long. He, Lord Hungerford, Sir Thomas Fynderne, and others were found after Hexham hiding in a wood, and were taken to Newcastle and executed at the Sandhill on May 17, 1464. Sir Ralph Percy had already died in battle, believing that by his return to his Lancastrian allegiance he had 'saved the bird in his bosom'; Somerset was beheaded immediately after the battle; and Roos's kinsman Sir Philip Wentworth was executed at Middleton. The fortunes of the Roos family were crushed with the Lancastrian defeat, and with the execution of Thomas, Lord Roos; in spite of his tragic end, he remains somewhat colourless, a type-character, 'a Loyal Lancastrian'.

Edmund Roos is said to have fled abroad and lived there; he was

---

[1] *Paston Letters*, No. 413.   [2] Scofield, *Edward IV*, I, 154–5.

C

overseas when Henry VII in 1485 annulled the Act of Attainder but kept the Roos lands reserved to himself. By 1492 the unfortunate Edmund was found to be insane, 'not of sufficient discretion to guide himself and his livelihood, or able to serve his Highness after his duty'. His brother-in-law, Sir Thomas Lovel, was granted custody of his lands, and Edmund lived at his Tiptoft manor of Elsing, near Enfield; lingering on till over the age of sixty, he died in 1508. His mother, Philippa, had outlived by many years two more husbands, Sir Thomas Wingfield, who was with the Duke of Norfolk at the siege of Caister, and Edward Grimston, who succeeded for a short while to Sir Robert Roos in ambassadorial duties.[1]

The wide Roos lands had been divided among many Yorkist owners. William, Lord Hastings, reveals himself as an enemy by his treatment of Belvoir; Leland[2] later described its state: Hastings had

apon a raging wylle spoilid the castelle, defacing the rofes, and takyng the leades of them. . . . Then felle alle the castelle to ruine, and the tymbre of the rofes onkeverid rottid away, and the soile betwene the waulles at the last grue ful of elders, and no habitation was there tyl that of late dayes the Erle of Rutland hath made it fairer than ever it was.

Hamlake was granted to George, Duke of Clarence, and later, in 1478, went by purchase to Richard, Duke of Gloucester;[3] Henry VII in 1487 gave the stewardship of it to Charles Somerset, illegitimate son of Henry Beaufort, the third Duke of Somerset.[4] Gradually under Edward IV certain fiefs came back into the main line: Philippa Roos was allowed several manors,[5] probably through the influence of her Yorkist brother, John Tiptoft, Earl of Worcester; her brother-in-law, Richard Roos, Esquire, was allowed to enter on his inheritance, the Norfolk manors of Holt and Cley; and even collaterals gained back Roos lands, like Eleanor Roos, daughter of Sir Robert Roos of More End, who by marrying a Haute entered the circle of Queen Elizabeth Wydville's kinsfolk and influence (see below). Edmund's elder heir, his sister Eleanor, had in 1469 married a Yorkist, Sir Robert Manners of Etall, at Wressel, where she was *domicella* in the household of the second Earl of Westmoreland,[6] one of the Lancastrian Nevilles, with whose second wife, Margaret Cobham, the Roos family had distant connections, as we have seen. The interpenetration of Yorkist and Lancastrian families

---

[1] *Verulam MSS., Hist. MSS. Com.* (1906), pp. 2–5, 8–12.
[2] *Itinerary*, ed. L. Toulmin-Smith, I, 98.
[3] *Yorks. Archaeol. Soc.*, XXIV, 332; V.C.H., *Yorkshire*, III, 410.
[4] See *D.N.B., s.n.*, Charles Somerset, Earl of Worcester.
[5] Anstis, *Register of the Order of the Garter*, I, 226.
[6] *Test. Ebor.*, III, 340.

may explain here as elsewhere the concessions made in the later years
of the reign of Edward IV.

V. RICHARD ROOS, ESQUIRE

Hitherto we have traced the Roos family through its baronial succession,
and have been dealing with the heads of the house. The fortunes of
younger members in this century were often equally varied and interesting. The life-story of Richard Roos, younger son of Thomas, eighth
Lord Roos, and of Eleanor Beauchamp, is perhaps the most unexpected
in these family annals, although such as the troubled times must have
often known. This is the Richard Roos who in literary studies has been
regularly mistaken for the poet, his uncle, Sir Richard Roos.

Born on March 8, 1428/9, Richard Roos, Esquire, disappears from
our view in English records till 1463 when he emerges at the age of
thirty and over, claiming his paternal inheritance, and subsequently
being objected to as an impostor by the then head of the family, his
nephew, Edmund, Lord Roos. Nothing in the legal documents explains
this long gap or Edmund's action; and we might still be at a loss, did
we not get a clue from the *Chronicle* of Georges Chastellain. From him
we learn that 'Maistre Ros' was for ten years the prisoner of no less a
person than the famous Seneschal of Normandy, Pierre de Brezé, Lord
of Varennes, trusted councillor of Charles VII, and friend and supporter of Margaret of Anjou. Roos comes into Chastellain's narrative
just at the turn of De Brezé's fortunes when his beloved master, Charles
VII, had died, and his enemy, Louis XI, had succeeded to the French
throne. De Brezé, conscious of his danger, took leave of his family and
retainers; but conscious also of his rectitude, he would not flee the
kingdom, but withdrew to his newly-built house at Nogent-le-Roy near
Chartres:

en laquelle avoit un sien prisonnier anglais dès la prise de Rouen, nommé
maistre Ros, demi-frère au duc de Sombreset de par mère, homme de
grant los et de pris en beaucoup de qualités.

The speech that de Brezé is made to address to 'maistre Ros' proves
at least his appreciation of his prisoner's personality:

Or ça, maistre Ros, vous estes mon prisonnier, et vous ay jà nourry par
l'espace de dix ans à mes despens, non pas si bien que je voudroie et à
vous appartient, mais au mieux que j'ay pu. Vous estes du royaume
d'Angleterre, et moy du royaume de France, ennemis l'un à l'autre; mon
heur est tel aujourd'huy ou que je suys banny du royaume, ou que je le
seray dedens une heure . . . et à vous qui estes gentilhomme et mon

ennemy à cause de la nation, je viens mettre ma vie en vos mains et en vostre conseil, et par vous seul et par vostre sçu je veux faire et moy conduire en tout ce que auray à faire.

Maistre Ros, 'un sage seigneur, moult entendant et profond', manifests his quality by his instant response:[1]

Regardant et voyant que ce noble chevalier, son maistre, après avoir eu tant de gloires . . . s'estoit venu rendre en sa main pour conseil de sa vie, certes commença à larmoyer des yeux, de la pité qu'en avoit.

He realizes that it is a moment for chivalrous loyalty (indeed the whole scene might come out of Arthurian romance), and he follows de Brezé into hiding in the forests of Normandy. When at last the hunted man gave himself up in Paris, and was imprisoned in the grim fortress of Loches,[2] Roos was not involved, but seems to have returned to Nogent-le-Roy. There he had a chance to speak for his honoured captor, and took it. The Comte de Charolais, the king's brother-in-law, appointed Governor of Normandy in de Brezé's place, stopped and lodged for a night at the château. In the absence of Jeanne de Brezé, 'maistre Ros' seems to have done the honours of the house and its master:[3]

[il] fit les contes de son maistre; comment il s'estoit venu rendre en sa main, et les beaux et piteux mots qu'ils eurent ensemble. Donc, pour finablement conclure, le glorifia pour un des plus vaillans et sages chevaliers du monde, et en qui plus avoit de vertu.

The narrative is fairly definite, and can be trusted, since Chastellain had been in de Brezé's service before he transferred to the court of Burgundy, and would be likely to have inside information, probably gained at first hand later. The identity of 'maistre Ros' is fortunately clear through the reference to the Somerset connexion; the Duchess had only two sons by her first marriage, Thomas the heir, and this Richard. Thomas was with his stepfather Somerset when the latter yielded Rouen in 1449 to the army of Charles VII, and was for a short time a hostage, with other young men of rank. But as a hostage he would be and was returned; and as we have seen, his life and doings in England, and the births of his daughters, can be traced during the ensuing decade until his death after Hexham in 1464.[4]

Of the manner of Richard's capture we know nothing. How it was that he was not ransomed we can only conjecture. His family may have been ignorant of his survival; Edmund's objection to him as an impostor

---

[1] G. Chastellain, *Œuvres*, ed. Kervyn de Lettenhove, IV, 175–8.
[2] *Ib.*, pp. 181–4.   [3] *Ib.*, pp. 189–90.
[4] These facts invalidate de Lettenhove's identification of 'maistre Ros' with his elder brother, the head of the family.

suggests that he was believed to be dead. Yet de Brezé knew his identity, and was in touch with English leaders, and had once in 1444 sat on a commission of truce with his prisoner's uncle, Sir Robert Roos.[1] Again, he was in correspondence with Margaret of Anjou and latterly working to serve her as in his raid on Sandwich.[2] If Richard's family knew of his survival and whereabouts, they were probably unable to raise his ransom; the frequent minorities of Roos heirs, and the consequent sustentation of dowagers (there were three alive all at one time), must have depleted the family exchequer.[3] Sir Richard the poet was always short of money; and the enormous sums which Edmund, Duke of Somerset, was mulcted of by the victorious French would cripple even his vast estates,[4] and limit his wife in any attempt to ransom her son. However this may have been, Richard Roos remained in de Brezé's hands throughout his twenties, and it is a pleasing picture which Chastellain draws of the friendship and esteem between captor and prisoner. Young Roos was indeed fortunate to have fallen into the hands of a man of this calibre; de Brezé was not only a gallant soldier and valued counsellor, but also one who partook of the splendours of medieval life. He fought in tournaments, as in those at Nancy after the departure of Margaret of Anjou for England, when he defended the daisy against all comers. A patron of writers, he was himself the centre of a poetic legend of *amour courtois*, on all counts 'l'homme le plus complet de l'époque'.[5]

How much longer the fortunes of 'Maistre Ros' and de Brezé were interwoven, it is difficult to say. Louis XI, realizing the unpopularity of his action, released his prisoner after four months. In apparent continuation of his father's policy, he gave de Brezé charge of the French expedition, assembled on behalf of Margaret of Anjou, but with so few men that Chastellain brutally says, 'il l'envoyoit ainsi que Peleus Jason en Colcos, pour en estre quitte'. As 'conduiseur de sa querelle', de Brezé accompanied Margaret on her entry into Rouen in July, 1462, with 'maistre Ros's' stepbrother, Henry, Duke of Somerset,

[1] *Rolles Gascons*, ed. Carte, II, 310.
[2] Ramsay, *Lancaster & York*, II, 201–2.
[3] See H. L. Gray, 'Incomes from land in England in 1436', *Engl. Hist. Rev.*, 1934, XLIX, p. 616.
[4] G.E.C., *Complete Peerage*, XII, i, 51.
[5] He is probably the hero-lover of Chastellain's *L'Oultré d'Amour*; he is twice invoked as arbitrator in poems of amorous debate (*Le Débat de l'estrange et de l'escondit*, and *Débat du vieil et du jeune*; see *Le Jardin de Plaisance*, ed. Piaget and Droz, vol. II, p. 258); and René d'Anjou refers to him in *Le Cœur d'Amours Espris* as a great lover. See Kenneth Urwin, *G. Chastelain; La Vie, Les Œuvres*, Paris, 1937, pp. 56–7.

in her train, probably too his cousin, Sir Henry Roos.[1] When her ill-fated expedition to the north coast of England was scattered by a storm, she and de Brezé gained Berwick in a fishing boat. In the castle-sieges that followed, Somerset and Lord Roos yielded Bamborough, but de Brezé's son, Jacques, helped to defend Alnwick until de Brezé and the Earl of Angus relieved it from Scotland.[2] From the time of de Brezé's joining Margaret till they left England in the late summer of 1463, de Brezé had been in touch with the elder brother of his prisoner.

In that same summer, on June 8, 1463, Richard Roos, Esquire, was granted by patent the Norfolk manors which had been demised to him in infancy by the will of his father Thomas, eighth Lord Roos; these lands were no longer in his elder brother's control, since all Roos manors had come to Edward IV by the attainder. The royal favour that Henry, Duke of Somerset, enjoyed after his surrender at Bamborough was probably taken advantage of by Duchess Eleanor on behalf of her long-lost Roos son. Master Richard certainly had a deed of release, with a warranty made to him by his mother. This we learn from the petition of Edmund, Lord Roos, against his uncle's claim,[3] which charged the self-styled Richard Roos with forging not only the deed of release but also the will. The petitioner, 'vexit and troubelet', saw himself barred and 'disheiret', and asked for the cancelling of the documents. The petition, which is imperfect, is not dated, but its address to the Chancellor, the Archbishop of Canterbury, limits it to the time of Morton, who, alone in the period after Edmund's resumption of the barony, filled both offices, from March 1487 to September 1500. A downward limit of date is set by Edmund's lapse into insanity, to which possibly these vexations conduced; the petition can therefore be assigned to between the years 1487 and 1492. By that time, Richard Roos had already enjoyed his inheritance for some two decades (with one interval), and had been recovering the years that the locust had eaten. In 1463 he received the hereditary Roos manors of Holt and Cley, Hackford, Whitewell and Watton.[4] But there were still vicissitudes in store. In July 1469, the Yorkist Lord Scales (Anthony Wydville) summoned Mr. Roos with others to Middleton; this was shortly before the battle of Edgcote.[5] On April 25, 1470, his name is found in the long list of 'rebels', all of whose possessions were to be seized; obviously he was among those suspected of complicity with Clarence and Warwick, prob-

---

[1] Chastellain, *op. cit.*, IV, 227, 230, 279.
[2] Ramsay, *op. cit.*, II, 291–4.   [3] Early Chanc. Proc., III, 158/13.
[4] *Cal. Pat. Rolls*, 1461–7, 285–6.
[5] *Paston Letters*, No. 613.

ably with the Lincolnshire rising of Lord Welles.[1] If he fell into Tiptoft's
hands, he escaped the 'dysordinate dethe' that Tiptoft meted out; we
may guess at a reason—his sister-in-law, Philippa (Tiptoft), Lady Roos,
was the Earl of Worcester's sister, and her second husband, Sir Thomas
Wingfield, was an adherent of the Yorkist Duke of Norfolk. With the
Re-adeption of Henry VI, we find Richard Roos, Esquire, kept busy as
an accepted Lancastrian as a Commissioner in Norfolk together with
his wife's kin, the Knevitts, and with the two Paston brothers.[2] One
of Sir John Paston's letters from London to his brother, in November
1470, urgently begs that Mr. Roos, 'olde Knevett, ye, and the worshyp-
fullest that wyll do for owr sake, as Arblaster' (etc.), should present
the Pastons' case to the Earl of Oxford at Norwich, presumably against
the Duke of Norfolk; the Mayor of Norwich will owe good will to Mr.
Roos.[3] With the end at Tewkesbury of Henry's brief resumption of
the crown, Roos must have had to lie low for a while. He did not get
his pardon till March 3, 1474, two years after the general pardon of
1472;[4] in November 1472, he went up to London, probably to plead
his case.[5] In 1474 he is called late of Holt, and again, late of Norwich.[6]

It was in Norwich that he found a wife. Some time after 1467 (the
year of his mother's death), he married Jane or Joan Toppes, widow of
the recently dead Robert Toppes, four times mayor of Norwich.[7] She
had a more than merely civic background. The Toppes family were
armigerous, with a canting coat quartering the arms of Blakeney;[8] a
John Blakeney, usher of the king's chamber, was one of those safeguarded in the Act of Resumption of 1450.[9] Jane was the daughter of
Sir John Knevitt of Norwich, and of Elizabeth Clifton.[10] Through her
mother, she was also the niece by marriage of that famous soldier, Sir
Simon Felbrigg of Felbrigg, whose first wife had been a Silesian lady-
in-waiting to Anne of Bohemia. His second wife was Catherine Clifton,
widow of Sir Ralphe Greene (son of the unlucky favourite of Richard II),
and daughter of Sir John Clifton of Buckenham Castle, Norfolk; her
mother was a Cromwell, her grandmother a De La Pole.[11] When

¹ *Genealogist*, N.S. Extra vol., 1903 (Wrottesleys), pp. 225–6; *Cal. Pat. Rolls,
1467–77*, p. 218.
² *Cal. Pat. Rolls, 1467–77*, pp. 245, 247, 249.
³ *Paston Letters*, No. 656.   ⁴ *Cal. Pat. Rolls, 1467–77*, p. 424.
⁵ *Paston Letters*, No. 705.
⁶ *Cal. Pat. Rolls, 1467–77*, pp. 424, 432.
⁷ MS. Harl. 4031, fol. 190 v.; Early Chanc. Proc., III, 210/21.
⁸ Blomefield, *Norfolk*, III, 257.   ⁹ *Rot. Parl.*, V, 192; cf. 216.
¹⁰ *Vis. of Yorks.*, 1563, p. 177; MS. Harl. 4031, fol. 190 v.
¹¹ St. John Hope, *Garter Stall Plates*, Plate XVIII; G.E.C., *Complete Peerage*,
III, 307–8.

Catherine Felbrigg died in 1459, she left a silver girdle to her niece, Jane Toppes.[1] The family connexions touch the Roos clan at more than one point: another niece and legatee of Catherine Felbrigg was Elizabeth Copledike,[2] whose kinswoman, Alice Copledike of Boston, married William Roos of Dowsby,[3] of a collateral line; and another legatee (receiving a gold cross) was Isabel, Lady Morley, who was mother-in-law of Elizabeth Roos, Sir Richard Roos's eldest sister. Anne Toppes, Robert's and Jane's daughter, married Sir Thomas Lovell, and her son, Sir Gregory, was either brother or cousin of that Sir Thomas Lovell, K.G., confidant of George, Duke of Clarence, and favourite of Henry VII, who married (as third husband) Edmund Roos's sister Isabel.[4] Anne Toppes is one of the children whom we can dimly discern through the gaps in an almost perished Chancery document: Richard Roos and his wife, Jane, sued the executors of Robert Toppes for their exorbitant claims for the cost of boarding the Toppes children. The sum demanded, unfortunately illegible, was utterly refused as 'aynste all reson and conscience'.[5]

Thus Richard Roos, Esquire, by marrying Jane Toppes, married in the outer circle of his family's kin, and into a large Norfolk connexion. This included the Pastons; Margaret Paston in July 1451 had been to dinner with her 'cosyn Toppys', and she tells her husband that 'my Lady Felbrygg and other jantyll women desyryd to have hadde yow ther. They seyd they shuld all abe the meryer'.[6]

The Rutland Papers preserve some letters which throw light on Richard Roos's intercourse with his loftier family connexions, the Dukes of Suffolk and Norfolk. The former, writing from Ewelme in the 1480s, calls him 'Trusty and entierly welbeloved cousin', and deprecates his displeasure against a chaplain of his at Holt market; the cousinship was on Jane Roos's side. The Duchess of Norfolk sends him messages by William Paston, and would gladly see him, writing to him as her dear cousin;[7] she was in fact his first cousin, his mother and hers having been Beauchamp sisters. William Paston, who writes to Master Roos at Refeham two long letters of business and of family talk, had become a connexion about 1470, when he married Lady Anne Beaufort, Richard's stepsister. The familiarity of the group is manifested by

---

[1] Blomefield, *Norfolk*, VIII, 110.   [2] *Genealogist*, I, 369.
[3] *Lincs. Pedigrees*, III, 830.
[4] W. Robinson, *Hist. & Antiquities of Enfield*, I, 138; *Lincs. Vis.*, 1562, p. 30; Blomefield, *Norfolk*, V, 16.
[5] Early Chanc. Proc., 54/187. Cf. also 135/94; 210/21 and 22.
[6] *Paston Letters*, No. 167; cf. 163.
[7] *Rutland Papers* (Hist. MSS. Com.), I, 10, 11; IV, 188.

William Paston's tale of the practical joke played on him by Lady
Norfolk and Lady Anne (also first cousins); with the help of the Bishop
of Ely (Morton) they sent him a pretended *subpoena* to appear before
the king before Christmas, on pain of a fine of £1000:

and I would nat be in the case that I was in t[w]o dayes tyl I knew the
mater, nat for xx *li.*

Lady Norfolk held the sweet jest up till he had actually sent his servants
to London; then she told him all, and 'tornyd to a jape that was ernest
with me afore'.[1]

It is noticeable that all these correspondents, like de Brezé earlier,
address Master Roos in terms of great respect. William Paston one
Christmas begs his company on a visit, part business, part pleasure, to
Lady Norfolk's; later he assures him that John Heydon, in a case pend-
ing between Roos and the elder Heydon,[2] is 'ryth conformable to do yew
plesore, and ryght reverent in hys utteraunce with all dew reveraunce
accordyng'; Heydon indeed addresses him as 'My wurchepful and
spesial gode maister'.[3] He seems to have been able to impress his
personality on his neighbours.

With all this intimacy it is not surprising that Lady Norfolk in 1492
made herself responsible for the marriage of Roos's two daughters,
Mary and Elizabeth. That same petition of Sir Thomas Lovel which
took measures for the 'guyding and governaunce' of his brother-in-
law, Edmund, the now insane Lord Roos, also safeguarded to Richard
Roos, Esquire, the peaceable enjoyment for his lifetime of £40 rental
from the manors inherited from his father. An equal rental was to be
paid to Elizabeth, Duchess of Norfolk, or her executor:

for and to th'use of the Marriage of Mary and Elizabeth, Doughters to
the forsaid Richard Roos, and of the longest lyvers of theym.[4]

How much longer Richard Roos lived is not stated, nor whether his
wife survived him. They were still alive in January 1493, when they
presented to the rectory of Cranwich.[5] There is an undated, but surely
much earlier letter from Jane Roos, one Michaelmas when she was very
ill, to an unnamed nephew in high place, perhaps an ecclesiastic ('Right
reverent and worshipfull Sir'), anxiously begging his help with her money
affairs, especially her many debts, and with the Toppes money due

---

[1] *Ib.*, I, 11–12.   [2] *Ib.*, I, 10, 11.

[3] In 1575 the arms of Roos, Felbrigg and Heydon were still to be seen in the
east window of St. Andrew's Church, Holt (L. B. Radford, *Hist. of Holt*, 1908,
p. 9).

[4] *Rot. Parl.*, VI, 453b.

[5] Blomefield, *Norfolk*, II, 225.

to her daughter Anne; there is no mention of her Roos husband.[1] Mary Roos was a lady-in-waiting to Elizabeth, consort of Henry VII, and married after 1494 Hugh Denny(s), son of Morris Dennys and Alice Poyntz, and squire of the body to the king. Soon after his death in 1511, she married Sir Giles Capell of Rayne, whose son and grandson both married Manners daughters.[2] Elizabeth's fate I do not know, but it is through her that we get a clue to Sir Richard Roos's reception of his lost namesake nephew. He must have been friendly to him, since in his will of 1481/2 (see below, Ch. II) he left a gold chain to Elizabeth Roos, his [great] niece, dwelling with lady Suffolk. Elizabeth could not then have been more than eleven or twelve years old.

This story of Richard Roos, Esquire, has been told in detail, partly because it has never been told before, but more particularly in order to make clear how different was the course of his life from that which will be traced for his uncle, Sir Richard Roos, the poet. Born in 1429, the nephew was too young to profit by or to contribute to the obvious revival of court literature after the Anjou marriage in 1445; he was then only sixteen. Four years later, as a prisoner, he was cut off from England and English influence and letters from the age of twenty to over thirty. One of the manuscripts important for his uncle's work is dated 1450; the nephew was then newly in captivity. There is nothing in the records of his own time to identify him with the poet, the 'chevalier'. The confusion between them was first created in the mid-nineteenth century, and has become worse confounded; it has continued long enough.

There remain now to be recounted only the lives of the two youngest sons of William, sixth Lord Roos, Sir Robert and Sir Richard Roos. Sir Richard the poet is reserved for a separate chapter. The career of Sir Robert, his nearest brother in age and intimacy, is traced here, together with the lives of his two children.

VI. SIR ROBERT ROOS OF MORE END (c. 1408–48)

Robert Roos was about six years old when his father died in 1414, and he came under the guardianship of the Duke of Exeter, Thomas Beaufort, then Earl of Dorset. He was still only a boy when his two

---

[1] *Rutland Papers*, I, 12–13.

[2] *Vis. of Gloucs.*, 1623, p. 50; D. Warrand, *Hertfordshire Families*, p. 84. An inscribed presentation copy to Mary Roos from Queen Elizabeth and from her mother-in-law, the Lady Margaret Beaufort, was sold at Christie's from the Chatsworth Collection on June 30, 1958; it was de Worde's edition (1494) of Hylton's *Scala Perfeccionis* (*Times Lit. Suppl.*, July 18, 1958).

eldest brothers fell at Baugé; but when Thomas, eighth Lord Roos, was drowned at Paris in 1430, he was a young man of twenty and upwards, and may well have been squire to his brother. His later guardian, Humphrey, Duke of Gloucester, seems to have remained on terms of some intimacy with him, for one of the Duke's French books bears the inscription, 'Cest livre est A moy Homfrey duc de Gloucestre, du don mess. Robert Roos, chevalier, mon cousin'.[1] Yet another manuscript, Royal 19.A.xx, bears the signatures of both men, but here the Duke was probably the first owner, since his name and motto are on fol. 2, 'Mon bien mondain Gloucestre Au duc' (erased); Robert's inscription does not come till fol. 152 v.: 'Ce liure de linformacion des princes est a moy Robert Roos chivaler'. Only the name is autograph. Robert was knighted before May 1433, and the inscriptions must post-date that event.

The first documentary notice of Robert Roos shows that he sued one of his father's executors, William Hoton, for his share of the estate of Thornton in Craven, and of Mapersalfe in Uffington, Lincolnshire. It is a useful document,[2] since it makes clear the order of Lord William's sons, better than did the will itself, and proves that William was indeed the second son. It also confirms that the third part of Lord Roos's 'moeble goods' was to be divided between the three youngest sons, Thomas, Robert, and Richard. There is no date, but the reference to Thomas as having issue proves it to have been written after 1427, when the little heir, Thomas, was born; it may even be later than the elder Thomas's death in 1430. Sir Robert is already a knight. The first known official recognition of his knighthood is his first half-yearly payment (May 1433) as one of the four King's Carvers,[3] together with Sir Edward Hungerford, Sir William and Sir John Beauchamp. They had been appointed not later than October 20, 1432.

In 1433, Sir Robert Roos married a young widow, Anne de Bohun, whose seventy-year-old husband, Sir John de Bohun of Midhurst, had died in January 1432/3, after a brief marriage of three or four years. She was the daughter and heiress of John Halsham, Esquire, of West Grinstead, by his second wife, Maud Mawley.[4] Robert Roos and Anne

---

[1] It is a French translation (now only fragments) of Aegidius Romanus, *De Regimine Principum*, and Vegetius, *De Re Militari*, now Camb. Univ. Lib., MS. Ee.2.17. See Vickers, *Humphrey, Duke of Gloucester*, pp. 417, 435, and P. Meyer in *Romania*, XV, 264–5.　　[2] Early Chanc. Proc., 39/143.

[3] Devon, *Issues*, 421. For the importance of this office, see Nicolas, *Journal of Thomas Beckington*, pp. 109–10.

[4] G.E.C., II, 201. No connexion is known between these Bohuns of Sussex and the great Humphrey de Bohun, Earl of Northampton, father-in-law of Bolingbroke; but Sir John called his heir Humphrey, and this suggests kinship.

had three children, Eleanor, Henry the heir, born in 1439, and John, mentioned in his father's will, but otherwise unknown. Anne Roos long survived her husband, till after 1486, when she was still presenting to the church of Weston Corbett in Hampshire, in a de Bohun manor, which may have been part of her dower.[1]

When next we hear of Sir Robert Roos he is fighting in France. French documents[2] show that on December 5, 1435, he took over from Talbot as Captain of Château Gaillard of which his eldest brother had been the first captain after its recovery under Henry V. Talbot had had a garrison of five 'lances à cheval', ten 'lances à pied', and forty-five archers. In October 1436 Sir Robert was still there, and in June had been given a reinforcement of seven more 'lances à cheval' and three more archers. Whether or not he was obliged to cease from fighting at a still early age we do not know but there is only one further reference to him as a soldier in these military records. For the rest of his life he is active in civil employments, though it is true that on one embassy he saw as much fighting as diplomacy.

In 1439 Henry VI had granted the survey and governance of vert and venison in the Forest of Rutland to Sir Ralphe Cromwel for life; but early in 1440 it was transferred to Sir Robert Roos (or his deputy) equally for life. The deer and game had been much diminished for lack of proper survey.[3] Evidently Sir Ralphe had taken his duties lightly, and evidently Sir Robert fulfilled them well, since in 1442 he was given the much more responsible office of Keeper of Rockingham Forest,[4] that great royal forest, stretching 'between the bridges of Staunford, and the gate of Oxford', and centring in Rockingham Castle, 'the Windsor of the Midlands'. The early Norman and Angevin kings had frequented it, but in the fourteenth and fifteenth centuries royal interest had waned, though the castle itself was later granted to Margaret of Anjou, and passed from her to her successor, Elizabeth Wydville. In 1475, Lord Hastings was its constable, one of the chief opponents of the Roos interest. This care of forests was no new thing to the Roos family; as far back as 1236, an earlier Robert de Ros was appointed 'justicer of the forest' from Nottingham to Northumberland and Cumberland,[5] and Sir Robert's father had been Master Forester of Pickering Forest.[6]

---

[1] V.C.H., *Hampshire*, III, 388.
[2] Bibl. Nat. MSS., Pièces Originales 2541, dossier 56856 (Roos), fol. 2–3.
[3] V.C.H., *Rutland*, I, 255.
[4] *Cal. Pat. Rolls, 1446–52*, p. 217. Cf. Alice Dryden, *Memorials of Old Northamptonshire*, pp. 11, 110; Charles Wise, *Rockingham Castle*, 1891, p. 15.
[5] *Cal. Pat. Rolls, 1232–47*, p. 169.   [6] Wylie, *Henry V*, II, 179–80.

About the same time, Sir Robert began that series of journeys as envoy or ambassador, for which he is chiefly known in English and French records; it was probably with a sense of these services that he was twice nominated (1445 and 1447) for the Garter, though without election.[1] In 1440 together with Lord Fanhope and Garter King, he escorted Charles d'Orléans to Burgundy on his liberation, an event at which Robert's patron, Duke Humphrey, showed his displeasure by remaining aloof on his barge during the farewell ceremonies. The English envoys stayed for the marriage of Charles and Marie de Clèves, and were treated with 'tres grant honneur et joyeuse chiere', and allowed to go abroad at will. They witnessed the jousts in the market-place of St. Omer,[2] and marvelled at the state and splendour of the Duke of Burgundy in the Chapter of the Golden Fleece, when Charles was made a knight of the Order. Fanhope then returned home, but Roos,[3] who was charged with letters to the French king, stayed to accompany the Duke and Duchess on their progress from Burgundy to Paris; he only quitted them when they cautiously decided to avoid the suspicious French king and to make straight for Orléans and Blois.

In 1442 came one of the most interesting episodes in Sir Robert's life, and the one of which we know the most, thanks to the journal[4] kept by a clerk for Thomas Bekynton, secretary to Henry VI, and former Chancellor to the Duke of Gloucester, recounting the journey to Bordeaux, on an embassy to the Count of Armagnac. With Bekynton and Roos were Sir Edward Hull, squire of the king's body, and Nicholas Husee, who was at one time Lieutenant of Guisnes, and was a personal friend of Sir Robert, and later one of his executors. Sir Robert was summoned on June 15 from Basingstoke, and joined Bekynton at Exeter on Sunday morning, June 24; the next day he rode to Powderham, and spent the night with Sir Philip Courtenay. On embarking at Plymouth, he must have witnessed the curious rites with which the future Bishop of Bath invoked the Blessed Virgin's aid for a favouring wind, which promptly came. On July 16 they landed at Bordeaux and found it in a state of siege; the delicate and tortuous dealings with the Count began, complicated by the successful attacks of the French. Henry VI, desiring an alliance with the Count, had demanded faithful portraits of all three of his daughters, 'in their kerttelles simple, and

---

[1] J. Anstis, *Register of the Garter*, II, 128, 133.

[2] Waurin, *Croniques 1431–47* (Rolls ser. 39d), II, 296, 301, livre VI[e].

[3] Monstrelet, *Chronique*, transl. Johnes, III, 310–11.

[4] *Official Correspondence of Thomas Bekynton*, ed. G. Williams (Rolls ser. 56), II, 177 ff.

their visages, lyk as ye see their stature and their beaulte and color of skynne and their countenaunces, with almaner of fetures'. On the Count objecting that he had no craftsman fit for the work, Sir Edward Hull in November brought from England 'vng overir', one Hans the artist, probably a Fleming. Still there were delays; the cold weather 'prevented his colours from working', and only one portrait was finished.

Meanwhile Sir Robert Roos had early been appointed regent or governor of Bordeaux, and found himself as much occupied with defending the town against the French as with diplomatic fencing. A royal letter promised that the Earl of Somerset (John Beaufort) would come with 'right a noble puissaunce of men of werre'; but still the Count prevaricated. Some successful forays did not prevent the general deterioration of the English situation, and in mid-January 1442/3 Bekynton and Roos left Bordeaux, still without the portraits, and promising to return. Charles VII forestalled them, however, and took the Count prisoner. Sir Robert was then employed in negotiations with France. He had already, in May 1441,[1] been sent with John Sutton, Lord Dudley, to France, to open negotiations for peace. In the important embassy that was commissioned (Feb. 22, 1444) to make peace with France, the three leaders, Suffolk, Moleyns, and Sir Robert Roos, are all entitled *Regii Consiliarii*; with them went Sir Thomas Hoo, and John Wenlock, with whom Sir Richard Roos was later to have to do.

Sir Robert seems to have taken part in all the ambassadorial arrangements[2] for the king's marriage with Margaret of Anjou, just as his younger brother was to do on the Escort. He was sent over in August 1444 with letters to the king's 'best beloved wyf the quene',[3] so styled after the proxy betrothal of May 24, 1444, at Tours. In the summer of 1445 he was one of those who with state and ceremony met and escorted the ambassadors of Charles VII on the Rochester road: 'vindrent audevant deux messire Thomas Hou et messire Robert Ros, en grant abillemens de robes et de chevaux harnaches dargent'. Nearer London, the greater men, the Marquess of Suffolk, the Earl of Somerset (Edmund Beaufort), and Lord Scales, rode out to join the cavalcade.[4] In August 1448[5] we find Beaufort, now Duke of Somerset, referring the questions of Valois Herald to Moleyns, and to 'messire Robert Roos, qui avoit plus grant congnoissance du fait des dites treues quil navoit'; but Roos, with Moleyns, was then in Brittany.

[1] Dep. Keeper of the Publ. Records, *48th Report*, p. 347.
[2] Sir Robert Roos's expenses and payments on various journeys are to be found in Exchequer Accounts, 323/25, 26, 27, and 324/8, 9, 13.
[3] Stevenson, *Wars in France*, I, 460.   [4] *Ib.*, I, 154–5.
[5] *Ib.*, I, 213, 215.

Records in France give further details of Sir Robert's activities.[1] In March 1445/6 one of the commissioners appointed to the government of France and Normandy was 'nostre amé et feal cousin Robert Roos chevalier'; the document by a fortunate chance preserves intact his seal quartering the arms of Roos and Badlesmere, and with the Roos crest, the peacock with trailing feathers. On this service he went in February and March 1446/7 on a tour of inspection to Argentan, and thence to Caen, 'pour mettre en regle de bon gouvernement grant nombre de gens d'armes et de trait qui vivoient sur le pays'. He is again styled captain of Gaillard. On May 29 he received 'lettres closes' sent urgently ('hastivement') when he was at Alençon.

All through the spring and summer of 1447/8 he was crossing to France, and in November he took part in the conferences at Vaudreuil. This was his journeyings' end. He must have returned home a sick man, for on December 28, 1448, he made his will,[2] and died two days later. He was spared seeing Rouen yield to the French, and popular fury fall on his associates, on Moleyns, murdered in a year's time (January 1449/50), and on Suffolk in the following May. He might well have shared their fate, as he shared their obloquy in popular rhyme, 'Suffolk, Moleyns, and Roos, thes thre'.

During these years of increasingly successful political service ('grans et honnorables services . . . plusieurs notables et grandes ambassades'), Sir Robert had been stabilizing his private affairs, and trying to safeguard his heir's prospects. As early as 1442 (Feb. 24) he had been allowed to lease Uffington in Lincolnshire during the minority of the fifteen-year-old heir Lord Thomas, with a safeguarding of his younger brother Sir Richard's right to a £20 annuity from the estate, a charge of which Robert was then 'wholly ignorant'.[3] In 1445/6 he was granted, with reversion to his son Henry, the chamberlainship and customs of Berwick-on-Tweed.[4] When he was made Keeper of Rockingham, he and others obtained seisin of some dozen manors,[5] among them that 'fair Benefield' which Drayton was to praise as the jewel of Rockingham:

> A Forest and a Chase in everything so fit
> This Island hardly hath. (*Polyolbion*, xxiii, 322)

Finally in 1446–7, after the embassies to France, he obtained a grant

[1] Bibl. Nat., Pièces Originales 2541, dossier 56, 856 (Roos), fol. 4. *Chronique du Mont Saint Michel*, ed. Siméon Luce, S.A.T.F., Paris, 1879–83. II, Nos. 256, 257.
[2] Lambeth Palace Library, Stafford 170. Printed in *North Country Wills*, No. 28, pp. 49–50 (Surtees Soc., 116).
[3] *Cal. Fine Rolls, 1437–45*, p. 209. [4] *Cal. Pat. Rolls, 1441–46*, pp. 402, 410.
[5] *Cal. Close Rolls, 1441–47*, p. 76.

of the castle and manor of More End, and 'of profits and commodities therefrom, for himself and his heirs, to be held of the Crown by fealty only'.[1] Plainly this was to be his home, pleasantly near the rides of Yardley Chase and Whittlebury Forest, and within easy distance of many country gentry of the Lancastrian interest, the Greenes of Greens Norton, or the Wydvilles of Grafton Regis. But death intervened; and his heir, Henry, had hardly reached his majority when the Yorkist attainder swept his possessions from him. Now at More End no trace of castle or manor remains.

Sir Robert Roos's will, like his father's, shows first his devotion to the Church. Three Northamptonshire foundations received gifts of plate, St. Mary's, Southwick, St. Catherine's, Castor,[2] and especially the Cistercian abbey of Pip(e)well,[3] lying to the north-east of More End. The Roos interest in Pipewell Abbey was probably of long standing, since it lay only some half a dozen miles from Stoke Albany, for long an important manor of the Roos family. The fourteenth-century Lord William had been present at the consecration of its church, St. Mary's,[4] Pipewell, and at Stoke Albany Sir John Roos, 'le bon compagnon', lies buried. The silver cross and candelabra, and the gold and red vestments that Sir Robert left to Pipewell suggest that he had a chapel at More End.

The only fief mentioned in the will is Gayton, in a village not far to the north of More End; this goes to Dame Anne Roos. Sir Robert makes provision for his servants and retainers, for the payment of debts, and finally, with the residue of all his possessions, for the 'sustentation and subvention' of his three children; his wife is given sole charge of them. The names of two of his executors recall Sir Robert's military and political experiences. Nicholas Huse (Hussey) was associated with him in the embassy to Bordeaux, and was a member of Margaret of Anjou's Escort; his name often occurs in Roos business documents; later (1460) he was Lieutenant of Guisnes.[5] John Merbury was probably a kinsman of the more notorious Sir Richard Merbury,

---

[1] Bridges, *Northamptonshire*, I, 319; *Cal. Close Rolls, 1447–54*, p. 391. In the will of Henry VI, of March 12, 1447/8, Sir Robert Roose, Knight, is the thirteenth out of fourteen names of those to have reversionary interest in various castles and lordships (Nicolas, *Test. Vet.*, I, 23).

[2] Now St. Kyneburga's, but with a fourteenth-century fresco of the martyrdom of St. Catherine.

[3] This is the abbey which a contemporary poet, probably Richard Spalding, celebrated in acrostic in a hymn to the Virgin (Carleton Brown, *Rel. Lyrics of the XVth Century*, pp. 56, 304).

[4] V.C.H., *Northamptonshire*, II, 118–19.

[5] G.E.C., VII, 11 note.

formerly captain of Pontoise, who, having married a Frenchwoman, surrendered Gisors in 1450 and became a French subject, in return for the freeing of two of his children, and for the enjoying of his wife's lands.[1] Two further names will recur together later in considering a manuscript, the third executor, Robert Wesenham, a Huntingdonshire neighbour,[2] and Robert Lathbury, one of the witnesses (see below, Chapter III). Anne, widow of 'the King's Knight, tenant in chief', was granted the wardship and marriage of her son, and the keeping of Rockingham Castle, lordship and forest during his minority. In this the experience of William Austyn, who was added to her advisers, would be useful, since he was Keeper of Moulton Park.[3] It is noticeable that Sir Richard Roos, the one surviving Roos uncle, was not appointed guardian or executor, but during the 1450s and again at his death he was in touch with Henry and Eleanor. Their course can be traced with some continuity, though not always in detail. With that kindness which the Lancastrian royal house always showed—and rightly—to the Roos family, Margaret of Anjou soon attached the two young people people to her Household. Their names occur in a list of 1452–3, Henry as *armiger*, and Alienora Roos as *dauncell dñe Regine*,[4] and in the next year they received gifts. Henry had been at the court as a boy, probably with his father, in 1446–7 and 1447–8, and had been given a bracelet and a brooch.[5] Presumably their home was at More End when they were not at court.

VII. SIR HENRY ROOS OF ROCKINGHAM (1439–1504)

With the beginning of the civil war, Sir Henry was in the fighting and was at Towton in Yorkshire on Palm Sunday, 1461.[6] For that he was forthwith attainted together with Lord Roos, his cousin, and with him went north to Scotland.[7]

The best that we know of Sir Henry is his long adherence to Margaret of Anjou in her exile and misery; he was with her at Sluys, and with the poverty-struck band of exiles whose privations were described by Sir John Fortescue.[8] He fought at Tewkesbury in 1471 and was reported

[1] Stevenson, *Wars in France*, II, 622; Waurin, Rolls ser. 39, V, 138.
[2] *Visitation of Huntingdon*, *1613*, *s.n.* Cotton (Camden Soc., No. 43).
[3] *Cal. Pat. Rolls*, *1446–52*, pp. 216, 217.
[4] Duchy of Lancaster Accounts, Various 5 (Sept. 1452–Sept. 1453).
[5] Jewels Accounts, E.101.409/14, 17; 410/11.
[6] Cotton, *Abridgement*, etc., 1657, p. 671, item. 671.
[7] Stevenson, *Wars in France*, II, ii, 778, 781.
[8] 'Lord Clermont', *Hist. of the House of Fortescue*, I, 21, 24.

D

killed, but was spared after the battle by a special petition;[1] it is not surprising to find him pardoned and restored in blood and lands, in the next year, 1472–3.[2] His mother and sister were still alive, and Eleanor's Yorkist connexions through her husbands may have been a help to him. He was later made useful in musters and commissions.[3] His uncle Sir Richard's legacy to him, in March 1482, of the collar of the king's livery, shows him to have accepted Edward's favour.

Some time after 1480 we find Sir Henry Roos married, and after 1495 settled in West Grenstead, where he inherited manors from his kinswoman on his mother's side, Joan Lewknor, *née* Halsham.[4] His wife Maud was already twice a widow; John Harbord (Herberd), Esquire, had left her with two daughters, Anne or Johanne and Maud, and a son, Thomas.[5] Her second husband, Richard Gorges, was a son of Sir Theobald Gorges of Wraxall, Somerset, and of his second wife, Joan Beauchamp of Lillesden, and had lands in Horsington and Sturminster. He died in 1480, leaving Maud with a son aged eight, Marmaduke Gorges.[6] Sir Henry thus inherited two families of stepchildren, with some of whom he had legal quarrels. In 1500 his stepdaughter Anne (Joan) and her husband, John Stepneth, sued him and his wife for refusing to pay her father's legacy of £20.[7] Dame Maud may have been the offender; after Sir Henry's death in 1504, her two Gorges granddaughters, Elizabeth and Maud, sued her for detaining the deeds of Horsington manor in Somerset, and for allowing their West Grenstead messuage to fall into dilapidation.[8] Similarly earlier, one William Morgan had complained that Sir Henry and Dame Maud had so per-

---

[1] 'Lord Clermont', *Hist. of the House of Fortescue*, I, 21, 24, 38.

[2] *Rot. Parl.*, VI, 25.

[3] *Cal. Pat. Rolls, 1467–77*, p. 551; *ib., 1476–85*, pp. 397, 447, 489, 575.

[4] *Cal. of Inquisitions, Henry VII*, I, 461. Cf. G. C. Elwes, *Castles (etc.) of West Sussex*, 284. The *Shropshire Visitation for 1623*, p. 105, gives to Margaret Touchet, widow of Sir Richard Grey, Lord Powys (died 1466), and of Sir Roger Vaughan, and possibly of Lord Berkeley, a third or fourth husband, *Dominus Henricus Roos*. No other allusion has been found, and this marriage is not accepted (G.E.C., VI, 140). But if the dates allow it (and she died before Feb. 2, 1480/1), there is nothing inherently improbable in it. Richard Grey and Henry Roos were nearly the same age; Margaret was a step-niece of Sir Robert Roos, through her stepmother, Margaret, *née* Roos. Sir Henry and she were therefore step-cousins. And her mother-in-law, Antigone Grey, Lady Powys, had been long acquainted with Sir Richard Roos (see below, Chapter V).

[5] *Sussex Rec. Soc.*, LXII, 236 (Will of Dame Maud Roos).

[6] *Ib.*, XIV, 104 (*I.p.m.* of Marmaduke Gorge); and Phelps, *Hist. of Mod. Somerset*, I, 315.

[7] Early Chanc. Proc., IV, 245/79–81.

[8] *Ib.*, 136/7. Cf. *State Papers of Henry VIII, For. and Dom.*, I, 321, Items 546–51.

sistently refused the evidence on his lands at Chepstow and on the marches of Wales that he did not even know how many deeds there were, or whether they were in 'bagge, boxe, or chest'. Further, Dame Maud, though having only the use of the freehold, had made 'voluntarie wast in plukking down of a barn' to sell the timber and stonework; worst of all, she had sold 'a mill and its grinding stones'.[1] Perhaps it was with an uneasy conscience, and in a restitutionary mood, that Sir Henry in his will left handsome legacies to his stepchildren, and that Dame Maud in her turn in 1511 made gifts to the Gray Friars of Chichester, and to the Friars of Sele Priory.[2]

Sir Henry Roos's will,[3] dated October 1, 1504, is chiefly concerned with the gifts of money to the Herberd girls (£40 and £20), and of land to Marmaduke 'Georg', the manor of Griffens in West Grenstead, and of Slotthouse in Slaugham. Others go to his wife, 'Bowbers' in West Grenstead (presumably their own residence), and Nuntham in Horsham. Only one new friend appears, Magister Gerard Burrell,[4] the well-known archdeacon of Chichester, who gets a small parchment missal; only one possible echo sounds from the past in John Horneby, who is given the manor of Gretefullowes in West Grenstead. A Peter Horneby had been in the retinue of Thomas, eighth Lord Roos, in February 1426/7;[5] this John may be a descendant, a retainer still attached to the Roos interest.

After the accession of Henry VII, Sir Henry was not fully restored to his former rights. His emoluments from Berwick went to Robert Clifford,[6] and Rockingham never came back into his hands. But he had some useful appointments as commissioner for the census of arms issued to Sussex in 1488, together with his Lewknor cousins, and in the next year as commissioner of the peace, and of oyer and terminer, and again as late as 1503.[7] He put in an occasional appearance at court, in 1488 at the coronation of Elizabeth,[8] in 1494 for the creation of Prince Henry as Duke of York, though he did not take part in the jousts,[9] and as late as 1502 at the betrothal of Princess Margaret Tudor to James IV of Scotland.[10] In 1486 his family ties had been recognized by making him, with Sir Thomas de Burgh, surveyor and steward of the lands of

---

[1] Early Chanc. Proc., 215/29.   [2] *Sussex Rec. Soc.*, XLI, 114 and 364.

[3] P.C.C. Wills, Holgrave 15.

[4] See J. H. Cooper in *Sussex Archaeolog. Collections*, XLIII, 1 ff.

[5] Dep. Keeper of the Publ. Rec., *48th Report*, 246.

[6] *Materials for a History of Henry VII* (Rolls ser., 60), I, 388.

[7] *Ib.*, II, 387, 477. *Rot. Parl.*, VI, 541.

[8] Leland, *Collectanea*, ed. T. Hearne, 1774, IV, 231.

[9] *Letters and Papers, Richard III to Henry VII* (Rolls ser., 24), I, 403, and App.

[10] Leland, *op. cit.*, IV, 260.

Edmund, Lord Roos;[1] this was part of the process of restitution. There is no sign in his will, or in any other transaction, that he had kept up with his sister Eleanor, or with the Haute family.

VIII. ELEANOR ROOS

Eleanor Roos, only daughter of Sir Robert Roos of More End, may well have been older than her brother Henry, who was not born till six years after his father's marriage. She must be distinguished from others of her name in the century; from Alienora Roos of Ingmanthorpe who died in 1438;[2] especially from Alienora Roos, her elder second cousin, daughter of Sir Robert Roos of Hunmanby, who had a dispensation to marry (1448) Humphrey Sutton, son of John, Lord Dudley;[3] and from her younger second cousin, daughter of the last Lord Thomas Roos, who married Sir Robert Manners of Etall, and was finally heir to Belvoir and the title.

After her father's death, Eleanor was *domicella* to Margaret of Anjou, certainly in 1452–3, and again in 1453–4, and probably continued at court till her first marriage to Robert Lovell,[4] son of William, Lord Lovell, and brother of William Lovell, Lord Morley in right of his wife Eleanor, Lady Morley. This marriage was evidently a family arrangement, since Eleanor Morley was the daughter of Elizabeth Roos (elder sister of Sir Robert), the fruit of her brief three months marriage with Robert, Lord Morley.[5] Hence two cousins of Roos descent, Eleanor Morley and Eleanor Roos, married two Lovell brothers; between bride and groom there may have been some discrepancy in age.

Probably the first marriage was by family council, and the second by Eleanor's own, perhaps wilful, choice. By 1466–7 she had married Thomas Prout, the 'king's squire', the king being now Edward IV. The pair were involved in Chancery suits with Lord Morley and the other brothers of Robert Lovell, concerning Eleanor's rights in manors in Northamptonshire, Hertfordshire and Wiltshire. It looks as if the marriage had taken place some little time previously, since Thomas and

---

[1] *Materials for . . . Henry VII*, I, 388.

[2] *Test. Ebor.*, II, 65, No. 49.

[3] *Ib.*, III, 330. See below, No. 83 (f).

[4] William, Lord Lovell died between June 5 and Sept. 1, 1455. His third son Robert is not described in his will as having issue. Probably the marriage took place soon after Lord Lovell's death (*Early Lincoln Wills*, ed. A. Gibbons, 1888, p. 186).

[5] G.E.C., IX, 219. Robert Morley's wardship and marriage had been granted in 1436 to Edmund Beaufort, Count of Mortain, the second husband of Elizabeth Roos's sister-in-law.

Eleanor had required the lands of the defendants 'often tymes sethyn the espousell had betwen them'; it also looks as if they may have married secretly, since the Lovells speak of 'the comynycacion of the saide mariage had'.[1] It is not clear whether this Thomas Prout is the same as the Thomas Prud who was sheriff of Oxfordshire and Berkshire in 1470.[2] There were Proutes in Kent,[3] and Pruddes of Bradden, Northamptonshire, Roos land, not very far from More End.[4] But documents show Thomas Prout, the king's servant, petitioning for the lordship of Cradley, holding lands of the king at Hagley, both in Worcestershire, and dying in 1474, when the Hagley lands reverted to the king.[5] The coincidence of this date with that of Eleanor's remarriage is significant. Her third alliance was both the most influential and also the most interesting.

On July 3, 1474, Edward IV made a grant for life to Richard Haute the younger, Esquire, and to Eleanor his wife, the daughter of Sir Robert Roos, of the manors of Ravensthorp and Boltby in Yorkshire, forfeited by Thomas, Lord Roos.[6] This control regained over some of the former Roos estates is an interesting example of the conciliatory policy of Edward IV after the decisive battle of Tewkesbury. During his reign Eleanor's course is set fair, and she has entered the temporarily powerful circle of the Wydville connexion. Richard Haute was a son of Sir William Haute and of Joan Wydville, the queen's aunt; he was therefore a first cousin of the queen and of her brother Anthony, Earl Rivers.[7] Eleanor herself could claim a distant connexion with the queen's first husband, for Sir John Grey's grandmother was a Margaret Roos, sister of William, sixth Lord Roos, Eleanor's grandfather.[8] We know a little of Richard Haute's doings in this decade. In 1475, when the long haggling between Edward IV and Louis XI over Margaret of Anjou's ransom came to an end, and she was sent over to France, Richard Haute was her escort to conduct her to the coast at Sandwich.[9] Did his wife, we wonder, have any intercourse with her former royal mistress? She was after all a daughter of the loyal house of Roos. She certainly would be a spectator when her husband won honours at the

---

[1] Early Chanc. Proc., C1.31/254; 33/74–84; 38/248. (Cf. Inquiry of 1468, facs. in J. R. Scott, *Scott of Scot's Hall*, p. 142.)

[2] *Ib.*, 64/4.

[3] Hasted's *Kent*, II, 815.   [4] Baker, *Northamptonshire*, II, 37.

[5] *Cal. Pat. Rolls, 1467–77*, Feb. 10, 1474, p. 419. V.C.H., *Worcestershire*, III, 133.

[6] *Cal. Pat. Rolls, 1467–77*, p. 460.   [7] Baker, *Northamptonshire*, II, 166.

[8] Nichols, *Leicestershire*, III, ii, 682 and 662 (for William there read Thomas, Lord Roos); cf. G.E.C., *Complete Peerage*, VI, 157–8.

[9] Scofield, *Edward IV*, II, 158.

grand jousts held for the marriage of the two tiny children, Richard, Duke of York, and Anne of Norfolk. Richard Haute 'came into the feild horsed and armed', and his horse was 'trapped in blew and murrey enramplished with roses of silver in suns of gold', Yorkist emblems; he won the prize for tilting in 'Osting Harnesse', an E of gold set with a ruby.[1]

Early in 1482, Eleanor's last link but one with her father's generation was broken. Sir Richard Roos died, and left her a jewel and a small piece of plate:

Also I biqueth to Alianore hawte my Nece, suster of the saide sir henry Roos, my litle Roos of golde sett and garnysshed with a Ruby and viij perles and my litle potte of siluer and parcell gilte withoute foote and coueryng.

His third gift still survives:

my grete booke called saint Grall bounde in boordes couerde with rede leder and plated with plates of laten.

Eleanor wrote her signature in it in a large sprawling hand, 'Thys boke is myne dame Alyanor Haute'; later she presented it to the queen (who also wrote her name), and thereby probably ensured its preservation in the Royal Library, intact, but shorn of its red leather and pewter plating, still one of the best known manuscripts of the Grail legend.[2] Evidently Eleanor Haute and Henry Roos had kept in touch with Sir Richard Roos and his wife.

In 1482, exchanging jousting for real fighting, Richard Haute accompanied Richard, Duke of Gloucester, on the expedition to Scotland; on St. James's Eve he received knighthood there from the Duke[3]— ironically enough, for it was through Gloucester that he came suddenly to his end. On the death of Edward IV, he had reached his highest responsibility and honour, Treasurer of the Household to the boy king Edward V, and steward of Gowerslands during the minority of the little Duke of York.[4] The swift *coup* in the early summer of 1483 by which Gloucester seized the person of the king, took prisoner his guardians, Anthony, Lord Rivers, Sir Thomas Vaughan, and Sir Richard Haute, charged them with treason, and had them beheaded forthwith at Pomfret, 'guiltles, god wot'—all this is matter of history.[5] What Eleanor did after her husband's taking-off, and during the brief reign

---

[1] *Narrative of the Marriage*, etc., ed. W. H. Black, Roxburghe Club, 56, pp. 28, 35, 40.
[2] See below, Chapter II.   [3] Shaw, *Knights of England*, II, 18.
[4] *Cal. Pat. Rolls, 1476–85*, p. 288.
[5] *The Great Chronicle of London*, ed. A. H. Thomas and I. D. Thornley, pp. 232, 435–6; Ramsay, *Lancaster & York*, II, 479, 492.

of Richard III, we do not know; perhaps she took refuge with her brother, more probably with her mother. She survived to re-appear in the court of Henry VII, like her brother; among the ladies present at the christening in 1486 of Prince Arthur was 'my Lady Dame Elyonor Haut'.[1] The young Sir Richard Haute who also appears at court early in the reign of Henry VII may have been a step-son of Eleanor; he could have hardly been her son.[2] Already in mid-1486 he is a knight, one of the king's Carvers, and is being rewarded with a £40 annuity out of lands in Lincolnshire for 'true and faithful service to the king'.[3] He accompanied Henry on his first progress to York and the North,[4] and was at Kenilworth with him when news came of Lambert Simnel's landing; there is an oddly sporting air about the description of the royal force setting out to meet the rebels:[5]

Sir Richard Haut, with many other Galants of the Kings Howse wer the For Ryders, and also the Wyng of the Right Hand of the Fowarde.

Sir Richard was equally in evidence at great functions, and was with the court at Christmas, Easter, and Hallowe'en festivals at Sheen and Westminster, at Hertford and Windsor.[6] He was one of the four knights who at the queen's coronation in 1486 bore her canopy 'from Mark Lane to Grasshe Chirche'.[7] He was at Princess Mary's christening;[8] and in 1492 he rode to meet the French ambassadors coming to make peace.[9] He married Katherine Boston, twice a widow; they both died in 1493.[10] He is not called a 'king's knight', but, as will be seen, his duties and activities at court, and his doings in the field, are very like those of Eleanor Haute's uncle, Sir Richard Roos.

This account of the family of Roos of Hamlake and Belvoir, even for

---

[1] Leland's *Collectanea*, ed. Hearne, 1774, IV, 206.

[2] Three Richard Hautes of this period are difficult to disentangle: (*a*) Richard Haute, Esquire, Senior, who married Eleanor D'Arcy, *née* Tyrrell of Heron, and died in 1487 (*I.p.m. Henry VII*, I, no. 373). His heir Edward Haute married Elizabeth Frogenall, and died in 1537; (*b*) Richard Haute, Esquire, Junior, later Sir Richard Haute, who married Eleanor Roos, and was beheaded at Pontefract in June 1483; (*c*) Sir Richard Haute, the younger, as above, whose wife Katherine Boston was the widow of Walter Writtell (d. 1473), and of John Grene (d. 1485/6). The *Visitation of Kent* started the confusion by ignoring the Roos marriage, and marrying the widow D'Arcy to the victim of Richard III (Harleian Soc., 42, p. 213).

[3] *Materials for a history of Henry VII* (Rolls ser., 60), I, 454.

[4] Leland, *op. cit.*, IV, 186.   [5] *Ib.*, IV, 210.

[6] *Ib.*, IV, 243, 246.   [7] *Ib.*, IV, 221-3.

[8] *Ib.*, p. 255.

[9] *Letters & Papers, Richard III & Henry VII* (Rolls ser., 24), II, 291.

[10] *Cal. of Inquisitions, Henry VII*, I, Nos. 895, 86, 152, 50. Cf. *Genealogist*, New Ser. 4 (1887), p. 203.

one century only, has involved much detail and the introduction of many subsidiary persons. Yet so close-knit was this Lancastrian party, the fighting knights, the great nobles, the court, the royal Household, and the civil functionaries, that it will be found that few names have been mentioned which have not some bearing on the life, or some significance for the poetry, of Sir Richard Roos. To us now, who lack intimate letters and memoirs, they may remain as flat as figures in a tapestry or fresco; but to the poet this was his living, active background, the men and women who with others even more important moved around him giving him love, or good will, or indifference, who intervened in his doings, and affected his whole chequered course of life.

CHAPTER II

Sir Richard Roos (c. 1410–81/2): Gloucester's Man and King's Knight

T HE life of Sir Richard Roos, fifth and youngest son of William, sixth Lord Roos, and of Margaret Arundel, falls easily into four periods: his childhood and boyhood; his early manhood, from about 1430 to 1442, when he was under the patronage of Humphrey, Duke of Gloucester; his middle years, when he was a King's Knight, and saw service at court from 1442 to about 1460; and his last twenty or so years of life to his death at the end of March 1482.

Of the first period nothing personal is ascertained, and we can only set him against the background of his family's doings. The exact date of his birth is not recorded; it was probably about 1410,[1] so that he was still a little boy when his father died in September 1414.

His father's will of February 1412/13 made provision for the education and upbringing of the three youngest sons, Thomas, Robert, and Richard; but Richard was too small to benefit yet by the chantry chaplain's instructions in 'discipline and grammar'. He almost certainly remained for some years in the care of his mother who never remarried; and this would entail staying with her at Helmsley in Yorkshire since it seems to have been used as the dower-house of the Roos ladies. Life probably ran a similar course for him, with his mother and her ladies, whichever of the family's two Norman castles he lived in. But in Yorkshire he had a different countryside around him, a country not of hill and fen, but of moor and dale and 'holtes hore' and he would hear

---

[1] Thoma s, the third son, was born in late September 1406 *Yks. Arch. Soc.*, 59, 174 ff. *I.p.m.* of John, Lord Roos); Richard was born before Feb. 1412/13. In the intervening six and a half years, Robert was born, and perhaps others (daughter; or infant not surviving). The central point in this period, 1410, is a useful approximation.

a different speech on the lips of the peasants and yeomen, and of the men-at-arms of local stock, different sounds and forms and words.

His childish mind was all too soon made familiar with the fact of death and with its pomps and ceremonies. His father's funeral may have been one of his earliest memories, and on revisiting Belvoir, probably yearly, he would see the fine alabaster monument erected to him.[1] He may have been at Helmsley when his grandmother, Lady Beatrice, died there in May 1415; but there is no mention of her grandchildren in her will, nor any proof of familiarity with them. Probably soon after his seventh birthday he returned to Belvoir to benefit by the chantry priest's tuition, in company with his next two brothers, Thomas and Robert. Lessons were learnt against the excitement of his eldest brothers Sir John and William going with the king to fight, at Agincourt, and at the siege of Rouen with the family's guardian, the Duke of Exeter. Young Richard would hear the news, as it was brought back by personal messengers, of Sir John becoming Marshal, and Lord of Bacqueville, and later Captain of Château Gaillard, and of William being knighted by the Duke of Clarence before the walls of Angers.

The news suddenly altered, and the boy of eleven must have felt the shock of insecurity and change when tidings came that his two brothers had died fighting at the battle of Baugé (1421), trying first to save the life of the Duke of Clarence and then to avenge his death. He would be there when Sir John's body was brought home to be laid beside their father's; he would see his mother's grief. Then would come the change in Thomas's status, Thomas his fellow-pupil who was to have been the *clericus* of the family; now he had to fit himself quickly to become the head of a fighting race, and in five years' time he was knighted, and then went out to France with the Duke of Bedford. It is possible that Richard was now cast for the clerkly rôle that Thomas had had to relinquish.

One event, probably about 1423, broke the tenor of his days. The completion and dedication of the great St. William window in York Minster which was given in memory of William, Lord Roos, would bring a family gathering, at which probably the Roos's of Ingmanthorpe joined the Roos's of Belvoir. It would be an occasion of ecclesiastical ceremony, mingling the glowing colours of the glass above, and of the vestments and banners below; an occasion too of both family pride and sadness: pride in the array of kneeling figures, the eldest sons in armour under their heraldic mantles, the youngest with dagger and belt and with the marks of cadency; but sadness at premature loss, so that

---

[1] Now in Bottesford Church; see A. Gardner, *Alabaster Tombs of the Pre-Reformation Period*, Camb. 1940, Plate 204, also Plates 20 and 175.

the window had become a memorial to three of the Roos men and not to one alone. Richard's own kneeling image is portrayed with his next brother Robert, with surely the intention at least of true likenesses, his aquiline features very different from Robert's round and boyish face.

The next family excitement would be his brother Thomas's marriage after 1423 to Eleanor Beauchamp; and one must believe that this girl, impulsive and quick-witted, as Thomas Basin later depicts her, made a difference in the predominantly masculine life of Belvoir. It certainly brought the Roos's into closer contact with that picturesque and striking figure, Eleanor's father, Richard Beauchamp, Earl of Warwick; probably he was godfather to Thomas and Eleanor's second son, little Richard. This is the Earl who became almost a figure of legend to his time, as the last of the English knights errant. Malory's master, he may be perpetuated for us as Beaumains. He jousted his way across Europe with heralds going before, and issued challenges to Christian and pagan, and sought out 'pas d'armes', like Jacques de Lalain of a younger generation.

Whether Robert and Richard served their brother Thomas, the head of the house, as pages and then squires, is not recorded, but it is very probable. If so, they may have been with him when as a young knight he went to Rouen in 1427 in the Duke of Bedford's train, and again when he accompanied the little king to Calais in April 1430. They may even have taken part in Lord Roos's entry with music into Paris, and in the ill-fated *sortie* of two days later, when their brother was swept down in the waters of the Marne.

Be this as it may, 1430 ended a period in Richard Roos's life, a period in which we can see him only through and in his family. Robert and he were the only sons left to his widowed mother; but there was the baby head of the house to be trained up, and Belvoir and Helmsley would still be his family background. In the thirties, however, documentary evidence begins to reveal him moving independently in a wider world. No provision had been made by his father for his later sustenance, and he had his way to make. For the next decade he fights, and writes poetry, and makes love.

A document among French records shows Sir Richard Roos, chevalier, on garrison duty in France at Gisors. This was under the great Talbot in December 1436,[1] and Sir Robert was not far away, captain in his turn of Château Gaillard. The younger brother is only a 'lance à cheval', but he is already a knight, and this presupposes some

---

[1] *Chronique de Mathieu d'Escouchy*, ed. G. du Fresne de Beaucourt (1863), II, 555. Cf. Stevenson, *Wars of the English in France* (Rolls, 22), II, 283.

experience in arms. There is no record of his knighting in England; probably the accolade was given him on the field, as Clarence had conferred it on his brother William before Angers, and as his nephew, Thomas, Lord Roos, was to give it to Sir Thomas Babthorpe after the battle of Wakefield.[1] To serve directly under Talbot was an honour for a young knight, and we remember that Talbot's wife, Margaret Beauchamp, was Eleanor Roos's elder sister.

Gisors, the capital of the Vexin, in the 'Pays de Conquête', was a notable feudal fortress to be stationed in. The castle, with its spacious *enceinte*, had been largely built by the English Angevin kings. Two donjons dominated the castle and the town, one within, of English building, the other without, added by King Philippe Auguste, after Richard Cœur de Lion had ceded him the town. A gilded statue of the Blessed Virgin stood at the head of the bridge over the river Epte, and is still to be seen in the town.[2]

How long Sir Richard Roos was kept at Gisors is not known. By May 1439 Talbot had reduced the 'lances à cheval' there from 40 to 15, as sufficient for its 'safe custody'; yet the 'lances à pied' and the archers remained the same.[3] Sir Richard may have been moved elsewhere; but he is not recorded as captain of a town. Certainly he was at times in England, and was benefiting from the interest shown in him by Humphrey, Duke of Gloucester. His mother, Margaret Roos, died in 1438, on July 3,[4] and on August 11, at the instance of the Duke, Sir Richard was granted a £20 annuity out of the family property of Uffington in Lincolnshire,[5] a fact which he did not disclose to his elder brother, Sir Robert. In the next year (Oct. 21, 1439) Sir Richard and three others were enfeoffed by the Duke of manors in Penshurst, Kent.[6]

All this may have sprung from pure benevolence on Gloucester's part; after all he had mulcted the Roos estates of 1000 marks annually as guardian.[7] But there is another possible explanation, and for this one must look back a few years into the Duke's history. His desertion in 1428 of Jacqueline of Hainault, and his marriage with his mistress, Eleanor Cobham, step-cousin of Sir Richard, had brought him to the nadir of his repute. But by 1431, in spite of his perpetual strife with Cardinal Beaufort, he had regained sufficient prestige and influence to

---

[1] W. C. Metcalfe, *A Book of Knights*, p. 2.

[2] *Soc. Hist. de Pontoise et du Vexin*, VII, 53.

[3] Stevenson, *op. cit.*, II, 302–3.

[4] Her whole will is not in print, but only the portion that relates to Belvoir Priory (Nichols, *Leicestershire*, II, i, App. p. 19, No. 69).

[5] *Cal. Pat. Rolls, 1436–41*, p. 185.

[6] *Ib.*, p. 386.

[7] Rymer, *Foedera*, X, 268.

get his salary as Regent raised, at the instance of Lord Scrope, and early in 1432 he was strong enough to dismiss officials who were against him, and to put his own men in their places. Thus Lord Scrope became Treasurer; Sir William Phelip, Lord Bardolf, took Lord Cromwell's place as Lord Chamberlain; and Sir Robert Babthorpe Lord Tiptoft's as Steward of the Household.[1] In the next year the Duke began to transform into a palace the manor at Greenwich, which had been the home of Thomas Beaufort, Duke of Exeter, and which Duke Humphrey had acquired by 1429. His frequent visits to it (and thence to Penshurst) show that it was his favourite abode, his Plesaunce.[2] Humphrey's influence with the young king was considerable, and the Duchess's was increasing; in 1436 she was given official recognition by being sent her Garter robes for St. George's Day.[3] Bedford's death in 1435 left Duke Humphrey as the leader of the war party against the increasingly pacific policy of the rising man, the Duke of Suffolk. Duke Humphrey's military expedition to Calais in 1436 against the Duke of Burgundy greatly heightened his prestige, though the work had been done before his arrival by Edmund Beaufort, Count of Mortain, and Richard Beauchamp, Earl of Warwick.[4]

In November 1436 Gloucester contrived to get that bone of contention between the two parties, Charles d'Orléans, transferred to Stirborough Castle into the charge of his father-in-law, Reginald, Lord Cobham, and away from Suffolk's care; there Charles was kept for eighteen months, till July 1438.[5] And here comes the possible explanation of the Duke's favours to Sir Richard. When one observes that two of Sir Richard's co-feoffees at Penshurst were Sir Reginald Cobham and Sir Thomas Cobham, one cannot help wondering whether these enfeoffments were the reward for services to Gloucester in connexion with Charles d'Orléans. In 1440 Sir Robert Roos was one of the three escorts of Charles on his liberation and it is possible that Sir Richard was in attendance with his brother.[6] It may have been in connexion with this new property at Penshurst that he went there some time between 1435 and 1439: Sir Richard Roos, reports the Keeper, '*nuper hospitatus fuit*' in the 'Cornertowre', which now needs repairs.[7]

The first check to Gloucester's policy came in this liberation of

---

[1] Ramsay, *Lancaster & York*, I, 439.

[2] *Cal. Pat. Rolls, 1429–36*, pp. 240, 250. For a full history of Plesaunce, see Hasted's *Kent*, I, 53–6.   [3] Vickers, *Humphrey, Duke of Gloucester*, p. 248.

[4] Ramsay, *op. cit.*, I, 484–8.

[5] Steele, *Engl. Poems of Charles Orleans*, 1941, p. xiii.

[6] See above, Chapter I.

[7] *Manuscripts of Lord De L'Isle & Dudley* (Hist. MSS. Comm.), I, 234.

Charles d'Orléans, of which he utterly disapproved. The next year, 1441, brought him a more bitter blow, in the accusation and trial of the Duchess, for sorcery and for attempts on the life of the young king. The miserable affair dragged on for four months, and culminated in three days of public penance through the streets of London.[1] Then Eleanor Cobham, stripped of her honours, and with her marriage dissolved, passed to imprisonment for life, chiefly in the towering sea fortress of Holm Peel; she outlived her husband, whose dark star she had been,[2] and died in 1454.[3] The Duke withdrew more and more from public affairs, and occupied himself with learning and literature.

Whether or not this withdrawal helped to bring about the change traceable in Sir Richard Roos's course of life, we do not know. The patronage of Gloucester, and his kinship with the Duchess, and, one may assume, his own talents, must have given him the entrée to that centre of elegant and cultured living, Plesaunce. It was there, as I hope to show later, that his early poems were produced, and for that circle chiefly that he began to write. Plesaunce was not, however, Roos's exclusive subject, since he wrote several poems for his sister-in-law Eleanor and her second suitor, Edmund Beaufort, poems which show a long connexion in friendliness. But neither that, nor his brother Robert's marriage in 1433, nor his mother's death in 1438, so often inspired him to poetry as did his devotion to a girl of the Plesaunce circle, Elizabeth Phelip, only child of that Lord Bardolf whom Gloucester had made Lord Chamberlain. There is no documentary evidence of this; the unsuccessful courtship of a younger son, his hopeless worship *par amours* of a lady who for him is Bounty and Beauty, is seldom documented; it does not get into the lawyer's hands for marriage settlements. The evidence lies in the poems themselves, as will be seen. Equally in the poems we find two of his sympathetic confidantes in this love-affair, Ismania Scales, wife of Thomas, Lord Scales, and Margaret Stanlow, wife of John Stanlow, treasurer of the finances in France. Both later were members of Queen Margaret's Escort, and of her Household. Both, through a long connexion of nearly thirty years, were celebrated by Roos as women of character, kindness, and grace. Elizabeth Phelip married, about 1433–4,[4] Sir Richard's brilliantly suc-

---

[1] Ramsay, *Lancaster & York*, II, 31–5; Vickers, *Humphrey, Duke of Gloucester*, 269–79.

[2] The Cobham arms were 'Gules, on a Chevron or, three Estoiles sable'.

[3] G.E.C., *Complete Peerage*, V, 736.

[4] Her eldest son, Henry Beaumont, who died *vita patris*, was seven years old and more in Oct. to Nov. 1441, according to the *I.p.m.* of her father, Lord Bardolf (G.E.C., *Complete Peerage*, I, 421, note C).

cessful kinsman of his own age, John Beaumont, soon to be created Viscount Beaumont. In 1441, before October 30, and in the year of the Duchess of Gloucester's trial, Elizabeth Beaumont died. Thus two links of the Plesaunce chain snapped for Sir Richard by the autumn of 1441. He paid his tribute, I believe, to the Duke and Duchess, in grave and moving laments and in one of his few religious poems. It was probably a relief for him to turn his back on Plesaunce, and to take up new duties, even though he left youth and early manhood behind him.

We first find Sir Richard called the King's Knight in a document of February 24, 1442, a patent which gives Uffington in Lincolnshire to Sir Robert Roos during the minority of young Thomas, Lord Roos, but safeguards Sir Richard's annuity from it.[1] The duties of King's Knights do not seem to be clearly defined; originally they were selected as eminent fighting men, fit for responsible posts such as captains of Norman fortresses. But by this time, they appear to partake also of the character of the chamber-knights whom Sir Simon Burley organized for Richard II. They are now also a personal bodyguard, 'a special reserve of the court party', always to be trusted to further the wishes of the sovereign, professional leaders of the Household.[2] For such work Sir Richard, scion of a house of undeviating Lancastrian loyalty, was apt and capable. I have not found further record of him on military service; it is possible that he may have been disabled, for he could hardly be considered too old in his early thirties; more probably it was desired to use his special talents for the young king. For some two and a half years, while his brother, Sir Robert, was making his reputation as an ambassador, there is no sign of Sir Richard's doings. I suspect that in the comparatively dull court of the pious young king he found the days hang heavy, and turned more to the craft and practice of poetry; I would assign to this period some of his translations from the French, and some adaptation of earlier poetry.

In 1444, an event of importance for the king and the nation affected Sir Richard directly—the marriage of Henry VI with Margaret of Anjou, which Suffolk, Molins, and Sir Robert Roos had laboured to bring about. In November 1444 a great train of English notables went to France to witness the proxy wedding, to provide a retinue for the bride, and to escort her to England; it passed through Cheapside, and so went over the sea 'in the moste riall astate that myght be . . . with newe chares and Palfrayes'.[3] Leading the expedition were the Marquess of

---

[1] *Cal. Fine Rolls, 1437–45*, p. 209.
[2] Tout, quoted by A. Steel, *Richard II*, p. 114; cf. pp. 128, 220–1.
[3] Caxton, *The Chronicle of England*, ch. 252 A.

Suffolk, and his lady, *née* Alice Chaucer. Among the forty-six names of those under them in due order of rank,[1] some may be signalized. The peers were Thomas, eighth Lord Clifford, a second cousin of Sir Richard Roos;[2] Ralph, Lord Greystoke (Clifford's cousin), and James Butler, Earl of Ormond. A dowager peeress, Beatrice, *née* Pinto, Lady Talbot, was probably chosen for her experience of foreign courts; Lady Scales was one of Sir Richard's chief friends. Among the knights, 'Ri*cardus* Roos, miles',[3] comes fourth after two of the king's carvers, Sir Edward Hull and Sir Robert Hungerford, and after Sir William, later Lord Bonvile (who became a Yorkist, and was executed after the second battle of St. Albans at the instigation of Queen Margaret herself); the younger ladies-in-waiting were Lady (Elizabeth) Hull and Lady (Elizabeth) Grey—not Elizabeth Wydville as is sometimes said, but the widow of Sir Ralph Grey of Heaton, who was still a lady-in-waiting in 1453.[4] Then come the two waiting gentlewomen, Rose Merston and Margaret Stanlow; Rose Chetwynde (Lady Beatrice Roos's will shows that she had been friendly with some Chetwyndes) had been attendant on Queen Katherine, on whose death she was begged by the Lords of the Council to marry according to the king's intent; she obediently married John Merston, who had acted as Queen Katherine's executor and was later keeper of the king's jewels; probably she was chosen now as having experience of a young French princess.[5] Margaret Stanlow was for long a regular member of the queen's household, appealed to in 1453 as experienced in ceremonies for the birth of the heir to the throne.[6] She was probably the wife of John Stanlow, who was Treasurer of the English finances in France, as Sir Richard Roos was to have occasion to know. Then come the squires of the king's body, among whom Edmund Hampden is noted here, because, like Sir Henry Roos, he accompanied Queen Margaret to Scotland, and to Sluys in 1463; he was killed at Tewkesbury.[7] Nicholas Husee was later to be an executor of Sir Robert Roos's will. At the very end of the list comes George Ashby, Writer to the Signet to Margaret of Anjou, known to us as a would-be poet. With all these people, the Household, Sir Richard and Sir Robert Roos would be on varying terms of acquaintance

---

[1] Brit. Mus., Add. MS. 23938, Brekenoke's and Everdone's accounts of the expenses.

[2] Clifford's grandmother was Elizabeth Roos, Sir Richard's aunt.

[3] MS. cit., fol. 5, 13 v.   [4] *Cal. Pat. Rolls, 1441–6*, p. 353.

[5] *Ib., 1436–41*, pp. 47, 48, 91, 121, 347.

[6] MS. Pepys 2516, fol. 117 v. Cf. *Letters of Margaret of Anjou*, Camden Soc., LXXXVI, p. 115.

[7] *Paston Letters*, Nos. 413, 671; Stevenson, *Wars in France*, II, 781.

or intimacy, that revealing intimacy of a palace coterie which enables a ready writer to compose pen-portraits, and satires. I believe that Sir Richard took the opportunity; certainly George Ashby had not the requisite quickness of wit or lightness of touch.

The comedy of the delayed wedding played itself out. For nearly two months the Queen's Escort kicked its heels in Rouen, and then for a month in Nancy, while Charles VII and René d'Anjou were encamped before the walls of Metz, whose rebellious citizens had taken the opportunity of seizing the baggage-train of Queen Isabelle of Anjou, and had to be disciplined. The delay was an anti-climax to King Henry's eagerness, and to the excitement of the magnificent preparations. Even when the embassy went to Nancy in early January 1445, in daily expectation of Margaret's arrival from Anjou, it was fully a month before she appeared. Then in a week the proxy marriage was celebrated in the cathedral of Nancy, the bride in white powdered with golden daisies. The spontaneously joyous air of the proxy betrothal was not to be repeated; then, at Tours in May 1444, the ceremony was accompanied by shouts of 'Noel' from a delighted people longing for peace, by feasting at which the bride was already given the honours of the queen of England, by archery-contests between French and English, by a duel of giants on camels, and by a great Maying in which a company of three hundred knights and squires accompanied the French queen.[1] Now René d'Anjou, a stage-manager of practised skill, had prepared jousts and winter spectacles; after Margaret's departure he continued them to celebrate another marriage, that of his elder daughter, Yolande, to Ferry de Vaudémont of Lorraine.[2] Meanwhile Margaret was on her slow journey, 'handed along' by her father to Bar-le-Duc, then by the French king through Paris, and finally committed to the charge of the English at the frontier town of Pontoise. There (supreme irony) Richard, Duke of York, met her with a great company of archers; and there she said farewell to her elder brother John of Calabria and other kinsfolk, and set her face towards England's guardianship. At Mantes she took boat, and while she came down the winding river, the cavalcade went ahead (along a road which runs not far from Gisors and therefore familiar ground to Sir Richard), for a dress-rehearsal of the state entry into Rouen.[3]

---

[1] Bodl. Lib., Digby MS. 196, fol. 155 v.–156.

[2] See below, No. 67.

[3] This is my suggested explanation of a procession which has puzzled commentators because of the absence of Margaret, although she was not then indisposed. The five empty saddles point to the absence of the French suite. Even now, all state processions tend to be rehearsed.

E

Sir Richard (Messire Richard Rioz) is included by name in the chronicler D'Escouchy's description of that rehearsed procession; he was in the vanguard of lords and knights, escorted by four hundred archers in fighting grey. Then came the squires with two hundred archers of the Royal Guard in rich livery, with a golden crown on the sleeve. Six pages, all sons of knights, followed on horseback, in rich black robes and hoods with silver-gilt braiding. The first page led a saddle-horse, with trappings of gold, the king's gift to the queen; the other horses had gear of silver-gilt. Then followed the queen's chariot, sent by the king; nothing like it had come out of England for long. Richly fitted and adorned, ornamented within and without in many colours, it was covered with cloth of gold displaying the arms of England and France, and was drawn by six fine white horses. In this rode the Marchioness of Suffolk, 'en l'estat de la Royne pareil que le jour qu'elle espousa'; with her, as 'dames d'honneur', were Lady Talbot and Lady Salisbury. On either side of the chariot as outriders, rode the Duke of York and Lord Talbot, 'tenans maniere comme se la Royne eust esté dedens'. Before rode the Marquess of Suffolk, as in the person of the king, and after him thirty-five horsemen in crimson with his arms. Behind the chariot were five horses (evidently meant for other important but absent members of the queen's suite), in trappings of damask of cramoisy or of crimson velvet powdered with golden roses. Other ladies rode behind the royal chariot, and still others were in another richly adorned chariot, which brought up the rear of the cavalcade.

Et en ce point, ils entrèrent par bel et honnourable arroy en ladicte ville . . . là où il y ot de grans honneurs et esbatemens par diverses manières, tant de jour comme de nuit.[1]

The queen herself entered Rouen on March 22 in this guise like a princess in a fairy-tale, to be met by Talbot, and feasted during Easter week. On March 31 she went by boat to Harfleur, but there the storms that were long remembered as portents of evil delayed her, 'twice by awkward wind from England's bank Drove back again'. Illness and the after-effects of her bad crossing kept her resting at Southampton, and it was not till April 23, on the well-omened day of St. George, that the wedding was celebrated at Titchfield Abbey. Thither the people of the southern counties came with gifts, among them the unhandy one of a lion; there too Humphrey, Duke of Gloucester, accepting the *fait accompli*, rode with five hundred liveried retainers to welcome her.

[1] *Chronique de Mathieu d'Escouchy*, ed. G. Du Fresne de Beaucourt, 1863, I, ch. 12, pp. 84 ff.

Throughout May, the fifteen-year-old queen journeyed slowly on to London, and at last halted at the royal palace of Eltham. At Blackheath, on May 28, the civic dignitaries and liverymen met her, and escorted her among divers pageants (compositions credited to Lydgate) to the Tower where the king awaited her. The next day, all in the white and gold of her daisy emblem [1] she went to service at St. Paul's, and the City entertained her with yet more shows and spectacles. Finally, on May 30 she was crowned in Westminster Abbey with all the splendour that could be devised. [2]

In all these ceremonies Sir Richard Roos must have taken part; and it is likely that his skill was called upon to 'devise sports', to relieve the tedium of the escort's preliminary waiting, and to beguile the queen on her slow journey. In this enlivened court, to which again a young queen and her ladies, French and English, brought a new air of youth and gaiety, Sir Richard Roos must have felt a fresh impulse to write; he certainly had fresh material. Now there was encouragement not only for ceremonial but also for the lighter side of life and poetry, a king eager to please his bride, a queen the daughter of the most many-sided *dilettante* of the arts in France, and herself with a flower name and emblem which would revive the poetic cult and the strife of the Flower and the Leaf.

Sir Richard now experienced a period of unwonted prosperity. The first reward for his services came in June 1445, when he was appointed for life Constable of St. Briavel's Castle in Gloucestershire; [3] it had been relinquished by Henry Beauchamp, stepbrother of Eleanor, Duchess of Somerset, and of Margaret, Countess of Shrewsbury, probably because of failing health, since he died the next summer. [4] It is not likely that Sir Richard deserted London and the court to immure himself in the Forest of Dean, in a Norman castle built to overawe the Welsh; he probably put in a deputy. Nevertheless he must have visited it occasionally in his sixteen years of tenure; and there were two Welshmen in his household at his death. His salary was probably about £100 of our money. [5] Nor was this all. In August 1446, as the King's Knight, yet having no fee of the king, and his livelihood not being sufficient to maintain his rank, he was given annual grants of £25 each

---

[1] The French colours for the marguerite are white and gold; the English represent the small pink-tipped daisy by red and white, or red, white, and green.

[2] Ramsay, *Lancaster & York*, II, 63–4; Hookham, *Margaret of Anjou*, I, 260–75.

[3] *Cal. Pat. Rolls, 1441–46*, p. 355.

[4] Doyle, *Official Baronage*, III, 144.

[5] Cf. Peck, *Desiderata Curiosa*, I, 71.

from the customs of Kingston-on-Hull and of Southampton.[1] In November of the same year, he signed and sealed a receipt for 1500 *livres tournois* in lieu of 250 marks sterling. This was a grant from the king (over and above his daily half-crown as a knight of the Escort), for

bons et bien aggreables services que nous a faiz le temps passé en maintes manieres nostre amé et feal Richard Roos, chevalier.

Then follows a formula:

fait continuellement de jour en jour et esperons que encore face ou temps advenir.

The purpose of the grant is to defray his daily expenses and charges, and especially those incurred

ou voyage derrain fait en France pour la venue de nostre tres chere et tres amée compaigne la Royne ouquel voyage par nostre ordonnance il fut lors commis et envoyé.

The grant is dated December 2, 1445; it was nearly a year (Nov. 21, 1446) before Sir Richard signed the receipt for it. These documents, fortunately preserved in French records,[2] give one of the only four signatures of the poet so far discovered; his accompanying seal shows that, like his brother Sir Robert, he quartered the gemel bars of Badlesmere with the water bougets of Roos, and like his father and his eldest brother, Lord John, displayed the peacock crest with trailing feathers.

Against this material prosperity must be set a material misfortune. On November 14, 1445, his house in the parish of St. Andrew by the Wardrobe, in Baynards Castle Ward, was burgled, and goods to the value of £40 were taken, including two covered cups of silver gilt, a holywater stoup with a 'strynkell' of silver, and a silver ewer of twenty pounds weight. Sir Richard had reason to believe that the goods were taken to Oxford to the house of Richard Bertelot, goldsmith, who bought them for cash on November 20, though he knew the men to be thieves, 'customers to stele and bryng godes so stollen to him'. As Roos did not know the names of the thieves, he had no 'remedye herof at the comon lawe', and accordingly petitioned the Lord Chancellor, Archbishop Stafford, to examine Bertelot. Another petition states that Bertelot would neither confess the names of his accomplices nor give up the goods, to the owner's 'greate hurt'; Sir Richard therefore asked for a writ against the delinquent.[3] Whether he recovered his silver, does not appear. Richard Bertelot, goldsmith, had been *vnum ministrum*

---

[1] *Cal. Pat. Rolls, 1441–6*, p. 457.
[2] Bibl. Nat. MSS., Pièces Originales 2541, dossier 56, 856 (Roos), fol. 5, 10.
[3] Early Chanc. Proc., Bundle 107, No. 21; 17, No. 128.

domini Regis as a tax collector, and in 1428 had been the centre of an affray, probably of 'town and gown'; in the exercise of his office he was assaulted by a crowd of clerks, and his black hood, worth 6/-, stolen. In December 1434, although of 'good repute and honest conversation', he was excommunicated by the '*commissarius*', John Burbage; whereupon Burbage and the Proctors were summoned to appear at the Court of Arches. And in 1448-9 (after this charge of receiving stolen goods) Bertelot was a royal collector of a fifteenth and a tenth;[1] evidently he had influential backers. Probably Sir Richard never saw his plate again. The nature of the pieces seems to show that he had set up house, and perhaps had a chapel. The parish of St. Andrew by the Wardrobe was in Baynard's Castle Ward, a district, like the Elizabethan Strand, of great town-houses of the nobility, Beaumont's Inn, Scrope's Inn, Burley house, Baynard's Castle itself, which Duke Humphrey had built anew after a great fire in 1428; and his 'Little Wardrobe' of which all plate and books were given to King's College, Cambridge, at his death; and finally a waterside tower (later Legate's Inn), given by Edward III in 1328 to William, second Lord de Ros of Hamlake, for a quitrent of a rose. Probably this was Sir Richard's dwelling; Blanch Apelton, a manor belonging to Thomas, Lord de Ros, in the reign of Richard II, was near St. Andrew Undershaft, but that was in Aldgate ward;[2] the special devotion to St. Andrew evinced in Sir Richard's will may date from this period, when he was a parishioner of St. Andrew by the Wardrobe. The vicinity of the royal wardrobe, and of the great houses, probably brought the district into favour as a place of residence for knights and squires of the Household.

An unforeseeable and curious circumstance now brought Sir Richard Roos back to the scene of his earlier life and poetic inspiration. The arrest and death of Humphrey, Duke of Gloucester, in February 1447 could not but affect his sensibility; it had an external effect also. King Henry granted Plesaunce to his queen, and Margaret took possession of it by Easter of the same year. She stripped its windows of Gloucester's symbols, replaced them by the royal badges, Henry's hawthorn buds and her own daisies, and embarked on a big project of modernization and extension which lasted for several years (see below, No. 70). Sir Richard Roos, possibly a prey to mixed feelings, must have often found himself accompanying the king to Plesaunce;

---

[1] *Oxford City Documents*, ed. J. E. T. Rogers (Oxf. Hist. Soc., XVIII), pp. 180, 105. *Munimenta Civitatis Oxonie*, ed. Salter (Oxf. Hist. Soc., LXXI), p. 201.

[2] Stow, *London*, ed. Kingsford.

in the early summer of 1450 the king took refuge there when Jack Cade threatened the city. It may have been an after-effect of this rebellion which sent Sir Richard 'Roese' and Sir John Wenlock, the queen's chamberlain, down to Staundon in Hertfordshire to arrest the vicar there on July 18, 1451.[1]

A more personal loss even than that of Duke Humphrey was the death of his brother, Sir Robert, in the winter of 1448–9. Sir Richard was not made an executor, nor even mentioned in his brother's will; it is possible that there was some coolness between them after 1442 and the matter of Uffington. But Sir Richard plainly remained on friendly terms with his nephew and niece; he would be in touch with them later at court in the 1450s. He seems too to have had some concern with the business of Rockingham Forest, since in the same period Queen Margaret paid him £60 for loads of charcoal ('subbostos et Aridos lignos') from Rockingham, Whittlebury and Saucy (Salcey).[2] The queen had been given the forest as she had been given Plesaunce. In the year 1451–2, Sir Richard and his young nephew, Henry, purchased the manor of West Wardon, Northamptonshire, from Nicholas Griffyn.[3] Sir Richard's and Sir Henry's rights had been safeguarded in the Act of Resumption of 1450, and were so again in 1455.[4] In 1454 Sir Richard was Alnager for Northamptonshire and Rutland;[5] and in that same year we find him taking part in complicated transfers of property in Fleet Street, and in Kent.[6] It looks as if he was becoming involved in trade, was 'going into the City'. Very possibly he wanted to augment his income.

One cannot disguise the fact that Sir Richard Roos did not have an outstandingly successful career. The prosperity and promotion of 1445–6 had not led to anything more. Whereas his brother was evidently a rising man, whose successful embassies might soon have led to a title, had he lived, Sir Richard remains a King's Knight. While John Beaumont, Wydville, Sir John Stanley, all outstrip him in honours and position, he is left in the same status. The reason is not easy to discern. Possibly he was dismissed by the fighting men as a mere word-spinning poet; possibly some of his satiric shafts struck home, and made him enemies. Whatever the reason, Sir Richard by the end

---

[1] *Cal. Pat. Rolls, 1446–52*, p. 478.
[2] P.R.O., Duchy of Lancaster Accounts, 5/8, fol. 17 v.
[3] *Cal. of Inquisitions, Henry VII*, I, No. 37, p. 16.
[4] *Rotuli Parl.*, V, 193a; VI, 453b.
[5] *Cal. Fine Rolls, 1452–61*, p. 103 and Index (Dec. 30, 1454).
[6] *Cal. Close Rolls, 1447–54*, pp. 495, 515; cf. *Cal. Plea and Memoranda Rolls, 1437–57*, V, p. 136.

of the reign was exactly where he stood in 1446. The death of his last remaining brother, the closing through the loss of France of all avenues to military promotion, the decline in popularity, and then in 1455 the death in battle, of his most influential connection by marriage, Edmund, Duke of Somerset, all these may have warned Sir Richard to look more hopefully to the city than to the court. There were Roos's engaged in trade, even a Richard Roos, mercer,[1] who may have been a distant (or left-handed) connexion of the Belvoir family. Sir Richard, impecunious in youth, and probably extravagant, may have been dazzled by dreams of wealth by merchandise.

There was yet another reason for this desire for money. By 1455 Sir Richard Roos was married. According to that sixteenth-century genealogy which gives unusually full information on the younger sons of the Roos family,[2] Sir Richard married Margaret, daughter of Sir Richard Vernon, knight. This is supported by a reference in Roos's will to his wife's niece, Mary Vernon. Sir Richard Vernon of Haddon (who died between April and June 1451)[3] had more children than appear in most of the genealogies. In addition to the heir, Sir William Vernon of Tonge, he had a son Roger, another son Foulke who was a member of the Escort, and several daughters (of whom more shortly), among them this Margaret. A document of 1455 connects her also with another family, and makes it probable that she had first married a Longueville. In 33 Henry VI (1455, 20 June), John Haldenby of Haldenby and John Haldenby of Isham demised the lordship of Wotton, Northamptonshire, to Sir George Longueville for life, with remainder to Margaret, the wife of Sir Richard Roos, for her life, and with reversion to the heirs of Longueville. Accordingly on Sir George's death in 1458, Dame Margaret Roos succeeded to Wotton.[4] This arrangement looks like part of a dower settlement, and may probably be thus explained: that Margaret Vernon had been the wife (possibly the second wife) of Richard Longueville, the eldest son of Sir George and of his first wife, Elizabeth Roche, who had died before February 4, 1435/6.[5] Richard Longueville's marriage was granted in March 1443/4 to Sir Richard Vernon and Sir Edmund Hungerford, King's Knights.[6] His consequent marriage with Margaret Vernon probably

---

[1] He is traceable in the *Cal. Pat. Rolls* for the 1430s.

[2] MS. Harleian 4031, fol. 190 v.

[3] 'French Rolls', Dep. Keeper of the Public Records, *48th Report*, pp. 386, 388.

[4] Bridges, *Northamptonshire*, I, 392; cf. V.C.H., *Northamptonshire*, IV, 294.

[5] *Cal. Close Rolls, 1435–41*, p. 15.

[6] *Cal. Pat. Rolls, 1441–46*, p. 326.

took place forthwith. He inherited his mother's property of Whitacres in Warwickshire. His death is not recorded, but it was probably before 1449/50.[1]

This identification of Margaret is supported by references in the queen's Jewels Accounts. The name Margaret Longueville makes a solitary appearance in the list of September 1449 to September 1450; whereas Domina Margareta Roos first appears in the Jewels Accounts in 1452–3, and again in 1453–4,[2] when Sir Richard Roos and she receive identical gifts, though their names are not coupled; first, silver-gilt salt-cellars, and then silver-gilt goblets with a scallop pattern. In the analysed list of the queen's ladies of December 12, 1452, her name, Domina Margareta Roos, comes fourth in the list of five ladies, headed by Ismania, Lady Scales.[3]

These dates fit with other indications. In the Act of Resumption of 1450,[4] when Sir Richard Roos's annuity from Uffington and his grants from the customs are safeguarded, no mention is made, as is usual with other men, of a wife or heir. The date of the marriage, between the Act and the Longueville document (1450 and June 1455), can be narrowed by reference to the Jewels Accounts and the list, to the two years between September 1450 and December 1452. If the Jewels Accounts for 1450 to 1452 were not unfortunately missing, we could probably narrow it still further.

Sir Richard Vernon, Treasurer of Calais at his death in 1451,[5] and earlier known as Speaker of the Parliament at Leicester in 1426, was a fairly well-known figure. He and his son Roger seem to have done some high-handed acts and breaches of the peace in the Peak district.[6] The family had not yet acquired the prestige that it was to

---

[1] A younger Richard Longueville died between Aug. 20 and Oct. 26, 1458, in the same year as Sir George, leaving, according to his will, a widow Anne, and an infant son (P.C.C. Stokton 26, fol. 206 v.–207. Cf. *Cal. Fine Rolls, 1452–61,* p. 223).

[2] P.R.O., Jewels Accounts E.101, Bundle 410, Nos. 2, 8, 11. It has been assumed that the lady was Lady Margery Roos, widow of John, seventh Lord Roos, who married Roger Wentworth, and later seems to have married a Hopton (*Paston Letters,* No. 219). But documents distinguish fairly clearly between Margeria and Margareta, as with Margaret, Lord William's widow; in the 1430s the two dowagers needed to be thus distinguished. It is true that Sir Philip Wentworth's name also occurs in the Jewels Accounts of 1453–4, and that in 1447–8 he was a squire of the Household. There is no sign of his being of the Household later; he may have paid a visit to Court (see *Paston Letters,* No. 207, for his visit to London in June 1454).

[3] P.R.O., Duchy of Lancaster, Accounts, Bundle 5/8, fol. 11.

[4] *Rot. Parl.,* V, 193a.

[5] Dep. Keeper of the Public Records, *48th Report,* p. 365.

[6] *Derbyshire Arch. Journal,* 1913, XXXV, pp. 227–30.

gain in the next century under Sir George Vernon, the hospitable
'King of the Peak'; but it contrived to keep clear of embroilment in
the Wars of the Roses.[1] Sir Richard's daughters, Margaret Roos's
sisters, married country gentry, and some of them settled in the
south-west of Derbyshire. Elizabeth married Sir John Stanley,[2]
Benedicta (named after her mother) was contracted in November 1441
to Thomas Charleton, Esquire;[3] Agnes married John Cockayne of
Ashbourne;[4] and Anne married John Bradbourne of Hough (now
Hulland).[5] All these names are found indicated in two poems in
MS. Ff. 1.6 which Sir Richard Roos evidently wrote for his sisters-in-
law, probably at their demand. The children of these families intermarried with Willoughby of Risley, Gresley of Drakelow and Fitzherbert
of Norbury. Sir Richard Roos was making a suitable, but not a brilliant
match; his most distinguished new connexion was Richard Longueville's
maternal aunt, Ellen, Lady Ferrers of Chartley.[6] One may hope that
he was following his heart. Certainly his grandmother, the matriarch
Lady Beatrice Roos, would have approved of this marriage, since Sir
Richard Vernon was heir to her dear friends the Pembridges. By a
later alliance with the family then at Belvoir, the 'elopement' of Dorothy
Vernon with Sir John Manners, Haddon Hall and Belvoir together
have added to the English store of romantic family legend.

Sir Richard the poet found it convenient on occasion, as did Edmund
Spenser, to have his queen and his wife bear the same name, as will
be seen. Certainly in the 'daisy' poems, there is some repetitiveness,
though it is generally easy to differentiate by the tone and handling.
His finest, and, I believe, his last ceremonial poem, written in the
early summer of 1458, was a Plesaunce poem (see below, No. 72); and
so his poetic cycle ended where it had begun. Within three years of
that 'joust of peace', all his family were attainted, and the time for
writing poetry of courtly compliment and Lancastrian symbolism was
over. Yet there was an aftermath.

Our knowledge of the last period of Sir Richard Roos's life, the twenty
years and more from the outbreak of the Wars of the Roses in 1460 to
his death in London, between March 8 and April 1, 1482, is scanty,
and would be still scantier if it were not for his very full and detailed

---

[1] C. Hussey, 'Haddon Hall', in *Country Life*, Dec. 16, 1949.
[2] *Shropshire Visitation* (Harl. Soc.), pp. 471–4.
[3] *Cal. Close Rolls, 1441–7*, pp. 42–3.
[4] Glover, ed. Noble, *Hist. of County of Derby*, II, 33; A. E. C. Congleton,
Cockayne Memoranda, 1873, pp. 193–9.
[5] *Derbyshire Arch. Journal*, 1936, LVII, 113–16.
[6] *Cal. Pat. Rolls, 1436–41*, pp. 502–3.

will. This proves, by some of its provisions and legacies, that by 1482, when he was over seventy, he had some post at the court of Edward IV. But what were the stages of this transference of loyalties, and what its inner compulsions, there is very little to show. The Act of Attainder (1461) destroyed for nearly twenty-five years his family's wealth and prosperity. As a King's Knight, and as connected with the Household, he would naturally accompany the royal army, unless disabled or a prisoner. But his name is not recorded with his kinsfolk in Scotland, or in the queen's flight abroad; and after the execution in 1464 of his nephew Thomas, Lord Roos, Sir Henry appears as the only prominent member of the family. Sir Richard seems to have been in prison, like Sir Thomas Malory, but in Windsor Castle; this was probably between 1468 and 1470, when the prisoner's poem of appeal to John Vere, Earl of Oxford, to strike a blow for the Lancastrian cause, must have been written (see below, No. 100); it is certainly his composition. The blow was struck, and helped on the brief Readeption of Henry VI in 1470.

It is probable that Sir Richard Roos, like Sir Henry, made his submission fairly soon after Tewkesbury; but his name is not, I believe, included in King Edward's amnesty and general pardon of 1472. After the murder of Prince Edward at Tewkesbury, and the complete subjugation of Queen Margaret, few Lancastrians felt that there was any immediate call on their allegiance; Henry Richmond, a boy of sixteen, was hardly yet accepted as a claimant. Possibly Sir Richard's way was smoothed by the two Yorkist marriages, by 1466–7, and again by 1474, of his niece Eleanor. A late cryptogram in a verse translation, which unites the name of her third husband, Richard Haute, with those of Antony Wydville, Fitzlewis, and Stafford, seems to show Roos in contact with the Wydville or queen's party, especially where it touched the families of the descendants of Eleanor, Duchess of Somerset, who had died in 1467/8 (see below, No. 102). Anthony Wydville's patronage of letters would make him an inevitable mark for Roos's interest; besides, he had married the daughter of Roos's tried friend, Lady Scales. He would be a natural bridge back to a court where the king was posing more and more as a man of culture. It is possible that when Edward IV in 1478 tried to set his Household in order and to curb its waste and extravagance, the opportunity may have been made to include an old and experienced courtier, skilled in the ways of a royal meynie. Whatever was the sequence of events, Sir Richard Roos before his death had changed the Lancastrian collar of SS for the suns and roses of the Yorkist collar of the king's livery.

Sir Richard Roos's will[1] was drawn up on March 8, 1481/2, he being 'hole of mynde and in gode memory', and was proved on the following April 1. He was then a parishioner of St. Peter's the Little in Thames Street; but he desired to be buried in the church of the White Friars in Fleet Street. To these two foundations he gave rich gifts in return for their prayers for his soul: to the first, 'an Image of o^r ladie of silue^r and gilte'; to the Carmelites, his 'Tablett of the coronacioun of our ladie made of the moder of perle garnysshed and sett in silue^r and gilte and w^t a fote therto of silue^r and gilte'; also £40, and in addition £5 for an 'honest obite' annually for six years. St. Andrew is the only saint named of 'all the hole courte of heven' to whom Sir Richard commits his soul; and we remember that he had earlier lived in the nearby parish of St. Andrew by the Wardrobe, in the adjoining Baynard's Castle Ward.

The family bequests are the most interesting and informative to us. To his wife, Dame Margaret, and to her heirs and assigns, goes the only land mentioned in the will, a messuage with a garden adjoining at East Greenwich, lately purchased of John Bellacourte. There is no disposal of the house in Thames Street; perhaps it was leased, perhaps it was his wife's dower; Stow notes that Richard Longueville, grandson of Sir George Longueville, had a messuage in Thames Street in 1459.[2] To his wife's niece, Mary Vernon, are bequeathed with circumstantial detail a jewel, a bed, fur and a gown:

a Be for her nek sett with ij diamondes and a Rubie and a perle and the white bedde complete that the same mary is wonte to lie inne and a furr of beale menyver which lieth in my gowne of blue velwett and my gowne of chamelett lynyng and all to make her a kirtill.

There is a familiar, affectionate tone in this; Mary Vernon, daughter of Sir Richard Vernon's younger brother, Thomas, was an acceptable visitor, or more likely inmate. She did not, however, get the blue velvet gown itself: that went to the Carmelites, presumably for a vestment.

Sir Richard's own relatives are well remembered: first Sir Robert Roos's children:

to sir henry Roos my nephieu my coller of golde of the kinges lyvery and my Ring of golde sette *with* a camahewe that I was wont to wer and my Sparver of silke that *se*rued me in the kinges courte.

Later bequests to servants make plain that this is indeed the contemporary court of Edward IV, where he and his man had a lodging:

to howell vaughñ the clothe of my sayde blak gowne furred w^t blak lambe being in the kinges courte;

---

[1] P.C.C. Wills, 5 Logge.   [2] Stow, *Survey of London*, Tower St. Ward, *ad fin.*

to John Richardeson that kepith my stuff in the saide courte my shorte gowne lyned that I was wont to ride inne and the stuff of the bedd that the same John was wonte to lie inne himsilf that is in the court.

In any case Sir Henry Roos had been reconciled since 1472, and could properly wear the Yorkist collar.[1] Henry's sister, Eleanor Haute, is given a jewel and a small piece of plate:

my litle Roos of golde sett and garnysshed w^t a Ruby and viij perles and my litle potte of siluer and parcell gilte w^{t}oute foote and coueryng.

Above all she received 'my grete booke called saint Grall', still extant as Royal MS. 14.E.iii, and to us the most valuable of Sir Richard's possessions.

The testator took thought for two of his young great-nieces. There is no gift to his nephew Richard Roos, Esquire; but to his little girl, Elizabeth, 'dwellyng w^t my ladie of Suffolk', goes the pretty present of a flat gold chain with a borage flower and a diamond. To another young great-niece whose christian name he evidently could not give, 'the wif of william parker draperer my Nece', goes a richly bound little book of prayers, 'closed in plates of siluer and eneled w^t an Image of the Crucifixe on the oon side and an Image of our ladie on the *other* side'. This bequest must have taken Sir Richard's memory back to his eldest sister Elizabeth, who probably helped to bring him up. She married rather late in life, in 1442, the much younger Robert Morley, fifth Lord Morley, whose marriage had been granted in 1436 to Edmund Beaufort, then Count of Mortain. It was a brief union, and the only child, Eleanor Morley, was born posthumously; she married William Lovell, and left two children, Henry Lovell, eighth Lord Morley, and Alice Lovell, both born in the 1460s. Alice Lovell was already married to William Parker, earlier than has hitherto been realized.[2] Little is known of Sir William Parker; he was an important member of the Drapers' Company, and was knighted by Richard, Duke of Gloucester, in Scotland in July 1482. He remained his adherent, and was his standard-bearer at Bosworth.

The Countess of Oxford to whom Sir Richard left his 'Tablett of Ivorie wrought *with* Imagery' was the wife of John Vere, thirteenth Earl of Oxford. For fully seven years he had been a prisoner in Hammes Castle, while his wife was reduced to great poverty; she was a Neville, and the sister of Warwick the Kingmaker. How the Earl of Huntingdon

---

[1] 'Item, that every Lord, Knight, and Esquire, . . . within the Household, wear daily a collar of the King's livery about their *nekket* as to them appertaineth' ('Liber Niger', quoted by Samuel Pegge in *Curialia Miscellanea*, 1818, p. 75).

[2] G.E.C., *Complete Peerage*, IX, 220, where her date of marriage is given as 'before 1486'.

(William Herbert) came to borrow £15 of Sir Richard is not explained, but the debt is recorded; a humbler debtor, Anneys, who had laid to pledge a rosary of coral gaudied with silver and gilt for a loan of 13/4, was to pay the money back before she could get her rosary; but she had also as a free gift, 'that narrowe cors girdull of silke travuersed *with* siluer'.

Of Sir Richard's quite numerous household, his two executors, under his wife, must be specially mentioned: Sir Roger ap Thomas, his chaplain, who was given 20/-, 'so that he contynnewe still in seruice with the saide dame margett my wife after my decesse', and also a psalter clasped with silver, and a chalcedony rosary; and Robert Stephenson, probably a steward, who was to have a furred gown, a black velvet doublet, a trussing-spoon of silver with a knop at the end, also 'myn own sadill that I was wonte to ride inne and a bridell so that the same Robert be reddy atte all tymes to ride for the erandes of the saide dame margarett'. Sir Richard's knightly care for his horses comes out in the special reward to 'Edward my seruaunt that kepith myn horses, mor thanne anny of his feleship', out of the proceeds of the sale of the other 'hors harneys'.

The Roos household had about a dozen other servants, including another Welshman, Howell Vaughan; Maude Wadiluf and Margaret Merysete (?) may be kinswomen of Thomas Wadeloue, *garcio*, and Robert Merefeld, *armiger*, both in Queen Margaret's household in 1452–3; so too George fferby may be a son of Robert Ferby, another *garcio*. Thomas Foxe's name throws a little light on the purchase of the East Greenwich messuage from John Bellacourte; in 1432 when Agnes Fox of East Greenwich conveyed a tenement and garden to Thomas Ferrour, the witnesses were John Fox and John Belacourt. The servants received generous gifts of furred gowns, girdles, a knife, or a coral rosary 'gaudied w^t calcedonyes'; the money gift is generally 6/8.

Towards the end of the will, which has several afterthoughts, such as the 'blue Veluett' gowne to go to the White Friars, comes a detailed inventory of Sir Richard's plate, and a general statement of his other household goods, for his wife. This comprises all the stuff that belongs to the buttery and the kitchen, all his other bedding, all the stuff and the ornaments of his chapel and closet, viz., 'chalice, cruettes, belle and paxe, the lesse masboke and the portuous'. Some of the goods bear interesting emblems, such as the covered salt cellar of silver gilt, 'made w^t colombynes'; columbines were a Lancastrian emblem,[1] as was

---

[1] Cf. Fabyan's account of the wedding-feast of Henry V, and of the dishes ornamented with columbines, with hawthorn leaves, and with Henry's word 'Vne sanz plus' (*Chronicle*, 1542, p. 366a).

the borage flower of the flat gold chain. The 'bedde of silke made w^t white hartes' must surely have been a legacy from Sir Richard's mother, formerly lady-in-waiting to Anne of Bohemia. In addition there were a covered standing cup, silver gilt, two basins of 'parys siluer', another covered salt with an emerald on the knop, a silver bowl of 'Roone making', and silver spoons long and short handled, a half dozen of each. Sir Richard is evidently reasonably well provided with horses, household gear, bedding, plate, and especially clothes, the furred and lined gowns of age, though hardly of infirmity since he was still riding; he was a man of sufficient 'moebles', but of hardly any land.

It is a naturally expressed and intimate will, and reveals much of Sir Richard's disposition. He evidently had complete confidence in his wife, in her fair dealing and 'gode discrecioun' as 'principall executryce'. Thoughtful for her future welfare and comfort, he tries to retain in her service the same chaplain and steward. There is no reference to direct heirs, children or grandchildren; presumably Sir Richard and Dame Margaret were childless now, if not always. Sir Richard was a considerate uncle, and evidently he (and his wife) chose the nieces' legacies with care, also those of the upper servants, such as Elyn Hannyng who had the silver fittings of a girdle, and the cloth of a gown to make her a kyrtell. Like his father, he provides for the payment of 'all and singuler', his rightful debts, so that his creditors shall be 'truly paied and contented'; and although ready money was probably short with him (as always), he spares 20/- for distribution among the poor 'by penny mele'.

Nothing is said of personal books or manuscripts, but this is hardly surprising; Sir Richard's writings had nearly all been 'poèmes d'occasion', and most of those occasions belonged to another life, almost to another era. As will be seen later, many of the manuscripts containing his poems were in the hands of members of the Lancastrian Household and adherents and were dispersed like their owners. Only one seems to have passed from his own house into the keeping of family friends and connexions (MS. Ff. 1.6). There is no bequest to Queens' College, Cambridge, although in 1448 he had been among the 'promoters of the establishment' and as such is still remembered in the service of Commemoration of Benefactors; probably he had been present when in the same year Sir John Wenlock laid the first stone of the fabric.[1] Had he lived three or four years longer, Fortune might have turned her wheel for him, as it did for Sir Henry Roos. Only in one way does the wheel seem to come full circle; his solitary purchase of land is made almost under the shadow of Plesaunce. Belvoir was in ruins, and

[1] For this information, I am indebted to the late President of Queens' College.

Hamlake had gone into the hands of Richard of Gloucester; Plesaunce was the property and resort of another queen, Elizabeth Wydville. Perhaps it was there that Eleanor Haute gave her Sir Richard Roos's 'grete booke'. In thinking of his spiritual welfare, Sir Richard looks back still further than Plesaunce, to his early youth, and begs his wife to 'ordeigne and dispose for my soule and for the soules of my fader and moder and all my gode frendes soules and all x^{ten} soules'.

Mary Vernon, daughter of Thomas Vernon, evidently unmarried in 1482, must soon have married Reginald Leigh of Egginton, a descendant of the Cheshire family of Adlington, and with Stanleys behind him on the distaff side. Their son Robert Leigh married Anne Lathbury, also of Egginton.[1] When Mary died is not recorded; her husband Reginald lived on to great age in the reign of Henry VIII,[2] and in 1508 he asked legal advice of Humphrey Newton, whose poems have recently been recovered for us.[3]

What happened to Margaret Roos, I have not discovered. Very probably she went back into Derbyshire, to be among her own people at Haddon, at Ashbourne, or Hough, or Egginton.[4] The 'Vernon policy of non-belligerency', their avoidance of involvement in dynastic struggles, and their position as 'territorial chieftains in the Derbyshire dales'[5] spelled security and peace for the members of their family. Margaret is probably the Margaret Roos, widow, who in 1485 sued Thomas Worth, late of Uttoxeter, to render a reasonable account for the time that he was the receiver of her money.[6] She carried out her husband's wish for burial in the White Friars; the name of 'Sir Richard Derois, knight' is in the list of those buried in the 'new choir', built sixty years previously. The friary was surrendered to Henry VIII, the church pulled down, and by Stow's time, the site was built over with 'many fair houses'. Whatever monument or memorial there may have been to Sir Richard Roos, it has perished. For nearly five hundred years his name and his writings have suffered eclipse.

---

[1] *Derbyshire Visitation Pedigrees*, p. 54. MS. Ashmole, 798, fol. 41.

[2] Earwaker, *East Cheshire*, II, 250–1.

[3] R. H. Robbins, in *P.M.L.A.*, 1950, LXV, 249.

[4] There is in Egginton church a recumbent figure, unfortunately defaced, of a lady in a mitre head-dress, clasping in her hands what appears to be a heart. The general treatment resembles that of the fifteenth-century figures in Ashbourne church; one may conjecture either Margaret Roos or Mary Leigh, *née* Vernon.   [5] C. Hussey, 'Haddon Hall', in *Country Life*, Dec. 16, 1949.

[6] Plea Rolls, De Banco, Trin. 3 Richard III, cited in *Hist. Collections for Staffs.*, VI, pt. i, New ser., p. 160. In 1498 a Robert Worth of Crich had land dealings with Raynold Legh, presumably Mary Vernon's husband (Jeayes, *Derbyshire Charters*, No. 638); and in the sixteenth century a Dorothy Vernon married a Jasper Worth (Earwaker, *op. cit.*, II, 337).

CHAPTER III

'La Belle Dame sans Merci', its transmission, and its implications

I N the life of Sir Richard Roos, as it has been narrated in the preceding chapter, there were two successive periods particularly favourable to the writing of poetry; his early twenties to thirties (c. 1432–41), when he was in touch with the circle of the Duke and Duchess of Gloucester at Plesaunce; and his mid-thirties to forties (1441/2–1460), when he was connected with the court, and from 1444/5 onwards had the opportunity of writing poetry for Margaret of Anjou.

Hitherto there has been only one fixed point for any ascription to him of a poem; it is a *point d'appui*, it can also become a *point de départ*. That is, the statement appended in one manuscript (Harleian MS. 372) to the English version of Alain Chartier's *La Belle Dame sans Merci*: 'Translatid out of Frenche by Sir Richard Ros'. There has been no dispute on this ascription; it carries conviction by its very unexpectedness. Roos is not a popular name to be assigned casually, like Lydgate's. Yet the ease which distinguishes the verse and its poetic technique, and which Professor C. S. Lewis was the first to recognize, justifies the reader in assuming that this is by no means prentice-work. It is obvious that this supple translator of some eight hundred lines, and writer of eight original stanzas (preface and envoy), was no stranger to poetic composition. He must have had much practice already in translation, and he had probably written other work under French influence.

We have a little documentary evidence for Sir Richard Roos as a man of letters and a lover of books. We know that he wrote a book hand which was notably practised, small and neat. His formal signature to the French receipt at the age of about thirty-six is very different from the hand of his brother Robert at about the same age, and from

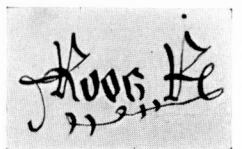

FROM A FRENCH RECEIPT

(b)   (c)

FROM MS. ADD. 30,864   FROM MS. 9, SPENCER
                              COLLECTION, N.Y. PUBLIC LIBRARY

THREE SIGNATURES OF SIR RICHARD ROOS

ARMS OF ROOS, QUARTERING BADLESMERE

the almost childish scrawl of his niece Eleanor Haute; it is distinguished, elegant, even mannered with its fine hair-lines, though not in the least eccentric. His probably later hand in his valued volume of the *Grail*, though thicker and stiffer, has the same careful appearance to match the precision of the statement: 'The begynnynge of this first boke . . . And after that the boke . . . And after that the mort darthur', etc. Altogether it is a hand compatible with a writer of conventional elegance. In two manuscripts of *Les Vœux du Paon* there is a Roos signature accompanied by a motto which can fairly be assumed to be his, since the manuscripts also bear signs of Manners ownership; after the scribe's final 'Amen. Amen' is written, 'A moy le mieulx. Roos R.' (Add. MS. 30864, fol. 79 v.); and on a flyleaf: 'Roos a moy le mieulx' (New York Public Library, MS. 9). Of all the members of his family he would be the most likely to adopt a French motto, for use in love and poetry and joust. There is then nothing in what we know of Sir Richard, his penmanship, and his handling of books, to make us feel that a writer's craft is beyond his tastes and powers.

Before we consider the manuscripts of the English version of *La Belle Dame*, there is a cognate enquiry to be made. No one yet seems to have looked for a copy of the original French poem in England;[1] there is certainly one such manuscript, Royal 19.A.iii. This manuscript is of considerable interest. It is a collection of eight French poems of the mid-fifteenth century; it contains Chartier's *La Belle Dame sans Merci*, now dated 1424, and his *Le Bréviaire des Nobles*; Baudet Herenc's *Les Accusacions contre la Belle Dame*;[2] Michaut Taillevent's *Le Débat du Cueur et de l'Œil*;[3] and four anonymous poems, *Le Congié d'Amours*,[4] *Le Seruiteur sans Guerdon*,[5] *Esbatements entre l'Homme et la femme* (a dialogue), and finally *Le Pris donneur*, which its anagrams show to be in honour of Margaret of Anjou,[6] and of which this appears to be the only copy known. This French manuscript was at one time in contemporary English hands; at the end of *La Belle Dame* is inserted a leaf of vellum, on one side of which is a fair copy of English verses, two stanzas of rhyme royal with a short-line conclusion. It appears to be another envoy to *La Belle Dame* ('Vnto suche fayre þt Do excile pite'),

[1] Piaget in the introduction to his edition of Chartier's *La Belle Dame* cites MS. Lansdowne 380, fol. 137 ff. The poem is certainly not there nor, as far as I can discover, in any other Lansdowne manuscript.
[2] See *Le Jardin de Plaisance*, fol. cxxxix–xlij v.
[3] *Ib.*, fol. lv–lx.
[4] *Le Congié d'Amours*, anon., begins 'En ce temps de joieux este'; also in MS. Arsénal 3523/321, but not the same as the poem of the same title (? by Taillevent) in MS. Arsénal 3521.   [5] *Le Jardin de Plaisance*, fol. clxij–iiij.
[6] See my *Studies in Villon, Vaillant and Charles d'Orléans* (Oxford, 1957).

F

a more intimate alternative to the ceremonious '*Verba translatoris*' of the English version (see below, Nos. 59 and 81*a*). The manuscript is an unpretentious volume, of paper except for this one leaf, without rubrication or ornament, but for a few flourished capitals; it looks like an unostentatious personal collection, almost one might say a working copy.

The assumption that Sir Richard Roos was the owner of this collection and the writer of the envoy on vellum would seem to be justifiable even if the latter's anagrams did not confirm it (see below, No. 81*a*). Any poet interested in *La Belle Dame* would also be interested in another poem here, one of the many to which Chartier's portrayal of a marble-hearted lady gave rise. It is not often enough remembered that *La Belle Dame sans Merci* was not an isolated and disregarded squib, but a firework that caused a blaze of poetic remonstrance. Chartier was condemned by the ladies of the court of Charles VII in a literary tribunal, and had to write his humble *Excusacion*. The presence in this collection of Herenc's *Les accusacions contre la belle dame sans merci*[1] is therefore understandable. Again, Sir Richard Roos would have special facilities for acquiring *Le Pris donneur*, the only known copy of a poem obviously to Margaret of Anjou on the question of her marriage. In addition, a fourth poem here, *Le Débat du Cueur et de l'Œil*, is the only copy known in England of the original French, which Champion has also connected with the court of Anjou. This poem too was translated in the fifteenth century, and the only known copy of the English version, *The Eye and the Heart*, is in MS. Longleat 258 which includes the English *La Belle Dame*. This may well lead to the suspicion that Sir Richard Roos also translated this poem.

If we are to seek for other poems by Sir Richard Roos, whether original or translated, the first obvious field of enquiry is the group of those manuscripts which contain the English *La Belle Dame sans Merci*. A second line of enquiry will arise from Roos's evident familiarity with the work of earlier and contemporary French poets; their methods and habits, even their tricks, may be imitated by him elsewhere. Now that we know that Sir Richard was personally acquainted with France, as a soldier, and as a member of Queen Margaret's Escort, this familiarity is easily explained. The third line of enquiry is on metre and poetic style.

I. MANUSCRIPTS

The manuscripts of *La Belle Dame sans Merci* in English are six in number: British Museum, Harleian MS. 372; Bodleian Library, Fairfax 16; Cambridge University Library, Ff. 1.6.; Longleat 258;

[1] See *Le Jardin de Plaisance*, fol. cxxxix–xlij v.

Trinity College, Cambridge, 599 (or R. 3.19); British Museum, Sloane MS. 1710. All these except the first and last are great and representative collections of English Chaucerian poetry. It is noteworthy that the poem does not occur in three other important fifteenth-century collections, Bodleian 638, Tanner 346, and Digby 181.

All these manuscripts are well known to fifteenth-century students; it remains to review them shortly again in this particular connexion to see if they throw any light on Roos problems, especially whether they can be traced to owners likely to have knowledge of the poet.

The most important manuscript in one way is MS. Harl. 372, as alone containing the Roos ascription—an explicit statement, part of the title, and in a contemporary hand. In other ways it is the least interesting. It is a composite volume of two unlike parts, an odd combination of moral and of courtly poetry, the latter as an afterthought. Eight moral or religious short poems, mostly Lydgate's, are followed by *Anelida and Arcite* and *La Belle Dame*, all in the hand of one scribe; the conjunction of these two poems is interesting, as will be seen. Another copyist adds a religious poem, and yet another begins Hoccleve's *De Regimine Principum*; a sixteenth-century satiric poem completes the volume. The date 1422 appears twice, but has little significance, since it accompanies Lydgate's verses on English kings, which end with Henry VI. Nothing indicates a possible originator or owner, and it is curious that parts of *La Belle Dame* are in wrong order. Relations of the manuscript with Fairfax 16 and with Harleian 7333 have been pointed out by Miss Hammond.[1]

MS. Fairfax 16 is the most impressive of this group.[2] It is an 'omnibus' volume of poetry, and contains *The Boke of the Duchesse*, and *The Legend of Good Women*; some of its fifteenth-century poems are either not known elsewhere (e.g. *How a Lover Prayseth hys Lady*, and the group of connected *Balades*, etc.), or else known only in one other manuscript (e.g. *Reson and Sensuallyte*, *The Chance of the Dice*, *Ragman Roll*); other more popular poems are reproduced in some half-dozen manuscripts, such as *The Black Knight*, and *The Temple of Glas*.

The manuscript gives clear evidence of its period and ownership. The date 1450 is written in a small contemporary hand on the flyleaf; this date, five years after the Anjou marriage, comes in the middle of the period in which Sir Richard Roos, the king's knight, seems to have been continuously in London and about the court. It is an upward date for a manuscript which may have taken some time to be completed. The heraldic shield at the foot of a fine frontispiece painting points to

[1] *Chaucer Bibliography*, pp. 328–9. [2] *Ib.*, pp. 333–9.

a Stanley of Stourton and Hooton as the owner, since it quarters the arms of Stanley with those of Hooton. The most important member of these Cheshire Stanleys in 1450 was undoubtedly Thomas, Lord Stanley (1405–59), an almost exact contemporary of Sir Richard Roos, and, like him, a member of the Escort. In 1446, Lord Stanley was put in charge of Eleanor, Duchess of Gloucester, and was for many years her keeper at Peel Castle. In April 1439, he was appointed Comptroller of the Royal Household; but in 1451 he fell under suspicion, and Parliament tried to force his dismissal. He then openly joined the Yorkists and under York's Protectorate was made Lord Chamberlain in 1455; he died before the worst of the conflict broke out.[1] For many years, then, he was an official of the Household in a position to have close knowledge of Sir Richard and his doings. There is a minute piece of internal evidence that the manuscript passed from Lancastrian to Yorkist hands; at fol. 332 v., beside the statement on Henry VI, 'By just tytle born by enherytaunce', a later hand has written 'Negatur'.

There were also family connexions between Stanley and Roos. Lord Stanley married Joan Goushill (b. 1401), a great-niece of Sir Richard's maternal grandfather;[2] Lady Stanley and Sir Richard were therefore in some sort cousins. The family connexions continued in curious and roundabout fashion, since a younger son of Lord and Lady Stanley, Sir William Stanley of Holt, married after 1443 Joyce Charlton, widow of John, Lord Tiptoft, and mother-in-law of Thomas, ninth Lord Roos, Sir Richard's nephew.[3] Not only so, but Joyce's daughter Philippa Tiptoft, widow of this Thomas, Lord Roos, married after 1464, as second husband, Sir Thomas Wingfield, a nephew of Joan Goushill, being the son of her sister Elizabeth Goushill, who had married Sir Robert Wingfield.[4] There are therefore throughout the fifteenth century three channels of family interest between Roos and Stanley such as might lead to the acquisition by a Stanley of a poem or poems by Sir Richard Roos. The third channel probably points to the later transmission of the manuscript, since on an end fly-leaf (fol. 333 v.) there are three Jacobean signatures:

Rob. Wingfield
14 Oct. 1612.

Olij Nicholaj
8br. 14to 1612.

Arma virumq. cano
Ferdinando Knyghtley.

[1] G.E.C., *Complete Peerage*, XII, i, pp. 250–1; Earwaker, *East Cheshire*, II, 602. [2] Ormerod, *History of the County Palatine and City of Chester*, III, 577.
[3] Earwaker, *loc. cit.*
[4] G.E.C., *Complete Peerage*, XI, 106; John M. Wingfield, *Some Records of the Wingfield Family*, 1925, pedigree; *Vis. of Huntingdon*, Camden Soc., XLIII, p. 128.

Sir Ferdinando Knightley was a fighting member of the famous family of the Knightleys of Fawsley; Robert Wingfields were many in the enormous Wingfield clan.[1] Without any definable relationship between these two young men, there were yet enough marriage links between the two families to warrant their mutual interest. Here they write as in an *album amicorum*, with a tag from Virgil.

The manuscript probably passed from Stanleys to Wingfields, perhaps already in the fifteenth century; at some later time it went through Stow's hands, but it was not necessarily in his possession. In 1612 it was being handled by a Wingfield. Then somehow it got to Gloucester; two hundred years after its inception, Charles Fairfax the antiquary noted in it:

I bought this att Gloucester 8 Sept. 1650 intendinge to exchange it for a better booke. Note that Joseph Holland hath another.

From Charles Fairfax it passed as a legacy to his nephew, Sir Thomas Fairfax, and so into the Bodleian. Notes in another Fairfax manuscript (Fairfax 3, Gower's English works) connect Sir Thomas Fairfax of Denton with his grandmother, Isabel Thwaites, and so bring the manuscript back into the Roos field; for Isabel Thwaites, the heiress, married Sir William Fairfax, son of Elizabeth Manners, daughter of that Eleanor Roos who was the great-niece of Sir Richard Roos.[2] We may then wonder whether Charles and Thomas Fairfax may have been aware of a family, as well as an antiquarian, interest in the contents of Lord Stanley's manuscript, Fairfax 16.

The third manuscript of *La Belle Dame* is in many ways the most interesting of all, Cambridge University, MS. Ff. 1.6, a paper manuscript of varied contents in several hands, 'all latter fifteenth century, if not later, and all slovenly, current and untidy'.[3] It is not an elegant and well-preserved manuscript like Fairfax 16, but a common-place book which has passed from hand to hand, and been added to casually, and probably lain about on window-seats, and suffered in consequence, especially from scribblers. Names or mottoes of copyists (hardly to be called scribes) have been noted: Nicholaus *plenus amoris*, leweston, W. Caluerley. Names occurring together in a coherent memorandum

---

[1] Oswald Barron, *Northamptonshire Families*, 1906, pp. 181–4, 197.

[2] *Herald & Genealogist*, VI, pp. 395 ff.

[3] Hammond, *Chaucer Bibliography*, p. 343, where a list of the contents is given, as also in J. O. Halliwell, *The Thornton Romances*, Camden Soc., No. 30, 1844, pp. xlv–l; see also R. L. Greene, *The Early English Carols*, p. 340, and the examination by L. F. Casson in his edition of *Sir Degrevant*, E.E.T.S., No. 221, 1949; and especially R. H. Robbins, 'The Findern Anthology', *P.M.L.A.*, LXIX, June 1954, pp. 610–42.

are Richard Lathbury, John Wilson, and Master Fynderne. Casual names set down are Thomas Kotin (fol. 139 v.), Elizabet Koton and Elizabet Frauncys (fol. 109 v.), Anne Schyrley (fol. 118), Margery Henckford (not Hungelford as Halliwell read it), followed by the motto, 'w^{t}owte variaunce' (fol. 20 v.). To these may be added some hitherto unrecorded: ric^d ayckyn (fol. 95 v.); and, in 'looking-glass writing' two names, 'Sharesmyth' (twice) and Willes (fol. 19), and two phrases, 'be [y]owe in hert', in the same hand as 'Sharesmyth', and, in a smaller, closer hand, 'and neu[er] repente' (fol. 10 v.). On these last I have nothing much to add, but all the rest are worth consideration.

First the Finderne reference (fol. 59 v.):

A rekenyng betwene John wylsu*n* and mest^r fyndyrne I*tem* fyrst tyme that I went into lestershyre w^t richard lathbery I spent iij^d for my-selfe and for my hors Ite*m* iijd anoder tyme wen I went to mester richard w^t for. . . . (fol. 70) Nota that theys be the p[ar]cellys of clothys at fyndyrn.

Findern is in Derbyshire, at the southern end, not far from the Leicestershire border, and not far from the homes of the Vernon girls (see above, p. 173). The Findernes, a family now long extinct, were faithful Lancastrians, and Sir Thomas Finderne was captured and executed after Hexham with Thomas, Lord Roos.[1] He had earlier followed Margaret of Anjou into France, again like Lord Roos.[2] The family prosperity was then eclipsed; his wife Catherine and his son, Sir William, survived him,[3] but not till the first quarter of the sixteenth century do we find a member of the family again buying land. The will (July 10, 1525) of Thomas Findern Esquire of Radcliffe on Soar, Nottinghamshire,[4] shows that he had been purchasing property in three counties. He may well be the 'mester fyndyrne' of the memorandum quoted, since he bequeathed to 'Richard Lathebere a blake stalkyng mare which is in the handes of Roberte Fyndron'.

From these memoranda, Professor Robbins calls the manuscript 'the Findern Anthology' and goes so far as to say that it was 'made by many hands at the country house of Findern'.[5] As will be seen, the Roos and other connexions of the jotted names are too complex for any such single assignment; there is no doubt, however, that it was long kept within a twenty-miles radius of Findern, and was familiar to many dwellers in

---

[1] Ramsay, *Lancaster & York*, II, 302–4.

[2] Scofield, *Edward IV*, I, 252.

[3] *Genealogist*, New ser. XXIII, p. 243. It may be of interest to note that Sir Thomas Elyot's mother was Alice Fynderne, a niece of Sir Thomas Fynderne (*D.N.B.*, Elyot).

[4] *Test. Ebor.*, V, 208.

[5] *Secular Lyrics*, etc., p. xlvi.

the district at the junction of Derbyshire, Leicestershire, and Notting-hamshire.

The mention of a Lathbury has a particular interest here, since Robert Lathbury, *armiger*, was a witness of Sir Robert Roos's will in 1448. The Lathburys were a Derbyshire family who by marriages had migrated also into Leicestershire. They do not seem to have been of the fighting caste, but rather of civilian employment; one John Lathbury was auditor to the Duchy of Lancaster in 1452;[1] Robert Lathbury, *armiger*, was almost certainly the son of John Lathbury of Egginton, Derbyshire, and the father of Agnes[2] who married Robert Staunton of Staunton Harold,[3] Leicestershire, eight miles south-west of Findern.

Another family at Staunton Harold was the Shirley family which inevitably intermarried with the Stauntons. Thomas Staunton,[4] the son of Robert Staunton and of Agnes Lathbury, left a young widow, Joan (*née* Meinill),[5] who then married Sir Thomas Clinton, Comptroller of the Household to Henry V. Her Staunton daughter, Margaret, married in September, 1423, Ralphe Shirley;[6] her Clinton daughter, Anne, married Robert Frauncis of Foremark, Derbyshire, lying half-way between Findern and Staunton Harold.[7] Lady Clinton's will of 1457[8] shows that Anne Frauncis had six children of whom one was Elizabeth. She became a nun; but Robert Frauncis, by his second wife (also Elizabeth), had another daughter Elizabeth who married John Finderne of Finderne, and his sister Anne Frauncis married Robert Staunton.[9] Thus the Staunton, Finderne, Shirley, Frauncis, Lathbury families are fairly closely interlinked.

The Cottons have not yet come into the picture; when they do, they involve yet another name of Roos interest, the Wesenhams of Conington, Huntingdonshire. Robert Wesenham was one of Sir Robert Roos's executors in 1448. In 1428 we find Robert Wesenham, together with John Basset and Thomas Braunspath, *esteantz ouec le Sire de Roos* (Thomas, eighth Lord Roos), and being given by the boy-king silver

---

[1] P.R.O., D.L. Accounts, 5/7, fol 23.

[2] Nichols, *Leicestershire*, IV, ii, 577; III, ii, 703.

[3] Agnes Staunton died in 1458 according to her brass and her husband's in Castle Donnington church, Leicestershire (*Leics. Arch. Soc., Trans.*, I, 382–5).

[4] John, according to E. P. Shirley, *Stemmata Shirleiana*, p. 47.

[5] Another Derbyshire name. The personal squire of Maria (*née* Percy), Lady de Ros, was Richard Menell (*Test. Ebor.*, I, 202; and see below, p. 109).

[6] Nichols, *Leicestershire*, III, ii, 703.

[7] *Derbyshire Visitation, Pedigrees*, ed. W. C. Metcalfe, pp. 38–9.

[8] *Test. Vetusta*, I, 284–6; *Cal. Close Rolls, 1447–54*, pp. 426–7; Nichols, *Leicestershire*, III, ii, 709.

[9] *Derbyshire Visitation, Pedigrees*, ed. W. C. Metcalfe, p. 38.

collars of his livery.[1] Robert Wesenham, with Thomas Heton and others, was made trustee for the younger Richard Roos's manors by the father, this Thomas, Lord Roos; he claimed and secured them for Richard Roos, Esquire, in 1463.[2] He seems to have acted as man of business for the Roos family. This is the Robert Wesenham who in 1460 succeeded to his childless brother Thomas,[3] and himself died childless in 1477. His niece and co-heir, Mary Folvile (whose hundred years of life spanned the whole fifteenth century), married William Coton, brother of John Coton of Ridware, Staffordshire. After his death at the second battle of St. Albans in 1461, she married twice again, and is generally known as Mary Billing. Her son, Thomas Cotton of Conington, some twenty miles south-east of Rockingham Castle, was the first of a line of four Thomas Cottons. The fourth Thomas, father of Sir Robert Cotton the antiquary, married c. 1565 as his first wife Elizabeth Shirley, daughter of Francis Shirley of Staunton Harold,[4] great-grandson of Ralphe Shirley and of Margaret Staunton. Ralphe Shirley's son by a second wife, another Ralphe, had married a Sussex heiress, and had started a collateral line there at Wisteneston.[5] His son Thomas Shirley of West Grinstead in the early sixteenth century married Elizabeth Gorges, step-granddaughter of Sir Henry Roos.[6]

Margerie Henckford of the scribbled name may come in here; I have not traced her among the Hankefords, but they had connexions with Frauncis on the one hand, and on the other side with Gorges, and so distantly with Sir Henry Roos. Sir Richard Hankeford (1397–1430/1) married *en secondes noces* Anne Montague (see below, No. 77), daughter of John, sixth Earl of Salisbury, and of Maud Fraunceys, daughter of Sir Adam Fraunceys, Lord Mayor of London in 1352–4 and knighted in 1381.[7] Adam Francis does not appear in the pedigree of Francis of Foremark, but an Adam Francis of the late thirteenth century was buried at Great Barlow, a Derbyshire village. Sir Richard's sister, Joanna Hankeford (mentioned in the will of her grandfather Sir William Hankeford[8] in 1423), married as first wife Sir Theobald Gorges. Sir Theobald by his second wife was the father of that Richard Gorges

---

[1] Rymer, *Foedera*, x, 387.   [2] See above, p. 38.

[3] Thomas Wesenham was one of those to whom was assigned the safe custody of Eleanor, Duchess of Gloucester, in 1441. His name occurs in a clerical capacity in the accounts of Margaret of Anjou in 1447–8 (Devon, *Issues*, II, 447–8; Exchequer Accounts, E.101, 409, No. 16).

[4] V.C.H., *Huntingdonshire*, III, 144, *s.n.* Conington. See also *D.N.B.*, *s.n.* Sir Robert Cotton; and his memoranda, *Misc. Gen. et Heraldica*, New ser., I, p. 338.

[5] Nichols, *Leicestershire*, III, ii, 717.   [6] *Sussex Visitation*, p. 7.

[7] G.E.C., *Complete Peerage*, V, 505.

[8] Jacob, *The Register of Henry Chichele*, II, 290–3 and 656.

whose widow Maud married Sir Henry Roos, and whose granddaughter Elizabeth Gorges married Thomas Shirley mentioned above.

Some more minute connexions between MS. Ff. 1.6 and the Roos clan can be suggested. The 'looking-glass' scribble 'Sharesmyth' shows a name with Derbyshire connexions. A Richard Scharesmyth was one of the jury for the *I.p.m.* (1432) of Constance Sutton, *née* Blount of Barton, Derbyshire. She was the mother of that Humphrey Dudley (Sutton) whose marriage to one of Roos's cousins is celebrated by a poem in this manuscript (see below, No. 83*f*).[1] Again, the copyist here of *The Parlement of Foules* was W. Calverley (fol. 44 v.). A Sir William Calverley married Elizabeth Middleton of Yorkshire and another Middleton girl, probably a niece, married Robert Roos of Ingmanthorpe, who founded the line of Roos of Laxton, Nottinghamshire.[2] Thus among a collateral Roos family in a neighbouring county there were Calverley connexions. Finally, the motto 'desormais' at the end of a ballade (fol. 140) is that of the Cliffords, whose Roos connexions go back to Sir Richard's aunt, Elizabeth Roos (see above, p. 25).

Thus marriage connexions which at one end start with an executor of Sir Robert Roos the father, and with a witness to his will, come at the other end to the step-granddaughter of Sir Henry Roos the son. One might well suspect that this very unprofessional manuscript, Ff. 1.6, which contains so many names of Roos interest, drew some of its material from poems to be found at More End. But one need not rest there. An even closer connexion with Sir Richard Roos himself can be suggested.

All these Derbyshire families lived very near the homes of the married sisters of Dame Margaret Roos, *née* Vernon; and at Egginton, barely half a dozen miles from Findern and Foremark, lived her niece Mary Vernon after her marriage with Reginald Leigh. Their son Robert Leigh (who died 1524/5) married Anne Lathbury, also of Egginton. She was a great-niece of that Agnes Lathbury who had married Robert Staunton.[3] MS. Ff. 1.6 may therefore have had not only an indirect Roos interest, but rather a direct link with Sir Richard's own household at his death in 1482. Moreover, a nephew of Margaret Vernon, John Bradbourne (son of Anne Bradbourne, *née* Vernon), married Isabelle, daughter of Richard Cotton of Ridware.[4]

The occurrence in MS. Ff. 1.6 of the fourteenth-century romance, *Sir Degrevant*, written by a man of some education who knew *Les Vœux*

---

[1] Salt Soc., 1888, IX, 54–5. [2] Camb. Univ. MS. Dd. III, 88, Item 9, fol. 4 v.
[3] *Derbyshire Visitation, Pedigrees*, p. 54; MS. Ashmole 798, fol. 41.
[4] MS. Ashmole 798, fol. 9 v.

du Paon, is not without significance for Sir Richard Roos and his familiarity with alliterative verse. Its only other known copy is in the Thornton manuscript, believed to emanate from Robert Thornton of East Newton in the North Riding;[1] this hamlet is less than five miles south-east of Hamlake. On the other hand, the motto 'Theynke and thanke' written in a later hand after the title in MS. Ff. 1.6 (fol. 96) brings us back to the Derbyshire *milieu* and its families. One can fairly assume that it was written in by one of the neighbours whose motto it was, the Tates of Delapré, who in the mid-sixteenth century set up a branch at Sutton Bonington,[2] just over the Nottinghamshire border, across the river Soar, and on the edge of the twenty or so square miles in which these families lived.

Again, the purchaser of the manuscript had local interests, John Moore, Bishop of Norwich, from whose great collection it passed to Cambridge in the early eighteenth century.[3] Moore was a Leicestershire man, and his mother was a girl from the Vale of Belvoir; he was born at her home within sight of the castle, and had his schooling in south Leicestershire.[4] He might well pick up this shabby worn manuscript in the neighbourhood, his eye caught by the familiar Midlands names scribbled in it.

For all these reasons, I would prefer to call MS. Ff. 1.6, not 'the Findern anthology', but 'the Roos scrapbook', and to see it as containing many lyrics, short poems and fragments of Roos's composition, which were in the possession of his widow and then of her niece, Mary Leigh, *née* Vernon. Through Mary's daughter-in-law, a Lathbury, it was available for scribbles to the fifteenth and sixteenth century descendants of the Lathburys and the Stauntons, Shirleys, Cottons, Frauncis's, and Findernes, all in one way or another aware of Roos of Belvoir. The two poems that by an anagrammatic braid of initials indicate the names of the husbands of the Vernon sisters[5] (see below, Nos. 83*d* and *e*) are

---

[1] *The Romance of Sir Degrevant*, ed. L. F. Casson, E.E.T.S., No. 221, 1949, p. ix.

[2] Bridges, *Northamptonshire*, I, 36.   [3] Casson, *ed. cit.*, p. xi.

[4] See *D.N.B.*

[5] One of these husbands, John Stanley, who married Elisabeth Vernon, connects possibly with the copyist of Items xviii and xix, 'Leweston'. A Philip Leweston, gentleman, or Le Weston, called Sheriff of Surrey in the Patent Rolls for May, 1442, can be traced through the Close and Patent Rolls, of 1429 to 1461. He is acting in land transfers with John Stanley in 1440 and 1441 (*Cal. Close Rolls, 1435–41*, pp. 378, 460), and again in 1461 (*Ib., 1461–8*, p. 58). In February 1442/3 he witnesses a charter involving Richard Beauchamp, Earl of Warwick, and Sir Thomas Kyriel (*Ib., 1441–7*, pp. 134–5); and in 1446, he and a John Leweston, son of Roger, lease land in Wimbledon.

proof presumptive of Sir Richard Roos's authorship and ownership. What other versifier in the length and breadth of England would have been interested in this group of historically unremarkable country gentry, or would have coupled their names with that of Margaret Roos? These poems, as undistinguished as their subjects, and several others in the manuscript with anagrams of Roos interest, are found nowhere else, and seem never to have been put into circulation. They were poems of private and family reference. Possibly too they are early drafts which the poet hoped to amend or complete.

The contents of MS. Ff. 1.6 comprise 62 items, as listed by Professor Robbins, ranging from a proverbial scrap to a complete verse-romance (*Sir Degrevant*), and including excerpts from *Confessio Amantis*, and *The Fall of Princes*, and several poems of moderate length such as *La Belle Dame*, *The Cuckoo and the Nightingale* and *The Parliament of Love*; also some two dozen lyrics, the majority not known elsewhere. Of these, I would assign 39 items to Sir Richard Roos, including almost all the lyrics, some poems hitherto attributed to Chaucer (e.g. *The Deth of Pyte*), and the translation from *Les Vœux du Paon*, 'Cassamus roos'. As Professor Robbins demonstrates, the volume is not a collection of independent fascicules, but was probably 'purchased as a blank commonplace book'. The Roos poems are not in order of date; thus Item x (*The Cuckoo*, etc.) dates from the early 1450s (see below, No. 82*b*), but it lies between lyrics of the 1430s and Item xxx, *La Belle Dame*, dating from before 1441. Near the end, 'Cassamus roos' (lx), is, I believe, an early work. And in a sequence of Roos's lyrics (xxxi–xliii) there is no chronological order from the mid-1430s to the mid-1450s. Two things will at once strike the reader of these short poems: that many are put into the mouth of a woman (who can be identified as Margaret Talbot, or Eleanor Cobham, or one of the Vernon sisters); and that the two most frequent themes are parting or separation, and complaints against Fortune.

Several of the short poems were printed in *Reliquiae Antiquae*, others in *Nugae Poeticae*; several more have been printed (or reprinted) lately by Carleton Brown in *Religious Lyrics of the Fifteenth Century*,[1] by Richard L. Greene in *The Early English Carols*;[2] also by Professor Robbins in *Secular Lyrics of the XIVth and XVth Centuries*,[3] and in *P.M.L.A.*, June 1954, LXIX, 610–42.[4] The texts have thus fortunately

---

[1] Nos. 32, 125, 166, 169, 170, 173, and 178, including the three Fortune poems.
[2] Nos. 442, 469.　　[3] Nos. 164–9, and No. 171 from an Oxford manuscript.
[4] Nos. in the MS., 8, 9, 17, 23, 31, 32, 36, 37, 40, 50, 52, 53, 57.

been made more accessible for scrutiny. For the rest, the manuscript contains five tales from Gower, Hoccleve's popular *Letter of Cupid*, a few pieces from Lydgate, including stanzas from *The Fall of the Princes* (fol. 150), some of Chaucer's undoubted shorter poems, such as *The Parlement of Foules*, one or two political poems including the verse-chronicle of the kings (stopping short of the Yorkists), and a long lament against Fortune. In short, it is just such a collection as a poet in Roos's situation might well make, so much so that, if the manuscript is accepted as a combined commonplace book and notebook of Sir Richard Roos, it is found to accord well with his taste, and with what we gradually discern of him in his circumstances and his writing. Thus Chaucer's *Compleynt to his Purse*[1] would strike convincingly on the ear of a poet always in like case; and two extracts from Gower's *Confessio Amantis* concern the behaviour of the Lover, his alternating hopes and fears and jealousies, just such variations of feeling as the lover-poet displays in *The Isle of Ladies*.

The fourth manuscript in order of interest and importance is Longleat 258. This contains *La Belle Dame* and, among other poems, *The Assembly of Ladies*, *The Temple of Glas*, and the unique copy of *The Eye and the Heart*; according to its early index, it once had *The Flower and the Leaf*, of which no manuscript is now known. It is judged to be a manuscript of about 1460 to 1470; its owner signs, 'Constat John Thynne'. This John Thynne may be a fifteenth-century owner, but he is more likely to have been the wealthy Sir John Thynne, the builder between 1567 and 1579 of Longleat. Sir John owed his advancement at court to his uncle William Thynne, the editor of Chaucer, and later harboured at Longleat William's son Francis, when he was in straits. Miss Hammond affirms that the errors of *The Assembly of Ladies* in Thynne's edition of 1532 reflect the mistakes of Longleat 258; and it would appear fairly certain that William Thynne used this manuscript in preparing what Skeat calls his collection of Middle-English poems.[2] Nevertheless there is no sign in it of his ownership, and for family reasons Sir John Thynne was a likely person to be interested in the manuscript.

The early family history of the Thynnes is obscure. Some would take it back to Matthew Paris's story of Geoffrey de Botteville, the Gascon who aided King John, and as a reward was made governor of Belvoir

---

[1] Written, I believe, to Henry IV, on his accession, a time when Sir Richard's father was in close contact with him (see *Medium Ævum*, 1957, XXV, 173).

[2] Hammond, *Anglia*, vol. 34, 235 ff.; Schick, *Temple of Glas*, pp. xxiv-v.

Castle, earning by his good behaviour the friendship of its d'Albini owner. Older genealogists (including Francis Thynne, Lancaster Herald) traced the Thynnes from this Botteville and his brother Oliver.[1] Modern scholars, such as J. H. Round,[2] will not admit the fusion of the two families; otherwise one might suggest that an ancestral connexion with Belvoir, rather than with the De Ros's, might cause Thynne's interest in a manuscript of *La Belle Dame*. There is also a more direct family interest. Sir John Thynne's mother was Margaret Heynes,[3] whose great grandmother Joyce Burley was a niece by marriage of Lady Beatrice Roos. Not only so, but she was the daughter of Alicia (or Amicia) Pembridge, sister of Sir Richard Pembridge,[4] and the Pembridges were among Lady Beatrice's dearest friends, seeing that she included them with her two last husbands in the arrangements for her St. Paul's chantry.[5] And if this seems to be too early and far away, there is a nearer link, in Sir John Thynne's second wife, Christian Gresham. She was a great granddaughter of James Gresham of Holt, who was both cousin and youthful clerk to Judge Paston, and man of business throughout the century to the family, including Sir William Paston, who married a daughter of Eleanor, Lady Roos and Duchess of Somerset,[6] and who was in touch with Master Richard Roos also of Holt. The material for a selective collection such as Longleat 258, in which the 'uniformity of taste suggests the possibility that the copyist was also the owner',[7] may well have been drawn from circles cognizant of the Roos family and its doings. Sir John Thynne's son Edward was to marry Theodosia Manners, daughter of Sir Roger Manners of Uffington,[8] an alliance which might confirm the Thynne interest in Belvoir, but is too late to affect a manuscript used already in 1532.

The fifth manuscript, Trin. Coll., Cambridge, 599 (R. 3.19),[9] used by Stow as is proved by his notes,[10] is a large and very neat and clean collection of Chaucerian verse, with no long poem by Chaucer himself except

[1] Beriah Botfield, *Memorials of the Families of De Botteville, Thynne, and Botfield*, 1858, pp. 15–18.

[2] In *Genealogist*, New ser., XI, p. 193.

[3] *D.N.B.*, John Thynne: Botfield, *op. cit.*, pp. 56, 58–9.

[4] *Topographer & Genealogist*, III, 486.   [5] *Cal. Pat. Rolls, 1408–13*, p. 40.

[6] *Miscellanea Genealogica et Heraldica*, New ser., IV, 117, 253; L. B. Radford, *History of Holt*, 1908, p. 98.

[7] E. Hammond, in *M.L.N.*, 1905, XX, 77–9.

[8] Botfield, *op. cit.*, pp. 54–5.

[9] M. Rhodes James, *The Western Manuscripts in the Library of Trinity College, Cambridge*, II, item 599, p. 69 ff.

[10] See P. Simpson, *Proof-correcting,* etc., pp. 59–60, for this manuscript as 'copy' for Stow's edition of Chaucer, including *The Court of Love*.

The Parlement of Foules. The other long poems, in addition to *La Belle Dame*, are *The Assembly of Ladies*, and *The Court of Love*, still largely an enigma,[1] and probably the latest poem in the collection. Two shorter poems are also in Fairfax 16 (*The Ten Commandments of Love*, and *The Nine Ladies Worthy*), which is dated 1450. *The Craft of Lovers* is dated internally 1448. The *Balade* in praise of the daisy is obviously to Margaret of Anjou, 'La bele Margarite . . . exalted of natife kind'; it refers to February, April, and May (the months of the proxy wedding, the actual wedding, and the coronation), and bears all the marks of the stiff and lumbering style of George Ashby, who was in her Escort. His prison poem is also here. Skeat's contention (accepted by Rhodes James) that the author of *A Balade Pleasaunte* was fifteen years old in 1403 at the wedding of Queen Joan of Navarre,[2] is not supported by the text. What the mocking poet says in st. 6 is that the elderly lady whom he is satirizing must have been fifteen already by 1403, i.e. that she was born about 1386 (see below, No. 88). The volume is therefore very largely a collection of mid-fifteenth-century poems, and it is the source of Stow's 'heap of rubbish'. The many poems in it that I shall be assigning to Roos cover a long range of dates from c. 1438 to 1450 to 1478–9.

This manuscript, together with Shirley's manuscript, R. 3.20, was presented to the library by an Elizabethan member of the College, George Wilmer (1583-1626); the Wilmer arms are stamped on the leather binding. The son of a wealthy merchant,[3] he married about 1606 Margery Thweng, daughter and heiress of Marmaduke Thweng, lord of the manor of Upper Helmsley, and representative of a younger branch of the Thwengs of Kilton Castle, Yorkshire. Upper Helmsley is some twenty miles south-east of Helmsley Castle; in the thirteenth century, a de Ros and a Thweng had married de Brus sisters, and Marjorie Thweng had conveyed land to her de Ros sister. In the sixteenth century, Thwengs were marrying Thwaites and Grimstons; and Margery Wilmer, as a widow, married Henry Fairfax, second son of Thomas, Viscount Fairfax of Emley, of the elder branch, collateral with the better-known Fairfaxes of Denton and Bilborough, who in the late fifteenth century intermarried with the Manners of Belvoir. Wilmer's wife was therefore in Yorkshire circles which would be familiar with the name of Roos of Helmsley or Hamlake. Whoever collected the poems had access to varied Roos material.

---

[1] See below, No. 103.   [2] *Chaucer Canon*, pp. 123–4.
[3] Jos. J. Green, *The Puritan Family of Wilmer. Congregational Hist. Soc. Transactions*, IV 3, Oct. 1909.

Wilmer's other presentation, MS. R. 3.20, copied by Shirley and annotated by Stow, contains French *balades* attributed to the Earl of Suffolk, and other fifteenth-century poetry. One cannot press the following point, since the name is so ordinary; but one may at least draw attention to a contemporary memorandum, 'p*er* me John Rychardson' (f. 93); this was the name of Sir Richard Roos's personal servant in the court of Edward IV, who 'kepte [his] stuff' there in 1481/2. Was MS. R. 3.20, a Shirley production, part of the 'stuff'?

The sixth manuscript, Sloane 1710, contains a large fragment, ll. 93–764 of *La Belle Dame* (fol. 164–76 v.; 'At my commyng . . . and fayre langage'). It is of paper, three stanzas to a page, in a very heavy thick hand, with the top lines of the pages flourished upwards in Chancery hand style. The rest of the bulky volume is incongruous, being a mixed collection of mainly seventeenth-century letters and documents, with nothing on the surface to indicate how this imperfect copy of fifteenth-century verse got into it from another volume, of which fol. 164 was formerly fol. 50.

Thus four out of the six extant manuscripts of the translation of *La Belle Dame* can be shown to have passed through, or remained in, the hands of persons so circumstanced as by immediate contacts, or by distant marriage connexions, or by their family locality, to have knowledge of the Roos family, or at least some interest in it. These four collections (Fairfax 16, Ff. 1.6, Longleat 258, and R. 3.19) will prove to have a considerable number of poems by Roos. The question at once arises, why is there no attribution to Sir Richard Roos in any of these? Aristocratic 'nonchaloir' is probably one reason; in general the courtly and personal poet did not blazon his name abroad as an author, but wrote for his own and his friends' pleasure. But here there is probably another and a stronger reason. The prestige of this Lancastrian poetry, personal and occasional as it will prove to be, was eclipsed for a quarter of a century; it became a liability, not an asset, to be concealed rather than claimed or acclaimed. For Roos in particular, the scattering of family papers may well have been almost fatal to any continuity of fame. More End, Belvoir, Hamlake, and presumably Sir Richard's own house, were all seized; Belvoir was laid waste, and it is possible that when its roofs were stripped, it was looted. It is also possible that just as the devoted neighbour tried to save the roofs, so Roos adherents may have tried to save other goods of value. It is noticeable that the Rutland papers now contain few personal manuscripts prior to 1460, though chartularies, charters, and other land documents survive in great numbers.

II. FRENCH POETIC DEVICES

The second line of enquiry based on Roos's translation arises from his proved familiarity with French poetry. French poets had certain marked habits in the late fourteenth and the fifteenth centuries. One of these is to name the poem not at the beginning nor by a title, but at the end in the last few lines or stanzas, sometimes following with an *Explicit*, or *Cy finit* repeating the name. Machaut, Caulier, Baude, Vaillant, all exemplify this method, and Chartier dismisses the hard-hearted lady thus:[1]

> Que ja nulle de vous resemble
> Celle que m'oyez nommer cy
> Qu'on appelera, ce me semble,
> La belle dame sans mercy.

Roos inevitably follows this, and shows that he recognizes the last line as the title by keeping it in French. *The Assembly of Ladies* also gives the name in French at the end; the narrator, in answer to the knight's query, 'tel me now, what ye the book do cal?', replies,

> of the name to tel the certeynte
> *L'Assemble de Dames*, thus it hight.

The author of *Le Songe Vert*, whether Gower or Froissart,[2] also answers a supposed question:

> Mais se nus hom par aucun tor
> Aucunement te demandoit
> Coment cez diz nomez seroit,
> Si lor respont tot en apert
> Qu'on l'apele *le Songe vert*. (ll. 1818–22)

Le Pris Donneur and *Sir Orfeo* also are named in the conclusion, and if this method had been realized, the true title of the much mis-named poem now called *The Isle of Ladies* would have been seen to be 'the yle of plesaunce'.

Another habit is that of concealing or half disclosing the name of the author. Chaucer does not, I believe, resort to this, but Gower does, clumsily and blatantly enough. Guillaume de Machaut delighted to

---

[1] *La Belle Dame sans Mercy*, etc., ed. Arthur Piaget, Geneva, 1949.
[2] See Ethel Seaton, '*Le Songe Vert*: its Occasion of Writing and its Author', *Medium Ævum*, 1950, XIX, 1–16.

puzzle his readers thus.[1] A surname which is also a recognizable word is almost too obvious a gift to a poet; Baude, with his hound's name, makes play with hunting and bushes.[2] A more artistic poet will not use it simply, but will probably combine it in some kind of phrase or motto. If it can be part-concealed, so that only the coterie smile over it, so much the better. Or if a motto is chosen, it may be worked into the sentence as it was worked into the patterned embroidery of a gown or mantle. Even so Chartier works his motto, 'Au povre prisonnier' into the first lines of his Rondel xv:

> Au povre prisonnier, madame,
> Donnez l'aumosne de liesce.

And Guillebert de Lannoy weaves his 'devise', 'Vostre plaisir', into the refrain of his seventh Balade: 'Vostre plaisir a mon leal pouoir'.[3] A translation naturally offers fewer opportunities; and in *La Belle Dame*, the line 'This woful man roos up in al his payne' (797) is an obvious rendering of 'Adonc le dolent se leva'. But line 3 of Roos's original prologue runs, 'Yet nat for thy I roos', and one wonders whether Sir Richard is taking advantage of the possibilities of his verb-like name, as did John Dowland later, with his motto 'Semper Dowland, semper dolens'. When this phrase is found conspicuously near the beginning (or end) of certain of the longer poems of the period, one guesses that it is intended as a private signature.

Yet another French method is the concealed or half-concealed indication of the persons for whom poems are written. The initial letter acrostic and the anagram are common in French poetry, whether in simple or complex forms, especially in the 'balades' of Eustache Deschamps. A delightful proof of the popularity of this game is found in the 'Heures de Marguérite d'Orléans', the beautiful gift *in absentia* of Charles d'Orléans to his sister on her marriage in 1426 to Richard of Brittany, Count of Étampes. In one charming margin, two women and two gardeners are sweeping up, as we might confetti now, letters large and small, red and blue, cramming them furiously into aprons and baskets.[4] In the wild confusion the repeated names of the bride and the groom can be picked out, but what else, whether 'devises' or names,

---

[1] For the complex methods of some French writers, see C. A. Robson, 'A Fifteenth Century Puzzle' in *Medium Ævum*, 1948, XVII, 15–20; and *Bibliotheca Pepysiana*, ed. M. R. James, III, p. 25, No. 1594.

[2] Champion, *Hist. Poét. du XVᵉ Siècle*, I, 241–2, 269; Plates xiii–xv.

[3] A. Piaget in *Romania*, XXXIX, pp. 329, 335.

[4] Jean Porcher, *Chefs d'œuvre de l'Enluminure française du 15ᵉ siècle*. Paris, 1951. Plate X. I owe this illustration to the kindness of Miss E. A. Francis, also that following from J. Renart.

G

has so far defied scrutiny. Again, words which conceal the name, or translate it, can be used, as Chaucer does at the end of *The Book of the Duchess*. Or words (or names) can be split into syllables, and these component parts read backward; Eustache Deschamps demonstrates this method in his poem to his patron, the Sieur de Coucy (poem 655):

> Les noms sarez du seigneur et servent,
> *Cou*vertement en ce rondelet *cy*,
> Maiz diviser les vous fauldra ainsi. . . .
> En reversent prendrez subtivement
> En derrain ver troiz petiz mos de li:
> *A ce eust* bien un autre defailli.

Cou-cy is clear enough; but Eust-a-ce might well escape even the poet's familiars.[1] Two centuries earlier Jean Renart had 'signed' his lays by a similar backward 'engin'—'procédé qui n'a rien d'extraordinaire au moyen âge'. Thus from 'il enTRA EN Religion' read Renart.[2]

A developed and complex version of a double acrostic anagram was known to Chaucer[3] and was largely practised, as I have found, by Charles d'Orléans and his friends,[4] and by those poets who came into contact with him, such as Villon, Meschinot, and Vaillant. The clearest demonstration of the method is given by the Breton poet, Jean Meschinot, in a 'Balade a lectres contrainctes' addressed to Marie de Clèves, Duchesse d'Orléans.[5] The first stanza shows the simplest form of acrostic; her name runs straight down the line-initials of the thirteen lines. It is also, less noticeably, repeated in the initial letters after the caesura of each line, thus:

> *M*ame angelique, *m*er d'honneur meliflue,
> *A*rbre de vie *a*pportant le doulx bame,
> *R*ecueil d'amour, *r*ose roial dont flue
> *I*nexfluxible *j*oie qui tous cueurs embame;
> *E*ureuse, eslite, *e*xcellente et grant dame (etc.).

This however is only a simple beginning. In stt. 2 and 3 and the Envoy,

---

[1] Edition S.A.T.F., IV, 114.
[2] See R. Lejeune Dehousse, *L'Œuvre de Jean Renart*, Liège, 1935, pp. 21–2.
[3] Ethel Seaton, '*The Parlement of Foules* and Lionel of Clarence' in *Medium Ævum*, 1957, XXV, 168–74.
[4] *Studies in Villon, Vaillant, and Charles d'Orléans*, Oxford, 1957.
[5] *Charles d'Orléans, Poésies*, ed. P. Champion, II, 601; see also pp. 623–4. The word 'contrainctes' appears to be a technical term in 'engins' of this kind. Bérenguier de Noya, a thirteenth-century troubadour, when providing the clue to a double acrostic (initial and final letters of lines) which gives his and his parents' names and places of birth, explains that in each line two syllables are 'costretes', i.e., enforced by the exigencies of the acrostic (see Ist van Frank, 'Un Message Secret de B. de N.' etc., in *Filologia Romanza*, I, 1954).

the corresponding letters are taken, two from each line, not in a straight acrostic, but anagrammatized. The resultant letters can be seen to repeat the name Marie de Clèves and to add Duchess d'O-lians, and also the poet's signature Mes-hinot, and the name of his most famous work *Les Lunett-s*. There is a residue of letters, most of them the letters of frequency; these in French are P and Q; in English they tend to be T, F, and W. In acrostics, initial letters of proper names may also be called into play, to ease the poet's difficulties; and, as always in French practice, a second or a third letter, or even a whole syllable or short word following on after an initial letter, can be used. An extreme example of this is seen in Deschamps' *balade* on his own name and that of his lady (Poem 540; S.A.T.F., III, 381–2).

Scrutiny of the original portion of Roos's *La Belle Dame* shows that he practised this complex double acrostic anagram. It was possibly through Chaucer's *Parlement of Foules*, probably through an early contact with Charles d'Orléans, that he became acquainted with it. Thus the four introductory stanzas yield: HOMF--Y; ALYAN. COBHAM; AnTIG., clearly indicating the Gloucester family. This and other examples in *La Belle Dame* will be fully gone into later (No. 59); suffice it here to say that this authenticated Roos poem gives evidence of his knowledge and practice of this hitherto unnoticed cryptogram.

Private methods of conveying names, such as those just described, can be reinforced, or hinted at, by heraldic pointers, such as badges, including flowers, crests, colours, mottoes, and 'devises'. These last were used in profusion in the courts of France and Burgundy on garments and hangings and jewels, for the eye, as well as in poems for the ear. When several of these pointers occur in one poem, as they sometimes do, they may well confirm each other; and such a poem may be found to act as a centre round which other similar or lesser lyrics may be grouped. All coterie poetry, as most of this period's lighter verse is (with a few outbreaks of naturalness), tends to divert its readers thus: even if there seems at first to be 'no consonancy in the sequel', they do well to wonder 'what should that alphabetical position portend?' We too must be prepared to play the poet's courtly game, to dance to his piping, and follow whither he leads us as he led his intimates and privileged contemporaries. If we hold aloof, we lose not only something of the atmosphere and the sport, but we miss sheer information too. The advantage to scholarship in such cryptograms of persons is plain. I had been inclined to date *La Belle Dame* after 1441 and the break-up of the Plesaunce circle, until Roos's original stanzas yielded up their secret of acrostic anagrams, the Introduction giving the names of the

noble family at Plesaunce, and the *Verba Translatoris* those of the Duke
and his treasurer, and other men of the group.   The powerful friends
who had demanded the translation from Roos, and whom he 'durst not
disobey', are therefore the Duke and Duchess of Gloucester.

III. METRE AND STYLE

The third line of enquiry, most debatable of all, is the criterion of metre,
rhythm, and style. *La Belle Dame* affords us eight stanzas of original
verse in rhyme royal, and a hundred eight-line stanzas of line-by-line
translation, rhyming ababbcbc as in the original. Whereas the French
is in octosyllabic lines, however, the English is in decasyllabics: 'Le plus
dolent des amoureux'; 'Of al lovers the most unfortunate' (l. 4 and l. 32).
Evidently the poet felt the need of elbow-room, and indeed the grave
compression of Chartier (who might for style and temper be called the
de Vigny of the fifteenth century) offers problems in elasticity to a
translator.   But the inevitable result of this lengthening is too much
padding, though one must admit the awkward necessities of rhyme.
The blessed word 'certeyn' is insertable anywhere, and as the rhyme
word it leads to frequent rhymes in -eyn; no less than thirteen of the
hundred stanzas have this final sound. Roos's trouble with rhymes is
shown by his tendency to insert padding at line-ends. Thus ll. 237-41
show the complete insertion of a triplet of rhyme:

> Though it be so that I can nat deserve
> To have your grace, *but alway live in drede,*
> Yet suffre me you for to *love and* serve
> Without maugre *of your most goodlihede;*
> Both faith and trouth I give *your womanhede.*

This is the best that Roos can do for a whole stanza (27) of word and
rhyme-play on forms of *servir*.   Again, elsewhere the word 'routh' for
miséricorde gives him the chance of an ever-useful rhyme, and by
translating 'loyauté' as 'trouth', he gets it. These two rhymes are constantly to be found again in other poems.

Tags and *clichés* abound, such as 'withouten fayle' (ll. 187, 469), 'in
this cace' (ll. 417, 445, 665), 'for wele or wo' (ll. 481, 632). Doublets
help to lengthen the line: 'my *lady and* maistresse' (l. 34); 'ful softe *and
demurely*' (l. 246); 'wepe *and waylen*' (l. 380). These do not always,
however, entail loss of energy; thus the lady's parting shafts are hurled
more vigorously in the translation:

> De vous mesmes juge soyez.
> Une fois pour toutes croyez

Que vous demourrez escondit.
De tant redire m'ennoyez,
Car je vous en ay assez dit. (ll. 764–8)

Be juge your-self; for so ye shal it fynde.
Ones for alway let this sinke in your mynde—
That ye desire shal never rejoysed be!
Ye noy me sore in wasting al this wynde;
For I have sayd y-nough as semeth me. (ll. 792–6)

The translator can enhance her energy of speech by judicious emphatic inversion: 'Free am I now, and free wil I endure' (l. 314, for 'Je suy franche et franche vueil estre', l. 286); or in the Rosalind-like observation 'Yet dyeth non, as ferre as I can see' (l. 616, for 'Mais je n'en ay veu nul mourir', l. 588). Occasionally the translation is so free as to have a different effect: 'Myself and I, me thought we were y-now' (l. 86) is of another temper than the French, 'En ung lieu tout coy et privé' (l. 58); and so is the expansion of 'Comme l'oisel au chant du boys' (l. 96) into

> Lyk as the sowne of birdes doth expresse,
> Whan they sing loude in frith or in forest. (ll. 123–4)

The close-pruned style of Chartier hardly admits of metaphors, however brief; Roos's additions often supply them: false lovers 'serve to boste, *to jangle as a jay*' (l. 744). Twice a hawking metaphor is inserted: Chartier's dissimulator 'A peine sa faintise queuvre (couvre)', Roos's 'fayned chere is hard to kepe in mewe' (ll. 310 and 338); the changeful lovers' hearts are 'bien reclamez'; in Roos they are 'wel reclaymed to the lure' (ll. 606 and 634). A military metaphor is enlarged: Refus had not only 'ses chasteaulx bastis' but also 'stuffed with ordinaunce' (ll. 790 and 818); a metaphor from feudal law is slipped into the line, 'La volonté franche et delivre', 'A wil that stant eneffed in fraunchyse' (ll. 336 and 364; cf. ll. 444 and 472). The English is seldom flatter than the French, though there are some lapses of the translation, as in st. 73, ll. 605 ff. An occasional misunderstanding, as at l. 331, is surprising, since the translation is generally not only adroit but exact.

Skeat remarked in 1897 on the smoothness and regularity of the metre; there are none of Lydgate's broken-backed lines (though l. 5 comes perilously near it), but skilful use is made of the variations established by Chaucer, such as the inversion of the first foot ('Ladies be nat so simple, thus I mene', l. 325). The shift of the pause is very free; the norm is after the fourth syllable, but it can come after the fifth (ll. 78, 106), or the sixth (ll. 147, 642), or even the third (l. 438), and there are frequent examples of that first foot caesura which checks and stiffens the too fluid line:

'With that, his heed he tourned at the last . . .
On her, the which his thought was most upon'. (ll. 141 and 144)

There can be more than one pause in the line, fitted easily into the syntactical structure: 'And sayd, Now deeth, com forth, thy self avaunce' (l. 801); sometimes with emphatic inversion: 'Wepe they, laugh they, or sing, this I waraunt' (l. 730); ejaculations can bring about frequency of pause: 'That fele, god wot, nat alther-grettest payne' (l. 298; cf. l. 428). Elision occurs occasionally, probably showing the normal development of pronunciation, as in *ever* (ll. 163, 172), *even* (ll. 266, 467), *cherissheth* (l. 415), or in a French word: 'And peraventure, I leve that it be so' (l. 710; cf. 105). The method of the original adopted in the translation precludes any run-on of stanzas, but there are three such links in the original verses—a practice rare in Chaucer. The easy run-on of lines is frequent, and there are some two score examples of a strong run-on needed to unite dependent parts of speech (e.g. ll. 31/2, 79/80).

The vocabulary is pure, without aureate or inkhorn terms, though with a natural fondness for words of French derivation, the expressions of *amour courtois*, and the literary standard speech of the period; such as *devoir, servage, maugre, juise*. Words in -aunce affect the rhymes as they do not in Lydgate; 'plesaunce (which occurs more than twenty times), semblaunce, desesperaunce, grevaunce, suffraunce'; 'alegeaunce' translates *alegement*, and therefore signifies 'alleviation', not allegiance (ll. 54, 725; cf. *Rom. of the Rose*, l. 4570). A form which has not survived is 'folily' for foolishly (ll. 490, 522). A few words occur of undoubted English background, but rare, or new, such as 'bakker-more', 'currish'. Skeat noted northern forms, 'longes, chase' (for 'chose'); we know how Sir Richard Roos came to have this range.

To sum up, *La Belle Dame sans Merci*, the one authenticated translation by Sir Richard Roos, gives evidence of a practised poetic style, and of familiarity with French poetry in general. In particular, it shows his acquaintance with the French poets' methods of dealing with their patrons and readers or auditors, of indicating their names and signing their own in a half-concealed manner. Several of the manuscripts of the poem can be traced to early owners who might be knowledgeable about Roos; one indeed shows clear signs of being a personal collection, started in his own household, and passing down through the families of his wife's niece, her kinsfolk and descendants. These enquiries must now be extended further.

CHAPTER IV

The Corpus *of Roos's Poetry*

THE conclusions drawn from Sir Richard Roos's translation of *La Belle Dame sans Merci* offer criteria which can be applied as tests to other poems of the century, both long and short. If a *corpus* of poetry by this obviously practised poet is to be found, it can be established only by close comparison with the English *La Belle Dame*. General observations here will run on the same lines of enquiry as in Chapter III, but in a more extended field, that is, 'signatures', concealed names, anagrams, *devises*, references and allusions to arms, crests and badges; metre and general style; and also manuscripts, other than those already discussed. One set of manuscripts, however, which involve special problems, will be reserved for separate consideration. At the end of this chapter a list will be given of the poems or groups of poems which on all these counts I would attribute to Sir Richard Roos. This claim needs the most careful substantiation if it is to win assent as establishing a *corpus* of his poetry. In the following chapters, each of these poems will be considered in detail, and the reasons of style, allusions, anagrams, etc., given for the authorship, and for the period or date, and subject or occasion assigned to each. The assumption that these poems are in fact by Sir Richard Roos of necessity underlies the general observations of this chapter; but it is recognized that this assumption is still *sub judice*, even in this study, until the detailed examination of individual poems is completed.

I. MANUSCRIPTS

A large proportion of these poems are to be found in four out of the six manuscripts which contain *La Belle Dame sans Merci*; several are in the three other collections already mentioned (see above, p. 83). Some, but not many, occur in Shirley's manuscripts, or in manuscripts derived from him. It will sometimes be found that, since we know the date of Shirley's death (1456), such occurrence or non-occurrence will help to confirm positively, or by inference, the approximate date suggested for a poem. Some observations on the provenance of these manuscripts are made here, first on manuscripts independent of Shirley, leading off with the two which, with Fairfax 16, form the so-called Bodleian Group, i.e. Bodleian 638 and Tanner 346.[1] Next to this group, and for the same kind of associative interest, stand Pepys 2006, and also Harleian 7578 which is related to Fairfax 16.[2] Certain manuscripts, which are concerned only or chiefly with one poem, will be dealt with under that poem, e.g. Longleat 256 and Add. 10303 under the *Isle of Ladies*. Two of Shirley's own manuscripts are involved, Add. 16165 and Ashmole 59; also two copied from Shirley, Add. 34360 and Harleian 78. Stow's great sixteenth-century collection, Add. 29729, is almost entirely a Lydgate *corpus*; but it contain's Stow's copy, made from Fairfax 16, of *Reson and Sensuallyte* (No. 61, below).

First, the Bodleian group; Tanner 346 is a Greystoke manuscript; it has 'J. Graystok' on the end flyleaves, and in the same hand within the volume. It is of vellum, with some modest but professional decoration, especially in the first part. It has the appearance of being composed of three fascicules, the first comprising *The Legend of Good Women*; the second containing Items 2 to 8, which include (3) *The Black Knight*, and (6) *The Deth of Pyte*; and the third with four more poems, including *The Temple of Glas* (State α). The second part especially is thriftily written; very little space is wasted, and the poems run across the quires. Parts II and III both contain scribbles, 'Penses J. G.' (fol. 73), and again 'J.G.' (fol. 80 v.), both in the hand of the last page, and on the flyleaf, the twice repeated 'J. Graystok'. On the last pages are also the names Philip Joisilyn and, in a later hand, Richard Justice. Another heavier hand has written 'Anne' (fol. 70) and 'only yorss. A.N.' (fol. 81).

The Greystokes were a Yorkshire baronial family, which early in the fifteenth century had intermarried with Clifford, Beauchamp, and Beaufort. There were two Lords Greystoke named John in the century, the fourth lord (c. 1390–1436), and his grandson, the sixth lord (d. 1500/1), son of Lord Ralph. Either of these might have been the scribbler, though the large sprawly hand is one more common towards the end of the century. If it was the earlier Lord John, his marriage with a daughter of Joan Beaufort would have relevance for the inclusion of a Beaufort poem. His mother was Katherine Clifford, whose brother

---

[1] E. Hammond, *Chaucer Bibliography*, pp. 333–9.   [2] *Ib.*, pp. 330–1.

Thomas, sixth Lord Clifford, married Elizabeth Roos (d. 1424), aunt of Sir Richard, and whose brother William married Ann Bardolf, aunt of Elizabeth Phelip. Lord Greystoke was Keeper of Roxburgh Castle, and was one of the commissioners to treat of peace with Scotland in 1430;[1] Thomas, eighth Lord Roos, was also appointed to this commission,[2] but hardly had time to do much on it before his sudden death. The later Lord John Greystoke married Cicely Herbert, daughter of William Herbert, Earl of Pembroke, and died in 1500/1. For neither John do the initials A(nne) N. have any obvious significance; but an Anne Greystoke, probably a daughter of the elder John, married a Bigod in 1432 (*Test. Ebor*, III, p. 226). There is yet a third possibility. From the choice of poems, all fashionable towards the middle of the century, the most probable first owner of the book might well be Ralph, fifth Lord Greystoke (c. 1414–87), the genealogical link between the two Johns, son of the one, and father of the other. He was a close contemporary of Sir Robert and Sir Richard Roos, and succeeded his father in 1436 at the age of twenty-two. Like Sir Richard, he was a member of the Escort for Margaret of Anjou.[3] There he was of course of higher rank than the Roos brothers, but it is possible that the three young men had been in contact previously as squires and knights, and he is the likeliest of these three Greystokes to have been interested in coterie poems by his elder contemporary and in some sort kinsman. Lord Ralph was a wavering Lancastrian, and later held office under Edward IV.

MS. Bodleian 638, though a slovenly and ill-treated volume of paper quires within vellum covers, is nevertheless considered by Miss Hammond to be occasionally better textually than its handsomer sister, Fairfax 16. Its contents are similar to those of MS. Tanner 346, and still more to those of MS. Fairfax 16. Watermarks and handwriting place it in the third quarter of the fifteenth century. An owner's name 'Gyl Astley' is followed by a date which looks like 1460; but since name and date are written on a *printed* page pasted in the cover, they must be considerably later. Nevertheless they may repeat and replace an inscription on the board, and the name is not without suggestiveness. Giles was a

[1] Dr. Hunt of the Bodleian Library has pointed out to me the difficulties in the way of taking seriously the scribble 'S W Anguis' beside the last signature of J. Graystoke. If it could be given the status of a name, it might indicate Sir William Douglas, nineteenth Earl of Angus, the elder Lord John's hostile neighbour on the Border, and, like him, one of the commissioners to treat of Anglo-Scottish peace in 1430. Contact between the two men might have occurred at any time from 1429 to 1430; during 1430 it is undoubted.

[2] G.E.C., *Complete Peerage*, XI, 104.

[3] *Ib.*, VI, 197–9; and see Chapter II above.

recurrent name in the well-known family of Astley in Warwickshire. In the early fourteenth century, Sir Giles de Astley was the head of the family; and although the next two heads of the house were Thomas and William, there was a younger branch, Astleys of Wolvey, which carried on the name. Giles Astley of Wolvey died in 1427; another Giles Astley was lord of the manor when Dugdale wrote in the seventeenth century.[1] 'Gyl. Astley' who in the later fifteenth century owned Bodleian 638, must be in that succession. His most famous kinsman was Sir John Astley, one of his cousins of Patshull, who fought duels and won honour, first in 1438 against a French knight in Paris, and then in January 1440/1 at Smithfield against a Spanish challenger. King Henry VI knighted the victorious Englishman on the spot, and granted him a pension of a hundred marks.[2] Nevertheless Sir John Astley turned Yorkist later, and was rewarded with the Garter by Edward IV in 1461.[3] The Astleys had earlier married in such a way as to cross the lines of Roos. William, fourth Lord Astley, left an only daughter Joan, who married *en secondes noces* Reginald, Lord Grey de Ruthyn. Grey's first wife, who died after a brief marriage, had been Margaret Roos, aunt of Sir Richard Roos.[4] The manuscript may have been copied later from material that was in the hands of these families in the middle of the century. The multiplicity of names and scribbles and of scraps of all sorts, sacred and profane, Latin and English, some dated in the sixteenth century, suggests that later it was in schoolboys' hands, perhaps in a monastery school. Of the many scrawled names, one, Humfrey Kyryel (fol. 127), leads on to the next manuscript to be considered, Pepys 2006.

MS. Pepys 2006, a paper manuscript, is in some half-dozen current hands of the fifteenth century.[5] It consists of at least two fascicules and three of the short poems are repeated towards the end. It contains, *inter alia*, *The Black Knight*, and *The Temple of Glas*. Two fascicules seem to have been gummed together; between pp. 377 and 378 is legible against the light the name 'Johes Kiriel', written 'in large black conventional script with long capital J'. John Kiriel (who had an illegitimate son, John) was a younger brother of the renowned fighting

---

[1] *Warwickshire*, fol. 45b.

[2] *Ib.*, fol. 72b–73a. Cf. Vlson de la Colombière, *Le Vray Théâtre de l'honneur*, 1648, II, 311–13.

[3] *Ib.*, fol. 73a.

[4] G.E.C., *Complete Peerage*, VI, 157–8.

[5] M. R. James, *Bibliotheca Pepysiana*, III, 60–3; E. Hammond, *Mod. Lang. Notes*, 1904, XIX, 196–8; Manly and Rickert, *Cant. Tales*, I, 406–9.

leader, Sir Thomas Kiriel. The Kiriel (Criol) family in its beginnings owned Croxton-Criol (now Croxton-Kiriel) some five miles south-east of Belvoir Castle, holding it of the d'Albinis, from whom they took their arms. Later the family moved to Kent, and held Bellaview (a name reminiscent of Belvoir), and Ostenhanger, now Westenhanger.[1] Sir Thomas made his name at Verneuil in 1424, and was the victor at Crotoy in 1435; he was Captain of Gournay (1437–9) when he is called a King's Knight, then Lieutenant of Calais (1440–1), and later of Gisors.[2] As Lieutenant of Calais he was associated with Sir Robert Roos, to receive there the repeated oath of Charles d'Orléans in 1440 on his liberation. In 1446 he fell foul of his superiors, Talbot, and John, Viscount Beaumont; 'feeling himself wronged', he appealed to the king; the appeal was referred to Adam Moleyns, and failed.[3] Nevertheless when, in early 1450, Henry VI took desperate measures to stem the tide of disasters in France, it was Sir Thomas Kiriel whom he sent out to Edmund, Duke of Somerset, with succours of men and material raised on money lent by Sir John Fastolfe. The succours never reached Somerset, since the French intercepted Kiriel at Formigni, defeated him in spite of his display of 'unheard-of personal valour', and took him prisoner:[4] 'Sir Thomas Keriel is take prisoner, and alle the legge harneyse, and abowte iij. ml. Englishe men slayn'.[5] He does not seem to have remained long in captivity, since from 1453 we find him involved in various of those complex transfers of land which were the chief fifteenth-century method of investment.[6] Earlier deeds show him as a witness together with Reginald, Lord Cobham, to a quitclaim made (1439) to John and Margaret Stanlow, who were members of the Household.[7] In 1446 he and Edmund, then Earl of Somerset, were heirs and assigns in a quitclaim by five Kentish gentlemen.[8] One of Sir Thomas's daughters seems to have married Sir John Stiward, who in 1441 was a member of the Household, and had Eleanor Cobham in his charge for some weeks; Stiward in 1447 left to his father-in-law a diamond ring which Eleanor had presented 'while she lived with me as my prisoner'.[9] Sir Thomas Kiriel's story ends in darkness. He turned Yorkist, bribed, it was said, by the promise of the Garter; it was a brief glory—elected K.G. on February 8, 1461, he was executed by February 19, after the

---

[1] *Misc. Gen. et Heraldica*, New ser., III, 239; Hasted, *Kent*, III, 438; cf. *D.N.B.*
[2] *Cal. Pat. Rolls, 1436–41*, 43, 62, 374.   [3] *Ib., 1446–52*, 6–7.
[4] *Misc. Gen. et Heraldica*, 5th ser., VI, 254–7.
[5] *Paston Letters*, No. 93 (ed. Gairdner, 1872).
[6] *Cal. Close Rolls, 1447–54*, 484–5.   [7] *Ib., 1435–41*, 260.
[8] *Ib., 1441–7*, 441.   [9] *Genealogist*, New ser., I, 154; II, 35.

second battle of St. Albans. He was adjudged to death as a traitor by Prince Edward, who, with his mother, witnessed the execution.

From 1420 to 1460, Sir Thomas Kiriel was moving in circles of interest which included the army, the garrisons in France, the Household, and, through Kent, and the Cobhams, impinged also on Gloucester's. It is possible that he was the first owner of MS. Pepys 2006, since his widow Cicely in her will in 1472 left all her goods and silver in the house at Westenhanger to her brother-in-law, John Kiriel, then apparently held in France, or, failing his return, to his illegitimate son John.[1] This manuscript may have been among the 'goods'. A later owner was 'William ffetypace, mercer'; a John Fetiplace was, like Henry Roos, one of the queen's squires in 1452–3.[2]

Before leaving Pepys's collection, one may note that another of his manuscripts (2516) can be traced back to concerns of the court of Henry VI. It is a collection of chronicles, and memoranda on court procedure; and it contains a part of a letter, unsigned and unaddressed (fol. 117 v.), which can be shown to date from 1453. The query has evidently been made, 'at what tyme the quene w^t chylde shall take hir chamb*er*'; the answer is, that the persons to be consulted are Margaret Stanlowe and Me Bromeley, and that the book of procedure in such matters was last in the hands of 'Hampton the Esquyer'. These names, and the reference to usage under Henry IV and Henry V, prove that the expected birth is that of Prince Edward, since Margaret Stanlow was one of Queen Margaret's gentlewomen, and John Hampden was the King's squire. The manuscript was given in 1597 by Daniel Hill to Coke. Its earlier ownership is not indicated; but evidently Pepys was buying manuscripts which came ultimately from Lancastrian families.

A few manuscripts do not contain *La Belle Dame*, yet prove to be of strong interest for Roos. The chief of these is Camb. Univ. Lib., MS. Gg. 4.27, a manuscript of *The Canterbury Tales* (mutilated), and *Troilus and Criseyde* (defective). The quire preceding *Troilus* contains six short poems, three of which prove to be by Roos, one written for Queen Margaret in 1445; this quire looks as if it had been added later (Manly and Rickert, I, 179). In the remaining poems, there are two remarkable features: the unique version (G) of the Prologue to the *Legend of Good Women*; and after *The Temple of Glas* (itself an important variant) the added *Compleynt*, an independent poem found elsewhere only in MS. Add. 16165 (Shirley's). Both these poems have particular

---

[1] *Misc. Gen. et Heraldica*, 5th ser., VI, 254–7.
[2] Duchy of Lancaster, (D.L.) Accounts, 5/8, fol. 11 v.

significance for Roos, and can be dated to 1450 as a *terminus ad quem*. The many peculiarities of spelling and the 'un-English miswritings' (Hammond, p. 191) of the scribe have given rise to the theory that the manuscript of the *Tales* may have been made for Jacqueline of Hainault, and was connected with her supporters of Flemish descent, the Robsarts. Too much should not, however, be made of the spellings (which continue even into the final *Compleynt*), since the majority of them can be paralleled in the Paston Letters, even in those of an educated man such as Friar Brackley; Norfolk has indeed been suggested for the dialect of the manuscript. An alternative theory, that the manuscript of the *Tales* was made for the Duke of Gloucester, is strengthened by finding superadded at beginning and end these poems with distinctive Roos features and variants, some of a date after the Duke's death. It seems possible that the manuscript may have come into Roos's own hand, and had these quires added.

MS. Harl. 7578 proves to be of considerable significance for Roos; its agreement with MS. Fairfax 16 in its texts and their grouping attracts our interest. It is a miscellaneous volume written in part in a 'late 15th century hand' (Hammond, p. 330). This accords with the date which I would assign to the second and fourth items, poems before the Wydville-Scales marriage of 1461. The two scurrilous poems (Items 3 and 5) involve one of the queen's foreign waiting women, and are of the 1450s; for three out of these four poems this is the unique manuscript. There is no long poem except Lydgate's *Summum Sapientiae*; some of the poems here that are now assigned to Chaucer and Lydgate I shall be claiming for Roos (*Newfangleness, Doubleness*). No notes of ownership earlier than the seventeenth century are found, but one memorandum of that period, concerning 'Francis Cartwright of Langeley, Derbie, gentleman', brings us back into the area of MS. Ff. 1.6, the 'Roos scrapbook'. Kirk Langley, half-way between Hulland and Egginton, was the home of the Meynells; in the fourteenth century, a Meynell had married a Roos of Belvoir, and two sixteenth-century John Meynells were to marry Maud Bradbourn (see above, p. 73) and Bridget Markham (see below, p. 513).[1]

A still later large collection of lyrics of very unequal value, MS. Rawl. C. 813, is of the Tudor period, as its poems on men in the service of Henry VIII prove. Nevertheless the Tudor collector had access to some Plesaunce material. Five lyrics in close proximity early in the volume (nos. 23, 24, 26, 27, and 32) have Roos anagrams on Plesaunce people, one (23) as late as 1450 to 1454. Item 10, an explicit elegy for

---

[1] Joseph Tilley, *Old Halls of Derbyshire*, IV, 97.

Eleanor Cobham, Duke Humphrey, and John Beaufort ('Musyng vppon the mutabilite'), though not by Roos, yet shows a throwback to interest in the period 1441–54. Many of the later lyrics are often reminiscent of Roos's style, though without his skill or elegance.

Two other 'Tudor' manuscripts of greater interest will be discussed later (Chapter XII).

The chief importance hitherto of John Shirley (? 1366–1456, October 21) has been as the authority for the Lydgate canon. This study will deprive Lydgate in Roos's favour of almost all the courtly poems, and Shirley's trustworthiness will inevitably be questioned and diminished. He acquires some fresh interest as a transmitter of Roos poems, but as completely in ignorance, for he never mentions him. His confidently worded headings on the persons concerned in the poems prove to be wide of the mark, for all their air of inside information. Nevertheless he helps to preserve some of the best of Roos's earlier work—as 'Lydgate's', or 'Chaucer's'. If he is the John Shirley who in 1431 was described as 'servant of Richard, earl of Warrewyk' (*Cal. Close Rolls, 1429–35*, p. 118), then he was early in touch with Roos connexions. Yet he does not transmit the Warwick family poem, *The Parliament of Love*, though he alone gives us the *Balade* made for the Countess of Warwick, ascribing it, however, to the Earl; both are Roos poems (see Chapter VI). His devotion to Lydgate might have brought him into contact with Gloucester; it might have made him aware of the undercurrent of enmity between Lydgate and Roos; but I know no proof of either connexion. His late and untrustworthy personal collection, MS. Ashmole 59 (c. 1447–56), has only two short Roos poems, and its text is full of slips. On two poems only does he unwittingly confirm my findings; by including *The Assembly of Ladies*, he supports my dating of 1451; and by omitting *The Flower and the Leaf*, he supports negatively my dating of 1458, eighteen months after his death at the age of about ninety.

In summing up these general observations on the manuscripts most significant for 'the Roos *corpus*', it is important to note that a proportion of them belonged either to members of the Court and the Household of 1430 to 1455, or to fighting families connected with it, and at least at that time Lancastrian. They were therefore in a position to know about Sir Richard Roos, a 'Gloucester's man', later a King's Knight and attached to the Household. Some of these manuscripts, except Fairfax 16 (and the later Trinity College, R. 3.20), are undistinguished productions. Just as the rise of the printed quarto was a concession to the modest purses of those who could not afford folios, so the same phenomenon of supply and demand may be seen in these smaller manuscripts, collections of the 'shorter poems of Chaucer' (not of *The Canterbury Tales*), and of poems of courtly love and of contemporary interest. One may question whether the theory of shop-production in bulk has not been pushed too far. These men of moderate means, the squires of the Household, the fighting knights, the younger sons, may not have had the long purses to command great manuscripts, but they did not necessarily always buy the ready-made, even in fascicules. Some copying was probably done to specification; and much by a private scrivener, or a friendly clerk, or even by friends and members of the family—as Robbins has suggested of MS. Ff. i.6. Personal taste and choice cannot be ruled out, nor the desire for a poem of immediate interest. All these points will be illustrated in the detailed survey of the poems of 'the Roos *corpus*'.

II. POETIC DEVICES

First, the 'signatures': *La Belle Dame* at l. 3 has 'I roos', and this with some variation recurs in another half-dozen or so of the longer or narrative poems of the century. In translation, 'I roos' is sometimes the inevitable rendering of 'Je me levai'. In *La Belle Dame* it occurs thus, but is supported by its repetition in Roos's own prefatory stanzas; in *The Romaunt of the Rose* the word 'anoon' takes the place of a detail in French, that the poet on rising put on his shoes. Four methods of this 'signing' emerge. First 'I roos anon', introduced as early as possible in the poem, and in one poem repeated near the end; this is prevalent in early works. It finds an unexpected confirmation on the flyleaf of MS. Ashmole 44, on which is written twice in an immature hand the letters R R, large and ornate; beside them slantwise in a different style of lettering is the word 'anon'. The manuscript is a rather well-worn small copy of the alliterative *Alexander*, and there are some curious parallels to be traced between its version and some of these poems; I believe that it was in Richard Roos's possession as an adolescent or young man. A second method of 'signing' is to spread this same phrase over adjacent lines; this method can be used independently of the first method, or in conjunction with it. Later, the word 'anon' is dropped; probably it alluded to some joke of his early coterie. I would hazard the guess that the poet was teased for his over-facile recourse to this ever-useful adverb and tag, and that later the jest lost its savour, possibly with the breaking up of this circle. Later he uses 'I roos' or 'up I roos'. In one poem, he introduces a fourth device, the capitalizing of words in a line; this occurs late in a long poem (*Reson and Sensuallyte*), and corresponds to a librarian's habit of stamping a book at p. 100 or p. 500. The words that strike the eye here are '. . . Roos vp a Knyght'. It is noticeable that the rose, the flower, is avoided. The only possible exception is in *The Romaunt of the Rose*, B., l. 3759, 'And to the Rose anoon wente I', but it is not very probable even here in a poem where the rose offers only too easy opportunities. It was never an emblem of the English line of Roos, though it was adopted by the Scottish line (Ross) which branched off in the thirteenth century. This seems to be a deliberate avoidance, which Lydgate may not have realized. Negative evidence may be found in the fact that these 'signature' phrases do not appear in any long poem claimed or signed by Lydgate, such as *The Sege of Thebes*, or *The Fall of Princes*. Yet another method of 'signing' can be found, a personal motto or 'devise' which comes to light among the anagrams which Sir Richard used in almost all his poems, 'J'ai tot forfait forfait'.

For the half revealing of the name of the subject of a poem, or of the person addressed, Sir Richard Roos shows extraordinary diversity of ingenuity, equal to that of the French poets, and certainly learnt from them, possibly also from Chaucer. In some of the early love-poems he makes use of a list of proper names, mainly those of the ladies of *The Legend of Good Women* (as later of the companions of Love in the Garden of the Rose), to form by initial anagram the names of his subjects. By this means he discloses (or conceals) in varying forms of the name (shortened, consonantal, or phonetic) his dedications to Elisabeth Beaumont (*née* Phelip), and to Antigone. Occasionally for Elisabeth, and for a few other persons, especially Ismania, Lady Scales, he imitates Deschamps in using a complex syllabic anagram,[1] a division of names or words, either read partly backwards, or the one name enclosing the other.

Above all, the method of indicating friends and dedicatees already seen in *La Belle Dame* can be seen in almost all Roos's poems whether long or short. He develops the double acrostic anagram used by Chaucer and later by Charles d'Orléans and his circle, with a complexity and variety which were probably intended to conceal as much as to reveal, to baffle undue curiosity, and to occupy pleasurably the leisure of the privileged and the initiated. He effects concealment by refraining from emphasizing or enlarging the line-initial, by shortened forms of the names, occasionally by omitting the tell-tale initial of the name itself, by complex interweaving of letters, overlapping from stanza to stanza,

[1] See above, Chapter III.

enfolding one name within the other, sometimes with a pretty love-symbolism, as of a bride and groom, a Homfrey Sutton-Dudley and an Eleanor Roos. For modern readers, whose mind and eyes expect normalized spellings, concealment lies also in the French forms of some names (Alianore, Artus), in medieval spellings (Homfrey), or in the phonetic renderings of names, so that Beaufort can appear as Bewfort, or Biaufort, Beauchamp as Bausham, Anjou as Anio(o). In long poems, Roos furnishes lengthy lists of names of a coterie or of the Household, 'braids' plaited and intertwined; here one suspects that to omit a name from the company would have aroused resentment (as if left out of the *Almanach de Gotha*) and laid up trouble for the careless poet. A large residue of unwanted letters may act as camouflage, often by an effective smoke-screen of one predominating letter, generally T, or W. The inner or secondary set of letters is generally worked in with the line-initials, and expands the skeletal names and adds others. But there are a few exciting instances where the important name is only revealed by reference to the less obvious caesural initials; thus the actual name of Lady Loyalty lies concealed in the conclusion of *The Assembly of Ladies*, to spring into view only when the caesural letters are brought into play. This refinement is not practised by Charles d'Orléans, as far as I know. Roos follows French precedent in allowing himself the occasional use of a second, even a third, letter of a word; the recurrence of 'For' at the beginnings of lines prepares for the word 'Forfait' which emerges as part of the signature-motto. There is no regularity in all this; he may, or he may not.

Two examples will show the working of this double acrostic anagram, in a short poem, and in separate stanzas of a long poem. The only English poem in the French collection MS. Royal 19.A.III has been referred to above as an alternative envoy to *La Belle Dame sans Merci*;[1] its anagram will reveal the dedication.

> O bewtie pereles and right so womanhod
> ffor the grete honour and vertue in you I see
> I you beseche of yor moste godelyhode
> This litill Boke it myght rehersed be
> Vnto suche fayre þt Do excile pite
> Whiche causeth their louers to morne with peinfull hert
> And not relesse them of their peynes smerte
>
> Other ther be with godely countenaunce
> that perse menes hertes right wt a sobre yee
> Their Bewtie is suche wt yke þe circūstaunce

---

[1] Printed in Robbins, *Secular Lyrics*, etc., pp. 206 and 288.

H

Whoo can refreyn þei most nedes loved be
A lady faire may not exile pite
Where bewtie is of right þere is pities place
Therfore alwey gode, Doo ye pray for grace

ffor he is true
And will pursue   } — in Hir seruice
Attendaunce due

[Let] hym not rue
his seruice true   } — [erased] ce
Do that exchue

Initial letters: o for i t v w an|o t t w a w t|for an a i [l] h d –.
Caesural letters: a an o i t t o|w r w t m o g.
This yields MARGA--T DAnIOW; LO--VI.; AI TOT FOrFA–T; thus,
O For I T V W An|o T T W A W t|F A a i L h D
A A O I T to| W R W t M o G|
There is a residue of letters, o w w t|a h|t o|w w t o; less than one-
third of the whole (11/38), a frequent proportion. The poem is a
rededication of *La Belle Dame* to Queen Margaret, with a slanting
reference to Roos's own lady, Margaret Longueville, and the request,

This litill Boke it myght rehersed be
Vnto suche fayre þt Do excile pite

Two separate stanzas portraying single characters in *The Chance of the
Dice* (see No. 71, below) will furnish clear and limited examples. One
is a compliment to a man seemly in all his doings (st. 22):

Wel oughte ech wyght desire youre semlynesse
God wolde that in youre ladyes eye ye were
As wel as thenketh me that ye kan dresse
Al maner thynge that longeth to your gere.
ffor leve hyt wel so hyt did yow no dere
Y wolde that I koude halfe your gouernaunce
So noble hyt is that moche hyt myght me avaunce.

Line initials: w g a a for y s
Caesural initials: d y t t s k t
This yields G–AYST–K; For–AYT; thus, W G A A For Y S
                                        d Y T T S K t.
Ralph, Lord Greystoke, was on the Escort with Sir Richard.
Another stanza ridicules a man for his sloth (st. 51):

Ryght wel prikked after by my trouthe.
Now softe awhile for ye haue ouertake
Hym that ye soughte your lustlesse maister slouthe.
Ye be to thryve as lothe as bere to stake.

But sothe ys seyde that man shal neuer make
Of pigges tayle good lyltinge horne to blowe.
Thus seyne al folke that wel your maners knowe.

Line initials: r n h y b o t
Caesural initials: b for y as t g t.

This yields G–OR, ASHBY; FOR––YT; thus, R n H Y B O T
b FOR Y AS t G t.

George Ashby, poet, and Clerk to the Signet, is the victim.

There are obvious dangers in all this for the modern solver of Roos's acrostic anagrams, especially in the looseness of the inner acrostic, where the place of the caesura may well be debatable. The solver must make it a rule never to tamper with the series of caesural letters, once carefully arrived at, in order to iron out a knotty solution. Another rule is not to use a letter a second time; yet I suspect that Roos occasionally did so, just as he made one name do for two ladies above, for the queen and for his lady-love. He may even have manipulated his anagram to appeal simultaneously to two groups of his friends, and I believe that twice he played this ingenious trick. He has some variations from the norm, as the use of three initials in a line, instead of two; or the use of anaphora to conceal the line-initial and remove it to the second word. His ingenuity is a constant challenge to tread warily, but boldly.

There are then difficulties, even dangers; there are also rewards. One may find that a poem, which has been merely a small piece of flotsam on the writings of the century, was launched at or after a definite date, generally a marriage, as of Homfrey Sutton-Dudley with Eleanor Roos of Gedney, or of Antigone with Lord Powys. Roos has a useful habit, possibly borrowed from Charles d'Orléans, and one which will endear him to the genealogist, of often indicating a married lady's maiden name: Cobham constantly (Roos's tie of kinship) for the Duchess of Gloucester; Whalesborough for Lady Ismania Scales, just as Charles d'Orléans in all his English poems gives Ann Molins Whalesborough for her sister.[1] Poems long thought to be Chaucer's are shown by the detail of the family names to concern men and women of fully half a century later. More than once the insertion of early titles of persons later, and by us better, known by a more exalted name helps to date the poem. These are sometimes French titles, not always so familiar to the English student, Mortain, Clermont, Eu. Late in life, Roos produces in the anagrams a fresh list of names which provides a clue to a later circle of his interest.

[1] See my *Studies in Villon, Vaillant and Charles d'Orléans*, Oxford, 1957.

'All anagrams', said Fuller in his miniature life of Queen Elizabeth,[1] 'must sue in Chancery for moderate favour.' The modern reader of poetry, inheritor of the Ages of Reason and of Romanticism, has lost interest in coterie writing, and in all the little 'politick arts' of ingenuity whereby the poet made of his verse a proffered bouquet or a parlour game. The lesser Elizabethan poets, such as Sylvester, with their loyal anagrams on Elizabeth, understood such poetic ploys better than we do. The seventeenth-century poets exalt the device, and require that an anagram of a name must be appropriate to the person to be celebrated; thus Isabella Lambard, *née* Garrard, marrying in 1638, was transmuted into 'A bride's all balm.[2] The anagram becomes 'an integral thematic part of the poem', which is then 'developed contrapuntally about it'. Sir Richard Roos, living and writing near the beginning of polyphonic music, cannot be expected to compose his poems 'in somewhat the way that Buxtehude and Bach composed their music'.[3] Yet one can hardly doubt that Roos felt some fugal excitement as his pen 'pursued transverse the volant' letters, some satisfaction and amusement at his own ingenuity—at first. Later on, his skill may have become burdensome, and enforced by unwelcome demand, as in the poems composed on the names of his four brothers-in-law.

We now feel almost revulsion (*crede expertae*) from the very idea of thus manipulating verse. Yet the anagram is of long and respectable ancestry in English, since Cynewulf turned thus one of his runic signatures. Certainly strong disbelief is felt that with such complex preoccupations the writer could produce poetry of any value. It is obvious that *The Flower and the Leaf*, Roos's finest poem, contains comparatively few, though sufficient, anagrams. But one cannot surely maintain that the freshness and élan of the May mornings in *The Romaunt of the Rose*, or *The Black Knight*, or *Reson and Sensuallyte*, suffer from the heavily interwoven anagrams. And the cloak of praise bestowed on Chaucer for the poems now shown by the anagrams to be of later date must rest henceforth on the shoulders of Roos. Again, the spectre of the Baconian cypher haunts the English scholar; but there is no comparison here. Just as Domesday Book or the Pipe Rolls were compiled for immediate use, not for the benefit of the future historian, so these anagrams were framed for the eye of the next day's reader, not to bemuse posterity. I have found that French scholars are as ready to credit the practice of these acrostic anagrams as their English counterparts are slow of belief. They realize that the ingenuity of Chaucer,

---

[1] *Holy State*, No. 80.   [2] Hasted, *Kent*, ed. H. Drake, I, 52.
[3] Arnold S. Jantz, *The First Century of New England Verse*, 1944, pp. 30–3.

Charles d'Orléans, and Roos in this kind in the fourteenth to fifteenth centuries has modified French literary history. The chief practitioners known so far, the Rhétoriqueurs such as Molinet, are later than these poets. Roos was perhaps not the only English anagrammatist of his time, though possibly the most skilful. The unknown 'Picard' (see below, No. 44) was ready to take a hand in the game. Again, Humfrey Newton, the Cheshire squire, of the next generation to Roos, writes three acrostic poems,[1] but does not, I think, practise the double acrostic anagrams, and an idle hand scratched an acrostic verse on a pillar in a Cambridgeshire church.[2]

These hidden references could be reinforced by the mention of livery colours (the red and white of Phelip, the blue and silver of Beaufort, the green and white of the Valois), badges (hawthorn, woodbine, the swan, the talbot, the anglehook), emblems (daisy, violet), crests (the peacock), and mottoes. French usage extravagantly introduced all these not only into poems and manuscripts but also into hangings, dresses, and robes of ceremony; here the plant design and the motto would disappear into or emerge from the seams of the garment with as fragmentary an effect as the shortened and partial anagrams.[3] We have the evidence of two manuscripts of *Les Vœux du Paon* that a personal motto of 'Roos R.' was 'A moy le mieulx'. It does not seem to be used in these poems, though one might expect it to be an answer to the common and popular 'De mieulx en mieulx'. Nor does it seem to have any relation to the obviously fighting motto of John Beaumont, husband of Elizabeth Phelip, 'Dessus eux heureusement'. Yet Beaumont may have used another, a personal motto, since the Stapletons, after a marriage with the Beaumont heiress, adopted the motto, 'Mieux je serra', which sounds like a retort to 'A moy le mieulx'.[4] Another personal motto for Roos the poet emerges out of the residue of many anagrams, both long and short, the ambiguous phrase, 'J'ai tot forfait forfait'. In the early love poems this enigmatic phrase probably expresses the humility of the devout lover, who confesses to every crime in love's calendar, who has transgressed all these statutes of Love which recur in the poems. It is then surprising to find it also in the cheerful and lively *New Year's Gift*. In later and more despairing Complaints, it may rather mean his loss as a player in the game of love; 'I have forfeited every pledge of love', a sad admission that for him love's labour

[1] R. H. Robbins, 'The poems of Humfrey Newton, Esquire, 1466–1536', *P.M.L.A.*, LXV, 249–81; and *Index*, Nos. 481, 737, and 2217.
[2] Robbins, *Secular Lyrics*, etc., No. 145.
[3] Joan Evans, *Dress in Medieval France*, 1952, ch. 4; and see Plate 26.
[4] *Excerpta Historica*, pp. 62, 170.

has been lost—he has played at forfeits, and Lord Love has swept up the stakes. It becomes a signature-motto, and its presence supports Roos's authorship; conversely its absence may lead one to doubt of his hand in an otherwise likely poem. It persists throughout the poems, often in fragmentary form ('tot forfait'), fading away like the fragmentary mottoes on robes.

The habit of adopting temporary personal *devises* for special occasions, such as weddings, jousts, or revels, adds to the difficulty of tracing them, as will be seen in *The Assembly of Ladies*. Those of royalty have often been recorded, Margaret of Anjou's 'humble et loial', or that of Henry VI, 'un seul', adapted from his father's wedding motto, 'une saunz plus'. Some grouping and coherence in the choice of mottoes and emblems may be traced; the *devises* may modify the family motto, just as the family arms were 'differenced' for a younger branch. Later members of a family may adapt an earlier famous example; thus Lady Margaret Beaufort's 'Souvent me souviens' responds to the 'Sovenez' of Henry IV as a Lancastrian theme; or the hawthorn buds of Henry VI, combining flowers and leaves, continue and yet contrast with the flowerless spikes of hawthorn of his father and grandfather. Too often our knowledge of *devises* and badges depends for their preservation on the legibility of a flyleaf, such as Eleanor Cobham's 'al en un', or on an illuminated manuscript, such as the Bedford Book of Hours, or on the memory of a chronicler, or the compliments of a poet. The intention of a motto was to be cryptic; the user might wear his heart on his sleeve, but it was not for daws to peck at. The peacock crest of the Roos family, still visible on their monuments, and used by Sir Richard himself in his seal,[1] probably accounts for his interest in the poem of the peacock vows. The adoption of the crest may date from the 1370s, when Thomas, fourth Lord Roos, fought under the Duke of Lancaster at the siege of Mont Paon. The livery and armorial badge, the Root of Bedford, the Swan of Bohun,[2] the Ragged Staff of Warwick, was known to all, as political poems show; but the personal badge, such as the Beaufort woodbine, had a private use and significance, and needed to be more delicately handled.

In all this ingenuity, the poet writing within an aristocratic coterie is balanced on a razor-edge; he must not betray to the outer world what yet must be clear to the discerning élite. Their secrets are not to be

---

[1] The Roos crest was the peacock 'à la queue traînante'; the Manners of Belvoir adopted instead the peacock in its pride.

[2] Eleanor Bohun, Duchess of Gloucester, owned a copy of *Le Chevalier a Cigne*, and Nicolas reminds us that the swan was the cognizance of her family (*Test. Vet.*, I, 148, xxix).

common property. After the lapse of centuries, however, the disclosure of their affairs makes the poems into social and personal footnotes to history, on the disposition, talents, and inner feeling of these personages of whom we know little beyond their actions. We learn of the pleasant and kindly impression that the elderly Anne of Woodstock made on a lovesick young poet, and we know now that Antigone sang charmingly. More seriously, we shall find that Eleanor Cobham in prison was reproachful of Antigone's neglect of her in her second marriage and departure to France. These poems, more even than the constant coupling of the two women's names in the Plesaunce poems, tend to confirm the historians' suspicion that the two were mother and daughter. If so, the connexion between Gloucester and Eleanor Cobham must have begun early in the 1420s. Antigone's son Richard Grey was born late in 1436; it is true that Sir Richard's poems for Plesaunce in the 1430s stress her youth. Similarly, if the poet is to be credited in a situation which is made use of in only one poem (see below, No. 77), Anne Montague in childhood had been the playmate of John Holland, and had conceived a devotion for him which outlasted her two other marriages, and was fulfilled only in their late middle age.

Doubtful points in genealogies seem to get confirmation in the anagrams: Antigone's second marriage to Jean d'Amancier has no English record, but has rested on the statement of the French historian Du Fresne de Beaucourt;[1] the name D'Amancier coupled with hers appears in the anagrams of many short poems. The marriage contract of the younger Benedicta Vernon to Thomas Charleton is not on record as having been fulfilled; but his name occurs in two poems among the names of Dame Margaret Roos's brothers-in-law (see below, Nos. 83*d* and *e*). One must not always, however, look to the anagrams to define or describe the circumstances of the persons named. Many of the poems are mere dedications of compliment or offerings of friendship, like the music of Elizabethan composers such as 'The King of Denmark's Galliard'. Yet we shall find that the anagrams reveal the value of some poems as autobiography, as personal confessions.

III. METRE AND STYLE

In the metres of the long poems, as we should expect from the original stanzas of *La Belle Dame*, rhyme royal holds pride of place—in *The Flour of Curtesye*, *The Black Knight*, *The Assembly of Ladies*, and *The Flower and the Leaf*. This Troilus stanza is almost inevitable for poems

---

[1] *Hist. de Charles VII*, V, 331.

of courtly love; in the poem to *The Flower of Womanhede*, the poet calls himself 'newe Troiles'. The eight-line stanza occurs for a use similar to that of *La Belle Dame*, in the line by line translation of *Le Cuer et l'Œil*; here again the octosyllabic line is lengthened into the decasyllabic. The octosyllabic couplet represents that of the French original in *Reson and Sensuallyte*, and in *The Romaunt of the Rose*; in a rougher, more rapid form in the *Compleynt* (No. 78) it is tossed off one April morning to lament the poet's unwilling departure

> in march now late
> Whan I tok leue now at the ȝate
> Of this goodly daysye (ll. 445-7).

There are signs that Roos's earliest verse was based on the native alliterative line. *How a Lover Prayseth hys Lady*, scornfully dismissed as four-beat doggerel, is more aptly to be called, as W. P. Ker might have called it, 'tumbling verse'; it comes down like the waters at Lodore:

> But throgh hope and grace ther spryngeth a well
> To paradys ledyth them out of hell. (ll. 77/8)

> Shynyng ful bryght by the sterred leme,
> Lyke a torche and the fresshe sonnys beme (ll. 123/4)

His extreme of alliteration is seen in such a line as

> Thrusshes, throstels and twytlyng goldfynche (l. 104);

often it is more diversified, and spread from one line to another. In all these poems, even the most polished, extra-metrical syllables are apt to crop up; sometimes they can be elided, as in *La Belle Dame*:

> That er the sonne to-morowe be risen newe (*Black Knight*, 655).

On the other hand, many decasyllabic lines could easily be read with no more than the four accents needed by the grammatical structure:

> My harm is hid, that I dar not disclose (*Flour of Curtesye*, 77).

The early poem, *For lac of sighte*, shows the difficulty that the yet unskilled poet found in forcing 'tumbling verse' to the five-beat line;[1] and the three short poems, that seem to be first drafts on their themes, *Hope* in MS. Harl. 7333, *Iuellis pricious*, and *The Flower of Womanhood*, in MS. Lambeth 306, show uncertainty of beat and syllable in many lines. In the same manuscript occurs in eight-line stanzas a *balade* that is found again in MS. Fairfax 16 in more polished seven-line stanzas. All this is evidence of steady self-training in craftsmanship, in the

---

[1] Cf. C. S. Lewis, 'The 15th Century Heroic Line', *Essays and Studies*, XXIV, 1938.

practice of the Chaucerian or syllabic metre, and in what Roos calls his 'peynted style'. The later mastery of lyric metres is therefore not surprising. The poet in the 1430s of the difficult but not always very musical variations of *A Compleynte to his Lady*, will be capable in the mid-1440s of the beautiful and complex modulations of *The Lover's Mass*. Run-on lines are as freely used in rhyme royal as they were in *La Belle Dame*; run-on stanzas, though very rare in the two simpler poems (there are none in *The Flour of Curtesye*, and only two in *The Assembly*), are increasingly frequent in the two more ornate poems, *The Black Knight* (fourteen links in 97 stanzas) and *The Flower and the Leaf* (twenty-two links in 85 stanzas).[1]

The rhyming is inaccurate by Chaucer's standards, as Skeat has shown in detail on *The Black Knight*, *The Assembly of Ladies*, and *The Flower and the Leaf*. An occasional assonance is left, though this may be partly due to French models, which allow of assonance more easily (e.g. named: attayned; remembre: tender, *Isle of Ladies*, 597, 1417; forjuged: excused; wreke: clepe, *Black Knight*, 274, 284). Imperfect rhymes are found, especially in the earlier works (e.g. destroid: conclude, *Isle of Ladies*, 735; ademant: foundement, *Romaunt of the Rose*, 4181). Certain rhyme-combinations are overworked: 'routh, trouth, slouth' are as useful to this poet as 'oght, noght' are to Chaucer in *The Boke of the Duchesse*; 'sterve, serve, kerve' are often recurrent. Another indispensable rhyme, indeed almost a hallmark of this poet, is 'goodlihede: womanhede', or either of these with 'seemlihede, dede, rede, mede', etc. The frequency of rhymes in -ayn is again noticeable, especially in *The Assembly* (in fifteen stanzas out of 108), and generally for the same reason as in *La Belle Dame*, the reliance on the tag '(in) certayn', also here because the word 'chamberlayn' often governs the rhyme.

Occasional but unmistakable northern forms have long puzzled those who attributed many of these poems to Chaucer, or to Lydgate; they are natural in the early work of a young man part of whose childhood was probably spent at Hamlake and York. Thus we have the northern present participle (e.g. seruand: lyuand, *Isle of Ladies*, 1629; doand, criand, sparand, *Romaunt of the Rose*, 2708, 3138, 5363); northern forms such as arn for are (*Romaunt*, 5484), duellys (*Reson and Sensuallyte*, 5046; cf. 359, 933), kirk (*Isle of Ladies*, 1308, 2067), thacke for thatch (*ib.*, 1773); and above all northern rhymes, such as mare with are, thar, and fare (*Rom. of the Rose*, 2215, 1852, 2079); maad: brad; trowe: lowe; wat: estate (*ib.*, 4199. 4531, 5399).

---

[1] Contrast this with 40 links in 1181 stt. of *Troilus and Criseyde*.

The poet's predilection for certain words is very marked in these poems. 'Plesaunce' is inevitably a useful word in all its meanings, with its rhymes, especially 'governaunce' and 'suffisaunce'; as in *La Belle Dame*, it occurs over a score of times in *The Isle of Ladies* (or *The Yle of Plesaunce*). 'Anon' is badly overworked, especially in the earlier poems, in a way which suggests that the first signature phrase 'I rose anon' was a gesture of mock defiance. A similar poetic self-assertion is heard in the earliest poem:

> fforthe sayl I wol and gesse yn my wyse
> As bayard the blynd trottyng on the Ise.
> When he is down ye iapen merely.
> fforthe I wol, lawghyt on, for so wol y.
> Ye laghe but selde [I] trowe at holynes
> But at me ye shal anon as I ges
> Ther shal neuer wyght gret thing atteyne
> That dret euery thing but ay lyf yn peyne.
>
> (*How a Lover Prayseth hys Lady*, 234)

Certain epithets are favourites, 'fresh, shene, kene', this last sometimes in curious applications, as in 'branches kene'. Syntactical inversions are a feature of the style and metre. In early work they can be awkward as in 'As yt please her may to devise', or 'Ye get have entre' (*Isle of Ladies*, 2202, 232); sometimes they obey the need of rhyme, as in '. . . to this bonde ever I me bynde' (*F. of Curtesye*, 249), or of stress as in 'But shal I thus yow my deeth for-yive' (*Complaynt d'Amours*, 31) or 'Among the busshes me prively to shroude' (*Black Knight*, 147).

No poem could be considered for inclusion in the 'Roos corpus', if its general style were impossible to be compared with that of *La Belle Dame*. A Roos style emerges from the 'signed' poems, and can be used as a touchstone for 'unsigned' short or lyric poems. When looking at the catalogue of Ashmole manuscripts, my eye was passing without much interest down a list of 'Tudor poems'; but half-way down I stopped and said 'But that sounds like Roos':

> Sauns remedye endure must I
> in paynes deadly for my *mistres*.

and so lighted on the dozen or so poems preserved by a Tudor copyist in MS. Ashmole 176, the anagrams of which attest Roos's authorship. The following passages, expressions of a lover's devotion, may be compared to show a common measure of Roos's style in this kind.

> Though it be so, that I can nat deserve
> To have your grace, but alway live in drede,
> Yet suffre me you for to love and serve

> Without maugre of your most goodlihede;
> Both faith and trouth I give your womanhede,
> And my servyse, withoute ayein-calling.
> Love hath me bounde, withouten wage or mede,
> To be your man and leve al other thing.
> $\qquad$ (*La Belle Dame*, 237–44, 'signed')

> And alder-last unto her womanhede
> And to her mercy me I recommaunde,
> That lye now here, betwixe hope and drede,
> Abyding playnly what she list commaunde.
> For utterly, (this nis no demaunde),
> Welcome to me, whyl me lasteth breeth,
> Right at her choise, wher it be lyf or deeth.
> $\qquad$ (*Black Knight*, 561–7, 'signed')

> For as me thynke I am ryght hylye bounde,
> To do that thyng whiche myght be her plesaunce,
> And her I thanke, yf in me may be founde
> O poynt of thryft or of good gouernaunce
> Or thyng that me to worschyp shuld awaunce;
> Thus haue I cause to serue her godelyhede,
> Constreynd of hert wyth stedfaste loue and drede.
> $\qquad$ (*Balade*, st. 2. MS. Fairfax 16, fol. 318)

This is a norm of his early style; but it is not without several variations. The early *How a Lover* may be ungroomed, but it is not unmusical, and the germ of the future style is there:

> Nowe of the baner of womanhede
> Whiche ys the geme of al goodlyhede
> The swete beaute of the visage whyte
> White as lyly when he ys yn hys delyte
> Most in the dry calme somer seson. (*How a Lover*, 270–5)

The later doggerel poem is written so for speed and urgency, the intentional choice of impatience and sincerity:

> I yow ensure, by myn trouthe,
> Thow that ye neuere haue on me routhe,
> Ne neuere ne wele me do mercy,
> 3yt schal I seruyn, tyl I dey,
> By god, on-to youre womanhede,
> How euere it falle that I spede. (*Compleynt*, 83–8)

Even in this poem of rough metre, there is more than one rhetorical catherine-wheel. The 'golden ease' seen in *La Belle Dame*, and again in *The Flower and the Leaf*, is a natural gift, heightened by art. Smoothness characterizes Roos's earlier poems in his 'peynted style' when he is aiming at 'coloures', in spite of his disclaimers:

> I haue slept out of the hul of parnaso, (*How a Lover*, 230)
> I aqueynted am not with no muse. (*Flour of Curtesye*, 182)

The early reading of alliterative poetry often leaves its trace in the syllabic verse, e.g. 'Of beaute for to bere the belle' (*Reson and Sensuallyte*, 1946); whole stanzas of *The Eye and the Heart* shift constantly into very un-French alliteration:

> Thou scornest fals murtherer as I trowe
> Thou hast me smytte with a stroke mortall
> By thy fals loke thou hast me ouer throwe
> I wende full litell thou hade be suche at all
> Thou hast me cast withoute the castell wall
> Of good comfort and oute of al gladnesse. (st. 37)

Later, the device will be controlled and euphonious; the stanza on the fountain in *The Assembly of Ladies* by its sibilants lets the plashing of the water fall on the ear:

> The flore beneth was paved faire and smothe
> With stones square, of many dyvers hew,
> So wel joyned that, for to say the sothe,
> Al semed oon (who that non other knew);
> And underneth, the stremes new and new,
> As silver bright, springing in suche a wyse
> That, whence it cam, ye coude it not devyse.
>
> 　　　　　　　　(*Assembly of Ladies*, 64–70)

Finally, it would be difficult to set bounds to Sir Richard's variety in lyric metres. The patterned French Balade, Rondel and Virelay, and the Petrarchan sonnet (see Chapter XII below), are as the formal flowers, tulips or lilies, central to a garden. They are surrounded by every kind of bloom, less noteworthy, but delicate as the 'souvenez', hardy and plain as the borage or marigold, 'perjink' as the columbine, evocative and unforgettable as the 'povre pensees'. Not forgotten either are the vigorous wildings, common to the simple seasonal rejoicing of both people and court:

> Up, sun and merry weather,
> Summer draweth near!

The ponderous technical names of these many metres cannot extinguish the brilliance and buoyancy, the impetuous movement, the spendthrift vitality of Roos's outpourings. He may and does practise himself in his art, not only polishing but constantly experimenting. There is no limiting him to a single type of lyric expression.

IV. THE *CORPUS* OF ROOS'S POETRY

The information assembled in these four chapters on Sir Richard Roos, his family, his patrons, the circles that he frequented, and his familiarity with the methods (and tricks) of French poetry, has been applied to much of the courtly verse extant in fifteenth and early sixteenth century manuscripts. As a result, and on the evidence of style, anagrams, allusions, and devices of various kinds the following list of poems has been drawn up as constituting the *corpus* of Roos's poetry. It is arranged in accordance with what is known of the course of his life and with the detailed study of these same poems in Chapters V–XII.

A. The Plesaunce Period, c. 1432–42: Plesaunce poems (see Chapter V)
  1. *How a Lover Prayseth hys Lady.*
  2. *The Isle of Ladies.*

Poems for Elisabeth Bardolf, Lady Beaumont.
  3. 'For lac of sighte'.
  4*a*. 'Hevy thoughtes and longe depe sykyng'.
  4*b*. 'Honnour and beaute, vertue and gentilnesse'.
  5. *The Flour of Curtesye:* 'Lydgate's'.
  6. *Ballade of her that hath all Virtues:* 'Lydgate's'.
  7. *A Lover's New Year's Gift:* 'Lydgate's'.
  8. 'Iuellis Pricious'.
  9. *Complaynt ageyne Hope* (Forms A and B).
  10. *Merciles Beaute:* 'Chaucer's'.
  11. *Balade of Compleynte:* 'Chaucer's ?'
  12. *The Deth of Pyte:* 'Chaucer's'.
  13. *A Compleynte to his Lady:* 'Chaucer's'.
  14. *Complaynt d'Amours:* 'Chaucer's'.
  15. i–xviii. Balades, Complaints and Letters in MS. Fairfax 16, fol. 318–25: 'Suffolk's' (see also No. 63).
  16*a–g*. Lyrics in MS. Ff. 1.6.
  17*a–d*. Lyrics in MS. Ashmole 176.
  18*a–c*. Lyrics in MS. Ashmole 191.
  19–34*b*. Lyrics in various manuscripts.
  35*a*. 'Horns Away': 'Lydgate's'.
  35*b*. 'When the wyntar wynddys'.
  36. *Ragman Roll.*
  37. *A Mumming at London . . . of Dame Fortune:* 'Lydgate's'.

Poems for the Duchess of Gloucester.
  38. *Womanly Noblesse:* 'Chaucer's'.

71. *The Chance of the Dice.*
72. *The Flower and the Leaf.*

E. The King's Knight: Personal Poems (see Chapter IX)

Poems upon Lord Fawcomberg, the Beauforts, and others.

73. *The Compleynt of Mars:* 'Chaucer's'.
74. *Anelida and Arcite:* 'Chaucer's'.
75. *Ballad of Good Counsel.*
76a. *The Legend of Good Women:* 'Chaucer's'.
76b–d. *Dido's Lament:* 'Pridioxe'.
  The Letter of Dydo.
  Cronycle made by Chaucier.
77. *A Gentlewoman's Lament:* 'Lydgate's'.

Poems chiefly for Margaret Vernon and her family.

78. *Compleynt.*
79. *The Temple of Glas:* 'Lydgate's'.
80. *Reson and Sensuallyte* contd.: 'Lydgate's' (and see No. 61).
81a. 'O bewtie pereles'.
81b. 'I hard lately to a ladye'.
82a–b. *A Seying of the Nightingale:* Roos completed by Lydgate.
  The Cuckoo and the Nightingale: 'Lydgate's'.
83a–f. Lyrics in MS. Ff. 1.6.

Poems for Eleanor Cobham and Antigone d'Amancier, c. 1450–4.

84. *The Complaint of Venus:* 'Chaucer's'.
85a–f. Lyrics in MS. Ff. 1.6.
86a–f. Lyrics in other manuscripts.

F. Satirical Verse (see Chapter X)

87. *Balade against Woman Unconstant:* 'Chaucer's'.
88. *A Balade Pleasaunte.*
89. 'Welcom be ye whan ye go'.
90. *The Servant of Cupyde Forsaken:* 'Lydgate's'.
91. 'Of their nature they greatly them delite'.
92. *In Praise of Woman.*
93. *Balade of a Reeve.*
94. 'To Burgeys'.
95. 'Loke wel aboute'.
96. 'O mossie quince'.
97a–b. Poems in MS. Ashmole 176.
98. *The Hood of Green.*
99a–b. Two Verse Letters in MS. Rawl. poet. 36.

G. The Last Years (till 1482) (see Chapter XI)

    100. 'The Prisoner to Vere': 'Rothley's'.

    101*a–e*. Poems for Anthony Wydville.

        (*a*) 'Al hoolly youres'.

        (*b*) 'Of gretter cause'.

        (*c*) 'Myne hert is set vppon a lusty pynne'.

        (*d*) 'Somewhat musing|And more mourning': 'Wydville's'.

        (*e*) 'Honour and Ioy, helth and prosperyte'.

    102. *The Romaunts of the Rose*, Fragment C: ? 'Chaucer's'.

H. The Tudor Aftermath (see Chapter XII)

    103. *The Court of Love:* Roos and 'Philogenet'.

    104. Lyrics in the 'Egerton' and 'Devonshire' and other manuscripts, and in *The Courte of Venus*, ascribed to Wyatt.

    105. Lyrics ascribed to Surrey.

    106. Lyrics ascribed by Tottel to 'Uncertain Authors'.

Out of this mass of work, a *corpus* as large as that of Chaucer, but with a very high proportion of brief lyrics, certain poems stand out. What may well come to be considered as typical of the century, and the flower of Roos's non-lyric work, are the poems forming a quincunx with *La Belle Dame sans Merci*: earlier, *The Black Knight*, and *The Isle of Ladies*; and later, The Prologue to *The Legend of Good Women*, and *The Flower and the Leaf*, three of them hitherto anonymous. Much translation is assigned to him, notably 'Chaucer's' *Romaunt of the Rose*, 'Lydgate's' *Reson and Sensuallyte*, and some less known pieces. Other shorter poems filched from Lydgate may arouse little objection, though in effect almost all his courtly poems are stripped from him. Some short poems of 'Chaucer' will cause regret, such as *The Deth of Pyte*. Alarm and revulsion will probably greet the claim for *The Legend of Good Women*, and horrified incredulity the chapter on 'The Tudor Aftermath'. It is for the scholar to judge whether, or how far, the cumulative evidence carries conviction.

CHAPTER V

The Plesaunce Period, c. 1428–41: Plesaunce Poems

I. THE PLESAUNCE SCENE

WE probably cannot estimate to the full the effect of contact with Humphrey, Duke of Gloucester, and with the life at Plesaunce, on a young man brought up in a predominantly military family, himself a soldier, but obviously capable of literary interests, certainly sensitive to poetry, and perhaps intended earlier for a clerkly career. Duke Humphrey's brilliance is dimmed for us now, and he appears erratic and ineffective; but he was then the highest representative of culture in England, the Maecenas of poets, scholars, and physicians, and he is the still-remembered patron of the University of Oxford. Eager for knowledge, a lover of books and fine manuscripts, gathering around him men of talent, feeling the first breath of the new learning from Italy, he added to all this the *éclat* of royal rank, and of power only just below the throne.[1] Early dealings with such a man, his notice and favour, might well be intoxicating to a young aspirant.

There were also claims of kinship; Eleanor Cobham, gradually given recognition as the Duchess of Gloucester, was a step-cousin of Sir Richard Roos on his mother's side, the only parent whom he knew intimately. Eleanor has been called a stupid and weak-minded as well as an unscrupulous woman, on the score of her admitted necromantic practices. Waurin in his first account of her draws a different picture:

Alyenor de [Cobham], une moult noble damoiselle et de grant lygnage, laquele il eut depuis espousee comme vous orez, quy estoit venue avec madame Jaqueline la ducesse sa femme ou pays de Henau par maniere

---

[1] R. Weiss, *Humanism in England*, chs. III and IV; H. S. Bennett, *Medieval Men and Women*.

de desbat, ainsi que jeunes damoiselles sont voullentrieues de veoir
nouveaulx pays et marches estranges, car aussi elle estoit belle et plaisant
a merveilles, si se moustroit de bon courage en divers lieux.

(Cronique, Rolls ser., 39c, vol. I, p. 176)

This sets her in another light from the poor waiting-gentlewoman,
daughter of a 'Gloucester's man', orphaned of her mother, who, when
aided and sheltered by Jacqueline of Hainault, turned like a snake and
betrayed her benefactress. Even the 'Solitary' of Lydgate's lament for
Jacqueline, who already accuses Eleanor of practising vile sorcery in
order to seduce Humphrey's heart, never charges her with base ingratitude. To him she is

> a myrmayde
> Ressemblyng vn-to a chaunteresse,
> Of faace lyke a soreceresse. (*Minor Poems*, p. 610)

A stupid woman would hardly have held the volatile Duke for fifteen
years; and her spells must have been supported by feminine powers of
charm and personality. Her later household probably assumed the proportions of a court, to match and uphold the Duke's prestige: 'Strangers
in court do take her for the queen' (*2 Henry VI*, I, iii, 82). When Anne,
Duchess of Bedford, 'bonne et belle et bien amée', died in 1432, Eleanor
became the first lady in the land:

> Amonge alle women magnyfyed,
> As Lucyfer felle down for pryde,
> I felle ffrom alle felycyte. . . .
> That hade alle London at my cure
> To crok and knele, whan I wold calle.
> (Wright, *Polit. Poems*, II, 206)

Shakespeare violates chronology by representing Eleanor face to face
with Margaret of Anjou in a clash of will-power; they never met thus.
But he remains true to the character of each woman, to Margaret's
jealous pride, and Eleanor's 'aspiring humour'. Whether after the death
of Bedford in 1435 Eleanor looked askance at the young king as the one
remaining obstacle between herself and the crown, and actually began
to plot his death, will perhaps never be certainly known; it remains a
possibility. Unlike Lady Macbeth, she would probably have concealed
her intents from her husband, 'infirm of purpose'. In the early 1430s,
however, a decade before this crisis, there was enough in the state
kept by the ducal pair to dazzle a young man brought up in the probably
old-fashioned household of his widowed mother and his fighting
brothers.

There was yet another cause of interest and excitement. To a youth whose home background had been the massive Norman castles of Hamlake and Belvoir, it was probably a revelation of elegance and modernity to watch the transformation of the old riverside manor of Bellacourt at Greenwich into the ducal palace of Plesaunce; it would be Roos's first close acquaintance with the practice of 'the mistress art' of architecture:

> I se castels, I se eke high toures,
> Walles of stone crested and bataylled,
> Medes, welles, river, sote floures,
> And many paleys fressh apparayled,
> Devises new vncouthely entayled. (*For lac of sighte*, ll. 9–13)

Not much building was done in the early reign of Henry VI, other than a few ecclesiastical and collegiate constructions. Only five licences for crenellating were issued during the whole reign, and one of these is to Duke Humphrey for Plesaunce which was in his hands from 1428 (Vickers, p. 444). Although Protector, he observed the due forms. The erection of Plesaunce was a joint project of the Duke and Duchess, 'Eleanor his wife' as she is named in the licences issued in 1433 and 1434: to impark two hundred acres, to build a tower of stone and mortar in the park; later, to make an underground conduit from a certain well of theirs in Greenwich called 'Stokwell' across the highway which ran between their garden and their park, in order to bring water from the well to their manor or inn there; and to enclose a way south from the highway to the river.[1] One may be assured that these grandiose plans without doors were matched by beauty and elegance within, by rich hangings and heraldic glass. Shakespeare repeats the charge of extravagance:

> Thy sumptuous buildings and thy wife's attire
> Have cost a mass of public treasury.
> (*2 Henry VI*, I, iii, 133)

An early poem by Sir Richard Roos reflects these new interests in a three-fold whirl of excitement: the varieties of knowledge and the beauty of the visible earth, the splendour of park and garden and of brave new buildings, and lastly the charm of women and especially of one woman, the whole conceived against the background suggested by *Le Roman de la Rose* and by the precepts and practice of Geoffrey de Vinsauf. Interspersed are *bravura* passages of youthful satire, with fitful meditation, and poetic self-assertion: 'fforthe I wol'.

---

[1] *Cal. Pat. Rolls, 1429–36*, pp. 240, 250, 369.

No. 1. *How a Louer Prayseth hys Lady:* a poem of 467 lines in rhyming couplets (with one triplet) of irregular, 'doggerel' verse.

> *Incipit.* When the son the laumpe of heuen ful lyght
> Phebus with hys eye ful gret round and bryght
> In the lyon rent yn hys domynacion
> *Explicit.* Let other amende hyt that better kunne
> ffor kunnyng in me was neuer kunne none.

Miss Hammond's judgment that it is certainly not Lydgate's is indisputable, and it has remained 'anonymous'. She suggested the date c. 1450, from its manuscript; hers is the only edition (*Mod. Phil.*, XXI, 379–95). I suggest Sir Richard Roos as the writer, and would date it certainly after Christmas 1433, probably in the high summer of 1436.

The unique manuscript copy is in MS. Fairfax 16; there it follows the only independent copy of *Reson and Sensuallyte*, with which it has much affinity. The owner of Fairfax 16 was Lord Stanley, who had final charge of Eleanor Cobham, Duchess of Gloucester; it is possible that this 'Plesaunce' poem came into his possession from her belongings. The poem is not 'signed', though the phrase 'anon aryse' (l. 299) may be an adumbration of the developed 'signature'. The astronomical opening has parallels in a French poem possibly known to Roos, *Le Congié d'Amours*, included in MS. Royal 19.A.iii (see above, Chapter III):

> En ce temps de joieux este
> Que Phebus est en sa hauteur,

and in the first lines of *The Flower and the Leaf:*

> When that Phebus his chaire of gold so hy
> Had whirled up the sterry sky aloft
> And in the Bole was entred certainly.

There are four pointers to a date in the mid-thirties. One occurs in the subject of polite conversation made by the knights under the shady trees as they

> rayl fresshly vp and down
> With ladyes ful of youthe and plesaunce
> And them tel how the reliquez com yn to fraunce (ll. 68–70)

The boy king, after a hastily prepared coronation at Westminster on November 6, 1429, had crossed to France at Easter, 1430 (Lord Roos was in his train), and after long delays, had been crowned again in Paris in December 1431. Lydgate had written for the king, for a Christmas mumming at Windsor, probably in 1429, the history of 'howe þampull and þe floure delys came first to þe kynges of Fraunce by myrakle at Reynes' (*Minor Poems*, pp. 691–4): the golden ampulla brought from heaven by a dove for the conversion and anointing of King Clovis; and the azure shield with three *fleurs de lis*, presented by an angel to replace the three toads of the king's pagan arms. This was for the little Henry's instruction probably before the coronation in France; and as was noted by the chroniclers,[1] a great point was made of the sacred relics kept for the French kings being brought out for Henry. These matters were therefore topics of polite talk about this time. The young poet may also be indulging in an absurd *double-entendre*, which may well have been a jest of the period. 'Relike' is used as a term of reverential endearment in *The Romaunt of the Rose* (ll. 2673, 2907), and also in the prologue to *The Legend* (F. l. 321), where the god of love calls the daisy 'my relyke, digne and delytable'.

The second indication of date comes in the comparison of the lady's beauty with that of

> a pryncely cristemesse
> In the tyme of glorious Calamon
> Cirtys Artour or els kyng John (ll. 195–7).

'Cirtys Artour' (which defeated Miss Hammond) might stand for 'Courteous Arthur'; but 'Cirtys' is probably a more topical reference, a 'modern instance', comparable with King John. King Henry spent the Christmas of 1433 at the famous Abbey at Bury St. Edmunds, Lydgate's monastery; its noted Abbot was William Curteys, who gave the young king so much princely entertainment and spiritual satisfaction that he stayed long, and returned for the whole of Lent.[2] Duke Humphrey joined him for Easter, and may have been there at Christmas also.

A third pointer tends to indicate August 1436 as the season of the poem. In the central anagram occurs the name JAC–V–TTA WYDVY. Jacquetta, Duchess of Bedford, had become a widow on September 15, 1435. Her secret marriage with Richard Wydville, the future Lord Rivers, took place some time before March 23, 1436/7, when she obtained pardon.[3] This is an August poem, and 1436 is more probable than 1437. The son of Humphrey's illegitimate daughter, Antigone, Lady Powys, was born on November 5, 1436,[4] and the poem is, I believe, written chiefly for her. The stress on fecundity in the description of nature supports the idea that it is a poem to a young wife.

---

[1] As by Monstrelet, *Chroniques*, ch. 109.
[2] Vickers, *Humphrey, Duke of Gloucester*, p. 241.
[3] G.E.C., *Complete Peerage*, XI, 21.   [4] *Ib.*, VI, 139.

Finally, the references to necromancy, carefree in tone, could not have been written after the autumn of 1441, when Eleanor's circle realized fully with what edged tools she had been playing; even here, the poet reassures himself on the innocence of these pursuits:[1]

> Ther was als a myrrour of wonder engyne
> Ipolysshed by Intellygence devyne
> Made by sterred astronomye
> By spirytes of the eyre and nygramancye
> In whom ye myght truly byhold and loke
> In thexemplayre of deuyn boke
> How your frendys fare yn euery contre
> And how your selfe yn parfyt hele may be
> And also by vertue feythe hope and cheryte
> By our fredom and vertues doyng
> With the prince of pees to abyde euer duryng. (ll. 131–41)

In a poem so diffuse and unpolished one is chary of looking for fully developed anagrams; only two brief passages, satisfactorily self-contained, yield recognizable names. The description of the magic mirror, just quoted, gives: A–IAn. –OBHAM; and in skeletal form it indicates one of her accomplices: BO–InB–O. The first twenty lines on the lady's appearing yield the names of the Plesaunce family, HO–F–Y; AlIAn. COBHA.; ANTIGONe; also JAC–V–TTA WYDVY., and the poet's 'devise' shortly, ForFA–T. This last recurs in the concluding eight lines, and makes the poet's claim to authorship, ForFA–T

Since the poem is not familiar, a short *résumé* is desirable, though brevity is difficult with verse which darts from point to point, like a dragonfly on a stream. The poet celebrates the heat of summer, when Phebus and 'diane echates', 'the flode and sees quene', combine to bring calm weather and maturing heat to all living creatures. He seeks a garden, walled, with towers of crystal, where grow all healthful and pleasant herbs and flowers:

> They lawghden on men ful pleasauntly
> And pirwynked on youthe ful nysely (ll. 21–2).

He names the trees, the fruit, and the herbs of healing 'Sent fro the Caan and preter John' (l. 38). Every sense is pleased, sight and hearing and taste. Men wander in the shady alleys, discussing with their ladies the French relics, or ardently making love. The wounds of love can be cured from a well, and by the medicinal herbs, tended by the master

---

[1] Eleanor's two chief associates, Southwell, and Roger Bolingbroke or Oonly, were clerics; Bale credits the latter with an apologia, *De Innocentia Sua.* Roos will allude to them covertly in *The Romaunt of the Rose* and elsewhere.

gardener, 'Old ypocras', aided by Galen, Apollo, and Avicenna. At their command music, gay or warlike, fills the garden, and so does 'The chirme of briddys feir and swete'. There follows a list of such birds as please the ear and also the eye; another pleasure of sight lies in jewels 'commyng out of Inde'. The nearby river is full of merchant ships, 'Of al the world fro Capses vnto ffrise' (l. 118). A fresh conduit flows with healing balms, and near it is the magic mirror. Abruptly, as if afraid of having said too much, the poet leaves the mirror, and describes the park with all its horned beasts (including unicorns), 'Iclosed with marble xxti myle a boute' (l. 144). A great city is nearby, fairer and richer than any ancient or modern city from Rome to Cologne. Then follow a score of lines of high idealism (or inverted satire) describing the *mœurs* of the inhabitants:

> Ther was withoute envy religion,
> Hygh lordshypp with oute extorcion (ll. 156–7)

This lofty tone is not sustained; and the poet includes 'Wydwes that neuer lysteth a man to kys' (l. 168). Soon he abruptly bids farewell to the garden, but turns back to describe the dwellers in it. These are the people of the Rose, but touched on with commendable brevity:

> I sey youthe that neuer hopyth to deye
> And rychesse that al the world doth gye. (ll. 178–9)

They are seen as in the magic of a time-defeating dream:

> Stondyng on a brygge ouer a ryuer
> ffastned with no thing but wyth a brer
> Sum byheld the gardyn iiijxxti yer and mo
> Sum an hour lyke the shadowe wer ago
> So me semed that suerte ne substaunce
> Myght not stond with sodeyn varyaunce
> Wel ys hym that syker and yn Joy ay may dwele
> That ys not yn erthe see neyther helle. (ll. 182–9)

The poet shakes off his musing fit: 'That lesson foryate I and lokyd aboute'; and in looking he comes to his supreme experience, the sight of the lady 'daunsyng yn the route', fairer than the sun in spring, or the planet Venus, 'fayrer than fayrye', or than 'esperus the day ster'. He invokes the aid of the rhetoricians, Tully and Geoffrey de Vinsauf, of Chaucer, Gower and Lydgate, of poets ancient and medieval, from Virgil to Alanus de Insulis. But 'al ys yn veyne'; he is no favourite of the Muses, but a 'dulle asse'. Yet he will try again: 'I haue ben out of my wey'; and from his digression he returns to his theme. Aided now by rhetoric, he works steadily through the lady's beauties: '*descripcio capitis'* (l. 248); *descripcio crinium* (l. 258), 'gylt tressys' fairer than those of 'yong absolon, Estrild, Eleyne, or fresshe Polexene'; then the countenance,

> the baner of womanhede
> Whiche ys the geme of al goodlyhede. (ll. 270–1)

For her fair eyes and her sweet breath, he has recourse to detailed medical and anatomical statements. For her smooth forehead he fortunately returns from book-learning to his own keen observation:

> No thyng pynchyd lyke a nonnys wymple
> Ne forowyd drye lyke a nabbesse gymple (ll. 326–7).

The lady's lovely proportions, the sweetness of her expression, all this is 'beaute wedded vn to delyte':

> O lytel mouthe, o leder of the daunse
> Louyers to wound with fyry pleasaunce (ll. 342–3).

Only Homer and the Muses could do justice to this non-pareil, the effort of whose making must have wearied Nature (cf. 'did tire the enginer'). The poet, inspired by *Architrenius*, ponders how and why such beauty can both bring a young man to mania, to 'sorowful passyon', and also cure his hurt; but, like him, he modestly leaves the theme. It is reserved for 'wedlok, the sacrament of grace', and he himself 'had neuer experience'. He ends the poem rather flatly with the fifteen beauties of woman (l. 446), summed up in her who 'All was beaute and parfyte wommanheed'. Let another do better than can he with his simple wit.

It is obvious that the poet has done much reading, starting with the older poetry, even ballads, for such phrases on the lady as 'lyke the bournyd white whalys bon' (l. 275; cf. l. 358), or 'whitter than swannys kynde' (l. 402). He invokes 'Moral gower, lydgate, Rethor and poete', and above all

> mayster Chauser sours and fundement
> In englysshe tunge swetely to endyte.
> Thy soule god haue with virgynes white (ll. 219–21).

He draws on *Le Roman de la Rose* for the general description of the walled park, the river and the well, the fruit-trees and the birds, but he never copies slavishly. His epithets are original and racy: 'twytlyng goldfinche' (l. 104); a 'crane bekyd' nose (l. 335); 'my flewmy wyt' (l. 381). From this parallelism with the source-poem spring other likenesses to poems equally dependent on it: to *Reson and Sensuallyte* (or rather to its French original) for the delight in the variety of nature;

to *The Court of Sapience* for the lists of birds and jewels, but those of
The Court are informative and pedantic, while these are gay and
sparkling, with names strung like glittering beads. Yet even these are
not merely wild and whirling words; the precious stones are carefully
chosen for their suitable properties (ll. 112–16). Ruby, the royal gem,
brings regard, honour and grace to the wearer; the sapphire vanquishes
envy. The jacynth achieves one's wishes, and enables safe going into
all lands.[1] The carbuncle shines by night, and the topaz feels the
moon's influence; it also keeps a man chaste. The adamant wins one's
husband's love; moreover, both the adamant and the diamond are of
use to enchanters, 'aydable as enchaunteurs'.[2] This last convinces that
the list of jewels is devised for the mistress of Plesaunce, owner of the
magic mirror, worker by night and moonlight; it even suggests that
Eleanor's plea at her trial, that her only aim was to keep her husband's
love and fidelity, may have been true, or at least believed by her friends.

Other authorities are closely followed, especially Geoffrey de Vinsauf.
From his *Poetria Nova* (ll. 563–613) the poet takes and expands much
of the description of the lady's beauty; he borrows the 'conceit' of her
mouth:

> tanquam praegnantia labra tumore
> Surgant, sed modico rutilent, ignita, sed igne
> Mansueto. (ll. 574–6)

> A wyght to fyre with out eny fyre. . . .
> Whos lyppys wyth chyld ben by maydenhede
> Swol and engreyned wyth rosys rede. (ll. 344–7)

And to the *De Arte Versificandi* he is indebted for the description of the
spring of water, and for the stress on the pleasure of the senses:

> Gustus et olfactus, oculi pascuntur et aures;
> Omnis ibi sensus est satiata fames (ll. 13–4, sect. 19).

So in *How a Lover*:

> Sum gladed the syght with staryng cher
> Sum therys by oft relacion
> Sum the mouthe by gret delectacion
> And ful many the hert yn especial. (ll. 54–7)

The *De Planctue Naturae* of Alanus de Insulis Roos might have been led
to by Chaucer; but Gervaise of Melkeley with his *De Versibus Edendis* is
a rarer bird; his *Pirame et Thisbe* describes feminine beauty in the same

---

[1] Paul Studer and Joan Evans, *Anglo-Norman Lapidaries*, Paris, 1924,
pp. 126, 98, 169.
[2] *Ib.*, pp. 110, 100, 97, 119.

way as does Vinsauf, but it is Vinsauf that the English poet follows. One might have doubted whether he was equally well acquainted with 'Archytreny' since he seems to class him with the masters of rhetoric, when he is in fact the name-character of a poem. Actually Roos borrows largely from the *Architrenius* of Johannes de Altavilla. A line like that on the lady's eyes, 'Lyke a smaragde or a cler saphire' (l. 294), illustrates Roos's conflation of borrowings: the first jewel is from Vinsauf's *Luce smaragdina* (l. 570), the second from Altavilla's *in quo saphyri flammata diescit* (p. 254). The expansions of the description are often indebted to *Architrenius*: the nose,

> Not apysshe short, signe of hastynes,
> Nor crane bekyd, to shewe manysshenes. (ll. 334-5)

is Roos's own application of *Excursus aquila nescit, vel sim[i]a recursus.* Some, but by no means all, of Roos's medical statements are due to *Architrenius*, such as the teeth 'Without ake or putrefaccion' (l. 359), for *qui nec livescere morbo | Erubet, aut putris olida ferrugine sordis* (p. 256).[1]

The fifteen beauties of woman, enumerated by threes, occur in more than one form of the French poem *La Louenge des Dames*, of which one was printed in Paris in 1500. Another, much more like this whole English poem, *La Louenge et Beaute des Dames*,[2] credited to a writer under François I, must surely have a much older basis. Its imagined state of perfection in all nature (the stones all jewels, the nettles all lavender, the ravens all nightingales, and the hail all pearls) springs from an ideal not unlike Roos's exaggerations:

> Et tout cueur d'omme sans durté
> Sans cruaulté, sans tricherie. . . .
> Et tout fust bon qui est mauvais
> Et toute haine vraye paix.

Plesaunce is indeed 'A plot of heuen made by angels devyse' (l. 175), a *locus amœnus*.

It may seem unwarrantable at this stage to suggest a parallel between the timeless dream on the bridge quoted above (ll. 184-9) and the annihilation of time in Petrarch's *Trionfo della Eternità*, ll. 62 ff.:

> Un'ora sgombra
> Quanto in molt'anni a pena si raguna. . . .
> tutti in un punto passeran com'ombra.

---

[1] E. Faral, *Les Arts Poétiques du XII*e *et du XIII*e *Siècle*, Paris, 1923, pp. 194 ff. Thomas Wright, *The Anglo-Latin Satirical Poets*, 2 vols., 1872, Rolls ser. 59 a and b. Vol. I, *Architrenius* (see especially the end of Bk. I and beginning of Bk. II); Vol. II, *De Planctu Naturae* (see especially *Prosa Prima*).

[2] Montaiglon, *Recueil de Poésies françaises*, etc., Vol. VII, pp. 287-301.

But it will be seen later that Roos, frequenter of Plesaunce, may well have acquired considerable knowledge of the Italian tongue and of Petrarch's poetry.

Yet all this parade of learning cannot dull the vitality of the poem. It has a living background, the river seen from the park; and the Thames at Greenwich is still one of the finest and most stirring views in England, not a stream, but a tidal estuary alive with shipping and the actuality of traffic. The neighbouring city's identity with London is not disguised by the inclusion of the name among the towns that it excels. And in Greenwich is Plesaunce; Leland will later break into verse on the splendour of Greenwich:[1]

> Quae turres, vel ad astra se efferentes!
> Quae porro viridaria, ac perennes
> Fontes. Flora finum occupat venusta. (*Itin.* ix, 16)

Eustache Deschamps had already provided Roos with a model for local poetry in his praise of Beauté-sur-Marne[2] and its inhabitants. In Plesaunce too there were notable people: first the Duke, who probably told this untrained young poet to study the rhetoricians; perhaps he weaned him from his alliterative verse, and taught him to 'metur make', as he did the anonymous and grateful translator of Palladius, who could only 'soso' counterfeit him.[3] There also was Gilbert Kymer the Duke's physician, a future Chancellor of Oxford, who probably inspired the technical descriptions of the eye and the epiglottis (ll. 308 ff.; 348 ff.); perhaps too he recommended study of the *Ortus Sanitatis* for the properties of herbs. There too were Roos's kinswoman, the Duchess, and the young Antigone, singing and dancing; above all, there was the lady, his 'own herts quene', Elizabeth Phelip, whose initials peep out from the names '*El*eyne or fresshe *Pol*exyene'. It is no wonder that the young poet is intoxicated with the earth's plenitude, and its teeming fecundity ('Ther was no tre mayde ne steryle', l. 59). The multitudinous activity, the sense, 'How good is man's life, the mere living', prevent any mechanical uniformity of thought or rhythm. The poem might be the work of a gifted student, a pupil of the unknown and learned author of *The Court of Sapience*, turning all his lessoning into life and gusto. Like Sapience herself, this young 'bachelier' 'rejoices in the habitable part of the earth'. Like Herrick, he indulges in 'cleanly wantonness'; unlike

---

[1] Plesaunce or Greenwich will come into literature again as the 'Mirefleur' of *Amadis de Gaule*, a 'little castle two leagues from London, on the side of a hill surrounded by forest, orchards and flowers, and watered by great fountains' (transl. Antony Munday, 1619, Bk. II, p. 64).

[2] Ballade 61.   [3] Hammond, *From Chaucer to Surrey*, pp. 202-5.

Herrick, he draws back here from grossness. Miss Hammond's appreciation of this rough and neglected jewel, the matrix of poetry if hardly yet a poem, is just and discriminating on the poet's 'direct and lively perceptions', his geniality and satire; 'a personality makes itself felt'.

A second poem shows us Plesaunce at one remove—as the imagined scene of a dream romance, invented to amuse its inhabitants, and to plead the poet's love.

No. 2. *The Isle of Ladies:* a narrative and dream poem of over 2200 lines, in octosyllabic couplets. At the end is a six-line decasyllabic stanza (aabbcc), an appeal to the lady; then a *balade* in three stanzas of rhyme royal with refrain; and finally an octosyllabic couplet which picks up a line of the *balade*.

Incipit.	When flora the quene of plesaunce Had hol acheued th' obeissaunce Of this freshe and new season.
Incipit of stanza.	Fayrest of fayer and goodlest on lyve.
Incipit of balade.	Go forthe, myn owne trew herte innocent.
Refrain of balade.	Geve the the blisse that thou desiryers ofte.
Final couplet (ll. 2234–5)	Ye that this balad red shall I pray you kepe you from the fall.

The poem is now considered as anonymous. Brandl,[1] and following him its editor Jane Sherzer,[2] date it 1420, and connect it with the marriage of Henry V and Katherine of France. Unfortunately this induces the identification of the elderly lady of the island's court with Katherine's mother, Queen Isabeau; to be equated with this friendly, sociable lady, would have astonished and affronted the redoubtable and none too reputable Isabeau of Bavaria, queen of Charles VI. Fortunately, it is this very lady whose anagram enables us to date the poem with some precision. Her description (ll. 91–122) yields AnN STAFFOr. WO-DSTOC., BOWCHI.; EW; IAY TOT FOrFAIT FOr-A-T. Anne, grand-daughter of Edward III, daughter and surviving heir of Thomas of Woodstock, married in 1398 Edmund, fifth Earl of Stafford, a nephew of Lady Beatrice Roos. Soon after his death at the battle of Shrewsbury (1403), she married Sir William Bourchier, Count of Eu. Her death, October 16–24, 1438, near the age of sixty, gives a downward date for *The Isle of*

[1] A. Brandl in *Archiv*, CXII, pp. 197 ff.

[2] Ed. Jane B. Sherzer, Berlin, 1903. Also printed by Chalmers, *English Poets*, I, 378–94 (as 'Chaucer's Dream'). See E. Hammond, *Chaucer Bibliography*, 429–30.

Ladies;[1] and a lady who has been merely a matriarchal name in genealogies is here given a full and rounded character. She is growing old with gaiety and grace, praised by a young poet who, like this dreamer, has experienced her courtesy and kindliness:

> on[e] the coni[n]gest creature
> She was and so sayd everychone . . .
> for she was sobre and well avised,
> and from every fault disguysed,
> and nothinge vsed but faythe and trothe.
> That she nas younge, hit was great routhe
> for every where and in eche place
> she gouerned her, that in grace
> she stod alwaye withe pore and riche
> that in a word was none her liche,
> ne halfe so able misteres to be
> to suche a lustye company. (ll. 110–22)

Historians have not hitherto connected Anne of Woodstock with Gloucester's circle, but the two were cousins, both direct descendants of Edward III, she by one generation the nearer in blood. Moreover, each was a child of a Bohun sister and coheiress; in 1431 they were sorting out Bohun dower lands (V.C.H., *Wilts.*, VII, 100). Her eldest son, Humphrey, later first Duke of Buckingham, was in her lifetime a mediator between Cardinal Beaufort and Gloucester; but three years after her death he served as one of Eleanor Cobham's secular judges.

There are two manuscripts, Longleat 256 (now containing no other work), which Francis Thynne had seen, and which wrongly calls the poem *The Temple of Glasse;* and Add. 10303, a late sixteenth-century manuscript, which calls it *The Death of Blaunch*, etc. Both ascribe it to Chaucer. Speght, the first to print it in 1598, called it *Chaucers dreame*, and distinguished it from *The Boke of the Duchesse*. Bradshaw seems to be the inventor of the title used now, *The Isle of Ladies*; the title intended by the writer was probably *The Ile of Pleasaunce* (l. 2199; and see above, p. 96). Speght was responsible, without citing his authority, for the view of it as a 'covert report' of the love-stories of John of Gaunt with Blanche of Lancaster, and of Chaucer with a lady unknown. Tyrwhitt rightly repudiated this unauthorized suggestion as a 'mere fancy'; it is a back-formation of conjecture.

The poem is 'signed' at its centre with the extended 'signature' phrase:

> And I as hole as any wyght
> vprose withe Joyoux harte and light . . .

---

[1] G.E.C., *Complete Peerage*, XII, i, 181.

And to my ladye where she playd
I went annone. (ll. 1203–8)

Another pointer is the introduction of Eleanor Cobham's motto, 'al en un', into one description of the queen of the island; her restrained behaviour is 'all in on[e] to euery wyght' (l. 672). Plesaunce is a word uppermost in the poet's mind; it occurs twenty-two times as the rhyme word, in all its meanings; and the slouth: trouth rhyme is not only recurrent, it also represents a dominant idea, a contrast in the service of love; thus the god of love promises to favour those

that seruethe trewlye witheout slowthe
and . . . auanced be by trothe (ll. 1057–8)

The anagram devoted to Anne of Woodstock has already been pointed out. Two anagrams at the beginning and the end indicate the full Plesaunce circle: the introductory passage (ll. 1–70) gives: HOMFREY; AlIAN.COBHAM; ANTIGONA POWYS; ELISABeTH BEWMONT, BA–DO–F; ISMANIA SCALYS; STYWA–D; BABThO; AY TOT FOrFAIT FOrF. The final *Balade* repeats some of this with the addition of 'Artus' the Duke's illegitimate son: HOMFr–Y GLO.; AlYAn.; AnTIGO.; ARTW.; BABThO.; whIT–––AM; IAY TOT FOrFAYT. The description of the poet's first awaking (ll. 1301–31) yields: HOMFR.; A–IAN. –OB–AM; ANTI––NA; AnN STAFF––D; KATH. whITT. His second sleep in the painted room gives two men's names: RAUF BABTHO.; ROBe–T whITTI––HA–; these are probably the younger men, the esquires who had been Roos's natural companions at Plesaunce. Sir John Stiward, an anglicized knight of Scottish birth, was later to be one of Eleanor Cobham's keepers; her gift to him of a diamond ring has already been cited (see above, p. 107); he may very well have been a friend of Plesaunce days.

The poem is then the work of Sir Richard Roos, with his 'signature' and 'devise', a Plesaunce poem by many signs and by the anagrams; it must be dated before October 1438, but not before 1435–6, since Antigone is already married.

The poem is in two parts, two wish-fulfilment dreams, with an introduction and a connecting passage. The poet, in a hunting lodge in May, dreams, and finds himself mysteriously transported to an island with walls and gates of glass, inhabited only by ladies. An elder lady challenges his presence pleasantly but firmly; he must leave. Their talk is broken off (l. 265) by the unexpected arrival of the queen of the isle; to the ladies' astonishment she is accompanied by an unknown knight, and to the poet's rapture by his own dear Lady. The queen tells (l. 315) of her customary journey every seven years to fetch the three apples which ensure the lasting youth and beauty of her subjects. This time its sequel was alarming; she found the Lady already picking the fruit, and was then carried off to a ship by a strange knight. The Lady rescued her, and all three have now journeyed in her ship to the isle. The knight, remorseful for his violence, swoons (l. 511), and prays for death; the queen, unrelenting, is determined to send him away.

A great fleet now appears (l. 693), and the ladies prepare to resist it; it is the navy of the god of love, who comes on a punitive expedition against these rebels. He meets them in high displeasure, rebukes the hardhearted queen (l. 763), and gives her a wound of love. But to the poet's delight he shows great favour to the Lady:

> And made her chere as a goddesse
> And of beutye cauled her princesse
> Of bountye eke gave her the name. (ll. 805–8)

He recommends her to pity her lover. The queen and her ladies submit themselves to Lord Love (l. 911); the next day, sitting throned on high among flowers, Love ordains the future government of the island; he then departs. The following morning (l. 1101), the Lady takes her leave, and the poet in despair runs into the sea after her ship, and is dragged aboard; the Lady revives him with the magic fruit, and is kind. They arrive at her home—and he wakes (l. 1301), to find himself faint and drenched with tears, in a room full of smoke. This ends the first dream.

The poet leaves the smoky chamber, gropes his way up a winding stair, finds a quiet room painted with old stories, lies down, and goes over his dream. Again he dreams (l. 1341), and is forthwith back in the island. The knight is taking leave of the queen, to visit his own country, where he is a prince, and to prepare for their wedding. He promises to return within ten days, but to his distraction, his lords delay him for fifteen days (l. 1491). He returns as he had gone in the queen's magic barge. He finds the isle in sad plight (l. 1597), filled with ladies clad in black and mourning for the queen, who has died 'for sorrow of your great vntrothe' (l. 1646), and now lies in state. The prince embraces her body (l. 1713), and straightway kills himself. The ladies bring the bodies to the royal burial place, an abbey of black nuns, and keep vigil. In the morning a wonder befalls (l. 1813). A bird flies against a window, and falls dead; but another bird brings a potent herb, and three of its seeds revive the dead bird. The abbess (l. 1882) takes the herb to the queen's bier; the miracle is repeated, and the queen, and then the prince, are restored to life. Amid great rejoicings (l. 1965) their wedding preparations go forward; but they insist on the Lady's presence (l. 1993), and she is fetched. After three months of festivity (l. 2069), the queen and the prince persuade the Lady to have pity on the poet (l. 2080). Their marriage is celebrated, but at the feast the loud music troubles the poet—and again he wakes (l. 2165). He looks round at the hunting scenes on the walls, and realizes his misfortune; weeping bitterly, he cries to dream again. He writes the poem to beg his Lady to turn dream into reality.

Miss Sherzer, the only modern editor of the poem, suggests as its sources Chaucer and *Le Roman de la Rose* in general; Claudianus, *De Nuptiis Honorii et Mariae* for an isle of Venus with a golden wall; Ovid's *Metamorphoses* X, for the magic fruit; Machaut's *Le Dit dou Lyon* for an island reserved for loyal lovers and reached by a boat which goes of itself; and finally Marie de France's *Eliduc* for the recovery from death through a plant. This last is the most important analogue, since the whole poem, with its simple, rapid style of telling, and its constant use of magic, is very like an extended Breton *lai*.

There are also other themes; the Amazonian parallel is the most comprehensive; Chaucer's 'Knight's Tale' had already introduced English readers to Hippolyta, the Amazon queen. The isle is a world of ladies, a regiment of women, ruled under the ordinance, 'That no mane here amonge vs dwell' (l. 246). There is a closer parallel in the alliterative *Alexander* in MS. Ashmole 44. Here Alexander, having taken the city of King Porrus of India, and viewed his wondrous palace, comes to the Caspian Gates, and summons Calistride, the 'mode quene of Amazoyne', to pay him tribute. She defies him and tells him of their state:

> Oure inhabetting, ser, is in an Ilee, & amed as a sercle,
> With rynand all aboute oure erd an endles wattre[1]
> . . . A preue planke is at a place to pas & to entre. (ll. 3736–40)

Alexander laughs at the defiance of these twenty-four thousand ladies, and offers them a safe-conduct:

> because we lufe ȝour comyng we consall ȝow blyth
> To pas out with ȝour paramours & pere vs be-forne.
> On Amon oure athill sire an athe I ȝow make, . . .
> Bathe oure gold ȝow to gefe & of oure gud kniȝtis
> To mary to ȝoure maidens & make þam a-vaunced.

The Amazons accept their destiny:

> Dame Calistride þe conquiris comes with hire ladis,
> Mas hire pes with oure prince & pas to hire landis (ll. 3778–9)

---

[1] So too Mandeville (ch. 50) says 'this lande is all environed with water'.

This would seem to be the stock on which the romantic love-story has been grafted.

The magical fruit is a Christianized form of the Hesperidean apples, kept, not by Virgil's witch, but in a 'hevenly armitage'. There is too the ancient theme of 'la princesse lointaine', for the knight has long loved the queen from afar:

> . . . thowgh he me never had sene
> yet had I longe his Lady bene (l. 385).

The angry god of Love is arbiter and judge in a Court of Love, even as we meet him in Herenc's *L'Accusacion de la Belle Dame sans Mercy* (which is in MS. Royal 19.A.iii). There Love's royal 'siege' is composed of flowers; so is it in *Le Cœur et l'Œil*, where too it is raised high in the air. In a sense the poem is of the Flower allegiance, but only in a general way, flowers being Love's livery:

> To-morne, here in this playne
> I woll ye be, and all yours
> that purposed bene to were flowers
> or of my lustye collours vse. (ll. 950–3)

Nevertheless, in spite of all these sources and analogues, the poem remains as original as one of Chaucer's, partly because fresh effects are gained from the derived material, partly because the impress of the writer's personality is on it. The best example of this is in the parallel to *Eliduc*, the restoration from the dead. Marie de France's forsaken wife revives her supplanter with a red flower which a weasel brings to restore its mate to life. Here the 'vermin' is replaced by a lovely bird,

> . . . all fethered blewe and grene
> withe bright arrayes lyke gold betwene (l. 1823).

It alights on the queen's hearse, and sings its song thrice 'full lowe and softelye'. Then a most ordinary happening startles it; an aged knight, absorbed in grief for his lord, hastily pulls off his hood to salute a prince passing by. Away goes the bird, and dashes to death against a window 'richelye painte'. A choir of birds assemble to sing its requiem; but one wise bird brings the magic herb,

> flowerles, all grene,
> full of smale leves and plaine
> swerte and longe withe many a vayne (ll. 1862–4).

The marvellously rapid flowering and fruiting of the plant take place, like the mango-plant trick, beneath the eyes of all. The bird rises and preens itself. The abbess then takes charge, and the process is repeated. Thus a new and very pretty incident has been made out of the old,

K

with the natural and the supernatural finely and convincingly blended. Some of the description is indebted to the alliterative *Alexander*: the magic birds of Porrus's palace are of gay colours, and sing as 'merry melody' as in May or at midsummer; and the Phoenix on the Dry Tree has

> frekild pennys,
> Of gold graynes & of goules full of gray mascles (l. 4988).

As in the poem *How a Lover*, the poet evinces a sense of wonder; but whereas there it was directed to the objects of the senses, here it transforms them. Thus the magnificent sight of Love's navy coming over the wavy flood, 'withe large toppes, and mastes longe' (l. 711), makes the poet's heart beat for joy. But the sails are full of flowers, and from time to time small birds descend in flocks on the ships, and sing 'withe voice full owt'. Again, the assembling of the prince's train on the seashore is told by one who must himself have taken part in the embarkation of a great host:

> . . . fewe was ther that night that slepte,
> But trussed and purueyed for the morowe. . . .
> waxinge the see, cominge the flode,
> was cryed, 'To shipe go everye wight'.
> Then was but hye, that hye myght.
> Unto the barge, me thowght, echeon
> they wente, witheout was lefte not one,
> Horse, male, trusse, ne baggage
> sallet, spere, gardbrace, ne page . . .
> Forthe goethe the shipe, sayd was the crede. (ll. 1544–69)

But he would have us suspend disbelief, and pack all this great array into the one magic barge, so that all were lodged as 'in a towne'. Yet he can be severely practical. He knows how a conquered town is pacified and due measures taken: Love

> gave his statutes in papers
> And ordayned diuerse officers (ll. 1097–8).

Again he explains carefully (perhaps to reassure the Lady) that his marriage in a tent was no hole-and-corner-affair, because the

> tente was churche perochiall,
> ordeyned it was in especill
> for the feast and for the sacre
> where arshebyshope and archedyaker
> sunge full owt the seruice (ll. 2135–9).

His varied experiences colour and give credibility to his dream-world.

The poet has a power of romantic vision, wild and strange, as in the description of the hermitage,

> wiche on a roche so highe stondes
> In strange se, out from all londes,
> That to make the [pilgrimage]
> Is caled a longe perileuse viage (ll. 331-4).

There is something in this anticipating Keats, and indeed the whole poem is of such a kind as *The Eve of St. Mark* might have become; Keats may have read *The Isle of Ladies* in Chalmers's edition of 1810, and have caught from it its atmosphere—and also his trick of 'so very' ('si tres'). Occasionally too there are anticipations of a stronger style, as in the concise line, 'Ther riches was ther olde seruice' (l. 1402), or the almost Shakespearean description of the great cry that rises from the prince's host at his suicide:

> That to the heven hard was the sowne,
> and vnder the arthe as far downe
> that wild beastes for the feare
> So sodanlye aferde a were, . . .
> They sowght, and rane as bestes blind,
> that clene forgetten had ther kynd. (ll. 1727-36)

In the night that passes before Love holds his court, some of the company compose virelayes and lays; the poet takes a romance and reads till sunrise (l. 977). Before writing *How a Lover* the poet had been reading the rhetoricians; before writing this poem, he has indeed been reading the romances, and especially the *Quête del Graal*. There he would find the 'castiaus as puceles' where 'couroit une euwe forte et rade'; and the barren islet rock where Perceval was tempted; and ships which move magically behind the whirlwinds. We know that Sir Richard Roos possessed in old age a fine copy of the *Quête*; perhaps it had earlier belonged to Duke Humphrey, as had one of his brother Robert's books (Royal 19.A.xx).

To this young poet, preoccupied as we have already seen with thought and time, the magic ship becomes a symbol of thought's control over time:

> Wiche barge was a manes thowght
> After his pleasure it him browght . . .
> Hit sayled by thowght and by pleasaunce
> Witheowt labor, est or west (ll. 1377-86).

The apples are another such symbol, defeating the ravages of time; they keep

> youthe ay durable
> bewtie and hele ever in one (ll. 348-9).

Thus the whole island illustrates the axiom, 'Thynke and have, hit cost no more' (l. 135), but with one limitation:

> Had thay been of ther lyves certaigne
> thay had been qwyt of every payne (ll. 165-6).

To return to the background of the poem. This is, plainly, a story written to divert the ladies of Plesaunce, which, if not an island, was yet an isolated palace beside the tidal river, with its walls and towers, and 'smale turrets hie', where nothing lacks 'wherein plesaunce might be'. The ladies' state is temporarily man-less (anticipatory of *The Assembly of Ladies*), perhaps when Gloucester was in France in 1436 for the siege of Calais. The queen of the isle regulates her demeanour by the motto of the Duchess. The 'counseler, seruant of loue' who speaks so wisely and faithfully, is a character who will appear again in Roos's portraits. The final couplet (ll. 2234-5) may be not by the poet, but by some satiric friend, perhaps that Picard who added the riddling stanza to 'My Lady Dere'. The Lady is formally given by Love the name of Bounty, by which name she will be celebrated and elsewhere identified with Elizabeth Phelip. If her name is found written 'in booke or els vppon a wall', the lover will reverence it as he would her own person, and as if it were of talismanic virtue, as one might a text or a maxim; so Lydgate in 'Thonke God of Alle', reads a 'blysfulle word' 'That welle was wrytyn on a walle'. Contrary to the necessities of the tale, the Lady is from the start 'in one clothinge' with the queen; this suggests a livery, as of a 'demoiselle de compagnie'. Her identification will be devised by various means in several other poems.

These two poems, neither of which is a negligible composition, seem to set the stage for Roos's courting of Elisabeth Phelip—the stage of Plesaunce, a place of beauty like the garden of the Rose, a centre of gaiety and civilized living, a court in which a lover could dream dreams, and read and write romances.

II. LADY BOUNTE

> 'She sweeps it through the court with troops of ladies,
> More like an empress than Duke Humphrey's wife',

says Shakespeare's Queen Margaret angrily of Eleanor Cobham, and it was probably true. *How a Lover* has painted the Plesaunce scene for us, and has peopled it with knights, and with 'ladyes ful of youthe and plesaunce', singing and dancing in the hot summer days. Who these ladies may have been, no one seems to have enquired; yet we know something of Gloucester's adherents. First there would be the Cobham ladies; Lord Cobham, Eleanor's father, remained high in favour with the Duke, and there is no reason to doubt his womenfolk's complaisance. His second wife (c. 1427) was Anne, daughter of Thomas Bardolf, Lord Bardolf,[1] the rebel of the reign of Henry IV. Eleanor's eldest brother, Sir Reginald Cobham, had married, first, Anne Beaumont, and then Thomasine Chideock. As he died in 1441/2, in his father's lifetime, his daughter Margaret took the title, and later married Ralph Neville, second Earl of Westmoreland. Eleanor's sister, Elisabeth Cobham, was to marry about 1439 Lord Strange of Knokyn, and her youngest sister Margaret married Reginald Curteys.

The Bardolf connexion spread farther. Anne Lady Cobham's sister, Joan Bardolf, had married before 1407 Sir William Phelip of Dennington, Suffolk, who became Lord Bardolf, *jure uxoris*. He was a valued servant of Henry V, K.G. in 1418–19, and Treasurer of the Household at the king's death in 1422. He became an adherent of Gloucester, who rewarded him with the office of Chamberlain at his anti-Beaufort *coup* of 1432. At the same time Lord Scrope replaced Hungerford as Treasurer, and Sir Robert Babthorp (d. 1436), one of the executors of Henry V, replaced Lord Tiptoft as Steward of the Household (Vickers, pp. 229–37). The bonds of fidelity of these men and their families would thus be strengthened. It is true that their tenure was short, as in 1433 Bedford dismissed some, but not Lord Bardolf, who, as one of the Duke of Exeter's executors, had Beaufort connexions—as had Sir Richard Roos. Lord Bardolf's wife, Joan, and his only child, Elisabeth Phelip, would be of this company, and it is Elisabeth whom Roos singles out for special devotion. She married, however, John, Lord Beaumont, by early 1433, her eldest son, his grandfather's heir, being seven years old and more in October 1441; the second son, who succeeded, was baptized on St. George's Day, 1438; Elisabeth's father died in June 1441, and she also between May and October of the same year. The members of Gloucester's household would add others, such as the enigmatic Antigone, illegitimate daughter of the Duke, probably daughter of Eleanor Cobham. Antigone married the blameless nonentity, Henry Grey, Lord Powys and Earl of Tankerville; their son, Richard, was born in 1436.[2] There might occasionally be also some Roos ladies,

---

[1] Anne Bardolf's first husband was William Clifford, younger brother of that Thomas, Lord Clifford, who married Elizabeth Roos, Sir Richard's aunt (Bodl. MS. 5043, fol. 131 v.).

[2] Very soon after Lord Powys's death in 1450, as will be seen later, Antigone married Jean d'Amancier, Master of the Horse to Charles VII, an alliance utterly alien to her dead father's policy (Beaucourt, *Charles VII*, V, 331). Sir Richard Grey, Lord Powys, turned Yorkist, as did many of Gloucester's adherents, and died in 1466.

since Gloucester had been the family's guardian, and was still its patron: Dame Anne Roos, *née* Halsham, wife in 1433 of Sir Robert Roos; Eleanor, *née* Beauchamp, widow after 1430 of Thomas, Lord Roos, until her Beaufort marriage; and possibly her elder sister Margaret, Lady Talbot. The military leaders, when in England, would come with their wives and daughters to pay their respects to the Protector; thus Lady Scales's name often appears in the anagrams among the Plesaunce ladies. In the same way, the fighting men of any rank in the Pays de Conquête were sure to have some contact with the Duke of Bedford's court at Rouen. The parallel is with the later days of English rule in India; Rouen was not only the New Delhi of the English, but also the Poona, and the centre of all civil and military government. Whatever the differences of policy between the two Dukes, there would be constant coming and going between Rouen and London—and Plesaunce. Of all the 'troops of ladies' involved we have here most to do with Antigone, with Lady Ismania Scales, and above all with Elisabeth Phelip, to whom in *The Isle of Ladies* Roos has given her poetic name, Lady Bounte, itself an anagram of Beaumont, Beu–ont.

No. 3. 'For lac of sighte': a Complaint of eight eight-line stanzas, with a four-line envoy to a lady. It was probably intended, as MacCracken points out, for a triple roundel with three different refrains, but one stanza of the first three is missing. (Printed by MacCracken in Herrig's *Archiv*, CXXVII, 326–7, as an anonymous and undated poem.)

 Incipit. For lac of sighte grete cause haue I to pleyn.
 Refrains. (i) Of my desire that I may se righte noghte.
      (ii) ffor cause onely my ladi is absent.
      (iii) Mi souereyn lady so fer is out of sighte.
 Lenvoye. Princes of beaute myrrour of godelyhede
      When so befall this dite that ye se
      Disdeyneth not but of godelyhede
      Haueth thereon mercy and pite.
         Explicit quod—

I suggest that the poem is by Sir Richard Roos, and is close in date to *How a Louer Prayseth hys Lady*. The idea of the poem, with its reiterated phrase 'I see', contrasted with the lack of sight of the beloved, probably comes from Oton de Graunson's *Complainte de Saint Valentin*, which opens thus:

    Je voy que chascun amoureux
    Se veult ce jour apparier,
    Je voy chascun estre joyeulx,
    Je voy le temps renouveller,

Je voy rire, chanter, dancer,
Mais je me voy seul en tristesse etc.

There are two manuscripts, Tanner 346, fol. 74 v.–75 v., the Greystoke
manuscript; and Ff. 1.6, fol. 19–19 v., the 'Roos scrapbook'. In Tanner
346 this and the companion poem 'As ofte as syghes' (No. 45, below)
defeat the contemporary indexer, who leaves a blank space, without
even giving the first lines. In MS. Ff. 1.6, the fourth stanza of MS.
Tanner 346 is lacking, that on 'instrumentis in her armone'; as this
manuscript is nearer to a Roos basis (see above, Chapter III), it may
represent a stage of unfinished composition.

The double acrostic anagram is both more extended and more concentrated than that of *How a Lover*; it shows that Plesaunce is again
the background, and allows us to conjecture the poem's date: HOMFR–Y,
ALIan COBHaM; AnTIGONA POWIS; A–TVS; MA DAM ELISAB–TH BA–DOLF
BeWMO–T; WIL–IAM B––DOLF; BABTHO; ISMAnIA SCAL–S; An. STAFFOr–;
WHITT.; WIMBISH; TOT FOrFAIT FOrF––T. The name Antigona Powis
suggests that the sumptuous occasions described by the poet may be
part of the wedding festivities of Antigone to Lord Powys. The Duke
had made the marriage contract in January 1434/5; the wedding must
have taken place before the early spring of 1436. The time of the poem
is 'Auguste this lusty fressh seson', the August probably of 1435. The
Duke and Duchess are joined, as often, with Antigone, and, as less
often, with Artus, who, though spelt thus or as Arteys in the few documents that mention his existence, is called Arthur by historians;[1] the
poet uses the French form of his kingly name. Elisabeth Phelip, already
married, is here one among many; other poems will isolate her name for
special devotion. Sir William Phelip, Lord Bardolf, is not mentioned
again in anagrams; but he may well have been at Plesaunce for a special
event; his daughter's absence is the cause of the poet's lament. Lady
Scales (*née* Ismania Whalesborough) will often recur in these anagrams;
Anne Stafford, or Anne of Woodstock, will again be more particularized
in the next poem. 'Whitt.' is probably Catherine Whittingham, who
often is coupled with Elisabeth Phelip. Babthorp references are many in
these anagrams, and are either to Sir Robert Babthorp whom Gloucester
made Steward of the Household in 1432, or to his son Ralph, nearer to
Sir Richard Roos in age. Wimbish, another name that often recurs in
Plesaunce poems, and in anagrams of other connexions, such as
Beauchamp and Beaufort, seems to be Nicolas Wimbish, a well-known
'Civil Servant', a Clerk to the Treasury, who had played a minor part

---

[1] In a pardon granted on July 14, 1447, to Gloucester's adherents after his
death, he is called Artus de Cursy (*Cal. Pat. Rolls, 1446–52*, p. 68).

in that same *coup* of 1432. He was liked for himself, as a compliment to
him in *The Chance of the Dice* shows; it is possible that his presence as
a Treasury officer at ceremonial contracts was obligatory as well as
acceptable. He is the only Nicholas among the people of Roos's anagrams; he may then be the copyist in the 'Roos scrapbook' (MS. Ff. 1.6,
fol. 64–7 v.) of the 'Legend of Pyramus and Thisbe'; it is signed as by
'your devoted Nicholas': *Nomen scriptoris nicholaus plenus amoris.* The
poet's 'devise' is given nearly in full.

'For lac of sighte' repeats much of the material of *How a Lover*, but in
a minor key and in brief. The lady is absent; and though all the
pleasures possible are presented to the eye, ear, and taste, they lack
savour. Stanza by stanza the poet enumerates them. He sees castles,
and high towers, he sees archery contests, or hunting and the deer
pulled down, he hears 'lusty trumpetes and lyght clariouns', he listens
to talk and stories of noble princes and chivalry, and songs made of
paramours; he tastes honey and spices, and wines of Gascony and
France: 'But in all this I fynde no plesaunce'. He sees some men laugh
for gladness, and others weep; others are struck low by Cupid's dart,
and such a lover in distress is he. The lady is not only absent, but also
disdainful: 'Disdeyn so thik his haburion hath mayled'. The final
prayer to her is, 'Disdeyneth not, . . . haveth mercy and pite'.

Two ballads similar in tone and rhythm are dedicated in the anagrams
to Lady Bounte by her maiden name.

No. 4 (*a*) *Incipit.* Hevy thoughtes & longe depe sykyng.
    Explicit. as knoweth owr lorde, swete Iesue,
        Whome [*sic*] preserue my loue wher-euer she goo.

This Balade is in three eight-line stanzas, of which the third is an envoy,
'Goo, lytle byll'. It is in the sixteenth-century collection, Rawlinson
C.813, fol. 44 v.–45 (*Anglia*, XXXI, pp. 356–7, No. 24). The rhyme
scheme is a little unusual, with seven rhymes instead of the conventional
nine in three stanzas; the second stanza harks back to the first, and so does
the third, thus: ababbcbc | dbdbbebe | cfcffgfg. The anagram runs:
st. 1, PHYLIP; ALIAn.; st. 2, CO.; wh–TT.; stt. 2–3, AnTIG; ISMAnY
SCA–IS; TOT For–A–T. The Balade begins with a lachrymose stanza, and
repeats the phrase 'my eyes tweane'; the devise-like phrase, 'neuer
change hur for noo newe' will recur with variations. The other Balade
is yet more ingenious in structure, and also a better poem.

No. 4 (*b*) *Incipit.* Honour and beaute, vertue and gentilnesse,
        Noblesse and bounte of grete valure.
    Explicit. Witnesse thowe I doo in this scripture
        Pity Savyng, ye want nothyng certeyne.

It is a Balade of three eight-line stanzas with a four-line Envoy, and a refrain. Its unique manuscript is Arundel 26, fol. 32 v.; MacCracken has printed it (*P.M.L.A.*, XXVI, 179–80). The second part of each stanza and of the Envoy holds in some form the anagram of Phelip; st.1, PHE–YP; st. 2, PHYL–P; st. 3, P–YLIP; Envoy, P–Y–IP. The remainder of the lines give a Plesaunce setting: HOMFr.; COBH–M; ANTYG. POWIS; MAVD. Antigone's marriage was some time after January 1435/6. The second stanza recalls six of the 'ladies worthy', Lucresse, Tesbe, Medea, Guinevere, Penelope, also Alcesse whose virtue is Bounty; but their initials do not here seem to contribute to the anagram or to form a separate one. Maud is Maud Stanhope who will often reappear.

The poem is headed 'Balade coulourd and Reuersid', a heading unique as far as I know. French 'vers retrogrades' of the sixteenth century were generally readable from the end word by word, preserving sense and syntax. This poem has all its *lines* end-stopped and structurally self-contained; and in stt. 1–3, sense can be found if the lines are read in reverse order.

III. LADY BEAUMONT

For Roos, the central attraction of the Plesaunce coterie was Elisabeth Phelip, both before and after her marriage to Lord Beaumont, and the great majority of shorter poems and lyrics of this period are written to, for, or about her, even though she is often, when the length of the poem permits, set against the background of the figures of Plesaunce. Only on very broad lines does it seem possible to draw conclusions on the dates of these many poems from the forms of the names used. The marriage of neither Elisabeth nor Antigone can be dated with precision, though Elisabeth's was certainly earlier by at least two to three years. Again, the name Bardolf seems to have been retained by Elisabeth even as Lady Beaumont; she was the Bardolf heiress. The omission of any one name may have been accidental, or due to the exigencies of composition. Often in these Plesaunce 'braids' Lady Stafford's death in October 1438 is the only firm date, and that only a downward one. In grouping the poems, I have therefore paid little regard to exactitude of date, and have used other convenient divisions: poems which use also the cryptogram based on names of the ladies of *The Legend of Good Women*; poems of Chaucerian attribution; poems in certain manuscripts; or poems about Elisabeth, but addressed to others, such as Lady Scales, or Margaret Stanlow.

The first group, with the proper name cryptogram, comprises *The Flour of Curtesye, Ballade of Her that hath All Virtues, A Lover's*

New Year's Gift with its companion poem, 'Iuellis Pricious', and *Complaynt ageyne Hope*.

No. 5. *The Flour of Curtesye:* a poem of 38 stanzas of rhyme royal, including a final 'Balade Simple' of three stanzas ('With al my mighte, and my beste entente'), two of which have the refrain, 'Upon the day of saint Valentyne singe'. *Lenvoy* of four lines (abab) is addressed to the 'Princesse of beautee'. (Printed in Skeat's *Chaucer*, VII, No. ix.)

> *Incipit.* In Fevrier whan the frosty mone
> 　　　　　Was horned, ful of Phebus fyry light.
> *Explicit.* Of herte and wil faithful in myn entente,
> 　　　　　Lyk as, this day, foules herde I singe.

No manuscript is now known; it was first printed by Thynne in 1532, and first credited to Lydgate by Stow in 1562; Stow's attribution, though unsupported by evidence, has been accepted. Skeat dated the poem 1401, and Schick 1400–2.

I would suggest that the author is Sir Richard Roos, that its date is in the 1430s, and that it is addressed to Elisabeth Beaumont. The poem is 'signed' at l. 33, 'I roos anon and faste gan me hye'. The reasons given for the early date are so flimsy as to be almost irresponsible. 'Chaucer is deed' (l. 236); ergo, he must be lately dead. But Lydgate is still saying 'Chaucer is ded' in *The Fall of Princes*, for which the date 1430–2 is established on internal evidence. Again, this is a simpler and less ambitious parallel poem to *The Black Knight*; ergo, it must be dated earlier; as if a poet advanced steadily by arithmetical progression. Both poems are indeed by one poet, and very close in date, but those dates, by internal evidence, are in the 1430s.

The poet represents himself as listening sadly on St. Valentine's day to the birds joyfully singing their praise to Venus. He determines to write in honour of his lady. This inner poem (l. 113) recites the lady's super-excellent qualities. He compares her (l. 190) with the ladies of old, especially those of the song in *The Legend of Good Women*. He stresses her properties of bounty and beauty (ll. 215–24), and wishes that he had Chaucer's power of 'fair making' and his 'gaye style'—but the Muses' well is now run dry. The Balade Simple gives the birds' song of faithful and devoted love, and the Envoy begs the lady to accept 'this simple dyte'. The Balade is in fact not so simple metrically, since all three stanzas have identical rhyme sounds for the a and b rhymes as well as for the c or refrain rhymes.

Skeat noted (*Chaucer*, VII, 509) the association of 'the whyte Antigone' of Troy with the Ladies of *The Legend*, and referred to

Troilus and Criseyde (II, 887), where 'fresshe Antigone the white' is
Criseyde's niece; a little earlier (II, 824) 'Antigone the shene' has sung
to Criseyde and Pandarus a lovesong composed by an unknown lady.
The strong presumption that the 'whyte Antigone' (the only explicit
naming of her in all these poems) is the Antigone of Plesaunce is supported by having found her name with Duke Humphrey's in anagrams
already; when in later poems a girl's sweet singing is commended, her
name is a constant in the anagram.

In this poem, most of the covert references are devoted to the Lady
of *The Isle of Ladies*, on whom Love had bestowed the name of Bounty.
The theme of Bounty and Beauty is insisted on here:

> For bountee and beautee ar togider knet
> In her persone, under faithfulnesse. (ll. 171–2)

and again

> bountee and beautee bothe in her demeyne,
> She maketh bountee alway soverayne.

> This is to mene bountee goth afore . . .
> And beautee folweth, ruled by her lore . . .
> So that in one this goodly fresshe free
> Surmounting al, withouten any were,
> Is good and fair, in oon persone yfere. (ll. 216–24)

This follows four stanzas devoted to the Ladies of *The Legend*, and of
'The Franklin's Tale': Policene, Helayne, Dorigene, Cleopatre,
Antigone, Hester, Judith, Alceste, Marcia Catoun, Grisilde, Ariadne,
Lucrece, Penelope, Phyllis, Hipsiphilee, Canacee, Dydo, Medee. From
among the initials of these can be arranged MA DAME PHELIP. Further-
more, two names conjoined here, as they are not in *The Legend*, by their
very sound suggest Philip: 'Phyllis and Hipsiphilee' (l. 204). The two
first halves give Phyl-Hip; the two last letters of each give le-is or Elis.
This syllabic division with back and forth reading, Deschamps' method,
is found again, and with other names, in *The Black Knight* and *The
Chance of the Dice*. The descriptions in *The Legend* of these two ladies
unite the motifs of bounty and beauty: Hipsiphile acts so as 'to don
plesaunce Of verrey bounte and of curteysye'; Phyllis is 'fayrer on to
sene Than is the flour ageyn the bryghte sonne' (*Legend of Good
Women*, ll. 1477–8, 2425–6; see below, No. 76).

This elaborate structure of reference and name-cryptogram is supported by the double acrostic anagram. In the *Proem* (ll. 1–28), it
yields E–ISAB–TH (ph)Y–IP, BARDO–F, BeWMO–T; CATh. wh–TT.; AI TOT
FOrFAYT FOrFA––. The description of the Lady (ll. 113–74) repeats this

with additions: ALIAN.; ANTIGO.; E–ISAB–TH PHIL., –ARDO–F, B–WMONT; WHITT.; STAFFOrD WOODSTO.; C–IFTO.; ROOS; JAY TOT FOrFAIT FOrFAIT. So again in the names of the Ladies (ll. 190–245): ALIAN. COBHA.; ANTI.; STAFFOr., WO–DST.; ELISAB. BARDOLF. B–WMONT; KATH. WHITT.; STYWA.; AY TOT FOrFAIT FOrFA–T. The 'Balade Simple' is more complex; the line-initials give PHYL.; W–ITT.; ISMANIA; the caesural initials –EWFO–T MORTAIN. This last, together with a rather different set of references, must wait for later comment. The name of Gervaise Clifton, the Duke's Treasurer, seldom appears in these lists, and the letters C–IFTO. above probably indicate his gentle wife Isabella Fitz-Herbert, widow after 1433 of William Scott.[1]

Roos has been reading not only Chaucer, but also a Lapidary, as before *How A Lover*, hence his praise of the ruby, which

> hath the soverainte
> Of riche stones and the regalye;

Cest li sire des peres . . . la gemme des gemmes'.

No. 6. *Ballade of her that hath all Virtues:* a poem of six stanzas of rhyme royal with *Lenvoye* as a seventh stanza. The refrain of stt. 1–4, 'Al þis haþe nature sette in youre ymage', gradually shifts to the last line of the *Envoy*: 'Which haþe alle vertues sette in hir ymage'. (Printed in MacCracken, *Minor Poems of Lydgate*, II, 379–81.)

> *Incipit.* Fresshe lusty beaute, ioyned with gentylesse,
> Demure appert, glad chere with gouuernaunce.

The two manuscripts constitute only one authority: MS. Trinity College, Cambridge, R. 3.20 (a Wilmer manuscript, see above, Chapter III), is Shirley's collection, and has the title, 'Loo here begynneþe a balade | whiche þat Lydegate wrote at þe request of a squyer þat serued in loves court'. This text is copied faithfully into MS. Add. 29729. The attribution to Lydgate therefore rests on Shirley alone.

I suggest that the poem is by Sir Richard Roos, and is near in date to *The Flour of Curtesye*. Being a short lyric, the poem is not 'signed', but the same method of cryptogram is used. The lady is like Alceste, 'Of bounte, beaute, having þexcellence'; and in st. 4. her beauty and her 'hye bountee' are praised together with other virtues. Stanzas 2–4 name the Ladies of *The Legend* and others. Initial-letters from the list give PHE–IP BARD.; ANTIG.; the missing letter L would have been

---

[1] Her brass (1457) at Brabourne, Kent, recorded that she was one *Qui nulli nocuit sed Domino placuit* (Jas. R. Scott, *Memorials of the family of Scott of Scot's Hall*, 1876, p. 44).

supplied if the poet had used Helayne instead of Hester. Only one
name, Cleopatra, is left unused. These names are reinforced by the
double acrostic anagram: ALIAn. –OBHAM; AnTIGO. POWYS; E–ISABeTH
PHYLYP BARDO–F BeWMO–T; WH–TTI–GHA.; BABTh.; TOT FOrFAI.
The poem is slight, no more than a *balade*; it praises the lady's
'avysinesse', steadfastness, and all the exemplary virtues, 'with al þe
surplusage', except mercy and pity. It is interesting, and sufficiently
rare in Middle English poetry, to possess another poem, a variant on
the same theme; this example on the virtues is shorter and lacks the
name-cryptogram.[1] Amusingly enough, the anagrams show that it was
written for a different set of people (see No. 49, below).

No. 7. *A Lover's New Year's Gift:* a poem of twenty-three stanzas of
three lines (aaB), generally fourteeners, the whole introduced by a
couplet probably meant for a refrain, especially as it introduces the B
rhyme of the rest.

Incipit.   In honnour of þis heghe fest, of custume yere by yere
            Is first for to remembre me vpon my lady dere.
            For nowe vpon þis first day I wil my choys renuwe.
Explicit. Now vpon þe first day of þis Ianuarye,
            And conferme fully vp my choyse ay frome yere to yere.
                                                    Explicit.

The only manuscript is Add. 16165 (fol. 253 v.–254 v.) from which
MacCracken prints it (*Minor Poems of Lydgate*, II, 424–7). This is
one of the chief of Shirley's collections, and he is responsible for the
title, 'Amerous balade by Lydegate þat haþe loste his thanke of wymmen'.
This title is more than usually inapplicable and inept, as the tone of
the poem is cheerful ('Hit voydeþe al myn hevynesse'), even apart from
the choice of a metre of (to us) rollicking effect. MacCracken convincingly suggests (*ib.*, I, xxii) that the title was intended for the next
poem in the manuscript.

Shirley's attribution has been accepted, though Miss Hammond
doubted that the poem could be Lydgate's (*Anglia*, 1909, XXXII,
190–6). I suggest that it is by Sir Richard Roos, and dates from the
1430s. It is not 'signed'; st. 5 contains, however, the rhyme of 'aroos'
with 'cloos', a rhyme which will recur in a very similar couplet (*Reson
and Sensuallyte*, ll. 89–90). The poem is vigorous in style; 'þis gladde
tyme' sets the note of hopefulness. The theme is the New Year renewal
of vows, with alternations of hope and fear (stt. 6–9), and with rehearsal

---

[1] Robbins prints these two allied poems without comment on their similarity
Secular Lyrics, Nos. 131 and 190).

of the lady's virtues (stt. 11–14). The poet laments that he has no gift to offer except the 'lytel symple gifft' of his song and his undivided heart; he sends them both forth to remain with her from year to year.

The lady's name is indicated in cryptogram (stt. 11.14), again through the initial letters of the Ladies of *The Legend*, here in rather more consecutive sequence: DAME P–ElIP; the first two halves of the first two names, Isaude and Eleyne, would also give IS–El, i.e. Elis. on Deschamps' method. The anagrams confirm the lady's name, and set her in the Plesaunce group: AlIAN. –OBHAM; ANTIGONe; STAFFOr.; –LISABeTH PHILI., BA–DO–F, BeWMONT; KATh.WHITT.; WIMBISH; BABThO.; IAI TOT FOrFAIT FOrFAIT.

The style of the poem is consonant with Roos's characteristics: the frequency of 'goodlyhede' and 'womanhede' (stt. 3, 9, 10); the use of 'shene (st. 5); the vivid phrase, 'þe frosty moone with hir pale light' (st. 4); and the word 'surplusage' (st. 21), common in contemporary French poetry. Reminiscences of *The Isle of Ladies* are found in the lover's being 'brought on bier' by the lady's hardness of heart (st. 6), and in the image of the sea-passage (stt. 8 and 22).

As with *All Virtues*, so with the *New Year's Gift*, there exists a related poem.

No. 8. 'Iuellis Pricious': a poem of four stanzas of rhyme royal with a concluding couplet. It is the first poem of a group of four in MS. Lambeth 306 (fol. 136v.); Furnivall prints it as anonymous. (*Political, Religious, and Love Poems*, E.E.T.S., 15, 1866 and 1903, pp. 66–7.)

> *Incipit.* Iuellis pricious cane y none fynde to Sell
> to sende you, my Souerein, þis newe yeres morowe.
> *Explicit.* For this hath loue and trouth y-lerned me þe lore,
> Euermore without chaung for euer
> til body and soule parte and disseuere.

The theme is the same as that of the preceding poem; for lack of other or richer gifts, the poet sends to his 'Dere heret' his own heart, and begs her acceptance. The insistence here throughout on the irrevocability of the gift expands what is lightly touched on in the *New Year's Gift* (st. 18): 'And vnto hir I gif hit al withoute repentaunce'. So Palamon gave his heart to Emelye, 'ne repentide it'. Here too the lover is following the annual custom.

The anagram shows that this poem also is addressed to Elisabeth Phelip: CO–HAM; ANTIG.; E–ISABeTh PHYLYP BARD., BeWMONT; CATH. WhYTTY– – –AM; WYM–YS. TOT FOrFAYT. In spite of the Beaumont anagram, there are one or two parallels with *The Black Knight*, a poem for another pair of lovers: the phrase 'Seynt Iohn to borowe' (l. 4; *B.K.*, l. 12); and the reference to Palamon (l. 19; *B.K.*, l. 368). The poem does not seem to be finally polished. The first rhyme in stt. 2 and 4 is faulty; in st. 2 it needs only the change of 'cane' to 'may'; in st. 4 'to chast' should perhaps read 'to shift' in order to rhyme with 'gyfte'. The fourth stanza is very irregular in line length. The poet does not sustain the excellence and promise of the opening line, which, however, gives rise to some relative considerations. The two finished poems (Nos. 6 and 7) are not particularly Lydgatian in tone, in spite of their attribution to him; but the two corresponding poems (this and No. 49), though less polished, could never be taken for Lydgate's work. They are not only both better and worse than Lydgate's stuff, they are different; and they throw into relief the differences between Lydgate and Roos. A line like 'Iuellis pricious cane y none fynde to Sell', with its typical inversions, is striking, rich and strange; but it has neither Lydgate's heavy ornateness, nor his occasional solid impressiveness.

One cannot leave Roos's cryptograms here without a word on Lydgate's occasional inclusion of the Ladies' names; a difference will at once be seen. Lydgate uses these and similar names in five poems of which I do not challenge his authorship; probably the earliest was that in honour of Gloucester and Jacqueline of Hainault, where he had a perfect opportunity for this kind of parlour-game. Seven names occur of famous ladies (st. 11), but have only a forced relation to Jacqueline; so too have the ten heroes' names to Humphrey of Gloucester. As this poem was written in the lifetime of Henry V (st. 7), Lydgate must get the credit for first introducing this kind of complimentary reference; it is characteristic that he did not see what further could be done with it. Three others of these poems can be dated, at least with a downward limit: first, the *Ballad to Henry VI* upon his coronation (1429 or 1430), in which Lydgate trumpets forth the names of twenty-one emperors, kings and worthies, almost the whole alphabet from A to Z, a criss-cross-row too near completeness to be significant. Two poems to Queen Katherine must antedate her death in January 1437: in the Haymaking poem, the poor lady was not allowed to walk in her sports in the new-mown hay without being preached to, 'That now is heye some tyme was grase', and reminded of the transience of beauty, witness Polixene, Crieseyde, Helene, Dido, Hester, and Gresylde. The second, and more ambitious, poem to the queen is a *Valentine* of the Blessed Virgin Mary, where Lydgate assembles twenty-one of the stock names of Ladies and goddesses, naturally only to reject them and to replace them by the Virgin and the saints, a most unsuitable place for a secular cypher. One poem which carries no exact evidence of date, *Timor Mortis* (MacCracken, p. 828), contains eight of the stock names, and words like 'Dame' or 'Phelip' could nearly be made out of them; but a didactic lament is not promising material for complimentary cyphers.

It looks as if Lydgate knew what was being written for the 'sorceress's' circle, imitated the method without realizing the concealed meaning, and finally wrote a counter-blast, a Valentine exalting the Virgin, and addressed it to the other, the Queen-Dowager's, court at Hertford or at Eltham. The unfortunate man had no flair for fortune's favourites; Jacqueline's marriage had ended disastrously; and he must have been horrified, when the secret of the queen's Tudor marriage came out, to realize the double life that his 'noble pryncesse' had been leading, she 'So weel avysed, so prudent, and so wys'. It is improbable that Eleanor Cobham forgave Lydgate for 'The Solitary's' abuse, or would accept poems of compliment from him. The Duke magnanimously set him to work on *The Fall of Princes*, which he could write in his monastery. It is unlikely that he frequented Plesaunce, and we can probably rule out any cryptograms in Lydgate's poems.

Yet another poem exists in two forms, this time definitely in two metres, of which one is evidently written earlier. This is a verse-letter, on a dialogue with Hope, again introducing the theme of all the virtues.

No. 9, A and B. *Complaynt ageyne Hope:* a poem in fourteen eight-line stanzas and a one-stanza envoy; the rhyme structure (ababbccb), with the second quatrain enclosed, is not common in this poetry.

> *Incipit A.* As that I me stoode in studeying loo Aloone
> Astonyede Right soore in studyes ful oolde.
> *Explicit A.* I leve þat hope tellithe me
> Bette þan þat I *with* eyene see
> hope in hope owte þus cane offte fooles feede.
> *Incipit B.* As I stoode | in studyinge alloone
> Astonyed in studye | wel colde
> *Explicit B.* I leve bette | that hope telleth me
> Thane I doo | that I with eyene se.
> hope | in | hope | out | thus kane ye foles fede.
> Explicit.

The two forms have been edited by Kenneth G. Wilson.[1] The poet, in unhappy solitude, despairs, and reproaches his lady for her indifference, and Hope for his false promises. He protests his innocence

---

[1] Univ. of Michigan, Contributions in Modern Philology, 1957. For the measure of my agreement and disagreement with Professor Wilson, see my review in *Medium Ævum*, 1958, XXVII, 206–8.

in love to the god of love, 'ryche Juge of loues Joyes alle'. He prays
to pass from Wanhope to Hope; Hope appears in the moonlight, and
defends both himself, and the lady of 'beaute clarefied'. The lover
admits her beauty, but as for her virtue, she has two great faults,
'Vnmerciable and parfite pitelees'. Hope silences him, and helps him
to write a letter, since 'Yt shal be long er I my lady se'. After fourteen
stanzas, he is interrupted, 'letted . . . by comyng of men'.

Form A occurs only in MS. Harleian 7333, fol. 135, the large collection derived from Shirley's material, and with much from Chaucer
and Lydgate. Form B occurs in the two important and allied manuscripts, Fairfax 16 (Stanley's) and Bodleian 638 (Astley's). In all three
it is immediately followed by the *Complaynt d'Amours* (see No. 14).
The poem bears several marks of Roos's style, the routh: trouth rhyme
(st. 3), and the goodlyhede: womanhede rhyme (st. 11). The lady sur-
passes 'both Creseyde and Eleyne' and is 'pitilees'.

Hope A is, I believe, the first draft, showing the poem as early work,
with its heavy alliteration, and its irregular number of syllables in the
four-beat line. But even here the last three lines (ccb) are shortened to
eight syllables, an effective change. The second draft clears away many
unstressed words, tightens the line, and so gets rid of the rocking movement. Altogether *Hope* B is tauter, more stream-lined in effect. Yet it
keeps much of the alliteration ('as mery as any vnder moone'), and also
retains the colloquial phrases which are more common here than in
most of Roos's verses: 'Now may I wistle in my fyste' and 'syng of
had-y-wiste'; 'a lytel cromme of routhe'; 'I moote forthe the candel
holde'. The dialogue ends with an unusually violent expression:

'Thow and I, we wanhope wol outlawe'.
'Nay, quod I, hange we him and drawe'.

The differences between the two forms inevitably affect the anagrams.
The line-initials show ten differences of letter, the caesural initials
considerably more; it is indeed difficult in the long lines of Version A
to be certain of the caesural pause. In Version B, with its stricter
syllabic method, the caesura is carefully indicated throughout. The
anagrams of the two versions, though both Plesaunce 'braids', differ
considerably, and Version A gives the impression that Roos is not yet
very skilful in handling them. There may well be more names there
than have been discerned. Version A yields: HOMFrEY; ALIAn. COBHAM;
ANTIGONA; ELISABeTh BA–OLF, BEW–ONT; ISMANYA SCALYS, WHALES-
BOROVGH; WI–BISH; IAI TOT FOrFAIT FOrFAIT. This is the core of the
Plesaunce group, with Lady Beaumont and Lady Scales both given their

maiden names; possibly both had only recently been married. Version B has a much longer result: HOMFR–Y; ALIAN. COBHAM; ANTIGONA POWYS; A–TVS; ELISABeTH BARDOLF BeW–ONT; ISMANIA S–AlYS WHAlI–BO–OVGH; IAQV–TTA BEDFOr–. ISABEL CLIFTON; MAVD WYL–OWBY; BABTHO.; WIMBY–H; IAY TOT FOrFAIT FOrFAIT. The interesting additions here are the names Powys and Jacquetta Bedford, indicating a date probably 1436 or after; Maude Stanhope's marriage to Lord Willoughby has not been precisely dated.

The subject, Hope and Wanhope, has a close parallel in the first lines of Jean de Meun's continuation of *Le Roman de la Rose* (ll. 4059–99), which forms part of *The Romaunt of the Rose*, Fragment B (ll. 4430–81). Here the lover threatens to fall into despair after the capture of Bealacoil, but reproves himself as 'Ungracious and unworthy'. Love had promised him the comfort of Hope's continual presence. Yet she is wayward, and has failed or beguiled many; thus the lover is tossed up and down. The poem on Hope, as a verse-letter, takes a different course; it is more dramatic, and in it Hope is a masculine figure. Points of style link the English treatments of the theme: the phrase 'faire beheste' (*Hope*, st. 4) which in *The Romaunt* (l. 4446) translates the colourless 'sa promesse'; the trace in *The Romaunt* of alliterative phrasing: 'my baalis beete' (l. 4441); and the use of the Saxon words Hope and Wanhope to translate and counterbalance Espoir and Desespoir.

IV. CHAUCER OR ROOS

The next few poems lead to debatable Chaucerian ground.

No. 10. *Merciles Beaute:* a triple roundel, or possibly three separate roundels, since the third is quite different in tone and temper from the first two.

> *Incipit.* (i). Your yen two wol slee me sodenly
> (ii). So hath your beautee fro your herte chaced
> (iii). Sin I fro Love escaped am so fat.
> *Explicit.* Sin I am free, I counte him not a bene.

The unique manuscript is Pepys 2006, the Kyriel manuscript, the contemporary index of which supplies the title.

The poem is doubtfully ascribed to Chaucer in Skeat's, Pollard's, and Robinson's editions, chiefly because it is preceded by several genuine poems in the manuscript, but also because the opening line recurs in *To my Soverain Lady* (l. 21) then assigned to Lydgate, and it was assumed that Lydgate could only be quoting Chaucer. I suggest that it is by Sir Richard Roos, and that he will later quote himself, picking out an effective line from this outdated roundel to grace a ceremonial poem of 1445.

The anagrams are a little unusual: the line initials give (i)–(ii) PHI(L)IP; (ii) PHY(LL)IS; (iii) HIPSIFILA, a play on names which we have already seen (No. 5). The caesural letters yield: E-ISA-ETh –EWMONT; ISMANY S–Al–S; TOT ForF–IT ForF–IT.

It is quite possible that French lyrics lie behind the roundel. Various poems by Deschamps and Guillaume d'Amiens have been suggested (see *Chaucer*, ed. Robinson, p. 982). To these I would add the second stanza of an anonymous lyric preserved in the great collection of fifteenth-century French poetry, *Le Jardin de Plaisance* (fol. cv), which begins 'Gente de corps, miroir qui mon cueur art':

> Naure mauez de vostre amoureux dard
> Qui mon cueur a enflambe et fort espris
> Par vng brandon tue dung doulx regard
> Dont iay este soubdainement surpris.
> Medecin nest en lamoureux pourpris
> Qui peust curer mon dueil aucunement.
> Pour tant vous prie affectueusement
> Que y pouruoyez ma dame desiree
> Durer ne puis ne vuire longuement
> Se vostre amour ne mest brief accordee.

The first line of the third part of the English poem undoubtedly translates, as has been pointed out, the first line of a poem contributed by Jean, Duc de Berry, to *Les Cent Balades* of Jean le Seneschal, a volume in which occur early examples of the use of the double acrostic anagram. Charles d'Orléans had a paper copy of *Les Cent Balades* with him in England,[1] naturally, since his father had much to do with it; Sir Richard Roos may well have seen this copy. The poem occurs in all manuscripts of *Les Cent Balades*, including that which belonged to René d'Anjou and bears his arms. This gives added force to the fact that the opening line was to be repeated in the poem that Roos later wrote for René's daughter, Yolande (see below, No. 67). It is of interest too to find that de Berry was one of those who practised the double acrostic anagram; and 'Puiz qu'a Amours suis si gras eschapé' preserves, like flies in cloudy amber, the names of his two wives, Jeanne d'Armagnac and, nearly thirty years later in 1389, Jeanne de Boulogne: st. 1, MESDaM–S; st. 2, LES; st. 3, P––NCESSES; stt. 1–2, JEAnNE; stt. 1–2 and 5, –OVLO–NE; st. 6, DA–MA–NAC. Jeanne de Boulogne was a child,

---

[1] P. Champion, *La Librairie de Charles d'Orléans*, pp. xxvii (Item 34) and 30.

and that may account for the mockery and absurdity of the poem.[1] The theme of the lean lover is fully developed in *Le Roman de la Rose* (ll. 2543–57), with the implication that only the false lover 'escapes so fat'. One might suspect that this third part is not only a separate roundel, but is also by a different author. It sounds as if some teasing friend had completed the triple roundel with a mocking reversal of the poet's sentiments, the same sort of addition as was seen in *The Isle of Ladies*, and will be found again in *My Lady Dere*. Part iii fits in with the anagrams of the whole, but it contributes two names independently (Hipsifila and Elisabeth).

The remaining short poems here develop the theme of Lady Bounte.

No. 11. *Balade of Compleynte:* a balade of three stanzas of rhyme royal without refrain or envoy.

> *Incipit.* Compleyne ne koude, ne might myn herte never
> My peynes halve, ne what torment I have.
> *Explicit.* I yow beseche, myn hertes lady, here,
> Sith I yow serve, and so wil, yeer by yere.

The only manuscript is Shirley's collection, Add. 16165, where there is no indication of the author. Skeat, discovering it, attributed it to Chaucer, but later recanted. Pollard and Robinson both include it as 'doubtful'. I suggest that it is another of Sir Richard Roos's poems to his Lady Bounty:

> Myn hertes lady, as wisly he me save
> That bountee made, and beautee list to grave
> In your persone, and bad hem bothe in-fere
> Ever t'awayte, and ay be wher ye were (st. 1).

The second stanza protests his devotion to her who is

> Myn heven hool and al my suffisaunce
> Whom for to serve is set al my plesaunce.

The anagram gives: AlIAN.; E–ISABETh; CATh.whITTIN––AM; and also ISMAN., this last tucked into the last three lines; the 'devise' is lacking. The concluding couplet suggests that the poem may have been yet another anniversary gift; but it is very like the conclusion of a later *Compleynt* (No. 78, below) which is a poem to Margaret Vernon on parting in March.

No one will grudge to Roos the *Balade of Compleynte*, but the next

---

[1] See *Medium Ævum*, 1957, XXV, p. 169.

two poems, *The Deth of Pyte* and *A Compleynte to his Lady*, are jewels
so firmly embedded now in Chaucer's crown that any attempt to prise
them out is likely to be strongly opposed; they must be considered in
close detail.

No. 12. *Complainte of the deathe of pitie* (Stow's title); *A Complaint of
Pitee* (Shirley's title); *The Exclamacion of the Deth of Pyte* (MS.
Trin. Coll.): a poem of seventeen stanzas of rhyme royal, comprising
a prologue (8 stt.) and 'The Bille of Complaint' (9 stt.). The second
line of the prologue is also the last line of the Bille.

> *Incipit.*   Pite, that I have sought so yore agoo
> With herte soore and ful of besy peyne.
> *Explicit.*   Thus for your deth I may wel wepe and pleyne
> With herte sore and ful of besy peyne.

The attribution to Chaucer is Shirley's, and has been followed without
question. There are nine manuscripts. Four of these are manuscripts
which also contain *La Belle Dame* (see above, Chapter III), Fairfax 16
(Lord Stanley's MS.), Longleat 258 (Thynne's MS.), Camb. Univ.
Library, Ff. 1.6. (the 'Roos scrapbook'), and Trin. Coll. Camb.,
R. 3.19 (a Wilmer MS.). Two manuscripts are of the related Bodleian
group (see above, Chapter IV), Bodleian 638 (the Astley MS.), and
Tanner 346 (Lord Greystoke's MS.). Another manuscript which bears
relation to Fairfax 16 is Harleian 7578, which gives no clue to its
fifteenth-century owners. The two remaining manuscripts are Harleian
78 (in Shirley's portion, with his title), and Add. 34360, derived from
a lost Shirley manuscript; these two tack on to *The Deth of Pyte*
the *Compleynte to his Lady*.

My attribution to Sir Richard Roos is based on the 'signature', 'But
up I roos' (l. 17); on the repetition of the theme of Bounty and Beauty;
on parallelisms with other poems; and on the anagrams. The two parts
of the poem have independent anagrams. Part I, the Prologue, yields:
E-ISABeTH PHILI., BA-DO-F, BEWMONT; KATh. WHITT.; STAFForD;
ISMAN-A SCAl-S; STAN-OW; WiMBYS; IAI TOT FOrFAIT FOrFAYT. Part II,
the Bille, gives: HOMFR-Y; AlYAN. COBHAM; AnTIG. P-WYS; ELISABETH
BA--O-F, BeWMONT; KAThE-IN WHYTTY---HA.; ISMAnIA SCAlE-;
STAN--W; BABTh.; and again IAY TOT FOrFAYT FOrFAYT. It is not probable that the poem is really an elegy on the death of Elisabeth
Beaumont, since that would destroy the allegory of her 'ruthlessness'.
Again, unless Lady Stafford is included merely in sad reminiscence,
the poem was written between 1435–6 (the Powys marriage) and October 1438. Lady Beaumont and the Plesaunce family were the main

objective; the names of Lady Scales and (Margaret) Stanlow appear only in the caesural letters.

It will be seen later that the death and coming to life of Pity is one of Roos's chief contributions to the myth and allegory of *amour courtois*. The poet, having composed a complaint to his rigorous lady, takes it to Pity to beg her help; but he finds Pity dead and on her bier, and in despair he puts away his now useless complaint, yet not before communicating it to the reader.

In the first part, 'Bounte parfyt, wel armed and richely, And fresshe Beaute' are the first two of the allegorical figures who stand near the hearse, rejoicing at Pity's death. In the Bille (stt. 2–3) these are two of the lady's own chief qualities:

> your contraire, Crueltee,
> Allyed is ayenst your regalye,
> Under colour of womanly Beaute, . . .
> With Bounte, Gentilesse and Curtesye,
> And hath depryved yow now of your place
> That hyghte 'Beaute apertenant to Grace'.
>
> For kyndely, by youre herytage ryght,
> Ye ben annexed ever unto Bounte . . .
> Ye be also the corowne of Beaute;
> And certes, yf ye wanten in these tweyne,
> The world is lore; ther is no more to seyne (ll. 64–77).

The language of the poem is so simple as to be almost colourless, and there are few characteristic words and phrases; 'regalye' is the most striking, a word not found in Chaucer, but occurring fairly often in the fifteenth century, used of kingship, and, as we have seen, of the royal gem, the ruby. Roos's favourite rhyme-sound (-eyne or -ayne) recurs in seven out of the seventeen stanzas. The description of the dead body on the hearse and of the effect on the swooning poet is like that of the dead queen and the knight in *The Isle of Ladies*. The puzzling crux, the appeal to 'thow Herenus (heremus, heremius) quene' (l. 92), found in the six most important manuscripts (which has been ironed out to 'vertuous(e)' by Shirley and Thynne), can best be explained by comparison with *The Black Knight*, ll. 619 ff., and *To my Soverain Lady*, ll. 83–91. The poet is appealing away from the cruel lady to Venus herself. This is common form, even in poems where Cupid or Love himself has been in action, as in *The Eye and the Heart*, or *The Parlement of Cupid*. 'Herenus' is, I believe, a misreading of Hesperus; the 'goodly brighte sterre . . . I mene Venus' of *The Black Knight* (612), the 'Willi planet, O Esperus so briȝt' of *The Temple of Glas*.

The whole poem has a manuscript connexion, and some intimate parallelism, with the next poem.

No. 13. *A Compleynte to his Lady* (Skeat's title); 'Balade of Pite' (Shirley's title): a poem of four sections, the first consisting of two stanzas of rhyme royal; the second of eight decasyllabic lines, apparently *terza rima* but lacking a line; the third, of seventeen lines of *terza rima* with some irregularity; the fourth, of nine stanzas of ten lines each (aabaabcdcd); the second stanza makes sense, though lacking lines 3 and 6; the ninth stanza is found only in MS. Add. 34360. It might be thought with Miss Hammond (p. 411) that these sections are separate poems, or attempts at poems; but the anagrams show them to be, though independent, closely allied.

> *Incipit.* The longe nightes whan every creature

The whole production is found in two manuscripts only, Shirley's portion of Harleian 78, and Add. 34360, derived from Shirley. In both it continues straight on from *The Deth of Pyte*, and in Harleian 78 has the same running title as it, i.e. 'The balade of Pytee by Chaucier'. In Add. 34360 it has a probably later colophon, ascribing it to 'Chaucier lauceire'; Skeat took this for 'lautour'; it might equally well be 'laureire'. Stow, first printing the poem in 1561, follows this attribution.

The poem is not 'signed'; short lyrics seldom are, and the 'signature' in *The Deth of Pyte*, is probably due to the narrative opening of that poem. The anagrams contain the 'devise', and run as follows: section i gives HOMFr., AnTIGON.; TOT FOrFAIT (the omission of Eleanor Cobham is surprising, and may indicate the loss of a third stanza); section ii (the single stanza) yields CATh. WITT., T–T FOrF–IT. Section iii (terza rima) is the core of the poem: ELISAB–TH BEAUMUNT; WHITT.; a large residue may point to some struggle with the unfamiliar and exacting form. Section iv (nine stanzas), which may be an independent poem, yields little at first, but stt. 5 and 6 give STAFFOr–; BABTho.; and AY T–T FOrFAIT FOrFA–T, and stt. 8 and 9 give –LISABeTH BAR–OLF, BeAUM–NT. There are similar references in the poem, especially in the opening lines of section iii:

> Now sothly, what she hight I wol reherse.
> Hir name is Bountee, set in womanhede,
> Sadnesse in youthe, and Beautee prydelees
> And Plesaunce, under governaunce and drede;
> Hir surname is eek Faire Rewthelees,
> The Wyse, yknit unto Good Aventure.

Here the Lady's poetic name is Bountee, allied with Beautee; if for her surname, Faire Rewthelees, is substituted Fair Pitiless, we get the probably intended suggestion of the sound of Philip(s). Plesaunce may have more than one meaning; and 'In goode aventure' was one of Gloucester's early mottoes, *testè* Lydgate in his poem on Gloucester's marriage (l. 160).

Chaucerian scholars will ill brook the depriving Chaucer of his one experiment in *terza rima*; but his fame as a metrical inventor stands so deservedly high that he, better than most, can spare one experiment, even if it be of this extreme interest. It is true that we have other direct evidence for Chaucer's knowledge of the *Divina Commedia*, and we have none for Sir Richard Roos. But there is no case for denying it to a young poet under Gloucester's influence. Gloucester presented books to the University of Oxford in 1435, and again more munificently in 1438; one of those was a copy of Dante's works with a commentary.[1] It was in the mid-1430s that the Duke was seeing in England Italian notables and men of letters, such as Zeno Castiglione, Bishop of Bayeux, or Piero del Monte; and his Italian correspondents were many. In 1436, his secretary was Tito Frulovisi, schoolmaster and dramatist.[2] Any young poet frequenting his company might well hear talk of Italian poetry, and be encouraged to experiment in Italian metres.[3] It is precisely in a passage of *terza rima* (section iii) that the poet makes his appeal to Lady Bounty.

Other sections have parallels with other Plesaunce poems. Sleepless love-longing (section i) is the connecting thread of *The Isle of Ladies*. Pity, mercy, and grace (l. 17) are the trinity to whom appeal is made elsewhere, as in *All Virtues*, and also in *The Black Knight* (ll. 479 and 679). In section iv the lady has 'a herte of stele' (l. 56) as she has in *A Lover's New Year's Gift* (l. 23), and in *My Soverain Lady* (l. 12); and there is a non-Chaucerian rhyme, Imis:y-wis (ll. 43–4).

No. 14. *Complaynt d'Amours:* a poem of thirteen stanzas of rhyme royal; the last stanza turns it into a Valentine.

> *Incipit.* I which that am the sorwefulleste man.
> *Explicit.* And love hir best although she do me sterve.

The *Complaynt d'Amours* is still classed as doubtfully Chaucer's, and is so printed by Pollard and Robinson. Skeat maintained it to be Chaucer's;

---

[1] Vickers, *Humphrey, Duke of Gloucester*, p. 403.
[2] R. Weiss, *Humanism in England*, chs. III and IV.
[3] See also Chapter XII below.

Brusendorff denied it to him. Koch connects it with *A Compleynte to his Lady*, just considered, accepting both as Chaucer's. I suggest that it is by Sir Richard Roos.

There are three manuscripts: MS. Fairfax 16 and Bodleian 638 (which has one 'author's variant'), both significant manuscripts for Roos; also Harleian 7333, an elegant folio manuscript, probably derived from Shirley, and distinguished by long, discursive, and informative headings to some of the poems. The heading to this poem raises more problems than it solves: 'made at Wyndesore in the laste may tofore novembre'. The fact that st. 13 makes a Valentine of the poem does not necessarily invalidate this statement, since it may have been tacked on to adapt a poem not otherwise dated internally. 'In the laste may tofore novembre' does indeed seem nonsense; but the misreading of one word could cause it. The scribe of Harleian 7333 (or Shirley himself prior to him) may have misread his copy's 'nig(ht)' as 'may'; 'The last night tofore November' as a method of designating a date, comparable with dating by the eve of an ecclesiastical feast-day, may be exemplified by Oton de Graunson, writing *La Complainte de l'An Nouvel*:

> Au boiz alay jouer et solacier
> La nuit devant que l'an doit commencier. (ed. Piaget, p. 199)

There is nothing in this English *Complaynt* of reference to Hallowe'en. A looser way of dating is seen in Poem xviii of the *Balades and Complaints* in MS. Fairfax 16 (No. 63, below), which starts, 'Not far fro marche, in the ende of feueryere'; and a later *Compleynt* lays constant stress (ll. 248, 259, 585) on the last day of March as its date (No. 78).

There is no 'signature', but the anagrams contain the full 'devise'. The typical rhymes are frequent, 'rewthe: trewthe (ll. 6–7); sterve: serve (ll. 34–5, 90–1); womanheed: deed (ll. 39–40); rede' (ll. 65–7). The Chaucerian parallels that Skeat noted are well within Roos's range, especially that with 'The Franklin's Tale', since he brings in Dorigen in *The Flour of Curtesye* (l. 192). But to see, as Skeat does, an allusion to the Isle of Naxos here seems forced:

> Ye han me cast in thilke spitous yle
> Ther never man on lyve mighte asterte. (ll. 12–13)

It has little relevance to the story of Ariadne, but much more to some rigorous isle, like that of *Le Dit du Lyon*, or *The Isle of Ladies*. The line, 'Whan every foughel chesen shal his make' (l. 86), is an obvious borrowing from *The Parlement of Foules* (l. 310); Roos is more likely to be making use of Chaucer than Chaucer needing to adapt himself.

The main theme of the poem is the thrice-repeated charge by a devout and submissive lover that it is the lady's 'pley to laughen whan men syketh' (l. 62; cf. ll. 10, 48–9). The general expression of the poem is fully in Roos's manner. The anagrams are strung down through the stanzas thus:

AlYAn. COBHAM (stt. 1–2); HOMFrEY (5–7); E–ISAB–Th BARDO–F, BEWMONT, PHILIP (7–8); STAn——W (7–8); STYW–D; WYMBYSS (10); ISMANYA SCAl–S, whAl–SBO. (12–13); whITTIN–HAM; BABTh.; IAI TOT FOrfAIT FOrfAIT.

V. LYRICS IN MS. FAIRFAX 16

The next group of short poems occurs only in MS. Fairfax 16, which contains *La Belle Dame sans Merci*, and which will increasingly be seen as a very important manuscript for Roos. It consists of eighteen Balades, Complaints, and Letters (together with two other poems, see below, Nos. 64, 65). The collection was printed by Professor MacCracken (*P.M.L.A.*, XXVI, 155–75), who assumed the poems to be by William de la Pole, Earl of Suffolk, chiefly because he believed Suffolk to be the translator of poems by Charles d'Orléans (whose keeper he was for a time), and because one of the poems of this series is also found in Orléans's personal manuscript. Miss Hammond considered this theory inconclusive (*From Chaucer to Surrey*, p. 198); and it has now been discredited by Robert Steele's proof of Orléans as the author of his English poems. No translator is in question. The result is that now we have no English poems by Suffolk to take as a yardstick for this group, but only a few French poems. Some of these may be by Sir Othes de Holande, brother of the Fair Maid of Kent, according to the running title in MS. Trin. Coll., Camb., R. 3.20. If so, even the French poems attributed to Suffolk are reduced to a very small number; and in the complete absence of accredited English poems, it is impossible to assert that the Fairfax group is in Suffolk's style, since we are in ignorance of his English style, if any.

I would suggest that the poems are by Sir Richard Roos. The anagrams of the eighteen lyrics bring them into the Plesaunce group and period. I have numbered them as eight groups, following the items of the contemporary index (fol. 2 v.):

[1] The iij balettes þt þe lover made to his lady.
[2] The ij complayntez þt [etc.].
[3] A letter þat [etc.].
[4] The vij Complayntez þat [etc.].
[5] The supplicacion that the [etc.]. (This counts as the seventh Complaint.)

[6] The letter þat the [etc.].

[7] ij Complayntez þat [etc].

[8] A letter and a complaynt that [etc.].

No. 15. Balades, Complaints and Letters (MS. Fairfax 16, fol. 318-25).

[1] *The iij balettes;* fol. 318 r.-v.

Incipits. No. i. To fle the sect of alle mysgouernaunce
  Refrain. Constreynd of hert wyth stedfast loue and drede.
    (3 stt.)
  No. ii. And os for yow that most ar in my mynde (4 stt.)
  No. iii. O lord god what yt is gret plesaunce (3 stt.)

[2] *The ij complayntez;* fol. 319 r.-v.

Incipits. No. iv. Now lyst fortune thus for me to purueye
  Refrain. And so I lyue almost out of byleue. (4 stt.)
  No. v. Knelyng allon, ryght thus I may make my wylle (3 stt.)

All five poems are in rhyme royal.

These five poems are in Roos's style, especially the first three, with the rhymes 'gouernaunce: plesaunce: remembraunce; and drede: womanhede: goodlyhede'; and with the expression 'So full of bounte' and reference to Lucresse and fair Eleyn (No. iii). No. v is a Testament, bequeathing the lover's heart and will, 'Euer to be suget to your seruyse'.

These poems differ little from poems of the early Plesaunce period, except perhaps in a certain flatness of tone; they are devout professions of faithful service, 'Not for to chaunge for erthely creature' (No. v).

The double anagrams of Group 1 concern Lady Beaumont and the Plesaunce set: (i) CO–HAM; WHITT. (st. 1); ALYAN; WHA–IS–ORO. (2–3); COBHAM (3); (ii) –LISAB–TH B–WMONT, BARDO.; WHITT.; I ROS ANON (it is very rare to find the 'signature' instead of the 'devise' in the anagram); (iii) (EL)ISAB–TH BEWMO–T; ISMANY SCALYS; ALIAN; ANTIGO.; FORF–IT FOR––IT. Group 2 has some variations: (iv) BEWMONT; ALIAN.; WHITTIN–HAM; TOT FOR–AIT, and also YSMAN–A SCAL., WHA–––BO.; in (v) st. 1., KATERIN is a straight acrostic hitherto unnoticed; the rest of the anagram gives WHITT.; B–WM––T, BARD.; WYMBYSS; TOT FOR–AYT.

[3] No. vi. *Lettyr;* fol. 320.

  Incipit. Ryght goodly flour, to whom I owe seruyse.
  Explicit. And god I pray, that worshypeth alle mankynde,
    That lord aboue, that syteth in his empire,
    He send yow Ioy of alle that ye desyre.

Here there is a marked change of tone, far greater vigour, and sureness of touch. The Flower is introduced, but there is here no opposition to the Leaf, and it is used absolutely, as in *The Flour of Curtesye*. The lady's young and 'tendir age' is the theme of a stanza; the lover longs to see her, and begs her to think upon his heavy state. The pious expressions ('that grace that god to yow hath sent') of st. 3, and the concluding prayer, are not common in secular love-poems.

The anagram reads: BEWMONT, BARDO.; WHYTT.; STAnHO.; BABTHO.; there is a large residue, and no 'devise'. If, as I believe, the poem was altered later in 1444/5 (see No. 63), necessary letters may have been lost then.

[4] *The vij Complayntez and the Supplicacion;* fol. 320 v.–323.

No. vii. O wofull hert prisound in grete duresse (3 stt.)
No. viii. O thou Fortune whyche hast the gouernaunce (4 stt.)
No. ix. O cruell daunger all myn aduersarye (3 stt.)
No. x. Now must I nede part out of your presence (3 stt. and envoy)
No. xi. What shuld me cause or ony wyse to thynk (3 stt.)
No. xii. Walkyng allon of wyt full desolat (3 stt. and envoy)

[5] *Supplicacion.*

No. xiii. Besechyth mekly in ryght lowly wyse (3 stt.)

The anagrams of groups 4 and 5 run as follows:

(vii) –LISAB–TH B–W–ONT; WHITT.; STANHOP.; TOT FOr–AYT.
(viii) Line initials, AN MO–INS WhA––SBOR.
　　　Caesural initials, B–WM–T; KATh. WhITT; IAY TOT FOrFAIT.
 (ix) E–ISAB–TH BeWMO–T, BA–D.; WHITT.; STAnHO.; BABTh.; IAY TOT FOrFAYT.
  (x) –LISABeTH BeWMONT, BA–D; ANTIG. POWY–; WHITT.; BABTH.; TOT FOrFAIT.
 (xi) B–WMO–T; ISMAnIA WhA–––BOro.; WhITT.; BABThor; and (caesural) TOT FOrFAIT.
(xii) COBHAM, ELISAB–TH BeWMO–T; KATh. WhITT–––HAM; TOT FOrFAIT.
(xiii) (Supplicacion) HOMF––Y GLOST.; AlIAn. C–BHA–; ANTIG. P–WIS; BABTH. (no 'devise').

Nos. vii, viii, and ix are the complaints of a humble lover, doubtful of finding favour in his lady's eyes, and resentful of Fortune and Daunger. No. viii is the poem also found in the personal manuscript of Charles d'Orléans (ed. R. Steele, p. 223); but the anagrams prove Roos's authorship, and are very cunningly contrived. They seem to show that Roos wrote it out of compliment to Charles, and during the years 1438–40 when Charles wrote his English poems to Lady Moleyns, *née*

Anne Whalesborough;[1] Roos includes also his own lady's name. Nos. x, xi, and xii are heavy complaints of 'wykkyd tonges', of slander, and of hindrance by adversity. No. xii addresses a prayer to the god of love, and a protestation of true meaning. No. xiii, the *Supplicacion*, is addressed to the Gloucesters, as the anagrams show; it imitates a formal petition, and seems to show that there has been some coolness. The poet has been 'hyndyrd to your grace' by false reports; he protests his innocence, and begs 'That he always may to your grace resort'. The pious expressions recur: 'So wolde criste, for hys hye pyte' (No. xi).

[6] No. xiv. *Letter;* fol. 323 v.

Incipit. Myn hertes Ioy and all myn hole plesaunce (3 stt.)

This poem is of unusual interest, because it is the first dated poem here, and because it exists in another metrical form. Here, like all these poems, it is in rhyme royal. In MS. Lambeth 306, fol. 137, it is the second of that group of four poems, two others of which are Beaumont poems (see Nos. 8, 23). There it consists of three eight-line stanzas with a four-line conclusion of short lines as a fourth stanza. This envoy is not in MS. Fairfax 16, which I take to be the later version, reversing the judgment of Carleton Brown and Robbins (*M.E. Index*, Nos. 2182 and 2247). In st. 1 the last two lines of the longer stanza have been cut in halves and run together; in l. 6 'symplesse' replaces 'som plesaunce' with better sense. Pious wishes are found in both versions, and in both the poet is an absent lover. The chief change is at the end of st. 3, where the address to 'my Souerein' is removed, and a date substituted:

> Go lytill byll and say thou were wyth me
> Of verey trouth, as thou canst wele remembre.
> At myn vpryst, the fyft day of decembre (MS. Fairfax 16).

> go, litil bill, and say thoue were with me
> this same day at myne vp-Ryssinge
> where that y be-sought god of merci
> tho to haue my Souerein in his kepeing (MS. Lambeth 306).

The anagrams of both versions yield Plesaunce names, but the metrical and verbal variations cause some differences:

MS. *Lambeth* 306. AlIAN.; AnTIG.; E–ISAB–Th BEWM–NT, BARD.; whYT–InG–AM; BABTh.; STIWARD; ToT For–AI.

MS. *Fairfax* 16. AnTIG.; –ISABeTH BeWMONT; whYTTInG–AM; BAB.; ForFAYT. The fuller list of the Lambeth manuscript is cut down,

---

[1] See my *Studies in Villon, Vaillant, and Charles d'Orléans*, No. 3.

probably fortuitously, through the later adapting of the poem to another purpose, as seen in the Fairfax manuscript (see No. 63, below).

[7] *Two Complayntez;* fol. 324.

Incipit. No. xv. The tyme so long the payn ay mor and more. (3 stt.)
No. xvi. What shall I say, to whom schall I complayn?
Refrain. Thus to endure yt is a wondir thyng. (3 stt.)

No. xv is very conventional in expression; its first line adapts the opening of *The Parlement of Foules.* Its theme, the healing of the wounded lover, with the lady as his leech, is reminiscent of the stress on healing in *How a Lover, The Isle of Ladies,* and *Fabula . . . Mercatorum.* No. xvi is narrative, and more unusual. The lover comes into a goodly plain, and kneels among a company of 'fair peple' to pay his vows; they break suddenly into singing, and pay no heed to him. He returns home in despair, and communes with his heart, which yet will wear blue for 'stedfast lyuyng'. The inconsequence suggests the telling of a dream; the colloquy with his heart is very much in the style of Charles d'Orléans. The anagram of No. xv looks at first sight unpromising, with the plethora of line initials in T; nevertheless the variety of the caesural initials brings –LISAB–TH BeWMONT, BA––OLF; whYTT., and TOT FOrFAIT. No. xvi yields: –LISAB–TH B–AUMONT, WHYTTIn–HA–; also AlIAN; and TOT FOr–AIT.

[8] *Letter and Complaynt;* fol. 324 v.–325.

Incipit. No. xvii. My best belouyd lady and maistresse (4 stt.)
No. xviii. Not far fro marche in the ende of feueryere (5 stt.)

The Letter is a good example of the close-packed complaint of a 'wofull wyght' in Roos's most fluent and easily commanded style. The last lines date it on 'our lady day'; the point of this and the next poem's dating will be discussed later (see No. 63). The Complaint describes how the lover has walked beside a river 'fayr and clere' to comfort his spirits, but in vain; 'Pyte is lost' and trouthe brings no routhe. The anagram of the Letter is restricted to Lady Beaumont and her companion: B–WMO–T, BA––OLF; whITTIn–HAM; TOT FOrFAIT. The longer Complaint is a Plesaunce 'braid', which includes Antigone's married name, and (less usually) Jacquetta, Duchess of Bedford: ANT. P–WYS; –LISAB–TH B–W–ONT, BARDO.; CATh. whITT.; SCA.; IAQU–TTA; and the 'devise' IAI TOT FOrFAIT.

This group of poems was written chiefly for Lady Beaumont; a few include the Plesaunce family, one (No. xiii) indicating an estrangement. The inclusion of Antigone's married name points to a date about 1436; we know that Roos was at Gisors in December 1436, and most of these poems lament the writer's absence. One of the poems (xiv) was certainly adapted; and it will be argued later that some years after Lady Beaumont's death (1441) they were furnished with dates, and pious expressions, for royal purposes (see Chapter VIII, No. 63).

VI. LYRICS AND POEMS IN MS. FF. I.6, ETC.

More than a dozen 'Elisabeth' lyrics are found in various manuscripts; of these the most numerous and most important are those in MS. Ff. 1.6, the 'Roos scrapbook', not in a cluster, though three are in the centre (fol. 136 v.–140). They are arranged here in alphabetical order.

No. 16*a*; fol. 138 v.: printed by Robbins, *P.M.L.A.*, 1954, LXIX, 635–6.

> *Incipit.* Alas, what planet was y born vndir.
> My hert ys set thus veray feythfully.
> *Explicit.* Ther ys in me for wo no certaynte
> ffor lacke of gr*a*ce thes parties shal y flee.

The poem is in three stanzas of rhyme royal; there is no 'signature', but the 'devise' appears in the anagram. The lover laments his ill-starred destiny, protests his constancy and his despair, and begs for grace; the style and rhythm are those of Roos. The anagram gives: ElsAB–TH B–WMO–T; WHITT.; also AlIAN COBHAM; AnTIGO.; and T–T FOrFAYT.

No. 16*b*; fol. 154 v.

> *Incipit.* As in my remembrauns non but ye alone.
> *Explicit.* ffor, alas, departyng hath my hert schent.

Robbins, printing these two stanzas of rhyme royal (*Secular Lyrics*, No. 168), emends the first word to 'Is'. Absence and separation are the theme. The line-initials give ISMANY. WHA––S; the caesural anagram adds B–WMONT, and nearly completes FOr–AIT.

The next two poems are in a light and popular style, justifying Greene's inclusion of them among his 'Amorous Carols' (Nos. 442 and 469).

No. 16*c*; fol. 136 v.

> *Incipit.* Some tyme Y loued as ye may see.
> *Explicit.* With joy there lyues lede.

The poem is in nine quatrains, of three octosyllabic lines and one of six syllables (aaab); the b rhyme is identical throughout, to accord with the second line of the refrain:

> Who so lyst to loue,
> God send hym right good spede.

At the end is 'Amen pur Charyte'. The narrative tells of a fall from the lady's favour, and of her disdain and unkindness; the lover still hopes to be recalled. The anagram includes one of the Ladies of *The Legend*, as does 'Your yen two', and yields: AlYAN.; BeWMONT, BA–D--F; HYPSIF.; IS–ANYA S–A–YS; FOrFAIT.
The next carol celebrates an even more carefree mood.

No. 16*d*; fol. 139 v.

> *Incipit.* Somtyme Y louid, so do Y yut.
> *Explicit.* This song with vs in fere.

The poem is in eight stanzas with a verse and rhyme structure similar to that of the preceding. The enemy here is Daunger, but the lover has escaped 'from his band', and his laughing freedom is enhanced by the gay and charming refrain:

> Vp, son and mery wether,
> Somer draweth nere.

At the end is 'desormais'; this is the motto of the Cliffords who were connected by marriage with the Roos family. Here it may indicate a friendly copyist. The anagram gives the familiar names: (E)–ISAB–Th B–WMONT, BA–D–LF; also AlYAN. COBHA–; ANTIG.; ISMAnIA SCAlYS; FOrFAIT. The initial of Elisabeth is doubtful and rests on an emendation of 'ascapid' (st. 7); the spelling throughout is not Roos's norm (yut, dude, ar for ere).

The following poem is one of several on Fortune in MS. Ff. 1.6 and as such was printed by Carleton Brown in his *Religious Lyrics*, No. 166.

No. 16*e*; fol. 53 v.

> *Incipit.* There schapeth [i.e. escapeth] nought from her entent.
> *Explicit.* As hyt comyth so lete it go.

The refrain needs to precede the stanzas, since it contains the grammatical subject:

> When fortune list yewe [? yeve] here assent,
> What is too deme þat may be doo?

This 'schort aviseament' on the control of Fortune over high and low consists of two quatrains of octosyllabic lines (abab), and may be a fragment merely; certainly the anagram names are skeletal: B–AU–O–T; wHYTT.; A–TYGO.; but FORFAIT is clear and compact in the first stanza.

No. 16*f*. Another scrap, a quatrain invoking fortune and addressed to a lady, yields even in this brief compass the anagram ISMAn. SCA–Y–; 'Sith fortune hathe me set thus in this wyse' (printed by Robbins in *P.M.L.A.*, LXIX, 635).

The last poem to be considered in this group runs straight on, in the same hand and ink, from Robbins's No. 169 (No. 41*a*, below) but they are two different poems, as the anagrams show.

No. 16*g*; fol. 20 v.: printed by Robbins, *P.M.L.A.*, LXIX, 632.

> *Incipit*. Where y haue chosyn stedefast woll y be,
> Newyr*e* to r*e*pente in wyll, thowth, ne dede.
> *Explicit*. syn þat ye wote þat sche ys merceles.

The poem is unfinished, since after two stanzas of rhyme royal, there is a fragmentary stanza of four lines. Nevertheless enough is left of this assertion of unswerving devotion to give a full anagram: E–ISAB–Th B–WMONT, BAr.; wHIT.; SCAl–S; TOT FOr–AIT.

A few 'Elisabeth' lyrics are to be found in a tiny anthology, a collection, in a sixteenth-century hand, inexplicably inserted among personal and astrological papers of Lilly and Ashmole, MS. Ashmole 176, foll. 97–101. I believe that they are not in print.

No. 17*a*; fol. 99 r. and v.

> *Incipit*. Ah my hart ah this ys my Songe / w*i*th weping eyes nowe and
> the*n* among
> *Explicit*. or elles wyll death be myne extremytye that ah my hart ah.
>   fynis.

This is catalogued as poem 10; actually it and the preceding couplet form the eighth poem, the refrain being,

> Adewe pleasure, welcome mo*u*rnyng, alas all payne nowe ys my p*art*
> for I see well yt my sweeting doth not consyder my true hart.

The Tudor copyist, accustomed to the long fourteener, or frugal of paper, wrote the poem in these abnormally long lines with internal rhymes; their straggling disguises the short staccato lines:

> I see of love
> she ca*n* no skyll

M

> and yet nedes must
> I love her styll
> for I cannot
> withdrawe my good wyll
> that ah my hart ah.

Read thus, the poem consists of seven stanzas of seven lines with a refrain; the rhyme scheme is abcbdbE.

The song reproaches the lady for her hard heart; she has reclaimed the lover 'to her lure', but without kindness or comfort, and he prays for death. The anagram yields: BeWMONT, BARDO.; WiTT.; ISMANIA SCAl–S; STAn–OW; IAY TOT FOrFAIT. The next two poems, celebrating Phelip, not Beaumont, may be early.

No. 17*b*; fol. 99.

> *Incipit.* Though ye my love were a ladye fayr
> Passing all other in bewty to ensue.
> *Explicit.* except I knowe a better assurance
> nay my Love nay farewell a dewe. finis.

Though catalogued as poem 7, it is actually poem 6, since the preceding couplet ('poem 6') is in fact the refrain:

> Lost ys my Love farewell adewe, lost ys my Love farewell adewe
> Ive the proofe she wyll not be true, lost ys my love farewell adewe.

There are three quatrains, of lines basically four-beat, but of seven to ten syllables, with a close rhyme structure: abaB, cbcB, dbdB. It is a simple song of grief and farewell. The anagram gives: FYLIP; IS–ANYA SCALES; ST–NL–W; TO– F––F.

No. 17*c*; fol. 100: catalogued as Poem 12, actually Poem 10. There are four stanzas, of which the first is probably the introductory refrain:

> Parting parting | I may well synge | hath caused all my payne
> From her to part | yt greveth my hart | ye wot not whom I meane.

If so, the poem proper begins at st. 2.

> *Incipit.* A mos[t] fayre and true | ye cause me rue | your absence ys my peyne.
> yet youe to love | by god above | I cannot me refreyne.
> *Explicit.* of my poore Love | by god above | ye shalbe ever sure. finis.

Again the two long fourteener lines with internal rhymes are meant to be read as four lines of four syllables, and two of six, an 'hour-glass stanza' (aabccb). The poem has, I think, been tampered with, perhaps altered by a singer, with an introductory 'Ah' before st. 1, and an explanatory but unnecessary 'which' ('for ye were she *which* comforted me') in st. 2. The rhyme-sound of the refrain is not continued beyond st. 1. The acrostic needs the deletion of both these extrametrical interpolations, and then gives: PHILY., B–WMO., BA–D.; SC––YS; FOrFAYT.

Finally there is a single octosyllabic quatrain, a small posy for Lady Scales alone.

No. 17*d*; fol. 99: catalogued as Poem 8, actually Poem 7.

> Alas myne eye whye doest y^u blynde bringe
> allwayes my hart in payne and woe
> Sythe thowe me rulest in everye thing
> whye art thou thus my mortall foe

The acrostic letters A.A.S.W.

           W.I.I.M.

give ISMA–IA with a residue of W.W. The eye and heart controversy finds full expression in one of Roos's translations of this period (No. 58, below). The first reading of 'bringe' as 'blynde' in l. 1 proves a mistaken but quite intelligent copyist, if proof were needed with this neat secretary hand of the early sixteenth century.

Other poems in the anthology concern Roos's other friends; and attacks on his *bête noire* of Queen Margaret's court show that the little group ranges to the 1450s (see below, No. 97*a* and *b*).

A group of six short songs with their musical settings is found in a large and varied volume, MS. Ashmole 191, as the fourth out of five manuscripts bound together. The first song, 'Now wold I fayn sum myrthis make', also occurs in MS. Ff. 1.6, the 'Roos scrapbook'; it is written later for Sir Richard's sister-in-law, and will be commented on in the next chapter. Four others have traces of Roos anagrams, and are probably by him. All are printed by Robbins in *Secular Lyrics*.

No. 18*a*; fol. 194: Robbins, *Secular Lyrics*, No. 154.

Incipit. Thus I complayn my grevous hevynesse.

This six-line stanza is of varying line-length in alternate ab rhymes. It is a rather listless appeal for help from one who knows the truth of his intent. The anagram gives ISMA–YA.

No. 18*b*; fol. 195: Robbins, *Secular Lyrics*, No. 156.

Incipit. Alas, departyng ys ground of woo.

This is an eight-line stanza with four-beat lines of slight syllabic variety (ababbcbc). The lover's heart is pierced by the memory of the 'bitter teris' of her weeping at their parting. Even this one stanza yields two names: B--MO-T; SCAlYS.[1]

An 'Antigone' stanza is added here for completeness, but one for Lady Willoughby is deferred till Chapter VI.

No. 18c; fol. 192 v.: Robbins, *Secular Lyrics*, No. 155.

Incipit. Go hert, hurt with aduersite

This is an unusual five-line stanza of octosyllabic lines (aaabb). The line-initials give ANTIG.; the caesural initials (with two capitals added) give I–MAN–A. George Cely learnt it in Oct. 1475.[2]

Another 'Antigone' stanza, but uniting her with Elisabeth Beaumont, is found among the sixteenth-century names on fol. 3 of William, Lord Arundel's volume (Royal MS. 17.D.vi), which also contains signatures of Roos interest on its flyleaf.

No. 19. 'Goo, lytell ryng, to that ylke suehte': a stanza of octosyllabic lines but rhyme royal in structure (printed in Robbins, *Secular Lyrics*, No. 95).

The double anagram reads ANTIGO. (ll. 1–3); BE–MONT. The ring is sent to Elisabeth who has his heart 'in hyr demaeyne', with the message, 'My masster wold that he wer I'; but it is sent under cover to Antigone.

Another stanza is sent to Lady Scales for Elisabeth.

No. 20. 'I ne haue Ioy'.

Incipit. I ne haue Ioy, plesauns nor comfortt
In yowre absenss, my verrey hertes quene.

It is a stanza of rhyme royal, but with a last line of fourteen syllables; printed in Robbins, *Secular Lyrics*, No. 159. The only manuscript is MS. Rawlinson poet. 36. The anagrams give B–WMO–T; IS–A–Y.

The lover is a prey to contrariety: disport becomes teen, laughter is from the spleen, and his cheer is at once sorry and glad.

No. 21. A more vigorous poem than the emotional songs of MS. Ashmole 191 is preserved in MS. Ashmole 1113, fol. 129. I believe that it is not printed; it is not in the *Index*.

Incipit. Yf onely sight suffyse
My hart to lose or bynd

---

[1] Another eight-line song in a Burgundian 'chansonnier', badly mangled by the foreign copyist, is printed by Robbins, No. 157; his reconstituted lines give the anagram AlIAN.; ISMA–I; FOrF--T. Its. l. 5, 'The ground of Wo I fele departyng', inverts l. 1 of this song (No. 156, unamended text).

[2] See A. Hanham in *R.E.S.*, 1957, N.S. VIII, 270–6.

> What Avaylethe it to move debate
> Wher in no peace I fynde.

Explicit. Vnto her selfe A lone
> Whose favor I Require
> for none shall knowe her name for me
> to maistere my desyer.

The poem is in eight quatrains (abab; 6686); a blank space is left between stt. 7 and 8, as if the copyist hoped to be able later to fill in a ninth stanza. The lover, having thrown 'the dice of love', is content to wait 'the doughtfull chance', and by steadfastness to overcome jealousy and envy. He has an unusual metaphor for this:

> As feble is the wyre
> that fyrste now is be gon
> so tender flaxe will bere no stren
> before that it be spunne. (st. 6)

Meantime he will not betray the lady's name. The anagram, however, reveals: –LYSA––TH BAR––LF. BeAUM––T; wHITT.; AnTIG.; T–T FOrF––T. R.R. A rather large residue suggests that the name of Wymbysshe was also intended: WYM––S.[1]

Roos does not always choose to write ornately for Elisabeth Beaumont; there is an almost deliberate naïveté in the thirteen simple quatrains of the following poem.

No. 22. 'A Heartless Mistress': Robbins's title, *Secular Lyrics*, 138.

> *Incipit.* Now fresshe floure, to me that ys so bryght,
> Of your louely womanhode I pray yow of grace
> *Explicit.* ffor your loue my deth ys dyght,
> My soule to god standeth in dyspeyre.
> lothe to offende.

The only manuscript is Trin. Coll., Camb., R. 3.19 (fol. 157), where it is written continuously. The lines are four-beat with variation of seven to eleven syllables. The stiffness and awkwardness of many passages may point to an unpolished poem; the reference to Cato is pedantic in tone, and the Ladies named are not 'Cupid's saints', but Kateryn, Elene and Margarete. If it were not for the Plesaunce anagram with the full 'devise', one would almost expect a less practised writer than Roos. The names are: ALYAN COBHAM; E(L)ISABeTh BEWMONT, BA–DO–F; Kateryn wHYTTIn–AM; ISMAnIA S–AlES; Margarete STAN–OW; WIMBIS;

---

[1] There is also a considerable number of 'Elisabeth' poems, with similar anagrams in MSS. Add. 17492 and 28635, and Egerton 2711, which will be discussed in Chapter XII.

IAY TOT FOrFAIT FOrFAIT. The final motto may be the poet's or a copyist's but it is more probably the poet's, since it recurs in the last lines of the next poem to be considered, a poem of similar anagrams.

No. 23. 'Frische flour of womanly nature': a lover's complaint in four eight-line stanzas, with a couplet as envoy. (Printed by Furnivall, *Pol. & Rel. Poems*, E.E.T.S., 15, p. 69.)

> St. 1   Frische flour of womanly nature
> ye be fulle gentille and goodly one to se
> And all so stedfaste as any criatur
> that is lyuynge in any degre
> fullfyled with alle benyngnete
> And an Exsample of all worthynes
> And they that to you haue nessesite
> be gracious euer thorough your gentilnes.
> *Explicit.* lothe to offende so y may my lady pleas
> welcome payne, And Fie one esse.

There is no 'signature', but the 'devise' is found. The only manuscript is Lambeth 306; like the three other poems there, it is rather rough, but I know no corresponding polished version, though there is a general parallelism with No. 22. The first stanza is not only cut to the pattern of the idealistic characters of women in the two game poems, it is even similar at points to stanza 24 of *Ragman Roll*, and stt. 9 and 44 of *The Chance of the Dice*. The anagrams run down the stanzas thus: HOMFr-Y; ALIAn COBHAM; (E)LISABeTH BeWMONT, BA(r)-O-F; SCALi., ISMAnY; WhYTTIn-AM; TOT FOrFAIT (R.R.). The motto 'lothe to offende' recalls the preceding poem; and a variant of this line (33) is found scribbled in two forms in MS. Bodleian Lyell 34, a version of the contemporary 'English Chronicle' to 1461.

To turn now to lyrics almost as much in the alliterative style as is *How a Lover*. One such poem had been written without any reference to Plesaunce.

No. 24. 'O lord of loue'.

> *Incipit.* O Lord of loue here my complaynt
> *Explicit.* Intoloreable ys here trespasse—
> [That fygure fresch that ys so fayre].

The last line is the unvaried refrain; there are five eight-line stanzas, in octosyllabics (ababbcbC); in st. 4, l. 4, assonance replaces rhyme. The only manuscript is Cotton MS. Vespasian D.ix, which also contains a

Roos lyric written for the Bedfords, as will be seen (No. 56a, below). Robbins prints 'O Lord of loue' in *Secular Lyrics* (No. 128).

The detailed description of the lady, 'so myld a mayde', of 'commely countenance' and 'stedfast stature', is in a style already archaic in the 1430s. For once Elisabeth Phelip's name does not emerge from the anagram, which is confined to ISMANIA SCAlIS, WHALYSBO-(R)O.; STAN-OW; IAY TOT FOrFAIT FO-FAIT (R.R.). Nevertheless she is probably the object of the complaint; Lady Scales and Margaret Stanlow seem to have been Roos's lifelong confidantes. The anagram is very clear, even omitting as it does all the refrain letters, T.

It is, I believe, for Plesaunce's amusement that we find Roos mocking this style by exaggeration. There are two lyrics which begin almost identically: 'Excellent soueraine, semely to see'; and 'O excelent suffereigne, most semely to see' (Robbins, *Secular Lyrics*, Nos. 205 and 130). The likeness can hardly be accidental; the first has no anagrams, the second is a Plesaunce 'braid'. The first opens thus:

> Excellent soueraine, semely to see,
> Preved prudente, peerlees of pris,
> Bright blossome of Benyngnyte,
> ffigure fairest, and fresshest of devys.

and closes with,

> ffarewell prymerose, my plesaunce.
> Explicet Amor.
> per ducem Eboracensis nuper factus.

The poem straggles on for thirty-four quatrains of alternate rhymes and a norm of eight to ten syllables; it is fairly regular in rhythm and accent, and is not without an artless charm, as when the lover longs 'a bird invisible for to be', to visit his lady unseen (stt. 15–6). The stiff aureate style of the thirteen stanzas of farewell, comparisons to flowers and jewels, tires by excess. The only manuscript is Douce 95, said to be of Yorkist provenance. If the poem was really the work of Richard, Duke of York, of the falcon and fetterlock (and the 'ffarewell faucon' of l. 116 supports this), it may have been meant for Cicely Neville, whom he married probably in 1438. *The Craft of Lovers*,[1] with which this poem has parallels ('O rubicunde rose'), announces itself as written in 1448 (not 1348, as Skeat showed in the *Chaucer Canon*, p. 120), and

---

[1] A. K. Moore sees *The Craft of Lovers* itself as 'a parody of grandiose diction' ('Some Implications of *The C. of L.*', *Neophilologus*, 1951, XXXV, 231–8). It is not, I believe, by Roos.

is in the same excessively ornate style, of which one fully sees the absurdity in the scene of St. Mary Magdalen *in gaudio*, in the play of her name. It is that style that we shall see Roos mocking.

No. 25. 'O excelent suffereigne'.

> *Incipit.* O excelent suffereigne, most semely to see,
> > bothe prudent & pure, lyke a perle of prise,
> > also fair of fygure & oreant of bewtye
> *Explicit.* my harte ye haue to kepe,
> > by god that made thys day.

The poem, a 'symple letter', consists of six stanzas of the antique bob-and-wheel stanza, but with a rhyme royal as the base before the dissyllabic bob, and the final quatrain of six-syllable lines (deed). The only manuscript is Rawlinson C.813 which Robbins describes (*Secular Lyrics*, p. xliv) as a 'miscellaneous Aureate Collection' written in the early sixteenth century. Robbins's dating of the poem (*ib.*, No. 130) as late fifteenth century is negatived by the Plesaunce anagram. This also allows us to see the poem as a direct gibe at the Duke of York's verses, indeed as a pastiche of the style. The close correspondence of the first lines is apparent; and there are other hallmarks of the style, the 'Ruby-counde Roose' and the 'trew turtyll' together with extravagances which Bottom would have enjoyed:

> . . . your rollyng eyes whyche ar as glasse clere,
> & your strawbery lyppes as swete as honye;

and some prettinesses:

> & your-selfe as swete as ys the gelyfloure
> or any lauender sedes strawen yn a cooffer
> To smell.

Indeed, the joke is enhanced by Roos's awareness of his own style in *How a Lover*; here again the lady's neck is 'as whyte as whalles bone' and her breath sweeter than 'balme, suger, or lycoresse'. For four stanzas the poem rollicks along in this vigour and gaiety, with rhymes like some in *The Craft of Lovers*, and unusual in Roos ('correction: derectyon; vareatyon: negatyon', stt. 3 and 5; cf. stt. 2, 6, and 8 of *The Craft*). In the last two stanzas the parody dies down, and the poem ends in the authentic tones of Roos:

> and neuer to change yow for no newe,
> but daylly for your grace to suye.

The double anagram yields: HOMFR–Y; AlYAn COB–AM; ANTI–ONA; BeW–ONT, –A–DOLF; WhYTTIn; ISMAnYA; STIWA.; –AUD WYL–WBY; IAY

TOT ForFAYT ForFAYT (R.R.). Maud Stanhope's marriage to Lord Willoughby is not precisely dated; but this poem is evidently later than *Ragman Roll*, where she is given her maiden name.

Roos gives further proof of his virtuosity in a different kind in two macaronic poems, love letters in French, English, and Latin.

No. 26.

> *Incipit.* (*a*) A celuy que pluys eyme en mounde
> Of alle tho that I have found
> *Carissima.*
> (*b*) A soun treschere et special
> Fer and ner and overal
> *In mundo.*

They are respectively in twelve and nine stanzas of six lines, aabccb, the b rhyme being always a short Latin word or phrase, and the longer lines alternating French and English. They are found together in two manuscripts, Camb. Univ. Library, MS. Gg. iv.27 (the first section), an important collection for Roos, and Harleian 3362, fol. 90 v.–91; they are printed in *Early English Lyrics*, Nos. 8 and 9. In MS. Gg. iv.27 they are headed *De Amico ad Amicam*, and *Responcio*, but this is probably dramatic. The anagrams show that the Plesaunce ladies are involved. They run: (*a*) stt. 1–2, P–ELIP; stt. 2–3, ELISA–ETh; stt. 3–4, BARDOLF; stt. 1–3, STAN–O; st. 5, SCALE–; stt. 6–7, COB–AM; stt. 6–8, ELI–BETh; stt. 7–8, MAVD; stt. 8–9, ANTIG.; stt. 10–11, ISMAnIA; stt. 11–12, PHE–JP; stt. 10–12, –YDVILE; st. 12, JAQueTTe; stt. 9–11, TOT For––YT; (*b*) stt. 1–2, JAQUeT; stt. 2–4, WY–VI–E; stt. 2–3, MAud S–A––OPE; stt. 3–4, SCALIS; stt. 4–5, ISMA–IA; BA–DOLF; stt. 5–6 AlIAN.; stt. 6–7, A–TIG.' PHELIP; stt. 8–9, –AVD STAN.; JACET. WYDVI.; diffused, TOT For–AJT.

Lady Beaumont's married name is not given, but this cannot indicate an early work, since Jacquetta of Bedford is by now married to Sir Richard Wydville; this dates the poems after March 23, 1436/7. The desire to include her name probably accounts for the admixture of French, giving easily the letters J, Q, and V. There is a fair residue of letters in both poems, and the arrangement of the names, somewhat broken by the French and Latin lines, has not Roos's usual smooth fluency, nor is the 'devise' clear and concentrated.

A poem in Roos's richer style on the theme of 'bounty and beauty' has escaped notice by being tacked on, even in a recent printing, to another poem; the anagrams show that they should be split apart.

No. 27. 'Now fayreste of stature': four stanzas of rhyme royal, a complaint in something the form of a letter.

>　*Incipit.* Now fayreste of stature formyd by nature,
>　　of beaute the merrour, and grond of gentylnes.
>　*Explicit.* The xvi day of the month of stedfastnys,
>　　The xxiij yere of polycy and southnes.
>　　　Penses de moy.

The only manuscript is Cotton MS. Vespasian D.ix, where on fol. 188 v. it runs straight on from a four-stanza poem, 'Exemplye sendynge to you', which by references and anagram proves to be addressed to the Duke and Duchess of Bedford (see below, No. 56). Both are printed by Robbins, *Secular Lyrics*, No. 198.

The poem is a direct appeal of the lover to the causer of his pain, 'Bounte, beaute and perfyte whomanhode'. It is written in 'thys nobyl and lusty may'. The year-date at the end (xxiij) is suspect because of the extra-metrical and awkward line; if it is meant for the regnal year, the omission of one numeral (x) would restore metre; the thirteenth regnal year, 1435, suits the Plesaunce references of the anagram. If it is meant for Roos's own age then twenty-three brings us to about 1433, also a possibility. This method of dating a poem like a letter recurs in the *Balades*, etc. of MS. Fairfax 16. The anagram, a little sketchy, gives: E–ISA––Th B–WMONT, –ARDO––; wh–TT–––HAM; ISMANYA; MAR. STAn–OW; TOT FOrFA.

There is more life and ease in this poem of octosyllabic stanzas.

No. 28. 'Thayr ys no myrth'.

>　*Incipit.* Thayr ys no myrth vnder the sky,
>　　Harpyng, lutyng, nor no mery dance.
>　*Explicit.* When I think apon your love so fre—
>　　By trew, lady, for I you truste.

The last line is the unvaried refrain of all the six eight-line stanzas (ababbcbC); Robbins, who prints the poem (No. 136) from the unique manuscript (Arch. Selden, supra 52, fol. 168 v.–169 v.), notes that it is added in a late fifteenth-century hand on the fly-leaf of a work on Biblical history. In stanzas 1–3 and 6, the rhyme with the refrain is replaced by assonance (e.g. 'inbraste: truste').

The lover celebrates his 'birde of all Plesance', and his tone is confident in spite of his admonitory refrain. The anagram is a full Plesaunce 'braid': HOMFrEY; AlYAN C–BHAM; ELISABeTh (P)HELIP, BeWMONT, B–RDOLF; whYTT–N–M; YSMANY; STYWA–T; BABTh; WYMBYSH (R.R.); T–T FOrFAIT FOrFAYT.

No. 29. A small roundel at the end of the collection in Trin. Coll.,

Camb. MS. R. 3.20 is an appeal for comfort in extremity, when nigh 'þe pittes brink'. 'Fresshest of colour and moste amyable' is addressed to IS–AnIA SCA––S; TOT FOrFA–T.

She is coupled with Lady Beaumont in No. 30, 'My Joye it is ffrome her to here' (Harleian 3362, fol. 90; printed (shortened) by Ritson, *Ancient Songs*, 1877, p. 165), a poem of five quatrains in an ingenuously simple style. The variants in Add. 18752, fol. 139 (Reed, *Anglia*, XXXIII, 366), do not damage the rather loose-knit anagram: B–WMO–T, BA–DO–F; ISMAnIA; FOrF–YT. The unusual wish that the lady's portrait were hung where the lover would constantly see it is reminiscent of *The Isle of Ladies*, where the beloved name might be written on a wall:

> Chryst wolt the ffuger of hur swete face
> were pyctored wher euer I dwell
> yn euery hall from place to place.

Several songs of Roos's are found set to music by Tudor composers in later collections. Such is the pretty song, No. 31, 'When fortune had me Avaunsyd' in two stanzas of rhyme royal, found in MS. Roy. Ap. 58, fol 21 v. It reminds the lady that 'hur trothe to me was fyauncyd' but her disdain has exiled truth; 'welcum payn' is the burden of the song. The poet's self-consciousness is expressed in a full 'devise': TOT FOrFAIT FOrFAIT; E–ISA––Th B–WMONT.

No. 32*a* and *b*. Lady Beaumont governs a song for which Robert Fayrfax the composer made the music (Add. 5465, fol. 26 v.—the Fayrfax manuscript). It is a single stanza of rhyme royal, so precisely in Roos's Plesaunce manner on 'bounte, beaute, and womanhede', that it might be a sample of his style; it may well be taken out of a long poem. 'Most clere of colour and rote of stedfastness' gives the names BeWMO–T; PH. Another poem set to music in the same manuscript (fol. 11 v.) is a tiny gift to Lady Scales; 'Loue fayne wolde I|yff I coude spye'; the single anagram of the eight short lines is S–ALYS.[1]

No. 33. A long complaint in seven romance stanzas renews the theme of the ruthless lady. 'Complain I may' (printed, Hawkins, *History of Music*, iii. 27) deplores that a true man should be driven 'in the wildernes' by a 'Dame Pitiles'. The single anagram gives her name with that of the poet's confidante: stt. 1–2, IS–AnIA SCAL.; stt. 4 and 6, B–WMOnT; stt. 5–6, S–AlIS; diffused, TOT FOrFAI– FOrFAI. The seventh stanza carries no anagram, and may be an addition; its lines, 'I trow a Jew|On me wold rew', do not sound like Roos.

[1] For these songs I am indebted to Mr. P. J. Frankis.

Another variation on the same theme is a complaint of devotion offered to one only love, but refused and disdained.

No. 34a.

> *Incipit.* Compleyn I may wher-soo-euer I goo.
> *Explicit.* Whome of all creatures I trustyde most.

It is a ballade in three stanzas of rhyme royal, without envoy, and is in MS. Rawl. C.813. One might be tempted to reverse stt. 2 and 3, leaving stt. 1 and 2 with the refrain, and ending the poem with the valediction, 'Farewell my loue & worldly feere'; but the anagrams run more smoothly with the present order: st. 1, AlIAN.; stt. 1-2, SCAlIS; STANH.; stt. 1-3, ISMANIA; stt. 2-3, B-WM-NT; st. 2, TOT FOrFA-T. In stanza 2, the rhyme 'refusyde' gave Roos trouble, and he produced 'illusyde' (deceived), and 'subtrusyde', rather oddly used apparently for 'thrust down'. The immediately preceding poem in MS. Rawl. C.813 (*Anglia*, XXXI, p. 358, No. 26) is also addressed to this group.

No. 34b.

> *Incipit.* O my dere harte, the lanterne of lyght.
> *Explicit.* To my swete harte, whome I loue best,
> Whome I pray God gyffe hur & me god reste.

It is a verse-letter, in five stanzas of rhyme royal, with a four-line envoy, 'Farewell, swetharte'. It does not speak of absence, but protests entire devotion:

> My loue ys lockyd vnder your lace,
> My body ye bereyd withyn your bowre.

But the lady does not respond, so that the lover is like a prisoner despairing of liberty:

> bowndon yn cheens, lyke to be dede,
> not yn parradyse, butt yn purkatorye.

The anagram shows at once who the sweetheart is: ELISAB-TH; BEWMONT; S-ALYS; whALISBO.; ISMANY; BABTh.; WILLOBY; FOrFAIT. There are several lines of anaphora on 'Your' and 'My', but Roos does not apparently here, as he will later, transfer to the initial of the second word to serve his anagram.

No. 35a. In another Plesaunce poem, 'Horns Away', Roos, who has already in *How a Lover* hinted at his dislike of artificiality in feminine appearance, openly attacks the fashionable horned head-dress in set terms.[1]

> *Incipit.* Off God and kynde procedith al bewte.
> *Explicit.* Be example of hir your hornes cast away.

It is a poem of nine eight-line stanzas with a variable refrain; the last four stanzas form the envoy. As Miss Hammond points out, it is a 'tour de force' on three rhymes throughout. There are ten manuscripts, of which only one, Trin. Coll., Camb., R. 3.19 is significant for Roos (see above, Chapter III). Shirley's MS. Ashmole 59 attributes it to Lydgate, and it has been unquestioningly accepted as his (MacCracken, p. 662). The anagrams are clear and simple:

st. 1, ll. 1–4, COBHAM; stt. 1–2, B–RDOL; st. 2, B–W–O–T; st. 3, AlIAn. COBHA.; stt. 3–4, HO–FRI; AnTI(G)ON.; (PHeL–P); st. 5, ELYSAB–TH; TOT FOrF–IT; *Envoy*, stt. 6–7, MAVD STANHOPe; st. 7, ISMANY– S(C).; st. 8, PHI–IP; stt. 8–9, B–RDO.; WH––––BO–OH; st. 9. BeWMONT.

The structure of the poem is unusual in the length of the Envoy. The first part, with its semi-philosophical tone, its stress on jewels, its appeal to Alain de L'Isle, its list of the Ladies, is in the now familiar manner of Roos; the envoy begins conventionally with its address to 'Noble pryncessis', but then devotes three stanzas to praise of the humility and simplicity of the Blessed Virgin, who 'wered a kourcheef, hornes wer cast away'. These last three stanzas, except for the link of the refrain, might almost form a separate Balade, and I expected a cessation of the anagrams; but these continue, without however a repetition of the poet's 'devise'. It is, I think, a fairly early poem, conceived under Lydgate's influence in the devotional portion, and in rhythm and phrasing, also with two direct borrowings: the contrast of gold and gossamer (l. 5; cf. Lydgate's *Letter to Gloucester*, l. 26); and the praise of the Virgin as the rose of Jericho (l. 62; cf. Lydgate's *Queen of Heuene*, l. 27). But there is much that can be paralleled in Roos's work, such as the indebtedness to 'Aleyn', and the well-informed reference to the properties of jewels, as in *How a Lover*. More important is the repetition of two themes in one later passage; the contrast between horns on women and on beasts (l. 34), followed by the appeal to the example of the Virgin, recurs in conjunction in one of Roos's original contributions in *Reson and Sensuallyte*, the Eighth Pawn, ll. 6546–66.

The reader soon realizes that the poet's objection to horns is as much one of fastidious taste as of morality. *Le Roman de la Rose* and *Les Echecs Amoureux* give him a precedent for his dislike of cosmetics, of

---

[1] On this fashion, see Hammond, *From Chaucer to Surrey*, pp. 110–11.

'papphing' and 'windring', and he expresses it in *How a Lover* (ll. 330–1; cf. the approval of unpainted nails, l. 408); and in *Reson and Sensuallyte* (l. 1368) he praises Nature, who 'neded noght to papphe hir face'. A lyric discussed later suggests another reason for disliking the 'horn'; its wearer could adjust its veils so as to conceal her face from her lover (see below, No. 105).

No. 35*b*. A longish poem in MS. Ashmole 48, fol. 88–90 v., is in praise of women, often with some ambiguity.

> *Incipit.* When the wyntar wynddys ar vanished away
>   Then the byttar blastes be ovar blowe.
> *Explicit (and refrain).*
>   For all the falsshede that man can comprehende
>   Fyrst sprang owt of a womans truthe.
>   Finis quod Johan Walles

It is in ten stanzas of twelve lines of uneven length, with a good deal of alliteration ('flowars florisshing'; 'Joconde and jollye, jenttele and goode'), and with an unusual rhyme scheme (abababababcdcd) which suggests a curtailed sonnet. In each stanza the last two lines form the refrain, with variation of the second half of line 11. The poem is printed in T. Wright's *Songs and Ballads*, pp. 145–9 (Roxburghe Club, 1860). John Wallis, probably a professional, contributes several poems to this Tudor collection of minstrels' material. I had been prepared to find that he or another had added stt. 8 and 9 with their unusual allusions to 'Cocke Lorrels bote', 'Sknoballys chyldren', 'the viij. chapter of Isopes fables', and 'blessyde sent Renolde'; but the anagram (of Lady Scales's name) continues through these stanzas unimpaired. The reference to 'the chanche of dyce' (st. 3) is in line with Roos's later game-poem. The writer declares in st. 5, 'We nede no auctors here in this matter', but later he has recourse to 'good auctors in bookys and in tables', 'our holly fathars', and Esop (st. 9). Cock Lorel's boat is not, I believe, known to us before the poem printed by Wynkyn de Worde (1510); it would be interesting if it can be found to precede Brant's *Narrenschiff* as a conception of a crew of fools.

The reference in the anagrams to Jacquetta of Bedford gives us her first marriage on April 20, 1433, as an upward date for the poem; the inclusion of Anne of Woodstock (Stafford, Bourchier, Eu) gives as the downward limit October 1438. The anagram is a full Plesaunce 'braid', and adds Eleanor Beauchamp:

Stt. 1–2, A–IAn; AnTI–On.; MA–D STAn–OP WI–OBI.
Stt. 2–3, B–WMO–T, P—LIP, BAR–O–F; JA– – –TTA Be–For–.

St. 4, YSMAnYA S-Al--; BABThO.; ForF-IT.

Stt. 4-5, E-ISABETh. stt. 5-6, AlIAn.BEAS--M.

St. 6, AN -TAFFOr.; EV; BO.

St. 7, AnTYGON.; ISMAn. st. 8, SCA(L)-(S); ForF-YT.

Stt. 8-9, WHA(L)(IS)BO(R)O--H.; TOT ForFAYT.

St. 10, MA-D STAnHOP. stt. 9-10, WILOBY; TOT ForFAYT For---T.

VII. PLESAUNCE REVELLING

Poems of spring and summer rejoicing, such as *How a Lover*, would not be the only call on Sir Richard's talent for easy versifying. Revels and pastimes at all seasons, especially at Christmas and Twelfth Night, would offer opportunities of a different kind. Two such poems, half guessing game, half personal reference, whether flattering or satirical, are, I believe, by Roos. He would probably be conversant with some of the rhyming games of this long tradition, such as Christine de Pisan's pretty rhymes for a pedlar of love; in these *Jeux à vendre*[1] the objects for sale may be useful like woollen gloves, or abstract like 'Du pré d'Amour l'usage', or symbolic like 'La fleur d'ancolie', or heraldic like 'le cerf volant', these last doubtless directed at certain individuals. In *Les Vœux du Paon*, though not now in the copy that bears Roos's signature (MS. Add. 30864), the company plays the game of 'Le Roi qui ne Ment', a 'society game cleverly combined with intrigue', as it has been described.[2] Crowning their chosen king (or queen) with a diadem of rushes, the players submit to the chartered libertinage of his 'demandes d'amour',[3] and in their turn subject him to the same ordeal. Within the game, the knights offer themselves to the ladies, who, as in a cotillion, are free to accept or refuse. The licensed freedom of frank criticism, the home-thrusts getting between the joints in the armour of rank, reputation, or self-complacency, all these are a boon to a close society. The more piquant the allusions and descriptions, the greater the fillip given to the success of the revel.

Two poems, *Ragman Roll* and, later, *The Chance of the Dice*, are, I believe, Roos's contribution to this tradition, and to the gaiety of Plesaunce, and of the Lancastrian court. Neither poem is 'signed', but the overlapping of some characters points to the one poet for both; and the style of *The Chance of the Dice* especially is markedly Roos's. Finally the anagrams, with the 'devise', confirm his authorship; and he

---

[1] Ed. M. Roy, S.A.T.F., I, 187-205 (1886).

[2] *Hist. litt. de la France des Bénédictins*, 36, p. 8 (Paris, 1927).

[3] How libertine the 'demandes' could be is shown in Jean de Condé's *Li Sentiers Batus* (ed. Schéler, II, 299-303).

has shown elsewhere full command of the two stanza forms. *Ragman Roll* is confined to a small company of twenty-three women, is rather stiffly written as if it were a first essay in this kind, and is mechanically constructed, with a regular alternation of complimentary and uncomplimentary portraits. *The Chance of the Dice* is much more ambitious in range. The two poems have hitherto been taken to represent type-characters; in spite of the exigencies of the game, the stanzas will be seen to portray individuals. The applications in *Ragman Roll* could conceivably be 'cooked', with its drawing out of little rolls, like cracker-mottoes, or forfeits.[1] It is not so easy to see how the fall of the dice could be manipulated, yet it is there that the descriptions are more markedly idiosyncratic. Roos proves himself capable of the compression of the one-stanza portrait. A common method is to display the subject not only as a person, but also as a member of a group, by showing his or her effect on others.

No. 36. *Ragman Roll:* a poem in twenty-six eight-line stanzas of which the first three form the writer's address to the company; the remaining twenty-three are feminine characters.

> *Incipit.*   My ladyes and my maistresses echone
> Lyke hit vnto your humbylle wommanhede
> *Explicit.* And sythen ye be so jocunde and so good
> And in the rolle last as in wrytynge,
> I rede that this game ende in your hood.
> Explicit Ragman roelle.

The poem is not 'signed'. There are two manuscripts: MS. Fairfax 16 (fol. 214 v.–218 v.) where it precedes *La Belle Dame*, and from which Wright printed it in *Anecdota Literaria* (pp. 83–8); and Bodleian 638 (Astley's manuscript) where it precedes *The Temple of Glas*. These are sister manuscripts, both important for Roos. They are connected with the Household rather than with Gloucester's Plesaunce; yet the poem is of this early period. It was presumably meant to enliven some occasion as purely feminine as was *The Isle of Ladies*; the characters are mostly drawn with more general strokes than are the later portraits of *The Chance of the Dice*.

The anagram of the three introductory stanzas helps to date the poem: HOMFR–Y; ALYAn COB–AM; ANTI–O. POWY–; ARTV–; STAFFOrd; KATh whIT.; AY FOr–AY–. Antigone became Lady Powys in 1435/6; Lady

---

[1] A. Långfors, *Un jeu de société du Moyen Age*, '*Ragemon le Bon*', Helsingfors, 1920. Reviewed by G. Huet in *Le Moyen Age*, 1921, XXXII, 185–6. A twentieth-century daughter of Belvoir has recounted how she benefited from a 'cooked' drawing of lots.

Stafford died in October 1438; the occasion of the poem lies between these dates. Yet in spite of the introduction, only one of the characters (st. 12) is attached to the family at Plesaunce. Perhaps they kept their state, and allowed Lady Beaumont to be the chief lady of the revel. The first character begins in high style:

> O worlde thogh thou be large in circuyt
> Within thy bowndes nys ther creature . . .
> As this lady. (st. 4)

It is plainly meant for the poet's chief lady; in shape and beauty she is Nature's pattern. This non-pareil is E--SABeTH BeW-ON-. By the antithetical arrangement, the next character is one so unlovely as to be a fit mate for the fiend. The third is charming, but too much controlled by Daunger; the fourth, a winebibber, is too 'fre and lyberalle'. Stanza 8 praises a faithful home-keeping wife, who is content to grow old gracefully; she is An STAFFor-, IU. The next stanza depicts a hideous hag, 'longe sydyde as a loppe', who dances determinedly at every revel. The lady of st. 10 defends 'the digne and puyr estat of virgynite' against the snares of the fiend; her contrast is a flatterer of all kinds of men. The twelfth stanza paints a golden girl, like the lady of *How a Lover*, whose sun-like beauty fills all men with gladness. And so the contrasted pairs continue, with an increasing tendency to start the satirical stanza with an apparent compliment:

> O constaunt womane, stabill as the mone (st. 15);
> O fayr lady, hewyd as ys the geet (st. 21).

The last lady, graceful in dance and song, and true in love, is joyfully hailed as the fitting conclusion of the game.

As far as I know, no lists of the Duchess's household exist, as they do of Queen Margaret's, and many identifications of the anagrams are necessarily conjectural, even for the good characters; the bad, who are probably also of inferior rank, are less likely to be recoverable. Some, however, are fairly clear. Lady Scales (*née* Whalesborough) is the loving, constant wife of st. 14: ISMAn.S-A-S, WHA---O-O; and also the lady under Daunger of st. 6: YSMAny SC. Roos's sister-in-law is the well-bred lady, slow to think evil, of st. 16: A-YAN.B-WFOrT. In st. 22 he presents two bouquets at once, in the one character of the lady generous and benign, to JOAn BARD--F, and An COBH., the two sisters, Lady Bardolf and Lady Cobham, mother and aunt of his Lady Bounte. The lady of st. 18, endowed by Mercury with eloquence, is Maud Stanhope (MAW.STAnH.) as she will be again in *The Chance of the Dice*, st. 12. The benevolent and highborn lady is Anne Montague (AnNe

N

MONTA--W, 24) for whom Roos will later write a poem (see below, No. 77). The lady of st. 9, aged but skittish, appears to be a Willoughby (WY--UHBY; AY FOrFAY.), probably Lord Willoughby's first wife, Elisabeth Montacute; the too easily pleased lady of st. 11 looks like a Knollys (KnOLYS; FOrF--T FOrF--T)—Sir Robert Knollys of Sculthorpe had dealings with the Duke.[1] The modest girl of st. 10 seems to be EL–SABETh –OBHA–; FOrF--T; Elisabeth, younger sister of the Duchess, will be met again later, in a somewhat different character. The golden girl of st. 12 is again, as in *How a Lover*, AnTI(G)–NA --WIS. There is a Jaquetta in the *Roll*, a lively demure soubrette, obviously of lower rank than the Duchess of Bedford (st. 17, JAQU–TTA), possibly Jaquetta Stanlow who will turn up in the queen's Household later. The glutton of st. 23 might be ALYAN.SWYN---TUN (with a pun on the name); and in st. 21, the swarthy dame might be a WORMIN–TON; the circumspect, distrustful lady of st. 20 might be a NAnFAnT; but of these I have no explanation. The last charming girl (st. 26) is IOAN F–SLOWES; she will have Fitzlowes kinswomen at the queen's court. Finally the picture of the termagaunt (st. 19) amusingly suggests that KATH. WHYT–YN–H., so often coupled in these poems with Lady Beaumont, was not only *dame de compagnie*, but also duenna and dragon.

The poet professes himself to be merely the instrument of destiny:

> Kynge ragman me bad sowe in brede
> And cristyned yt the merour of your chaunce.
> Drawith a strynge, and that shal streight yow leyde
> Vnto the verry path of your governaunce.

Like Malvolio, he asserts that 'all is fortune': 'Pray hir of helpe, ye hange in her balaunce' (but the anagrams belie him). He will be delighted if they are lucky; and is probably sincere in protesting, 'For ay lest ye mysdrawn I me drede'; Alain Chartier had experienced the wrath of court-ladies affronted.

No. 37. An entertainment of a very different character, 'moral, plesaunt, and notable', was provided by Roos for a Christmas in London: 'þe deuyse of a desguysing to fore þe gret estates of þis lande', known now as *A Mumming at London*.

> *Incipit.* Loo here þis lady þat yee may see,
> Lady of mutabilytee.
> *Explicit.* Lat Fortune go pley hir wher hir list.

It is a dramatic poem of 342 lines in octosyllabic couplets, to accompany the entry of Lady Fortune, and of her four opponents, the ladies

---

[1] Vickers, p. 315.

Prudence, Rightwysnesse, Fortitudo (or Magnyfysence), and Attemperaunce. There are two manuscripts, both attributing it to Lydgate, Trin. Coll., Camb., R. 3.20 (a Shirley manuscript), and Stow's manuscript, Add. 29729, a collection of Lydgate's didactic poetry, but containing *Reson and Sensuallyte*, also Roos's. Sieper noted (*R. and S.*, p. xvii) that the 'desguysing' was not only in the same metre as the translated poem, but also very much resembled it in other respects. Brusendorff (p. 389) thought that Lydgate must have had access to a part of the translation of *Le Roman de la Rose* (see below, No. 60). Neither noticed the equally plain parallels with *The Isle of Ladies*. Lydgate's authorship, stated by Ritson, and apparently confirmed by the manuscripts, has been unquestioned (MacCracken, pp. 682–91). The anagrams, with the 'devise', indicate Roos as the author.

The anagrams are unusually interesting. I had expected to find the five allegorical figures yielding the names of the ladies impersonating them; this would have been a pleasant indication that Anne of Denmark was not the first great lady to participate in court pageants. But the many names in each figure point away from individual impersonators, and give instead examples of men (and women) either embodying the virtues, or experiencing the caprices of Fortune. The references, laudatory or otherwise, have historical and political rather than courtly interest. The anagrams of the descriptive introduction on Fortune begin with the ladies of Plesaunce, and then, with the classical examples of her victims, Julius Caesar, Gyges, and Croesus, shift to satiric interpretation. Prudence, with her power to control past, present, and future 'by goode avysement', yields the names of financial officials of Gloucester's party; Righteousness, who is Justice with her balances, covers a list of judges past and present; Fortitude, or Magnificence, openly refers to 'prynces of latter date' (266) fit to be set beside the Nine Worthies, and especially to Harry the Fifth; accordingly the passage encloses the names of nine great soldiers of the time; only in Attemperaunce, 'Humble, debonayre and sadde of cheer' (282), do the names of the Plesaunce ladies recur; and the poem ends with the ducal pair, and the promise of a prosperous year brought by the four Ladies' sojourn in the household; the 'disguising' closes with a new song (unfortunately not given) sung round the fire, the singer being Antigone.

These anagrams run as follows:

Ll. 1–66, Fortune and her ambivalent dwelling: SCAYL–S, WHAL–––
––OR––H; MAVD STAnHO., WILL.; FOrFAIT; ISMAn–A; B–WMOnT,
BA–DOLF; COB–AM; B–AVFORT; ISMANIA SCA–IS, WHA–ESBOROVH.

Ll. 67–80, Julius Caesar's life and death: IOH. A(R)Vn–EL, TOV–AIn; MAU. STAFF.

Ll. 81–93, the two tuns: CHA. DOR–EAnS; FOrFAIT.

Ll. 94–101, Gyges: FAW–OMBE–(G). ? ASHFOrTH.

Ll. 102–32, Croesus and his daughter: CA–D(I)NAL HeNRY B–AVFO–T; (I)OAn STRADLY-G, A–VnDE.

Ll. 139–72, Prudence: SCRO(P); BARDOL(F), (P)HE–I(P); CHAWO–TH; BABTHOR(P); TOT FOrFA–T.

Ll. 172–220, Righteousness: WIL––AM GAS–OIN; –OHAN FOrTES––W; WM. BABYNTON; N–CHO–A– WIMBISH; R. NEWTON; IOHN HODI.

Ll. 221–80, Fortitude: B–A–ShAM, WArWIC; TOT FOrFAIT FOrFAIT; TAlBOT; HO––AND, EXceST–R, SOM––S–T; (P)LAnTAge––T; B–WFOrT; FAn(H)OP; HOMFRI; IOHAn BeDFOr.; A(R)Vn–EL.

Ll. 281–310, Attemperaunce: IS–AnYA S(C)ALIS; PHELi.; An. STAFFOrD; HOl–AnD; –AVD STAnH.

Ll. 311–19, Summing up. WhA–ISBOrO; (P)HI–I(P).

Ll. 319–32, the conditional promise of prosperity: HOMF(R)Y; AlIAN. –OBHAM; AnTI––NA; FOrFA–T.

Ll. 333–42, Conclusion with a song: An–IG. P–WYS; S–ALES.

Some of these names are novel in Roos's anagrams, and mark the special occasion. John, Earl of Arundel (made Duke of Touraine in 1434), had ended a brilliant career by dying a prisoner in French hands on June 14, 1435; his widow Maud, formerly Lady Stafford, survived him less than a year. She was the Lady Beauty to whom Charles d'Orléans devoted his early French poems, hence the introduction of his name in the succeeding passage; Charles, as Duke, and then as prisoner for twenty-five years, had indeed tasted of both sour and sweet. Roos will often satirize Lord Fawcomberg; but nowhere else, as here on Gyges, is there the charge of murder implied against him. The residue of letters might form 'Ashforth'; I have no explanation. Roos will again make the wealthy Cardinal Beaufort the target for his satire, and the subject of his narrative; the story of his natural daughter, Joan Stradling, *née* Arundel, is told fully below (see No. 76).

With Lady Prudence, Roos celebrates three of Gloucester's nominees in the political coup of 1432; Lord Scrope of Masham, who was made Treasurer; Sir William Phelip, Lord Bardolf, father of Lady Beaumont, who became Chamberlain; and Sir Robert Babthorp, who was made Steward of the Household, as he had been under Henry V. Sir Thomas Chaworth of Wiverton had no official post, but as a prominent land-owner in Nottinghamshire, he was a member of commissions to raise loans for the king, and himself once contributed £40; hence probably his inclusion among the financially prudent.[1] Also he was father-in-law to Lord Scrope.[2]

The concealed roll-call of upright judges begins with the incorruptible William Gascoigne; the tradition of the episode with Prince Hal may well have descended in the Roos family from Lord William, associated with Gascoigne over the Scots prisoners (see above, Chapter I).[3] John Fortescue was beginning to make his name, and in 1440 he supported Duke Humphrey against Cardinal Beaufort.[4] When Sir John Hodi died in December–January 1441–2, Fortescue immediately succeeded him as Chief Justice of the King's Bench. William Babington retired on the score of age in 1436 from being Chief Justice of the Common Bench, though he lived for nearly twenty years more. Richard Newton was made Chief of the Common Pleas in 1439.[5] Nicholas Wimbish, often mentioned in Plesaunce poems, was Master in Chancery, 1424–51.[6]

With Fortitude we are warned to expect nine great soldiers, 'modern instances'. The first is the father-in-law of John, Lord Roos, Richard Beauchamp, Earl of Warwick (d. 1439). Beauforts figure largely; Thomas Beaufort, Duke of Exeter (d. 1426/7); John Beaufort, Earl of Somerset; and another Beaufort (as Hector), probably the Count of Mortain, the 'Black Knight'. Sir Richard Roos had been under Talbot at Gisors in 1436; Lord Fanhope, long retired from fighting, was one of the keepers of Charles d'Orléans; Lord Arundel, 'the English Achilles', recurs; Holland may be that John Holland, Duke of Exeter, for whose third wife Roos will later write a poem (see below, No. 77). Finally the two Plantagenet dukes, Bedford and Gloucester, are signalized. The equating of Fortitude with the philosophers' virtue of Magnificence is unexpected. Reference is made to the steadfastness of Plato and Socrates, but not to Aristotle; yet the description of her labours, 'For to maynteyne þe goode comune', and her undertaking of great emprises (ll. 231–9) is reminiscent of Aristotle's Magnificence in the *Ethics* (IV, iii). One should remember that Duke Humphrey admired (1433) Leonardo Bruni's Latin translation of the *Ethics*, and asked him to translate the *Politics*: also that in 1437 Frulovisi, Italian secretary to the Duke, was

---

[1] *Cal. Pat. Rolls, 1429–36*, pp. 467, 126, 529.

[2] Thoroton, *Nottinghamshire*, I, 198.

[3] The friendship between the Roos and Gascoigne families appears in the will of the judge's brother, Richard, Feb. 3, 1422. He left money for prayers for the souls of Lord Thomas and Lady Beatrice de Ros (*Test. Ebor.*, I, 403, No. 286).

[4] Plummer, *Fortescue*, p. 134.

[5] For these names see Foss, *Judges of England* IV, 163–70 and 283–349.

[6] *Ib.*, IV, 222.

engaged in writing for him his *Vita Henrici Quinti,* in glorification of
Henry's French wars, and therefore of the Duke's policy.[1]

The comely and sober virtue, Attemperaunce or Moderation, brings
back at first Roos's best friends among the Plesaunce ladies. When the
strong protective powers of the four Virtues are invoked, the naming
of the Gloucester family is clear; the injunction to avoid Fortune's
'double varyaunce' must be an intentional warning, the poet attaching
his 'devise' by way of signature. Then the tone relaxes for the cheerful
conclusion, and the promise of a song inevitably brings in Antigone,
now Lady Powys. Her name and that of Lady Stafford help to date
the poem closely; her marriage took place 1435-6, and Lady Stafford
died on October 16, 1438. The Christmas festivities of 1436 or 1437
seem to be indicated.

Sir Richard Roos, faced, possibly at short notice, with the writing of
the libretto for a disguising, had recourse to Jean de Meun's description
of Fortune in *Le Roman de la Rose.* It is derived from the *Anticlaudianus*
of Alain de L'Isle, but Roos is verbally indebted to the French (e.g. l. 47,
'Daubed of clay is that doungeoun'; cf. 'D'autre part sont li mur de boe',
Roman, l. 6106; and contrast the more generalized *vili materie* of
Anticlaudianus). The whole passage proves that Roos's acquaintance
with de Meun's work went beyond the point at which Fragment B of
the translated *Romaunt* stopped (see below, Nos. 60 and 102). Roos
turns the barren rock in the sea to account also in *The Isle of Ladies.*
His addition of bird-song (ll. 20-3; 34) to the flowers and trees of de
Meun is in tune with his bird poems (see below, Nos. 68 and 103).
Obviously the poem was spoken and visually presented and Roos skilfully varies the substance and tone of the verse, shifting from description
to story, from didactics to the classical *exemplum* and the modern
instance, knitting up the whole with the final blessing (like Puck's) on
the household, and the song by the fire. Fortune is vigorously defied.
And when later the copy was in the Duchess's hands, the ladies of
Plesaunce would be kept busy and amused till Twelfth Night working
out the anagrams.

VIII. THE DUCHESS OF GLOUCESTER

It is not likely that this poet of the Plesaunce circle could or would
neglect the claims of its mistress, his kinswoman, the Duchess. The
Duke's name and hers have been found in the anagrams of the majority
of the poems concerning Elisabeth Beaumont. There is at least one

[1] R. Weiss, *Humanism in England,* pp. 47, 42-3.

poem addressed directly though not solely, to her, 'Womanly Noblesse'.
Another allows of some conjecture as to the poet's intercourse with her;
one of the Complaints in MS. Fairfax 16 seemed to point to a period of
coolness and disfavour, and there is another here, 'O Mestres whye
Owtecaste am I?' The poet, who has profited by this atmosphere of
modernity and culture enough to cut away the crudities of his alliterative
style, would have suffered in every way by exclusion from Plesaunce.
Translations from the French undertaken at this period may well have
been suggested by these patrons; one indeed, *La Belle Dame*, was written
at their instance.

No. 38. *Womanly Noblesse* (Skeat's title, taken from l. 24, *Chaucer*, IV,
25) or, *Balade that Chaucier made* (MS. heading): A balade of three nine-
line stanzas rhyming aab aab bab; the a and b rhymes are identical
throughout (-aunce and -esse). *Lenvoye* of six lines ('Auctour of norture,
lady of plesaunce') introduces a third rhyme (acacaa), but in the final
couplet repeats the opening lines of the poem. Line 5 of st. 2 is lacking.

> *Incipit.* So hath myn herte caught in remembraunce
>   Your beautee hoole and stidefaste governaunce
>   Your vertues alle and your hie noblesse.

This *Balade* is known only in MS. Add. 34360, a collection derived
from Shirley. It immediately precedes *The Question of Halsam* [*squire*],
which is also found in full in MS. Fairfax 16 (Carleton Brown, *Religious
Lyrics of the Fifteenth Century*, No. 171). This Halsham may very well
be the John Halsham, Esquire, whose daughter Anne married Sir Robert
Roos in 1433. *Womanly Noblesse* was accepted as Chaucer's by Skeat,
Kittredge, and Robinson; Koch refused to endorse it; Pollard included
it in the Globe Chaucer as 'doubtful'. It would seem very probable
that the experimenter with the metres and effects of Nos. 13 and 69
is also the writer of this unusual stanza of exacting rhyme-structure.
No rhyme comes easier than -aunce to Sir Richard Roos.

The tone of this poem is more weighty, formal, and reserved than is
that of many of these early pieces, and I do not take it for a love-poem.
The first line of *Lenvoye* is, I believe, literally intended, and the poem is
addressed to the 'Lady of Plesaunce', the Duchess of Gloucester, as the
poet's 'auctour of norture' or patroness. The compliments are extreme
to our taste, and the terms are not far from those of a lover; but they
may well apply to the service of a young kinsman, desirous of favour
and patronage from a lady of 'hie noblesse', promising to serve her with
all his 'plesaunce', all his 'besynesse', to conform to her 'ordynaunce'

without 'unbuxumnesse', and in general paying her the flattering homage due from a young knight to the greatest lady in the land. It is to be remarked that in two of the three Ladies' cryptograms, the name of Cleopatra is included, but the initial is not used as if the name were to be isolated, and in *The Flour of Curtesye* she comes next to Antigone. One may guess that Cleopatra was the coterie's name for the mistress of Plesaunce. According to the *Balade* in *The Legend of Good Women*, Cleopatra was celebrated for 'passyoun', 'trouthe of loue', and for 'renoun'. In her 'Legend' the tribute paid to the mutual passion of Antony and Cleopatra (ll. 599–615) expresses the idea familiar later that they counted the world well lost for love. The application to the Duke and Duchess does not seem to be far-fetched (see below, No. 76). These conjectures are confirmed by an unusual anagram. The line-initials of stt. 2 and 3, with two other letters, give ALYAn COBHAM fairly obviously. The caesural initials (and the place of the caesura is never in doubt here) yield the full 'devise'. It seems as if the poet were thrusting the poem on the Duchess's notice. Actually however, the anagram also contains less obviously the names ISMANYA SCALIS and M. STANLOW. Possibly, this, if realized, gave offence to the Duchess. Certainly another poem to be considered shows that offence had been taken.

'Auctour of norture'. The phrase recalls another poem addressed to 'Moder of norture, best beloved of al'. Is this meant for the same 'lady of plesaunce'? Skeat, printing *A Goodly Balade* (*Chaucer*, VII, No. xxii), pointed out that the central section of the poem was addressed to a daisy and that with a little manipulation the stanza initials indicated Ma Dam Jacq. He therefore very plausibly conjectured a Margaret Jacques as the lady of the poem. For long I accepted this[1] (though puzzled by the strong Roos echoes in the phrasing); but the double anagrams of the poem draw a very different picture, forming a Plesaunce 'braid' plaited with some care through the stanzas. A reconsideration of the poem is needed.

No. 39. *A Goodly Balade:* a triple balade in rhyme royal with Envoy; the sixth stanza is lost. The first and third Balades have refrains; the two remaining stanzas of the second have only a half-line repeated.

---

[1] Among the many Jacques or Jakes of the Midland and East Anglian counties there are two Margaret Jacques, the widow and the daughter of John Jakes, gentleman, of Ashen, Essex, who, dying in Oct. 1438, left his daughter Margaret twenty marks to her dowry (P.C.C. Wills, 25 Luffenham).

Incipit. Moder of norture, best beloved of al
And fresshest flour to whom good thrift god sende.
Your child, if it list you me so to cal.
Explicit. Now forth; I close thee, in holy Venus name.
Thee shal unclose my hertes governeresse.

No manuscript is known, and the sole authority is Thynne (1532), who attributed it to Chaucer. Skeat called it 'manifestly Lydgate's'; but MacCracken (*Minor Poems*, I, xlix) with remarkable prescience denies it to him, and says 'it might have been written by any one of the Chaucerian school, the poet of MS. Fairfax 16, for example'. There is no 'signature', though the phrase 'anon it ryseth', or 'roseth' (Skeat's emendation, l. 59), gives one pause; the 'devise' occurs in the Envoy. The anagrams yield: stt. 1–2, H–MF--Y; AlIAn; stt. 1, 2, and 5, COBHAM; st. 2, ISMANYA: st. 3, WYMBIS; stt. 3–4, BA–DO–F; stt. 4–5, B–WMONT; stt. 5–8, PHY–YP; stt. 7–8, E–ISABETh; ANTIG.; stt. 8–9, IAQu–TT. BEDFOrD; st. 9, ISMANYA; Envoy, TOT FOrFAIT FOr–AIT.

The person addressed in the first balade is manifestly the Duchess; the poet calls himself her 'child', and the stress is on 'governaunce'; so too the envoy, which contains the 'devise', sends the poem to 'my hertes governeresse'. Is it possible that after the death of Margaret, Lord William Roos's widow (July 1438), the Duchess had promised 'to be a mother' to her young kinsman? It may be suggested that this reference lies beneath the central balade to the 'Daisy of light, very ground of comfort'. There was no Margaret in the Pleasaunce circle; nor need there have been any exact allusion. But if one observes the elegiac undertone of Balade ii, and the resignation of the opening of Balade iii, one wonders if they reflect emotions rising from the illness and death of the poet's mother, and this in spite of their containing the 'Elisabeth' anagrams. The daisy, 'my lyves lady dere', closes with the setting sun, and misty clouds oppress true, humble hearts; but may she 'disclose and sprede'. Here the lack of the sixth stanza is deplorable. The third balade begins with a sigh cut short, and with pious reflections:

> *Je vouldray:*—but gret god disposeth
> And maketh casuel by his providence
> Such thing as mannes frele wit purposeth;
> Al for the best, if that our conscience
> Nat grucche it, but in humble pacience
> It receyve.

I interpret this poem therefore as referring to the death of Sir Richard's mother, the only Margaret so far at the heart of his life, and as addressed to his friends of the Pleasaunce circle, the Duke, Antigone, Lady Beaumont, Lady Scales, and above all the Duchess, to whose service his good will 'fayn wolde entende'. But he fears that his writing is more acceptable than his presence:

> What ye said ones, myn herte opposeth,
> 'That my wryting japes, in your absence
> Plesed you moche bet than my presence'.

The French phrase, *Mieulx un*, which recalls Roos's motto, *A moi le mieulx*, may be a complimentary fusion of that and the Duchess's *Al en un*.

No. 40. 'O Mestres whye Owtecaste am I': a lyric of four eight-line stanzas of four-syllable lines (aaabaaab or aaabcccb). It has been printed frequently, in *Reliquiae Antiquae*, I, 255–6, in Fluegel, *Neu-engl. Lesebuch*, p. 140, in Chambers and Sidgwick, *Early Eng. Lyrics*, p. 76, in Robbins, *Secular Lyrics*, no. 137.

The only manuscript is Harleian 2252, which was owned by a London merchant in the time of Henry VIII. The single acrostic anagram of the short lines reads: stt. 1–2, HOMFr–Y, AlYAn; –OOS; stt. 2–4, BABThor.; and diffused, TOT FOr–AIT. It looks as if the poet thinks of being outcast from Plesaunce the place, as well as from the favour. The third stanza has a rather puzzling allusion: the lady is as strange and haughty as if she possessed

> þat nobylnes
> To be dochess
> Of grete Savoy.

Amadeus of Savoy, Burgundy's ally, had in 1435 tried to marry his widowed daughter Margaret to the widower Charles d'Orléans; his wife, Marie of Burgundy, was niece of John of Bedford's first wife. The names would therefore have been perfectly familiar to Roos; but this hardly explains the slightly acid flavour of the stanza. It looks like a hint at the pretensions of the Duchess of Gloucester; after all she was not the consort of a duke regnant, but only the wife of the king's uncle. Possibly her associates knew of what Shakespeare was later to call her 'canker of ambitious thoughts'.

Roos probably changed his *venue* from Plesaunce to the young king's court after Eleanor Cobham's fall in the autumn and winter of 1441 —perhaps even before that. But he does not forget Plesaunce. He would indeed have been hard of heart, if he had left this reversal of fortune unsung. Many poems, several in MS. Ff. 1.6, are written about this event, most of them dramatically, as if spoken in lament by the Duke, or more often by the Duchess. Some are devout prayers. The anagrams enable us to divide these poems into two periods: a few belong to the 1440s, but the greater number, by introducing the name of Antigone's second husband, prove themselves to be composed after Lord Powys's death in 1450, and before the Duchess's death in 1454. These later poems will be discussed in Chapter IX; three of the early poems are in MS. Ff. 1.6 ('the Roos scrap-book'), and nowhere else.

No. 41*a*.

> *Incipit.* I may well sygh, for greuous ys my payne.
> *Explicit.* Wyth alle my myght to be bothe true & playn—
> Alas for woo, departynge hath me slayn.

The poem (MS. Ff. 1.6, fol. 20) is in three stanzas of rhyme royal, with a refrain; it is so printed by Robbins (*Secular Lyrics*, No. 169). Miss Hammond (*Chaucer Bibliography*, p. 344) attaches to it two and a half stanzas which appear to run straight on, but they are part of an 'Elisabeth' poem (see above, No. 16*g*). The speaker, in a heavily burdened tone, takes farewell of 'my myrthe & chefe of my comfort', 'lady souerayn'. He will take their misfortune 'ryght pacyently', and will never change. The anagram is rather unusual: H–MFR–Y; MADA. ALYAn. MA FAM.; ANTIG.; TOT FOrFAY– FOrFAY–.

No. 41*b*.

> *Incipit.* Most glorius quene, Reynyng yn hevene.
> *Explicit.* Torne all my woo into Ioy and gladnesse.

The poem (MS. Ff. 1.6, fol. 146) consists of three stanzas of rhyme royal; it is printed by Carleton Brown in *Religious Lyrics*, No. 32, and entitled *An Orison to Our Lady by the Seven Joys*. A dignified devotional poem, it pleads for comfort and mercy for one 'that lythe in grete dystresse', in a case where 'mane can schape no remedy'. The line-initials of st. 3 form HOMFR–Y with a little rearrangement and one caesural initial, and the double acrostic anagram yields: AlIAN. C–BHAM; ANTI. POWYS; TOT FOrF–YT. It is the most affecting of the three poems.

No. 41*c*.

> *Incipit.* A mercy, fortune, haue pitee on me.
> *Explicit.* Then torne thy whele and be my frynde agayn
> And sende me Ioy where I am nowe in payn.

The poem (MS. Ff. 1.6, fol. 178) is in three stanzas of rhyme royal with a couplet refrain; it is printed in Carleton Brown's *Religious Lyrics*, No. 170. The speaker protests innocence of offence, and deplores the dividing 'Of ij trewe hertis louyng feithfully'. The anagram is skeletal, but is supported by the suggestion ('Alwey in on') of Eleanor's motto, 'Al en un'; HO–FR.; ALIAn. –O–HA–; ANT.; AI TOT FOR–AIT.

Three poems I have from their contents and their anagrams assigned to the autumn of 1441, while the issue of the charges brought against Eleanor Cobham was yet unknown.

No. 42*a*.

> *Incipit.* My ryght good lord, most knyghtly gentyll knyght.
> *Explicit* (st. 8 as in MS.)
>> For all good cher on evyn and on morow
>> Wyche then was made now tornyth me to sorow.
> *Explicit as rearranged* (st. 6 of MS.)
>> And to yow trew as evyr was hert and pleyn
>> Tyll cruell dethe depart yt vp on tweyn.

The poem, of eight stanzas of rhyme royal, is known only from the collection of the Paston Letters (Add. MS. 43491, fol. 27–27 v., much corrected; ed. Gairdner, 1875, III, pp. 302–3, No. 870). It has no title; its first editor, Fenn, called it, 'Verses written by a Lady in the reign of Henry VI or Edward IV to an absent Lord with whom she was in love'. This describes the substance. The writer has no 'lycence' to address his lordship, but like a sick man taking the nearest way to his cure and balanced between life, death, and desire, she longs for his presence as the only remedy (stt. 1–4). She remembers disports and pleasures past, the knights at the archery or at the 'Paame', the ladies in their wonted walks; now all is deserted (stt. 7–8). She bids farewell, envying her 'rude byll' for coming to her lord before she can; she commits it and her service to him, protesting her fidelity till death (stt. 5–6).

The poem is a verse-letter, but the form is obscured by its wrong order; when rearranged, with stt. 7 and 8 following the opening stt. 1–4, and with the farewell of stt. 5–6 transferred to its proper place, the end, its conformity to the typical verse-letter is seen (cf. below Nos. 99*a* and *b*.)

The anagram is clear enough in the printed form, but the names run more smoothly in the rearranged stanzas:

Stt. 1–2, HOMF(R)I; A–IAn. COB–AM; ANTIGONA. Stt. 2–3, MAWD STAnH. St. 3, WIMBIS. Stt. 3–4, ISM–N. Stt. 4 and 7–8, wHA––-BOrO., S–ALeS. Stt. 5 and 8, E–IS–(B)–Th BEWMONT. St. 6, STIWA–D. Stt. 4 and 7, FOrFAIT FOrf–IT. Stt. 5 and 8, TOT FOrFAIT FOr–A–T.

These familiar names, together with the sorrow for enforced absence and the entreaty to be visited, and with the regrets for the former pleasures of a social group (cf. 'For lac of sighte', No. 3), point to the changed circumstances of Eleanor Cobham in 1441. Yet there is neither personal anxiety nor the note of despairing penitence, voiced in the next poem to be considered. This points to a date fairly early in her imprisonment, possibly near to 25 July, her first examination. She spent most of the following months at Leeds Castle, in the charge of Sir John Stiward.

The expressions of the poem are possible to Sir Richard Roos, though not strikingly so. The image of sickness, and of the cure to be found only in the loved one's presence, is frequent in all this poetry. So too is the complaint of absence; and for the exclamation, 'O owght on . . .', cf. No. 62 below, ll. 561–3. The phrase 'Tyll cruell dethe depart' is common, both as Lady Talbot's 'raison', and as a typical sentiment. The words 'by aventure' in the middle of the Gloucester family's anagram are reminiscent of one of Duke Humphrey's mottoes, 'In Good Aventure'; and for the rhyme 'aventure: cuyre', cf. No. 79 below, ll. 589–90. For 'empryse' here and for 'presumptuousnesse' cf. *The Black Knight* (No. 43), ll. 416 and 429 (presumpcioun). The reference to the walks frequented by ladies and knights reminds one of *How a Lover* (No. 1), and the later *Assembly of Ladies* (No. 70); and the mention of the 'Paame' play (Jeu de Paume) will recur much later (see below, p. 501). The dramatic writing as by a woman is frequent in these poems, especially for Eleanor Cobham (see below, Chapters IX and XII); and several such lyrics occur in MS. Ff. 1.6, the 'Roos scrapbook'.

This would seem to be a sufficient explanation of the poem, in line with many other 'Plesaunce' poems. There is, however, an unusual circumstance which complicates the issue. This is the only fifteenth-century manuscript in this 'Corpus' which has all the appearance of being an author's draft.[1] There are many corrections, all in the same hand as the poem itself, some apparently made *currente calamo*, some affecting whole or half lines. A superficial conclusion would be that this is a sheet of Sir Richard Roos's own composition (and we know of his redrafting his poems), strayed somehow among the Paston papers. The point of contact might lie in Anne Beaufort, daughter of Roos's sister-in-law Eleanor, and wife before 1470 to William Paston, the Judge's son. The obstacle to this conclusion is the identification of this sheet as a holograph of John Paston the youngest, a prolific letter-

---

[1] For this information, and for the loan of a reproduction of the manuscript, I am indebted to the kindness of Professor Norman Davis.

writer, who wrote (says Professor Norman Davis) a characteristic and easily recognizable hand. Of Roos's handwriting, on the other hand, we have at present only formal specimens, signatures or short inscriptions, and nothing of a cursive or casual character. There appear then to be two conflicting forms of evidence, the only occasion in Roos's lifetime that a clash so direct is found.

There is, however, a possible explanation, in line with those poems of later transmission which will be discussed in Chapter XII. There the phenomenon is often seen of a Roos poem being copied out, and then corrected, polished, even adapted by the copyist, who thereupon appears to assume responsibility for the poem, if not to claim authorship (see below, Chapter XII, especially pp. 458-9). The same thing may well have happened here. By some means John Paston had procured a Roos poem written for Eleanor Cobham. Ignorant of the anagrams, and seeing only a poem to hand for his needs, he set about altering it. It is not probable that he meant it for Margery Brewis; more likely it was for his 'Lady', the Duchess of Norfolk, for whom its elevated style and courtly references were suitable. If so, the occasion was probably the absence of the Duke on that expedition to France in June to September 1475, which ended ignominiously in the Treaty of Pecquigny (August 29). The Duke's following, forty men-at-arms, and three hundred archers,[1] was large enough to leave behind a general sense of solitude and dullness.

A reader of the poem, ignorant of the real situation (a woman in prison under a heavy charge, writing to her husband in despair of his coming, and feeling she has outlived the world's joys), could well interpret it more superficially thus: the mistress of a castle, left behind while her husband has gone off with his retinue, writes foolishly and unadvisedly, and complains of the dullness of her life.

Can it be claimed that the corrections aimed at toning down the grief, and adapting the sentiment to this more common situation? The boldness of the writer is originally 'Growndyd on foly, and on Insolence'; this latter phrase is toned down to 'for lak of provydence' (l. 6). The line 'Ryght so I, whyche dayly do endure' becomes the conventional 'And Ryght so I, so it yow not dysplease' (l. 13). The complaint, 'I dyspeyryd am of your heare comyng', not applicable to a soldier on service, becomes 'of your soone metyng' (l. 27). Finally the too poignant line, 'I leefe to long, Alas what remedye', a sentiment paralleled in many Eleanor Cobham poems (see Nos. 42b, st. 4 and 42c), is erased and not

---

[1] Scofield, *Life and Reign of Edward IV*, II, 117.

replaced (st. 7, l. 3 MS.). Thus the general effect of all but the most trivial changes is to lessen the weightiness of the poem.

One may then assume John Paston to be both copyist and corrector; how many of his drafts lay between this manuscript and the original poem we cannot tell. It is remarkable that the anagram is as little affected as it is; but this is often so. In nine lines only out of the fifty-six do the changes affect the line-initial or the caesural initial; thus the (R) of HOMF(R)I is supplied only in the original form of l. 13 'Ryght so I' etc.; but HOMF–I is a form often met with, and the letter R is a letter often avoided in the anagrams. In st. 7, original A, I, and al become I, Al, d; the d is not wanted. Three stanzas (4, 6, 8) are left intact.

I would suggest that the original author of the poem was Sir Richard Roos, writing for Eleanor Cobham in mid-1441; that John Paston thought to please the Duchess of Norfolk in her husband's absence in 1475, and altered the poem chiefly to that end. Whether or when he finished and presented it we do not know; the Duke's sudden death, a few months after his return (Jan. 1475/6), would demand a poem in another tone.

No. 42*b*. A longer, and less known, complaint is more interesting in its anagrams. It is the *Complaint of a Prisoner against Fortune* in twenty-one stanzas of rhyme royal. The plaintiff, suffering in prison, appeals (stt. 1–5) against Fortune, who roundly answers that sin is the cause and that adversity in this world may bring salvation in the next (stt. 6–7). The plaintiff now calls on the three Fates by name, deplores the loss of fame and 'good los', and laments the indifference of former friends (stt. 8–18). The conclusion is a devout prayer to the Blessed Virgin for all Christian souls, for Holy Church, and for the penitent suppliant (stt. 19–21).

> *Incipit.* Fortune alas, alas what haue I gylt
> (*or* Alas Fortune etc.)
> In prison thus to lye here desolate.
> *Explicit.* Now lady swete I can no more now say
> But rew on me, and helpe me when I dey.
> Explicit le compleint again ffortune.

The poem is found in three manuscripts: Add. 34360, fol. 19; Harleian 2251, fol. 271; and Harleian 7333, fol. 30 v. From the last Miss Hammond printed it (*Anglia*, 1909, XXXII, 484–90); it is also in *Originals & Analogues* (Chaucer Soc.), App., pp. i–vi. All three manuscripts have Shirley in their background, and the variants of the text are slight and have very little effect on the anagrams; st. 4 ('Why nad I rather died an Innocent|Or seke in bed ful ofte whan I haue layne', etc.) is found only in Harleian 7333. It is not a highly polished poem; and it has some phrases not common in Roos: two moral Latin lines spoken by Fortune, and somewhat in Lydgate's style; the courtly phrase 'I was . . . in bounchief' (78); and 'I se now at eiȝe' (120). But the phrase 'synke or saile' (84) parallels 'flete or synke' of *The Deth of Pyte* (110). The anagrams run as follows:

Stt. 1–5, the opening complaint: AlIAn.; TOT ForFA–T; ANTI–ONA; IS–AnIA S–ALES; AnTIG.; whA–ESBOrO.; COB.; BO–INB.

Stt. 6–7, Fortune's answer: ChIChE–E; wy–BISH; STEWAd; ?KeMP.

Stt. 8–12, the Destinies: stt. 8–9, BO(L)InB–OC.; stt. 9–12, MA–IOrI IOrDEMAIN.

Stt. 12–14, Desertion by friends: ChETWIN; STANH.; STANLOW; I–MANI; wh(E)ThA–ST.; FO–F–IT.

Stt. 15–16, complaint, AlIAN.; THO–AS S–VThWE––.

Stt. 17–18, MA–IOrY IOV–––MAIn.

Stt. 19–20, Prayer for Holy Church: BOLInB–OK.; TOT ForFA–T.

Stt. 20–21, Prayer to the Virgin: ALIAN. –OBHA–; (ch)I–HeLe.

These names, some of them not occurring elsewhere in the anagrams, are of great interest as suggesting that the poem was written in 1441, during the actual course of the Duchess's trial. Archbishop Chichele, and Kemp,[1] his brother of York, conducted the enquiry, Chichele withdrawing after October 21. Sir John Stiward was Eleanor's first Keeper; and Nicholas Wimbish, her legal friend, may have been one of her realistic advisers.

The introduction furnishes the usual Plesaunce ladies, with the addition of the Duchess's evil genius, Roger Bolingbroke. The very moving stanzas (12–14) on her friends' neglect of the prisoner contrast former approval and flattery with present avoidance:

> Thei wold me onys not yeve a draught of drynke
> Ne say ffrend, wilt þow aught with me.

The names are those of Lady Scales, Maud Stanhope, Margaret Stanlow, and a Chetwynd, who may be Rose Chetwynd, of the queen dowager's household, who in 1437 had married John Merston. Added to these is Whethamstede, Duke Humphrey's well-known friend, the Abbot of St. Albans. I had expected to find the Duke's name at the lines (83–4):

> And he þat seid [he] wold me neuer faile,
> I myght for him [chese to] synke or saile.

---

[1] I am not quite sure of Kemp's name in stt. 6–7; if there, it is partly on Deschamps' method, by reversing the word EKE, a word frequent in this poem.

But the writer has not dared so far. The stanza (15) on Christ's action with the accusers of the woman who 'take was in spouce breche' might suggest a similar charge against Eleanor; but the chroniclers (and there are no documents extant) do not allude to it. This and the following stanzas (15–20) of lament, and of repudiation of Fortune and the Fates, cover the names of the Duchess's three 'familiars'; Thomas Southwell, canon of St. Stephen's, Westminster, Roger Bolingbroke or O(o)nly, an Oxford priest, and Margery Jo(u)rdain or Jourdemain, known as the Witch of Eye, were all to suffer in 1441 the extreme penalty that Eleanor was spared. The phrase (120) 'Ther is no more I se now at ei ʒe', in the witch's anagram, is clearly placed thus emphatically of set purpose. The final submission to Holy Church brings in again the Archbishop's name, and the prisoner's. It is difficult to see the purpose of these names, or to assume that the prelates would be interested in the anagram, or affected by the inclusion of their names. More probably the poem was meant to give the imprisoned Duchess sympathy, and a familiar occupation to relieve her misery and tedium.

No. 42*c*. A third poem is meant chiefly for the Gloucester family.

> *Incipit.* Grevus ys my sorowe
> Both evyne and moro
> *Explicit.* Pray for this ded body
> That your unkyndnes haith slayne
> Finis. Amen.

It is in fourteen stanzas of eight short lines, the fifth line lengthening from six to eight syllables. The fourth line of st. 13 is lacking. The last half of each stanza constitutes an unusually long and variable refrain, though the rhyme-scheme of the whole is unaffected (aabbcdcd). It is found in MS. Sloane 1584, fol. 85, and was printed by Ritson in *Ancient Songs*, p. 171 (1877), and by Halliwell in *Reliquiae Antiquae*, I, 70–3.

There is no mention of prison; the lament is personal, and formally elegiac. The bold charge,

> And he that love[d] me beste
> Hyme selfe my deth haith dreste, (st. 7)

is pointed by preceding the only occurrence in the anagram of 'Humphrey'; the Duke's helplessness in face of the situation has long been remarked. 'Alas, I lyve to longe' is again the sad conviction, and the prisoner is facing death. The poem turns into a 'last wyll' (st. 8), the heart being left to him 'that is my deth', since he is heartless; she begs

o

forgiveness for him. Her tomb is to be in the blue of constancy, and her mourners will sing 'Placebo, dilexi'.

For the anagram, ingenious use is made of the long and changing refrain. In the first stanzas the name Alian. Cobham is repeated very sketchily; but as the variations in line-initials increase, so the name recurs more fully and clearly, and is accompanied by Homf(re)y (once), Antigona (twice), the 'devise', and at last by Stanhope. A four-line anaphora ('Wo worth', st. 4) adds two less obvious but useful letters. The anagram runs thus: st. 1, Al–An.; 1–2, AnT–G––A; 3, AlYAn. ––BHAM; 4–5, AL––N. –––HAM; 5, Al–An.; 5–6, ForF–IT; 6–7, AlIAn. COBHAM; 7, AlIAN.; 8, Al–An.; 8–9, HOMF––Y; 10, COBHAM; 10–11, ANTY–ONa; 10–12, COBHAM; 12–14, M–U. STAnHOP; ForF–IT TOT.

The experience of Plesaunce had been to Sir Richard Roos a mingled yarn, of good and ill together. He had known love and disappointment, fighting and ease after war, revels and quiet reading, and friendships with men and women which would last long. Finally he had lived at the very centre of a 'modern instance' of tragedy as his world and time knew it, a 'fall of princes', which might well have involved him in its ruin. Fortunately for him, he had, as will be seen, other resorts and resources.

CHAPTER VI

The Plesaunce Period,
1432–c. 1442: Beaufort and
Beauchamp Poems

DURING the time that Sir Richard Roos was courting Elisabeth
Phelip, Lady Beaumont, he had other calls on his poetic energies.
The Black Knight and other lesser allied poems, though written within
the decade of the 'Elisabeth' poems, do not originate in Plesaunce, but
rather from the opposite camp. There were family claims on Sir
Richard's talent. I know of no poems obviously written for his brother
Robert's wedding in 1433; but the influential marriage of his widowed
sister-in-law, Eleanor Roos, *née* Beauchamp, called forth one of his
more ambitious efforts. This and allied poems can be assigned to the
years 1433–8.

No. 43. *The Complaint of the Black Knight* (Thynne, 1532), or, *The
Complaint of a Loveres Lyfe* (Fairfax 16, Bodleian 638, Wynkyn de
Worde), or, *The man in the Erber* (Digby 181), or, *The maying and
disport of Chaucer* (Arch. Selden B. 24, and Chepman and Myllar, 1508),
a poem of ninety-five stanzas of rhyme royal, with an envoy of two
eight-line stanzas. It is not a dream poem, but a lover's complaint for
his lady's coldness, overheard by the poet, himself an unsuccessful
lover; it is set within the compass of an ideally lovely forest and park,
and follows the course of a day in May from dawn till evening star.

> *Incipit.* In May, whan Flora, the fresshe, lusty quene,
> The soile hath clad in grene, rede and whyte.
> *Explicit.* Recure to finde of myn adversite.

The author has been generally accepted as Lydgate, on the strength of Shirley's attribution to him in MS. Add. 16165. The date assigned by Skeat and Schick is 1402, and 1402–3 by Krausser who dismisses as too late the suggestion of 1430 (*O.E.D.*, *s.v.* celure). The reasons for this early date are similar to those used for the companion-piece, *The Flour of Curtesye*, and are equally arbitrary. Even when based on linguistic or metrical usage, they are conditioned by the assumption that the poem is Lydgate's; it cannot be later than his *Pilgrimage*, or his saints' legends, *ergo*, it must be early; it is rather good, *ergo*, it must be by the young Lydgate, before he got elderly and dull. I would assign the poem to Sir Richard Roos, and date it between 1433 and 1436–8, probably 1434–5, for reasons that follow.

The popularity of *The Black Knight* is attested by its being found in eight manuscripts, and in two early black-letter editions. Three of the manuscripts are of the important family of manuscripts (Fairfax 16, Bodleian 638, Tanner 346); one, Pepys 2006, can be traced to a person interested; so also, in another way, can the Sinclair manuscript, Arch. Selden B.24; the title given in Digby 181 is of some significance; Add. 16165 is Shirley's collection; and the Asloan manuscript has only a fragmentary portion.

The poem is 'signed' twice, at l. 22, and again near the end at l. 646, with the precise phrase, 'I roos anon'. The 'devise' appears in the anagrams.

The question of date is bound up with that of the identity of the Black Knight, which no one since Tyrwhitt seems to have tried to discover. Nevertheless, several pointers within the poem combine to indicate Edmund Beaufort (c. 1406–55), Count of Mortain, later Earl of Dorset, then Earl and finally Duke of Somerset.[1] This is the nephew of Cardinal Beaufort, and the younger brother and heir of John Beaufort, Earl of Somerset. Before March 1438, he had married Eleanor, Lady Roos, daughter of Sir Richard Beauchamp, Earl of Warwick, and widow of Thomas, Lord Roos, Sir Richard Roos's elder brother, who was drowned in the Marne in August 1430. She was still unmarried on July 5, 1433;[2] the birth of the Beaufort heir is conjectured as in April 1436.

The first pointer to this identity is the reference to the woodbine: the complaining knight lies between 'an hulfere and a wodebinde' (129), an unequal juxtaposition which strikes by its oddity. The woodbine is a constant in all the manuscripts; but the hulfer or holly appears as

[1] G.E.C., *Complete Peerage*, XII, i, 49–51.
[2] *Cal. Close Rolls, 1429–35*, p. 249; *Cal. Pat. Rolls, 1436–41*, p. 160.

'hasell' in Shirley's manuscript, as 'lorere' in Arch. Selden B.24, and as 'hoser' in Chepman and Myllar. Only one great noble of the century used the 'bine' as a badge; in a sixteenth-century list of fifteenth-century badges, in MS. Ashmole 763, fol. 191, the Duke of Somerset is credited with three personal badges, two obviously warlike, the cresset and the helmet, and one obviously civil, the 'beanestalke'.[1] It is possible that it was originally a personal Beauchamp badge, since Joan, widow of William Beauchamp, Lord Abergavenny, had bed-hangings of black and red, embroidered with 'wodebynde floures of sylver'.[2] If so, Edmund Beaufort had taken his lady's badge in the true tradition of chivalry. The choice of the woodbine as a badge of love can probably be traced to Chaucer's description of the embraces of Troilus and Criseyde:

> And as aboute a tree with many a twiste
> Bytrent and writh the swote wodebynde,
> Gan ech of hem in armes other wynde. (III, 1230–2)

The herald's 'beanestalke', with its harsh consonants, is understandably replaced by the poet by the more euphonious word, woodbine; the basis of both is the 'bine', or clinging tendril.

The second pointer is more closely concealed, and indicated in another way. At l. 575 the important manuscripts Fairfax 16 and Bodleian 638 (and Wynkyn de Worde's edition) have the marginal note, *Nota perseueranciam amantis*. Coming as this does at the end of the knight's complaint, it seems inept; but it may be intended to draw attention to something else. Three lines further down (l. 578) occurs the phrase 'mortal payne', a phrase ordinary enough, though it is found only rarely in this *corpus* of poetry. It will be seen, however, to include within Count Edmund's title 'Mort-ain', the letters 'al p', which may possibly stand for Alienora, princess. After the marriages to foreign princes of the daughters of Henry IV, until the later days of Edward IV, there were no young princesses at the royal court; and the term princess was freely and inexactly used for great ladies of high rank, who often were of royal or semi-royal connexion, as for instance Alice, *née* Chaucer, Duchess of Suffolk. Such a manipulation of names has already been seen in *The Flour of Curtesye*. A third pointer is yet better obscured

---

[1] In the same list, Lord Roos's badge is given, not as the peacock or the water-bouget, but as the portcullis, the family badge of the Beauforts, assumed to show his personal connexion with the leader of the armies in France, his step-father, Somerset.

[2] *Register of Henry Chichele*, II, 537.

in the generalizations of the description of the Black Knight's many excellences of person and disposition:

> So wel y-mad by good proporcioun
> If he had be in his deliver strengthe (ll. 163–4),

phrases which are merely expansions of 'beau' and 'fort'. Chaucer has already done this kind of thing in *The Boke of the Duchesse* (ll. 1318–1319).[1]

The fourth pointer is the 'erber'. An 'erber' is common enough in courtly settings to disguise the fact that here it may have some significance. The Knight lies weeping in 'an herber grene', 'ful of floures inde' (blue) (125–7). When he leaves it he goes to 'a logge . . . ther besyde' (585), where he was wont to spend the month of May. To any Londoner of the period, the words 'The erber' had as precise a significance as, say, Apsley House, or Holland House, had to the Victorians. The Erber was a famous mansion near the church of St. Mary Bothaw, called from it Bothaw by the Erber. Stow gives us the history of this 'ancient place' and 'great old house', occupied in his day by Sir Francis Drake. It had been given by Edward II to Geoffrey Scrope, and passed then to the Nevilles of Raby, and later to Richard Neville, Earl of Warwick.[2] In the reign of Henry VI it was in fact the great town house of the numerous clan of the Nevilles. The connexion between Edmund Beaufort and the Nevilles was fairly close about 1436, since Elisabeth Beauchamp, Eleanor's younger sister, married in 1436/7 George Neville of Raby, Lord Latimer. The Nevilles of the second family were always supporters of their kinsfolk the Beauforts. It is quite possible that at about the period of the poem the Count of Mortain was indeed visiting his cousin and prospective brother-in-law at the Erber; his own dwelling in Southwark would be just across the river *via* London Bridge. This connexion was probably known to the unidentified owner of MS. Digby 181, who entitles the poem 'The man in the erber'; for him the name had point. The double anagrams in the course of the poem confirm this identification of the poet's subject: stt. 2 and 3 of the introduction yield A(L)IAN. B–WFOrT; B–SHAM(P), MOrTAyen; TOT FOrFAIT; ll. 155–68, describing the hero, again give B–WSHA–, B–WFOrT; WI–BISH; ll. 491–511, on the Lady, give AlIAn BeWCHA(M)P; –D(M)–N(D) (M)OrTA–N; TOT FOr–AIT. The poet's prayer to Venus (ll. 617–44) couples the two significant

---

[1] Spenser also will occasionally give punning translations of names: e.g. Mordant, 'that death does give'; Amavia, 'her that loves to live' (*F.Q.*, II, i, 49–55; see R. H. Super in *Explicator*, Mar. 1953).

[2] See *Cal. Close Rolls, 1447–54*, p. 509. April 2, 1454.

names in different form: ALEAN. BEA(V)CHA(M); E–M(V)–D –EA(V)FOTT, and adds TOT FOTFAIT FOTFAIT. Similarly in the Envoy, ALYAn. BEA–SHAMP; BEAUFOTT, (M)ORTAY–; and FOTFAIT FOTF.

This identification of the Black Knight fits with the many references to him as a fighting man, who 'proved was, ther men shulde have ado' (161), who had experienced 'grete empryses', 'sheding of blode', 'ofte woundinge at sautes by distresse' (416–18). Edmund Beaufort was then at the height of his soldierly reputation: knighted at twenty-one, captain of Gisors in 1430/1 (some years before Sir Robert Roos), he took a leading part in 1436 in Duke Humphrey's expedition for the relief of Calais and Harfleur. These successes he was never to repeat; and as Lieutenant-General of France, he was chiefly responsible for the loss of France in the disastrous years after 1448.

A stronger light is now shed on the Kyriel ownership of MS. Pepys 2006. Sir Thomas Kyriel, who, as we have seen, was the more important brother of John Kyriel, the owner, had military and personal connexions with Edmund, Earl of Somerset. Especially he had cause to associate him with the disastrous mischance of his defeat and capture at Formigni. The Kyriel family had reason enough to be interested in a poem on the early life of Edmund Beaufort.

Again, the occurrence of *The Black Knight* in the Sinclair manuscript (Arch. Selden B.24), in close proximity to the unique copy of *The Kingis Quair*, is extremely interesting. The English bride of James I, Joan Beaufort, was the elder sister of Edmund Beaufort; it is very natural that she should possess a copy of a poem about her brother's wooing. The ridiculous colophon title, 'here endith the maying and disport of Chaucere', of which all three nouns are incorrect, is probably a scribe's muddle; to judge from his many attributions, Chaucer is the only English poet whom he (whether James Graye or another) has ever heard of. All this has its bearing also on *The Kingis Quair* and its authorship.[1] The occurrence of copies of the two poems in this late fifteenth-century manuscript belonging to the eminent and semi-royal Sinclair family strengthens the argument for the material for the manuscript having formerly been in royal hands. A sister of James I was grandmother to Henry, Lord Sinclair, a later owner,[2] and this provides a channel of transmission. Both poems are in a sense Beaufort poems; the one concerns the wooing of the elder sister, the other the courtship of the younger brother. The text of *The Black Knight* here, though lacking

---

[1] See below on *The Temple of Glas*, No. 79.
[2] Alexander Lawson, *The Kingis Quair*, p. lii.

one stanza, has some sound readings,[1] as if the scribe had a good copy. It has the spelling 'roos' in the first 'signature' (l. 22).

MS. Digby 181 also contains Peter Idley's *Instructions to his Son*, now dated between 1445 and 1450. Peter Idley of Drayton, Oxfordshire, had been bailiff for the honour of Wallingford Castle when Sir William Phelip, Lord Bardolf, and Suffolk had been jointly Constables. His wife was a member of that family of Drayton from whom Sir John Wenlok also chose his wife. In July 1453 Idley became the king's gentleman falconer, a post under the Household, and three years later he was appointed controller of the King's Works for the whole kingdom.[2] He is later found having dealings with Edmund Hampden, squire of the body, and with John Merston, formerly Treasurer of the Chamber and husband of Rose Merston, who in 1453 was still one of Queen Margaret's attendants.[3] Miss Hammond asserts the relationship of MS. Digby 181 to the Oxford family of these manuscripts.[4] It probably had its origin among the Household; whoever had access to *The Black Knight* might have access to the *Instructions*. Miss d'Evelyn, Idley's biographer, will not accept his connexion with the Idle(y)s of Kent, but does not disprove it.[5] William Idle, son of John Idle, was heir to a manor (Easture) near Chilham Castle, which was a Roos fief, inherited through the Badlesmeres.[6] One minute sign that Peter Idley had read *La Belle Dame* comes in his second Book (l. 296, p. 163); the line, 'Not fully aslepe, but half wakyng', turns around Roos's opening line, 'Half in a dreme, not fully wel awaked', and also measures the difference between Idley's metrical stiffness and Roos's grace and rhythm.

To sum up on the manuscripts of *The Black Knight*: only one manuscript unites it and *La Belle Dame*, but that is Lord Stanley's manuscript, Fairfax 16. Of the remaining seven, four were owned in Lancastrian families connected with the court and the army. Two are Scottish manuscripts, one connected with the royal family, and therefore with Joan Beaufort. Shirley's handwriting in the seventh attests the poem's priority to 1458. The interest of the owners, only one of whom was at all closely associated with Sir Richard Roos, would be centred in the identity of the Black Knight; one of them had been a comrade in arms.

The Black Knight has obvious parallels in theme and method with

[1] E.g. ll. 90, 101, 184, 360, 461–2, 665, and one variant line, 553.
[2] Charlotte d'Evelyn, *Peter Idley's Instructions to his Son*, 1935, pp. 4–5, 12–13.
[3] Duchy of Lancaster Accounts, 5/8, fol. 11.
[4] *Chaucer Bibliography*, pp. 339–40.
[5] *Op. cit.*, pp. 1–3; but see F. St. John Brooks, *Times Lit. Suppl.*, Sept. 12, 1935.
[6] *Cal. Fine Rolls, 1430–7*, pp. 20–1.

Chaucer's *Boke of the Duchesse*, and in general mental attitude with Chartier's *La Belle Dame sans Merci*; but though Death is called on he is kept out of the poem. Skeat pointed out many details drawn from the English *Romaunt of the Rose*; these and parallelisms with *The Temple of Glas* will be mentioned later. Two French poems should be cited, Machaut's *Le Dit dou Lyon*, and the anonymous *Le Chastel de Joyeuse Destinee*. *Le Dit dou Lyon*, which has already been traced in *The Isle of Ladies*, furnished the poet here with material for the Knight's complaint (ll. 407–34) of the success in love of the false flatterer and the failure of the worthy lover with all his past prowess. This is very like the description in *Le Dit* (ll. 1348 ff., 1488 ff., 1587 ff.) of flatterers, and verbally close to the achievements of worthy knights.

Le Chastel de Joyeuse Destinee is a more difficult problem, since Droz and Piaget, the editors of *Le Jardin de Plaisance* (1501),[1] date it at about 1460, but without offering detailed proof. This poem, of which the rhymes point to a Picard author, is not mentioned in the century, and not found in any manuscript; it is a long and inordinately repetitive poem of some four thousand lines, and might be three poems tacked together. The chief reason for the date, c. 1460, seems to be the sections on 'vauderies' or attacks by witches and heretics against Love, which make the modern historian turn to the great 'vauderie' or witch-terror of Arras of 1459–61. But the references to Souppeçon, the leader of this witches' sabbath, never as a sorceress, but as a 'vaudoise', 'prageoise', and 'de Bohéme', point rather to the conflicts with the heretics (who were always accused of witchcraft), and especially to the war against the Hussites in Bohemia. This would have greater interest then for a Beaufort or for Roos than would the Vaudois, because of Cardinal Beaufort's campaign in person against the Hussites in the late 1420s. Sir Edmund Beaufort of Southwark went in his uncle's retinue in the summer of 1429.[2] There is no reference to this episode in *The Black Knight*, but in the allied short poem, 'As ofte as syghes', there is a fleeting allusion to Bohemia: 'In sondry londys fro cartage vnto prage'; Carthage is a common terminal in all this poetry, but not Prague.

The parallels in *The Black Knight* are drawn from the first and third sections of *Le Chastel*, an argument possibly for the unity of that poem. The first section describes how the poet finds himself in a beautiful region which delights his senses, and takes from him all need of food; the beauty of flowers, trees, and bird song, of grass and clear streams,

[1] *Le Jardin de Plaisance*, ed. Droz et Piaget, Vol. I (1910), fol. xxv–lv; Vol. II (1925), notes and summary, pp. 90–4.
[2] *48th Report*, etc., pp. 262, 263.

is in itself a refreshment. He hears the sighs of a young lover, and finds him in a place

> clos de toutes pars
> De fueilles largement espars
> Et separe de tous esgars
> O fin millieu de la forest (fol. xxvii).

The lover arraigns Fortune in a long complaint. The sympathetic poet approaches and finds the lover

> mort a demy,
> Descouloure, fade et froidy.

He lies on

> la terre dure et farouche
> Qu'il touchoit de sa belle bouche (fol. xxviii).

The poet remonstrates with him, and at last rouses him. He finds him to be a man of sense, 'mondainement saige', and recognizes in him a former friend:

> . . . luy qui tant honneur scauoit
> Et en qui tous biens on trouuoit
> Et qui par sus tous don auoit
> De bien parler (fol. xxix).

Here the two poems part company for a while; the French poet and the lover visit the Castle, and are feasted by Doulx Regard, Espérance and Loyaulté. Under the safe conduct of Hault Vouloir and Bon Advis, they journey on to the country of Souppeçon, and there, with Love and his forces, are attacked by her 'vauderie'. They beat off the 'vaudois', and are entertained at night with 'une morisque' of characters in dialogue, song, and dance, 'gorgiase et frisque'. The next day, they come to the Tower of Cold, where a lover ('froit à oultraige') is imprisoned:

> Son corps alloit tousiours tremblant
> Pour laspre froit de mesprison . . .
> Vous loyssies dung loing trembler
> De froit et tout son corps mouuoir
> Et dent contre dens marteller. (fol. xl v.)

This compares with the opening of the Black Knight's Compleynt, in which he describes his feverish access of

> the cold of inward high disdayne
> Cold of dispyt and cold of cruel hate (ll. 239–40).

The Knight's ensuing complaints of the conspiracy of false 'Envye, Wrathe, and Enmite', of the slanders of Male-Bouche and others of his

kind, including Fals-Suspeccion, have their parallel in the letter of
credit given to the lovers (fol. xxxviii v.–xxxix) to warn them against
Dangier and his supporters, Souppeçon with her 'langue volaige',
Parler Mençongier, 'oultrageuse Envie', and 'Haine mesdit et fole
ialousie'.

In the third section, a third unfortunate lover, 'Lamant sans Partie',
complains (fol. xlii v.) against Fortune and Love, while the travellers
listen in hiding. The burden of his complaint is the same as the Black
Knight's—that he is a true lover, of long endurance and many rigorous
sufferings, 'mainte dure mal adventure', but Love has no regard for
his service:

> Amours ne me veult a mercy
> Prendre n'entendre ma requeste (fol. xliii v.).

He will accept his death if the lady exacts it, as will the Black Knight:

> Et certes mieulx vouloye mourir
> Quen riens son deshonneur souffrit
> Son ennuy ne sa desplaisance (fol. xliv; cf. *B.K.*, ll. 549 ff.).

The French poem now continues at inordinate length with yet another
attack by 'la vieille enragée vauldoise' and her troops; her prisoner,
Le Vray Amant, argues against Envy and Lying, and a great battle is
described at length (fol. l–liii). The poem ends with a vision of Love's
Paradise, a castle filled with feasting and music. This last part of the
third section, repetitive and artificial, differs entirely from the natural
beauty of the ending of *The Black Knight*, where sunset, twilight, and
the rising of the planet Venus, 'So glad, so fair, so persaunt eek of
chere', bring the poem to a harmonious close.

Some of this parallelism between the French and the English poem
is due to the background common to both, *Le Roman de la Rose*, but
by no means all of it. There are, too, signs of familiarity with other
French conventions: the poet in the failing light hastens to set down
the Knight's Complaint: 'A penne I took, and gan me faste spede'.
So too the poet of *Le Povre Amoureux* has just carefully chosen a pen
out of half a dozen when he perceives a lamenting lover, and hears first
a complaint, and then a dialogue like that of *La Belle Dame*. The poet
listens from behind an old hanging, and at the end joyfully seizes paper
and his 'plume fendu' to set it down (*Le Jardin de Plaisance*, fol. cxxix).
It is clear that the poet of *The Black Knight* is in touch with contemporary
French poetry, its themes, style, and conventions.

The Black Knight is a full-dress compliment to Edmund Beaufort, as the wooer of Eleanor, Lady Roos. It is not the only poem on the subject; a *balade* celebrates the same courtship in simpler style.

No. 44. *My Lady Dere:* a lyric of fifteen eight-line stanzas of octosyllabic lines, rhyming ababbcbc, with the refrain, 'Whane that I se my lady dere', with variation of the first words. The fifteenth stanza is *Lenvoye*, 'Go lytel bille in lowly wyse'. A sixteenth stanza in one manuscript only is headed 'Devynayle par Pycard', and professes to explain the identity of the lady.

Incipit. Euery maner creature
Disposed vn-to gentylesse.

The poem was attributed to Lydgate by Shirley in an otherwise erroneous title, and is accepted and printed as Lydgate's (MacCracken, *Minor Poems*, II, 420). I suggest that it is by Sir Richard Roos, and is a slighter companion piece to *The Black Knight*, written about the same date, between 1433 and 1438.

The poem is not 'signed'. It occurs in three manuscripts, Add. 16165, and Ashmole 59, both Shirley's, and in Stow's miscellaneous collection, Harleian 367. Ashmole 59 heads it 'a compleynt made by Lydegate for the departing of Thomas Chaucier in-to ffraunce by hes seruauntz vp-on the kynges ambassate', and has corresponding running titles. Add. 16165 makes the same statement in shorter form; Harleian 367 has this heading, and Stow obviously copied from Shirley. The three manuscripts therefore constitute only one authority. MacCracken points out that this title is really that of the preceding poem in Add. 16165, which actually does deal with Thomas Chaucer's embassy of 1417; there is no temptation to deprive Lydgate of this poem.

The very first lines point at once to the lover's identity with that of the Black Knight, Edmund Beaufort, Count of Mortain; an acrostic in ll. 1–6 gives ED. B-WFort, quite in the manner of the acrostics of Eustache Deschamps. Again, the lover has vowed to wear black till he sees his lady; another pointer is the repetition of the phrase (116), 'mortel peyne'. The anagrams fully support all this. One might infer from the concentration of the manuscripts in Shirley's hands that the poem was not in wide circulation at the time of its writing. This is consonant with the result of the anagrams, which suggest a family gathering as the occasion of the poem. The full double anagram omitting the 'Devynayle' brings in a long braid throughout the poem, not only the lady by her maiden name, but also her father and stepmother, the Earl and Countess of Warwick, her two sisters, Margaret and Elisabeth, and their husbands, Lord Talbot and George, Lord Latimer; also Roos's own lady, Elisabeth Beaumont (in a stanza on the lover's paradise and purgatory), and his friend, Lady Scales: St. 1, ED. B–WFort; stt. 1–2, ALIAnO. BeWCHAM; stt. 2–3, E–IS–BeTh; st. 3, (P)HI–(P), B–WMO–T; stt. 4–5, MARGA–ET, IOHAn, TAlBO.; st. 6, RI–HA. WARWI.; stt. 6–7, ISAB.; st. 7, ISMAnIA; stt. 8–9, WHA–ISBOrO.; st. 9, SCA–IS; stt. 10–11, EDMVn.; st. 11, SOM––S–T; LATIMIR; stt. 10–11, ––ISABeTH; st. 12, MorTAIn; st. 13, B–WForT; stt. 13–14, WIM–IS; stt. 14–15, (G)–O–G.; st. 15 (Envoy), Lady A–IAn. ROOS; stt. 2–3, ForF–I. ForF–I.; stt. 8–9, TOT ForFAIT. The second 'Edmund' (stt. 10–11) is run straight down the caesural initials of four lines. The 'devise' is not so full as frequently, probably because 'For' is needed for the name Beaufort. If Somerset denotes Edmund's elder brother, John Beaufort, the third earl, then we get closer to the probable date. After sixteen years as a prisoner in France, he was released in May 1438. The Earl of Warwick died on April 30, 1439. These would seem to be the limiting dates. There is a curious phenomenon in this anagram. The caesural initials only, without the line initials, give a different result, an almost complete Plesaunce braid: –LISA––TH BeWMONT, BArDO–F; AlIAn COBHAM; HOMFRY; AnTIGO.; ISMANIA SCAL–S; CATh. WHITTInHAM; IAI TOT ForFAIT. Roos seems to have been playing a double game. Finally the last stanza, the 'Devynayle par Pycard', is a hard nut to crack; even Miss Hammond did not solve it. Now that we have the clues, it can be forced to give up its secret:

> Take the seventeþ in ordre sette
> Lyneal of þe ABC,
> First and last to-geder knette
> Middes e-ioyned with an E,
> And þer ye may beholde and se
> Hooly to-gidre al entiere
> Hir þat is, where-so she be,
> Myn owen souerayne lady dere.

If we take the seventeenth letter of the medieval alphabet, R, and then the last, Z, we are still faced with the question of the connecting vowel which should apparently rhyme with C, se, and be. MacCracken printed E, and offered no suggestion as to identity. Furnivall printed G, another consonant. A glance at the only manuscript, Add. 16165, appears to justify MacCracken, the letter is a very odd E, with a curving line down the right-hand side, rather like a mirror-reflection of the new moon with the old moon in her arm. It is in fact O, overwritten as E, and we realize that Shirley fell into the trap prepared. It is a trick of the same order as Hamlet played when he produced 'pajock' as the rhyme to 'was', and Horatio commented 'You might have rhymed'. Hamlet avoids the insulting word of the true rhyme; Picard prepares for the wrong vowel-sound, E, and then furnishes the true one, O: an inversion of Hamlet's method. He trusted that no scribe would believe his eyes, and Shirley did not. ROZ is the name of the 'lady dere'. He also uses the double anagram to give in this one stanza the fuller name, LAdy ALIAn. B–W–H–M. The shift of caesural stress to the word 'lady' only here and in the Envoy is intentional for the formal naming of the heroine.

Who was this knowing rhymester, Picard? The Pic(h)ards of Ocle Pichard in Herefordshire were armigerous landed gentry, sheriffs and knights of the shire, from the time of Henry III.[1] Probably of this family was that Henry Pichard, vintner, and former Lord Mayor of London, whose magnificent feast to Edward III and three other kings has almost passed into legend. Stow describes how after the feast he 'kept his hall for all commers that were willing to play at dice and hazard. the Ladie Margaret, his wife, kept her chamber to the same effect'.[2] Henry Pichard, from his *Inquisitio post mortem*, died early in 1362; Margaret Pychard married, secondly, Sir Bartholomew de Burgersh, and thereby became a great-aunt by marriage of Maud Burgersh, Thomas Chaucer's wife. She died in 1393, when her son, John Pichard, was aged thirty.[3] Margaret Pychard is said by Dugdale to have been born a Badlesmere; if so (and G.E.C. does not accept it),[4] then she was a kinswoman of the heiress Margaret Badlesmere, who married William, second Lord Roos, and whose arms the Roos main line quartered with their own water-bougets. However this may have been, any fifteenth-century Picard could be on terms of sufficient equality with Sir Richard Roos to tease him by giving away the answer to his riddles.[5]

The *balade* describes the joy of all kind of creatures, the sun and stars, the birds in the air, the deer in the forest and marsh; it is an orchestration on the theme 'Sumer is i-cumen in'. But the lover is like a fish dying on dry land when he cannot see his lady. He needs her as the jewel needs its setting, or the flowers the sunshine. All this is the natural language of the poet of *How a Lover*, and in its stanza-form the

---

[1] Duncumb, *Hereford*, II, 140 ff.
[2] *Survey of London*, 'Honour of Citizens', I, 106.
[3] Hasted, *Kent*, I, 4, note 3 (pedigree).
[4] G.E.C., *Complete Peerage*, II, 427.
[5] There was also a Pycard, known from the Old Hall Manuscript of Late Plantagenet music as a composer of very complex Church music. He might have had some contact with Roos.

poem achieves a similarly light and rapid tone. That of the third poem of this group, under the gusty sighs which are its ostensible theme, is even more light and rapid, a kind of *moto perpetuo* of comparisons.

No. 45. 'As ofte as syghes': a poem of thirteen eight-line stanzas, decasyllabic; the thirteenth stanza deserts the framework, 'As oft . . . so oft . . .', and takes the form of an Envoy, asking mercy of Fortune. The refrain, 'So ofte and ofter I sygh for youre sake', is varied in the tenth and thirteenth stanzas.

> *Incipit.* As ofte as syghes ben in herte trewe
> And cristall teres on dolefull chekes trill.

The poem, like its companion, 'For lac of sighte' (see No. 3 above), is found in two manuscripts, Tanner 346, Lord Greystoke's manuscript, and Camb. Univ. Library Ff. 1.6, the 'Roos scrapbook', and was printed by MacCracken, *Archiv*, CXXVII, 323. There is no obvious 'signature', but the 'devise' is given in full. The double anagram is similar to that of *My Lady Dere*, though with some interesting variations: EDMUND; ALIANOr; BeWFOrT MOrTEIN; ISAB. WA–WIC.; E–ISABETH BeAVSHA–P, G(E)Or. N–VI(L), LATYMER; IOHAN TA–BOT; MAr–ARET BeA(V)-CHA–(P); A(L)IAn; –ORTAIN; I ROOS AnON; AI TOT FOrFAIT FOr–AIT.

It is very unusual to have the poet's full 'signature' phrase in the anagram as well as his 'devise'.

The poem consists of a rapid succession of similes, four or five to a stanza, with an effect which would be overpowering if it were not almost ridiculous. Individual prettinesses, the honey-drops distilling from the comb, or Hesperus westering under the waves, are lost in the relentless accumulation of conventional comparisons. This is indeed the poet of *How a Lover* with as strong a sense of the earth's beauty and variety, but with far less vividness and tact; one almost suspects a skit of the conventional simile:

> As fele sithes in forest or parke
> Ar nombre of bukkes, or do, or hert, or hinde,
> Or sondry trees ben closid vndyr barke.

The writer may have been hampered by the necessity for introducing complimentary allusions to the objects of his poem, The inept statements just quoted lead up to the tender branches of the 'wodebynde'; the only one of the Ladies Worthy named is Penelope, who 'renewed her werke in the raduore', a tactfully suitable choice. Penelope, as a widow, denied herself to suitors; Eleanor Roos, remaining a widow some years before remarrying, was certainly unusual in her generation, and a *rara avis* among the younger Roos ladies. The next simile is 'As there be pleyntes vndyr clothis blake' (st. 12). The earlier reference (st. 9) to Venus's 'thoghtfull seruaunts with herreos yshake' probably insinuates the two meanings of love and heroism for such a figure as Edmund Beaufort (see below, No. 62).

The earlier references of the poem concern colours and badges; the first flowers mentioned are no longer white and red, as they were in the poet's proem to *The Black Knight*, but as they are in his 'erber', 'floures ynde' or blue. Here Flora's embroidery is white and blue:

> The daise ycrowned white as lake
> And viilettis on bankes be bedene.

When white and red flowers occur (st. 4), they are roses and are joined with 'flouredelis plesaunt and delectable' (cf. 'The lylyes and þe swoote roos, The dayeseyes who taketh hede', *My Lady Dere*, ll. 83–4). All this is heraldically correct. Roos's own colours, and fortunately for him those of Phelip, were red and white; when the Beauforts were legitimated, they bore the Royal arms, quartering England with the lilies of France, differenced by a gobony border of argent and azure. Their colours were therefore blue and white. Hence the suitability of blue, the colour of fidelity, for 'The trewe man, that in the herber lay' (l. 637). Here too comes in the delayed explanation of the otherwise puzzling allusions in the 'Balade simple' that closes *The Flour of Curtesye*. Why at the end of that poem to Elisabeth Phelip should there be the Beaufort allusions of 'wodebynde' and 'fetheres ynde'? These occur only in the song of the satisfied and happy birds whom the poet hears and envies:

> And over this myn hertes lust to-bente
> In honour only of the wodebynde. (ll. 260–1)

It is the poet's suggestion to his lady (as it will be Donne's to the 'Queen of Hearts' in his most romantic *Epithalamium*) to imitate these birds of 'devout herte'. A similar criss-crossing of allusions is found also in *The Black Knight*, where the poet, in enumerating the qualities of the Knight's lady, makes a rapid passing obeisance to 'bounte' and 'beaute' (l. 498) as the two prime qualities, and in his symbolic trees includes the story of Phyllis and Demophoon (ll. 68–70). All this goes to show that the two poems are not to be kept in water-tight compartments; their streams mingle, and they flow at the same time. It might be argued indeed that the Beaufort allusions of the 'Balade Simple' prove *The Flour of Curtesye* to have been written after the betrothal of Eleanor Roos and Edmund Beaufort; this would reverse the accepted order of the two poems. Certainly the 'Balade Simple' gives evidence that in these productive years the two circles of Roos interest intersected.

The *Black Knight* is a fine and carefully-wrought poem in the high tradition of *amour courtois*. Its brilliantly written setting is verse that anyone might be glad to claim. It has its weaknesses; nevertheless a stronger, tougher fibre runs through it than through many of its kind. The poet is not here bewailing his own hopeless love, though the proem shows him to be an unsuccessful lover, nor is he writing to please his lady. He is writing of another man, a soldier as well as a true lover; soldierly references abound, and the stress on truth, true meaning, and true men, gives force to the Knight's complaint; there is a constant, antiphonal balancing on false and true:

> To slee the trewe, and false to respyte . . .
> To save the false, and do the trewe deye. (ll. 403–6)

A similar independence in poetic expression, and a like impersonality of tone, inform the two shorter lyrics. Cheerfulness keeps breaking in with the swing and rhythm of *My Lady Dere*; in 'As ofte as syghes', the fun of piling up comparisons becomes almost hilarious. The very similes that have been seriously used in *The Black Knight* are here poured out pell-mell, good and bad, sometimes with a flatness of expression which only the speed of the whole can overcome. The poem could easily pass for a skit; in the long development of English verse, it looks forward to the ironic sentiment and the patter of Gilbert and Sullivan's songs.

No. 46. A poem intended chiefly for the three famous Beauchamp sisters is found in MS. Arch. Selden B.24, fol. 217, which with its inclusion of *The Kingis Quair* and *The Black Knight* has close Beaufort connexions. The spelling has been scotticized, but this does not affect the anagrams, and some rhymes can only be southern or midland, e.g. st. 18, with words in o.[1]

> *Incipit.* Befor my deth this lay of sorow I sing
> *Explicit.* Of him, the quhich enherytt hath þe vent
> Of fair langage to all þe worldis ere.

It is a poem of 185 lines and of nineteen stanzas, the last stanza being an envoy of ten lines. Most of the stanzas are of nine decasyllabic lines (aabaabbab), the stanza of *Anelida and Arcite* (see No. 74). Two stanzas, however (stt. 8 and 18), are of sixteen lines with the rhymes reversed (aaabaaab|bbbabbba); these are octosyllabic, and play a special

---

[1] Printed by Kenneth G. Wilson, *Speculum*, 1954, XXIX, 708–26.

part in the anagram. A pointer to the dedication of the poem is markedly
given in the arrangement of the anagrams in st. 1

The double anagram runs thus:

St. 1. line-initials, BEWFOrT; caesural initials, SOME–S–T. stt. 1–2,
––AVCHAM, AlIAN.; stt. 3–4, E–ISAB–Th LATI–Er; IS–ANIA SCAl–S; st. 4,
FOrF–IT; stt. 4–5, FOrFAIT; stt. 5–6, whAlISB––O–H; B–WCHAM AlIAN.;
stt. 7–8, MA–D STAnHO.; st. 8 (shortened), TOT FOrFAIT; –LISABeTh
Be–MO–T; BABTho.; st. 9, TAlBOT; stt. 9–10, IOHAN; stt. 10–11,
FOrNYVAL; stt. 9–10, MA–Ga––T; stt. 10–11, BeAVSH.; stt. 11–12, Geo.
LATYMy–; st. 13, N–VI–.; stt. 14–16, no anagrams; stt. 17–18, AlIAN.;
st. 18 (shortened), SOM––set, B–A–SHA–; MO–TAIN; FOrFAIT; stt. 18–19,
E–MVN–; st. 19, *Envoy*, PHE.; B–WMO–T; TOT FOrFAYT.

It is clear that the poem is a braid chiefly of the three Beauchamp
sisters and their husbands: Margaret, and John Talbot, Lord Furnival;
Eleanor, and Edmund Beaufort, Count of Mortain; and Elisabeth, and
George Neville, Lord Latimer. Added to these are Lady Scales and
Maud Stanhope. The first pair of shortened stanzas (8–9) are devoted
to Lady Beaumont, with Roos's confidant, Babthorpe. The second pair
at the end show clearly that the 'Black Knight' and his lady are the
important persons, but the Envoy makes Lady Beaumont, who has
'commanded' the poem, the recipient. The poet's 'devise' is scattered
throughout. The anagrams seem to cease in three central stanzas;
M is generally a rare letter, yet it recurs seven times in two stanzas
(17–18). The opportunity to use the sisters' 'raisons' is not taken,
though Lady Latimer's 'Till my lyves ende' may be suggested in her
anagram stanza (4) in the line, 'Non othir ende Is schapin me bot ded'.

The poem is a lament by a woman for the absence and estrangement
of her lord and for the uncertainty of love; it is a careful and dignified
production, a worthy companion piece to *The Black Knight*. Its general
ideas and its phraseology are typical of Roos (e.g. disauenture, plesaunce,
womanhede, euer in one, recure, all my cure). But whereas its similes
are almost as many as in 'As ofte as sighes', they are used here with
propriety and due weight, and some are unusual in his body of work.
Yet they are not outside the scope of his interests, whether hawking
('Bot brok is now bell and ges' etc., st. 8), or chess ('In couert thus
ʒe matit haue my play', l. 88), or archery ('As doith the bow þat will
nocht cast, bot frete', l. 128); or of his expression elsewhere ('so thrillith
me that thorne', l. 27; cf. 'So thirleth with the poynt of remembraunce',
Anelida and Arcite, l. 211, see below, No. 74). Other expressions are
novel in his poetry: 'my cristenmess Is turnit Into lent' (17); 'ʒe haue
brokin þe balance|Of my resoun' (148–9); 'In my garding quhare I

sewe|All paciens, now fynd I nocht bot rewe' (51–2); or the northern proverb, 'Bot all to late to stek þe stable nowe' (84); and, finest of all, in the Beaumont stanza, 'The ruby fall Is fro þe ryng' (69). The Envoy is much more humble than is Roos's wont on the poem's shortcomings; it is rude and 'vncorrek', abridged and with borrowings here and there, not to be compared with the work of the great inheritor of fair language, presumably Chaucer. This deprecation is excessive.

Another poem in somewhat simpler style again sets Eleanor Beaufort against the background of her family, in a feminine group.

No. 47. *The Parliament of Love* (Furnivall's title): a poem of 108 lines, chiefly of octosyllabic couplets, but containing a song in rhyme royal (ll. 25–31), and 'a litle bill' in the form of an Envoy of three stanzas of rhyme royal (ll. 88–108).

> *Incipit.* What so euyr I syng or sey
> My wyll is good too preyse here well.
> Now ȝee that wull of loue lere
> *Explicit.* For sche þat is the floure of wommanhede
> At her oown leyser schall the syng and rede.

The poem is known only in MS. Ff. 1.6. (fol. 51–3), the 'Roos scrapbook', and was printed by Furnivall in *Political, Religious and Love Poems* (E.E.T.S., 15, 1866 and 1903, pp. 76–9). It is not 'signed' but the 'devise' appears in the anagrams.

A parliament of ladies and lovers is depicted, summoned by Love, presided over by Venus, and held in 'a castell feyre ande stronge' (*beau* and *fort*), a pointer to the coterie involved. After a short song, or prayer, to the god of love, the debate is set. But the poet leaves this theme and the debaters, and applies himself to describe a lady young and fair; he withdraws into a corner to write the envoy in her praise.

The double anagram of the first ten lines names the lady, A–IANO–B–W–HA.; the description of the company (ll. 11–24) indicates the chatelaine, ISA––L WAR––C, and gives the 'devise', TOT FOrFAYT FOr–A–T. The Song (ll. 24–31) introduces Lady Talbot as STRANG–, one of Lord Talbot's many titles. The description of the Lady (ll. 43–73) names her by all her designations, and again indicates her elder sister: ALYAn. B–AVSCHAM, WARWIC, –OOS, B–WFOrT, MO–TAYN; TA–BOT, St–AnGE. In the Envoy (ll. 88–198) the poet again names the lady, and signs his 'devise': ALYAn. B–WFOrt MOrTAY–, TOT FOrFAIT FO––FAIT.

The whole brief poem is like a very simple and slight fore-runner of *The Assembly of Ladies*. There is the same division according to rank into ladies, married and unmarried, and 'gentyll wymmen of lower degre', with the addition here of 'all þo men þat louers were', and of 'marchauntz wyfes' with their attendant maids. This may indicate a City gathering. The later *Parlement of Cupid* and *Assembly of Ladies* will keep more strictly to the form and matter of a debate; this poem resolves itself into a compliment to one lady, Eleanor Beaufort.

No. 48. 'Beware of Doublenesse': a poem of thirteen stanzas of eight octosyllabic lines (ababbcbc), the last stanza being an envoy.

> *Incipit.* This worlde is ful of variaunce
> In euery thing, whoo taketh hede.
> *Explicit.* Sette on your brest, your-self tassure,
> A myghty shelde of doublenesse.

There are four manuscripts: Fairfax 16, an important manuscript for Roos; Add. 16165, in which Shirley names it 'Balade of wymmens constaunce', but gives no author; Ashmole 59, a late and unreliable Shirley manuscript, which asserts Lydgate's authorship in four forms; 'Nowe here foloweþe a balade made by Lydegate of wymen for desporte and game per Antyfrasim'; 'Balade made by Lydgate'; Running titles, 'Lidegate of doubilnesse', 'By Lydegate poete'; Harleian 7578 (c. 1450?), a miscellaneous volume with a good many Roos poems. To these can be added a fragment in Ashmole 39, a Bourchier manuscript; on the flyleaf, under signatures of Anne, Isabell and Thomas Bourchier (see below, p. 487) is written in a minute hand the Envoy of the poem, with a few variants. (Printed by Skeat, *Chaucer*, VII, p. 291; and by MacCracken, *Lydgate, Minor Poems*, II, 438.)

The ascription to Lydgate (by Shirley, Bale, MacCracken, and Schirmer) is not surprising, since the poem is certainly ambiguous in tone. The argument that women, naturally true and 'entiere', are justified in assuming 'A myghty shelde of doublenesse' against the wiles and assaults of men, does not gain in force by the appeal to Delilah's truth and innocence. Shirley would inevitably interpret it *Per Antifrasim*, as he does; at l. 32 the annotator of Fairfax 16 does the same. Ambivalence will be seen in the anagrams also. But the lightness and speed of the verse, like that of *My Lady Dere*, are not Lydgate's, nor is the slyness of the humour his:

> What man may the wynde restreyne
> Or holde a snake by the tayle,
> Or a slepur eele constreyne
> That yt wil voyde, withoute fayle? (ll. 49–52)

The comparisons with Fortune's wheel, with the steering of a ship, with the chance of the dice (st. 10), are casual and debonair in tone, and are not in Lydgate's ponderous style. Possibly it was early taken for a companion poem to Lydgate's 'This worlde is ful of stabulnesse', an expansion from the French.

The double anagram yields a braid of Beaufort-Beauchamp names: AlYAn BeWForT BEA–CHAM; ED–VND MOrTAYN; ISABEL WA–WYC; MArGA–ET TAlBOT; ELISABETH LATIM.; AI TOT ForFAIT ForFAIT.

Even in the anagrams, 'doubleness' in the poem's sense is to be found, and counterpoints the meaning. The line-initials alone give the Beaufort braid recognizably, and the caesural initials merely serve to fill out the names. This is probably because the caesural letters, if kept separate, can yield a totally different anagram, a Plesaunce braid: A–IAN COBHA–; HOMF–EY; ANTIGONe POWYS; ELISABETH BeW–ONT BA–DO–F; WHITT.; TOT ForFAIT.

For the second time, and as in *My Lady Dere*, Roos is balancing on an anagrammatic seesaw between the two circles of his readers. His poem may only just keep on the hither side of doggerel, but it implies real virtuosity to get any meaning into it at all.

No. 49. 'Unto my Lady, the Flower of Womanhood' (Furnivall's title): a poem of six stanzas of rhyme royal, of which the last stanza is an Envoy: 'Go litill bill with all humblis'. No author is indicated; its editors, Furnivall (*Political . . . Poems*, E.E.T.S., 15, p. 71) and Robbins (*Secular Lyrics* etc. No. 190), leave it anonymous and undated.

> *Incipit.* That pasaunte Goodnes, the Rote of all vertve
> *Explicit.* hir louynge a-lone—not schanginge for no newe.

The only manuscript known is Lambeth 306 (fol. 137 v.), where there is a little cluster of four poems, three of which, including this, are twin poems to others better known. The manuscript is a very mixed and nondescript collection, most fully described by Greene (*Early English Carols*, p. 334); I have not been able to discover anything about its background.

The parallelism with the 'Ballade of her that hath all Virtues' (No. 6, above) is obvious, first in theme:

> Nowe lady myn in whome Vertus Alle
> ar Ioyned and also comprehendide (st. 5)

and also in expression; the second line of Poem No. 6,

> Demure appert, glad chere with gouuernaunce,

is an improved version of the heavier first line of st. 2 of this poem:

> Youre sade Demewre appert goueronance.

There are other parallels also: stt. 3 and 4 describe the poet's nightly dreams and visions of the lady, his troubled waking ('Bute whan y wake, ye Are away'), his despair, and sense of 'mortall langoure', all in a manner reminiscent of *The Isle of Ladies*, of the poet's thwarted dream-marriage, and also of the prince's despair and suicide:

> Hit is nat so it is fantasticall
> the whiche my herte with þe swarde mortall
> that nothinge is saue uery Dethe   (st. 4).

The faulty syntax and metre point to an unrevised poem; so do the irregular lines of the last stanza, some long and lolloping, others too short.

> And if sche wot nat whoo it is, bute stonde in erore,
> Say it is hire olde louer þat loueth hire so fre, trewe.

Stanzas 3 and 4 show signs of the poet's attempting a higher style, with such fine words as 'noxiall' (for 'by night'), 'memorall', and 'fantasticall'; in *How a Lover* the distinction had been made between 'memor', and 'fantesye', 'ymagynyng', and 'mannye'. French words are rather frequent: 'pasaunte', 'magrie', 'sauns coloure'. The style shows the general manner of Sir Richard Roos, with one novelty, that here he calls himself 'newe troiles'; but this does not recur in the poem to Elisabeth Phelip, his 'Faire Rewthlesse'.

The anagrams show that this little poem was indeed addressed to the opposite camp: ALYAn B–AVForT MORTAIN; (R)I(C)HA(RD), ISAB. (WAR.); E–YSAB–TH B–WCHAMP WArWY., (GE)O(R). N–VYL LATYM; WIM–ISH. There is no 'devise', perhaps another sign that the poem was not yet ready for publication.

A poem in the high style, and set to music, similarly celebrates the same pair:

No. 50. 'So put yn fere I dare not speke': a ballade in three stanzas of rhyme royal. It is a man's lament on the hackneyed theme of the deep wound from the eye to the heart, and the need for the lady to cure it. It is in the manuscript of Tudor music, Add. 5665 (the Ritson manuscript), and is printed by B. Fehr in *Archiv*, CVI, pp. 48–70, no. 86.[1]

The anagrams intertwine the names, running thus: st. 1, A–IAn.; SOM–(R)S–T; stt. 1–2, –DMVnD; ––AVshAM; stt. 2–3, B–AVForT; stt. 1–3, MORTAYn. There is no 'devise', but it is thoroughly in Roos's style. The last line, 'And neuer to chaunge hyr for no new', incorporates, as

---

[1] For this reference I am indebted to Mr. P. J. Frankis.

does that of 'The Flower of Womanhood' (No. 49), Eleanor Beauchamp's 'raison', 'Never new'.

The theme of *The Black Knight* is repeated in a short poem written in a more popular style, which has found its way into the small collection of fifteenth- and sixteenth-century verse bound up in the alchemical and astrological manuscript, Ashmole 176.

No. 51*a*. 'In a garden vnderneth a tree': a poem of six stanzas (fol. 100) copied on a space-saving method by a Tudor copyist accustomed to the long fourteener as if each stanza had three lines. Actually each stanza has six lines generally of eight syllables (aaabab).

> *Refrain.*
> *Incipit.* This nyghts rest, this nyghts rest
> adewe farewell this nights rest.
> In a garden vnderneth a tree
> To g[a]ther ye floures y^t grewe therby.
> *Explicit.* I can no more but ever one
> adewe farewell this nyghtes rest.

I know of no other copy; it is not included in Carleton Brown and Robbins's *Middle English Index*. The poet describes his finding a man lamenting on the ground; he asks the cause, and the lover tells of his unhappy love:

> She hathe reclaymed me to her lure
> to say farewell this nyghts rest.

The anagrams run thus: B–WFOrT, MO–TAIN; ALYAN. BeAWSHAM; IAY TOT FOr–AIT.

Another short poem in the same collection, Ashmole 176, fol. 99 v., is a more careful piece of work.

No. 51*b*. 'Sauns remedye endure must I': a poem written as 12 lines of sixteen syllables. The apparent four-line stanzas have internal rhymes, and the poem is an example of the older fashion of short lines in 'rimes couées', on a highly complex rhyme structure which binds the three stanzas together thus:

St. 1. aaab. aaab. cccb. dddb.
St. 2. aaae. fffe. gggh. iiih.
St. 3. bbbk. aaak. aaab. aaab.

Something of the same effect will be found in *The Lover's Mass* (No. 69). The end here of st. 3 not only returns to the first rhymes, but repeats the opening lines with variations.

Incipit. Sauns remedye endure must I
in paynes deadly for my mistres.
Explicit. alas y^t she doth not petye
of her bountye and great goodnes.
finis.

The theme is that of a sleepless lover, racked with the pains of love for an unpitying lady. From the forty-eight initial letters of these short lines there emerges a Beaufort anagram: from st. 1, ED. B–AUFOrT (reading 'unlesse' for 'onlesse'); from stt. 3 and 2, ALIANO– B–A–CHAM; and from the remaining letters, MOrtAIN, DO–S–T, SO–––SET. This leaves a residue of twenty letters which give IAY Tot FOrF–IT FOrF–IT. These names help to date the poem. Edmund Beaufort, Count of Mortain, and later Earl of Dorset (August 1441), succeeded his elder brother John in May 1444, as Earl of Somerset, and was created Duke of Somerset in March 1448 (G.E.C., IV, 417). The upward date for the poem would therefore be May 1444. As the married pair seem to have led a very united life, the mournful sentiments probably have no direct reference to them; a lyric in fashionable style is dedicated to them in compliment.

No. 52. 'Ffair fresshest erthly creature': a poem of six stanzas of nine lines, chiefly octosyllabic, but with a few lines of four, six, and ten syllables (ababcbdddb, but with variations); printed by Robbins, *Secular Lyrics*, No. 199.

Incipit. Ffair fresshest erþly creature
that euere the sonne ouer-shone
Explicit. Certes y can-not elles sayne
but deþ y may not a-stert.

The unique manuscript is Douce 95 (fol. 3 v.). This is a Yorkist manuscript; but the early Neville-Beauchamp-Beaufort alliances would make it easy for the poem to find its way into such a collection. It is difficult to know whether the metrical roughness is due to an original not yet polished, or to faulty copying; regularity could be easily restored in places, e.g. in l. 7.

The poem calls itself a little letter; it expresses ardent devotion to a most beautiful lady. The anagram covers the names of the three Beauchamp sisters, but the one that appears obvious in the line-initials of stt. 2–3 is Latimer (T..Y..MYRLA); the lady addressed is probably the youngest sister: ISABEL LATYMYR, NEVIL; MAR–A––T TALBOT; ALIA––Or BEUForT, BeWCHAMP; MOrtAIn; RICHA–D; AY TOT FOrFAIT F––FAYT.

No. 53. It is unusual for a short poem to unite the names of Elisabeth

Phelip and of Eleanor Beauchamp, but this occurs in a five-stanza song, 'If I had wytt for to endyght' (Add. 31922, fol. 34 v.; with music in Roy. Ap. 58; *Early Eng. Lyrics*, No. 26). The pointer to the latter is in st. 3, 'Nor for no newe me change doth she', which disguises her 'raison', 'Never Newe'. The anagram runs: stt. 1–2, SOM--S-T; stt. 1–3, B-WSHAM; stt. 3–5, B-AUFOIT; stt. 4–5, PHELIP, FOR--IT. The determination not to reveal the lady's name reminds us how the officious Picard divulged it at the end of *My Lady Dere*.

No. 54. *Balade for the Countess of Warwick:* a poem of sixty-one lines in stanzas of four lines, with one extra line in conclusion; the stanzas have three octosyllabic lines, and one of four syllables, and the rhymes are linked (aaab bbbc cccd, etc.).

> *Incipit.* I can not half þe woo compleyne
> þat doþe my woful hert streyne
> *Explicit.* Myn hert and al my bysynesse
> Haue I gyve
> For euermore whyles þat I lyve.

The unique copy is in MS. Add. 16165 (fol. 245 v.–246 v.), and Shirley's hand has added later to the title 'Balade' the information, 'made of Isabelle Countasse of Warr. and lady Despenser by Richard Beauchamp, Eorlle of Warrewyk'. MacCracken accordingly printed it as 'The Earl of Warwick's *Virelai* (*P.M.L.A.*, XXII, 597–607). Shirley is proved right as to the subject of the poem, for the anagram of the line-initials, with a minimum of recourse to the caesural initials, gives: MA DAM ISAB. COWNT–SS OF WA–WIC; RICHA. BEWSHAMP; IAY TOT FOrF–IT FOrF–YT.

If the earl is to be credited with the authorship, then he must be added to Chaucer, Lydgate, and probably Duke Humphrey, as one of Roos's masters in versification. This would be possible on the facts. Richard Roos was about seventeen years old when his brother Thomas's marriage to Eleanor Beauchamp brought the Roos family into the orbit of this dazzling figure of the time. But no other poems are attributed to the earl; and this poem, in addition to the 'devise', has many marks of Roos's style: his rhymes (plesaunce: allegeaunce: governaunce; kerve: sterve: serve: swerve); his phraseology, and above all the run and rhythm of his verse, with all the mingled grace and brilliance of his idealistic love poetry. The poem must have been written before 1439, the year in which the earl and his widow both died.

In addition to the more elaborate Beaufort poems, there are some short poems and stanzas found only in MS. Ff. 1.6, the 'Roos scrapbook'.

Various pointers and the anagrams proclaim them as fragments of the Beaufort sequence.

No. 55*a*. 'Continuaunce': a tiny lay (fol. 138 v.–139) (printed by Robbins, *P.M.L.A.*, June 1954, LXIX, 636).

> *Incipit.* Continvaunce
> Of remembraunce
> w⁺owte endyng

Between this and the preceding poem, written large and with an ornament, are the words 'Crocit dytyn'. These have been read as a signature, possibly disguised; it seems more likely that they are the descriptive title of this poem: a 'crossed ditty' with 'rimes croisées'; the recurrence of rhymes in these eighteen lines is emphasized here, as often elsewhere, by the brackets: aabaab|ccdccd|eefeef.

The single acrostic anagram (the lines are too short for a caesural acrostic) reads: ED. B–WForT, cont. of M––TAIN; For–AIT.

No. 55*b*. 'His Mistress, his Comfort' (Robbins's title, *Secular Lyrics*, No. 164): two stanzas of rhyme royal (fol. 28 v.).

> *Incipit.* As in yow resstyth my Ioy and comfort.
> *Explicit.* And to be releuyd of all yowre grevaunce.

The writer protests a desire to have reassuring news of the sufferer's recovery from malady; the phrase, 'Youre dissese ys my mortal payne', is reminiscent of *The Black Knight* and *My Lady Dere*. The anagram is B–W–O–T, MorTAIn, SOM––SeT (I have corrected the copyist's faulty 'Ar' in l. 6 to the required 'Or'); there is no 'devise', but this is probably an uncompleted balade. The name Somerset dates the poem after 1444 when Beaufort succeeded his brother.

No. 55*c*. The same phrase governs a tiny poem, possibly a scrap from a longer one, and indicates the same connexion.

> *Incipit.* Yf I had space now for to write
> my mortall Paynes to Endite.

Even in this single 'hour-glass' stanza of eight lines, the anagram gives: (E)DM–N–; ForF–IT. It is in MS. P.R.O., S.P. 1/246, fol. 28.[1]

Another poem in MS. Ff. 1.6 which connects with the same families is a woman's lament at her lover's long absence:

No. 55*d*. 'My woofull hert': a poem of twenty-one lines on two rhymes,

---

[1] For this reference I am indebted to Mr. P. J. Frankis.

aab (886) (fol. 69 v.) (printed in *Reliquiae Antiquae*, I, 169, and by
Robbins in *P.M.L.A.*, LXIX, 633).

> *Incipit.* My woofull hert thus clad in payn
> Wote natt welle what do nor seyn
> *Explicit.* I gaue hitt hym with-owte constrayn
> euyr to contenwe so.

The lady protests her fidelity and her longing for a sight of the absent
one. The phrase 'ffor lakke of syght' recalls the opening of another, a
Plesaunce poem in the same manuscript (see above, No. 3). The
protestation 'tyll deth departe us t[w]o' points to Eleanor Beaufort's
elder sister, Margaret Beauchamp, Lady Talbot, whose 'raison' was
'Til deth depart' (i.e. divide). The double anagram yields the names:
IOHaN TAl--T, CLE-MONT, WAT--ForD; MA-Gr-T B-WCHAM. Sir Richard
Roos had been under Talbot at Gisors in 1436, but this poem must be
later; Talbot was created Count of Clermont-en-Beauvoisis in 1434,
and Earl of Waterford in 1446. The 'longe absens' bewailed in the poem
may be merely his fighting in France, or it may be the subsequent six
months as a prisoner in French hands, from the fall of Rouen (Nov.
1449) to that of Falaise (July 1450). (Ramsay, *Lancaster and York*,
II, 100, 110.)

No. 55*e*. 'A Pledge of Loyalty' (Robbins's title, *Secular Lyrics*,
No. 171); a poem which occurs in Ff. 1.6; and also in MS. Ashmole 191,
fol. 191, with music as a song.

> *Incipit.* Now wolde y fayne sum merthis mak
> Al only for my lades sak
> *Explicit.* And that y may in her seruice
> euer to amend

This is a pretty trifle of six five-line stanzas of varying line-lengths, one
of the poems of Roos's for which a setting survives. The lover, absent
far away, denies the truth of the proverb, 'seldyn seyn is sone for-geit',
and asserts the resolve 'neuer to chaung for no newe'. This prepares us
for the double anagram giving Eleanor Beauchamp's names: AlIAN.
BEUForT, B-AUSHA-, SO---SET, and also the 'devise' in full: IAY TOT
ForFAIT For-AIT.

These last short poems have gone beyond the Plesaunce period, into
the later married life of Edmund Beaufort and of John Talbot, and into
Roos's service as a King's Knight. The last two poems to be considered
here return to the middle years of Plesaunce, and are written for

Humphrey's elder brother, John, Duke of Bedford, Regent of France, and his second wife, Jacquetta of Luxembourg.

No. 56*a*. 'To his Mistress, Root of Gentleness' (Robbins's title, *Secular Lyrics*, No. 198): a poem of four stanzas, of rhyme royal. Robbins, following the manuscript, attaches to it another poem of four stanzas of rhyme royal, 'Now fayreste of stature formyd by nature', but that is a poem for Elisabeth Phelip, as the references and anagram show (see above, No. 27).

> *Incipit.* Exemplye sendynge to you, rowte of gentylnes,
> Bothe true and trusty stok of all nature.
> *Explicit.* that lustyth not to offende hys souerayn lady.

The only manuscript is Cotton MS. Vespasian D.ix. The copying is very faulty: the second and fourth stanzas have lost lines and this spoils the rhyme structure; words have been misunderstood, e.g. 'the bon-ayre' for 'Debonayre' (l. 3), and 'wyked' for 'wyht' (l. 24).

The opening lines point to Bedford's famous badge of the dry stock, or as it was better known, the Root ('The Rote is ded, the Swanne is goone'). The poem celebrates his second wife, Jacquetta of Luxembourg, whose brief marriage lasted from April 1433 to September 1435. The double anagram yields: I-HAn BeDFor-, JA-VETTA; IOYWS Re--S, and the poet's 'devise', Ai TOT For-AIT; the name of Bedford's house in Rouen was Joyeux Repos.

The poem purports to be an answer to a letter, but this does not rule out Roos's authorship. Among John of Bedford's many fine qualities, we have no warrant to include proficiency in versifying; it would be quite in order for the young squire or knight to put his talents at the Regent's service. More than once he includes Jacquetta's name in a Plesaunce braid; later he will write of her again in Queen Margaret's court. For her alone, without her husband, he composed a macaronic poem in French and English.

No. 56*b*.

> *Incipit.* En Iesu Roy soueraign | you lady fair and fre.

The solitary copy of this macaronic love-song is in the Yorkist manuscript, Douce 95, fol. 6; printed in Robbins, *Secular Lyrics*, No. 172. In its nine quatrains, a very obvious single anagram is devoted to scAIy- (stt. 1-2); IsMAN(I) (stt. 8-9); in all the central stanzas the anagram gives: IAQuETT. BEDFOrD, LVSSeMB-(R). One can guess that it was written soon after her first marriage, while she was yet unskilful in English; possibly Lady Scales was instructing her. We have seen that she was involved later, as Jacquetta Wydville, in two macaronic verse-letters (Nos. 26*a–b* above).

These poems of the early period, but not written for the people of Plesaunce, do not, with one exception, reach the varied excellence of the Plesaunce poems. The exception, *The Black Knight*, remains one of Roos's best works, superior to *The Flour of Curtesye*, with which criticism has always paired it. The rest, except 'Befor my deth', are weaker and less vigorous. It is not surprising. Eleanor Roos's marriage into the famous and semi-royal family of Beaufort must have brought problems for the young poet. He suffered from a divided allegiance. It could not have been easy for a 'Gloucester's man', kinsman of the Duchess, and satirist of the Cardinal (see below, No. 60), to turn to eulogy of the Beauforts. Indeed the majority of these poems are meant for the Beauchamp family at Warwick Castle, with whom he had probably been familiar from boyhood. A Beauchamp poem, 'I can not half þe wo compleyne', is the finest of these shorter poems. There is no doubt that the personal ardour, the fervour of his writing, is reserved for Elisabeth Beaumont, Ismania Scales and Antigone; 'For lac of sighte' is a far better poem than 'As ofte as syghes'. Among the Beaufort and Beauchamp poems, in spite of the sombre impressiveness of 'Befor my deth' (No. 46) there is nothing to equal the sparkle of *How a Lover*, the romantic dreaming of *The Isle of Ladies*, or the poignancy of *The Deth of Pyte*.

CHAPTER VII

Early Translations

THE Plesaunce poems have shown Sir Richard Roos, from c. 1432 to c. 1441, training himself away from alliterative lines of an irregular number of syllables, to the smooth regularity of lines modelled on Chaucer's usage and on the French. In these, sometimes at the cost of complete rewriting, he gains the skill to compose a longish romance in the octosyllabic couplet, and many lyrics and descriptive poems after the French pattern, and even, once, in *terza rima*. Acquaintance with these foreign models, and perhaps also increasing intimacy with Chaucer's work, he probably owed to Duke Humphrey; possibly later Charles d'Orléans widened his French knowledge. From them, and perhaps from other contacts made in Normandy itself, he had the notion to develop his skill by translating French poems of some length, some too long-breathed indeed for him ever to complete the translation. Six such poems owe their inception to the Plesaunce patrons, though not necessarily their continuation, for in some the references of the anagrams change and develop.

The poems are 'Cassamus roos', *The Eye and the Heart, La Belle Dame sans Merci, The Romaunt of the Rose*, Fragments A and B, *Reson and Sensuallyte*, and *Fabula Duorum Mercatorum*. The whole forms a very respectable achievement, and testifies to the young knight's industry in his twenties, and to his competence in the French language.

No. 57. 'Cassamus roos', or 'King Truthteller': an anonymous translation in seventy-one eight-line stanzas (ababbcbc) of that portion of *Les Vœux du Paon* which describes the scene of the game, 'Le roi qui ne ment', ending with a few stanzas which lead back into the narrative.

Incipit. Cassamus roos aftre this talkynge
And took yn counsel Ydore and Betys.
Explicit. But Porrus of al was helde the beste knythe

Large he was of body and ther-to ryght my3te
Men seyde of these iiij was a noble sy3te

The unique manuscript is Ff. 1.6, the 'Roos scrapbook', where it is the last item but two in the collection (fol. 166–77 v.). The writing is small, neat, and regular; the pages are not defaced by scribbles or signatures. The word *Explicit* is written small and like a catchword, as if leading to a colophon.[1]

The poem is not 'signed' with the usual phrase, and the 'devise' is not obvious in the anagrams; but the occurrence of 'roos' as the second word may be significant, and be one reason for the poet's starting at this point. The version has not the life and spontaneity of Roos's better work, such as *La Belle Dame*; it sounds like an early experiment made before he had formed his individual style. On the other hand, the skill needed to transform the long *laisses* of alexandrines (between 25 and 90 lines) into eight-line decasyllabic stanzas is already in Roos's control. On the whole, I would place it before *The Eye and the Heart*, which is in the same stanza.

Two external considerations affect the assigning of this version to Sir Richard Roos: first, the evident attraction of this French poem for his family with its peacock crest, and the existence of two manuscripts of it with the signature, 'Roos R' (see above, p. 81); second, the occurrence of the translation only in that manuscript which has very particular connexions with the poet (see above, Chapter III). The Plesaunce anagrams are a third reason. The first four stanzas again set the stage there: HOMF–EY, AlYan COBHA–, ANTI–ONA, E–YSAB–Th BA–DOL–, SCA––S. The description of the beauty of Edes (st. 8) gives E–YSAB–TH; that of Phesonas (st. 40) gives YS–An–A S–ALYS. The anagrams are comparatively few, as if they were a new venture, and do not seem to include the name Beaumont; this supports the early dating; in *The Eye and the Heart*, the lady's married name occurs.

The poem has some of Roos's characteristics: the awkward inversion, often for rhyme ('3ow to serue hedyr be come al we', l. 510 and cf. ll. 24, 173); the 'routh : trouth' rhyme, but only once (st. 38; the copyist has miswritten 'trouth' as 'thou>e'); the frequency of 'fresh' as an epithet; the Kentish form 'shette' to rhyme with 'lette, bet, met' (st. 36, but the copyist has written 'shitte'; cf. 'smet', ll. 61, 76); the occasional identical rhyme ('frend', st. 68; 'trewly', st. 23); the syllabic variation of lines, especially towards the end; and above all the frequency of syntactical run-on between stanzas, a marked metrical peculiarity of

---

[1] The edition by Rosskopf (*Editio Princeps des Me.* 'Cassamus', Erlangen, 1911) was brought out before the folios of the manuscript were renumbered.

Roos's 'signed' poems; here there are eleven such links in seventy-one stanzas, an extreme example being 'therfore wolde I be | Enformed sekirly . . .' (stt. 50–1).

The exigencies of translation result in words not often used by Roos: 'entrecomuned' (l. 448); 'sauerous' (328), 'celenesse' (431), 'mawdysour' (434), 'amerousté' (451), 'perygal' (526); but with 'amonesté' (310) compare the 'bien monesté' lady of *The Assembly* (l. 675), and with 'stodye' (288), the first line of *Hope* (No. 9, above).

Though the vocabulary and style do not markedly suggest Roos, the matter and the themes are such as he will constantly use. The parlour-game, obviously the object of this extract, recurs in less refined forms in the two game poems (see Nos. 36 and 71); the tongue-tied lover reappears in *The Compleynt* (No. 78); the 'king' defends the joys of that Secret Thought which is alluded to in *The Parlement of Cupid*, and which derives from *Le Roman de la Rose*; and the visitation of Hope (ll. 320–35) is the theme of a whole poem.

No. 58. *The Eye and the Heart*: a translation of *Le Débat du Cueur et de l'Œil*, in 103 eight-line stanzas (ababbcbc).

> *Incipit.*   In the first weke of the saisoun of May
> Whan the wodes be couered al in grene.
> (En may la premiere sepmaine
> Que les boys sont pares de vert)
> *Explicit.*   . . . and who the chappellet playne
> Shal gete than to loue for him I pray
> That to al his desires he may attayne.

The translation is apparently anonymous; its editor, Miss Hammond,[1] and Professor MacCracken[2] agree in not ascribing it to Lydgate, the latter thinking that its rhymes show a younger hand than Lydgate's. The French original is also anonymous. One of its manuscripts ascribes it to Alain Chartier, but it has not Chartier's plainness and gravity. Two manuscripts give it to Michaut Taillevent, the Burgundian poet, and he is accepted by Champion, and by Droz and Piaget.[3] Champion dates it after 1445, and refers it to various Burgundian tourneys and 'pas d'armes'. Droz and Piaget, on the other hand, point out the lack of definite internal evidence; the reference to a 'locksmith from Portugal' might indicate after 1429, when Philip the Good, Duke of Burgundy, married Isabella of Portugal. They date it soon after 1430, when Taillevent was in his thirties. He was 'farceur' (1426), and later 'valet

---

[1] *Anglia*, 1911, XXXIV, 235 ff.   [2] *Minor Poems of Lydgate*, I, 1.
[3] *Le Jardin de Plaisance*, II, 96; text, I, fol. lv v.–lx.

de chambre' to the Duke, and died in 1458. A date in the early thirties is supported by the English anagrams of the translation.

I suggest that the translation was probably an early attempt at the art by Sir Richard Roos, in the Plesaunce period, after the marriage of Elisabeth Phelip. It is a line by line translation, substituting decasyllabic lines for the octosyllabic of the French, as will be done again later in *La Belle Dame sans Merci*. The channel of transmission to English knowledge was probably Bedford's wife, Anne, sister of Philip of Burgundy; Thomas, Lord Roos, had been under Bedford from 1427 till his death in 1430, and it is possible that his younger brother was his squire.

The unique manuscript of the translation is Longleat 258, one of the family of manuscripts which also contains the English *La Belle Dame*. The only manuscript of the French original known in England is the collection of French poems, Royal 19.A.iii (fol. 29–41 v.), which also contains the original *La Belle Dame*, and which may have belonged to Sir Richard Roos (see above, Chapter III). The translation is not 'signed', but the 'devise' appears in the anagrams.

The problem of the anagrams in these long poems appears formidable; actually the method employed is similar to that traced in poems of medium length. The introduction will contain the names of the group who will be the readers; the Lady of the poet's devotion will be found (but not exclusively) in the description of the chief lady of the poem. The conclusion will repeat any or all of these names, with possible additions; and the poet's 'devise' will be threaded through the relevant stanzas, generally most prominent in the first or the last. So it is here. The opening stanzas 1–3 yield ALIAn. –OB–AM; AnTIG.; BEWMONT; st. 4 completes the 'devise' IAI TOT FOrFAIT FOr–AIT. Stt. 6–8 repeat AlIAn. and also give –LISAb–Th –EuMONT; ISMANIA; WYM–YS; and TOT FOr–AIT. The description of the Lady (stt. 16–18) repeats B–WMOnT, BA–DO.; AnTIG.; ISMAnYA S––L–S; TOT FOrFAIT. The last three stanzas (101–3) again give COBHA–, E–ISA–ETh BEW–OnT; S(C)Ales. We are therefore again in the Plesaunce coterie, with its mistress, Antigone, Elisabeth Bardolf, now Lady Beaumont, Lady Scales, and Nicholas Wymbysh.

The poem is divisible into two parts, a setting (stt. 1–27) describing a hunt, and a dream (stt. 27 to the end) showing to the narrator the strife between his Heart and Eye. The poet hunts a stag, and falls in with a bevy of ladies singing and dancing, who courteously include him in their sport. One lady walks musing apart, and his eye and his heart are drawn to her. A running stag breaks up the company, and the poet

Q

renews the chase. He loses his way, despondent at having also lost
sight of the lady, and sleeps; in a dream he sees his Heart and his Eye
debate, quarrel, and finally fight. The judge, Ardent Désir, takes them
before the god of love. Lists are prepared, and the symbolic supporters
of the combatants, and their fantastic trappings, are described. As the
fight grows fierce, Dame Pity intervenes, and takes the champions before
Venus. The goddess reconciles them, since she has equal need of both.
She has the case recorded, to be submitted to all true lovers; whoever
adjudges it aright will be rewarded with a chaplet of roses and his
heart's desire.

The translator makes only one change of statement, but that is significant, and in accord with the anagrams; the French hunter finds by
the fountain under the shady pine-tree 'dames sans nombre' of

> atour notable
> Et doulce beaulte tresmondaine,

accompanied by 'hommes gentilz bien habillez'. His English counterpart finds only ladies with their gentlewomen. The men are temporarily
eliminated (though they intrude in st. 15) as they are in *The Isle of
Ladies*, and will be later in *The Assembly of Ladies*. The translator's
attraction to the poem probably lay in this group of courtly ladies; the
description of the scene is the best part of the work and of the translation,
and has something of the grace of a 'fête champêtre'.

After this attractive prologue, the original poem is not very distinguished in style; the Burgundian tone and taste become pronounced,
a mixture of ostentation and absurdity. The poet describes the lists
of gold covered with tapestry, gates of jasper and crystal, barriers of
coral, a dais of amber, a chair of estate of beryl, supported by four
golden sparrow-hawks, and illuminated by six carbuncles. Love's robe
glitters with emeralds and pearls, his crown (unfortunately 'gown' in
the English) is adorned with cameos and sapphires, very different from
the god of the Rose, with his robe of flowers, and his halo of fluttering
birds. The flowery robe Taillevent transfers to the combatants, and
by excess makes it ridiculous. The poem becomes like a Carnival, a
Battle of Flowers; not only do chaplets of roses, lilies, and lavender
adorn the supporters, but the tents are made of roses or of gillyflowers,
the seats of eglantere or woodruff. The officers of the lists are armed
with marguerites and spears of laurel, coursers are in trappings of
marjoram, and their riders in robes of periwinkle. In this riot of
flowers and of symbolic heraldry, blazons of sighs, tears, and groans
('De gemissemens dyapree'), the reader finds with relief that Venus's

litter is merely of gold and blue enamel, though the ostriches (possibly heraldic) that draw it are original enough.

The poem is not improved in the translation, which is stiff and clumsy, with many lines of thudding monosyllables, as in stanzas 27 and 28. The intention rather than the achievement of grace is felt in the first part; yet in the duller matter of the second part, one occasionally begins to hear by sheer momentum the easier rhythms of Roos's future writing, as in stanza 96 and onwards. Stanza 29 is completely after his method. His best and liveliest work here describes action, as where the stag, having taken soil, breaks away:

> And whan this hert aspied wel his tyme
> He leped lightly oute of the fontayne clere.
> My wery houndes laide theim stille by me
> ffor noon of theim might noo thing nigh hym nere.
> He brake the busshes so bothe here and there
> He went his wey withouten any arrest
> And rennyng forth amonges the bowes shere
> He scope vs fro and toke the thik forest. (st. 22)

The translator here falls back instinctively on alliteration; elsewhere he is too dependent on clumsy padding, especially 'anon' with which his stanzas are powdered. His plain sense revolts at some of the more fantastic symbolism; and when the Heart casts down a sigh as his gage of battle, he refuses that fence utterly (l. 371). Oddly enough, similar extreme fantasies Roos could find in the alliterative *Alexander* in MS. Ashmole 44; there Hercules' statue is crowned with a hat 'Of palme and of peruy[n]k & othire proud blossoms' (l. 4541); and the description of Love's jewelled robe is no richer than the English alliterative poet's addition on those of the Jewish priests (ll. 1513-72).

Roos's own imagination is in truth richer and stronger than the prettiness and silliness of *Le Cueur et l'Œil*, as *The Isle of Ladies* shows, especially in its parallel description of Love throned on high. There is here an anticipation of the coming theme; the champions are taken before Venus, to

> a straunge yle
> That was made right stronge aboute w^tall [d'ung mur]
> Of brennyng brondes by craft right habile. (st. 81)

Roos will make a more living poem out of this idea of the strange isle. So too later in *The Flower and the Leaf*, he will take up again and glorify the theme of opposition that ends in reconciliation because all the time both parties are on the same side, both serving the one power; the threatened 'joûte à outrance' becomes a 'joûte de paix'.

La Belle Dame sans Merci, already considered as a touchstone for

Roos's work, must now be fitted into the mosaic pattern of his poetic development; by comparison with these forerunners, it rises in our estimation.

No. 59. *La Belle Dame sans Merci:* a poem of 856 lines, comprising four original stanzas of rhyme royal as introduction; a hundred eight-line stanzas translated from Alain Chàrtier, including his envoy of two stanzas; and *Verba Translatoris,* or an envoy to the translation, four original stanzas of rhyme royal.

> *Incipit.* Half in a dreme, not fully wel awaked,
> The golden sleep me wrapped under his wing;
> Yet nat for-thy I roos, . . .
> *Incipit of translation.*
> Nat long ago, ryding an esy paas.
> *Explicit of Verba Translatoris.*
> I pray god sende hem better aventure.

The poem is accepted as the work of Sir Richard Roos, on the evidence of the statement in MS. Harleian 372, fol. 61: 'Translatid out of Frenche by Sir Richard Ros'. Skeat first dated it at 1410, then, in mistaken attribution to Richard Roos, Esquire, at 1450–60. The date of the French original is 1424. The anagrams of the original stanzas link the translation with Plesaunce, probably at the end of its period, possibly even the last few months. Chartier's poem would then particularly attract Roos, since he wrote as one grieving for a dead mistress, still holding aloof from merry company:

> Le plus dolent des amoureux . . .
> La mort me toulit ma maistresse
> Et me laissa seul, langoureux,
> En la conduite de tristesce.

He must abandon 'Le rire pour le lermoyer'. Roos enhances this melancholy statement:

> The deeth hath take my lady and maistresse,
> And left me sole, thus discomfit and mate,
> Sore languisshing and in way of distresse.

He must

> laugh no more but wepe in clothes blake,
> My joyful tyme alas, now is it slake (ll. 34–41).

It is possible that the translation was set as a friendly 'penaunce' (l. 9), to reprove him for moping, and to draw him back into activity, and into poetic expression on a congenial theme. The translation was commanded of Roos by them whom he 'durst nat disobey' (l. 7):

> At whos request thou mad were in this wyse
> Commaunding me with body and servyse (l. 848).

The 'signature' 'I roos' drops the word 'anon', as if the jest had worn out; but the 'devise' appears in the anagrams.

The double anagrams of the four original introductory stanzas give HOMF--Y, ALYAN. COBHAM, AnTIG., IAI T-T FOr-A-T. The *Verba Translatoris* give a more unusual result: GLOUC-ST., G. CLIFTO., BABThORP; WhITTIN. Gervaise Clifton was the Duke's treasurer; Sir Robert Babthorp, whom Gloucester had made Treasurer in 1432, had died in 1436. This must then be his eldest son, Ralph, who was killed at St. Albans in 1455; he was probably nearer Sir Richard in age and companionship, and the name Babthorp often occurs in these anagrams. As this seems to be a group of men, the name Whittingham here would indicate either Sir Robert, receiver-general to John of Bedford, or, again more probably, his son Robert, who was later a squire in the Escort. There are some anagrams also in translated stanzas: descriptions of the hard-hearted Lady yield B-W-ONT, FOr-A-T (st. 15), and -ARDO--, TOT FOr-AI- (st. 19); the *Verba Auctoris* unite B-W-ONT with Al-An COBHA-, and TOT FOrFAI- FOrFA. The Envoy repeats B-WMONT, -ARDOLF, with FOrFAYT FOrF-IT.

The manuscripts of the translation, and the significance of Royal MS. 19.A.iii, with its copy of the French and its alternative envoy in English, dedicated by anagram to Queen Margaret, have already been discussed in Chapter III. This manuscript contains another poem by Chartier, and may have been owned by Sir Richard. How he became acquainted with Chartier's work we do not know; possibly through Charles d'Orléans before 1440, possibly a decade earlier when Chartier went as French ambassador to Scotland. Thomas, Lord Roos, was in 1430 a commissioner for the treaty with Scotland, but hardly had the opportunity to go north before his death in August of that year.

Chartier is by no means the only contemporary French poet whom Roos had read. The first line of his introduction is on a pattern common in French poems, especially in those inspired by *La Belle Dame*. 'Half in a dreme, not fully wel awaked' is like the line 'Moittié dormant, moittié veillant', with which Chartier introduces the vision of Amours in his *Excusacion* for *La Belle Dame*, or like Achille Caulier's beginning of *La Cruelle Femme en Amours*:[1]

> Ne tout ayde ne tout greue
> Moitie en vie, moictie mort, etc.

The method of translation, the devices used to get round the difficulties of rhyme and line-length have already been discussed; they are

---

[1] *Le Jardin de Plaisance*, fol. cxlii v.

similar, *mutatis mutandis*, to those to be found in *The Romaunt of the Rose* and *Reson and Sensuallyte*. It is perhaps fortunate that this poem, the 'touchstone' for Roos's work, should be of this nature and character, a work of central date and typical subject, in no way unusual, but well fitted to be the yardstick of his manner and skill. It is not his most enthusiastic, like *How a Lover*, or his most romantic, like *The Isle of Ladies*, or his most glowing, like the opening of *The Black Knight*, or his finest, like *The Flower and the Leaf*. But it keeps a steady level of achievement, and shows his maturing powers, the competence of a good craftsman, the ease of a skilled poet.

No. 60. *The Romaunt of the Rose.* Fragments A and B.

Incipit. Many men sayn that in sweveninges

'Shall I therefore', said Bentley before his final audacity with the text of *Paradise Lost,* 'after so many prior presumptions, presume at last . . .?' It may be felt to be presumption to claim Sir Richard Roos as the translator of *Le Roman de la Rose.* Yet in fact Chaucerian scholars have been far from unanimous in assigning the extant translation to Chaucer; the greatest have vacillated in a way heartening (as well as exasperating) to the humble student. The daisy petals, 'He wrote it, he wrote it not', have been plucked bare; but editors of Chaucer always include the poem, though with cautionary notes. Skeat finally in 1891, after nearly fifteen years of oscillation, accepted Fragment A as Chaucer's, Lounsbury accepted the whole. So did Brusendorff, but postulated a northern transmitter with a bad memory, whose lapses he supplied with Bentleian confidence. Bradshaw, Furnivall, Ten Brink, Kaluza (who first discerned three Fragments) denied Chaucer's authorship. Other translators have been suggested: Lydgate for Fragment B by Lange, and for both A and B by Koch; King James I for B by Skeat.

Those who lightly assume that Chaucer, a busy official, set out to translate *Le Roman de la Rose* entire, might remind themselves that it runs to over 22,000 lines, of which less than one-fifth are by Guillaume de Lorris. It has been noted, though not enough stressed, that no part of this fragmentary translation really answers to the description given by the affronted god of love; none of this is 'an heresye ageyns my lawe'. Of the English *Romaunt* of nearly 7700 lines, 4429 are taken from Guillaume de Lorris; even Fragment B (ll. 1706–5810) is three-quarters de Lorris to one-quarter de Meun, and very mild de Meun at that. To all this the god could hardly take exception. Only Fragment C is from de Meun alone, and even this recounts at first Love's plan to storm the tower of Jelousie; but after this auspicious opening, there is a steady drift to theological controversy, discouraging to any courtly translator. Had he been Lydgate, no more congenial a subject than the rebuking of de Lorris's follies could have offered itself. It is obvious that the main interest of the translator is in 'Amour Courtois'.

I feel therefore free to claim Sir Richard Roos, on evidence similar to that previously offered, as the translator of Fragments A and B, and, in a later period, of Fragment C. Fragment A was begun during the contact with Elizabeth Phelip since it contains both a cryptogram and anagrams for her; it was probably continued during the period in which *The Black Knight* was written, i.e. between 1433 and 1436; there are several parallels of phrase. Fragment B may have gone straight on during the two years of Roos's probable contact with Charles d'Orléans, to mid-1438, and on over the change in Roos's life. Fragment C is shown by different cryptogram and anagrams to belong to a much later period, and will be dealt with in Chapter XI.

The accepted division between A and B is artificial; it does not correspond to any break in the French, and rests on the change of the word 'knoppes' to 'boutons' for the rosebud. This does not necessarily entail a change of translator. 'Knop' was a household word,[1] and certainly so in the Roos family: Lord William had an armorial silver cup with 'le bouse super le knop'; and Sir Richard at his death owned silver spoons with 'gilte knoppes'. In the alliterative *Alexander* (MS. Ashmole 44) he would find 'knopis of perle' for curtain-ornaments (l. 4917). It was a very natural first choice; it is no wonder that he started with 'knoppes' for buds, and equally no wonder that after five instances he changed to 'boutons'. Attractive rhymes for 'knoppe' are limited: lop, crop; what else? hop, pop; 'babbling rhymes' indeed. One can imagine Charles d'Orléans laughing, as foreigners still do, at the funny little words in English, our famous Saxon monosyllables. Within thirty lines the poet discovers that 'knoppe' is 'a hard rhyme', does not use it in rhyme, and changes to 'bouton'. This has all the advantages; it is a sliding dissyllable, fore and aft accentually, with an easy final sound for rhyme (e.g. ll. 1761-2, 1845-6, 3473-4). It is true that the poet discards de Lorris's rhyme of 'bouton: mouton', and produces a more conventional line, 'Whanne thei ben faire in her sesouns' (l. 4012), thereby provoking Brusendorff (p. 331) to a flourish of his crook which brings back the strayed sheep. The so-called Fragments A and B are homogeneous in the English as in the French. It is convenient still to use the terms, especially since there were changes in the translator's

---

[1] See *Cal. Close Rolls, 1441-7*, p. 267.

circumstances. I propose to deal with A and B together; of the genuine Fragment C, only one point is noted here. The argument of easier rhyme holds good also for the change from Bialacoil in B to Fair-Welcoming in C. Of some four dozen times that Bialacoil is mentioned in the English the name is never rhymed: Fair-Welcoming occurs only four times but twice it is rhymed, with 'thing' and 'nothyng' (ll. 7521-2, 7639-40). This rhyming of the present participle inflexion is fairly common with Roos, as in the first two stanzas of *La Belle Dame* (wing: remembring; thing; musing: imagening). There is probably also another reason for the change (see No. 102).

A word must be said on Skeat's assigning Fragment B to James I of Scotland, on the score of parallels alleged in *The Kingis Quair* to *The Romaunt*, and in spite of his assumption that James would not be able to read the original French. It is a dangerous assumption to make of a Scottish prince who at his capture was on his way to France, and who was twice in northern France with the armies of Henry V. All Skeat's parallels, except one, are as much with *Le Roman de la Rose* as with the translation. Only one point needs further consideration, the occurrence in *The Kingis Quair* (st. 31) of the Kentish rhyme-form 'knet' for knit, as in *The Romaunt*, l. 1397. But since the rhyme-word 'knette' occurs elsewhere in Chaucer (e.g. *Parl. of Foules*, l. 438), James would have other warrant for the rhyme. The Kentish rhymes in Fragment B puzzled Skeat in the work of an assumed Northern poet; they need not puzzle us in a Roos of Hamlake, who was also a frequenter of Plesaunce in Kent.

The poem is 'signed' fairly early in Fragment A:

> And up I roos, and gan me clothe.
> Anoon I wissh myn hondis bothe (ll. 95-6);

probably again in Fragment B:

> Upon my fete I ros up than. (l. 1829)

There is no 'signature' in C. In A, as in *La Belle Dame*, l. 97, the English inevitably translates the statement of the French:

> De mon lit tantost me levai,
> Chauçai moi e mes mains lavai. (ll. 89-90)

But the statement is manipulated; the otiose words 'From my bed', and the detail of the shoes, are eliminated to make room for the word 'anoon'.

The proper-name cryptogram in honour of Elisabeth Phelip (Bardolf) is handled in a rather different manner from that of poems already considered. Sir Richard cannot here juggle with proper names at will;

he is perforce tied down to the *personae* of *Le Roman*. So little obvious is the result that he may have done it for his secret satisfaction. My impression is that he did not at first intend any attempt at the cryptogram, but that when he found himself in the Garden (ll. 1033–1211) with (in the French), Beaute, Richesse, Largesse, Fraunchise, all within two hundred lines, he saw that he had B–R––LF. By keeping the names in French, and by putting in 'Dame' before a later mention of Richesse (1129) where it is not in the French, he obtained the one missing consonant, D. He thus had the consonants of Bardolf. Only then, probably, did he look round to see what else he could do; it was not much, but at one point by careful translation he could suggest the lady's two other names. The translation (l. 415) of Papelardie as Poope-Holy, an inelegant word and incorrect derivative, has always puzzled students; he never has recourse to it again, or elsewhere, but uses Ipocrisy (l. 6112) or Papelardie itself (l. 6796). The last three of the painted figures (ll. 349–450) are Elde, Poope-Holy, Povert; from these Roos gets El. PH–lyP. Hence, I believe, his rather desperate choice of Poope-Holy in a list of names which was proving refractory. By using the 'Saxon' word Elde instead of Age or Vieillesse he gets the first letters of the Christian name. By all these ingenious expedients he succeeded in wringing his cryptogram out of a fixed list of names. It is difficult to see why Sir Richard Roos should have spent all this ingenuity on a name-initial cryptogram when the double acrostic anagrams are so numerous in Fragment A, becoming almost continuous in the Garden of the Rose. The character-portraits of the poem lend themselves to his method; as there are fewer in B, so there are fewer anagrams there. In A, however, he unexpectedly uses even the unattractive Painted Figures, for special purposes, some of historical interest.

The introduction on dreams (ll. 1–41, in Thynne only) sets the stage with HOMFr–Y, GLOST–R, ALIAn. COBHA., AnTIGONA, BA–Tho., TOT For–AIT, R.R. Following straight on with the description of May (ll. 49–70) comes the name of the Lady, discernible only in the caesural acrostic, E–ISAB–Th BAR–OLF, PHY., and WHITT–––AM, while IAI TOT FORFAIT is in the initial acrostic. Ydelnesse (ll. 538–84) covers AlIAn. –OBHAM ANT–G., and introduces ISMANIA S–A–ES and IAQueTTA STAn–OW, FULPOT, with ForFA–T ForFA. Gladnesse singing (ll. 745–58) is of course ANTIG. COBHAM, and the two dancers (ll. 776–92) unite IAQueTTA with some unidentified girls, IDONEA[1] and KATHer., and with TOT ForFA–T.

---

[1] Idoine FitzHugh, wife of Sir Geoffrey FitzHugh, is a possibility; he died about June 1436. His father, Henry, Lord FitzHugh, had been guardian to Henry VI, and a member of the Council under Gloucester until his death in 1424/5 (G.E.C., V, 421–3, 427 note *d*).

In Curtesie (ll. 793–814) homage is paid to the Duchess alone: ALIAN, COB–AM, DUC–ES. AI TOT FOrFAIT. Beaute (ll. 1006–32) brings in the Lady under her married name, BeauMONT, BA–DO–F, together with ANT–GONA and ISMAN–A (Scales) WHA––S; these are the poet's three Graces, 'linked in lovely wise'. With the long description of Largesse (ll. 1149–96), there is room for a suitable braid of Plesaunce names: HOMFR–Y GLOUC–ST., AlIAN CO–HAM, ANT., A–TWS, PHeli–., STAFFOr., STAnLOW, KATH. WHITTIN–HAM, TOt FOrFAIT FOrFAIT. Largesse's Knight (ll. 1197–1210) is confined to the ducal pair, interweaving HO–FrE–. GLOST. with Al–An. –OBHA. Fraunchise (ll. 1211–45) returns to the Ladies Beaumont and Scales: –LISAB–TH BARDO–F, BeW–ONT, ISMANYA S–AL–S WHA––SB–R–GH, with T–T FOrFAIT FOrFAIT. Fraunchise's Knight (ll. 1246–50) is BABThO., with AlIAN. included. Idilnesse and Youthe dancing (ll. 1273–1302) give, the one STAnLOW, FUL–POT,[1] and the other BeWMONT, BA–DO., ANTI–ONA, BABTH., KATH–––N WH–T., with FOrFAYT FOr–AIT.

Two figures, Sir Myrthe and Dame Gladnesse, are used to introduce another family, already known to Plesaunce and to the reader, the Bourchiers and Staffords. Myrthe himself (ll. 817–46) is HOMF. STAFFOrd (the fifth Earl) with his mother An. BOWCHI. (Anne of Woodstock, see above, No. 2) and his wife An N–––IL (Anne Neville, daughter of Ralph, first Earl of Westmoreland, and of Joan Beaufort). Gladnesse (ll. 847–76) brings in a younger stepbrother, IOHAN BOWSHI., in the Plesaunce set with ALIAN. COBHAM, ANTIG.; BABThO.; WIMBISH.

Yet another Plesaunce lady, a rarer bird in Roos's nets, is Curtesie dancing: ISAB. SCROO., C–AWOrTH, together with ISMAN., FOrFAIT. John, Lord Scroop of Masham, who had married Elisabeth Chaworth by 1418, was Gloucester's nominee as Treasurer of England in the 'Coup' of 1432; he was a grandson of a Roos girl, Maud, daughter of the fourteenth-century William, Lord Roos.

The Painted Figures show some very interesting departures from the Plesaunce norm. In Sorowe (ll. 301–48) Roos pays a tribute of sympathy to two widows, to his sister-in-law, as yet unconsoled for her husband Thomas, drowned in the Marne in 1430: AlIAN. B(E)AUSHAM, –OOS, FOrFAIT FOrFAIT; and to the widow, Maud (Lovell), of the famous soldier, Sir John, Lord Mautravers and Arundel, who died of wounds on June 12, 1435; she did not survive him a full year (May 19, 1436):[2]

---

[1] According to Roos's method, this and later Stanlow-Fulpot conjunctions imply a marriage, as if Margaret was a Philpot by birth, or Jacquetta Stanlow married a Philpot; there was a well-known city family of that name; but I cannot explain it more exactly.

[2] She was the Lady Beauty of Charles d'Orléans; see Steele, *English Poems*, etc., p. xxxiv.

A–UND–L MAW–A–S. In Elde (ll. 349–412), Roos remains in this circle
with the names of his mother and, curiously enough, of her mother,
who died before his birth: MAR. –OOS, ARUNDEL; AlIAN. MAWTRAUERS
COBHAM. Lady Roos must have been born not later than 1380, when
her father, Sir John de Arundel, was lost at sea; she was therefore sixty
and perhaps upwards at her death in 1438. Her mother, Baroness
Mautravers and Lady Cobham, was about the same age at her death
in 1404/5, an age then considered 'vieillesse'. She is probably introduced
here to stress the kinship of Cobham and Roos, as being the grandmother of both the Duchess and Sir Richard. Hate (ll. 147–61) seems
to give a skeletal and semi-concealed form of Willoughby (WY–––WBY,
FOrFAYT); I know no explanation of this unless it refers to the first
Lady Willoughby, who is unflatteringly portrayed in *Ragman Roll*, st. 9.
The remaining Figures give us Roos's comments on persons well known
in history. The first ten lines (with three more letters) of Coveitise
(ll. 181–206) give CARDI–AL ––AUFOrT, –InCHeST–R, FOrFAIT FOrFA–T;
Cardinal Henry Beaufort, Bishop of Winchester, is the typical rich and
grasping prelate of this century, as Wolsey is of the next. As Gloucester's
bitter rival, he would be a welcome subject for satire at Plesaunce. In
four Figures Roos comes nearer home, perhaps dangerously so. Felonye
and Vilanye (ll. 162–80) yield s–vThwel; HUH S–InF––T; BO–––––OC.
Avarice (ll. 207–46) gives BOLINGBROK, SOUTHW., AlIAN.; HWH SWINN-
FLET; HOMFR(Y); Envye (ll. 247–300) yields: ROGE– BO–INBrOK, THOMAS
SOUTHW(E)L, MA–GE–Y IO–DAIN, WIT–H OF EYE, SWINNF–(E)T. IAI TOT
FOrFAIT FOrFAIT. Here Roos is bold enough to display the character and
motives of the Duchess's band of necromancers, and to pronounce
judgment on the notorious trio, Thomas Southwell, Roger Bolingbroke
or Only, and Margery Jo(u)rdain, known as the Witch of Eye. Hugh
Swynflet, gent., had gone bail for Margery Jourdemayne in May 1432
(*Cal. Close Rolls, 1429–35*, p. 192). His name does not occur in 1441;
but Roos evidently connects him with the Duchess, and the necromancers. Roos has coupled Eleanor Cobham's name with Bolingbroke's
in the description of the magic mirror in *How a Lover*, in the *Complaint
against Fortune*, and will again thrice in *Reson and Sensuallyte* (see below,
No. 61); here in Avarice he adds HOMFRY at the end, possibly as a
warning to the Duke against his wife's dangerous practices. There
remain the Figures, Povert and Poope-Holy; for the first (ll. 449–74)
I have no clear solution.[1] For Poope-Holy, Roos turns to the Lollards,

---

[1] The anagram seems in part to cover, ANTIGONA (ll. 458–62) and [P]OWIS,
with AlIAn CO–HA., and with the 'devise' and a fair residue. Whether this is
ironical, or a plea for Lady Powis or for the impecunious Roos himself, as
impoverished, I cannot say.

and makes a braid of notorious names: OLDCAST., –OBHAM; WAW; PY; W(H)IT.; and sHARP WIGMO.; and adds TOT FOrFAIT FOr FA–T: Sir John Oldcastle, Lord Cobham, the only Lollard aristocrat to suffer the death penalty (1417); William Wawe, robber of a nunnery, but condemned as a Lollard plotter (1427); Pye and Whyte, who suffered in 1428; and 'Jack Sharpe of Wigmoresland', treated as rebel and heretic, and beheaded as recently as 1431. Duke Humphrey's prompt action in repressive measures against Wawe and Sharpe was celebrated in verse by yet another of his protégés, the laborious translator of Palladius (Hammond, *English Verse*, etc., pp. 204, 463).

Fragment A is thus made to form a kind of running commentary on the people of Plesaunce, their dispositions, their associates, their political interests. In Fragment B similar anagrams are found at first, but gradually the Duke and Duchess recede from view, and the centre of the stage is taken by Lady Scales and the Stanlow ladies. The first obvious opportunity for anagrams comes in the three gifts or solaces of Love. Swete-Thought (ll. 2791–824) runs on a very restricted range of letters (eleven only in 34 lines), yet its anagram reads STAnHOPe; TOT FOrFAIT FOrFAIT. Swete-Speche (ll. 2825–92) has the long Plesaunce braid: HO–FrEY, AlIAn COBHA.; AnTIGO.; BeW–OnT, BARDO–F; WHITT.; ISMAnIA SCAl–S; STAnHOP; BABTHOR; IAY TOT FOrFAIT FOrFAIT. Swete-Lokyng (ll. 2893–934) is confined to Roos's two chief ladies, PHY(L)IP, BARDO–F, BeWMONT, and ISMANYA SCAl–S, TOT FOrFAIT FOrFAIT. Bialacoil is always associated with the name Stanlow: STAn–OW, TOT FOrFAIT, (ll. 2981–7), MAR., JAQu–TTA, STAn–OW, PHI–P–T, TOt FOrFAIT (ll. 3066–84).

Most of the remaining figures of Fragment B are assigned to Stanlow and to Lady Scales, whether as doing or suffering. They must be felt as active in Shame and Chastite (ll. 3042–60), ISMAnIA S(C)AL–S, (S)TAn–OW, TOT FOrFA–T, R.R.; in Resoun (ll. 3193–216), ISMANY SCA––S WHA––S–BOR––GH, BABTH., TOT FOrFAIT FOrF–IT; (ll. 4615–28), ISMAnIA SCA–IS, STAn–OW, FULPOT. But they are surely the victims of the repulsive Daunger (ll. 3130–38), STAnLOW; of Wikkid-Tunge (ll. 3799–820), ISMAnIA SCA–ES WHA–E–BORO., STAn–OW, F––POT, FOrF–IT; and of Jelousie (ll. 4284–300), ISMAnIA SCAl–S, STAn–O, TOT FOrFAIT. When Roos is working on Freend, his thoughts recover the friends from what by now are surely the figures of earlier years, HOMFrI, AlIAn C–BHAM, IAI TOT FOrFAIT (ll. 3338–52), and again AlIAn. COB., AnT–G., EL–SABeTH BEW–O–T, TOT FOrFA–T (ll. 5201–20). In the description of the Rose in bloom, as in that of Beaute in Fragment A, the three ideal names again appear: B–WMO–T, IS–AnIA SCAl–S WhAL–SBO––GH, ANTIG. POWIS, IAY TOT FOrFAIT FOrFAIT (ll. 3627–66).

These anagrams give the impression that Roos is at first deeply involved with Plesaunce, but that by the end of Fragment B, Plesaunce and even Lady Bounte are becoming a memory, and in the forefront of his thinking are the women friends who console and advise him on the loss and then the death of Elisabeth Beaumont. In Fragment C, all these names are dropped, and persons of the 1470s take their place, some being members of the younger generation of Beauforts. In the same way, *Reson and Sensuallyte* will prove to have started in Plesaunce, to move with the translator to new experiences of 1445–50, and to break off after a mood of reminiscence.

The unique manuscript of *The Romaunt of the Rose*, MS. Hunter, Mus. V.3.7, in the National Library of Scotland, is an elegant and clean volume, in a style of execution pointing to a well-to-do patron. Its production was dated 'at the first quarter of the fifteenth century or so' by Brusendorff (p. 296), who considered Skeat's date 'about 1440' (*Chaucer*, I, 13) 'almost certainly too late'. Skeat is however nearer the mark for the translation of the first part of the poem at least; but Fragment C will be seen to point to a date in the 1470s. The relation of the manuscript to Thynne's edition of 1532 is debated; Thynne supplies to the poem the first forty-four lines, and later nearly a hundred lines, and again fifty lines, missing from the manuscript through loss of leaves. As we have seen (p. 92, above), Thynne seems to have had access to Roos material. Kaluza thought that Thynne printed from the Hunter manuscript; Brusendorff (Chapter V) argues for at least five other assumed manuscripts, not closely related textually, as the separate bases of the two texts (p. 297, footnote 3).

Parallel passages are of particular interest in dealing with this translation, and need to be considered in some detail. The parallels with Chaucer's works (Brusendorff, pp. 392 ff.) prove no more than that the translator knew his Chaucer well, as he was likely to do, and as it is obvious that Sir Richard Roos did. Not all of Brusendorff's parallels are convincing. The reflections on Time as spoken by the Host, and as translated in *The Romaunt*, are not 'rather close renderings', but quite independent, and different in tone. Chaucer's

> As dooth the streem that turneth nevere agayn,
> Descendynge fro the montaigne into playn (*Cant. Tales*, B.23)

is poetically in another sphere from the tinkling literalness of

> As watir that doun renneth ay
> But never drope retourne may (*Romaunt*, ll. 383–4).

Brusendorff's parallels on the spacing of the trees (p. 397) may be added to and taken further. In *The Boke of the Duchesse*, Chaucer, says Brusendorff (p. 397), was indeed ignorant in tree-planting of the meaning of *toise* (fathom, or over six feet); but there is another possible explanation. In *How a Lover*, Sir Richard had not specified the distance, and in *Reson and Sensuallyte* (l. 5145 ff.) he omits the vague statement of the original, 'Par ordre et par mesure'. In *The Romaunt*, he translates *toise* correctly, so that the tree trunks are between thirty and forty feet apart (ll. 1391–4). When he comes to write *The Flower and the Leaf*, having by then had some experience of Rockingham Forest, he reverts to Chaucer's method of description; in *The Boke of the Duchesse* (ll. 419–20), each spreading tree stood 'by hymselve', ten or twelve feet distant from its neighbour; so Roos's oaks, in what is obviously a plantation, stand 'with braunches brode' each eight or nine feet apart from its fellows.

Parallels here and there with Chaucer's poems are not proofs of Chaucer's authorship; but parallels with the tenor of these poems of 'Amour Courtois' just discussed have greater significance, because greater unity. Many have the 'signature' or the anagram, or both. Amusingly enough, Brusendorff himself is once very 'hot' in a footnote (p. 415, cf. p. 327, footnote 4) dealing with his Bentleian figure, the reviser whose 'local habitation must have been the North Midlands', and who must have belonged to

that Chaucerian tradition in the North of England during the first half of the fifteenth century, which is chiefly represented by the anonymous author of *The Ile of Ladies*.

'Reviser' must yield to 'translator', but he was certainly not, as Brusendorff thought, 'a person of a rather Puritan turn of mind'. It is obvious that the writer of *How a Lover* felt the stimulus of *Le Roman de la Rose*; the general picture of the garden and the well with its magic mirror, of the birds, and fruits, and trees 'sette yn rengys' (l. 30), proves that the poet knew de Lorris's work intimately. He has other sources also, however, and makes his own fresh lists with exciting names and words. The lady too is own cousin in her features to Ydelnesse, and in her disposition to Curtesye. At two places in *The Romaunt* the translator drifts into the lilt that is so marked in the 'doggerel' poem. Of Beauté, de Lorris writes delicately:

> Tendre ot la char come rosee;
> Simple fu come une esposee
> E blanche come flor de lis.
> Ele ot le vis cler et alis (l. 999).

The English author expands thus:

> Hir flesh was tendre as dew of flour;
> Hir chere was symple as byrde in bour;
> As whyt as lylye or rose in rys (l. 1013).

Then he modulates back into his usual rhythm with the line, 'Hir face gentyl and tretys'. The same kind of rhythmical shift is subconsciously induced by the word 'wimple'. Shame comes forth to defend Bialacoil,

> Humble of hir port, and made it symple,
> Weryng a vayle in stide of wymple. (l. 3863)

The 'doggerel' poet has already said of his lady's smooth forehead that it is

> No thyng pynchyd lyke a nonnys wymple
> Ne forowyd drye lyke a nabbesse gymple. (l. 326)

The rhythm, as much as the words, suggests the same poetic craftsman at work, and in a manner different from that of Chaucer. The first example above shows pleasure in tail-rhyme verse, which Chaucer treated only with derision. Chaucer uses alliterative metre very skilfully for two totally different effects, battles, as in the 'Knight's Tale' (ll. 2600–16), and Constance's prayer to the Virgin ('Man of Lawes Tale', 841 ff.). In the first, energy and speed are deliberately heightened; in the second, the rhythms of vernacular devotional lyrics to 'Mylde Marie, Moder and May' [1] increase naturalness and pathos.

In *The Isle of Ladies*, the poet is under the spell of *Le Roman de la Rose*, seen mainly in the outlook of romantic love, which was the Rose's legacy to later poetry. On the other hand, the linguistic likenesses of *The Isle* and *The Romaunt* are many, in northern forms and non-Chaucerian rhymes. In *The Black Knight* the close verbal parallels are of significance as Skeat showed (*Chaucer*, VII, xliv–xlv, and pp. 504–5), though with conclusions which no longer apply. The use in it of the words 'costey', 'attempre', and finally of the grass 'softe as veluet' (a comparison added in *The Romaunt*), Skeat took as proof that the author of *The Black Knight* 'was acquainted with Fragment A'. Krausser pointed out that Lydgate has used the last phrase for the 'yonge grene' in the *Troy Book*. It would seem that both in *The Black Knight* (also 'signed') and in *The Romaunt* Sir Richard Roos paid Lydgate the compliment of a borrowing from the *Troy Book*, translated in his childhood. A much

---

[1] See Carleton Brown, *Rel. Lyrics of the Fourteenth Century*, Nos. 26, 32, 110, 111.

more unusual and striking use of velvet is that in *How a Lover* to express the soft, rosy skin of the lady:

> The snowe iij partyes, the rose that other
> Held with crymysyn veluet ys brother (l. 282).

In the later *Flower and the Leaf*, he will use the actual stuff white velvet, for the rich dresses of the ladies, the heralds and the squires of the Leaf (ll. 141–233, 261). Like Keats, Roos was keenly alive to the sensuous delight of touch, to the feel of 'woof and texture'.

In *Reson and Sensuallyte* (also 'signed', and probably begun not long after the first part of *The Romaunt*) the likenesses to *Le Roman* are chiefly due to the close dependence on it of the original French poem, *Les Echecs Amoureux*, especially of the first part. The description of spring, and of the natural world, the seductiveness of Venus in person and speech, the arguments of Diana, who plays a part like that of Resoun, the garden of Déduit and its inhabitants, Cupid and his arrows, the Rose, the prison of Bialacoil, the well of Narcissus, all these are confessedly drawn directly from *Le Roman* already in the French. Parallelism with *How a Lover* is inevitable. Brusendorff here lends unwitting support (p. 388, footnote 2); he denies *Reson* to Lydgate, dismissing Sieper's parallels; and he shows that its translator knew *The Romaunt*, B, since he uses 'bouton' and Bialacoil, not 'knoppe' and Belacueil (ll. 5650, 6725, 6757).

It is Brusendorff also who in the same footnote lays stress on Schick's point that in *The Compleynt* (attached in two manuscripts to *The Temple of Glas*) a line of *The Romaunt* which is not in the French (l. 1971) is included: 'Withoute feynyng or feyntyse' (l. 477). *The Compleynt* is a personal love-poem by Roos, more original and naturalistic than some; but near the end its naïvety is heightened by a rhetorical catherine-wheel of antitheses, based on Resoun's definitions of love. This passage, which describes the lady's varied inspiration to the poet, is a continuation on similar lines rather than a translation, but it shows an echoing memory of the sound as well as of the meaning of some lines, as here:

> Myn fulle trust & myn grevaunce
> Myn seknesse, & myn hol plesaunce
> Myn myrthe & ek myn maledye   (*Compleynt*, ll. 497–9);

> It is sike hele and hool seknesse,
> A thurst drowned in dronkenesse
> And helthe full of maladie (*Romaunt*, B, ll. 4721–3).

The problem of how access to the English *Romaunt*, which does not seem to have been widely spread, was had by the author of *How a*

Lover, of *The Isle of Ladies*, and of *The Compleynt*, and also by 'Lydgate', is much simplified if we can assume that the author of these poems, and the translator of *Le Roman*, were one and the same. The occurrence of the northern forms and rhymes, which have forced critics into contortions of explanation, are not only explicable, but natural in the work of a Roos of Hamlake.

It is indeed extraordinary that the claim to Chaucer as the translator of this *Romaunt of the Rose* has so long survived in the face of all the evidence of non-Chaucerian rhymes, and northern rhymes and forms. It rests on our ignorance hitherto of any other poet of the necessary skill and accomplishment. Now that such a poet is known, that argument by default is no longer valid. Non-Chaucerian words also have to be admitted in sufficient number to give pause to the supporter of Chaucer. For some, another influence, a source, is available. MS. Ashmole 44, the alliterative *Alexander*, has been shown (see Chapter IV, section v) to be probably Sir Richard Roos's own copy; this will give us the non-Chaucerian words 'avenaunt', 'inde' (blue), and 'orfrays' (bands of jewelled gold embroidery). They seem to be words of earlier borrowing from the French, kept alive in the fourteenth century in the Romances, especially in the alliterative and the rhymed *Alexander*, neglected by Chaucer, but revived in this fifteenth-century poetry. The means of transmission to Roos would seem to be MS. Ashmole 44.

The pretty word 'avenaunt' is already there in a shortened form to mean 'courteous': 'For þe auaunt ser Alexander is all þe werd famyd' (l. 2387); its more feminine application is seen in *How a Lover*: 'a lady feyre, yong, and avenaunt' (l. 428). In *The Romaunt*, Curtesye is 'of body avenaunt' (l. 1263; the word is not in the original); and Resoun is 'of hir porte full avenaunt' (l. 4622); the two remaining instances show the word applied to seemly and suitable behaviour and feeling (ll. 2058, 3679). In *Reson and Sensuallyte* the word is used of the beauty of Mercury ('Hys body small and avenant', l. 1719), and of the fine fashioning of the chess-board ('Lusty to syght and avenant', l. 6047).

The connexion of 'Inde' (indigo blue) with sky-colour is suggested in MS. Ashmole 44, ll. 1523-4, when the walls of Jerusalem are hung for Alexander with

> webis of ynde
> Of briȝt blasand blewe browden with sternes.

So in Mandeville (ch. xii) the beak of the phoenix is 'coloured blue, as Ynde'. In *How a Lover* the poet does not use the word but compares the Lady's veins with 'fressher blue then swaged [?ewage] saphyre'

R

(l. 373). *The Isle of Ladies*, with very few colour-words, uses blue and green for the bright bird; whereas in *The Flour of Curtesye* the birds have 'fetheres ynde' (l. 257) and the flowers in the Black Knight's 'erber' are also 'inde' (l. 127). *Reson and Sensuallyte* has two significant examples: first, Juno's crown is 'Fretful of ryche stonys inde' (l. 1400; cf. l. 5750), though her jewels and her rainbow have 'blywe' colours; this recalls the list of jewels 'commyng out of Inde' of *How a Lover* (l. 112), and may have the same meaning as also in 'rubies and . . . stones of Ynde' (*Mars*, l. 246); in the poem 'As ofte as syghes' the poet passes from the 'goldy grauel' of Pactolus to 'Inde stones' that 'shynen with her lemys' (l. 59). Secondly, Diana's warning on the garden of Déduit describes the serpents lurking under flowers 'Yelwe, rede, ynde, and pers' (l. 4019). In *The Romaunt* there is the same collocation; the ground is clothed in 'gras and flouris, ynde and pers' (l. 67); the original line runs 'L'erbe e les flors blanches e perses' (l. 63); the translator has added 'ynde' to Chaucer's 'pers' for another shade of blue.

Another elegant word, 'orfrays', neglected by Chaucer, is found in MS. Ashmole 44; Candace's hall is adorned with 'orfrays & orient perles' (l. 5269). In Fragment A, Ydelnesse and Gladnesse wear chaplets and Richesse trimmings, of 'orfrays' (ll. 562, 869, 1076) as in the French.

It is in the siege accounts that we chiefly see some influence of a soldier's reading joined to his experience. The description of Jelousie's tower is very freely translated (ll. 4145–250B). Compared with the French (ll. 3796–920) there are several additions and omissions, and, more significant perhaps, the substitution of the particular for the general. Thus the couplet describing the mortar,

> Car l'en destrempa le mortier
> De fort vin aigre e de chauz vive (ll. 3840–1),

is expanded to

> The temperure of the morter
> Was maad of lycour wonder der
> Of quykke lym, persant and egre,
> The which was tempred with vynegre (ll. 4177–80).

A soldier in an army of occupation which never had enough funds knew the 'wonder der' expense of building and repairing fortifications, a continual necessity as castles and towns changed hands. 'Many a riche and fair touret' is built in addition to the four corner towers, which, on a square keep with walls of six hundred feet, would be too widely spaced for adequate defence. The vague phrase 'engin qui sache getier' is replaced by 'gyn, gunne, nor skaffaut' (l. 4176), and the

even vaguer 'engins de maintes manieres' become 'Spryngoldes, gunnes,
bows and archers' (l. 4191), and recall Alexander's siege of Tyre, when
the Greeks

> Strykis vp of þe stoure stanes of engynes, . . .
> Tilt torettis doun, toures on hepis,
> Spedely with sprygaldis (ll. 1415–19).

The building of Alexander's tower against Tyre, and his later siege of
Thebes, are equally forcibly described (ll. 1149–62, and 2209 ff.). In
The Romaunt, single lines here and there are added to or altered in a
way which suggests a soldier-translator. Thus the rather weak comparison of the sleepless lover with a man restless from toothache ('qui
a mal as denz') becomes the more forcible 'As man in werre were
forwerreyd' (l. 2564). He replaces (l. 3826) Etampes and Meaux by
larger towns familiar to Englishman of all ranks at home and in the
army, Rheims (Reynes is Lydgate's form of the name too) and Amiens.
There may be yet another reason; in August 1439, Talbot tried, but
failed, to relieve the siege of Meaux, and it was not a name of good
omen. The finest added line in the whole translation gives vividly the
gesture and contortion of a wounded man trying to pull out an arrow:

> The shaft I drow out of the arwe,
> Rokyng for wo right wondir narwe (ll. 1905–6).

The writer must have seen this bitter effort many times; he may have
had to make it himself.

Another revelatory addition is that to Love's recommendation to
the lover to ingratiate himself by knowing how to play and dance:

> Among eke, for thy lady sake,
> Songes and complayntes [se] that thou make,
> For that wole meven in hir herte,
> Whanne they reden of thy smerte. (ll. 2325–8)

It is the advice of a lyrical poet, and an appeal as well. So too the desire
that a reader should 'observe the stops' is that of a man whose work is
read aloud to a coterie audience, as ready to jest and jape as were the
courtiers in Theseus's palace:

> And poynte it as the resoun is . . .
> For a reder that poyntith ille
> A good sentence may ofte spille (ll. 2157–62).

Is there also personal experience, from the pupil's end, in this added
couplet?

> It is but veyn on hym to swynke,
> That on his lernyng wol not thinke (ll. 2151–2).

It may be argued that Roos possibly stopped at the end of de Lorris' poem, and only continued with de Meun at the later period when Fragment C was written. As well as the anagrams, two circumstances make this improbable: first, the occurrence of the later cryptograms in the first section of C, immediately after the long gap; and secondly, the close parallelism between the first lines of de Meun on Hope and Wanhope, and the poem on Hope (see No. 9, above), which in both its versions is evidently a fairly early production; this last goes to show that Roos had de Meun early in his mind. It is possible that the translation, begun for Plesaunce, was continued as a means of 'conditioning' the young king's mind towards love and marriage. The Lancastrian party increasingly desired an heir to the throne. Richard Beauchamp, Earl of Warwick, who since 1428 had been the king's tutor, and who had commissioned Lydgate to translate a defence of Henry's claim to the French crown, might well, before his death in 1439, have encouraged his daughter's brother-in-law, skilled in 'amour courtois', to introduce the king to these inevitable ideas by means of poetry, tempering them by moral insertions such as that on youth amending its foolish ways (ll. 3239–43), or on the true end of marriage (ll. 4821–5). At the time of the royal marriage, Roos, I believe, gave further help, culminating in the beautiful and tender *Lover's Mass*.

No. 61. *Reson and Sensuallyte:* an allegorical, narrative poem (a vision, not a dream), of over 7000 lines of octosyllabic couplets, freely translated from the first part (ll. 1–4873) of the anonymous French poem, *Les Echecs Amoureux*. It is difficult to place in any chronological survey, because its anagrams cover at least ten years of Roos's experience, as do those of *The Temple of Glas*. The wide range of Plesaunce references, both immediate and retrospective, will be explained in this, the main consideration of the poem; the remaining anagrams, dealing with Queen Margaret's court, and Roos's second wooing, will be picked up later.

> *Incipit.* To alle folkys vertuouse
> That gentil ben and amerouse.
> *Explicit.* Ther stood a poune of gret renoun
> Callyd delectacion,—

The translation thus stops short abruptly, early in the description of the poet's chessmen, before the game has actually begun; hence it omits the didactic conclusion of the poem on the contemplative and active life.

The translation has been accepted as Lydgate's at the instance of

Schick,[1] and was edited as such by Ernst Sieper.[2] Schick dated it 1406–8, and Sieper before 1412. Schick, considering it to be 'the only one of Lydgate's poems which we can read with real interest and enjoyment', put it later than *The Flour of Curtesye* and *The Black Knight*, both 'inferior'.

I suggest that the translation was by Sir Richard Roos and was begun towards the end of the Plesaunce period, probably soon after *The Romaunt of the Rose*, and resumed and continued till about 1450. It shows strong traces of the period of Gloucester's influence, and, in a tone of reminiscence, of Roos's courtship of Elisabeth Phelip. Opportunities for the cryptogram by the Ladies' names are not taken, but anagrams are very numerous, possibly more than I have discerned. A striking reference to Duke Humphrey is seen in the long interpolation of forty lines on the death of the Swan (ll. 1245–82). This is a deliberate and marked intrusion into the poem, slipped in quietly at first, but with an obvious ending, the relieved conclusion of one who has delivered his soul, and returns from his admitted digression. The Bohun badge of the White Swan was retained by the sons of Henry IV and Mary Bohun, of whom Duke Humphrey was the last survivor after 1435; it was identified with him in popular song, as the contemporary gloss on the well-known political poem of about 1450 shows:

> Bedforde   Gloucetter
> The Rote is ded, the Swanne is goone
> Excetter
> The firy Cressett hath lost his lyght.
> (Wright, *Polit. Poems*, II, 221)

The indisputable allusion to Gloucester is reinforced, as will be seen, by the anagram of the Duke and Cardinal Beaufort. The interpolation may be an elegy or a warning. One might well take it for the latter; true, the burden is *Respice finem*, but under the didacticism, there lies a *caveat*:

> So euery man, in caas semblable,
> Which is a best resonable,
> Shulde aduerte and han in mynde,
> And vnclose his eyen blynde,
> To sen aforn, it ys no Iape,
> How he the dethe may nat eskape,
> Whan Antropos the hour hath set. (ll. 1255–61)

After Eleanor Cobham's fall in 1441, Sir Richard Roos, the king's knight,

---

[1] *Reason and Sensuality*, Anglia, Beiblatt, VIII, 134 ff.
[2] E.E.T.S., Extra ser., 84, 89 (1901, 1903).

was in a position to hear court rumour; he may have tried to help his former patron. Certainly he dragged in this significant swan by the smallest feather of its wing, seizing the incongruous opportunity given by the French poet's description of Pallas haloed by a flight of cygnets. On the other hand, the later anagrams show Roos working at the poem from 1448 onwards; and the passage may lament the Duke's death in February 1447. If so, the introduction of the Cardinal's name shows Roos prepared, like others, to lay on him the guilt of Gloucester's death. Lydgate had as much reason as Roos to lament misfortune to Gloucester; but the attack on Lydgate revealed later by the anagrams puts him out of court as the translator.

Other expansions towards the end of the poem are quietly reminiscent of Lady Bounte, in a tone of emotion reflective rather than active. The poet expands into four hundred lines the forty lines describing the Maiden's pawns and queen;[1] he retains the symbols on the shields of the pieces, but moralizes them, with qualities of the beloved woman, and of the lover. These correspond to those allegorical significances given in a fifteenth-century French prose commentary on the original poem, which expand the symbolism of the chess-play of love.[2] There, or in a common source, Roos must have found the names of the maiden's pawns: Jeunesse, Beaute, Simplesse, Doux Semblant, Manere, Faiticete, Sens (which he calls Providence, i.e. Foresight), Bontez, Noblesse. When he describes the Second Pawn, Beauty or the Rose, his words are a plaintive reminder of its fleetingness and of the power of Age, echoing the style of Guillaume de Lorris muted by the sombre tone of Jean de Meun:

> Lat no woman ther-of han pride
> For yt wil no while a-byde
> But passe, as dooth a Rose flour,
> Al vnwarly with a shour,
> For age, or they taken kepe,
> Lyche a thefe wil vnderkrepe
> And appallen the beaute,
> From whos stroke they may nat fle (ll. 6221–8).

When he comes to Bounty, the panther, symbol of the irresistible attraction of the beloved, he drops back into the language of his Bounty-Beauty poems, though Bounty is here more closely equated with generosity, 'largesse', than it is elsewhere:

> Bounte, which ys of fredam welle,
> Al vertues dooth excelle,

---

1 Sieper, *op. cit.*, I, 202–3.
2 *Ib.*, II, 67, and Sieper, *Les Echecs Amoureux*, pp. 89 ff., 97 ff.

> And ys preferred of renoun
> In euery maner Region:
> Gretly in erthe magnefied,
> And in the hevene stellefyed
> Amongys goddys celestial
> As the vertu most Royal.
> And thys vertu specialy
> Ys apropred naturely
> Of Iuste reson to womanhede
> Oonly for ther goodlyhede.
> For fredam, bounte, and largesse,
> Worship, honour, and kyndenesse,
> Norture, and al curtesye
> Ben so nygh of hir allye
> That fro the welle of her goodnesse
> Springeth out all gentylesse,
> They be Merours of al bounte. (ll. 6449–67)

The poet continues with a long diatribe against those who deny this virtue to women.

For all these reasons, and because of the Plesaunce anagrams, I would put the inception of the translation at about 1438, broken off probably c. 1441 when Lady Bounty died, and with the Swan interpolation certainly after 1441, possibly after 1447. The anagrams of 1445–50 will show yet further re-working, but they do not necessarily fall in chronological order.

The anagrams start as usual at the Introduction (ll. 1–46), a dedication to lovers of chess-playing, with the Plesaunce braid: HOMF––Y, ALYAn COB–AM; ANTIG. POWIS; –LISAB–Th BeWMONT; ISMANIA; KATh. whITT; TOT FOrFAIT FOr–AIT. The name Powis gives the spring of 1436 as the upward date. The description of the fragrance that surrounds Dame Nature yields only the Lady's name and the poet's 'devise' (ll. 228–46): ELISAB–TH BeWMO–T; TOT FOrAYT FOrFAYT. The beauty of Nature gives ANTI–ON.; IS–ANIA SCA–YS WHA–––BO–OH; TOt FOrFAYT FOrFA–T (ll. 315–46). The Swan drives home its warning by the names (ll. 1247–74); HOMFR–Y, BOHAn, SWAn; HE––Y B–WFO–T; TOT FO–FAYT. The end of the passage on the power of Mercury (ll. 1699–1708) describes his 'sotyltes ful profounde', and the wisdom that he gives to philosophers and prophets:

> Of many merveyles and secretis, . . .
> And futire thingis oon and alle,
> To telle aforne, how hyt shal falle.

The anagram here is: AlIAn COBHA. Later Roos will be still more explicit. Diana yields the name of Ismania Scales, not surprisingly,

but the method is unusual; the name ISMANIA SCALES WHAlY–BORO–GH
is repeated four times, in varying forms threaded through some hundred
lines, with at the end the 'devise' also repeated. It is a method used by
Charles d'Orléans for her sister Anne,[1] but I do not know it elsewhere in
Roos's early work. Now the poet recurs three times to Eleanor Cobham's necromantic practices, and as in *The Romaunt of the Rose* he
implies a judgement on them. Among the 'meschefs' of the people of
the garden of Déduit, the cautionary tales told by Diana, comes that
of Phaeton, much enlarged from the original (ll. 4200–26):

> Make eke thy merour of Pheton . . .
> Al went to dystruccion;
> Oonly through his presumpsion,
> By disposicion fatal,
> And lak of counseyl caused al.

The anagram yields: HOMF–E.; Al–AN.COBHAM; Oonly, BOLYNB;–W–NFL–T;
TOT ForFA–T. This application of the story implies that Eleanor's fall
had already taken place. The word 'merour' prepares us for the recurrence of the allusion in the long sequence on the well of Narcissus,
the 'welle most royall', which reflected

> Al the estris environ
> By Apparence vnto the syght,
> Who that koude looke aryght (ll. 5758–60).

The first passage (ll. 5684–721) gives: A–IA(N). COBHAM; BO–IN–BROK;
SOVThWe.; MARGA––T; SWINF––T; TOT ForFAIT; also KATH. WHITT., and
AnTI(gone). The second passage (ll. 5751–75) repeats three of the
names: AlIAn. –OBHAM; BOLINGBR.; ThOMAS SOVThWE.; and adds
STAnHOP. Again as in *The Romaunt* the name Swinflet appears in this
group.

With the figures of the Garden, Roos revives some of the anagrams
of *The Romaunt*, even preserving the identity. Thus in *The Romaunt*
Isabella, Lady Scroop, *née* Chaworth, was Curtesye dancing; here she
recurs as Curtesye welcoming the poet to the garden (ll. 4995–5019):
ISABEL–A CHAWOrTH S––OO. And Gladnesse singing is again AnTI–ONA
with IS–ANIA SCALE(S) and TOT ForFAIT added (ll. 5247–61). When the
game of chess begins, and the lady, the poet's opponent, proves to be
Margaret of Anjou, an air of reminiscence comes over the passages that
still produce Plesaunce anagrams, especially in the brief original poems
that describe the Maiden's pawns. The First Pawn, Youth, yields
AlIAn. COBHA.; AnTIGONA; ELISABeTh BeW–ONT BARDOL. (ll. 6155–202).

[1] See my *Studies in Villon, Vaillant and Charles d'Orléans*, Blackwell, 1957,
No. 3.

The Second Pawn, Beauty (ll. 6203–52), again gives the bevy of Plesaunce ladies; ALIAn. COBHA.; ANTIG–NA; –LISABeTH Beau–ONT BA(R)DOLF; CATh. whITT. BOWNTY, BeWTY; ForFAIT ForFAYT. The Third Pawn, Symplesse (ll. 6253–72), turns to another lady whom Roos valued, his sister-in-law A–IANO– BeA–CHAMP, TOT ForFAIT. The Fourth Pawn, Doulz Semblant, with the rainbow distilling the 'dewe of goodnesse', 'holsom as the Aprile shour, Fallyng on the erbes newe', celebrates E–ISAB–TH BeWMONT BARDO–F; KATH. WHITT.; (I)S–ANYA SCAlis; TOT ForFAIT ForFAIT (ll. 6273–314). The Fifth Pawn, Port or Manere (ll. 6315–74), again combines ELISAB–TH BeWMO–T BAR–O–F PHELIP, with KATH WHYTTIn–HA(M), and also with AlYAn. BeAVSHAM SO(M)E–SeT; IAY TOT ForFAIT ForFAYT. This can only be after 1444, since Eleanor bears the Somerset title.

The Sixth Pawn, Foresight (ll. 6375–432), is a very individual treatment by Roos of the French *Sens* as 'Purveyaunce' or providence, 'To sen aforn what shal falle, . . . Of worldly mutabylyte'. To point this, the anagrams name four ladies who failed to stop their ears against the enchantment of sugared words, the deceit of flattery. They are AlYAn. and E–ISAB–TH –OBHAM; B–W–ONT PHI–IP; and ANT. POW(I)S DAMANS. Together with them are the men who deceived them: BOLINB(R)O., SOVTHW. for Eleanor Cobham; FAWCOMB(erg) for Elisabeth Cobham (see below, Chapter VIII); the name D'Amancier for Antigone must indicate a date after 1450. It is surprising to find Elisabeth Beaumont's name here, as if she had some voice in her marriage to John Beaumont. The poet's 'devise' completes the long solution: TOT ForFA–T ForFA–T. A still more unexpected direction is taken by the anagrams of the Seventh Pawn, Bounte. 'Lady Bounte' here is set aside, and the long passage of nearly a hundred lines (ll. 6433–522) is written in praise of the overflowing generosity and bounty of women, and in violent abhorrence of their detractors:

> I prey god yive hem evel sorwe
> And short her tongys with myschaunce
> Which ys y-whet with fals plesaunce
> For to a-peche her Innocence.

The ladies' names here are AlYAN. OBHAM; ANTIGONA DAMANSI.; but the obvious name is that of Lydgate: DAn IOHAn –IDGATE MONACH–S; and to him are joined two more important clerics; WIL–IAM CIRT–YS ABBOT OF BWRY; IOHAN WHETHAMST(E)De AB–OT OF ST AlBANS, with at the end AI TOT ForFAIT For–AYT. The anagrams pillory the rival, antifeminist poet, and two abbots who were favoured by the king and by

Duke Humphrey. The Eighth Pawn is the Eagle, signifying Noblesse and Auctorite, and for the royal bird Roos makes a roll call of the Lancastrian dynasty, both direct and legitimated, of his lifetime and knowledge: first the ancestors, PLAnTAGEn–T, BOHWN; then HENRY; IOHA(N) BeDFor.; HOMF(R)I G–OUCEST.; An STAFFor., WOO–STOK; IOHAn BEAWFort; AlIAn. –OBHAM comes in only by marriage; the whole is formally signed, IAI TOT FOrFAIT FOrFAIT (ll. 6523–86).

After this, the earlier references give way for a time to Queen Margaret's court. Not till the poet's First Pawn, Idleness, do they recur (ll. 6931–52): AlIAn.; ELISAB–TH BeWMOnT; (C)ATh. whITT. TOT FO–FAIT. The symbol of the dry tree is used for a confession of the poet's sense of wasted time and of 'fals delyte'; it is a self-judgment, a confession of some pathos in the man of middle age who looks back on 'false lights and wandering fires'. That is the last Plesaunce reference; it was probably meant to appeal to Margaret Vernon. The anagrams make it clear that the poem is becoming a personal confession; one can only regret that it stops short.

The poem is 'signed' twice, first at l. 904 with the phrase, 'I roose anoon'. This is much later in the poem than the usual first thirty lines or so, and the reason is amusing. The point of the first nine hundred lines is precisely that the poet is a sluggard; he has to lie and endure a long rebuke from Nature for his 'verray wilful ydelnesse'. He cannot rise. The second 'signature' is a new invention, found only here. At l. 3578, in the story of Jason and Medea (of which the anagrams have a quite different reference) occurs the line,

Euery tothe Roos vp a Knyght,

altering thus the 'geants' of the original French; on the page (MS. Fairfax 16, fol. 251) only two names, the epithet ('Impossible'), and these two words, have been capitalized and rubricated within the lines; they stand out noticeably.

There are two manuscripts of the poem, MS. Fairfax 16, fol. 202–300, where it precedes *How a Lover*; and Add. 29729, fol. 184–286 v. But since this latter manuscript is of Stow's copying in 1558, and since he obviously copied from MS. Fairfax 16, there is in fact only one authoritative text. This is reassuring for the deciphering of the anagrams. In Fairfax 16, nine pages are left blank at the end, as if the copyist still hoped to procure a full text, or, in a manuscript of 1450, to hear that the translator had gone on with, if not completed, his task. The scribe has omitted some sixteen lines throughout the poem, which have been supplied in the margin by another hand. Sieper conjectured the corrector to be Shirley,[1] but there is no other sign of Shirley in the manuscript. Stow's hand has supplied the title and ascription: 'Reson and sensuallyte compylid by John Lydgat.'; the title in the Index is both more descriptive and more precise, but lacks the ascription: 'The booke of þe Autoure how he plaid at þe Chesse and was mated of a Feerse'; the translation does not reach this checkmate.

The many marginal notes in MS. Fairfax 16 raise some questions, first, on the identity of their writer, and then on his personality as a commentator. The commentator is not the translator. The proof lies in his misunderstanding of the writer's intentions in the interpolations on the Maiden's pawns. Unable to believe that the extreme praise of women could possibly be intentional and not satiric, he starts by writing *'per Antifrasim'* (l. 6172), and again *'per contrarium* (l. 6202) against the First Pawn, Youth. Then he desists for a while, probably puzzled. At the Fifth Pawn, he writes an angry *'Cujus contrarium est verum'* (l. 6368) at the assertion of women's secrecy. But this is the last note of the kind, for in the middle of the Seventh Pawn, Bounty, he finds an obviously sincere curse pronounced against defamers of women:

> I prey god yive hem evel sorwe
> And short her tongys with myschaunce (ll. 6498–9).

That must have given the objector pause. In the Eighth Pawn, he is silenced by the identification of womanly noblesse with the Blessed Virgin:

> For the grete humilyte
> Of a woman, this no drede,
> The seconde persone of the godhede
> Took flessh and blood and be-kam man.
> Now as me semeth truly than
> Men sholde worshepe hem and preyse,
> Her honour eke exalt and reyse,
> Oonly for the sake of oon. (ll. 6546–53)

This evidence of 'mechanical thinking' on the part of the commentator, and of his complete misapprehension of the translator as a 'champion des dames',[2] is proof enough of his separate identity. It is pretty plain that he is a cleric, partly from the anti-feminine tone shown above, and still more from the gratuitous note on *Castitas*. Diana the huntress is complaining that 'Yn tyme of olde antiquyte' she was held in high esteem; her attack on lust does not come for another hundred lines, but the commentator anticipates it by the note (l. 3030): *'Castitas*

---

[1] *Op. cit.*, I, xii.
[2] His misapprehension is unfortunately shared by the poem's editor, Sieper.

quondam fuit magne reputacionis' etc. He is a learned man, and whereas some three-quarters of his notes are mere summaries of the substance of the verse, or guides and pointers to the reader (e.g. at ll. 552, 696, 724), about a quarter are true commentary notes, adding information drawn from the Bible (l. 3685 on Adonis), Ovid (l. 393), *Somnium Scipionis* (l. 823), Valerius (l. 3370), Isidore (ll. 3620–75, on Sirens), and Pliny (l. 2789 on ebony). One note which at first sight looks like the gloss of a foreigner proves merely that the writer did not recognize a term of falconry which was indeed slow in getting into literary English: 'soore i.e. flye' (l. 4176). This commentator, a learned, anti-feminist cleric, may possibly have been Lydgate; there is more than one sign that Lydgate and Roos knew each other's writings, and even occasionally crossed swords. If it was he, it is amusing to think that the anti-clerical anagrams of the Seventh Pawn were lying like an unexploded bomb under his hand. It is probable from the rubrication that the original notes were not written into Fairfax 16, but were already in whatever manuscript was the basis of Fairfax 16.

How did Roos get acquainted with *Les Echecs Amoureux*? Possibly through Charles d'Orléans. One of the extant manuscripts of *Les Echecs Amoureux* (Bibl. Nat. fonds. français, 143) contains also a book presented to Louis d'Orléans, Charles's father.[1] Was it then in Charles's possession? One of Charles's English poems, *Love's Renewal*, describes the changeable rainbow colours of the robes and mantle of Lady Fortune (ll. 4979–87, 4995–5005) in a way not unlike the briefer description of the changeable hues of Mercury's robe in *Reson and Sensuallyte* (ll. 1724–33); *Love's Renewal* is reminiscent here of *Le Songe Vert*, but there is nothing like this rainbow effect in that earlier French poem.

The relation of the translation to the vast French original is difficult to establish with precision, since the French poem is still unpublished; fortunately the samples furnished by Sieper throughout his study of *Les Echecs Amoureux*, and in his edition of *Reson and Sensuallyte*, enable a comparison of some crucial passages, and give a fair idea of the translator's methods. He, and not the author, gives a precise date for the day of his vision, 'Apprile . . . the firthe prime'. It is clear that he set out in an expansive mood, responding to the joys of spring:

> In a morowe so as I lay
> *In my bed wythin a cloos,*
> *Whan the clere sonne Aroos*
> In grene ver ful of delyt,
> *Which prikketh with his appetyt*

[1] Sieper, *Les Echecs Amoureux*, p. 97.

> *This lusty hertys amerouse,*
> *The seson is so graciouse,*
> For this seson, with-outen fayle,
> *Clotheth with newe apparayle*
> *Alle the erthe, this verray trewe,*
> *With many sondry dyuers hewe.*[1]

Similar additions expand the shortened account of the lover of the Rose. The translator's acquaintance with *The Romaunt of the Rose*, as his expansion of *Les Echecs* shows, is now understandable:

> Comment Il songa vne nuit
> Quil vint au vergier de deduit
> Et comment a pou de priiere
> Oyseuse qui en yert portiere
> Le mist ou bel pourpris quarre
> Par le petit guichet barre (*Les Echecs*, quoted Sieper, p. 201).

> The whiche drempte in his slepyng,
> How erly on A morwnyng
> He was vn-to this gardyn broght
> And so longe aboute hath soght,
> Til he fonde a smale wiket,
> The which ageyns him was shet;
> And fonde as thoo noon other weye,
> Til that he gan knokke and praye;
> And, without more delay,
> There was no wight that sayde nay
> Nor made thoo no straungenesse
> For the porter ydelnesse
> Lete hym in, and that in hast (*Reson*, etc., ll. 4819–31).

> Tho gan I go a full gret pas,
> Envyronyng evene in compas
> The closing of the square wall,
> Tyl that I fond a wiket small
> So shett that I ne myght in gon,
> And other entre was ther noon.
> Uppon this dore I gan to smyte . .
> Ful long I shof and knokkide eke, . .
> Til that the dore of thilk entre
> A mayden curteys openyde me (*The Romaunt*, ll. 525–38).

When he comes later to the mere list of the figures painted on the outer wall (l. 4943) he makes a masterly brief expansion, giving the gist of the portrait in a line or an epithet (crooked Age, 'Tremblyng as she wolde

---

[1] *Reson*, etc., ll. 88–98, and see p. 199 for the original French; the translator's additions are shown by italicizing.

dye', or Hypocrisy, 'Dedly of chere lyke a rynde'), and not here running
too close verbally to *The Romaunt*. It is noticeable that fewer of the
French names are translated here; thus Déduit and Doulz Regarde
remain, and are not transmuted to Myrth and Sweet Looking, Papelardie
is retained and the group that gave the letters B–RD–LF does not recur
here. As in *The Romaunt*, the pride of chivalry is exalted; thus the
Maiden's Knights are

> Made of Saphirs oriental,
> *Of chere and look ful Marcial,*
> *And bothe to myn inspeccion*
> *Ful knyghtly of proporsion,*
> *Of cher and port ful of pride* (ll. 6685–9).

In the original, it is the sapphire that is dwelt on. Native pride may
have prompted the added praise of Arthur's knights:

> the knyghtes of Breteyne,
> *Most renomyd and most notable,*
> *With Arthour of the rounde table,*
> *The myghty famous werriours* (ll. 3176–9).

Occasionally the translator airs his knowledge by giving in full a story
only touched on in the French; thus the three lines on Silla, faithless
daughter of Minos, become twenty-two in the English (ll. 4307–28).

All the usual expanding phrases, doublets, and clichés are brought
into play; Sieper's detailed analysis as for Lydgate, in Chapter V of his
introduction, could be paralleled at most points from Roos's other
translations; his favourite phrases are repeated here: 'did his (her) busy
cure (peyne)', 'in his (her, my) demeyne', 'holtis hore', euer in oon',
'to your plesaunce'. Yet one must admit that such expansions, found
also in translations by Chaucer and Gower as well as by Lydgate and
Roos, are almost inevitable in the transposition of condensed and easy
rhyming French into the looser and harder rhyming English. At one
point the translator here can be charged with a venial misunderstanding;
'Dauis' (king David), read as 'Danis', gave rise to the ingenious couplet:

> To wynnen euery pounde and marke,
> That the kyng hath of Denmarke (ll. 2711–2).

He evidently made it into a contemporary reference to Erik of Denmark
(died 1459), brother-in-law of Humphrey of Gloucester.

The unknown author of *Les Echecs Amoureux* combines the quality
and tone of Guillaume de Lorris and of Jean de Meun, tracing a
middle path between the enchanted garden of the one, and the thorny

thicket of the other. He is prepared for youth to enjoy the pleasures of the Garden with due moderation and afterwards to 'se ranger', if not in *vita contemplativa*, then in *vita activa*, useful to his Prince, and not ill-pleasing to God. The poem ends as an *Institutio*, and loses poetic force. The English version, never getting beyond the Garden, has inevitable parallels with the other poems of the Rose's inspiration. There is much of lowest common measure between *The Romaunt, How a Lover Prayseth*, and *Reson and Sensuallyte*. Common to all three is the joy in the diversity of the world, 'so lusty and delyciouse', and in the great rivers 'full of merchandyse',

> Somme so myghty and so large
> To bere a gret ship or a barge
> The which in many sondry wyse,
> Serveden for marchandyse,
> And wern also ful profitable
> And vn-to manne ryght vayllable. (ll 943–8)

There is a welcome intrusion here of common life into this rather re-fined literature, revivifying the verse. In the last two mentioned poems, and indeed in all Roos's poems, there are small strokes which show where references from *The Romaunt* stuck like burrs in the poet's mind, e.g. the reference to Caribdis, to Cartage; the early poems show the dislike of artifice in beauty, of 'wyndred browis', and 'popped' cheeks (*The Romaunt*, ll. 1018–20), of a 'papphed' face (*Reson*, etc., 1368), and, more originally, of finger-nails 'peyntyd as in spayne' (*How a Lover*, l. 408). It is to be noted that these scornful allusions vanish, except in satire, in his later, more sophisticated poems. One noun shows a clever adaptation from *Le Roman* (l. 3879), 'Peor rot grant conestablie', i.e. a garrison to guard the northern gate of the tower; in *The Romaunt*, this appears as 'the kepyng of the conestablerye' (l. 4218); in *Reson and Sensuallyte* (l. 1470), Venus is the leader of 'The amerouse constablerye'.

A straight and more humorous description of lovers playing chess, and using the moves to press their suit, Roos would have found in *Les Vœux du Paon*; though not now in the copy that bears his signature (MS. Add. 30864), it may once have been there. The alliterative *Alexander* in MS. Ashmole 44 may have given Roos a few hints for diverse subjects, such as the diamond broken only by goat's blood, explicit in *Reson and Sensuallyte* (ll. 6892–3), implicit only in *Alexander*, l. 3378. The long and repetitive description of the golden fruit in Diana's forest (*Reson*, etc., ll. 4380 ff.) as better than that sought by Alexander, and not found even on the trees of the sun and moon, could be substantiated from Ashmole 44; there the trees bear no fruit.

Diana's fruits in their effects are like the golden apples of the *Isle of Ladies*, and are

> confortatyf,
> To preserve a mannys lyf
> Longe from al corrupcion,
> By kyndly dysposicion. (ll. 4391-4)

Finally, Roos (and not Lydgate) may have the honour of first using in English poetry the word 'Ideas' in a Platonic sense; on Dame Nature's robes was wrought

> The resemblaunce and the fygure
> Of alle that vnto god obeyes,
> And exemplarie of ydeyes,
> [A lexemplaire des ydees]
> Full longe aforn or they weren wrought,
> Compassed in dyvyne thought. (ll. 358-62)

The verse of *Reson and Sensuallyte* shows a great advance on that of *The Isle of Ladies* in speed and lightness; the phrases may not be succinct, but the metrical movement can be as rapid and flitting as is the Fairy's speech to Shakespeare's Puck. The poet 'took hys wey towarde the herber of Deduit', a weighty choice, but his heart is light:

> Withouten any lenger space
> I gan on my waye trace
> And Diane anoon forsooke
> And forth the ryghte wey I tooke
> Bothe throgh felde and throgh forest,
> Forth ryght, as me sempte best,
> Gan to crosse dovne and dale
> And ouer-twerten hille and vale,
> The next wey as was myn happe,
> Spared nouther bussh nor gappe,
> Felte nowher no greuaunce
> For [my] ioy and my pleasaunce,
> Both in countenaunce and chere; . . .
> Til I kam vn-to the gate,
> This lusty herber delytable. (ll. 4779-97)

This joyous progress, as of a pilgrim of love with feet winged by desire, is beyond the powers of the slow-paced Lydgate. The poem, like Venus's 'gardyn of plesaunce', is 'gracious, Agreable and debonayre'. It could not long continue thus when the life of the actual Plesaunce came to an abrupt and tragic end.

Another poem which is not strictly a translation is added here, partly because it is directly dependent on a literary source (it is actually called 'my translacioun', l. 590), and is kept close to it, partly because it is clearly early work. It is near in style and theme to Roos's first treatment of the subject of *amour courtois*, though here in a bourgeois disguise.

No. 62. *Fabula Duorum Mercatorum*, or 'The Merchant of Baldok' (title in the table of MS. Rawlinson, poet., 32): a narrative poem of 130 stanzas of rhyme royal.

> *Incipit.* In Egipt whilom, as I reede and fynde
> Ther dwellyd a marchaunt of hih & gret estat.
> *Explicit.* This my desyr in al degrees of men;
> That it so be, I pray you, seith, Amen.

The poem exists in six manuscripts, only one of which, Harleian 2251, has much other connexion with Roos's work. They tend to be Lydgate collections. Thus MS. Harleian 2255 is a manuscript of high authority for Lydgate (E. Hammond, *Anglia*, XXVIII, 24–5) and the poem is found there among many of his pietistic works. MS. Harleian 2251 is another large Lydgate collection, but not exclusively so, as it also contains Roos's *A Lover's New Year's Gift* (Item 72), and his 'Allas I wooful creature' (Item 77). Allied to Harleian 2251 is Add. 34360 (fol. 4–18 v.) and both are judged to be derived from a lost Shirley collection. Leyden Vossius 9 (fol. 97–129) is akin in certain texts to Lansdowne 699 (fol. 3–18). The sixth manuscript is Rawl. poet. 32. (fol. 38–53) which now lacks the last two stanzas. Only Harleian 2255, which Schleich signalizes as the best manuscript, ascribes the poem to Lydgate (*Explicit quod Lidgate*). This ascription, and that in Bale's list of 1559 (No. 217), have been accepted without question by Zupitza, by G. Schleich who edited the poem from Zupitza's material (*Quellen und Forschungen*, 83, 1897), by MacCracken (*Minor Poems*, pp. 486–516; cf. p. xvi), and recently by Schirmer (pp. 207–8).

My ascription of the poem to Sir Richard Roos rests on a form of the signature dictated by the third-person narrative ('Rys vp anoon', l. 423; 'Anoon he ros', l. 428); on the frequency of the word 'anon', seventeen times in 910 lines, whereas it is rare in Lydgate—twice in *The Churl and the Bird* (385 lines), and not at all in *The Horse, Goose and Sheep* (659 lines); on the medical passage, unlike Lydgate's work, but comparable with that in *How a Lover*; on descriptions and words comparable with 'For lac of sighte' (e.g. stt. 25, 46); and finally on the Plesaunce anagrams, with various forms of the poet's 'devise'.

The double anagrams of the first three introductory stanzas yield B(E)WMONT, BAR-O-F, P-E(L)I-; AnTI(G)OnA; I(S)–AN(Y); and IAI TOT FORFAIT FORFAIT. The description of the month of May (stt. 16–17) gives

S

AnTIG., ISMAnIA, WHITT.; and the lament of the lovesick merchant proves to be a 'braid' of the Pleasaunce ladies: AlIAn CO–HAM; –LISAB–TH BeWMONT BA–DOLF; AnTIGOn.; ISMAnIA SCALYS, K–Th. WHITT., with TOT FOrF–IT FOrF–IT. The description of the ideal lady (stt. 54–6) produces BeWMONT BARDO–F PH––IP; AnTIGO–A; KATH. WHIT–In–HA.; with FOrFA–T. The praise of happy marriage and a good wife (stt. 68–70) gives BeWMO–T; WHITT.; ISMAnIA WHA––SBO. (cf. *Ragman Roll*, st. 14), with B–WSHA–P; TOT FOr––YT. The brief Envoy (st. 130) gives in skeletal form AlIAn. –OB–A–. The original passage on the stars, making the usual medieval fusion of Arcturus and Arthur as the steersman of The Plough, may be meant to include another figure of the Pleasaunce household, Arthur.

Whether the Duke or Duchess asked for the poem one cannot say. It is not like Roos to write of merchants, even if he exalts them into merchant princes; but after 1433 he had some probable contact with mercantile society. His sister-in-law Anne (wife in 1433 of Sir Robert Roos) had a stepson, Sir Humphrey Bohun of Midhurst, who married Margaret Estfeld (died before 1445/6), daughter of a wealthy mercer, who was twice Mayor of London, in 1430 and 1438 (G.E.C., II, 201). Roos constantly throws over the story the colouring of chivalrous life (as in the entertainment, stt. 22–5), and still more of love; the lover laments that love is all-powerful; he suffers from 'Amor erreos', that loftiest form of fever and love-sickness, never mentioned elsewhere by Lydgate, but twice by Roos, as in 'As ofte as syghes', 'Her thoghtfull seruaunts with herreos y shake' (l. 69); the Furies are invoked, Megaera, and Tisiphone; rhetorical catherine wheels of *anaphora* and *exclamatio* are frequent. Everything is being done to lift this bourgeois story to the knightly level and the high style. A little aristocratic grumble of no relevance to the subject is dragged in:.

> For now of trowthe no man can contryve
> A verray seel or thenpreent i-grave
> Withoute a label his armes hool to save (866–8).

Sir Richard's seal of 1436 shows no 'label'; it is not an idea likely to occur to Lydgate. The tale is more weighted by moralizing than Roos's usually are, but he reflects less on virtue than on love and fortune.

The story, a variant of the tale told later by Sir Thomas Elyot as 'Titus and Gesippus', was familiar to medieval readers; the interest even then would lie in the treatment. The colophons of two manuscripts refer to the *Gesta Romanorum*; Schleich (pp. lxxi–xci) had no difficulty in developing Warton's hint and showing that a fuller version, that of Petrus Alphonsi in his *Disciplina Clericalis* (Chapter III), was the direct source of the story. A copy of the *Disciplina*, in which a father sending forth his son gives him worldly wisdom by tales and proverbs, used to be at the Abbey of St. Edmunds, where King Henry spent Christmas and Easter, 1433-4; it is now MS. Royal 10.B.xii. For the medical interpolation, Schleich picked up a reference to 'Gyles' (l. 308), and traced it back to Gilles de Corbeil (Egidius Corboliensis). His *Viaticus: De Signis et Symptomatibus Ægritudinum* could give Roos all the material for his passage on fevers (stt. 40-50), on 'Effymera' (*Viaticus*, ll. 119-49), on 'Tres Ethicae species' (ll. 1950 ff.), on 'Putridus' and 'Synochi' (ll. 2245 ff.), and on melancholic mania and frenzy (ll. 202 ff.).

What Gilles does not include is 'Amor erreos' (l. 336) and its description. One might think that Roos need go no further than Chaucer's 'Knight's Tale' (ll. 1373-6); actually his description is longer (stt. 48-50), and in quite different terms, without localization in the brain cells. Roos's is a more psychological rendering:

> The roote wherof and the corrupcioun
> Is of thilke vertu callid estimatiff,
> As yif a man haue deep impressioun,
> That ovirlordshipith his imagynatif.

This is verbally close to Bernard Gordon's account in his *Lilium Medicinae*, as quoted by Livingston Lowes (*Mod. Philology*, XI, 499). Gilbert Kymer, the Duke's physician, a man eminent for learning, might well be the intermediary of such information and Duke Humphrey gave a copy of the *Lilium* to Oxford in 1439.[1] The description of Egypt and the fructifying Nile (stt. 3-6), Schleich could not trace; Roos, who knew his Mandeville (see below, Chapter XIII), would find the matter in Chapter 12.

It looks as if Roos had set out to write a *Fabula* in Lydgate's style, either deliberately, possibly by request, or because he had not yet fully formed his own stanzaic medium. Already his rhythms are lighter and smoother than Lydgate's. The parallels with the alliterative *How a Lover* suggest nearness in time to that Plesaunce poem. Certainly Roos has not yet developed his distinctive run-on between stanzas; there is only one weak example here (stt. 50-1). But the vocabulary is vigorous and individual, like that of *How a Lover*, and Schleich's glossary shows how independent it is of Lydgate's forms. Yet Roos is almost over-using learned and technical terms, preponderantly in the medical passage;

---

[1] Charles d'Orléans had a copy with him in England (Champion, *La Librairie de Charles d'Orléans*, pp. 14-15).

irrigat (24), interpollat (283), oppilat (325), as past participles; inexcusable (403), multipharye (530), mercymony (31), prymycere (685), overt (519); aquosite (327), vberte (613), tediouste (900). These are not Lydgate's words, nor will Roos use them again. His own simple style, based on French usage, begins to appear in the latter half of the poem. Some of his heightened words we have already heard elsewhere, 'memorial, fantastical' (ll. 55–6; see above, No. 49); Kentish forms 'vnshet' (60), 'i-knet' (427) are more characteristic of Roos than of Lydgate.

Whether or not Roos merits the name of 'grant translateur', there is no doubt that he becomes skilful in the art. In metre alone, his progress is obvious. In 'Cassamus roos', a stiff rendering yet shows skill in the reduction of the irregular paragraphs of the original to stanza form with fairly frequent run-on. In *The Eye and the Heart*, a better or an easier choice of stanza is imposed by the subject; the too close translation is neither varied nor supple. *La Belle Dame* is incomparably the best in stanza form; yet the original introduction in rhyme royal is superior to the translation in eight-line stanzas. Roos's undoubted success in translation is in the octosyllabic couplet, in the grace, ease, and lightness of the best parts of *The Romaunt* and of the more freely handled *Reson and Sensuallyte*. The metre is rare in Roos's original work, but in the *Compleynt* (see below, No. 78) it is equally light and fluid. Yet it is in these two translations that anagrams abound.

CHAPTER VIII

The King's Knight, 1442–61: Ceremonial Poems

H ow it was that Sir Richard Roos came to be a King's Knight and therefore in closer touch with the royal household, we do not know. Sir Robert Roos, King's Carver, may have had a hand in it; Gloucester himself may have aided the change, especially after the break-up of the Plesaunce circle. Richard Beauchamp, Earl of Warwick, father-in-law to Sir Richard's elder brother, and *magister* or governor to the king, may, before his death in 1439, have been anxious to secularize the mind of the young king, soon to attain his majority, and too much drawn to the contemplative life. It had been the earl's duty to teach the king to love, worship, and dread God, and to draw him to virtue. Henry's natural piety made this easy; but he was also to be taught 'nurture, lettrure, langage, and other man*n*er of cunnyng'.[1] In this a young and knightly poet could help.

The appointment was probably promotion in Sir Richard's career; it could hardly at first be of much help to him in his poetry. Unfortunately also it came at a break in his poetic inspiration. The two shocks that he had suffered in 1441, the death of Lady Beaumont and the disgrace of the Duchess of Gloucester, might have at once and immeasurably changed and deepened his writing, had he been a great poet. But Sir Richard's poems till now had almost all been of those 'floures rede and whyte' that close when darkness falls; it was to take longer for him to develop to full power. After the brilliance and feminine elegance of Plesaunce, the talk and learning, and the stimulating atmosphere, the young king's court, for all Warwick's efforts, must by contrast have seemed almost monastic in its sobriety. For some three years, Sir

[1] *Proc. and Ord. of the Privy Council*, III, 299.

Richard must have moved heavily, becalmed in a very doldrums of dullness and formality. He probably went on with translation, as of Fragment B of *The Romaunt of the Rose*; and he seems to have been in close touch with the Beaufort family.

I. THE ROYAL MARRIAGE: POEMS IN CELEBRATION

In the spring of 1444, there was a *reverdie*, a quickening. Sir Richard Roos would naturally be aware of the developments of the king's wooing of Margaret of Anjou. His brother, Sir Robert, was employed in the transactions, only second to the Earl of Suffolk and Adam Moleyns themselves. The court would be alive with rumours, agog with curiosity; after the betrothal at Tours in May 1444, tension would be relaxed. Immediately, however, preparations were begun for the next event, the wedding. King Henry borrowed money, bought furnishings and plate, sent out gifts to his 'dear wife and queen', despatched Sir Robert with letters, and, skilfully worked on by Suffolk, showed every sign of loverlike impatience. The Escort, of which Sir Richard Roos was a member, was commissioned in October, and the marriage was expected to follow speedily. Its delays have already been described. It is inconceivable that Roos should stop composing in all this ferment. One may fairly assume that he was expected to put his poetic talent and his knowledge of French poetry at the service of the royal bride. His writing of love poetry now took a new direction, and was tuned to conform to the whole effort of the court and the time. Some poems are shown by their anagrams to be concerned with the last days of the Escort in France.

No. 63. Before discussing these, I would first revert to the group of poems already discussed, the *Balades, Letters* and *Complaints*, which precede them in MS. Fairfax 16 (No. 15, above). These poems' anagrams reveal their Plesaunce connexion, and the references to Elisabeth Beaumont and to Eleanor Cobham prove them to have been written before the autumn of 1441. Nevertheless there are some odd circumstances not yet explained: one poem exists in two forms; another is also to be found in the personal manuscript of Charles d'Orléans; several contain devout expressions of a piety not found in Roos's normal love-poems; and three bear dates which are compatible with the later months of the Escort's *longue attente*. Finally, the series closes in MS. Fairfax 16 with two longer poems, one openly in praise of a 'flower', and the other, a *Parlement of Cupid*, summoned only to be deferred;

and here the anagrams relate to the royal party and the personnel of the Escort.

Of the *Balades, Letters* and *Complaints,* the poem in two metrical forms is No. xiv, a Letter in rhyme royal which exists also in MS. Lambeth 306, where it is in three eight-line stanzas with a four-line conclusion. Thus one at least of the group of poems was metrically rewritten. No. viii, the complaint against the governance of Fortune, is to be found also in the Orléans manuscript. The anagrams show it to have been written before 1440; but it is one of the latest poems written into the French manuscript. Orléans was at the proxy betrothal of Margaret of Anjou at Tours in 1444, having been instrumental in bringing about the alliance; Richard's brother, Sir Robert, was there as one of the envoys. In February, 1445, Orléans was with the wedding party at Nancy, and he and his duchess accompanied the bride on part of her journey.[1] Sir Richard could well have had some contact with the Duke in February to March 1445. If, as seems very probable, they had already met in England, Orléans was not the man to neglect a fellow-poet.

The pious expressions beyond the wont of secular love poetry are found in No. vi ('Ryght goodly flour to whom I owe seruyse'), with its concluding prayer; No. xi ('So wolde criste for hys hye pyte', st. 2); No. xiv ('I beseche the only trinite Yow kepe and saue', etc., st. 3); No. xvii ('That knowyth god, that made us euerychone; ... god in trinite He be your guerdon of hys goodnesse', stt. 3–4). Finally, the three dated poems are No. xiv, December 5, the date being found only in the version in MS. Fairfax 16, deliberately inserted; No. xvii, which closes thus,

> Wrytyn in hast of verey trouth to say
> At   vpon our lady day [the assūpcion].

The blank may be due to the scribe's failure to read his copy, or it may have been deliberately left to be appropriately filled at the last moment. Professor MacCracken, adapting to the Marquess of Suffolk, proposed 'Wallingford'; as good metrically would be 'Westminster'. The scribe has inserted the marginal note 'the assumpcion' but that is on August 15, a curious date to come between the dates of the neighbouring poems, December 5, and the end of February. There are three other lady days in the year, and February 2, the feast of the Purification, is an equally valid date, and suits the context better. The third dated poem is No. xviii, 'Not far fro marche, in the ende of feueryere'. These dates should be compared with the doings of the Escort: during

---

[1] Champion, *Vie de Charles d'Orléans*, pp. 344–9.

November and December it waited at Rouen; in January to February 1445 it was at Nancy; in the first week of February Margaret arrived at Nancy; Charles VII and René d'Anjou left Metz for Nancy on March 3, and the wedding was celebrated before March 12.

These considerations, together with the address of No. vi to the 'Ryght goodly flour', make me suspect that these poems, originally written before 1441 as personal love poems, were adapted by Roos to the needs of the Escort, and were even turned into love-letters such as the saintly Henry would wish to send to his betrothed. The king was incapable of writing poetry, let alone love poems. Sir Richard might well write them on his behalf, as naturally as a private secretary drafts a politician's speeches. Roos knows his royal master well enough to know just the pious recommendations with which he would fill a letter. Waiting in Rouen, Roos has heard that Margaret uses her name emblem; probably he knew of the great French volume (MS. Royal 15.E.vi) that the Talbots (his connexions by marriage) were having prepared as a wedding gift. Here daisies powder the pages, and appear scattered on the hangings and the mantles as well as on the ground; the bride's wedding dress was in fact so adorned. In No. vi, the poem meant for Roos's 'flower of womanhood' is turned to a poem of the Flower-cult, and revives it in England.

This hypothesis of adaptation would account for the flatness of tone that mars many of these poems. Nos. vii–x are especially stiff in expression and conventional in tone. No. x cannot refer to an actual visit by the king; it may be a missive sent after the leave-taking of an emissary, possibly Sir Robert Roos. The theme of Nos. xi–xiii is the hindrance perpetually suffered, 'the causys which that men do fynde To hyndyr me' (xi). The delays were indeed intolerable. The statement of Thomas Gascoigne[1] that Margaret was detained by Charles VII, and concealed from Suffolk in order to force the cession of Anjou and Maine, is not supported elsewhere, but there may have been some basis for it; it might explain the undue delays.

The two next poems in MS. Fairfax 16, more descriptively indexed ('How þe louer is sett to serve þe floure', and 'The Parlement off Cupyde, gode of love'), are of a very different character from the preceding eighteen. They do not read like substitutes for royal missives; they have life and actuality, especially the first. The lady of the flower has come, and is there to be greeted with vows of courtly devotion. They were probably written for pastime in February 1445, when Margaret, arriving early in the month, had to wait for her father's uncertain coming

[1] *Loci e Libro Veritatum*, ed. J. E. Thorold Rogers, pp. 109, 205, 219.

with the French king. Miss Hammond printed the former poem as 'A Reproof to Lydgate',[1] and Robbins entitled it 'In Praise of Margaret the Queen';[2] but it is regrettable to omit the cult of the Flower from the title, and misleading to detach the poem from *The Parlement of Cupyde*, which its last stanzas directly foreshadow:

> The court ys set, thy falshed is tryed . . .
> Lat thyn attournay sew and speke for the. (ll. 76–80)

It is true that no reference is made to Lydgate in *The Parlement*; but it is possible that the unique text gives us here only the framework of an evening's entertainment, similar to that which *The Assembly of Ladies* will later present in fuller guise. The date of *The Parlement* (Feb. 22) is about a fortnight after Margaret's arrival.

No. 64. *How þe louer is sett to serue þe floure* (title as in the manuscript Index; there is no title at the head of the poem); fol. 325 v.

In these twelve stanzas of rhyme royal, stt. 4 and 5 seem to have been transposed; stt. 3 and 5 constitute the appeal to Chaucer for inspiration; st. 4 begins with a lament for his death, and ends with the coldly-phrased address to Lydgate; st. 6 announces the charge against him which is continued to the end.

> *Incipit.* Myn hert ys set and all myn hole entent
> To serue this flour in my most humble wyse.
> *Explicit.* Haue mynde of this for now I wryte no more.

The first stanza in fresh and lively verse expresses the paradisal vision of the opening flower, 'Wyth colours fressh ennewyd white and rede'; it is obvious that a young queen with a flower-name is as much a gift to a court-poet as a politician with an exaggerated feature is to a cartoonist. St. 2 offers the poet's observance, his life-long service. The invocation to 'noble chaucer' is natural; it is also a delicate compliment to Chaucer's grand-daughter whose husband led the Escort. When the writer turns to Lydgate, his words at first are guarded:

> ffor thy connyng ys syche and eke thy grace
> After chaucer to occupye his place.

But Lydgate has dared to attack love, and to question women's steadfastness and fidelity: 'A, fye for schame, O thou envyous man'. He is bidden to repent and to prepare his defence. This comes naturally from the translator of *La Belle Dame sans Merci*, who would know how Alain Chartier had had to recant when rebuked by the angry ladies of the

---

[1] *From Chaucer to Surrey*, pp. 200–1.
[2] Robbins, *Secular Lyrics*, etc., p. 186.

French court. Is there also here a desire to discourage Lydgate from making a bid for the young queen's favour? 'Be not to hasty, com not in presence'. Professor MacCracken notes the lordly tone of this rebuke, which he ascribes to a patron, to Suffolk writing to compliment Margaret of Anjou; it may equally well be the tone of an aristocratic rival in poetry.

The anagram naturally has no reference to Lydgate who has been openly castigated, but reveals the group for whom the poem was written: ISABEL, MARGA–ET, YOLAND, DANIOW: BA–BAlIn, IAMONA. These are the royal Angevin ladies, the queen and her two daughters: Barbelina (Herberquyne) was a confidential attendant who accompanied the queen to England, and whom Roos pilloried in later poems; Jamona Cherneys married Sir Thomas Sharnborne of Sharnborne in Norfolk, and stayed in the queen's service. The remaining names refer to the Escort; the leader's wife, AlIC. POL. SUFFO.; an old friend of Roos's who was to become the queen's chief lady-in-waiting, ISMAnYA SCALES; also two of the gentlewomen, STAN–OW, wife of John Stanlow (treasurer in France), and later a permanent member of the Household; and KATH. WHYTTIn–HAM, friend of Elisabeth Beaumont; Robert Whyttingham the younger was an accredited squire of the Escort. Sir Richard threads his full 'devise' through the poem: IAY TOT FOrFAIT FOrFA–T, with some further repetition, FOrFA–T FOrFA–T.

No. 65. *The Parliament off Cupyde gode of love* (Index). *The Parlement* (title), fol. 327–9. Sixteen stanzas of rhyme royal with a four-line envoy (abab). Printed by MacCracken, *P.M.L.A.*, XXVI, 171–4.

> *Incipit.*   O ye louers which in gret heuynes.
> *Explicit.*   Lenvoye.
> O ye peple that louers yow pretende
> Prayeth hertly to Venus the goddesse
> Off your matters sych tydynges yow to sende
> That fro hensforth we take non hevynesse.

Cupid, sitting high on the daïs, opens his parliament, held by appointment at *Secret Pense* on February 22. A great crowd of suitors presses in, and Cupid gives his preliminary commands for the due ordering of the court. The suitors then kneel and present their bills; their complaints repeat those of the preceding group of poems, hindrance, absence, endurance, and the ill-will of Daunger. Cupid has to consult Venus (st. 13), and therefore adjourns the parliament to April 29 at *Vivre en Joye*. These place-names are in accord with the dates, and with the love-symbolism. In Roos's translation from *Les Vœux du Paon*, 'Cassamus roos', the 'king' defends the pleasure of Secret Thought, of unconfessed love; here it implies the encouraging hope, the unspoken thought, of maiden meditation; *Vivre en Joye* is consummated bliss, and hints at the marriage itself. On February 22 the poet is looking forward to the certain completion of the wedding festivities by the end of April. He could not foresee the delaying storms, and Margaret's unlucky bout of sickness. This gathering up of the themes of the Complaints suggests that *The Parlement* is indeed the last poem of this whole group.

The anagrams, with some variations from the Flower poem, show that the same group comes into play. The royal names recur, ISABEL, MARGA–Et, YOLAnD, DAnJOU, and the two important English ladies, AlIS POLE, SUFFOL., and ISMAnIA SCALES, WHAlSBO–OWGH. To them is added the dowager Beatrice, Lady Talbot, the Portuguese widow of Gilbert, fifth Lord Talbot: BeA––IS TALBOT, PInTO.[1] This is one of the only two occurrences of her name in Roos's anagrams. The two gentlewomen re-appear, STAn–OW, and CATH. WHITTIn–HAm; and MA–STO. is added for Rose Merston (*née* Chetwynde), wife of John Merston of the House-hold. A few men's names appear: c–IFFO., presumably for Thomas, Lord Clifford, a distant connexion of Roos; BO–V., for Sir William Bonvile. A few names are not those of the Escort, but seem to be put in for personal friendship: B–WFOrT (it is possible that Edmund Beaufort was present on February 22); BABThO., for Rauf Babthorpe, one of Roos's Plesaunce friends; and VAVASO.; a Vavasour will come into later poems. The 'devise' is only slightly shortened: TOT FOrFAIT FOr–A–T.

The presence of this collection of poems (Ballades, Complaints, etc.) only in MS. Fairfax 16 is understandable. Lord Stanley, its owner, and Comptroller of the Household in 1447–51, would have a special interest in acquiring these poems of the Escort of which he had been a member. There were three poets in that company: Suffolk, who wrote or translated French verse, but who, even if he did write English poems, would have been both too busy, and too exalted in his position as the royal proxy, to provide these pastimes; George Ashby, whose pedestrian verse could never rise to the elegance of these complaints, or to the disdain of the confident reproof to Lydgate; and Sir Richard Roos, the king's knight, whose good birth and social experience set him in exactly the right position, rather like that of an aide-de-camp, to put his skill at royalty's service. His mark is on every poem.

One name in the anagrams of these two Escort poems is rare in

---

[1] She did not long survive her duties with the Escort, but died two years later, and lies buried in stately fashion in East Shefford, the home of the Berkshire Fettiplaces, one of whose members she had married.

Roos's poems, that is the 'first lady' of the Escort, Alice de la Pole, *née* Chaucer, later Duchess of Suffolk. Another occurrence is in a somewhat ambiguous poem.

No. 66. 'Envoy to Alison':

> *Incipit.* O lewde book with thy foole rudenesse.
> *Explicit.* Now of al goode sith ye be best livinge.

It is a Balade of three stanzas of rhyme royal, with a six-line envoy. It occurs in the two related manuscripts, Fairfax 16 and Tanner 346 (Greystoke's), and in five sixteenth-century editions of Chaucer (Thynne, Stow, and Speght). The Envoy contains an obvious and straight acrostic, ALISON. This is supported and explained by a tangled acrostic (in stt. 1–3) of the line initials only: st. 1, SWFFOl.; stt. 1–2, AlISO.; FOrFA–T; st. 3, TOT. The caesural initials are apparently not called into play; there is no sign of Alice's other names, Chaucer, Phelip, Montagu or Salisbury.[1] If it were not for the anagrams in the two poems and in *The Birds' Praise of Love*, one would almost suspect that Roos was unwilling to allow to the lady knowledge of the double acrostic anagram.

The style is equally puzzling; 'a very poor piece', says Skeat flatly,[2] and the Balade is indeed a heavy prosaic version of Roos's usual phraseology. By contrast, the Envoy breaks out into extravagant and ridiculous aureate terms, a sixain of bombastic flattery. Were it not for the poet's 'devise', I should relieve Roos of it. Its forced and fantastic air must have had some cause or purpose; possibly a side-shaft at the ponderousness of Lydgate, possibly dislike of the lady; the caesural initials may then cover uncomplimentary expressions. I would date it 1445, the only period when Roos is known to have been in direct contact with the Suffolks; Lord Greystoke, presumed collector of MS. Tanner 346, was also a member of the Escort. I have no clue to the 'book' presented.

There are other poems pertaining to the early spring of 1445; Margaret was not the only prospective bride to be complimented.

No. 67. *To My Soverain Lady.*

> *Incipit.* I have non English convenient and digne
> Myn hertes hele, lady, thee with t'honoure.

---

[1] Harris Chewning (*Studies in Bibliography*, 1952, V), examining the seven texts, establishes 'the paucity of variation'. In the two manuscripts, the only variant affecting the acrostic is in Fairfax 16, which in the Envoy reads ALESON.

[2] *Chaucer*, VII, lxii.

Explicit. Ayeines seynt Valentynes day,
    For I have chose that never forsake I may.

The poem consists of sixteen stanzas of rhyme royal; of the 112 lines, about a dozen are in French. It is not 'signed', and no manuscript of it is known. Thynne, printing it in 1532, tacked it on to a poem in honour of the Virgin. It is noticeable, however, that the religious poem is found separately in two manuscripts, Sloane 1212 (Lucas's manuscript), and Ashmole 59, where Shirley attributes it to Lydgate (though it is more 'aureate' than Lydgate's usual style), but that neither of these manuscripts contains the secular poem. Skeat (*Chaucer*, VII, No. xi) was the first to show by these manuscripts the necessity of cutting the two apart, and to invent the title for the secular Valentine. He still assigned it to Lydgate; MacCracken excludes it from the Lydgate canon for lack of evidence.[1]

I suggest that the poem is by Sir Richard Roos, and was written in February 1445, just before the two Anjou weddings.

Skeat recognized that the poem was clearly written for a French princess ('this lilie'), and suggested Katherine, queen of Henry V, who arrived in England on February 21, 1421. The month date would fit, but the lady of the poem is also addressed as 'O violet, *O flour desiree*' (l. 96), an address which surely rules out Katherine as well as Margaret of Anjou. If the one term is heraldic, the other is probably personal, giving either name or devise. Two Angevin princesses combine these requirements in the century: first, Yolande d'Anjou, sister of King René, daughter of Louis II d'Anjou, and of Yolande d'Aragon, and granddaughter of Violante de Bar; secondly and more probably, her niece, Yolande d'Anjou (1428–83), elder daughter of King René. Immediately after Margaret had started for England, the wedding (after a twelve-year betrothal) of her sister Yolande to Ferry de Vaudémont, or Ferry of Lorraine, was celebrated amid fêtes and revels as animated as those of the earlier wedding. Jean d'Angoulême, younger brother of Charles d'Orléans, liberated at last by the English after an even longer imprisonment, was present. Almost certainly this younger Yolande (Violante) is the violet-lily of the English poem. The lines,

    With fervent herte my brest hath broste on fyre;
    L'ardant espoir que mon cuer poynt, est mort
    D'avoir l'amour de celle que je desyre. (ll. 99–101)

come naturally from a poet who has seen depicted René d'Anjou's favourite device of the flaming brazier with his motto 'Ardent Désir'.

---

[1] *Lydgate, Minor Poems*, I, xlviii.

They also suggest that the French lines may be quotations from some poems by the minor poet Pierre de Hurion, called 'Ardent Désir', who wrote for René d'Anjou, and who was considered 'Imitateur tressoubtil entre mille'.[1] The bridegroom's father, Antoine de Guise, was a poet of at least a dozen rondeaux, and he may have been pillaged. There are also clear echoes of Eustache Deschamps: his *Alleluia d'Amour* (poem 588) begins 'Or a mon cuer ce qu'il vouloit' and hammers on the first four words for five lines; hence Roos's lines here,

> *Ore a mon cuer ce quil veuilloit,*
> *Ore a mon cuer* the highest excellence. (59–60)

Again, a slightly distorted echo of Deschamps' refrain, 'Plorez, priez pour le vray amoureux' (poem 503), comes in *'Pleurez pur moi si vous plaist amorous'* (49).

The anagrams support this interpretation of the poem with unexpected precision: initials of six of the French lines give IOLO–DE; and the double acrostic anagram, running almost straight down the poem, gives ISAB–L (stt. 2–3); MA–GA–ET (st. 5); YOLAND (st. 6); DANIOW (stt. 7–8); RENE (st. 9); F–RY DE VAUDEMONT, MA–QUIS DE LOrAIN (stt. 14–16).[2] Ferry was actually only a count, but the higher title would probably not displease. Roos strings his full 'devise' through the poem, IAI TOT FOrFAIT FOrFAIT, and tucks in the name of his chief friend on the Escort, ISMAnYA SCALIS (stt. 4 and 11).

The dates given above fit these identifications. Margaret and her mother, and presumably her sister, arrived at Nancy early in February. If Roos wrote the Flower poem for Margaret's arrival, he might well write a Valentine for her sister. He is obviously not writing as in his own person. Just as Margaret could have poems as from King Henry, so Yolande may have a poem as from her betrothed, who was kept at Metz, fighting beside her father and the king of France. This dedication would account for the stately formality, 'English convenient and digne', with which the poet strives to invest the terms of love; the more passionate speeches are in French: *'Estreynez moy [ma dame] de cuer joyous'*. Even in the English lines, many words used are more French than English, 'digne, tristesse, esploit, renome' (instead of the more usual 'renoun'); a quick-witted French girl of sixteen, though with very little English, could pick out the sense of most of this.

Two of the lines of French will recur in *The Birds' Praise of Love*,

[1] *Le Jardin de Plaisance*, ed. Droz et Piaget, II, 51.
[2] The names of Yolande and Vaudémont are united in the anagrams of the poem, *Le Pris donneur*, in honour of Margaret of Anjou, found only in MS. Roy. 19.A.iii (see my *Studies in Villon, Vaillant, and Charles d'Orléans*, Oxf., 1957).

and link the two poems together as allied efforts although in very different styles; they are *'Jay en vous toute ma fiaunce'* (14), and *'Estreynez moy [ma dame] de cuer joyous'* (98). This last is octosyllabic in both poems, rightly in *The Birds' Praise of Love*, wrongly in *My Soverain Lady*. A favourite Roos phrase, 'hert of stel', occurs in both poems. He approaches the comparison with the famous Ladies, but sheers off from it, and cites instead Rosamond:

> For never non was [here] so faire y-founde,
> To reken hem al, and also Rosamounde (76–7)

'Alone I live, alone' is a phrase or sentiment which Roos could find in the English poems of Charles d'Orléans: 'Now may y say alone y goo alon' (l. 2046), or in his model, Christine de Pisan: 'Seulete suy et seulete vueil estre'. The ten lines beginning *'Salve Regina'* (83) are not, as Skeat thought, addressed to the lady, and a proof of her queenship, but the usual invocation to Venus, which in one guise or another heightens a love poem of any dignity, as it does *The Temple of Glas*, *The Black Knight*, and, I believe, *The Deth of Pyte*. Venus it is who is the 'refut in every payne' and whose mercy most avails to guide by grace (ll. 89–91).

The theme of the poem is the lover's longing to see the lady's 'goodly fresshe face' and the beauty of her 'eyen twayne'; hence the appropriateness of the line, 'Your eyen two wol slee me sodainly', which is also the opening line of *Merciles Beaute*. It would be perfectly proper for Roos to be quoting Chaucer here—indeed the opening line is from 'The Man of Law's Tale'—but it is equally possible for him to be quoting himself (see above, No. 10).

The Escort's departure from France would not put a stop to Sir Richard Roos's poetic compliments. The young queen's illness in April secluded her from activity until her wedding on St. George's Day. During May she journeyed slowly towards London through the southern counties; and a poem of birds singing in flowery springtime would be a fitting gift from the poet among the many presents that poured in on her. In *Reson and Sensuallyte* Roos had added to his original a line on the birds praising God in their morning-chorus:

> And herest, how the briddes synge
> For gladnesse of the morwenynge,
> Preysing god as they best may,
> *Syngyng ther hourys of the day.* (ll. 457–60)

Now the birds sing of devoted love. The poem was entitled by its editor, Miss Hammond,[1] 'A Parliament of Birds'. It is not a ritual, as is

---

[1] *J.E.G. Phil.*, 1908, VII, 105–9.

the 'Birds Mattins' in *The Court of Love*, simply a love argument, with the natural vigour of a dawn-chorus in spring; and the title given in the *Middle English Index* is preferable.

No. 68. *The Birds' Praise of Love:* a poem of fifteen eight-line stanzas (ababbcbc), of which the eighth line is in French, except in stt. 10, 12, and 14.

> *Incipit.* In may whan euery herte is lyȝt
> And flourys frosschely sprede *and* sprynge.
> *Explicit.* En dieu maffie sanz departer.

The poem is not 'signed', nor hitherto ascribed to any author. Its unique copy is in the Cambridge University MS. Gg. 4.27 (Item 4), a manuscript important because containing the G prologue of *The Legend of Good Women*. It is a mixed anthology of no certain provenance; the suggested connexion with Jacqueline of Hainault is not proved, but that with Humphrey of Gloucester is more likely; and we remember that he came in state into Hampshire to greet the young queen. The poem is among short poems in an extra quire added at the beginning of the manuscript (Manly and Rickert, *Cant. Tales*, I, 179–82).

The idea of a company of birds singing to the hero in romances was too austerely noted by Percy as an 'impertinent digression'. The Squire of Low Degree is comforted by them; so later is Spenser's Sir Calepine, who goes forth 'To take the ayre and heare the thrushes song'. It is a natural vivification from the mere lists of birds in *Le Roman de la Rose* and its imitations, such as *How a Lover*. Here the birds are more individually treated, leading off with a 'turtil trewe' which sang

> In frensch ho so þe rondele knew,
> Amour me fait souent pensere.

The poet walks in a wood in May, 'Pur moy ouhter hors de dolour'; he rests in an 'erber' and hears many birds sing of love. Cupid's bird, the nightingale, sits on a cedar (as in *Troilus and Criseyde*) and sings the traditional 'ocy, ocy'. 'Ner esperance mon cuer senbat'. A mavis utters a gnomic line, 'Qui bien ayme tard oublye', which is like the opening phrase of Machaut's *Le Lay de Plours*. The unmusical jay, and Watte the jangling magpie, sing 'Que je ne facece fors de bien aymmyer'. Robert redbreast and the wren protest their devotion to love: 'Biele a biels yeulx ou que ie soye'; the pheasant declares 'Ma esperaunce mad deceu'; the sad, complaining lark, the heir of Troilus in love, sings 'Car vene me ad purchace la mort'; a jolly goldfinch, 'frosch and gay', nevertheless sings a complaint, 'De iour en iour par languisaunce'. The

discourteous and sceptical cuckoo 'can no french', but the popinjay
rebukes him and sings to his love, 'Estreynez moy de cuer Ioyous'. The
rustic fieldfare realistically dismisses a hardhearted lady with 'adew,
adewe', but the starling, though unskilled in French, loves both the
pitiless and the pitiful. The titmouse counsels patience, hope, and trust:
'Je ay en vous tut maffyaunce'. The throstle sums up with a pious conclusion fit for Henry's queen, 'En dieu maffie sanz departer'.

French predecessors of the type might be known to Margaret; the
nearest English model for this kind of writing is *The Parlement of
Foules*, also in this manuscript. There are odd anticipations in the poem
of *The Assembly of Ladies* and *The Flower and the Leaf*. The style is
simple, with strong stresses and alliteration against which the French
lines stand out curiously:

> Myn sor for syghte to don socour
> W'inne a wode was myn walkynge
> Pur moy ouhter hors de dolour. (st. 1)

Some epithets have the sharp observation shown in *How a Lover*: the
'rusti chateryng' of the jay, the 'sunny federys' of the goldfinch; and a
sportsman's eye is seen in the close description of the pheasant:

> þe fesaunt scornere of þe cok
> Be nihyter tyme in frostis colde
> þat nestelyth lowe be sum blok
> Or be sum rote of bosschis olde. (st. 7)

The strife between those who speak English and those who sing in
French would have point for a French girl, needing to learn something
of the language of her new country. The birds of race and romantic
tradition, the turtle-dove, the nightingale and the lark, sing in French,
as can her poet, and so Margaret has a proverbial line from Machaut,
and two lines and many expressions which would take her mind back to
her sister's poem. But she is warned that the bucolic fieldfare will not
understand the refinements of courtly love; and the uncouth starling not
only 'can no skille of swich french fare', but positively has 'more deynte'
to speak English.

One might half expect the anagrams to hint at the identity of these
birds of differing views, but they do not. Yet they are worked on the
closer method whereby one name mostly derives from one or two
stanzas, with only very slight borrowing from neighbouring verses.
ISMANYA (st. 1), and FORFAIT FOR–A–T of the second stanza describing
the poet in the 'erber', indicate the writer and the lady who was the
probable intermediary to the queen. Stt. 3–6 give ISABEAV and YOLAnDE

T

ANIOU,[1] and stt. 7–8, MARGA–ET. Two of the French ladies recur, SHA––BOr. (i.e. Jamona, now Dame Sharnborne), and BARBAlINE (12–14). The remaining names are English: AlIS SVFFOL. (8–9); BEAVFORT, SOMErS. (9–11); WhYTTIN–HA. (15); and again near the end the poet's 'devise', with (unusually) his surname, TOT FOrFAIT FOrFAIT, ROS (11–12). The coupling of Beaufort-Somerset helps to give an upward date for the poem, since Edmund Beaufort only became Earl of Somerset after his brother's death on May 27, 1444; the reference may be to his wife, Roos's sister-in-law. The twelve French lines tantalizingly suggest a separate anagram, and one can certainly get DANJOU from the line-initials but the rest is confused.[2]

Any poem to the king (and he could hardly be left without a wedding-poem) would be as different from the queen's as his saint-like simplicity was poles removed from his bride's brilliant self-consciousness. The beauty and delicacy of the gift devised argue a real affection felt for the young king by his knight.

No. 69. *The Lover's Mass:* a poem of 145 lines in varying metres, with the headings *Introibo, Confiteor, Misereatur, Officium, Kyrie, Christe, Kyrie, Gloria in Excelsis,* and *The Oryson.* It is thus a series of love-lyrics within the framework of the service of the Mass; appended is a disproportionately long 'Epystel in prose' on the pilgrims of love.

> *Incipit.* Wyth all myn hool herte enter
> To fore the famous Riche Auter.

The only pronouncement so far on its authorship is its editor's denial that it could be by Lydgate.[3]

I suggest that it is by Sir Richard Roos, that it is the climax of these poems for the royal pair, and was written for the wedding day of Henry VI and Margaret of Anjou; it should therefore be dated April 1445.

The unique manuscript is Fairfax 16 (fol. 314), where it precedes the *ballades.* But the contemporary Index gives evidence of some uncertainty in its placing, since it is entered twice under different names. For its present position it is called 'The observaunce of Venus goddes of

---

[1] At l. 48 Miss Hammond read 'on ge ie soye', but the manuscript is quite clear with 'ou que ie soye'; it is a common phrase for the French lover, 'where'er I be'.

[2] For the connexion between this poem and 'The Birds' Mattins', see No. 103, *The Court of Love.*

[3] Hammond, *From Chaucer to Surrey,* p. 208.

love'. But after the entry, 'The Parliament off Cupyde gode of love', comes this precisely descriptive entry in another and probably later hand: 'The solemne service of a lover to his lady. The orison and Epistle in prose with other Balads'. In the text of the manuscript, 'The Parliament' is now the last poem, and is immediately followed by the much later prose notes on heralds and their duties.

The poem is not openly 'signed', but it has the movement and phraseology of Roos's poems, and the characteristic rhymes, 'slouthe: routhe: trouthe' (ll. 47–8, 91); 'womanhede: dede' (ll. 91, 93), and 'sterve: serve' (l. 93, internal rhymes). The couplet rhyming on 'shourys: flourys' (ll. 113–14) is very like one in *The Isle of Ladies* (ll. 913–14).

Miss Hammond rightly praised the interest and the skill of the strophic variation, which alone puts the poem out of Lydgate's reach. The first four portions are in octosyllabic couplets. For the *Kyrie* the poet achieves the difficult pattern of three eight-line stanzas, with a final-rhyme scheme bbcbbcbc, and two internal rhymes within each decasyllabic line, beginning aabccb, etc. The three stanzas are linked by repetition of a single word. The *Gloria* is almost equally complex, consisting of eight five-line stanzas (ababc), the short fifth line halving the octosyllabic line, and all fifth lines rhyming between themselves in pairs. *The Oryson* is an eight-line stanza of octosyllabic lines (ababbcbc). The successful handling of these complex structures with a total effect of simplicity and ease is sufficient proof of the poet's skill. We have seen Roos practising this kind of technique in a Beaufort poem written recently between 1443 and 1444. But in this poem there is more than mere virtuosity.

Miss Hammond was puzzled that the nearest parallel to this poem is a Spanish *Misa de Amores* by Suero de Ribera, who is said to have imitated a similar poem by his earlier contemporary, Juan de Dueñas, both men being poets of the reign of John II of Castile (1406–54). In view of the connexion of the English poem with the Anjou marriage, there is no need to hark back, as Miss Hammond does, to John of Gaunt and Constance of Castile. Juan de Dueñas, though a Castilian, fell out with John II, and fled to the court of Aragon, where Prince Ferdinand was *de facto* king.[1] But the titular queen of Aragon was the notable Yolande d'Aragon, mother of René d'Anjou. Brought up by her mother, Violante de Bar, at Barcelona, in the atmosphere of 'Cours d'Amour', she had been married at Saragossa to Louis II d'Anjou. Her grand-daughter, Margaret, had been in her care while René and his wife Isabelle were in Italy, and it was only some two years before the

[1] Puymaigre, *La Cour littéraire de Juan de Castille*, Paris, 1873, II, 185, 201.

girl's wedding that Yolande died in December 1442. Here then is a possible channel for knowledge of a Castilian *Misa de Amores* to percolate to Sir Richard Roos, through Aragon, through the titular queen, and finally through Margaret herself.

The trend of the poem suits with this identification of its subject. The lover's 'confession' accords with the situation of the modest and reserved bridegroom of twenty-two, marrying a girl of fifteen:

> Touchynge the grete tendyrnesse
> Of my youthe and my symplesse
> Of myn vnkonyng and grene age
> Wil lete me han noon avantage
> To serue loue I kan so lyte (17–21)

The verse on the winter's trials may be literal as well as symbolic:

> Affter gret wynd and stormys kene
> The glade sonne with bemys shene
> May appere
> To yive hem lyght affter dyrknesse
> Joye eke after hevynesse (115–19)

There is tactful encouragement (like gentling a nervous colt) to the almost monkish young king to learn the rites of married love:

> This the wyl of Dame *Venus*
> And of hyr Bisshop *Genius* (55–6).

This couplet sums up the *Misereatur*. The *Officium* is a protestation of sincere humility and devotion. The *Kyrie* in its rapid rhymes reflects the wavering flux of emotion:

> Now hope | now dred | now pensyffhede | now thought
> Al thyse yfere | palen myn chere | and hewe. (83–4)

The lovely *Gloria* is no more secular in tone than many carols (the reference to the 'herdys' sheltering from storm is carol-like), and has something of their pure, clear, singing note. The *Oryson* is expressed with piety so simple that with the change of one word it could be said in a church as well as in Venus's chapel.

The anagrams repeat the names of the royal pair in one or another form in every section of the poem; in the *Misereatur* and the *Gloria*, they are accompanied by the names of some of the chief nobles, the pillars of the state, and probably participants in the ceremony. In the *Kyrie*, the internal rhymes break up the apparently decasyllabic lines into three sections (4–4–2), so that each line has two caesural letters.[1] In all the

---

[1] It has been suggested to me by a medievalist that leonine rhymes probably gave the first suggestion for the caesural acrostic.

parts of the poem, the caesuras are carefully marked in the manuscript. The recurrence of the name Plantagenet is interesting; Ramsay maintained[1] that the surname Plantagenet, though 'suggestive of dynastic claims', was not heard of in English history from Geoffrey of Anjou till Richard of York's assumption of it in early 1446. The attaching of it to Henry's name in these anagrams in early 1445 by a poet of the Household suggests that Henry was known to consider it his dynastic name. The poet's 'devise' is not given in full, but insinuates itself throughout the poem. The anagrams run as follows:

Introibo: PLAnTAG.; –ARG. DAnIOW.

Confiteor: PLAnTA.; MAR. DANIOW; HOMF–Y; TA–BOT; TOT FOrFAIT.

Misereatur: P–AnTAGen.; (D)AnIO; TA–BOT; SWFFolk; BeA(v)–OrT, ByOUSHA(M); ROOS.

Officium: HEn–I; MA. DAnIOW; BeWFOrT; FOrF–IT.

Kyrie: FOrFAIT FOr.

Christe: HENRY PLANTA.; DANI–V.

Kyrie: KING HEn.; MA– – –ET; TOT FOrF–IT.

Gloria: P–ANTAG.; MA–GA– –T DANJOV; HOMF–I; SWFFO.; TA–BOT; BeAVSHAMP.

The *Oryson* has no obvious anagram.

The names of Suffolk, Talbot, and Edmund Beaufort need no notes; Beauchamp is not now the great Richard, Earl of Warwick, of former anagrams, the king's tutor, but his son, Henry Beauchamp, Duke of Warwick, who died in the following year, and whose sister and final heiress brought the Warwick title (by creation) to Richard Neville 'the Kingmaker'.[2] The 'Roos' that appears in the *Misereatur* is not probably a signature, but meant for the poet's nephew, Thomas, Lord Roos, a complimentary association of him with the foremost Lancastrian nobles.

The 'Epystel in prose' takes its pilgrim-simile from an interesting source, Laurent's French version of Boccaccio's *Fall of Princes*, the prologue to Book III (cf. Hammond, *op. cit.*, pp. 209 and 449). The vocabulary is close to Lydgate's translation ('fardels', 'the soot of myn inportable labour'), but perhaps only accidentally so; fardels is the natural translation of 'fardeaux', and is moreover almost a technical term in the equipment of a pilgrim.[3] The theme is converted here to that of the pilgrims of love. In the second part, the writer looks back on earlier pilgrims, and we find ourselves again in the company that

[1] *Lancaster and York*, II, 83.   [2] *D.N.B.*, *s.n.*, Richard Neville.
[3] See MS. Ashmole 1519, fol. 47 v., a permit from Richard III to one John Rede to go to France to visit Premonstratensians; he can go, 'with his fardells, males, Bogettes, Caskettes', etc.

Roos's Plesaunce poems celebrated: Troilus, Penelope, Polycene, Dido, Tristram and Ysoude, and the woeful Palamydes. It is plain that here not the king but the writer is the theme, 'the por plentyff in love wyth many yers of probacon professyd to be trewe'. The prose is not distinguished, it is too overloaded; but it is expressive, and at times rhythmical, and there is too little secular prose before 1445 for this fragment to be neglected.

The choice for the king of a 'Lover's Mass', which shocks some sensibilities, was daring but probably deliberate. The liturgical framework was to soothe by its familiarity; the devout phraseology was to insinuate the sanctity of these new emotions: 'Havynge ful gret repentaunce ... As my conscience kan recorde. ... Humble of herte, devoyde of pryde'. The touch on this 'tender youthe', this 'pure, honest, and holy creature', as his biographer called him, is supremely delicate, and the winning effect of the poem is enhanced by stately beauty and lyric charm. It is indeed a gift fit for a royal marriage.

These poems and pastimes, composed for the royal pair at the time of the marriage, were probably the 'bons et bien aggreables services' for which Sir Richard Roos was generously rewarded over and above the ordinary payment for the Escort. Returning to his duties as King's Knight in England, he would still have occasion for royal compliments and diversions. Two ceremonial poems survive, and one designed for a revel, which by their allusions indicate their court connexion.

II. POEMS FOR THE LANCASTRIAN COURT

No. 70. *The Assembly of Ladies:* a narrative poem of 108 stanzas of rhyme royal, with eleven stanzas of introduction and three of conclusion, the inner story occupying stt. 12 to 105 inclusive. A lady, spending an autumn afternoon with others in a garden, tells a knight her recent dream of a 'Council of Ladies'. She dreamt that a gentlewoman, Perseveraunce, summoned her with others to a council at Lady Loyalte's dwelling, Plesaunt Regard. She must wear blue, with a 'devise', and may present a petition. Another gentlewoman, Diligence, comes to escort her, and she finds a little company of four other ladies and four gentlewomen. After due preliminaries, they wait on Lady Loyalte in the presence-chamber, and present their 'bills'. These are read, and the petitioners are dismissed with an 'answer general', the promise of a 'court of parliment'. The lady is awaked by the fountain spray and writes down her dream; the knight commends it.

> *Incipit.* In Septembre, at the falling of the leef
> *Explicit.* Rede wel my dreem, for now my tale is doon.

The poem has been generally accepted as by an unknown poetess, who is also credited with *The Flower and the Leaf*. There have of late, however, been dissentients from both views. Skeat dated *The Assembly* as the later poem of the two, possibly in the last quarter of the century, after the Wars of the Roses (*Chaucer*, VII, lxvi, lxx)—wrongly, as will be seen.

I would suggest that the poem is by Sir Richard Roos, and that it may be dated between February 1447 (Gloucester's death) and 1456 (Shirley's death), probably after May 1450, when Suffolk was murdered. For reasons which will appear, I suggest 1451 as the probable date. The poem is not 'signed' but *The Flower and the Leaf* is, and in spite of divergences of style, I take them both to be by the same author, as do most critics.

The Assembly of Ladies is found in three manuscripts: Longleat 258, one of the important manuscripts for Roos, from which Thynne must have printed it in 1532; Trinity Coll., Cambridge, R. 3.19, a Wilmer manuscript (see above, Chapter III); and Add. 34360, Stow's manuscript, derived from a lost Shirley manuscript, where it precedes *The Deth of Pite*. Miss Hammond (*Anglia*, XXX, 320 ff.) compared the three texts, and found the text of R. 3.19 more akin, though inferior, to that of Longleat 258 than to that of Add. 34360; this is what one might expect from the background of the three manuscripts.

The arguments for a poetess were drawn from the simplicity of language and style, and still more from the interest in the detail of women's dress. The simplicity of style is probably intentional, and partly dramatic. The second argument, which seemed valid to an age of black broadcloth and stove-pipe hats, simply does not hold good of the Middle Ages, when men's clothes were as elaborate as those of women, and as much matter of ingenuity and interest: one has only to remember the Lover of the Rose, who sets out fashionably sewing in his sleeves as he goes;[1] *Li Biaus Descouneus*, written for a lady by a man (Renaut de Beaujeu), has many detailed descriptions of the two heroines' attire, some stereotyped, some more original; the figures in the illuminated manuscript of Creton's metrical history of Richard II (Harl. 1319) show the utmost extravagance of cut and brilliance of colour, and have inspired producers of Shakespeare's play. A later letter between men, describing the meeting in 1506 of Henry VII and Philip of Castile, gives in detail the dress, the jewels, the embroidery, the horse-trappings, of the two kings and their retinue (*Paston Letters*, No. 953). One might as well argue that the details in *The Assembly* on tapestry and buildings

---

[1] *Romaunt*, ll. 97-105.

prove the poet to have been a weaver or an architect. If a woman wrote these two skilful poems, why is not her name known for her very rarity, as are those of Marie de France, Christine de Pisan, Anne de Graville, or Margaret of Navarre? The fact that a woman is the ostensible narrator of the poem is no argument.

The poem is a daisy poem, and the flower indicates Margaret of Anjou as the Lady of the Assembly. This rules out any application to the two later queens, Elizabeth Wydville and Elizabeth of York, and therefore militates against the late date. Nor can it have been designed for Margaret of York marrying Philip of Burgundy in 1468, since it is not a wedding poem, or even a love poem, and the flowers and mottoes have Lancastrian significance. The Lady of 'greet estate' (97) is Lady Loyalte; Margaret's motto was 'humble et loial', and the word 'loyal' was incorporated in the mottoes of many Lancastrian families; the word 'humbly' (little though it may seem now to fit the queen) is used here to shew the graciousness of Lady Loyalte: 'Ful humbly she took' the petitions of the kneeling ladies. For this occasion her motto is 'A endurer', the theme of many of the *Complaints* in MS. Fairfax 16. The whole description of her is that of royalty, no less: her raised throne under a canopy, her state entry preceded by a mace bearer, followed by a noble company, herself clothed in cloth of gold (a royal prerogative), with royal ermine, and with a collar of

> fair rubyes
> In whyte floures of right fyne enamayl (533–4)[1]

Her speech is authoritative, with the royal plural, 'We wol'. The opening lines of the poem adapt the beginning of a French poem earlier addressed to her, *Le Pris donneur*, of which the only copy known is in MS. Royal 19.A.iii, a manuscript probably owned by Sir Richard Roos (see above, Chapter III, 1). The autumnal setting is rare in courtly poetry; here it had a French precedent, and probably also fitted the facts:

> Au moys que len nomme Septembre
> Ou fleurs es bois se vont retraire

> In Septembre, at the falling of the leef,
> The fressh sesoun was al-togider doon.

If Queen Margaret is Lady Loyalte, where then is Plesaunt Regard,

---

[1] Queen Margaret's badge was a golden crown raised off a fluted hat of green, and surmounted by five 'daisies pro*per*', the flowers, stalked and slightly inclined, are shown half-closed, and would therefore be pink-tipped (MS. Ashmole 1121, fol. 227). Here the tell-tale crown is replaced by a collar.

the place of assembly, an easy day's journey for those summoned to attend? The best commentary on the poetic description of this place was written contemporaneously in the accounts of the Clerk of the Works for the alterations made by Queen Margaret to Plesaunce at Greenwich.[1] Immediately after Duke Humphrey's death in February 1447, the king seized his London house, 'The little Wardrobe', for the benefit of King's College, Cambridge, and gave Plesaunce to the queen. She took possession of it with almost indecent haste, and by Easter 1447 the work of alteration and new construction had begun; it went on for some five years. Evidently Duke Humphrey had not kept the place up, for underpinning of the walls and battlements was needed, with much re-leading of roofs and windows, and a thousand elm planks were bought (for 20*s.*) for flooring rooms. One of the first actions was symbolic, to place an escutcheon of the king's and queen's arms in the great window in the queen's ward, and to 'flourish the white glass with the queen's margarites'; presumably the Duke's arms had been torn out.

The detail of the Accounts shows that the garden setting of the poem and of the dream-palace where the assembly is held are one and the same. The knights, squires, and ladies are walking in the 'crosse-aleys' as they were in *How a Lover*. The sunk fountain, with its spiral stair (54) going down from the 'herber', must be part of that underground conduit which the Duke made in 1434, and which gave its name to Conduit or Fountain Court still in the sixteenth century. The description of the outside of the dream-palace (160-5) is reminiscent of the Duke's Plesaunce, the 'toures hy' (Duke Humphrey's Tower was a feature of the landscape till it was pulled down about 1778 for the building of the Royal Observatory), the great wall of the park, and above all the bay-windows. These last were already there in 1447, and were only being re-glazed by the queen; there were two great bay-windows in the queen's ward, and one in her room, and she had another made (or 'bowed' in the Clerk's phrase) in a closet in 1452. This disposes of the argument for dating the poem late because bay-windows are a late architectural feature; they were in Plesaunce before 1447. The poem's palace is recognized in the chambers and parlours ('the parlours next the great garden', 'a parlour in the little garden', 'a royal closet for the queen'), and in the great hall with its tresans and dais and its new rails for the arras. The poet's stress on the floor 'paved faire and smothe' (64) of the fountain, with 'stones square' craftily joined, and again on the paved floor of the hall, 'The goodliest that any wight might see' (451-2), is

---

[1] Duchy of Lancaster Accounts, 28, 1/11. Printed in Hasted's *History of Kent*, ed. Drake, part i, pp. 55-6.

justified by the thousands of Flanders tiles bought for paving the queen's
room, the dais in the great hall, two bay-windows, and especially 'a
parlour in the little garden'. The most interesting object, still not fully
explained, is the maze, a casual part of the poem's setting, where the
ladies' behaviour is described with extraordinary truth to nature:

> Some went inward, and wend they had gon out,
> Some stode amid, and loked al about. . . .
> Other ther were, so mased in her mind,
> Al wayes were good for hem, bothe eest and west, . . .
> And some, her corage did hem sore assayle,
> For very wrath, they did step over the rayle. (ll. 34–42)

No maze is mentioned in the Accounts, but there are two possibilities.
Between Greenwich and Blackheath is Maze Hill (Mays Hull in an
early fourteenth-century document), and the name may commemorate
one of the ancient turf mazes. More probably a maze with low railings
was made in the garden of Plesaunce; the only hint of it is in the entry,
early in 1451, of six loads of rails for railing the vines in the great garden.
The idea of a built-up maze, novel in England, would be familiar to
Margaret, since her father, René d'Anjou, had one at Baugé (a name to
be remembered by Sir Richard Roos), which in 1477 needed repairs;[1]
presumably there too impatient ladies had stepped over the rail. As a
literary idea, a maze was familiar to Sir Richard from the legend of the
Minotaur, from Chaucer's *Hous of Fame*, and from *Reson and Sensuallyte*:

> For this the house of Dedalus
> Wyth the clowthy and the threde,
> Dedly perilouse, who taketh hede.
> It is so wrynkled to and froo
> That man not, how he shal goo (ll. 3604–8).

Another hint of the behaviour of the younger ladies lies in the 'pot of
marjolain' that stands on top of the winding stair of the fountain (l. 56).
Allusions in Northern French poems show that the nightly task of
bringing in the marjoram out of the cold was a recognized opportunity
for twilight snatches of lovers' talk and a 'baiser volant'; witness the
testament of Pierre de Hauteville:

> Je laisse aux amoureux ardans
> De nuit estre aux huys actandans
> Qu'on mette en sauf les marjolaines,
> Ilec de froit claquer des dens
> (*Le Jardin de Plaisance*, ed. Droz and Piaget, II, 306).

[1] W. H. Matthews, *Mazes and Labyrinths*, 1922 p. 112.

to this half-French court, the poet reveals his awareness of the trysting-place at the fountain stair.

Queen Margaret had taken care to put into the windows of her Plesaunce, not only the king's and her own arms, but also their badges:

fourteen feet of white glass eflu[r]oshyd with flowers of the King and Queene, viz., with hawthorn budds and margarits, placed in three lights in the baywindow within a closet.

In this manless poem, the king's hawthorn buds, which he had adapted from his father and grandfather, are omitted, but near the fountain the marguerites are given special prominence:

> With margarettes growing in ordinaunce
> To shewe hemself, as folk went to and fro,
> That to beholde it was a greet plesaunce (57–9).

With them are 'ne m'oublie mies' and 'sovenez', flowers of Lancastrian meaning, as in Henry V's motto 'Souvenez', and Margaret Beaufort's adaptation, 'Souvent me souviens'.

The next flower is of more general application:

> The povre pensees were not disloged there;
> No, no, god wot, her place was every-where (62–3).

Pansies, the flowers of regretful remembrance, are here not yet dislodged as signs of grief and affection. Two ladies of the court circle suffered loss in 1450: the assassination in May 1450 of the Duke of Suffolk must have brought as much horror and dismay to Queen Margaret as to his widow, Alice.[1] He could fittingly be referred to with just this passing tone of melancholy by the poet who had served under him in the Escort. Hard on this murder came another; on July 4, 1450, Lord Say, together with his father-in-law, William Crowmer, was killed by Cade's rebels. His wife, Emmeline, whose name is found in the earlier Jewels Accounts, survived this double loss for eighteen months. There is no reference to the woodbine, and one may infer the absence of the Duchess of Somerset. The Duke returned to England in the autumn of 1450, but was back in France in 1451. The Duchess's only recorded present from the queen was in 1452–3.

The reasons for suggesting 1451 for *The Assembly* are partly historical and political. Between May 1450 and 1456, the limits above referred to, hardly any other year would be propitious. The rebellion of Cade in

---

[1] In the same year, a curious and direct connexion is seen between Plesaunce, and Alice de la Pole and her son; furniture (tables, trestles and a bench) made for them out of the queen's store is entered in the Clerk's accounts. It may indicate that they had temporary lodging there, she as a 'King's widow'.

1450 was, it is true, suppressed in July; but it had disorganized court life considerably, and brought grief to the court circle. Early in 1452, York had collected an army, and it was a year of unrest, although the king and Somerset forced him to swear allegiance. 1453 began with disaster in the death of Talbot and the final loss of France, and continued with the king's mental illness from August for sixteen months. The prince's birth in October 1453 provided the desired Lancastrian heir; but the resultant protectorship of York, and the imprisonment of Somerset, were blows to the queen's policy, and were felt by her as personal affronts. Not till early 1455 did the king make a temporary recovery, and that year saw the outbreak of bloodshed in May, and the death of Somerset and of many Lancastrian supporters at St. Albans. 1451 was the only year in this period when the court and the Household were comparatively at ease, at least to outward seeming; in spite of ferment, the government was holding its own, secure in York's withdrawal to his estates on the Welsh border. Finally, Henry VI and the court were at Greenwich, September 1 to 3, 1451.

This date, 1451, can be partially supported by inferences of another kind, from the theme and personages of the poem. First it must be stressed that the poem does not conform in more than structure to the pattern of a 'Cours d'Amour'. Lady Loyalte is not arbitrating in a 'cas d'amour', as did the queen's ancestress in Spain. There is no mention, far less any appearance, of Venus, Cupid, Amour, or Love. The inexperienced narrator assumes that the goodly company are 'such folk ... That list to love' (353), but her informant's reply is non-committal, and in the 'bills' the word 'love' occurs only twice, and only once (668) seems to refer to love between the sexes. The ladies summoned to the 'counsayl' are to sue in any matter, grief, or offence wherein they feel their heart displeased (122–6). The Lady will gladly give them audience, and ease their disquiet. Actually no judgment is given; as in *The Parlement of Cupid*, the assembly is adjourned. The inconclusive ending may suggest reference to an actual situation. Of the nine petitions, eight are concerned with unfulfilled promises, insufficiently rewarded desert, insecurity of position, uncertainty of favour, 'no thank for al her good desert' (635), lack of appreciation of faithful purpose, 'good continuaunce', patient but unacknowledged fidelity. These are not 'the pangs of dispriz'd love'; they are much more like 'the spurns that patient merit ... takes', or like 'simple truth miscalled'. There seems to be more than one possible interpretation of the whole. The poem may depict no more than a storm in a Palace posset-cup, a flutter among the ladies of the Household, such as in another century only a Grenville, a Creevey, or a Horace Walpole could have done justice to, and there was none such to chronicle it in the fifteenth century. Or it may be a political allegory, and represent a test and a reaffirmation of Lancastrian loyalty; or it may have been meant to convey a warning of discontent. To get further with any such hypothesis, the structure of the household of Lady Loyalte needs to be studied. The strict observance of the grades must be realized before any conjectural identification is made through the anagrams and mottoes.

Three sets of people are distinguished. First, there are the regular officials of the Household, differentiation being duly made between the ladies and the gentlewomen, between such as a Paulina and an Emilia in *The Winter's Tale*. Among the former are Largesse, the Steward (317), Remembraunce, the Chamberlain (336), Attemperaunce, the Chancellor (507), and the Secretary, Avysenesse (337). Of the latter are Perseveraunce, the summoner (91), Diligence, the guide (133), Countenaunce, the portress (176), probably also Belchere, the marshall of the hall. There are also two women who flit across the scene without taking any part, Discrecioun, the Chief Purveyor, and Acquaintaunce, the Herbegere (260–70). In this group alone does the allegory lie, and it has been so sharply derided that its interest has been overlooked. This is the first courtly poem in English to get away from the figures of *Le Roman de la Rose*, and to call up qualities which distinguish professions.[1] Avysenesse, with its dual sense, could not be bettered for a secretary both well-informed and sagacious; Belchere is a practical external quality for a marshall of the hall, quite different from the psychological Belacueil. And in this well-ordered court, under that all-embracing virtue of Attemperaunce or Measure, the Chamberlain, there is no place for such discomfortable, disruptive persons as Daunger or Ydlesse. The poem is nearer a Morality in its allegorizing, and the poet may indeed already have seen some such Morality as *The Castle of Perseverance*. Or he may have known the religious allegory, *The Abbey of the Holy Ghost*,[2] of which Sir John Paston later owned a copy (Letter 869). There nineteen ghostly ladies, in pairs under the Abbess Charite, perform the duties of their covent, Curtasye as hosteler, Resone as purveyor, the lady Drede as porter who 'kepis besyly þe cloyster of þe herte', and the damsel Discrecyone who is 'witty and

---

[1] It is true that in *Le Chastel de Joyeuse Destinée*, Roos could find the Seven Virtues of Love, e.g. Esperance, Loyaulte, Atrempance, Diligence (*Jardin de Plaisance*, fol. xxxii). He may well have recalled them here.

[2] Ed. G. G. Perry in *Rel. Pieces in Prose and Verse from Robert Thornton's MS.* (E.E.T.S., O.S. 26, 1867 and 1889, Item 3, pp. 48–58).

... full ware' as Treasurer to 'luke þat all go wele'. At the Assembly of Ladies, however, there is no psychomachia.

If there is any undercurrent of discontent it is not in the loyal Household, but only in the second and third groups, the visiting ladies and gentlewomen. Here again the distinction of rank is duly preserved:

> We been, quod I, fyve ladies al in-fere
> And gentilwomen foure in company (407-8).

The narrator is the fifth lady, but she is unused to the court and her unaccustomedness and modesty draw on the clever description of the organization of a palace; it deserves more study by the social historian.[1] It proves the poet's complete familiarity with palace etiquette—with the way in which the stranger is first summoned, guided, then met and received at the outer gate, where the baggage is already waiting; with the proffered rest in an outer chamber, where the visitors remove the stains of travel; with the provision for their lodging, and the information given about the officials; in short, with the 'handing along' from one to another official in this system of jealous guarding of the privacy and safety of royalty. At length the Presence Chamber is reached; Lady Loyalte makes her impressive appearance, standing for an instant in the doorway under the arras held back; all fall on their knees, all rise as one. The chamberlain is summoned to control the undistinguished crowd of unnamed suitors; the Lady hands the petitions to the secretary, the chamberlain transmits her orders. The ladies proffer their 'billes' first, then the gentlewomen. The shy narrator, who has contrived to be passed over among the ladies, is gently encouraged, and with many false starts stammers out her sense of neglect. With the promise of a 'court of parliment' the petitioners depart, elegantly taking each other by the sleeve, like the ladies in *Les Vœux du Paon*. All is done with the courtliest propriety.

In turning to examine the text for possible identification of individuals by anagrams, we have the advantage of some documentary aid. We have met some of the future members of the queen's household in the Escort, such as Lady Ismania Scales, and Lady Elizabeth Grey.[2] Future gentlewomen were Margaret Stanlow and Rose Merston, wives respectively of the treasurer in France, and of the keeper of the king's

---

[1] Cf. M. St. Clare Byrne, 'The Social Background' in *A Companion to Shakespeare Studies* pp. 187-218.

[2] She was not the future Queen Elizabeth Wydville, as has been stated, but the widow of Sir Ralph Grey of Heaton, and a daughter of Lord Fitzhugh; her son Ralph was a king's squire in 1445 (*Cal. Pat. Rolls, 1441-6*, p. 353, June 27, 1445).

jewels. For the queen's establishment in England we have some documentary basis. The first analysed list of her household is found in 1452–3, possibly drawn up with a view to the economies which were effected during the king's illness in 1454.[1] Lady Scales and Lady Grey are joined here by Lady (Isabella or Elizabeth) Dacre (*née* Bucceley) and by 'Domina Margareta Roos', not, I believe, the elderly dowager, Margery Wentworth, widow since 1421 of John, Lord Roos, but Margaret Vernon, widow of Longueville, and recently the wife of Sir Richard Roos. Of the French gentlewomen, Barbelina, Dame Jamona Sharnborne, and Katherine Whittingham, *née* Gatevyne, are still there, and also Katherine Penyson of Provence. The English are the experienced two already mentioned, and with them are Matilda (Fitz)Lewis, Agnes Parre, and finally Eleanor Roos, daughter of Sir Robert who had died in 1449. Her brother Henry's name is among those of twenty-two squires. The three clerks still include George Ashby, the minor poet; grooms and pages fill up the tale. Many more names crowd the rolls of the Jewels Accounts.

The series of Queen Margaret's Jewels Accounts is unfortunately not complete, since those for 1448–9 and 1450–2 are missing, but there are extant five annual accounts between the years 1446 and 1454,[2] and these show the nature and the objects of the queen's 'largesse'. It embraced all the regular members of her own Household, and a great many of the king's servants, high and low. In addition there are gifts which are non-recurrent, and which seem to indicate the occasional visitors, some of whom came only once in half a dozen years; whereas repeated gifts show us others like the much-favoured Jacquetta, Lady Rivers, the Suffolks, or the Buckinghams, who were in frequent attendance, and would certainly be there for the great festivals. Special gifts for marriages and baptisms sometimes allow one to fill out the personal history of individuals. One category of temporary residents would be the 'King's widows' and the 'King's wards', the dependents of knights and gentry who were summoned to court until their estates were settled, largely as a safeguard against imprudent or unlicensed marriage; it is probably in that capacity that Margaret Longueville's name suddenly appears in the Jewels Accounts of 1449–50.

In addition to these there are entries in the Patent, Close, and Fine Rolls which specify holders of posts in the Household. Such are the documents concerned with the 'denization' of the queen's French

[1] P.R.O., Duchy of Lancaster Accounts, 5/8, fol. 11.
[2] P.R.O., E. 101/409/14 and 17; 410/2, 8, and 11.

attendants in 1449;[1] to the names we know are added Osanne (Heriman), Mary, Bastard of Anjou, Isabella Barbays, and Joan de Gragione. Many other deeds are gifts and appointments; the king's lavishness to his Household was one of the causes of general discontent beyond the confines of the court and its beneficiaries. From all these sources, and from the list of the king's Household in 1454, we can trace some of the names in Roos's anagrams, and gain some idea of the group of knights and squires, ladies, gentlewomen, and women of the chamber who surrounded the royal pair in a circumscribed sphere of elegant living.

One cannot but be amused in *The Assembly* at Roos's wariness and skill in avoiding pitfalls as he identifies his allegorical virtues with the regular members of the Household. He has many to compliment, and he is not to be lured into committing himself. The description of each personage is accordingly made to cover two or even three anagrams; and a second mention of the personage may be accompanied by yet another set of names. With the visiting ladies and gentlewomen there is more precision; and two persons are constants, the narrator and Lady Loyalte.

The poet opens with his 'devise' AI FO–FAIT (st. 1) and the last ten lines of the narrator's introduction give AlIAN. ROS (67–77). Then begin the multiple identifications of the allegorical persons. Perseverance (ll. 78–91) is triple, IAQUETTA STAnLOW, JAMOnA SHA–NBO., WHITT., TOt FO–FAIT; Dame Sharnborne is already familiar; Jacquetta Stanlow, probably a daughter of Margaret Stanlow, gets gifts in 1449–50 and 1452–3, and at the later date a silver gilt cup *ad maritagium suum*; Whittingham is not the earlier Katherine Whittingham, Elizabeth Beaumont's friend, but the French gentlewoman, Katarine Gatevyne of Anjou, who married Robert Whittingham, the King's Sergeant, Roos's friend of earlier days. She stayed on in the Household, and her name appears in all six lists, her married name first in the Jewels Accounts of 1449–50.[2] These two marriage dates, one upward and one downward, are additional reasons for dating the poem September 1451. Diligence described (ll. 127–40) yields again SH–RNB., IAQU–TTA STAn–OW, and adds OSAnA; Osan(ne), *Cameraria Regine*, is without surname even in the patent of naturalization, and so appears in the Jewels Accounts and in the lists until 1453, when she is casually called Osanne Heriman (D.L. Accounts, V, fol. 18 v.). Diligence in person (ll. 190–203) gives

---

[1] *Cal. Pat. Rolls, 1446–52*, p. 240.

[2] See also *Cal. Pat. Rolls, 1446–52*, p. 165, Feb. 10, 1448; and in the Jewels Accounts of 1452–3, is recorded a baptismal gift of £20 for the son of Robert Whittingham.

a very different pair, MATI--A and ISA. FI-LOWIS. Elizabeth or Isabella
FitzLewis appears in 1447–8 as *filia Leweys Capitalis domicella Regine*;
in 1452–3 she receives an odd gift, a ragged staff in gold, garnished with
a balays ruby and two pearls; it looks as if she were marrying a Beauchamp, and she disappears from the remaining lists. Matilda, probably
her sister, continues on into the last dated list. The FitzLewis or
FitzJohn family of Horndon, Essex, are difficult to trace, partly because
they continued the Fitz method of naming. These girls were probably
sisters of Sir Henry FitzLewis, a fighting Lancastrian, whom we shall
meet again later. The young woman passing by, Discrecioun, and the
unseen Acquaintaunce (ll. 260–73) conceal two names, IOHAn BATT–R--Y,
IAQu–TTA, with ForFAIT. Johanne Battersby occurs as a *cameraria* in the
list of 1452–3; there is no Jacquetta of lesser rank except Jacquetta
Stanlow in the Accounts. Countenaunce the portress (ll. 301–8) is
again WH–TT--GHAM, with, added, the place of her birth, AnIOU; this
was given at her naturalization. The lady Largesse, the Steward
(ll 315–21), is again another endenizened French lady, ISA. BA--AYS, yet
Isabel Barbays of Lorraine does not appear in the Accounts. With her
here again is whITT. It is probably Barbays who is sketchily repeated
(B--B–Y.) with I–QU–TTA ST----W for Remembraunce the Chamberlayn (ll. 330–7). Avysenesse the Secretary (ll. 337–50) is an English-
woman, ISAB. FFYeNIS; this is probably one of the 'King's widows',
Elizabeth Holland, whose husband Sir Roger Fiennes, Treasurer of the
Household in 1446–7, died in November 1449.

When we come to the petitioners, we realize that some at least are
visitors only dramatically, for the first Lady (ll. 582–8) proves to be
Lady Scales. For her Christian name, the word 'jamais' of her 'motto'
is to be read by Deschamps' backward syllabic method, 'ja-ma-is',
'Is-ma-ja'. Her surname SCAl. is 'got from the anagram, also a suggestion
of –TAn–OW; to these two friends Roos had written many poems in the
time of his 'Lady Bounte'. The second lady (ll. 589–95) is also indicated
partly by her motto, 'Une sanz chaungier'. 'Sans changer' is the motto
of the Stanleys, and Lord Stanley (owner of MS. Fairfax 16) was
Comptroller of the King's Household, 1447–c. 1451. His wife, Joan
Goushill, was a distant kinswoman of Roos; her anagram here is
STAn--Y, G–U–HI. The third Lady's anagram (ll. 596–609) is TA--OT,
CO–NT–SS OF SHROW., and for Margaret Talbot, Roos's connexion by
marriage, he adds his 'devise', AI ForFAIT ForF., and for her motto,
'Tyl deth depart', substitutes 'Oncques puis lever'. The fourth Lady
(ll. 610–23) is announced by an inversion of her first husband's motto:
'Entierment vostre' reverses the famous motto of John of Bedford, 'A

U

vous entier'; the anagram gives IA-----TTA BE-FOr., RI--RS. Jacquetta
of Luxemburg, now Lady Rivers, and aunt by marriage of the queen,
received fine gifts in 1447–8 and 1452–3.

Of the gentlewomen, the first petitioner (ll. 627–41) combines
STAnLOW and OSANNA. The second (ll. 642–58), MAT., E-LISABeTH,
FISLOWIS. The third (ll. 659–72) seems to be MARY BASTA---, AnIOO,
one of the 'endenizened' ladies, an illegitimate cousin of the queen,
whose name does not appear recognizably in the Jewels Accounts;
FOrF-IT is added. The fourth gentlewoman (ll. 673–9) remains puzzling;
the letters suggest MA-GA---T THWA-TS, but no Thwaites girl appears
in the existing Accounts. She might be a bird of passage. There were
two large families of Thwaites, one in Norfolk, and one more important
in Yorkshire, into which the Manners of Belvoir later married (see above,
Chapter III, MS. Fairfax 16). At last the fifth Lady, the narrator,
speaks (ll. 687–707), and the name is again ALYAN. –OOS, IAI TOT FOr-AIT.
The conclusion confirms this, with a final pretty trick. The initial
letters give ALIANOR, AI FOrFAIT; but with the caesural letters the full
anagram proves to be, MAR–AR–T (D)ANIOU. ALIAN., AI TOT FOrFAIT
FOrFAYT. That is to say, the poet finally signs with his 'devise', and
reveals that Lady Loyalte is indeed the queen, and the narrator his
niece Eleanor Roos, whose name appears in the list of 1452–3, and in the
next year's Jewels Accounts. She probably came to court early in 1450,
after her father's death, and so was well fitted for the role of an artless
ingénue.

The anagrams have shown the dramatic character of the poem, and
the mottoes confirm this. Only two of the Ladies have an adaptation of
their family or personal motto. The remainder are almost certainly not
heraldic or family mottoes, but 'devises' assumed for a special occasion,
as was customary. The mottoes of the allegorical persons indicate zeal
and devotion, and are in keeping with the poem's unifying stress on
loyalty, service, and desert: 'Tant que je puis', 'Bien et loyalment'.
Compare the Norris motto, 'Feythfully serve', which appears in the
windows of Ockwells Manor, where Sir John Norris perpetuated in glass
his Lancastrian loyalties and friendships, to the queen, to Edmund,
Duke of Somerset, the Duke of Warwick and others. Fortunately he
did not deface them when he became squire of the body to Edward IV.
Yet Alice Norris, his wife, and head of the queen's 'daumsells' in 1446–7,
does not appear in these anagrams. The mottoes of the four gentlewomen are comparatively colourless, 'soyes en sure', 'cest sanz dire'.
It looks as if the queen had indeed summoned at short notice a company
of intimates for a definite social occasion, perhaps a kind of house-

warming for the new Plesaunce. This may be a later record of the entertainment devised, or even, with its precision of detail, a libretto. The complaints need have no relation to the real situation of the individual 'visitors'.

It is not surprising that the old Plesaunce is in Sir Richard Roos's mind; for him there are ghosts and echoes of the past in these chambers and gardens. So he peoples the walls of the great chamber with personages whom he knows (as the two Margarets of his devotion may not have known) to be shadows from a former phase: Phyllis, who died for love of Demophoon, and Antony and Cleopatra (ll. 456–62). This artistically brief and wistful retrospect is for his private satisfaction. He inserts a special compliment for the queen. The acumen of Skeat suggested that 'Hawes the shene' (ll. 463–4) was a scribe's rationalization of the reading that Stow's manuscript garbled ('Enclusene'), and that beneath the mess lies the name of Melusine, and her story. As Skeat recalls, it was Melisende, a descendant of the legendary lamia, foundress of the House of Lusignan, who brought 'the uneasy crown of Jerusalem to the house of Anjou'.[1] Since too Geoffrey Plantagenet, Count of Anjou, was another of the serpent's descendants, the poet is hinting at the distant kinship of Henry Plantagenet and Margaret of Anjou.

The general situation of the poem might spring from memories of Roos's romantic *Isle of Ladies*, but on this manless assembly, with its actuality and its feminine fuss and flutter, the maturer poet cocks a whimsical eye, as in the innocent narrator's questions and their answers:

> Now yet, quod I, ye must tel me this cace
> If we shal any man unto us cal?
> Not oon, quod she, may come among you al.
>
> Not oon, quod I, ey *benedicite*,
> What have they don, I pray you tel me that.
> Now by my lyf I trow but wel, quod she,
> But ever I can bileve there is somwhat. (ll. 145–51)

Professor C. S. Lewis[2] was the first to give the poem due credit as an 'admirable picture of manners'. No woman who has ever attended her College Gaudy, or a women's conference, but will smile over the pertinent descriptions of the officials, as of the Secretary, who 'may do

---

[1] *Chaucer*, VII, 395, 537. *The Romans of Partenay or of Lusignen*, ed. W. W. Skeat, E.E.T.S., XXII, p. xi. At the jousts at Nancy, Charles VII had borne the image of Melusina on his shield, out of compliment to the Anjou bride (Hookham, *Margaret of Anjou*, I, 251).

[2] *The Allegory of Love*, pp. 249–50.

right moche in every thing' and is 'ful good and ful loving'. Throughout, compliments are heaped on the officials, even on the unseen 'herbegere', 'A woman of right gracious manere'.

The simplicity of the style has brought down hard words on the poem as the silliest stuff. In 1451, simplicity may have had a purpose, and be due neither to 'le faux naïf', nor to the 'niaiserie' of the writer. It was probably deliberately assumed for the French-born queen, and her half-dozen French attendants, nearly all of whom are complimented in the anagrams. The frequent question and answer are like those of a phrase-book, almost 'basic English':

> How fer, quod I, have we unto that place?
> A dayes journey, quod she, but litel lesse. (ll 213-14)

Monosyllables are many and even fill whole lines: 'For wit ye wel I wold be gon ful fayn' (l. 242). The many doublets often give French and English words together: 'ful sad and ful demure' (82); 'her devyse, her word' (207); 'a soft and esy pace' (219); 'departed was and gon' (275); 'her joy, her comfort and gladnesse' (604); 'sorowes and payn' (695). The French colouring of the courtly vocabulary is as strong as ever here. Thus to say of all this deliberately simplified style that it is impossible in the poet of the far richer *The Flower and the Leaf*, is to misunderstand the poet's intention and to underrate his powers: the gulf is nothing so wide as that between *The Queen of the May* and *In Memoriam*.

Under all this prettifying there may lurk, perhaps, a sense of personal or political grievance, certainly a serious comment: 'long to sewe it is a wery thing' (l. 420); it is the sentiment that Spenser will express more forcibly:

> What hell it is in suing long to bide,
> To loose good dayes that might be better spent.

Whatever may have been the political implications, loyalty is finally asserted, more confidently than the facts were to justify later:

> Submitting us lowly til her servyse.
> For as we thought we had our travayl spent
> In suche wyse as we helde us content (ll. 731-3).

The sudden spray of the fountain wakes the dreamer, but not before the dream has come to a seemly and orderly conclusion, a dream which for this courtly audience carries weight,

> passing good,
> And worthy to be had in remembraunce.

No. 71. *The Chance of the Dice:* a poem of fifty-nine stanzas of rhyme royal, of which the first three stanzas form the poet's introduction, and the remainder are characters: printed by E. Hammond in *Eng. Studien*, LIX, 5–16.

> *Incipit.* First myn vnkunnynge and my rudenesse
> Vnto yow alle that lysten knowe her chaunce.
> *Explicit.* ffor hasarde hath with maystry quytte me soo
> My while that I [ioyles] now leue in woo.
> Explicit the Chaunce of the Dyse.

There is no 'signature', but the 'devise' often occurs in the anagrams. The poem occurs in the same two manuscripts as does *Ragman Roll*, MS. Fairfax 16 (fol. 148–54), and Bodleian 638 (fol. 195–203 v.). In Fairfax 16, the first three stanzas are entitled 'Balade vpon the Chaunse of the Dyse'; in Bodleian 638, a leaf is missing between fol. 200 and 201, so that stt. 43–8 inclusive are lacking, also a part of st. 39. In the margins, three dice drawn in red beside each character give the numbers of the throw.

The style and metre are very markedly those of Sir Richard Roos, with the 'routhe: trouthe: slouthe' rhymes (four times), the 'sterue: serue' rhyme, and many rhymes in '-aunce'. The style is free-running and colloquial, as befits a revel:

> More rowm, for goddys love, why prese yee so,
> War, let this man here knowen his auenture (st. 49).

The writer has frequent recourse to common proverbs and popular sayings: 'as lyght as leefe on lynde' (15), 'ye wol wipe the stake' (25), 'the wheston kepe and bere' (25), 'when that most ys nede, Than boote ys next' (29). On the other hand, there are a number of literary allusions, to Jason (5), to Mercury, the disposer of eloquence (12), to 'Arthoures dayes' (33), to 'the cytee of new troye' (32), Troilus and Creseyde (20, 55) and Pandare (23), to 'Grisildes pacience' (30), the Wife of Bath's life as the only study for a shrew (43), and to 'Catoun the wise' for a gnomic saying (53). The whole effect is much more carefully wrought than that of the simpler *Ragman Roll*, and it is plainly intended for a more important company, a high revel, embracing all ranks; the anagrams, after an early false start, soon make clear that the company is the royal Household, and that the single stanzas portray individuals.

The introductory stanzas are evidently old material being used again; the anagrams are HOMFREY; AlIAN. –OBHAM, ANTI.; WI–BISH; V–V–S––R: TOT FOrF–IT. There are also two 'characters' which raise memories of that earlier circle. The delightful effect of a pleasant voice 'that fresshly kan synge' (20) has a parallel in *Ragman Roll*, st. 26; here it is pointed by a reference to Troilus and Creseyde, as if to prepare us for 'Antigone the shene'. The initials of lines 1–4, working upwards, give A–NT., and the full anagram is ANT. –OWIS. It is possible that Lady Powis attended court in her brief widowhood in 1450 before her remarriage in France. Stanza 50 is even more remarkable in this poem of the later Lancastrian court; it depicts a person unfortunate and pitiable:

> Allas allas why abyggen ye so dere
> That menen nought but trouthe and gentilesse.
> Why nad fortune taken hede of your sadnesse.

Yet the terms are too vague to prepare us for the anagram, ALIAN. COB–AM. Is it possible that the imprisonment of Eleanor Cobham became less stringent after the Duke's death (see below, No. 86c)? That of Isabella, queen of Edward II, was much relaxed with the passage of time.[1] But it is difficult to imagine the former Duchess of Gloucester making even a fleeting appearance at Queen Margaret's court; was she impersonated for this occasion?

Lancastrian references engage the remaining stanzas. The portrait of the chief lady does not come first, as it does in *Ragman Roll* (st. 4). But it is in similar terms (28), praising

> this creature formed so clene
> That of al beaute is chefe high toure.

The anagram is –NIOW. The terms of st. 18 have already made clear the reference to Henry (P–AnTAG.):

> O mekenesse of vertu princepal
> That may be founde in eny creature. . . .
> The lorde of vertu and al vices cure
> Perfit beaute grounded withoute envye
> Assured trust withoute gelousye.

The stanza is torn out of MS. Bodleian 638. The first character (st. 4), highly complimentary to a lady, indicates Lady Scales by several means. The anagram is IS–ANYA WhA– – –B–RO. The comparison with sweet cinnamon again employs the backward syllabic anagram, sy-nam-ome for ys-man (cf. *Assembly*, l. 583, *jamais* for is-ma-ja; the word is found also in Roos's list of spices and herbs in *How a Lover*, l. 351). The last clue is heraldic:

> To the orient perle as norisse is Cokille
> Ryght so ben ye to al vertu the rote.

The canting arms of Scales were three scallop shells or 'écailles'; scallop and cockle were names used interchangeably, and Lydgate had given

---

[1] Edward Bond in *Archæologia*, XXXV, 453–69.

warrant for making a cockle conceal a pearl (*N.E.D.*, *s.v.* cockle). At this period the pearl as clearly denotes Queen Margaret as Cynthia will later denote Queen Elizabeth I; and the line 'To the orient perle as norisse is Cokille' is a roundabout way of preparing us for Lady Scales, the chief guardian of the queen, *attendens arca personae*.

Lady Scales heads a bevy of virtuous ladies. She of st. 6, honest and active, a model of 'gentilesse' and honest disport, but shunning company, is YAC–TT. WYDV.; as the queen's connexion by marriage, Jacquetta, Duchess of Bedford, now Lady Rivers, was a favourite of the queen. The eloquent lady of st. 12 is M–UD STAnHOPE, as she was in *Ragman Roll*, st. 18; Mercury gave her a birth-gift of knowledge, and of the best way to express it. The lady charitable of speech (st. 40) is STANLOW; her kindly manners make her welcome in all company. She of the fair hands (st. 56) seems to be AlIS NO–––IS, the wife of Sir John Norris, Keeper of the Jewels. One who bears gracefully age and experience, after a well-spent youth, proves to be the queen's connexion, Mary the Bastard of Anjou (BAST–R– AnIOW, st. 26). One in whom 'spronge ys newe Grisildes pacience' (st. 30) is a FI–NNIS, possibly Emmeline Fiennes, widow in 1450 of Lord Say, possibly Elizabeth, wife of Roger Fiennes and the 'Secretary' of *The Assembly of Ladies*. The fresh and charming young person, whether boy or girl (st. 32), gives BEA–FOrT, FOrF–YT:

> throgh out al the cytee of new troye
> Of daunsynge and of freshnesse nys youre pere.

This must be one of the Beaufort young people, the children of Edmund and Eleanor; one of the Beaufort girls in 1446–7 was given by the queen an armilla garnished with pearls and a diamond. A lady gentle and humble (36) seems to be AVIC. BWT., or Avice Stafford (daughter of Maud Stafford, later Lady Arundel), who was the wife of James Butler, Earl of Ormonde; she died in the summer of 1457.[1] Stanza 38 gently chides one who has given harbourage to Daunger, a malady ('Colyk') from which the writer has suffered sorely; the lady seems to be AlIS (C)HAWO–Th; FOrFA–T. Sir Thomas Chaworth of Wiverton Park, Nottinghamshire, had several daughters by his second wife, and this shy, aloof lady may be one; his elder daughter Elizabeth, Lady Scroop of Masham, had been celebrated by Roos as Curteisie dancing in the Garden of the Rose. Another, perhaps slightly ambiguous, stanza (39) recalls the theme of the death of Pity; the generous lady who

> graunted soone with liberal entent
> As ye nought wist what any euel ment,

---

[1] G.E.C., *Complete Peerage*, X, 127–8.

proves to be CATh. whYTTI. This is probably at this date the French lady, Catherine Gatevyne, married about 1448-9 to the younger Robert Whyttingham.

Not all the women are praised. The indiscreet and boisterous giddy-pate of st. 13 is BA–BeLYN, Barbelina Herberquyne, whom Roos lets off lightly here with a contemptuous 'Lorde that youre brayn ys comen of gedy kynde'. A second Creseyde (55) who leaves her old and takes 'newe and newe', looks like A–IS CrO., FOrF–IT. Alice Crowmer might be either the wife (widow) or daughter of William Crowmer, who was murdered at the same time as his son-in-law, Lord Say, in 1450. A rich but ill-bred and repulsive person is given no distinction of sex (st. 11), but the anagrams seem to yield MA––A––T WENTW.; FOrFAY. There is no sign in the poems of liking or connexion between Roos and his sister-in-law, now Margaret Wentworth; her son, Philip, was about the court as an Usher of the Chamber, and like Sir Richard received a goblet in 1453-4. There is also a second Wife of Bath, who knows by heart the 'lyfe' of her model (43); she proves unexpectedly to be the French or rather Burgundian gentlewoman, Osanne Heriman, OSAn. HE–IM.; For––YT.

The list of the men praised must (after the king) be headed by the great soldier, the 'noble creature' highly favoured of 'Mars Armypotent' (42). Here Roos resorts to his method of twin anagrams, to honour his two connexions by marriage, the brothers-in-law, Talbot and Somerset (TA–––T; SOM––S–T; TOT FOrFA–T). Great praise is lavished on an all-round man, free from all despite and envy, and endowed with a comprehensive wisdom:

> Be hyt to speke of Musike or clergye,
> Of huntyng, haukynge, or of Cheualrye,
> Al in youre witte kan ye wel comprehende. (st. 34)

This is LOrde BOCIN–HA. Humphrey Stafford, first Duke of Buckingham, was the eldest son of Roos's old friend, Anne of Woodstock; his father, Edmund, Earl of Stafford, had been a nephew of Beatrice, Lady Roos, and he was therefore a second cousin of the poet. His wife Anne Neville received fine gifts from the queen. An honoured and faithful Lancastrian, he lost his heir at the first battle of St. Albans (1455), and himself was killed at Northampton five years later. A man seemly in all (st. 22) whose noble governaunce the poet envies (but it is hinted that he does not stand as well as he deserves in his lady's eye), is Lord Greystoke (G–AYST–K.; FOr–AYT). Ralph, fifth Lord Greystoke, had been on the Escort with Sir Richard Roos. He had married in 1436 Elizabeth Fitzhugh. He later turned Yorkist, and outlived Roos,

dying in 1487.[1] The deserving and trustworthy man (46), 'besy trouthe
to serue', is Thomas Montgomery, Marshal of the Hall (TH–MAS
MONT–OM––Y), who in 1449 had been appointed warden of the exchange
and mint in the Tower;[2] later he was a keen Yorkist, as references in the
Paston Letters show. A man plain of appearance but well-bred and
much liked ('Youre goodelyhed gladeth eche companye' (8)) proves to
be Roos's former friend Wymbyssh (WY–BYSS). A good man, steadfast
in love (14), is THO. THOR., Thomas Thorpe, the convinced Lancastrian
who in 1453 was Speaker; of his private life nothing seems to be known.
A man manly and much admired, pleasant and acceptable, is Thomas
Hotoft (TH. HOTOFT (54)), a Sergeant of the Hall. Two lesser members
of the Household win praise. The person of thrifty governance (44),
who for long has known his 'obseruance', is FISSEWYK, or Philip Fisshe-
wyk the Butler, who in 1446 had seen nineteen years' service.[3] The
skilful harp-player of st. 48 proves to be John Turges (YO–AN TW–GES):

> There ys no wyght that wolde haue in dispite
> Eche other melodye and freshnesse
> Whan in youre harpe ye compleyn your distresse
> So wel ye konne and eke so pitousely
> With goodely notes alle the strynges ply. (48)

Among the king's few musicians, there is no harper specified; but after
the queen's advent, John Turges is honourably mentioned. He was
safeguarded in the Act of Resumption of 1450 as 'Harpour with oure
moost deere and bestebelovyd wyf the Queene' (*Foedera*, V, p. 196A);
nine years later he was given an annual grant of 100s. 'for good service
to the king and queen'.[4] A Clerk of the Chapel, John Penant, may be
the sober man whose governance and consideration of others is such
that his service is much sought after (PE–AnT). Can this mean that he
looked after the choir boys well? The compliment of a lucky throw
(two fives and a six) is early bestowed on a particular friend of Roos's,
Whittingham (10; whYTTIn–Am; TOT FOr–AYT):

> ffor of counseyle in love ye so habounde
> That euery wyght yow holde as a prophete,
> To eche purpose youre wordes ffale so mete.

Evidently Robert Whittingham, now the husband of Katharine Gatevyne, was one of Roos's chief counsellors in his troubles.

The satiric stanzas on men are numerous, and most will prove to be
on minor members of the Household, but not all. The fickle Jason of
st. 5, the 'double creature', is Lord Fawcomberg (FA–OMBe.); here as

[1] G.E.C., *Complete Peerage*, VI, 199. [2] *Cal. Pat. Rolls, 1446–52*, p. 305.
[3] *Ibid*, p. 47. [4] *Cal. Pat. Rolls, 1452–61*, p. 458.

elsewhere he is coupled with Maud Stanhope (STAN–OP). His adventure with Lady Strange (see below, Nos. 73, 74) is alluded to almost enviously in st. 16; he is indeed lucky in love (F–W – – –B.; STRAN.; FOTF–YT.). The 'werray prevy shrewe' among lovers (st. 41) seems to be STAN– –Y, presumably Lord Stanley, the Chamberlain, and also the chief keeper of Eleanor Cobham. A man openly stigmatized presents some difficulties: 'Ther is no beter pandare, as I trowe' (st. 23). The name appears to be Maltravers in one of its many forms, MAWT–E–YSS, A–VN (cf. Marlowe's *Edward II*, where the Lord Mautravers of that reign is called Matreuis). The variant of the last line in MS. Bodleian 638 asserts, 'ffor al this londe throgh out suche be ye knowe', and this seems to point to a well-known person. There seems to be little doubt that William FitzAlan, Earl of Arundel and Lord Mautravers, is intended. The Mautravers male line had died out in the preceding century, and the title had gone through Lady Mautravers (Roos's maternal grandmother) to the FitzAlans. Such an insult to a man of rank is imaginable in the court of Charles II, but not of Henry VI; the term is not recorded for another century and a half in any general sense, as an encourager of baseness and evil in others. Is it possible that it is here used politically? By 1461 Arundel was fighting with the Yorkists. The whole stanza is contemptuous in tone.

Mere mockery and ridicule are the portion of many, as of the perverse and ill-regulated man (17), diligent of 'al vnthryft', who is Thomas Daniel[1] (THO. DANYAL), to whom the Yorkists objected as a member of the Household; or of the dissimulator (19), whose words are the falsest chapmen's ware, and who is John Daunt (I– –N DAUNT), groom of the Chamber. It may be more than the 'chance of the dice' that these two portraits flank that of the king; is Roos hinting at undesirable influences on the unsuspicious Henry? One stanza makes us think of 'joly Absolon', and the first line prepares us for a singing clerk:

> A prety propchaunt ye be for the nones
> And lustely ye praunsen whan ye ryde.
> Your make was neuer made of flessh and bones,
> A gentyl drury and a noble gyde
> Ye were to walken by a ladyes syde
> As folke were wonte in Arthoures dayes take
> With hem to Courte and hem felawe to make. (33)

This is no allusion to either the Drurys of Suffolk or the Propchants of Kent; Prop[er]chant here has its musical meaning, implying one who,

[1] See C. F. Bühler, 'Some New Paston Documents', *R.E.S.*, 1938, XIV, 131–4.

like Absolon, can sing lustily. The anagram gives BOWY.; Richard
Bowyer was a clerk of the chapel. Another dissembler, feigning friendship and impossible to deal with, is John Hampden, or Hampton,
(YOHAn HAM–DOn, 58). A fickle promise-breaker in love is Thomas
Pulford, (THOS. PW–FOrD, 27), yeoman of the chamber; and another
yeoman, Richard Fasakerley (FAS–KEr--Y), is pilloried (st. 49) for his
ill-favoured visage:

> He shulde ben by dome of fisnamye
> The gretest shrewe I sawgh this day with ye.

He came indeed to a shrewd end, being murdered by a wronged husband
at Ludlow in 1452.[1] George Ashby, Clerk to the Signet, gets no
appreciation from his fellow-poet (51, G–OR. ASHBY); he is mocked for
his sloth, with a variant of a common proverb suitable for one who
aimed at poetic utterance:

> Bot sothe ys seyde that man shal neuer make
> Of pigges tayle good lyltinge horne to blowe.

A malapert man and untrustworthy, but a lusty dancer, seems to be
William Beaufis, Clerk of the Cellars (7, WI. BIAWFY; FOr–AYT).

In five portraits Roos adopts a rather crude pun, twice reinforcing it
with the anagram, in the rest leaving the pun to have its effect. An
awkward, clumsy man (37) is told,

> Now trewly yow becometh al your gere
> As wel as Cowe a sadel to bere.

The anagram D–AN AYS(CO)W assures us that the final line really puns
on A(y)scogh. Robert Ayscogh was Dean of the Chapel in 1447.
Another man is so mastered by sloth that he moves as heavily as a
pudding shot 'out of Arwblaste' (31); the roll of the reformed Household
of 1455 reveals that Thomas Arblaster the elder remained one of the
twelve Squires of Attendance to Henry VI. The anagram gives TH.
ARBLA–T. A specious and casual creature (15) is told, 'Ye russhen
forthe as lyght as leefe on lynde'. The alliteration on 'l' may point to
ly-l-forthe; Robert Lilforth was a page of the chamber. Similarly a new
man currying favour by a show of zeal (29) is pilloried by the backward
syllabic method: 'Ye be ryght besy, fye on ydelnesse'. John Besynby
('besy-be-ye') was a groom of the chamber.[2] The only well-known
stanza of this poem (9) is that quoted by Stow (who worked over

---

[1] Gairdner, *Paston Letters*, 1872, I, cxlviii.
[2] One may compare here a pretty 'modern instance'; in the B.B.C. parlour
game 'Twenty Questions' (Sept. 1954) Mr. Richard Dimbleby's 'object' was
'A nimble bee'; he guessed it.

MS. Fairfax 16) in his *Survey of London* under Aldgate Ward. It compares a tall big man, 'stuffed bet of wine then brede' (and like a gurgling cask), with the maypole on Cornhill, and glances aside at the rival weathercock of St. Andrew Undershaft. Within a mile of that church lies Bread Street; and William Bredstrete was among the king's minstrels in 1451; the anagram gives WiL–AM BRA. and the words brede and strete occur in ll. 3 and 7. The crown of the joke is that he was a trumpeter, hence the evocation of the puffed-out weathercock, with head held high.

A few persons still keep the secret of their identity: the ardent ambitious youth, full of good will (24), may be a Fitzwaryn or a Fiennes (FISW––YN or FInNYS); a Robert Fenys was an usher of the chamber. The fun poked in st. 35 at the awkward manners and stiff bearing of one who apes 'the scole of clerkynwele' is probably a hit at the style of acting of the parish clerks' famous plays staged at Clerkenwell. No such play is recorded after 1411, but when the Guild of St. Nicholas of Parish Clerks received a charter in 1442, they probably celebrated it suitably; and at St. Margaret's, Southwark, the Clerks and players acted plays steadily from 1444 to 1457.[1] A malicious man (45) aims at hindering others 'With prevy rownynge . . . or lowde crye'. The poet compares him with the butcher-bird:

> The waryhungle thus ye haue in mynde
> That nyne shrewde turnes doth eche day be kynde.

Chaucer's Friar had said that the Summoner's tale was

> as ful of jangles
> As ful of venym been thise waryangles (D. 1407–8).

In the alliterative *Alexander*, Darius is deceived with a caricature of the conqueror, as

> an ape of all othire
> A wirling, a wayryngle, a wawil-e3id shrewe (ll. 1705–6).

This vigorous alliterative abuse might well stick in the mind of a young reader (or owner) of the poem. Ray in the seventeenth century located this name wirrangle for the nine-killer or shrike in the Peak of Derbyshire; it is also known in Yorkshire dialect, and contact with the Vernons may have revived the word in Sir Richard's mind. The anagram suggests Hayworth or Haywood but I know none such at the court. So too the anagram of one whose garrulity is a positive defect of nature suggests Swynnerton (SWYN–TON; cf. *Ragman Roll*, st. 23), but I know no explanation. A man of sense and substance, 'stuffed of purveyaunce' (52), eludes me, and also the suspicious, jealous creature (53), who might

---

[1] E. K. Chambers, *Mediaeval Stage*, II, 380–1.

be a Catesby (CAT–SBY, and see the reference to Catoun), but none is to be found at court in this reign. The man of the last and poorest throw, unrewarded for his desert, may be the John Penycoke (PANYQU., 59) whose name appears in the Jewels Accounts of 1449–50. There are two apparent references to Roos himself and his kin. The anagram of stanza 21 gives ALYAN.; TOT FOrF–YT; and one can only conclude that Sir Richard is teasing his young niece Eleanor Roos, telling her that she is lazy and eats too much (probably sweetmeats), and is altogether a sly puss ('a wyly pye'). In the last stanza (59), the poet consoles the player for an unlucky throw (three ones) by comparing his own lot:

> I knowe the bet by myn ovne gouernaunce
> ffor hasarde hath with maystry quytte me soo
> My while that I [ioyles] now leue in woo,

and 'signs', FOr–AYT FOr–AYT.

All these allusions have grouped themselves in the period after the royal marriage. *The Chance of the Dice* suggests the all-licensed foolery of a saturnalian revel, with shafts directed at high and low. Such a revel could hardly take place after the king's first illness of 1453, which weakened Lancastrian confidence, and cast a gloom over the court. The poet twice refers to his own state: he knows feelingly what it is to suffer from Daunger (st. 38); and he disarmingly associates himself with the ill-luck of the last throw; he has had ill-fortune, and now joyless, lives in woe. This, with the lack of any reference to Margaret Longueville (*née* Vernon), may describe the period shortly before his marriage. The year 1445 is the extreme upward limit of date; it can be brought down to 1448–9, when Robert Whittingham married his French Catherine (st. 39). For the latest possible date, the allusion to Eleanor Cobham points to before 1454, when she died; that to Antigone Powys (st. 20) to before 1451 and her second marriage. If Grisilde (st. 30) is Emmeline Fiennes, Lady Say, her death in 1451, a year after her husband's murder, again sets the downward date there. The period between 1448 and 1451 seems to be indicated.

The vividness and variety of the satire, as on liars, idlers, boasters, and worse, constantly surprises and stimulates. The many attacks on sloth make one realize afresh how high *Accidia* stood among the medieval deadly sins. The zest of a vigorous writer, enjoying his own fun, is felt in the absurd puns. By the end of this series, Roos reveals a considerable power of satiric portraiture, and steps into his place early in the long line of character-writers from Chaucer to Pope. His self-conscious and mistrustful man is a seedling for John Earle's 'Suspicious Man' (*Microcosmography*, no. 78), to laugh before whom is 'a dangerous matter, for it cannot be at any thing but at him, and to whisper in his company plain conspiracy':

> To euery wight ye haue suspecioun
> Ye ben so Jelouse and eke so contrayre,
> So surquedroux ys youre condicioun
> That whan ye seen folkes togeder apayre
> Ye wene there speche be but to yow empaire.
> Who gilty is so seythe Catoun the wise
> Demeth loo they my maners now dispise (*The Dice*, st. 53).

No. 72. *The Flower and the Leaf:* a narrative poem of eighty-five stanzas of rhyme royal, of which nineteen stanzas give the setting. A lady sets out on a fine May morning to enjoy the birds' song in a pleasant grove; she sees two splendid companies of knights and ladies enjoying their sports, the one of jousting, the other of dancing and singing. After a storm the two companies join in amity, and depart together singing. The meaning of the two parties, of the Flower and of the Leaf, is explained by a lady of the Leaf.

> *Incipit.* When that Phebus his chaire of gold so hy
> Had whirled up the sterry sky aloft.
> *Explicit.* Sith that thou wost ful lyte who shal behold
> Thy rude langage, ful boistously unfold.

The Flower and the Leaf is the only anonymous poem of the mid-fifteenth century which has won general approval, and the honour of modernization by one major poet, and of an appreciative sonnet by another. It is a pleasure therefore to claim it for Sir Richard Roos. So far it has won negative recognition as not by Chaucer, and not by Lydgate. Godwin assigned it to the 'unknown poetess' of *The Assembly of Ladies*. Skeat unfortunately agreed, and at one time saw no more in it (in spite of Keats) than the 'flashy attractiveness' of 'a tinsel-like glitter'. He suggested c. 1460 as the date. No manuscript is now known, though, according to the contemporary index of MS. Longleat 258, one of the inner group of manuscripts for Roos, it was once there; it was first printed by Speght in 1598. I would assign it to Sir Richard Roos, and on internal evidence date it certainly after 1454, and probably about Whitsun, 1458.

The poem is 'signed' at about the usual place, 'And up I rose'[1] (l. 24), and in the later formula, and the 'devise' is given in full in the concluding anagram. The arguments advanced above against the 'poetess' of

---

[1] Speght's reading; Skeat altered to 'roos'.

The Assembly hold good here also, and one more may be added, the reference to Livy:

> Witnesse of Rome that founder was, truly,
> Of all knighthood and dedes marvelous;
> Record I take of Titus Livius. (ll. 530–2)

Such a reference would come more naturally from a man than from a woman of the period, and especially from one who had had the run of Duke Humphrey's library. The Duke of Gloucester was in 1427 given by his brother Bedford a manuscript of the French translation of Livy's Roman History, a magnificent illuminated folio made for Charles V. In 1445, the Duke presented it to Alfonso of Aragon; now it is again in its country of origin.[1] Duke Humphrey referred to it in a letter of 1439, in the period in which Sir Richard Roos was still 'Gloucester's man'.[2] There is every probability that Sir Richard handled it and read in it, the more easily for its being French.

The lack of manuscripts of the poem may be partially explained by the late date, so near the downfall of Henry's throne. The upward date 1454 is pointed to by the pastoral references, most unusual at this period, but not at all improbable in one who would hear the talk of Queen Margaret's French ladies. It was in September 1454 that René d'Anjou consoled himself for the loss of his Queen Isabel by marrying Jeanne de Laval, and began with her that life of courtly pastoralism and elegant simplicity which was later to attract a less fortunate queen, and to culminate in Le Petit Trianon. Georges Chastellain[3] put it into verse:

> J'ay un roi de Cécille
> Vu devenir berger
> Et sa femme gentille
> De ce mesme mestier
> Portant la pannetière
> La houlette et chappeau,
> Logeant sur la bruyère
> Auprès de leur trouppeau.

Little of the heather was to be seen, however, in the 'Pas d'Armes de la Bergère', held at Saumur in 1455, where the court, though in pastoral guise, appeared glittering in gold and silver. 'Regnault and Jehanneton' are the hero and heroine of these pastoral delights, and of the poem *Les Amours du Berger et de la Bergeronne* (c. 1457). It is no wonder then that an English courtier introduces for the first time, into a poem of his

---

[1] *Bibliothèque de Ste. Geneviève*, MS. français, 777.
[2] Vickers, *Humphrey, Duke of Gloucester*, pp. 375, 438.
[3] *Œuvres*, ed. Lettenhove, VII, 200.

queen's daisy cult, a shepherd's song, a 'bergeret', sung in French by a
lady of the Flower:

> there began anon
> A lady for to sing right womanly
> A bargaret in praising the daisy;
> For as me thought among her notes swete
> She sayd, *Si douce est la Margarete* (ll. 346–50).

This is not the only, or the most important, way in which *The Flower
and the Leaf* differs from other poems of the cult. Although it is a
'daisy' poem, and culminates in the annual choice, the final compliment
this time is to the Leaf; 'Unto the Leef I ow myn observaunce' says the
poet finally, in answer to a direct challenge. It is the answer due from
a King's Knight; it acknowledges Henry of the hawthorn and yet it can
imply no rejection of the Flower-queen. Similarly the full significance
of the two birds perching in the trees (ll. 434 ff.) has been missed, partly
by taking 'medle-tre' as medlar; it is more likely medle or motley-
tree, i.e. the hawthorn (cf. 'the fresshe hawethorn In whyte motle', *Black
Knight*, ll. 71–2). The nightingale, the bird of devoted love, is of the
noble company of the Leaf, and sits in the laurel; the gay goldfinch,
pecking the hawthorn buds of the king's badge, yet belongs to the lady
of the Flower. This criss-crossing of the allusions is typical of the poet's
intention. The poem is indeed one of opposition without hostility, of
succours given compassionately to the Flower by the Leaf, of feasting and
song together, and of final amity and concord: 'They passed al, so
plesantly singing' (432). Only one period of the troubled years after 1454·
could be celebrated by so happy a reconciliation, the all-too-brief time
when Yorkists and Lancastrians had had a loveday, on March 25, 1458.
Led by the king and queen and the Duke of York, a great procession
went to St. Paul's, the Yorkist Earl of Salisbury paired with young
Henry, Duke of Somerset, and Warwick the Kingmaker with his rival,
the Duke of Exeter. Later on, as Fabyan tells us,[1] 'iustis of peace' were
held before the queen, first in the Tower, and then again, still at Whit-
suntide, at Greenwich or Plesaunce. Henry, Duke of Somerset (Lord
Roos's stepbrother), Anthony Wydville, and others unnamed, jousted
against the queen's squires, the royal hawthorn against the royal marguerite. At this date, the affirmation 'Unto the Leef I ow myn observaunce' had also a political significance; it could be a renewal of
Lancastrian troth to Henry of the hawthorn, rather than to Richard of
the falcon.

The references to badges in this poem of stately heraldic ceremony

---

[1] *Chronicle*, 1542, p. 417.

lend support to the connexion between this event and the poem. The royal hawthorn and the Somerset woodbine are united in a single line ('Some of hawthorn, and some of woodbind', l. 272); and the well-informed lady of the Leaf explains their significance to the enquiring narrator:

> And tho that were chapelets on hir hede
> Of fresh woodbind be such as never were
> To love untrew in word, thought ne dede
> But ay stedfast; ne for plesaunce ne fere,
> Though that they shuld hir hertes al to-tere,
> Would never flit, but ever were stedfast
> Til that their lyves there asunder brast. (ll. 484-90)

This stanza not only celebrates the fidelity in love of Edmund, Duke of Somerset, and Eleanor Roos (*née* Beauchamp), on which the records cast no shadow, it also paraphrases the well-known 'raisons' of the three Beauchamp sisters, Margaret, Lady Talbot's 'Till deth departe', Eleanor's 'Never new', and Elizabeth, Lady Latimer's 'Til my lyves ende'. The son of Edmund and of Eleanor must have accepted and continued the significance of his father's courtly badge, the woodbine.

The anagrams of the poem confirm and extend these conclusions. Just as the narrator of *The Assembly of Ladies* proved to be Sir Richard's niece, Eleanor Roos, so now his early-rising spectator of the poem's events is his wife. The five opening stanzas give her name, and that of an important participator in the action: ISA. FISleWIS; BEAUForT, SOM--S-T; and (stt. 3-5) MA-GAReT LongU-VIL, with For-A-T. The Ladies of the Leaf (ll. 134-54) cover (with considerable residue) the names B-W-ORT, B-WCHAm; and Diana herself (ll. 164-75) gives again E-ISAB-Th FIS-OWIS; SO-ERSeT, BEW---T. The Knights of the Leaf when jousting (ll. 274-322) afford a braid of Beaufort names: IOHAn Som--S-T; ALIAn B-WSHAM(P); HEnRI B-AUForT, some-S-T. The company of the Flower, suggesting the queen by their daisy song, confirm this in the same stanzas (ll. 337-50) by the anagram: MARGA-ET (in the caesural initials only), and AnIOW; Flora (ll. 379-86) is not the queen herself, but gives HOWTH, SO--R--T. The well-informed lady (ll. 456-66) yields MOWBRAI, TA(L)BO-, and in her praise of the followers of the Leaf, she introduces the paraphrase of the Beauchamp sisters' mottoes by a stanza (ll. 477-83) which gives BEAVCHA--. In her further explanation of the Flower and its pleasure-loving adherents, the name in anagram is A-IANO- BOTI(L)IR, SO---S-T. The two concluding stanzas of the poem again name IOAN HOUTh (who was Flora), and give the writer's full 'devise': IAI TOT ForFAYT ForFAIT.

All this, unexpected as some of it is, proves to be surprisingly
x

coherent; the poem is now seen as a Beaufort and Beauchamp poem of the second generation, a later companion poem to *The Black Knight*. Edmund Beaufort, Duke of Somerset, was one of the first Lancastrian victims of the war, dying at St. Albans in 1455. His widow Eleanor (*née* Beauchamp) long survived him; and his heir Henry was now Earl of Somerset, and taking his father's place in Lancastrian councils. He was beheaded after Hexham (1464), and a younger son, John, was to fall at Tewkesbury (1471). The five Beauchamp daughters were marrying, and one, Margaret Stafford, had already lost her young husband with her father in 1455 (see below, No. 103). Elizabeth married Sir Henry Fitzlewis, and we shall meet them and their son-in-law later; Joan was to marry an Irishman, Lord Howth. The anagrams suggest that with these two the betrothals at least had preceded the poem.[1] Certainly Eleanor Beaufort's marriage was in 1458, probably in April, to the rising royal favourite, James Butler, Earl of Ormonde and of Wiltshire. The three Beauchamp sisters are honoured in the stanza of paraphrased mottoes, and there is good reason why the speaker should know them, for though not a Beaufort, she is a Talbot cousin. Elizabeth Talbot, daughter of the great Talbot and of Margaret Beauchamp, had married in 1448 John Mowbray, he being then aged four; in 1458 his parents, the Duke and Duchess of Norfolk, were in attendance on the queen.

All this enables one to see the setting of this court poem in its true perspective. Although the king and queen, the Leaf and the Flower, are honoured, the main interest is in the Beaufort clan. Henry Beaufort led the jousters at Greenwich on the king's side; in these imagined jousts of the Leaf, he and his brother John are knights, likened to the Douze-Pairs, and their mother is mentioned for honour's sake, since Roos seems always to have had an affectionate regard for his sister-in-law. It is possible that the laurel-tree, to which all the company of the Leaf do reverence, signifies the illustrious family of Beaufort and its founder.[2] Henry's sisters have their parts to play in the imaginary

---

[1] There is a genealogical difficulty here. The anagram HOUTH is very clear; but Joan Beaufort did not marry Lord Howth till mid-1478. Yet there is a possible explanation. Robert St. Lawrence, who was twenty-eight at his father's death in 1462–4, married before 1459 Alice White of Killester, Co. Dublin. It is possible that his father, a favoured Lancastrian, had betrothed him as a boy to the youngest Beaufort girl; that as a young man and a Yorkist he broke the contract to marry a local girl at his own choice; but that twenty years later he carried out the original engagement. Very little is known of these early Howths (G.E.C., *Complete Peerage*, VI, 604–5).

[2] In *The Black Knight*, 129, the lover (Edmund Beaufort) lies between a woodbine and a laurel, according to that Scottish MS. (Arch. Selden B.24) which has Beaufort connexions.

celebrations, Elizabeth (FitzLewis) as Diana, and Joan (later Howth) as Flora. Evidently the queen, the genius of the Flower, kept her state, and the little girl was her deputy as Flora. The informative lady, a Talbot-Beauchamp cousin, still keeps the honour of the Leaf in the family. Most interesting of all is it to find, at the centre of Roos's warning how unreliable is the company of the Flower, the name of Eleanor (Beaufort), Countess of Wiltshire, for her husband was reported to have fled from St. Albans, to save his handsome looks. It may be true; he expiated his cowardice after Towton. Finally, Roos, in the person of his wife, presented the poem to the little girl, Joan, the queen's deputy.

In this, the last of the Plesaunce poems, the architectural excitements have died down, and the poem is taken out of doors, into a setting which recalls the royal parks of Plesaunce and (by its references to the Order of the Garter) of Windsor, perhaps also the forest of Rockingham, and the imaginary park of *The Romaunt of the Rose*. The trees are 'streight as a line', and the grass is thick as velvet, like the famous grass of Benfield in Rockingham, 'a grasse as softe as is the daintie sleave, And thrum'd so thicke and deepe'.[1] There are touches which remind us of the young poet of *How A Lover Prayseth hys Lady*, the sense of prevailing excitement, the heat of the summer sun, and the sweet scents which can bring relief to the heart overlaid with 'thoughtes froward and contrair' (l. 82). There are also two recognizable echoes: some of the ladies of the Leaf wear 'chapelets fresh' of *agnus castus* to signify their maidenhood (ll. 160-1, 475-8); again, the 'large wones' and all the treasury of 'Prester John' could not have bought a tenth part of the riches of the company of the Leaf (ll. 200-4). These two themes had been united in *How a Lover* (ll. 37-8, 47), for there 'agnus castus the grete' is one of the herbs of every region 'Sent fro the Caan and preter John'.

The poet's French reading enters into the poem. Reduced to its simplest terms of structure and theme, it is plainly based on the fourth *Lai* of Eustache Deschamps, as has been pointed out.[2] The *Lai de Franchise*, a daisy poem, describes 'uns mondains paradis', in which the poet, unobserved, watches a Maying by noble and beautiful ladies; a royal joust supervenes (ll. 144-69); after it, the ladies approach the jousters, and beg their company to the Valois palace of Beauté-sur-Marne. This is cordially agreed to, and the two companies join and go

---

[1] Drayton, *Polyolbion*, XXIII, 318-19. Skeat emends l. 53, 'That most lyke vnto grene wel wot I it was' to 'That most lyk to grene wol, wot I it was'; but 'welwet' is more likely; cf. *Black Knight*, l. 80, 'And softe as velowet the yonge gras', MS. Add. 16165.

[2] *Œuvres*, ed. De Queux de Saint-Hilaire (S.A.T.F.), II, p. 203, num. 307.

'cornant et dansant vers Beauté'. It is precisely this uniting of the two companies that supports (against Marsh's contention)[1] the poem as a source for the basis of *The Flower and the Leaf*: 'They passed al, so plesantly singing' (l. 432). Deschamps spoils the artistic unity of his poem by a didactic epilogue: the onlooker emerges, and finds Marion and Robin dining frugally and talking great good sense; he applauds them by contrast with the nobles. Roos does not thus turn his poem inside out.

The opening lines of *The Flower and the Leaf* recall the proem of *Le Congié d'Amours* (MS. Royal 19.A.iii):

> En ce temps de joieux este
> Que Phébus est en sa haultesse.

As in *Le Débat du Cueur et de l'Œil*, the poet is surprised to hear the singing of 'dames sans nombre', of 'A world of ladies', of whom one keeps apart, 'Sole by herself'.

A fresh inspiration can also be traced. This is a poem of magnificent ceremonial, of processions described with delight in their heraldic colour; in rich and royal stuffs, silk of Tartary, ermine, and cloth of gold, in jewels, the emeralds of the Leaf, with 'perle, ruby and saphere'; in garlands of leaves and chaplets of flowers. One prose romance above all others, *Perceforest*,[2] has this gusto for the trappings of chivalry, this air almost of exaltation, and there are signs that the poet had recently been reading or re-reading it. Within the scope of Chapters 34 to 42 of the First Book occur three points of his description. 'His 'okes grete, streight as a lyne', are not, as in the garden of the Rose, thirty to forty feet apart without regularity, but a plantation, 'an eight foot or nyne Every tree wel fro his felawe grew' (ll. 29-32). So in the forest of Darnant, the trees are

> plantez ordonnéement comme vne droicte ligne, et auoit entre chascun arbre bien lespace de dix dextres. (I, 34, fol. xxvii, v.)

The knights exploring there come soon to a clearing:

> Et veirent vng lorier dont les braunches estoient nourries et vignetées tout a lentour et estoit si grant que dessoubz le tour se fussent mis en

---

[1] George L. Marsh, 'Sources and Analogues of *The Flower and the Leaf*', *Mod. Phil*, 1906-7, IV, 296-9, 325-6.

[2] The edition cited is that of 1528, 6 vols. small fol., based on a copy made by David Aubert, for Philip of Burgundy. *Perceforest* still awaits its modern editors; see, however, Jeanne Lods, *Le Roman de Perceforest*, Soc. de Publications Romanes et Françaises, XXXII, Geneva, 1951.

lombre deux ce*ns* chevaliers et auoit audessoubz beau préau et sièges
ordonnez si noblement, que plus ne pouoit. (*loc. cit.*)

This is probably the ancestor of the 'fair laurer' which shelters first the
company of the Leaf, and then that of the Flower also:

> With leves lade, the boughes of gret brede;
> And to my dome there never was indede
> Man that had seen half so fair a tree;
> For underneth it there might wel have be
>
> An hundred persons, at their own plesaunce,
> Shadowed fro the hete of Phebus bright. (ll. 305–10)

Farther on in *Perceforest*, Alexander with his knight Floridas is exploring on a mountain-top; they find 'ung beau lieu peu hanté', since the
grass grows to the horses' knees; they then come to a hedge so thick
that they despair of penetrating it, but at last strike 'vne voye petite et
estroicte moult peu hantee' (I, 42, fol. xxxv. v.). The lady of the poem
finds among the trees at the last a path 'of litel brede . . . that gretly had
not used be',

> For it forgrowen was with gras and weede
> That wel unneth a wight might it see. (ll. 45–6)

She is fortunate enough to come to a 'plesaunt herber', with a quick-set
hedge, 'as thik as a castle-wal', a work of skill and art (ll. 49–66).
Much farther on in the romance (chapter 138, fol. cxix) is described the
building of a 'fueillie', a leafy tent or tabernacle on a grand scale, with a
central pole eighteen feet high, and a 'roe' or circle made of 'rains de
cordier fueillés'. In it the hermit and his twelve fair nieces sit to watch
the great tourney, 'en leur feuillie séant tout autour de la roe' (ch. 147,
fol. cxxxvii, v.). This enables us to correct an error in Speght's text:
Diana's roundel should read,

> Sous le feuillie de vert . . .
> Séant, et mon joly cuer endormi. (ll. 176–8)

'Seen' for 'Séant' is an English scribe's or printer's misreading. As the
course of the romance, and the detail of the hermit's tourney show, his
'fueillie' is like the thick hedge of the English poem, so made that no one
can see in but anyone can easily look out (ll. 67–71).

More important, however, than any detail in this absorbing romance,
Perceforest, is the effect of its heightened air, its atmosphere of magnificence: its wonders and marvels, its fire-charm and sleep-charm, its
invisible spirits and terrifying enchantments; its grand-scale ceremonies, coronations, feast, and royal baptism; its ladies who might be

'déesses ou fées'; its knights of unmatchable prowess, their ceremonial arming, their magnificent tourneys, so 'acharnés' that night falls on the contestants, and by torchlight Alexander must ride into the lists in great state to stop the fighting. As Gaston Paris summed it up: 'Le *Perceforest* paraît avoir excité les imaginations et fixé une mode qui regna longtemps dans les hautes classes'.[1]

That Sir Richard Roos might be attracted to *Perceforest* would be in keeping with his family traditions. The romance is an anonymous mid-fourteenth-century expansion of *Les Vœux du Paon*, two manuscripts of which bear the name Roos and a motto which may well have been Sir Richard's. He and his brother, and his father before him, bore the peacock crest, and used it in their seals. The romance brings into operation in Britain that Alexander saga of which Roos possessed a copy in alliterative verse. It certainly seems to have 'excité son imagination' when once he laid hands on it. Its knights in green, in 'fueilles de lyerre', its knights in white, the queen's knights of the silver rose, the procession of joyous feasters to the queen's rooms, headed by Alexander singing, 'Bien doit chanter ioyeusement', all these are in tone with this English poem of the open air 'between the forest and the sown', of knights and squires, heralds and pursuivants in white, jousting and singing; and of peaceable knights and ladies in green, dancing round the tuft of daisies in the mead.

Perceforest was the final and unsurpassed expression of fourteenth-century chivalry; *The Flower and the Leaf* is the swan-song of English courtly poetry. After that the shadows fall, and true chivalry dies in the bitterness of the Wars of the Roses. Sir Richard Roos, now in middle age, seems to have felt the cold breath, and to have wondered how the younger generation, inexperienced in war, the devotees of the Flower who 'loved idlenes', would stand before it:[2]

> And for the Flour within a litel space
> Wol be lost, so simple of nature
> They be that they no grevance may endure,

> And every storm wil blow hem sone away. (ll. 558–61)

Within fifteen months of the loveday, the storm broke over Blore Heath, and raged for nearly five years, till the Yorkist victories of Towton and

[1] *Esquisse historique de la Litt. Française au Moyen Age*, 1922, p. 213.

[2] According to Abbot Whethamstede, this had already been seen at St. Albans in 1455: effeminate knights, even of the Household, 'viri in se formae satis elegantis', but given to luxury like Paris, rather than to prowess like Hector, fled from the sight of bloodshed, 'ex mollitie spiritus' (*Registrum Abbatiae*, ed. H. T. Riley, I, 168–9).

Hexham decimated the Lancastrian ranks, and confirmed Edward IV on the throne. The tempest swept away many whose names have become familiar to us here: Lord Roos, executed with Sir Thomas Fynderne after Hexham; Henry, Duke of Somerset, son of Eleanor Roos; Sir Philip Wentworth, adored son of Margery Roos; Edmund Hampden, squire of the Household; and, on the other side, Sir Thomas Kyriel. Sir Richard, like Caxton later, realized the need of the time for men and women hardy and steadfast,

> very exemplair
> Of all honour longing to chivalry.

CHAPTER IX

The King's Knight, 1442–61:
Personal Poems

A<small>FTER</small> 1444–5, Sir Richard Roos was clearly the chief court poet of the young queen, Margaret of Anjou. In addition, in his years as a King's Knight, he wrote several poems on other subjects. Four chief themes will be discerned in this chapter: the scandalous doings of William Neville, Lord Fawcomberg(e); matters of family history, chiefly of the Beauforts; the poet's wooing of his future wife, Margaret Longueville, *née* Vernon; and lyric laments for Eleanor Cobham, after the second marriage in 1450 of Antigone, which took her to France, and so farther out of the prisoner's reach.

I. LORD FAWCOMBERG

A poem which by its anagrams establishes the existence of an intrigue between Lord Fawcomberg and Lady Strange of Knokyn will be considered first; other poems make references to the affair by the same symbolism, more or less incomprehensible until the story is known. Two other women are later involved with Fawcomberg, Maud Stanhope, Lady Willoughby, and Barbelina Herberquyne, the queen's 'Almain' waiting-woman.

No. 73. *The Compleynt of Mars.*

> *Incipit.* Gladeth, ye foules of the morowe gray.

Chaucer's authorship was stated by Shirley in Trin. Coll., Camb., MS. R.3.20: 'made by Geffrey Chaucier at þe comandement of þe renommed and excellent Prynce, my lord the Duc Iohn of Lancastre'; he proceeded to attach the poem to Isabella of York and John Holland, later Duke of Exeter. Lydgate's list of Chaucer's 'labour' in the Prologue to *The Fall of Princes* does not mention the *Mars* but devotes a descriptive stanza to a poem on the brooch that Vulcan wrought at Thebes. Chaucer himself does not mention the poem under either title.

There are seven manuscripts, and, to judge from a colophon to *The Legend of Good Women*, there was once another copy in B.M. Add. 12524. Two of these manuscripts also contain *La Belle Dame* (see above, Chapter III); Fairfax 16 (Lord Stanley's manuscript), and Longleat 258 (Thynne's manuscript, used in printing). One manuscript, Tanner 346, Lord Greystoke's manuscript, is of the related Bodleian group (see above, Chapter IV); MS. Pepys 2006 (the Kyriel manuscript) which has two copies of the poem, and MS. Arch. Selden B.24, also contain *The Black Knight*. One manuscript (R.3.20) is Shirley's; another is derived from Shirley (Harl. 7333, with an unfinished copy). The similarly entitled *Complaint of Venus* is in the same manuscripts with the exception of Longleat 258 (yet Thynne printed it) and Harl. 7333, and with the addition of Ashmole 59, Shirley's own collection, and of MS. Ff.1.6, the Roos scrapbook; but as will be seen later it has no direct connexion with *Mars*.

My attribution to Sir Richard Roos is based on what appears to be the poem's connexion with a group of people active in the fourth decade of the fifteenth century, as indicated by heraldic references, and by acrostic anagrams which include the 'devise', 'J'ai tot forfait forfait'. The symbolism of the poem seems to have been triple, astronomical, mythological, and personal, the last conveyed by crest and badge and anagram.

The poem consists of twenty-two stanzas in rhyme royal followed by sixteen stanzas of nine lines; a *Proem* of four stanzas is followed by the Story in eighteen stanzas. The actual 'Compleynt' spoken by Mars consists of a single-stanza *Proem*, and five sections of three stanzas each, like independent *balades*, but without refrains; the fourth of these compares the fatal beauty of Venus with the disastrous brooch of Thebes made by Vulcan.

The heraldic pointers are two, with other minor hints. The first is the reference to the white bulls with which Venus's chamber, chosen for her meeting with Mars, is 'depeynted', astronomically correct, since the lovers, as planets, are now in the house of Taurus; but the colour is unexplained. The second is the laboured simile in Section III of the lover likened to the unlucky fisherman who 'Baiteth hys angle-hok with som plesaunce'. These both point to the same person, Sir William Neville, Lord Fawcomberg(e) (Fawconberg(e), Falconbridge), son of

Ralph Neville, first Earl of Westmoreland, and of his second wife, Joan Beaufort. He was married c. 1422 to the Fawcomberg heiress Joan, who was an idiot from birth; he left no legitimate sons, and with his death in 1462/3 the title fell into abeyance. His crest, as it is seen on his Garter stall-plate, was a white bull, differencing by colour the Dun Bull of the Nevilles, famous in legend and ballad. His badge was the fish-hook or angle-hook, as political poets knew; 'The Fisshere hathe lost his hangulhooke', says the poem of c. 1449, referring probably to Fawcomberg's period of imprisonment in France. His renown as a fighter in the French wars, at Crotoy and Meaux, and at Harfleur which won him his K.G. in 1440, is quite consonant with his mythological and astronomical disguise here as Mars. The anagrams of the poem are unusually clear, since the small sections into which the whole is divided give the opportunity for short and repetitive solutions. In no other anagrams of this body of poetry do the operative letters recur with so little variation; one is reminded of a Sestine by Spenser or Sidney, where the identical rhyme-words click round; here the acrostic letters recur monotonously. Yet by a judicious omission of varying letters different forms of the names are presented, and obviousness is avoided. The letters betray not Fawcomberg alone, but also three other actors in the drama.

The anagrams run as follows:

Proem. FAW–O(M)B–R.; STRAnG; CO–HA. COLeP–PER. VAlAnc.;
    (v)A(v)ASUR; T–T ForFAYT F–FAYT.

The lovers' meeting, ll. 64–84.
    –AWCOM.; ELISAB–Th St–AN., KnokIn. ForFA–T.

Mars. ll. 113–19. (v)AlANS. ForF.
    ll. 140–6. (v)A(v)ASWR. VA–ANC.

Proem to Compleynt. –AW–OM.; –OBH–M, STRAN.

Section I.
    WI– – –IAM FAW–OMB.; E–ISAB–Th ST–AN.; AI TOT ForFAIT ForF–AIT.

Section II.
    Ne–ILe, FAW–OMB.; –UISBO–OU–H; –LISA– –TH ST–AN.; –OBHAM;
    TOT ForFAYT ForFA–T.

Section III. (the Angle-hook).
    WY– – –AM FAW–OMBe.; –LISAB–TH ST–AN.; TOT ForFA–T.

Section IV (Brooch of Thebes).
    E–ISAB–TH ST–An.; –OBHAM; T–T ForFAYT.

Section V. FAWCONB.; E–ISABeTH ST–An. KNOCIN. COBH–M; –AlAns; TOT
    ForFAYT For–AYT.

The lady's name seems to have been Elisabeth, and is linked with the names Cobham, Colepeper (once), and Strange of Knokyn. Her existence can be traced, but little else. Elisabeth Cobham, daughter of Sir Reginald, Lord Cobham, and of Eleanor Colepeper, and therefore full sister of Eleanor Cobham, Duchess of Gloucester, married, after March 1439, as second wife, Richard (Le) Strange, Lord Strange of Knokyn. He died in 1449, and she in 1453 (G.E.C., XII, i, 356), having apparently married Sir Roger Kynaston of Middle, and borne him an heir. Sir Roger's second wife (1465) was also taken from the Cobham group; she was Elizabeth Grey, sister of Richard, Lord Grey of Powis, and daughter of Antigone.[1] There is every reason why Sir Richard Roos could be cognizant of an intrigue involving the Duchess of Gloucester's younger sister; it is not known to history—why should it be? He had already given her a complimentary stanza in *Ragman Roll*, 10. Roos's habit of clarifying his references to a married lady by giving also her maiden name is particularly useful here. Cobham makes it clear which Lady Strange is intended, Colepeper stresses the full blood connexion with the Duchess, and perhaps placates Lord Cobham's second wife, Anne Bardolf, aunt of Sir Richard's 'Lady Bounte'. The dating is limited to the decade between March 1439 (the marriage) and August 1449 when Lord Strange died.

There were also reasons why Roos might have heard the tale from the other side. Guisborough Castle (cf. Section II), the Fawcomberg seat in the North Riding, where 'the Fisher' lies buried, is only twenty miles due north of Helmsley (Hamlake). Yorkshire gossip might well apprise Roos of the affair. There had been a marriage-connexion between the families in the preceding century, which probably accounts for the 'Fawconberge cup' left by Lady Beatrice Roos to Richard's father.

The other names in the anagrams are more puzzling, though not beyond resolving. Vavasour is a well-known Yorkshire name, the Vavasours of Hazlewood (West Riding); Sir Henry was exempted from county duties in this decade and had been a gentleman usher of the Chamber in 1442;[2] John Vavasour appears in the Jewels Accounts of 1446–7, presumably a Squire of the Household; and though not listed as a member of the Escort, yet his name gets into the anagram of *The Parlement of Cupid*. It looks as if a Vavasour had been in the confidence of his powerful Yorkshire neighbour. The name Valance is even more tricky and interesting; it may lead us to the fourth mythological person-

[1] *Vis. of Shropshire*, Harl. Soc., II, 295; see also W. Burson, 'The Kynaston Family', in *Shrops. Arch. Soc.*, 1894, 2nd. Ser., VI, 211.
[2] *Cal. Pat. Rolls, 1441–6*, p. 98.

age, Cilenius. Why should Mercury be given this name, less familiar, though astronomically valid? It can be read, on Sir Richard's 'back and forth' syllabic method, as U–LEN C–. With the name Valans in the anagrams, this points to one of two men well known to the Roos family. With the death in 1324 of Aymer de Valence, the tenth and last Valence Earl of Pembroke, the name was separated from the title. In the mid-fifteenth century, the heir-general was Lord Grey de Ruthin (Denbigh-shire), whose first wife was Sir Richard's aunt, Margaret Roos.[1] Another claimant, also through female descents, was Lord Strange of Blackmere, the great Talbot,[2] brother-in-law to Eleanor Beauchamp-Roos-Beaufort. The conflicting claims seem never to have been fully settled, but the epitaph on Talbot's monument at Rouen (now des-troyed) is said to have included among his many honours the title of Valence; this Shakespeare knew from Holinshed: 'Great Earl of Wash-ford, Waterford and Valence' (*1 Henry VI*, IV, vii, 63). In this poem of Yorkshire-Shropshire intrigue, one may suspect that Talbot was the kindly Mercury, who, 'rydinge in his chevache', was able to shelter Lady Strange as she fled from her husband, Venus escaping from discovery by Phoebus, whose beams 'knokkeden ful lyghte' on her chamber. In this decade, one does not expect the anagram to indicate the Plesaunce circle, even for a Cobham lady; was the poem then written to amuse Roos's other circle, the Beauforts and Talbots? After all, Talbot's other brother-in-law was George Neville, Lord Latimer, Fawcomberg's brother.

The Beaufort-Neville descent of Lord Fawcomberg gives some point to the presence of the poem together with *The Black Knight* in two manuscripts, in the Scottish collection for a Beaufort queen (Arch. Selden 24) and in Sir Thomas Kyriel's collection (Pepys 2006).

If Mercury is Talbot, one can narrow down the dating of the episode; he was almost continuously in Normandy in the earlier years of the Strange marriage, but not so in the later. The truce arranged at Queen Margaret's marriage (1445) was continually extended, and was not broken till March 1449, at Fougères. Talbot could thus be at home in Shropshire in a springtime of 1446-9. Another handling of the same matter supports this tentative dating. When in translating *Les Échecs Amoureux*, Roos comes to Diana's attack on Venus, he drags in Mars, not mentioned in the French, and enforces the allusion by the anagram: ELISABETH K–OKIn, FAW–OMB., VALAn., ForFAIT. Not content with this,

---

[1] G.E.C., *Complete Peerage*, X, 388, 396.
[2] *Ib.*, XI, 699.

he continues it in the following myth of Icarus, which he greatly enlarges: STRAN., KnO-In, CO-HAM, FAW-OM., FOrFAIT. The implication that Fawcomberg, like Icarus, flew too near the sun of powerful interests and singed his wings, is obvious, though the moral is tame: 'A mene ys good in alle thing'. Other allusions in the translation are to Roos's courting of Margaret Vernon, which culminated in their marriage between 1450 and 1452 (*Reson and Sensuallyte*, ll. 4127–54, 4155–99).

With the evidence of these anagrams before us, what then of Lydgate's and Shirley's statements? Lydgate's ascription, written in the early 1430s, must refer to another poem by Chaucer, supposedly a full-length account of the fatal Broche of Vulcan. He makes no reference to the Mars-Venus-Phoebus-Mercury story; and Roos's use of the jewel merely in three stanzas is now seen rather as an allusion to Chaucer's poem. Lydgate knew it, and presumably Roos did too; we now unfortunately do not. Shirley's note, that some men say the complaint was made on John Holland and Isabelle of York, has already been deflected by Manly to John Holland and his future wife, Elisabeth of Lancaster. It is possible that whoever gave Shirley the poem intentionally misled him, with harmless references to scandals of the past. The open use of the angle-hook, well known as Lord Fawcomberg's badge, shows clearly that great secrecy was not intended. The allusions would probably have been observed long ago, if Shirley had not led enquirers down false trails.

The poem treats the subject in the romantic style that Roos had earlier given to Edmund Beaufort's wooing of his sister-in-law, Eleanor. The willingness of critics to accept Chaucer's authorship is a testimony to the poem's excellence in its minor form. It is a trifle, composed in the same half-sympathetic, half-malicious spirit as is *The Rape of the Lock*, and perhaps with a similar purpose, to help smooth over a family scandal. It presents the lovers in the guise of planets inevitably following their appointed courses, and of deities, who yet are 'constreyned' by the all-powerful god of love. The brilliant spring description of the *Proem* minimizes the whole affair by presenting it as no more than a tale told by a mating bird on St. Valentine's day. The heraldic allusions were clear to the protagonists' friends, and are re-inforced by other hints: 'Venus, causer of plesaunce' (l. 46); 'Venus valaunse' (l. 145), still difficult of precise explanation, but perhaps showing her hiding under the curtain-wall of the Valence castle, 'Cilenios tour'; and the unexpected transference from light to sound when Phoebus' beams 'knokkeden' on Venus' chamber—the naughtiest touch of all for the suspicious Lord Strange of Knokyn.

Another and even more interesting poem continues in a similar vein on the further amours of Lord Fawcomberg.

No. 74. *Anelida and Arcite:* an unfinished poem of 357 lines, with an invocation of three stanzas of rhyme royal, the Story in twenty-seven similar stanzas, the 'Compleynt of Anelida' in fourteen stanzas of varied metres, and one stanza purporting to resume the narrative.

> *Incipit.* Thou ferse god of armes, Mars the rede.
> *Explicit.* That shapen was as ye shal after here.

The poem is not mentioned by Chaucer himself, but has always been accepted in the Chaucer canon, on the strength of Lydgate's inclusion of it in his list of Chaucer's works in the Prologue of c. 1432 to *The Fall of Princes*, Bk. I:

> Off Anneleyda and of fals Arcite
> He made a compleynt, doolful and pitous,
> And off the broche which that Vulcanus
> At Thebes wrouhte.

It is also attributed to Chaucer in three manuscripts, two of which (Add. 16165 and Trin. Coll. R.3.20) are by Shirley, but not in Harl. 7333, copied from Shirley; the third manuscript is Harl. 372, that in which Sir Richard Roos is named for *La Belle Dame*. There are eight manuscripts of the whole poem: Fairfax 16; Tanner 346; Harl. 372; Bodl. 638; Longleat 258; Digby 181; Add. 16165; Harl. 7333. Of these, the first five also contain *La Belle Dame*, three contain *The Compleynt of Mars*, and one has *The Black Knight*. In Fairfax 16 and in Bodl. 638, the 'Compleynt' comes first, and the narrative second. There are also four manuscripts of the 'Compleynt' only: Ff. 1.6. (the Roos scrapbook); Pepys 2006 (a *Belle Dame* manuscript); Phillipps 8299; and Trin. Coll. MS. R.3.20, a Shirley manuscript; in Add. 16165, the other Shirley manuscript, the 'Compleynt' occurs first, separated by some dozen folios from the narrative. As Miss Hammond says (*Chaucer*, p. 356): 'The independence of the Complaint, originally, thus becomes a possible question'.

I suggest, on the evidence chiefly of anagrams, that Chaucer's *Compleynt* 'off Anneleyda and of fals Arcite', mentioned by Lydgate, was indeed a complaint only, and that its remains may be traced now in Strophes 1 and 2, and in Antistrophe 1 of the existing 'Compleynt'. These are the only stanzas that do not carry fifteenth-century anagrams. The remaining stanzas of the 'Compleynt', including the Proem and the Conclusion, and the whole of the narrative, contain anagrams which make me assign these portions to Sir Richard Roos.

The anagrams run as follows throughout the narrative:

Invocation to Mars, ll. 1–21:

> Stt. 1–2: COBHAM; FAWCO(MBe); stt. 2–3: (EL)ISABeTh; TOT FOr–FAIT; st. 3: MAU. STANHO(PE), WI–By.

The Triumph of Theseus in Athens, ll. 22–42:

> ll. 22–8: HOMF–I; ll. 29–35: (E)DMOn. BeWFOrT, SOMe.; ll. 36–42: B–W(C)HA(M); WA–WI(C).

The destruction of Thebes: ll. 43–70: WILOBI; BEVSH(Am)P; (J)OH. B–WMONT; (TY)PTO–T; HON(Gre)FOr.; CRO–We– –; WHeTTInHA.; (C)A–AIS.

There are two threads of interest in the anagrams so far, the personal and the military. The personal, on the trio Elisabeth Cobham, Maud Stanhope, Lady Willoughby, and Lord Fawcomberg, is plainly indicated in the invocation to Mars. The military governs the beginning of the story. The three names hidden under the triumph of Theseus were only on one occasion so allied in fact, and that was at the Siege of Calais by the Burgundians in 1436. The laggard Duke of Gloucester went out in August, by which time Edmund Beaufort and the Earl of Warwick had already done the fighting. The further stanzas on Thebes and its princes give the opportunity for a roll-call of names from the English host. Such were the Lords Beaumont, Tiptoft, Hungerford, and Cromwell, and among the lesser men, Roos's friend, Robert Whittingham. (Stevenson, *Wars in France*, II, xlix–lii.) Lord Willoughby is not known to have been at Calais; he had been forced to surrender Paris in the preceding April. He may be inserted here as a connecting link between the two themes. The Beauchamp name here can hardly repeat the Earl of Warwick, or refer to his twelve-year-old heir, Henry; it may be meant for Sir William Beauchamp of Powick, Sir Robert Roos's companion as King's Carver. Some signs point to this passage being written much later than the event of 1436: Edmund Beaufort did not become Somerset till 1444; and the rare reference to Beaumont, husband of 'Lady Bounte', probably indicates a date later than her death in 1441.

The personal allusions, which certainly point to the mid 1440s, continue in the rest of the narrative and in the Compleynt:

Anelida described, ll. 71–84: (EL)ISA– –Th –O–HAm; ll. 78–84: STAN–OPe.

Arcite described, ll. 85–91: FAW–O–BE.

The New Lady, and Arcite's inconstancy, ll. 141–62: ll. 151–7: STAnHOP.; FOr–AIT; ll. 148–54: Faw–O–BArg; ll. 155–62: STAnH.; FAW–On– –R–; TOT FOr–A–T (diffused).

The new Lady's tyranny over Arcite, ll. 183–96: MAUD STANH.,
WI--UHB.; FAW--NB.

Anelida then is Elisabeth Cobham; the name had been Chaucer's
choice, but the form here given can be read in anagram as ALIENA(d),
i.e. Strange, the only reference here to her married state, except possibly
for lines 201–2:

> The kynde of mannes herte is to delyte
> In thing that straunge is, also God me save!

Maud Stanhope is also married by now; there may be a pointer to her
in her colours, which Arcite promptly adopted, 'Wot I not whethir in
white, rede or grene' (l. 146); Sir Richard Stanhope's arms were
'quarterly ermine and gules'; green is the colour of inconstancy, and the
avoidance here of blue has been noticed.

In the Compleynt, the personal names are repeated in a wider context. The Proem (ll. 211–19) gives the anagram, ALIAn.; FAW---MB.;
For--YT; STAnH.; the Plesaunce phrases in it, 'fals plesaunce', 'Alwey
til oon, and chaungeth for no newe', prepare us for the more extended
anagrams of Strophes and Antistrophes 4 and 5: AlYAn. –OB–AM;
MAU. –TAN–O.; I–MANYA.; AnTI(G)ONA COBHAM; IS–ANIA S–Alis,
whAlISBO--UH; AI TOt FOrFAIT FOr–YT. We remember that young
Elisabeth Cobham had been one of the girls of Plesaunce. In Strophe 3
and Antistrophes 2 and 3, Fawcomberg is the subject of complaint:
FAW–OMB.; FAU--MBe.; FAW--MB--G. In the sixth strophes and the
conclusion, the anagrams return fully to Lord Fawcomberg, and his
new lady. Strophe 6: FAW--MBe–G; STAN. Antistrophe 6: FA–OMB–R.;
STAN–H--; Conclusion: STANHOP; ISMAn.; FOrF(A)IT.

And what of Ermony, where Anelida was queen? I doubt if it
should be looked for 'outremer', or any further than the West Riding of
Yorkshire. Since Anelida is Elisabeth Cobham, and Arcite Lord
Fawcomberg, we remember his Yorkshire connexions, and his helper
in *The Compleynt of Mars*, a Vavasour of Hazelwood. In South Yorkshire, about twenty miles south-east of Hazelwood is the small place
now called Airmyn, but earlier known as (Great and Little) Armin,
Eyreminne, Ermenie, Ermenia.[1] This is some miles distant from the
Fawcomberg seats and manors in the North Riding (Skelton Castle,
Marske, etc.), but it is only half a dozen miles south of Wressel, the
chief Neville seat, and therefore certainly familiar to the boy William
Neville. The point of attaching Ermony to Elisabeth Cobham we can
only conjecture—was it for her a Rosamond's Bower? But we can con-

---

[1] V.C.H., *Yorkshire* (General), II, 270, 298.

jecture that, whatever its aptness, Roos would know of it through his friends of Plesaunce days, the Babthorps, for the Babthorp seat, near Drax, is only some half dozen miles north-west of Airmyn. Within an easy twenty miles' riding of Airmyn were the Vavasours, the Nevilles, and the Babthorps; and thirty miles to the north was Helmsley (Hamlake), with York half-way between. County and court gossip would make short work of these distances.

The poem thus appears as a companion poem to *The Compleynt of Mars*, commiserating with Elisabeth Cobham, Lady Strange, the Venus of that work, on Fawcomberg's neglect of her for Maud Stanhope, now Lady Willoughby. It takes the Rake's Progress a step further; the final stages will be treated, seldom in the high style, more often with bitter satire. Here the sympathy is reserved for the forsaken Elisabeth-Anelida. There may be some *Schadenfreude* in the poet's description of the apt-spoken Maud Stanhope's discipline of the false lover by her sharp tongue ('every word he dredeth as an arowe'), and by her ruthless display of Daunger: 'lest that he were proud, she held him lowe' (l. 192).

'The *Anelida* has long been a puzzle to the critics', says its latest editor, Robinson. The pompous epic beginning, the decline to a tale of sentiment, the 'meagre and ill-developed narrative', the highly elaborate complaint, have always been seen as parts without organic or even structural relation. 'Poor and conventional' in characterization, thin in substance, 'a tendency to poetic diction'—these express the general recent dissatisfaction. On the credit side come 'the swift and flexible narrative style', and the mastery of its very complicated metrical forms. These are merits familiar to readers of Roos's poems; and the complex rhyme structures of strophe and antistrophe have their parallels in *The Lover's Mass*. The cleavage in the interest is partly explained by the anagrams. Roos apparently began to write a heroic poem of compliment to celebrate the success at Calais in 1436, and the phrasing of the narrative shows him still under Plesaunce influence; this, I believe, remained unfinished. Later, in the 1440s he desired to write a personal poem condoling with an unhappy Plesaunce lady; and to hand he found a Complaint by Chaucer, brief and capable of expansion, and already coupling (possibly only in the title) the knight of Thebes, 'false Arcite', with a lady. It seems to have had no mention of the rival lady; to supply and characterize her, and to identify her by the anagrams, was Roos's chief addition. Thebes is the link between the two themes thus arbitrarily connected.

This explanation solves some of the difficulties, though not all; the
Y

reference to Corinne still remains unexplained. But indebtedness to Ovid and Statius, to Boccaccio and even to Dante, is far from impossible in a 'Gloucester's man'; this Italian touch we have seen before, and shall see again.

As for style, Roos is here often at his most impressive, whether in the close-packed line ('Withoute love, he feyned jelousye', l. 126); or the glittering description of the procession, and of Emelye's bright presence in it (ll. 38–42); or, above all, in the lovely couplet that picks up one of his favourite words:

> thou Polymya . . .
> Singest with vois memorial in the shade,
> Under the laurer which that may not fade.

Roos has the right to take to himself the praise of this poem written by Legouis for Chaucer:

C'est une belle chose malgré sa longueur monotone . . . il sait garder à la voix d'Anélida l'accent le plus vrai . . . les plus touchantes pensées.

No. 75. Yet another poem deals with Fawcomberg's 'affaires' in sober style, even though the third woman is indicated at the end: the *Ballad of Good Counsel*, or, as it is called in two manuscripts, 'A resoun *de fallacia mundi*'. It is a poem in nineteen stanzas of rhyme royal, with a variable refrain in the last couplet, and with an envoy to 'princes, cherisshers of vertue'.

> *Incipit.* Consider wel with every circumstaunce.
> *Refrain.* (Yet) suffre hem speke, and trust right wel this,
> A wikked tonge wol alway deme amis.
> *Explicit.* Withdraw your hering from al that deme amis.

The poem is known in seven manuscripts, two of which (of Shirley descent) ascribe it to Lydgate. It was printed without ascription by Thynne, but as Lydgate's by Stow; Skeat and MacCracken have no doubt of its being his work (*Chaucer*, VII, no. xii (from Thynne); *Minor Poems*, p. 839, from MS. Ellesmere 4). The most significant manuscripts for Roos are Ff. 1.6, where, as Item 44, it follows the central series of Roos's lyrics; and Trin. Coll., Camb., R.3.20.

The anagrams run as follows:

Stt. 1–2, SCA–IS, whA–I––ORO; TOT FOr–AIT; stt. 3–4, E–ISABETh; stt. 5–6, ST–An–E; st. 7, COB–A–; stt. 8–10, BeWFOrT; st. 10, sOMe––S–T; stt. 8–10, He––Y; –DM–––; stt. 10–11, B–WMO–T; stt. 11–13, KnO–In, E–ISA–ETH ST–An; FAW–OM.; stt. 14–15,

(SCAl)Y-, W(H)A----OrOH; stt. 16–18, (M)AV. STAnHO(P)E; stt. 16–17, (PHElJP); stt. 18–19, FAW–OM.; BARBAlINa; TOT FOrF–IT.

These seem to show that the poem is addressed to Lady Scales, and that it is a homiletic consideration of the ill repute of Fawcomberg's dealings with Lady Strange, Maud Stanhope, and even, slipped incongruously into the Envoy, with Barbelina. There is a large residue; the poet's 'devise' occurs only twice, at beginning and end. One stanza recalls Beaumont, and the names of the Ladies Worthy give Phelip; but no cryptogram seems to be intended in the list of great men (stt. 13–15). The opportunity of suiting the anagram to the sentiments is only once taken (stt. 8–10), where on the theme of great riches the clear names of Beaufort and Somerset are accompanied by the merest skeleton of the names Henry and Edmund; and one recalls the attack on the Cardinal as Coveitise in *The Romaunt of the Rose*, and that Edmund was heir to his uncle's wealth:

> And som wol sayen, that it cometh of fraud,
> Outher by sleight, or by fals chevisaunce;
> To say the worst, folk have so gret plesaunce. (52–54)

The stress on that last word must be intentional; this was indeed the view of the Cardinal taken at Plesaunce. Earlier, Roos had disavowed didactic poetry ('Counsell cordes not well in ryme'), and it is difficult to guess why now he chose to write on Fawcomberg in a subdued and moderate tone, with Lydgatian generalizations and heavy style, with words like 'equipolent, corpulent, vinolent'. Yet the social observation is basically as shrewd as in the lively individual comment of *The Chance of the Dice*, whether on the backbiter or on his victim (cf. *The Dice*, stt. 7, 45). Roos had made the Black Knight abuse Malebouche and all his attendant train; here there are no allegorical figures, but 'médisance' is displayed in all its phases of spite and detraction, its venomous perversion of good into evil:

> no man may eschewe
> The swerde of tonge, but it wol kerve and byte.

II. FAMILY HISTORY, BEAUFORTS AND OTHERS

No. 76a. Roos has now ridiculed Lord Fawcomberg under the guise of Mars and of false Arcite; and in *The Chance of the Dice* he has coupled him with another famous deceiver: 'Wher Jason falsed oon, ye falsen two' (st. 5, on Fawcomberg and Stanhope). The line is reminiscent of a charge against Jason in the 'Legend of Hypsipyle and Medea': 'There othere falsen oon, thow falsest two' (L.G.W., 1377). Closer scrutiny reveals that this whole passage of 'Reproach to Jason' in *The Legend*, which has no parallel in the sources, is another attack on Lord Fawcomberg, and brings in the third stage of the Rake's Progress. He has by now deserted Maud Stanhope for Barbelina (see below, Chapter X). This discovery forces us to a thorough examination of *The Legend of Good Women*, with results even more startling than those on *The Compleynt of Mars* and *Anelida and Arcite*.

There can be no doubt that Chaucer wrote *a* poem of good women (as he did *a* translation of *Le Roman de la Rose*); proof lies in his own references, in 'The Man of Law's Prologue', and in the 'Retractation'; also in those by his near contemporaries, the Duke of York, Hoccleve and Lydgate. These are sufficient guarantee.

But the poem that we have and know as *The Legend of Good Women* is not, I believe, the poem that Chaucer wrote as he left it. The presence in both the Prologues and all the Legends of many of Roos's anagrams forces one to this conclusion. They range from Plesaunce, to his period of courtship of Margaret Vernon, and still later to Anthony Wydville's wedding plans. Indeed, the question arises whether any of the existing poem is Chaucer's, or whether the whole of it is worked over, even written, by Sir Richard Roos. Certainly the two Prologues admit of no easy solution; but it is, I believe, possible to get a clearer view of the Legends.

These general assertions need now to be taken in more detail. First, Chaucer's undoubted authorship of a poem which seems to have been variously called 'the Seintes Legende of Cupide' ('Man of Law's Prologue'); 'The book of the xxv Ladies' (Retractation); 'prologe of the xxv good wymmen' (*The Master of Game*); [Cupid's] 'legende of Martres' (Hoccleve); and 'the Legend of Cupide' and 'a legende of parfite holines' (Lydgate). Two points strike us in these early names, the numbers, and the stress on Cupid's martyrs. The number xxv is general, but, probably through scribal error, not invariable; three manuscripts of *The Canterbury Tales* give x, ix, xv and 29 respectively (Cardigan MS., Lansdowne 851, and Harl. 1239). The manuscripts of *The Master of Game* vary almost half and half between xxv and xv (which Shirley in MS. Add. 16165 writes out, 'fyfftene'). Again, the name of the god, when cited, is always Cupid. The same is true even in Roos's own possible allusion, in the prose epistle to *The Lover's Mass* (1445), where, as pilgrim of love, he says that he 'rad also ful often in my contemplatyff medytacions The holy legende of Martyrs of Cupydo'. By implication too the devout wish for Chaucer in *How a Lover* (221), 'Thy soule god haue with virgynes white', must apply to Chaucer's

Legend. In these works, and in the many Plesaunce poems (c. 1435–41) that enumerate the ladies of the Ballade, Roos can hardly be intending his own Legends, which, as the anagrams show, come down to c. 1450, and probably later.

Contrast all this with the names of the existing poem in its manuscripts; within the poem itself (ll. 483–4) it is called the 'legende Of goode wymmen'; in MSS. Fairfax 16 and Bodley 638, 'the boke of the ix goode Wymmen'; in MSS. R.3.19 and Add. 12524, 'the legend of ladyes'; in Arch. Selden B.24, 'the legendis of ladyes'. Here only two allied manuscripts give a number, different from the other numbers, and exactly corresponding to the actual complement of tales. The terms, holy, and saints, are dropped, and martyrs are retained only in the headings to the Legends. Mention of the god is discarded, and in the course of the prologue he is never called Cupid, but always 'the (mighty) god of Love', or Love, as he is in *Le Roman de la Rose*, and in Roos's translation of it. With two exceptions, the term women is replaced by ladies— compare *The Assembly of Ladies* and its distinctions of rank. There is some justification here for thinking that the shift of title corresponds to a change of substance, and that we are dealing with two different sets of poems. It is quite possible that Chaucer's poem, if written for Richard II and his queen, was never put into circulation, and that a solitary copy remained in the Royal Library, or in Gloucester's hands, where Roos had access to it and was able to write the poem that we now possess.

This suspicion of two different sets of poems is aroused by the presence of many characteristic anagrams, and some peculiarly personal ones, covering Roos's range of interest for about twenty years. They are used in his usual manner, strung down through long passages, or introducing a name at a relevant description or allusion, such as the significant lady in the description of the heroine, or as the two Margarets for the honour of the daisy. The importance of this can only be properly estimated when the anagrams have been given in full. Only then too can the amount of Roos's work, whether partial or total, and the extent of a Chaucerian residue (if any), be estimated. I had hoped at one stage that the vexed question of the relative dating of the Prologues might be finally solved, but that is not so simple. More definite results can be got from the Legends, with some new variations and adaptation of anagrams to subject. The knowledge that Chaucer himself practised this particular anagram[1] complicates the enquiry, especially at points in the

---

[1] See '*The Parlement of Foules* and Lionel of Clarence' in *Medium Ævum*, 1953, XXV, 168–74.

Prologues, and even in one Legend, when names important to both poets, such as Beaufort, are involved.

The Prologues. MS. Fairfax 16; Gg. 4. 27.

Fairfax 1–16: E–ISAB–TH BerDO–F; ANTI.

Gg. 1–16:   E–ISAB–TH BeWMONT; ANTIGO.; FOrF–IT.

No conclusion as to priority in writing can be drawn here from the names Bardolf and Beaumont, since in the continuing lines, on books and their value to the world and to the poet himself, both versions have the later name 'B–wmont':

Fairfax 17–39: B–WMO–T; AnTIGO; ISMAnIA S–A––S; WHYTT.

Gg. 17–39:   B–WMONT; AnTIGO; ISMAN. WhA–––BOr–UGH.

The May morning passages begin to have greater variation, and at first the anagram is sketchy in both:

Fairfax 40–9: E––SA–ETh; Wh–TT.

Gg. 40–9:   B–W––NT.

The variations between the Prologues increase as the poet turns to the daisy, and from it to the theme of the Flower and the Leaf. Gg. 51–60 on the flower closed at eve, gives AnTIG.; FO–FAIT F–––AIT. The much longer passage in Fairfax, 50–72, on the daisy opening at dawn, provides a full braid of the Plesaunce ladies: AlIAn.; AnTi.; (E)–ISAB–TH BeW–O–T; YS–An. S–Al–S, whAl–S–OROH; KATh. WheT.; TOT FOrFA–T FOrFA–T. The famous reference to former poets, and the assertion of the poet's detachment from commitment to the Leaf or to the Flower in Gg. 61–80, gives the names of the Gloucester family: HOMF–EI; ALIAN.; ANTIGON.; with FOrFAIT. By contrast, the very different treatment in Fairfax, 73–82, with its affirmation of devotion to the Flower, carries a merely feminine anagram: AnTYG.; ISMAnY; FOrFAIT. The beautiful passage which is only in Fairfax, 84–96, 'She is the clernesse and the verray lyght', pinpoints the reference to Be–MO–T; YsMan. S–A––S; R.R.

When the two streams converge with the poet's recourse to the daisy, the evening flower of Gg. seen at the end of May (81–106) again celebrates the lord and lady of Plesaunce, together with the poet's lady, and his confidant: HOMF––Y; AlIAn.; [E]LISA––Th B–W–ONT; I–MAnIA whAl––OrOU.; TOT FOrFAIT FOrFA–T. The morning flower of May-Day in Fairfax 16 again omits the Plesaunce owners, and limits itself to the two ladies (97–114): E–ISA––Th B–WMO–T; ISMAnIA.

When the Gg. Prologue introduces the queen in her daisy dress (141–57), this again combines Roos's two ladies: ELISA––TH; ISMANYA WHA(L)––OR.; FOrFA–T FOrFA–T. Fairfax 16 on the other hand (210–25) omits Lady Beaumont, and gives Lady Scales only, by her triad of names: ISMAnIA SCA(L)., WHA–Y–OR––H; FOrFA–T FOrFA–T. A similar shift of emphasis is seen in the description of Love. Gg. 158–83 gives the two ladies: BeW–OnT; ISMAnIA SCA(L)–S, WHAlISBO––(G)H; FOrFAYT FOrFAIT. Fairfax, on the other hand, confines it to the Scales family: THOMAS (LO)–D SCAl–S; ISMAnIA WHA–YS–O–––H. FOr–AIT FOrFAIT. The nineteen ladies of Gg. (185–202) cover Lady Beaumont and Antigone: BeW–ONT, BA–DO–F; ANTIGO. The corresponding passage in Fairfax (270–99), which follows the song, gives prominence to Lady Scales: S–A(L)., ISMAnIA WHAlI–BO–OU(G)H; BeWMONT; TOT FOrFAIT FOrFAIT.

The two songs, though their lists of ladies are identical, have different refrains, and slight variations in line-initials. Gg. (203–23) gives: st. I., PH(El)Y.; AlJAN.; st. 2, (P)HELI.; st. 3, ELYSA–ETH BA(R)D–L. Fairfax (249–69) eliminates Eleanor Cobham, and inserts Lady Scales thus: st. I, PH(El).; YSMAN(J)A; st. 2, (P)HiL.; stt. 2–3, BA(RD)OL.; Y–MAN(Y)A; st. 3, ELYSA––TH.

Now comes the session, and the arraignment of the poet: in neither Fairfax (300–40) nor Gg. (224–53 and 254–316) do I find any anagrams. These are resumed, however, in the speech of Alceste (Fairfax 341–72 and Gg. 317–52) but with considerable differences. Gg. gives an almost full Plesaunce 'braid', the only omission being Antigone: HOMFR–Y; (Al)IAn –OBHAM; BA(R)DO–F; ISMANIA S(C)AlE., WHA(L)–SBOrO––H. Fairfax inserts Antigone, but omits Bardolf: HOMFR–Y; (C)–BHAM; ANTYGONA; ISMAnYA S(C)AlE., WHA–––BOrOUH; TOT FOrFA–T. I omit for the moment Alceste's political argument, as its anagram entails other considerations. The queen's concluding petition for the poet, identical in both versions, brings in the three chief ladies of the earlier period: (F. 431–41; Gg. 421–31) AlIAn.; B–W–ONT; wh(Al)I––OrO––H.

Love's answer to Alceste, with the poet's plea for pardon, is practically identical in both Prologues, and yields the same anagram: F. 442–54, AnTIGO.; BeWMO–T; ISMAN S–AlIS; Gg. 432–44, AnTIGO.; BeW–ONT; ISMAnI S–Al. F. 455–74 and Gg. 445–64: AlIAn.; ANT–GO.; B–W–ONT; ISMAN. S(C)A(L). Alceste's reply in Gg. 465–85 gives AlIAn CO.; AnTIG.; B–W–ONT; ISMANYA; TOT FOrFAIT. So does Fairfax, 475–97, except that the famous couplet on presenting the poem to the queen in one of her palaces, Eltham or Sheen, allows the addition of (S)CA–(E). Love's disclosure of the person of Alceste, with the poet's eulogy of the daisy, identical in both texts, shows itself as a late addition or reworking by its Margaret anagrams; the disclosure (F. 498 and Gg. 486) yields IS–AnYA SC(AlE)s, wHA(L)––BOrO––H; and the daisy, with a little help from the explanation: MAR–AReT DAn(JOv); VerNON, LON.; FOrFAIT.

Love's commission to the poet to write the poem, in the shorter and differing form in Gg., gives only ISMAnIA S(CAL)IS, WhA(Le)SBO–OUGH (523–45). The longer version of Fairfax agrees in IS–AnIA S(C)A(L)., WHA–Y–BO–OU–H (535–51); but the expanded recommendation to write gives the three chief Plesaunce ladies (552–67): AlYAn COBHAM; AnTIGO.; BEWMONT; TOT FOrFAIT. Finally it ends (568–79) with Lady Scales, and the poet's devise: S–AlIS, WhALys–OrO.; TOT FOrFA–T.

To revert now to the political passage in Alceste's plea, the injunctions to a god-like king to rule justly and to keep the support of the half-gods, his great lords. Here there are indeed anagrams, but they are not only possible to the 1390s, but also more suitable there. The names are these: Fairfax, 373–411, RYCHA.; LAn–AST.; HEN–Y BOLInB–OC; BOH–N; IOH. BeWFOrT; Gg. 353–97, RYCHA.; LAn–AST.; HEn–I BOLInB–OC; BOH–N; BeWFOrT; also P(L)ANTA. in ll. 360–4 which are not in Fairfax. The names of Lancaster, Bolingbroke, and Bohun are undoubtedly meant for King Richard's consideration:

> Al wol he kepe his lordes hire degree,
> As it ys ryght and skilful that they bee
> Enhaunced and honoured, and most dere.

It is a plea to him to live in amity with John of Gaunt, with Gaunt's son and heir, and that son's father-in-law, and with the second family, the Beauforts, legitimated in 1397. After all, they are of Plantagenet descent, and royal kinsfolk. The remainder of the advice, that a king ought to

> Shewen his peple pleyn benygnete, ...
> And here compleyntes and petyciouns,

is applicable to the resentful, difficult Richard II of the 1390s, but not at all to Sir Richard's king, the over-generous and complaisant Henry of the 1440s.

It seems then that if we look for the substratum of Chaucer's original in the prologues, this passage is one of the certainties. The other two, which have no anagrams, entail also other considerations. The praise of books is vouched for as Chaucer's in *The Master of Game*. Yet it is curious that the quotation is not only inexact (that might well happen) but also has no ring of poetry; it sounds like a prose sentence:

Be wryteng haue men of ymages passed for writyng is þe keye of all good remembraunce.

Finally, the enumeration of Chaucer's writings (F. 412–30; Gg. 398–420) can apply only to Chaucer. It is noticeable that it contains none of the titles that I have claimed for Roos, *The Compleynt of Mars, Venus,* and *Anelida and Arcite*; and Chaucer's 'Rose', which was 'an heresye' against love, must have been totally different from Roos's doings.

The anagrams are unfortunately too repetitive to make a clear-cut division of time between the two Prologues; but certain conclusions can be drawn. I believe that Gg. is the earlier, pre-1441, form, but that it had some re-working of the conclusion about 1449–50. The stress in it is on Plesaunce and its family, on Elisabeth Beaumont, and only secondarily on Ismania Scales. The Balade even celebrates Elisabeth only, by her maiden names. A later stage, after 1441, is seen in Fairfax, with three chief changes. First, Duke Humphrey is dropped from Plesaunce anagrams where there is re-working. The only passage in which Fairfax keeps him is in Alceste's first speech on false accusation, where there is very little alteration. Secondly, Lady Scales is steadily enhanced, so much so that in the first appearance of the daisy-queen she alone survives of a feminine trio; F. 210–14 are verbally altered in such a way as to eliminate ELISA-ETH. In the immediately following description of Love, a similar change takes place; BEW–ONT goes, and Lord Scales's name Thomas replaces it. He is very rarely found elsewhere in Roos's anagrams, indeed only in the poems for his daughter's wedding. With all this, it is curious that the refrain of the Ballade in Gg. has the name Alceste, whereas that in F. has not. One would expect the reverse; Skeat suggested that the name is suppressed in F. to heighten the final surprise. Or it is possible that Roos's original Alceste was Elisabeth Beaumont; that he saw the name to be an only too obvious anagram of Scales, and altered the refrain to protect the modest and retiring Lady Scales? A song was more liable to get out of its writer's control, to be set to music and be sung by all and sundry (see below, Chapter XII), than was seemly for a coterie poem. It is clear from the end that Gg. had some later revision, and Alceste's name may have been a late insertion; either situation is possible.

Thirdly, although Gg. has the reference dating from about 1449–50 to the two Margarets, it does not have two other similar references which are in F. alone. In ll. 175–86, on the daisy, 'The emperice and flour of floures alle', both Roos's Margarets are celebrated; and at ll. 496–7 comes the famous injunction to give the completed poem to the queen at Eltham or at Sheen. The legend that Sheen was destroyed after the death of Anne of Bohemia has died hard. But the itinerary of Henry VI and his court proves that it was visited occasionally by him after his marriage. In 1446 he went to both Eltham and Sheen. In 1447–8 when, as we have seen, Margaret was busy repairing Plesaunce, the neighbouring Eltham was thrice visited, for only one visit to Sheen in March 1448. In 1449 the king was at Sheen in July, in August, and in September; and in 1451 for a fortnight in April and a brief visit in August.[1] After 1451 Sheen understandably drops out of the account. The king's illness, and then after 1455 the resort to Coventry and the Midlands to rally supporters, took him away from the palaces beside the Thames. It looks as if the anagram of Margaret Vernon-Longueville, coupled with the visits to Sheen of 1448–51, indicates the period 1449–51 as the probable last date for the conclusion of Gg., and the final redaction of F.

Unless another manuscript turns up with Chaucer's own version of the Prologue—a consummation devoutly to be wished—this is perhaps as far as one can now get. I will venture the suggestion that it was a very different affair from either F. or G.—not a rejoicing daisy poem of the Flower and the Leaf, but perhaps a poem in memory of the dead queen, and certainly with a serious appeal to Richard II to read history and learn its lessons, and to avoid antagonizing his great nobles.

The Legends

There are nine Legends extant, praising ten heroines, since Legend IV covers two, Hypsipyle and Medea, both victims of Jason. Of the sixteen heroines named by the Man of Law, seven do not appear.[2] On the other hand, two extant legends, Cleopatra and Philomene, are not mentioned by Chaucer, although in both Prologues Cleopatra is specified by the god of Love as the first tale: 'At Cleopatre I wol that thow begynne'. We have seen that this line immediately follows a passage of some dozen lines which contains in anagram the names of the two ladies of Plesaunce. With this in mind we may study the anagrams of 'Cleopatra'.

Ll 589–615, description of Antony and Cleopatra (in order): HO–FREI; ANTIG.; AlIAn. (C)OBHA(M); E–ISAB–TH B–W–ONT; FOr–A–T.

Ll. 616–23, the poet's brevity on the wedding: ALYAn; TOT FOrFA–T.

Ll. 624–33, the two navies and the seafight: IOHAn ARUND.; AlIAn. –AUT(R)AUIS; TH––AS BAnAST.; IOHAn T(RO)–PInTOn.

This gives a very different and a surprising anagram, which needs explanation. Sir John Arundel and Eleanor Mautravers were the maternal grandparents of Sir Richard Roos. He is known to have been wrecked and drowned at sea in 1379. According to the account in the *Anonimalle Chronicle* (ed. Galbraith, 1927, p. 131), Sir John, together

---

[1] M. E. Christie, *Henry VI*, pp. 382, 385.
[2] Dianire, Hermyon, Erro, Eleyne, Brixseyde, Ladomya, Penelopee.

with two knights of John of Gaunt, Thomas Banastre and John Trumpington, ravaged the coast of Brittany, but was then caught in storms. Arundel reached the Irish coast and forced the master mariner to attempt a landing, against his better judgement. Sir John was drowned with his two chief associates and many sailors. The event alluded to befell in Chaucer's lifetime, but the unusually personal turn in the anagrams seems to be decisive for Roos's authorship; and the linking of his grandmother's name may hint that this is an account from oral family tradition. The source of this sea-battle, and its vivid detail on methods of fighting, have been sought in Froissart; they may come at first-hand from a survivor of the wreck, a Mautravers-Arundel retainer, whose racy speech Roos represented by modulating into the older alliterative rhythms.

Ll 653–705, the flight and death of Cleopatra (in order): AlYAn.; HOMF–I; (C)OBHA–; ELISAB–Th B(E)WMONT; ISMAnIA; AMAN(C)I(E)R, AnTIGONA; FOrFAIT FOr–AYT. Here the appearance of the name Amancier points to a date later than 1450; it seems possible that the Legend is indirectly an elegy for Eleanor Cobham who died in 1454:

> And she hire deth receyveth with good cheere,
> For love of Antony that was hire so dere.
> And this is storyal soth, it is no fable (ll. 700–2).

Thus one of the two Legends not claimed by Chaucer himself appears to be by Roos *in toto*; the other is VII, the 'Legend of Philomene'. The unusual and as yet untraced proem to this, with its philosophic loftiness, and its sudden venomous attack on Tereus, betrays at once by its anagram the *dramatis personae*.

Ll. 2228–43, *Deus dator formarum:* FAWCOM–Er.; STAnHO–E; whA–YS–OrOU–H. The poet's concern is the Fawcomberg-Stanhope affair, and he addresses the sympathetic ear of Lady Scales. Ll. 2244–59, Tereus weds Progne: and ll. 2260–9, Progne longs for Philomene: FAWKO(M)B–R(G) (J)OAN; STAnHO(P), WiLOB(I); S–Al–S; TOT FOrFA–T. The anagram here is firm, precise, and skilful. It is the first time that the name of William Neville's wife, Joan Fawcomberg, has been introduced into the anagrams; it appears that here she stands for Progne, the neglected wife.

Ll. 2270–95, Tereus goes to Pandion: MAU. STAnHO(P)., WILL–UGHBI; FAWKO–B––G; TOT FOrFA–T.

Ll. 2296–307, Pandion's speech, and Tereus's leave-taking: STAnHO.; IOAN.

Ll. 2308–41, Philomene in the Thracian cave: MAU. STAnHOP; FAW–O–B–(G); BA–BALIn HArB–––In; S–AlYS.

Ll. 2342–9, Tereus's return home: FA––B.; –TAnH–P.

Ll. 2349–70, Philomene weaving: STAnHO.; BA–BALIn; SCA––S; ForFA–T.

Ll. 2371–82, Progne finds Philomene: STANH–(P).; IOAn FAW–––B.

Ll 2383–93, Conclusion: –AUD STAN–O––; TOT ForFAYT.

The names are clearer to read than their application. Plainly Lady Scales is the interested audience. The main theme is Maud Stanhope's ill-treatment by Fawcomberg, and his desertion of her for Barbelina Herberquyne. The introduction of this hated name accounts for the violence of the poet's attack on the villain who 'Corrumpeth, whan that folk his name nevene', and whose ancient venom still affects the beholder. But the nature of the ill-treatment in this Legend makes one wonder if there is some sly malice in the choice of the story of the 'tongueless vigil'; if there was one thing that to Maud Stanhope would have been worse than death, it would have been the loss of her tongue. Again, did Lady Willoughby and Joan Fawcomberg, the 'idiota' wife, ever meet for mutual consolation? It seems most improbable.

One unexplained word here, 'radevore' (l. 2352), is now seen to be a Roos word, since its only other known occurrence is in 'As ofte as syghes' (see No. 45; 'Penelopye | Renewed her werke in the raduore'): Urry suggested 'ras de Vaur', cloth of La Vaur in Languedoc, not however known for tapestry. More probably it is 'ras de varwe', or dyed, coloured cloth, from the Flemish 'varwen', to dye.[1] Roos is then seen to be translating summarily Ovid's 'purpureasque notas filis intexuit albis' (l. 580). Roos was made alnager of cloths for sale in Northamptonshire at the end of December 1454, much later than 'As ofte as syghes', but possibly not far from the date of writing this 'Legend'. He probably first heard the term from his women friends.

Here then are two Legends not claimed by Chaucer, and full from beginning to end of characteristic Roos anagrams. The remaining Legends, all in the Man of Law's list, will be surveyed in order of their underlying themes.

Legend II, Thisbe, has anagrams as follows:

Ll. 706–36, the lovers' situation: –LISA(B)–Th; FAW–OMBE–G; BA–ByLeNa; STANHO(P); TOT ForFAYT For–A–T.

Ll. 737–71, the wall: –AUD STAn–O–; –AW–O–B–R–; Y–M–nIA WhALe–BOrO.

---

[1] G. de Poerck, *La Draperie Médiévale en Flandre et en Artois*, I, Glossaire flamande. Gand, 1951, *s.v.* varwe, etc.

Ll. 772–92, the fatal day: FAWCO–Be.; –AU– –TA(N)HO(P); TOT FOrFAIT FOrFAIT.

Ll. 793–804, Thisbe at the well: STAnH–P; FAW–O–B.; FOrFA–T.

Ll. 805–22, she flees from the lioness: FAW–O–B.; STAnHO.; ST–ANG–.

Ll. 823–52, Piramus comes, and kills himself: –TAnHO(P); –AW–OMB––G; BA–BAlINA.

Ll. 853–82, Thisbe finds his body: FAW–O–B.; STAnHO(P); BA–BAlINA HA–Be–QuIn; STAnHO(P).

Ll. 883–915, she kills herself: MAWD STAnHO(P); FOrFAIT; BA–BeLInA; FAW–OMB––G; STAnHO(P).

Ll. 916–23, conclusion: STAnH–P; FAW–O–Be––.

The relevance of the tale to Fawcomberg and Maud Stanhope is not easy to see, unless the implication is that she was prevented by a 'wrechede jelos fadre' from marrying where her heart was given, and so in a loveless match (Lord Willoughby was greatly her senior) more easily succumbed to Fawcomberg's wiles. The shadowy appearance of Elisabeth Strange looks back, but Barbelina's pervasive presence puts the composition after 1445. She is the disruptive *tertia quis*—like the lioness in the story. Lady Scales is involved probably as a sympathizer. One should note that 'Thisbe' is the only portion of the whole *Legend* that is in MS. Ff. 1.6, 'the Roos scrapbook'.

Legend IV, 'Hypsipyle' and 'Medea'. Fawcomberg is again the chief villain in this double Legend, but in the first story there are complications, arising from Roos's previous application of Hypsipyle to Elisabeth Bardolf, Lady Beaumont, dead in 1441 (see above, Nos. 5 and 10). The original opening attack on Jason, directed against Fawcomberg, has a verbal parallel in *The Chance of the Dice*, as has been seen; and the distinction drawn between love and lust has its longer counterpart in another Fawcomberg-Stanhope passage in *The Court of Love* (ll. 1066–77; No. 103, below).

The anagrams of 'Hypsipyle' run as follows:

Ll. 1368–95, the reproach to Jason: FAW–OM.; STANHOP; BA–BAlIN.; skAlIs whA–Y––Oro.; TOT FOrFA(I)T FOr–A(J)T.

Ll. 1396–1422, Pelleus's treachery to his nephew, Jason: E–(ES)A––TH KnO–IN CO–HAM; (P)He–I(P); FAW–O–BE–G.

Ll. 1423–38, the Golden Fleece: EL–SABeTH COB–AM, S(Tr)An.; B–W–ONT.

Ll. 1439–50, Pelleus incites Jason: MA–D –TANH–(P); AnTIG.

Ll. 1451–68, Jason sails in the Argo to Lemnos: FAWCO–B(Er).; LAdY STRAn(GE).

Ll. 1469–90, Hypsipyle welcomes Jason and Hercules: E–ISA––TH –T–AnG(E); B–AU–O–T; AnTIGO.; TOT FOrFAIT FOr–A–T.

Ll. 1491–1523, her hospitality: ELISAB(E)TH (C)OBHAM, ST–An–E; BeAUMONT; FOrFAYT.

Ll. 1542–58, Hercules in guile praises Jason to her: FAW–O–B–RG; BEAUMOnT; (E)LiSAB–TH STRAn.; FOrFAIT.

Ll. 1559–79, Jason's treachery, and Hypsipyle's constancy: COB–AM; BeW–OnT; STANHO.; WhA––SBOrOU––.

Here the chief stress is clearly on Lady Strange, with a secondary stress on Lady Beaumont, and with Maud Stanhope and Barbelina named in the introduction and conclusion to fill up the measure of Fawcomberg's enormities. Lady Scales and Antigone are probably interested listeners.

Legend IV B, 'Medea'. Here the double Fawcomberg-Beaumont reference yields to Fawcomberg with Maud Stanhope only, the name Medea probably suggesting 'Maud' to the anagrammatist. The lines on form and matter (1580–8) from Guido are parallel with those in the introduction to 'Philomene'.

The anagrams yield:

Ll. 1580–8, matter and form: FA–(C)O–––R.

Ll. 1589–1602, Jason at Jaconitos: MAU– STAnHOP (in line initials only); FAW(C)––B (in caesural initials only).

Ll. 1602–10, Jason described: (F)AWco–––g (three letters after anaphora of 'And'); S–ANH––.

Ll. 1611–19, Medea offers her aid: STA–HO.; TOT FOrFAI.

Ll. 1620–8, Jason's gratitude: FAW–OMB––G, Ne–I––.

Ll. 1629–50, their mutual troth: FAW–O–B–R; (M)AU– STANHO–.

Ll. 1651–61, Jason's betrayal: FAW(C)–(M)Be.; –TANHO–.

Ll. 1662–79, Medea's reproaches: FAW–OM––RG; STANHO.; TOT FOR–AIT.

In 'Hypsipyle' Roos has used the identity of names (Elisabeth) between Lady Strange and Lady Beaumont to keep Beaumont references running, and he has apparently made Jason's companion 'Ercules' stand for Lord Beaumont, thus, as often, covering two disparate references under one set of anagrams. In 'Medea', since here there had been no previous thought of Lady Beaumont, she vanishes from the anagram. It is a very cursory treatment of the legend, inferior to Gower's. The absence of Barbelina from 'Medea' may point to composition before 1445. She re-appears, however, in the first anagrams of the next legend devoted to Fawcomberg's villainy, the much finer 'Ariadne'.

Legend VI, Ariadne (Adriane). Here the story of Minos is taken further back (unnecessarily) to his gaining of the city of Alcathoe from its king Nisus through the treacherous aid of the infatuated princess, Scylla. The bird-transformation of the father and daughter, omitted here, will be found in the parallel story in *Reson and Sensuallyte* (ll. 4307–28); there it is greatly expanded from the French original, and given different anagrams which point to the date 1450 onwards. The origin and dual nature of the Minotaur is here passed over in silence, and, as has been noted, the expansion of the Ovidian legend owes much to 'The Knight's Tale'. The parallels that Skeat noted with Plutarch's 'Theseus' would not be impossible in Roos, since in 1437–8 Lapo da Castiglionchio sent to Duke Humphrey his Latin translation of some of the *Lives*, including 'Theseus'.[1]

The anagrams run as follows:

Ll. 1886–93, introduction: FAW(C)OMBe.; B---Be-JN.

Ll. 1894–1927, Minos aided by Scylla: -LES(A)BeTh STR(A)N. (C)OBHAM; (M)AU. STA-HO.; TOT FOrFA-T; BARB(Al)INA; FOrFA-T.

Ll. 1928–42, the Minotaur: FAW-O(M)-R.; (M)AUD -TAnHO.

Ll. 1943–59, Theseus in prison in Crete: MAU. STAnHO.; TOT FOrFAIT; FAW-OMB(E).

Ll. 1960-2024, Ariadne and Phedra plan help for him: IOAN -AWCO(M).; Le ST-AN.; COBHAM; (M)AUD -TANHOP.; PHeLY(P); FAW-O.; TOT FOrFAIT FOrFAIT; ISMAnIA WHA-ISBOrOUH; STAnHO.; FOrFAIT FOrFA-T.

Ll 2025-73, Theseus vows his allegiance to Ariadne: FAW-O(M)Be.; STRAN.; FOrFAIT; MA-D STAN-O-; FA-CO(M)B.

Ll. 2074-102, Ariadne accepts his faith: FAW---B--G; ST-ANG.; -AUD STAn-O.; FOrFAIT.

Ll. 2103-22, Theseus tells Ariadne of his seven-year-long fidelity: FA-OM.; BA---LIN(A); MAUD STAn-O.; TOT FOrF-IT FOrF-IT.

Ll. 2123-35, Ariadne's joy: ELISAB-Th; MA. STAN-O-.

Ll. 2136-62, Theseus overcomes the monster, and escapes: FAW-O(M)B--G; -TAnHO-(E); -TRAnGe; IS(M)An-A.

Ll. 2163-78, Naxos: STAnH.; FAWC.; FOr-AIT.

Ll. 2179-217, Ariadne deserted: FAW--MB.; MAUD STANH-P; STRAn., COBHAM; BAR-AlInA; TOT FOrFAIT FOr-AIT.

Ll. 2218-27, conclusion: FAWCOMB(E).; STANHO--.

Here, as in 'Philomene', the poet has introduced the name of Fawcomberg's wife Joan; and the long talk and planning of the two princesses

---

[1] R. Weiss, *Humanism in England*, pp. 50-1.

is made to cover the names of three victims of Fawcomberg's faithlessness, and of Roos's two particular friends Lady Beaumont and Lady Scales. Such, it is implied, has been the devoted support the wretch has always won from women.

In Legend VIII, 'Phillis', the last to attack Fawcomberg, we are again in a story formerly consecrated to Lady Beaumont; like Hypsipyle, Phillis had been a name which Roos had played with because of its likeness to Phelip, and he is fond of the story of her betrayal by Demophoon, son of Theseus (cf. *Flour of Curtesie*, 204; *Black Knight*, 380; *Assembly of Ladies*, 457).

It is not surprising to find that her Legend has some Plesaunce anagrams.

Ll. 2394–403, introduction, 'like father, like son': PHI., B--(D)O-F, B----NT; A-TIG.

Ll. 2404–26, Demophoon shipwrecked: (PHI)LI. BeWMONT; ANTI.; CO-HA.; IS-A(N)IA SCAL-S, WHAL-SBroUH.

Ll. 2427–38, he is cast on Phillis's land: MAU(D) STAnHO(P); FAW-O--(R).

Ll. 2439–53, he is received by her: MAUD -TANHO(P); FAW-O---R-.

Ll. 2454–71, like Theseus, he is false: FAWKO-B-RG; STAnHO(P).

Ll. 2472–93, he departs, and she laments: FAW---B-R.; MAV(D) STA-H-(P); Le STRAN-.

Ll. 2494–517, her letter (A): (PHIl)Y(P) B-W-ONT BA(RD)OLF; AnTIG.; S-AlYS, WHA---BOrOUH.

Ll. 2518–61, her letter (B), and conclusion: MAU- STANHOP, WI-BY; FAWCOmB.; BARBeLInA HA-B----In; TOT ForFAYT ForFAYT; YSMANY- WHAl-SBO-O.; ForFA-T.

These anagrams in their alternation of names suggest two stages of Roos's composition. Twice, in the shipwreck and the letter, the two sets of names appear, with the effect as of juxtaposition in blocks. After a Bardolf-Beaumont introduction, the Beaumont anagrams continue through the storm and the shipwreck. But when Demophoon comes to land, the Fawcomberg-Stanhope anagrams begin, and continue throughout the story till his desertion, with the single intrusion of the earlier victim, Lady Strange. In the first part of Phillis's letter, the poet reverts to Beaumont; with obvious repetitiveness the second part returns to Fawcomberg, and for the first time includes Barbelina. The concluding seven lines, with the famous injunction, 'And trusteth, as in love, no man but me', when added to the end of the letter, address the poem to Lady Scales. The two stages of the poem can be dated as probably before 1441 (an independent tale of Phillis for Lady Beaumont), and after 1445, an indictment of Fawcomberg for insertion into *The Legend*. It may be only by 'hindsight' that one feels a more supple rhythm and more moving tone in Letter B than in Letter A; the difference between the two shipwreck passages is not, I think, so marked.

Of the nine Legends, five have been seen to concern Lord Fawcomberg and his 'affaires'. One, on 'Thisbe' and the faithful but laggard Piramus, is as sympathetic in tone as is *Anelida and Arcite*. The remaining four, 'Hypsipyle' with 'Medea', 'Ariadne', 'Philomene', and 'Phillis', are covert attacks on him as Jason, or as Theseus or Demophoon. All five (but not 'Medea') introduce the name of Barbelina Herberquyne, and are therefore to be dated after 1445. Two of them, 'Ariadne' and 'Philomene', bring in Joan Fawcomberg, the *idiota* wife to whom Lord Fawcomberg owed his title. Lady Strange (Anelida) comes into all except the very brief 'Medea' and the fully handled 'Philomene'. The one constant name is Maud Stanhope, and there seems little doubt that she and her relations with Fawcomberg and her replacement by Barbelina are the chief reason for these attacks. The monotonous repetition of the three names when listed in the anagrams does not invalidate the poetic charm of many of the scenes painted, Ariadne on the rocky shore, Philomene at her coloured weaving, her radevore. It is however a relief to find that the remaining three Legends introduce, like 'Cleopatra', quite different personages and interests. In the arrangement, whether purposely or not, these Legends are at first alternated with the Fawcomberg subjects.

Legend III, 'Dido', an elaborate and ambitious tale, has not won ungrudging praise, chiefly because its flavour is medieval and non-Virgilian. It affords a very interesting and novel set of anagrams. Those of the introduction set the stage within the Chaucerian period, with John of Gaunt, Catherine Swinford, and their son, Henry Beaufort, the future cardinal. As the names that are further revealed are not familiar, this piece of secret family history should first be explained.

The Elizabethan antiquary, Rice Merrick, in his *Morganiae Archaiographia* of 1578 (ed. J. A. Corbett, 1887), in the course of a detailed pedigree of the Stradlings of St. Donat's, Glamorganshire, tells the following of Sir Edward Stradling, twelfth of the line, who was knighted in 1421–22:

This Sir Edward married with Jane, Daughter to Henry Beauford (after Cardinall) begotten before he was   upon Alice, one of the Daughters of Richard, Earle of Arundell.

The Alice FitzAlan in question must have been Alice, daughter of the
z

fifteenth Earl of Arundel (executed 1397), and of Elizabeth Bohun. She in 1392 married John Cherleton, Lord of Powys;[1] he died in 1401 without children. The date of Sir Edward Stradling's marriage to Jane (FitzAlan) is not given; he died in 1452–3, according to his *Inquisitio post Mortem*.

This odd piece of family history is supported by the anagrams of 'Dido'; all these names, Swinford, Henry Beaufort, Alis FisAlan Arundel, Cherleton, Powys, Joan Stradling, recur throughout. With them at beginning and end is a fifteenth-century name, a lady who might well learn this story, and even take a hand in its later developments, Margaret Beaufort, *née* Beauchamp, wife (c. 1442) of John Beaufort, third Duke of Somerset, nephew, like Edmund Beaufort of Mortain, of the Cardinal. She and her husband will recur in these anagrams. The story may help to explain the embittered enmity between Henry Beaufort and Archbishop Arundel, who was Alice's uncle. It must be remembered that Roos had marriage connexions on both sides: with the FitzAlan-Arundels through his mother, who was a first cousin of this Alice; and with the Beaufort-Somersets through his sister-in-law, Eleanor Beauchamp, wife of Edmund Beaufort.

The anagrams run as follows:

Ll. 924–57, the Introduction: Æneas leaves Troy (in order): GAV(N)T IOHAn; (on Creusa) CATHErIn SWInFor(D); HeN–(Y) BeWFOrT.; (diffused) (P)OW(YS); (M)A–(G)A–(ET) B–A(VC)HAM.

Ll. 970–1003, Venus appears: H(EN)–Y B–AUFOrT; –ATHErIn SWIn–Or(D); A(L)IS Ar(V)N(D)., FISALAn, CHE––TO., POWIS; AlIAN. B–W–HAM.

Ll. 1004–14 and 1035–43, Dido described: (C)Hir––TO.; ST––(D)–In., F–SA–An, IOAn.

Ll. 1060–77, Æneas described: ALis, IOAn ST–A.; HeN. BeA(V)FOrT. The stress in these lines on beauty together with 'braunes and . . . bones' is a pointer to Beau-fort, as in *The Black Knight*, ll. 163–4.

The long enumeration of Dido's rich presents to Æneas and of his return gifts has been remarked on as not in Virgil, and 'of a decidedly medieval cast'. If written after 1442, it had extreme, almost satiric relevance to the rich Cardinal Beaufort, whose enormous wealth enabled him by loans of money, plate and jewels, to be the financier behind the throne. Roos had already pilloried him secretly as Coveitise in *The Romaunt of the Rose*. The anagrams again name the protagonists. Ll. 1106–35: HEN. BEWFOrT; ALIS FISA–AN A–UN(D)E.; IOAN. Dido and

---

[1] Her father's will, later in the same year, shows marked affection for his 'dear daughter Charlton' (Nicolas, *Test. Vetusta*, I, 129–34).

Æneas on horseback, a passage of verbal correspondences so neat that it has the effect of two six-line stanzas, gives the ladies' names only, woven back and forth: ll. 1198–209: Al–S ArU–(DE)., POWIS; –OAn STRA–Li–G. The poet's reflections on Dido's trustfulness and the Trojan's courtship name all three again: ll. 1254–75: HEn–Y; A–IS FISA–An. A–UN.; JOAN (ll. 1273–4), ST–AD–IN; ForFA–T. Ll. 1277–89, Æneas's ingratitude and inconstancy: FISA–An CHE––TO.; For–AIT. Ll. 1290–1308, Dido's prayer to Æneas: B–WForT; Alis FISAlAn, CHA––TO. Dido's plea that she is with child (ll. 1314–24), not in Virgil though found in Ovid, gives only the name ST–ADLIN. Æneas's flight and Dido's grief (ll. 1325–42) repeat all three names: B–AUForT; ARUn(D). FYSA–An; (J)OAn ST–A(DL)in. The conclusion (ll. 1352–67), a passage easily detachable, repeats the name of the dedicatee: MAR–AReT Be–ForT, BeASH; and gives FISAlAN to indicate finally the writer of the letter, Dido; hence too the white swan, the *albus olor* of Ovid, is relevant also as her mother's badge, the White Swan of Bohun.

The constant introduction of the name Stradling prevents the assumption that the Beaufort-Arundel anagrams are Chaucer's work. The illicit connexion may have begun in his lifetime, but Sir Edward Stradling flourished under Henry V and Henry VI, and Joan (FitzAlan) could hardly have been old enough to be his wife before Chaucer's death in 1400. Margaret Beauchamp of Bletsoe was almost exactly Roos's contemporary, being eleven in 1420–1.[1] Her first marriage with Oliver St. John brought her into the neighbourhood of the Danvers of Berkshire who were to intermarry with another branch of the Stradlings, founded by Sir Edward's second son, those of Dauntsey.[2] She may also have had some contact with the Cardinal's daughter, after her marriage in 1442 to the Cardinal's nephew. She appears again more intimately in the anagrams of the Legend next to be considered.

Legend V, 'Lucrece'. The anagrams run thus:

Ll. 1680–1710, Introduction; the Romans talk of their wives: IOHN B–WForT; AQuiTA–N; BEWS–A–P; RI–HAR. IOR.; ROAN; CISLy N––ILL.

Ll. 1711–44, they go to Rome and visit Lucrece: MA(R)GA–ET St IOHAn, ––WSHA–P; B–WForT, SO–––S–T; IorC.

Ll. 1756–78, Tarquin's plan against Lucrece: Ry(C)HAR– YOR.; (R)OUAn; BeWForT; AQuiTA–N.

Ll. 1779–1824, the rape; Tarquin reproached: RI–HA–R. IOR.; B–WForT; AQu–TA–N; SIS(L). NeVilL; MA–(G)A––T B–AUshA., SOMe–S–T.

---

[1] V.C.H., *Beds.*, III, 41.
[2] F. N. MacNamara, *Memorials of the Danvers Family*. 1895, pp. 229, 235.

Ll. 1825–60, Lucrece's grief and suicide: IOHAn BEAUFOrt, SOM--S-T; YOr., NEUILE; B-WFORT, BEAUSHAM; FOrFAYT FOrFAIT.

Ll. 1861–74, the grief in Rome: (B)-ASHA-; YO(R)K; NE--(L)LE.

Ll. 1875–85, conclusion on faithful women: ISMANIA S(C)AL(IS); FOrFA-T.

These names are easily identified: John Beaufort, Duke of Somerset, and his wife, Margaret, *née* Beauchamp; the Duke of York, Richard, and his wife, Cicely Neville; the places Rouen and Aquitaine; and finally Lady Scales, the recipient of the concluding eulogy of faithful women of 'stable herte, sadde and kynde'. The interpretation of the situation is more difficult, until one realizes the ingenuity of the poet's application. He has taken the classic *exemplum* of a woman choosing to commit suicide rather than bear a dishonoured name; he has changed the sex, and applied it to a political suicide within his circle—the only one, so far as I know.

To understand what he is doing, one must sketch the unhappy history of John Beaufort, third Duke of Somerset, '*homo animo ultra modum elatus et presumptuosus, sed in opere et effectu vanus et inefficax*'. His misfortunes began at the age of seventeen when he was taken prisoner at Baugé. The reason for the length of his captivity (1421–38) is not stated. At his release he was knighted, then made Captain of Cherbourg, and K.G. in 1439. About 1442, he married Margaret St. John, *née* Beauchamp, and their daughter, the 'Lady Margaret' of the future, was born. In 1443 he was appointed Lieutenant General of Guienne and Aquitaine,[1] but to his mortification the Duke of York had in 1440 been preferred over him as Regent of France. Somerset's expedition against Guienne failed, and his evil genius prompted him, in August 1443, to pillage the frontier of Brittany, though an allied province. He then 'threw himself upon the hospitality of the Duke of York at Rouen'.[2] Returning home as a failure, he died in May 1444, 'by his own hand' in chagrin at his disgrace, '*non volente ipsius petulancia atque superbia . . . injurias ferre pacienter*'.[3] The poet would know the true story, if not at first hand from the Duchess, then from her sister-in-law and his, Edmund's wife Eleanor. The anagrams suggest the rivalry between Somerset in Aquitaine, and York at Rouen, with perhaps a hint of a political rape, of which the historians are ignorant. The introduction of the wives' names (Margaret Beauchamp and Cicely Neville) does not probably hint at any feminine complications in the rivals' relations,

---

[1] G.E.C., XII, pt. i, p. 47, and note (h).
[2] Ramsay, *Lancaster and York*, II, 55.　　　[3] G.E.C., XII, i, p. 48, note (b).

but are there simply for identification. Margaret Beauchamp's mar-
,riage had been brief; and this suicide directly affected the fortunes of
the Duke's brother and heir, Edmund Beaufort of Mortain. There was
every reason why Roos should be interested in this happening.[1]

With the last Legend (IX), 'Hypermnestra' (Ypermystre), left unfinished, the anagrams indicate a different circle and situation. They
are pervasive throughout; no passage is without them.

Ll. 2562–75, Introduction: AnTho. WY(D)UI(LE); SCA.

Ll. 2576–99, character of Hypermnestra: AnTHO. (WY)D(V)Y.; – –ISA–
– –TH SCA–YS; BO(V)R(S)HIEr; TOT FOrFA–T.

Ll. 2600–22, the marriage-feast: AnTho. W(YD)–IL(E); ELy–ABeTh
BOWR–HIR; Tot FOrFAIT.

Ll. 2623–46, Egistus's charge to his daughter: ANTHON. W(Y)DUI.;
E–ISAB–TH BOu–SHi.; TOT FOrFA–T FOrFA–T.

Ll. 2647–61, her terror: AnTHO. W(Y)D–I.; SCAlis, BU–GHSHI.; FOr–AI–.

Ll. 2662–76, the opiate: AnTHO. WY––(IL); S–ALes.

Ll. 2677–710, her resolve: ANTHON.WIDU–Le; BOrSHI.; ISMANYA
S– –LyS; TOT FOrFA–T FOrFA–T.

Ll. 2711–23, the flight of Lyno; conclusion. ANTONe W–D––L;
S–AlIs; FOrFA–T.

The circle is as clear as the situation is puzzling. In 1461, Anthony
Wydville married the Scales heiress, Elisabeth, widow since August
1458 of Sir Henry Bourchier, second son of Lord Bourchier (later Earl
of Essex). Roos was to write lyrics in connection with this Wydville-
Scales union (see below, No. 101*a*, *b*). This Legend cannot, however, be
relegated to so late a date as 1461, since there exists a one-stanza summary of it, also with the Wydville anagram, in Shirley's hand in his
manuscript, Ashmole 59; Shirley died in 1456 (see below, No. 76*d*).
The Legend must then refer to some period before 1456, probably near
the Bourchier-Scales wedding, the date of which is not known. One
must infer some connexion of the young Anthony Wydville with this
event.

The reasons for the poet's choice of this melancholy and not very
auspicious tale are not easy to find on the surface. The fine description
of the marriage ceremonies, and the fact that from Lynceus and
Hypermnestra there sprang a race of heroes, especially Perseus and

---

[1] A later poem, 'On the Mutability of Worldly Changes' (in MS. Rawlinson
C.813; *Anglia*, XXXI, 325–6), refers to John Beaufort's death as caused by a bull
('the bull to gronde hym cast cruellye', st. 6). Roos's 'Lucrece' justifies the
chroniclers, Ingulph and Basin. Perhaps the Bull (Neville) was used symbolic-
ally and heraldically; but York's Neville marriage hardly justifies this suggestion.

Hercules, hardly seem to be enough warrant. The tale breaks off with the imprisonment of the heroine, and never reaches its happy ending. Possibly Roos had thought to compliment the lady's mother, the loyal Ismania, by a tale of wifely constancy and devotion:

> syn I am his wif,
> And hath my feyth, yit is it bet for me
> For to be ded in wifly honeste
> Than ben a traytour lyvynge in my shame.

There is, however, another possible explanation, the clue to which lies in the original line, not found in any source, on marriage of cousins, within the degrees:

> To Danao and Egistes also—
> Althogh so be that they were brethren two,
> *For thilke tyme was spared no lynage,*
> It lykede hem to make a maryage etc. (ll. 2600 ff.)

The Legend may well cover another piece of private family history, not now known; there may have been an attempt, prior to 1456, at a contract between Anthony Wydville and Elisabeth Scales, which came to nothing, the reason (or excuse) being the prohibited degrees. The Scales heiress was then married off to one of the Bourchiers. I can find no proof of this consanguinity. The Wydvilles were an undistinguished family before the rise of the future Lord Rivers by his foreign marriage to the semi-royal Jacquetta of Luxembourg; and their English alliances are not well known. Even the baronial family of Scales kept little record of the distaff side in the thirteenth to fourteenth centuries. One must remember, however, that godparents in common were also counted as a bar. Even without any barrier of consanguinity, it is possible that the Scales looked down on the upstart Wydvilles, and that for that reason only Lord Scales 'killed' an early project, as Egistes would have killed Lyno, and 'imprisoned' his daughter in more suitable 'bonds of wedlock'. The most suggestive fact here is that within a year, possibly even within eight months, of Lord Scales's murder (July 1460), his widowed daughter married Anthony Wydville[1]—as if an obstacle had been removed. There is an almost comic circumstance here. Scholars have remarked that the poet has inverted the fathers, and made Danao the sire of the son, and Egiste the father of the daughter. Yet otherwise he adheres closely in these lines to the Italian version of the *Heroides* made by Filippo ?Ceffi–.[2] I do not know whether Roos could be aware that

[1] G.E.C., *Complete Peerage*, XI, 506–7.

[2] S. B. Meech, *Chaucer and the Heroides*, *P.M.L.A.*, 1930, XLV, 110–11, 123–4.

Danao signifies 'drought' (the Danaides with their leaking water-pots are obviously part of a rain and river myth), and with typical medieval subtlety applied it, *per antifrasim*, to Lord Rivers. If this bold suggestion is judged to hold water, then an upward date for the Legend is obtained; Richard Wydville was created Baron and Lord de Rivers on May 9, 1448.[1]

It is by now apparent that not only the two Prologues but also all the extant nine Legends carry anagrams of Sir Richard Roos's usual subjects, early and late, and also of some unfamiliar themes, personal to Roos's circle (Arundel, Scales), or intimately connected with the Beauforts. No room is left in the 'Legends' for even a small substratum of Chaucer's writing, such as was found in the Prologues.

It is noteworthy that there is no fourteenth- or even early fifteenth-century manuscript of *The Legend of Good Women*. This is compatible with the mid-fifteenth-century allusions in the poem. The majority of the manuscripts are those fifteenth-century collections, most of which are connected with members of the Lancastrian Household. Three of the manuscripts contain also *La Belle Dame*, Lord Stanley's (Fairfax 16), one of the Wilmer manuscripts (R.3.19), and 'the Roos scrapbook' (Ff. 1.6) with one Legend only. Three others contain also *The Black Knight*, a Beaufort poem, i.e. the Scottish manuscript, Arch. Selden B.24; Bodley 638 (the Astley manuscript); and Pepys 2006, the Kyriel manuscript; and it has been seen that there is important Beaufort matter in the 'Legends'. Several manuscripts of *The Legend* contain also other poems which deal with the Fawcomberg-Strange affair, *The Compleynt of Mars*, *Anelida and Arcite*, and *The Temple of Glas*. An immediacy of interest and appeal becomes apparent in the manuscript collections of 1440 onwards. The owners are not only collecting Chaucer and Hoccleve; they are securing the latest productions, and are probably as well aware of their topical interest as, for example, Pope's friends were on *The Rape of the Lock*. MS. Pepys 2006 is particularly interesting. Sir Thomas Kyriel, as we have seen, had reason to be curious about poems which concerned the Beauforts; and the occurrence in the manuscript of *Mars* and of *Anelida* suggests an equal interest in his other fellow-soldier, Lord Fawcomberg. But it is noticeable that Pepys 2006 has nothing after the first few lines of the 'Reproach to Jason'. This may be due to loss or excision; but it may also mean that the later 'Legends' were never collected. Sir Thomas Kyriel was a prisoner from 1450 (Formigni) to c. 1453.

The solitary version of the Prologue that is in MS. Gg. 4.27 is even

---

[1] G.E.C., XI, 20.

more of a mystery than the F. Prologue of MS. Fairfax 16 and the remaining manuscripts. There are others of Roos's poems in the manuscript: 'The Birds' Praise of Love' (item 4) and *The Temple of Glas* (item 10) with the *Compleynt* addressed to Margaret Vernon that is lacking in all other manuscripts of *The Temple* except one of Shirley's (see No. 78). *The Legend* is item 8. I have said above that I cannot agree with the idea that the manuscript was originally made for Jacqueline of Hainault, but that I think it may have had some connexion with Duke Humphrey. The G. Prologue is stronger than the F. in Plesaunce anagrams and colouring; on the other hand, the presence even in G. of anagrams for Margaret of Anjou and for Margaret Vernon, shows that the manuscript was added to after Humphrey's death in 1447. Is it possible that it came later into Sir Richard's own hands, or is at most at only one remove from him?

If then all the existing manuscripts of *The Legend* give us Chaucer re-written by Roos, what happened to Chaucer's own version? I have already suggested that there may have been only one copy. Although it is not certain now that the poem was commanded by Richard's queen, the prologue at least was probably meant for Richard, as the political and moral counsels show. So personal a royal poem would be in royal hands only; from the royal books it could come into Gloucester's possession, and so into Roos's hands for reworking. There can be little doubt that Roos is here deliberately imitating Chaucer far more closely than he usually does, especially in the use of final -e. His success is proved by the long sleep of critical suspicion, in spite of a general uneasy feeling that Chaucer did not seem to be here his characteristic self. Critical lack of interest has found it easy to attribute growing creative tedium to Chaucer, to account for the dropping of the annual scheme. This desire to imitate, and the necessity of writing on so many diverse subjects, and sets of people unfamiliar hitherto in Roos's poems, may account for what can be felt as some strain and difficulty in the anagrams, and occasional (but only occasional) unease in the narrative. Plesaunce anagrams drip fluently from Roos's pen; here careful manipulation is called for, and that in a metrical form still rare in him, the heroic couplet.

If we accept Roos as the author of *The Legend* as we have it, we find that a new light is shed back on those earlier poems, *The Flour of Curtesye* or the *New Year's Gift*, which about 1434-8 had played with the names of Ladies of the *Ballade*, turning them into the circle of Plesaunce. Just so *The Black Knight* had enumerated the men unhappy in love. In 1445, these men and women were still foremost in Roos's conception of the pilgrim of love, as his 'Epistle in prose' shows (see

No. 69). About the same period, the *Ballade of Good Counsel* (No. 75), directed against Fawcomberg, celebrates the 'trewe affeccioun' of Alceste, the 'virginal clennes' of Policene. Later still, in *The Assembly*, he will hark back to Plesaunce memories, adorning the walls with Phillis, Cleopatra, and Thisbe; and in the basic form of *The Court of Love* (1453-4) he will recall in one stanza his own creations Dido and Anelida (ll. 231-4), fair images in the bright windows of Love's temple (see below, No. 103).

Much of Roos's verse in *The Legend* is in his recognizable style, not only in details of rhyme and (once) of signature (1743), but of tone and handling. The antagonism between the subject and the poet's temperament that critics have felt of Chaucer does not apply to Roos. This is his proper *terrain*, this devout praise of the injured woman, this scorn of the perjured lover. Because Roos has so little need to force himself, passages in the F. Prologue are among his best writing; such is the miniature allegory which might be another poem for his myth of Pity:

> Al founde they Daunger for a tyme a lord,
> Yet Pitee, thurgh his stronge gentil myghte
> Forgaf, and made Mercy passen Ryght,
> Thurgh innocence and ruled Curtesye. (ll. 160-3)

or the praise of the Flower:

> She is the clernesse and the verray lyght
> That in this derke world me wynt and ledeth.
> The hert in-with my sorwfull brest yow dredeth
> And loveth so sore that ye ben verrayly
> The maistresse of my wit, and nothing I.
> My word, my werk ys knyt so in youre bond
> That, as an harpe obeieth to the hond
> And maketh it soune after his fyngerynge,
> Ryght so mowe ye oute of myn herte bringe
> Swich vois, ryght as yow lyst, to laughe or pleyne.
> Be ye my gide and lady sovereyne!
> As to myn erthly god to yow I calle,
> Bothe in this werk and in my sorwes alle. (ll. 84-96)

This may be largely translation from the *Filostrato*, and echoed from the French; but Roos makes a new and lovely thing here out of his attachment to his two ideal women, Elisabeth Beaumont and Ismania Scales. And the lines on his heart responsive as a harp show him turning to love that susceptibility to music which he confesses in praising the skill of the queen's harper (*Chance of the Dice*, st. 48). How much of the themes of the Flower and the Leaf, the May morning, and the daisy worship, can now be credited to Chaucer as originator, it is difficult to say. My own impression is, little if any part. I am not even sure that Chaucer it was who first invoked Alceste in the Prologue, when one sees that her name is itself a very fair anagram of Scales; his two undoubted references to her couple her with Penelope as if she were to be merely one of the 'martyrs', with a straightforward tale:

> . . . gladlier I wol write, yif yow leste,
> Penelopeës trouthe and good Alceste. (*T. and C.*, V, 1777–8)

As appendages to this reading of *The Legend of Good Women*, three poems fall to be considered here, confusing, and as poetry almost valueless, yet of great interest in that their anagrams largely confirm the allusions found in the Legends.

No 76*b*. *Dido's Lament*, a poem subscribed 'Finis Thomas Pridioxe' in MS. Add. 15233, fol. 47–47 v. It is John Redford's own volume, with his *Wit and Science*, and with organ-music by himself and others.

> *Incipit.* Behowlde of pensyfnes the pycture here in place.
> *Explicit.* bytrayne of hym whom I thought myne.

A poem of five six-line stanzas, the closing couplet in each being octosyllabic. The speaker is Dido. It is an undistinguished treatment of the twelve-syllable line, with an occasional fourteener in the third line. The anagram is the most interesting feature: st. 1, B(E)–FOrT; stt. 1–3, IOAn; A–IS; stt. 2–5, AR–N(DE)–; stt. 4–5, HEnRY B–WFOrT; diffused ST–AD.; TOT FOrFAIT. Stanza 5 begins with three initial O's; the initials of the ensuing words are r, c, d; these with one caesural initial give cArd. and are in the same stanza as the Cardinal's Christian name.

As the poem stands, it sounds like a typical 'drab' production; and I believe that Pridioxe, to suit the Tudor liking for strong alliteration, and possibly to fit the accompanying tune, inflated into the popular twelve-syllable lines a poem originally in decasyllables and octosyllables; this by the simple process of inserting alliterating epithets and padding phrases. The line thus blown out in one or other hemistich does not necessarily change the place of its caesura. Thus st. 5, with excrescences pruned away, provides the same letters for the anagram, with one unimportant exception; it even keeps, because of the alliteration, the three letters hidden after the exclamatory anaphora, thus:

> O ruthlesse hartes, your owne with spite to spill,
> O crewell men, how can you worke such ill.
> O deepe dispaier, ring out my endes knill.
> welcome, sweete death, my grave yt is my will

The words omitted are, l. 1, 'rockie'; l. 2, 'curssed'; l. 3, dolfull, carefull';

and l. 4, 'to me' (twice). It becomes a better poem; it also sounds much more like Roos.

Another poem with Dido as speaker, and again with the same anagrams as in 'The Legend of Dido', combines them (Beaufort, Alis Arundel) with those of Fawcomberg, and the two ill-treated ladies Lady Strange and Maud Stanhope.

No. 76c. *The Letter of Dydo.*

> *Incipit.* Folke discomforted | bere heuy countenaunce
> *Explicit.* you in any thyng | y^t ye haue done for loue.

The poem is found only in Pynson's blackletter edition (1526) of Chaucer, a mixed volume which also contains *La Belle Dame sans Merci* (as 'translate . . . by Geffray Chaucer'). No manuscript is recorded (see Hammond, *Chaucer Bibliography*, pp. 114, 436). It consists of 'the prologue of the translatour', nine stanzas in rhyme royal; then of the Letter to Eneas, in 242 lines of rough heroic couplets; and finally of 'Lenuoy of the translatour' in two stanzas of rhyme royal. There is no ascription. The poet announces himself as an unlucky lover, moved to fury by the perfidy of Eneas. He invokes Fame and the Muses, the Ladies Worthy, and finally Celeno (i.e. Mercury, represented by STANHOPE) to aid his lack of skill in translating French. In the ninth stanza he summarizes the story of Dido, down to the writing of her letter. His Envoy warns 'good ladyes whiche be of tender age' against deceitful lovers.

The anagrams run as follows:

Prologue, st. 1, some dissemble their grief: FAW–O–BerG.

St. 2, 'playnnesse is best': COB–AM; BEWsh–M.

St. 3, the unlucky poet pities Dido and hates Eneas: H(En). B–WForT; A–vn(D).

St. 4, he invokes Fame against Eneas: FAW–OMB.; A–vn–E–.

St. 5, the Muses and Juno cannot help: STAN(H)O.; ForFAIT ForF–JT.

St. 6, the Ladies Niobe, Myrra, Byblis, Medea and Lucrece cannot aid, and Venus, mother of Eneas, will not: YSMa(Ni). S(C)–(L)E–; (B)–W(M)ONT.

St. 7, he appeals to Celeno for help: –TANHOP; ForFAYt.

St. 8, readers must bear with his difficulty with French: STAN––P; whITTIn.

St. 9, after the fall of Troy, Eneas, at Carthage, breaks faith with Dido: ArV–(DE)–; BEWF––T.

The letter, ll. 1–12, Dido's swan-song: FAWC–M.; HeNRY B–WForT.

Ll. 13–32, Eneas's inconstancy in leaving Carthage: STAN–OPE; ST–ANG(E), COB–A–.

Ll. 33–54, Eneas as ruler of Italy: STAnHOP; KnOKYN, ST–ANG(E) COBHAM; AlIAn.

Ll. 55–78, appeal to Cupid and Venus: AlIS. A–Vn–(E)L; –A(V)D STAnHOP; COBHAm; ForFAIT.

Ll. 79–100, the dangers of the sea: BeWForT; –AWCO–B; STANHOP; ST–ANG(E).

Ll. 101–22, plea to Eneas to tarry: H(E). BeWForT; FAWCOMB.; ST–AnG–; TOT ForFAYT.

Ll. 123–46, if he is wrecked, her ghost will remind him of his falsity: STAnH.; ST–AN.; –OBHA–; ArV–D(E)–; BeWF––T; FAW––MBe.

Ll. 147–68, he should consider the safety of his son and his followers: ST–AnG–; STAnH.; FAW––M.; –OBHAM.

Ll. 169–85, Divine displeasure on Eneas: STAn–OP; –AW–OMB.; A––ND––.

Ll. 186–93, Dido muses on Eneas: STrAn––; HeN–Y.

Ll. 194–217, she again addresses him: BeA–ForT; A––N–EL; STAnHOP; FAW–O–Be; AlLYAn. COB.; For–AIT.

Ll. 218–30, the fatal sword: STrAn.; –TAnHO., WIL.; For––IT; IsMe–I.

Ll. 231–42, Dido appeals to her sister: A–Vn(DE)–; ST–AnG(E); STAnHO.; FAWCO.; FO––AIT.

Lenuoy. YS–AnY SCA–(E)S, WhA––SBorOU.; TOT For–AYT.

It is clear that, whereas the 'Legend of Dido' confined itself to the Beaufort-Arundel story, this poem makes one *exemplum* cover two villains and three deceived ladies; but there is no trace of Joan Stradling in this version. The Envoy denotes the dedication to Lady Scales.

As in *La Belle Dame*, the translator adds original stanzas at beginning and end of the translated epistle. Unlike *La Belle Dame* is the marked contrast in versification and style between the stanzas and the heroic couplet. The Prologue is reminiscent of Roos at every turn: in the appeal to the Muses (cf. *How a Lover*, *The Court of Love*); to the Good Ladies, who appear in many poems of the Plesaunce period; and to Celeno, the Cilenius-Mercury of *The Compleynt of Mars*; in the deprecation of his work; and in such a phrase as 'To purpose, lo' with its characteristic interpolation of 'lo'. One difference from convention is that his shaking hand shakes, not for nervousness, but in rage against the perfidious Eneas.

There is, however, one puzzling stanza, with the assertion,

> To translate frenche, I am nat redyest
> No marueyle is | sithe I was neuer yet
> In those parties | where I might lāgage gete.

We know that Roos was in France at Gisors in 1436, and that the Cobham-Knokyn marriage did not take place till 1439, the Stanhope-Willoughby one (referred to once in these anagrams) probably later still. The plea for lenient judgment of the translation is apparently a mis-statement. Perhaps Roos was drawing a red herring across his trail for the Cardinal's suspicions. Or he may be concealing that, as in the Legend, the source for the Epistles is the Italian version of the *Heroides* by Filippo ?Ceffi; for French should one read Italian? Perhaps the easiest explanation is that he is making use of earlier material, as in the introduction to *The Chance of the Dice*.

The *Letter of Dydo* has indeed a stiff and wooden effect, like other translations which I have for that reason assumed to be early attempts, 'Cassamus roos', and *The Eye and the Heart*. This may, however, be due to experimenting (for nearly 250 lines) in the heroic couplet with its exacting 'quick return' of rhyme. There is a great gulf between this *Letter* and the skilful, musical rhymed couplets of *The Legend*, written after Roos had immersed himself more deeply in Chaucer's living waters. The lines common to both in substance emphasize this, e.g. the opening of the Letter, and the conclusion of the Legend:

> Ryght as ye swan whan her dethe is nye
> Swetely dothe syng her fatall desteny
> Lykewise I Dido | for all my true loue
> Whiche by no prayer | can you remoue (etc.)
>
> (*Letter*, 1-16)

> Ryght so, quod she, as that the white swan
> Ayens his deth begynnyth for to synge,
> Right so to yow make I my compleynynge.
> Not that I trowe to geten yow ageyn,
> For wel I wot that it is al in veyn (etc.)
>
> (*Legend*, 1355-65)

The *Letter* may well be an experiment in a yet untried verse-form, but its anagrams show that it must follow in time Roos's early experience in France. A downward date is easier to determine, 1445; there is no reference to Barbelina, the German waiting-woman. The dedication to Lady Strange is characteristic of the early to mid 1440s. The Beaufort allusions in 'Dido' have thus been twice repeated in poems outside *The Legend*. A third poem confirms the anagrams of nine ladies.

No. 76*d*. *þe Cronycle made by Chaucier*, so called by Shirley in his manuscript, Ashmole 59 (the sole occurrence), with the misleading caption: 'Here nowe folowe þe names of þe nyene worshipfullest Ladyes þt in alle cronycles, and storyal bokes haue beo founden of trouþe of constaunce and vertuous or reproch[les] womanhode. by Chaucier'.

> *Incipit.* Grete Rayson Cleopatre is þy Kyndnesse
> Be putte in mynde | and also þyne hyeness
> *Explicit.* And lyche seemewes | transfourmed him and þee.

The poem was printed by Furnivall in 1871 for the Chaucer Society, *Odd Texts of Minor Poems*, Ser. 1, xxiii, App. pp. vi–viii. It consists of nine eight-line stanzas (aabbccdd), and celebrates Cleopatre, Adryane, Dydo, Lucresse, Philles, Thesbe, Isiphyle, Ypermistra, and nominally Alceste, actually Alcyone.

Shirley's attribution to Chaucer has been rejected by all scholars from Ten Brink downwards (Skeat suggesting Shirley himself as the author) because of the commonplace lines, and the 'atrocious rhymes'. Brusendorff, in pointing these out (p. 236), remarked on Shirley's great age when writing this unreliable manuscript (he died in 1456), and suggested that the poem was 'a late anonymous *rifacimento* of the *Legend*'. *Rifacimento* it probably is, but not quite in Brusendorff's meaning. Is this another instance of Roos's re-working of his material? In its seventy-two lines the routh:trouth rhyme occurs twice; one of the 'atrocious rhymes' ('prysoun:bycome', ll. 11–12) is really assonance such as Roos uses every now and then. Finally, there are the anagrams with the 'devise', agreeing in the main with those of the 'Legends'. Against Roos's authorship is, apparently, the Alceste-Alcyone confusion in the last stanza; also the heavy dullness of the verses, explicable, however, if they were produced to order as a kind of epitome, or quasi-guide to the long poem.

St. 1, Cleopatre: (CO)B–A–; AnTIG.; –AWT(RA)–(ER)S.

St. 2, Adryane: MA. –TAnH.; FAW––MB.

St. 3, Dydo: A–IS ARVn(DE)–; ForF––T.

St. 4, Lucresse: BeWForT; (R)I(C)HA––; ForF––T.

St. 5, Philles: (P)HE.; SCA–––.

St. 6, Thesbe: FAW–O–B.; BA–BEl.

St. 7, Isiphyle: FAWCO.; –(LIS)A––Th (CO)––A(M); IaQueTT.

St. 8, Ypermistra: ANTHO.WY(D)--LE; FOrFA–T.
St. 9, 'Alceste' (Alcyone): S–(Al)–S, whA------OVH.

The order is not that of *The Legend*, though Cleopatra still holds pride of place, and Alceste-Alcyone, taking priority over Philomene and Medea, is evidently intended as the conclusion. Any idea that the poem is an early attempt at short biographies of the Ladies so often used as *exempla* in the Plesaunce poems, is ruled out by the appearance in the anagrams of Barbelina (st. 6), and of Anthony Wydville. The anagrams are basically the same as in the longer accounts of *The Legend*, and corroborate those findings. Clear and striking is the identification of Dido as Alice Arundel; and also of Anthony Wydville in the Hypermnestra stanza (8). 'Cleopatre' holds also the name Mawtravers of Eleanor Cobham's maternal grandmother (and Roos's), found in the seafight in the 'Legend'. There are some interesting variations, as of 'Richard' in st. 4, more often called York in the 'Legend of Lucrece'. The chief differences are in 'Thesbe' (st. 6) and 'Isiphyle' (7); Barbelina had reared her head in the Legend of Thisbe; here she ousts Maud Stanhope altogether; in st. 7 here Fawcomberg is combined with Elisabeth Cobham, Lady Strange, whereas in the Legend of Hypsipyle a parallelism was maintained between Lady Beaumont and Lady Strange.

Finally, what is to be made of the curious combination, in a stanza yielding the Scales anagram, of the name of Alceste with the story of Alcyone? It goes down to the final bird-change, which Chaucer omits with apparent indifference from his version in *The Book of the Duchess*. If it were not for the anagram, and for one other shred of evidence, one might assume that this confusion cut the *Cronycle* apart from the writing of the Prologue to *The Legend*. That shred is a line in the Prologue, identical in both forms: 'I, your Alceste, whilom quene of Trace' (F. 432; Gg. 422). Skeat commented that Admetus was not king of Thrace (*sic*) but of Pherae in Thessaly; recent editors (Pollard, Robinson) ignore the mistake. Yet this is vestigial in the life-history of the poem, showing that the Alceste-Alcyone confusion is deep-seated. For Ceyx (Seys) was king of Trachis in Thessaly, the place-name that survived as Trace in this line. The *Cronycle* should then correspond to a form of *The Legend* in which the nine heroines were known by their anagrams but the Alceste-Alcyone confusion was embedded in the memory of the writer. By all the signs, even in a dull poem, that writer should be Roos; but he may not have added the last stanza (its anagram lacks his 'devise'); or Shirley may have fallen into some error. Yet mere scribal error seems to be ruled out by the rhyme Alceste: byheste.

This seems to be a major difficulty; but in spite of it, and of some minor ones in these three poems, the similarity of their anagrams with those of *The Legend* cannot be mere accident. It provides corroborative evidence, if not full confirmation, of the identity of the Ladies of the Legends.

As a parallel to the poems of family history embodied in *The Legend*, one may here consider a marriage poem of some historical interest.

No. 77. *A Gentlewoman's Lament:* a poem of seven stanzas of eight octosyllabic lines (ababbcbc).

> *Incipit.* Allas! I wooful creature,
>   Lyving betweene hope and dreed
> *Explicit.* To haue hooly my remembraunce
>   On his persone, so mychil I thynk.

The poem is found in three manuscripts: Trin. Coll., Camb., R.3.20, pp. 152-4; Harleian 2251, fol. 250 v. and 251 v.; Add. 29729, fol. 160-1. In this last it is attributed to Lydgate ('made by Lydgate'); it has been accepted as his and is printed by MacCracken, *Minor Poems,* pp. 418-20. I suggest it as Roos's on the evidence of phraseology and rhythm, and more especially of the anagrams and the 'devise'.

The 'gentilwomman whiche loued a man of gret estate' (MS., R.3.20) laments her long and secret devotion to her 'chosen knyght', dating from childhood, when they played together 'And gaderd flowres in þe meede'; even then, Love gave her 'A knotte in hert of remembraunce'.

The anagram is unusually plain, since each name is sufficiently indicated in the line-initials of one stanza, with a few supporting letters from the caesural initials, and from other stanzas: st. 1, AlIAn. HOL–AnD; stt. 2–3, An. STAFForD; 4, HAN–For–.; 5, For–AIT; 3–5, LOWIS IOHAN; 6, AnN MONTAGEW; 7, SA–ISB––Y; WIMBI–H; and, diffused, IAY TOT ForFAIT.

A good deal of family history underlies this chain of names. Anne Montague, daughter of John Montague, sixth Earl of Salisbury, and of Maud Francis, married three times: first, Sir Richard Hankford, who died in 1430/1; next, Sir Lewis John of Horndon, who died in 1442; and thirdly, John Holland, Duke of Exeter, who had become a widower in 1439. Anne and the duke must have been about the same age, he (born in 1395) probably a little the elder. The exact date of their marriage is not known; he died in 1447, she ten years later, and they were buried in St. Katherine's in the Tower. Anne's brother, Thomas Montague, seventh Earl of Salisbury, married first Eleanor Holland, third daughter of the second Earl of Kent; on her death he married before 1424 the child Alice Chaucer, already widow of Sir John Phelip, uncle of Roos's 'Lady Bounte'; on Montague's death, Alice married in 1430 William de la Pole, Earl of Suffolk. Eleanor Holland had thus been a young sister-in-law of Anne Montague; she was also a cousin of John Holland, and as such she may well have been a confidante of Anne, to be remembered here. John Holland's first wife (1427) had been Anne Stafford, daughter of Anne of Woodstock, probably also a friend of Anne Montague's girlhood.

It seems probable that this poem of love-longing was written for Anne Montague, before her wedding (after 1442) to the Duke of Exeter; it contains the names of her former husbands, of her father, of her former sister-in-law, and finally of the duke's first wife, Anne Stafford, this last perhaps a delicate hint of the direction of her thoughts. It is a distinguished company drawn from the semi-royal families descended from John of Gaunt, Thomas of Woodstock, and the Fair Maid of Kent. They are not Sir Richard Roos's usual associates, but he has affiliations with them, through his mother's family, through 'Lady Bounte', and through his old friend, Anne of Woodstock; and Thomas Montague it was who avenged Baugé, which to Roos had been a family as well as a national disaster. With all this in the background, and the suitability of the dates, one may hope that Sir Richard is doing a thing rare in this century, recording for us one of those private emotions which elude the annalist; and that Anne Montague in middle age was to know a few years of happiness with her 'chosen knyght', chosen from her 'tendre youþe'. Perhaps Roos's intention was to help on the marriage, as he had others:

> Wolde God the sooþe þat he knewe,
> Howe offt I sighe for his saake.

The occurrence of the poem in MS. R.3.20, where are some French lyrics said to be by Sir Othes de Holande, suggests that parts at least of that manuscript came from a Holland source.

III. MARGARET VERNON AND HER FAMILY

Just as Sir Richard Roos turned from writing poems for Gloucester's Plesaunce to celebrating his sister-in-law's wooing, so now, about 1450, he had occasion to turn from poems for the queen and court, and to advance his own wooing of his future wife, Margaret, whose name has already been found casually in anagrams. Two longish poems are involved, one translation, and a few lyrics and scraps. The tone is somewhat different from that of the earlier courtship. Roos is now a man of

A A

about forty, courting a young widow, as did Spenser his Elizabeth Boyle. This is not young love, and one may even suspect a Mirabel-Millamant wooing, with wilfulness and delays and 'perturbaunce'. Margaret Vernon, one of a family of at least half a dozen brothers and sisters, may well have been different in disposition and manners from the only child and heiress, Elisabeth Phelip. This is no serene and remote Lady Bounte, but a woman who, together with all the inevitable ideal qualities, is of a jesting humour, and keeps her lover on tenterhooks, 'Myn pley, myn penauns most Iocounde'. Certainly this new attraction can set the poet's emotions in a vertiginous whirl, even to incoherence, and can (again as with Spenser) sharpen his eye for natural beauty, for the 'hony-souklys in the mede' or for Phebus 'cler shynynge in his spere'. The *Compleynt*, with its rush of feeling and words, shows the fountain, sealed for some years, again flowing freely. It is a personal poem, explicitly to his daisy, his Margaret.

No. 78. *Compleynt:* a poem of 628 lines of rough and rapid octosyllabic couplets.

> *Incipit.* Allas for thought & inward peyne
> That myn herte so constreyne.
> *Explicit.* þis is al and some, my lady dere,
> And I youre man frome yere to yere.

The *Compleynt* is found as a continuation of *The Temple of Glas* in the only two manuscripts which have been fully adapted to make of that poem a 'Margaret' poem, i.e. MSS. Add. 16165 (S), and Camb. Univ. Lib. Gg. 4.27 (G) (see next poem). A passage of it (ll. 439–505 inclusive) is also to be found in one leaf of MS. Sloane 1212 (fol. 4). Shirley's manuscript (S) is more complete than G, since a leaf has been cut out of G, part of the description of the lady (ll. 255–330); G also lacks the conclusion (ll. 563–628). S however lacks twenty lines (ll. 157–76), probably through picking up from the wrong rhyme word. Shirley's text exhibits some shocking misreadings (e.g. ll. 362, 512). But it also shows signs of its 'copy' having been amended and polished; thus, in ll. 411–13, a rhyme on 'if' is got rid of by changes in the sentence structure and vocabulary, and one clumsy couplet (ll. 465–6) is greatly improved. In this couplet, Sloane 1212 is nearer G, though with a minute variant, such as is found some half a dozen times in the Sloane leaf. This *Compleynt* is openly a daisy and Margaret poem, and is a very personal love letter. Although tacked on to a poem assigned to Lydgate, these 'worthless rhymes' have never been foisted on him. I suggest that the poem is by Sir Richard Roos, and is a personal offering to Margaret

Longueville, *née* Vernon, recalling an actual parting. It is not 'signed'; there is no need for a code signature in a letter dashed off helter-skelter on the very day after the parting. Nor has the poet time to elaborate many anagrams, but he contrives to insinuate some few, brief but sufficient, in the introduction, in the description of the lady, and at the end of the praise of the daisy: MAR–A–ET LON–VI., VERNO. (ll. 4–27); IAI TOT FOrFAIT FOrFAIT (ll. 30–47); MA–A––T LON––VIL, VerNON, ISMANIA SCAlIS WHAlISBO–O–H (ll. 329–61); and again MArGArET V–RNON, ISMAnIA S–A–IS WHA–YSBOrO (ll. 395–445). This linking of Margaret Longueville with Lady Scales, Roos's trusted friend, might be a natural result of their association at the queen's court; Roos might well be asking Lady Scales's interest for his lady. There may be yet another reason, some slight tie of kinship between the two. Ismania's father, Thomas Whalesborough, had legal dealings in 1456/7 over a Devonshire manor, which was to remain to Elizabeth, who had been wife to Edmund Whalesborough, and now was wife to Thomas Vernon.[1] This was probably Margaret Vernon's uncle, father of the Mary Vernon mentioned in Sir Richard's will.

The lover describes his acute distress at parting on the last day of March from his lady. He longs to do her service, 'By sum offys or sum empryse' (l. 160), but she will lay no commands on him, she has 'no deynte' of his devotion. He begs her to have pity, and recalls his misery at parting, increased by the heartless shining of the sun and the perversely fine weather of the variable month of March. He describes the lady's virtues, offset by her hardness of heart. He reproaches Fortune in a rhetorical description of her mutability (ll. 362–93), and begs that his daisy, 'The wheche is callyd margaret', may indeed exemplify its name, 'petyt confort' and cure his wounds; he describes the flower in its idyllic surroundings (ll. 416–37). Again recalling his parting

> in march now late
> Whan I tok leue now at the ȝate, (ll. 445–6)

he begs Fortune for better luck in April. He appeals again to the lady to believe in him, and in a second rhetorical passage describes her complementary value to him (ll. 456–515):

> Myn Ioye, myn helthe & ek myn wo,
> Myn fulle trust & myn grevaunce.

Between these contraries, he has been in a continual fever ever since the

---

[1] 'Feet of Fines (iv)', ed. E. Green, *Somersetshire Record Soc.*, 1906, XXII, 203.

end of March; on that same day he wrote a ballad and this *Compleynt*. Deprecating what is amiss in it, he begs her to look at it, even if she then tears it up.

The poem bears many marks of Roos's manner and style. The 'routh: trouth' rhyme occurs four times, the 'goodlihede': woman-hede' rhyme five times. In general roughness and rapidity, and in its shift into an occasional decasyllabic line (ll. 335-6), it compares with *How a Lover*. The medical daisy-name, *petyt confort*, is a variant of the similar *petit consould*, found not in *How a Lover*, but in one of its analogues, *La Louenge et Beauté des Dames*. The description of the lady has close parallels with that in *The Flour of Curtesye*; Helen and Polixene are invoked in passing (l. 268), and bounty and beauty fleetingly appear again in the virtues of this Margaret (ll. 323-4). Like the Flower, she is 'Dotous of tungis that ben large' (l. 343; cf. 'Dredful also of tonges that ben large', *The Flour*, l. 157); like the Flower, she is 'As deth hatynge dyshoneste' (l. 347; cf. *The Flour*, ll. 160-1). An even more significant parallel with *The Romaunt of the Rose* has already been pointed out (see above, p. 256). As in *Reson and Sensuallyte*, Fortune's cask, of 'sharpe lycour so fel & egre', is introduced; and the ever-burning stone, Albiston, which gives light to Venus's oratory, is described (ll. 537-62) with more knowledge and detail (perhaps gained from Isidore of Seville) than in the reference to the horse of the Maiden's chessman king (*Reson*, etc., ll. 6847-51).

On the assumption that Roos is writing the poem to the Margaret whom he married between September 1450 and December 1452 (see above, p. 72), one may be able to get closer to the date from the astronomical observations. In this informal complaint, the elegant opening giving the season is lacking. But at l. 247, the poet hazards a guess that the gaiety of the sun on March 31 was due to the prospect of meeting Dyane, 'His owene lady & his quene', and being with her all night and even all the next day till eve. Near the equinoxes, the hour of sunset and the hour of a new moon setting can approximate closely; this must then have been a year when there was a new moon near March 31. The lover, parting at the gate, is more likely to have observed the real new moon than the new moon of the erroneous calendar. In March 1449, the real new moon was on March 24, the calendar new moon on March 27; either would apply here. So late a date in March for the new moon, whether real or calendar, does not recur for the next three years. March 1449 seems to be indicated as the year of the poem.

The *Compleynt's* only editor, Schick,[1] first perused it 'with many a

[1] *Lydgate's Temple of Glas*, E.E.T.S., Extra ser., 60, 1891, App. I.

deeply-heaved sigh', and apologized for publishing a poem 'so thoroughly stupid'. A polished poem it certainly is not, any more than *How a Lover*, but, like that early poem, it is full of felicities in the rough and of touches of nature, some of them none the worse for being reminiscent of *Le Roman de la Rose*; such is the lover's tongue-tied state before his lady:

> For al myn olde peyntede style
> Was clene a-gon & out of mynde:
> For I ne coude a word not fynde
> To speke to ȝow, I was so dul; . . .
> Whan I am come to ȝoure presence
> Farwel, speche & eloquence;
> A tunge I haue, but wordys none,
> But stonde mut as a stone
>   (ll. 38–41, 47–50; cf. *The Romaunt*, ll. 2523–36).

The pathetic fallacy makes an early appearance here in our poetry, when the poet chides the sun for daring to be cheerful instead of sympathetically dull, and March, which so easily can snow and hail, for being so contrarious. Twice he indulges in rhetorical set-pieces, first to illustrate Fortune's variable countenance:

> Now blak as ben the skyis donne;
> Now as the rose, frosch & newe,
> Now as the netyl row of hewe (ll. 372–4).

Further on, he imitates the definitions of love of Guillaume de Lorris (himself copying Alain de Lille) in what Schick calls an 'interminable litany of antitheses and oxymora'. Granted that Roos cannot excel Sir Walter Raleigh at his highest when adapting the same passage:

> Now what is Loue, I praie thee tell,
> It is that fountaine and that well,
> Where pleasure and repentance dwell,

yet he can at least recall him to our minds:

> Myn dredful pes, myn glade fyght,
> Myn quiete & myn busy werre,
> Myn pensyfhed bothe nygh & ferre,
> Myn softe salve, myn sharpe wounde,
> Myn pley, myn penauns most Iocounde. (ll. 508–12)

The lover's conceit of his burning heart, fired by Cupid's brand (ll. 554–61), is not surprising in one who had seen René d'Anjou's emblems (cf. *To My Soverain Lady*, ll. 99–100); and his final plea to the lady to tear up his poem if she will, but to tear it herself, with her 'owen handes sofft', is in the line of loverly exaggeration and poetic wit that runs from Philostratus to Ben Jonson:

> For youre touche, I dare wel seyne,
> Wel þe lasse shal ben his peyne.

For one quality here Roos needs no apologist, and that is the fresh-ness and charm of his nature description. He unerringly picks out the only pastoral lines in Chaucer's poetry,

> And pipes made of grene corn,
> As han thise lytel herde-gromes
> That kepen bestis in the bromes.
> *(Hous of Fame*, ll. 1224–6)

Just as Spenser will orchestrate that theme in his February *Eclogue*, so does Roos here; he bridges the gap of time between the two great poets, and writes the first 'pastourelle' passage in English poetry, in praise of his daisy:

> Where as it doth so fayre sprede,
> A-geyn the sunne in euery mede,
> On bankys hy a-mong the bromys,
> Wher as these lytylle herdegromys
> Floutyn al the longe day,
> Bothe in aprylle & in may,
> In here smale recorderys,
> In floutys & in rede sperys,
> Aboute this flour, til it be nyght;
> It makyth hem so glad & lyght,
> The grete beute to be-holde
> Of this flour & sone onfolde
> Hyre goodly fayre white levis,
> Swettere than in 3ynge grevis
> Is cheuyrfoyl or hawethorn,
> Whan plente with hire fulle horn
> Hyre sote baume doth out-shede
> On hony-souklys in the mede,
> Fletynge ful of sugre newe;
> Yit is ther non so frosch of hewe
> Nor half so fayr vn-to myn ye,
> As is the lusty dayesye,
> Whos frosche beute nygh me sleth. (ll. 415–37)

These are neither stupid nor worthless rhymes. In the pleading with the lady, the manner of expression may be repetitive of Roos's earlier work, but the stamp of sincerity and actuality is on these hurried accents, these urgent tones:

> [I] seye: 'allas what may this be?'
> Astonyd so in al myn blod,

> That I to symple—& ʒe to good—
> For ʒoure worthy excellence,
> That myn kendenesse yow doth offence, . . .
> What have I gilt, allas, allas!
> Othyr offendyt, in ony cas,
> ʒoure womanhed or ʒoure heyghnesse,
> Ageyn ʒoure trouthe & gentillesse. (ll. 108-18)

And the last lines are of appealing simplicity:

> And euer of mercy I you prey,
> Whedir þat I lyf or deye.
> þis is al and some, my lady dere,
> And I youre man frome yere to yere.

This Benedick, who has resisted love and marriage for nearly a decade, has yielded in middle age with the abandonment of one who may even have been surprised and delighted by the completeness of his surrender.

No. 79. *The Temple of Glas:* a narrative poem, a love-allegory and dream of 1403 lines with long passages of decasyllabic couplets, interspersed with still longer passages of rhyme royal.

> *Incipit.* For thouʒt, constreint, and greuous heuines,
> For pensifhede, and for heiʒ distres.
> *Explicit.* I mene þat benygne & goodli of face,
> Nou go þi way, & put þe in hir grace.

Two manuscripts (G and S) omit ll. 1380-1403, and end on the couplet:

> For loue of whome, so as I can endite,
> I purpose here to maken & to write.

The poem has always been accepted as Lydgate's on the strength of Shirley's attribution in his copy (S). Its editor, Schick (E.E.T.S., Extra Series 60, 1891), dated it conjecturally between 1400 and 1415, and from the astronomical opening suggested 1403. His arguments are closely connected with the assumption that Lydgate was also the author of *The Black Knight,* and *The Flour of Curtesye* (p. cxiii).

It would be tempting to argue that there was a short basic poem by Lydgate, begun in December 1419 (which also fits the astronomical dating), and altered in 1420-1 for the marriage and homecoming of Henry V and Katherine of France, a Valois bride, with the Valois colours green and white, allied to Henry of the hawthorn. This might account for the gloomy opening, and for some of the uninteresting decasyllabic passages. But this is a rather too easy solution, and the pervasiveness of the anagrams works against it. I suggest that the poem as we have it was by Roos, begun in December 1438, for the Plesaunce circle, and after divers alterations, adapted for his Margaret Vernon.

Of the eight manuscripts known, two are of the family of manuscripts of *La Belle Dame*, Fairfax 16 (F), and Longleat 258 (L.). Two more are allied to Fairfax 16, Tanner 346 (T) (Greystoke's), and Bodley 638 (B) (Astley's) which calls it 'The Temple of Bras' like Fairfax 16;[1] they also contain *The Black Knight*, similar at many points to this poem. So too do Pepys 2006 (P) (Kyriel's) and Add. 16165 (A) (Shirley's). Close to Shirley's copy is Gg. 4.27 (G). In addition there is Sloane 1212 (not known to Schick) where a paper manuscript of Hoccleve's *Regiment of Princes*, signed at the end 'Lucas endure 27', is enclosed in vellum leaves of a totally different manuscript, also with Lucas's name, and with many heraldic ornamentations, and assigned mottoes. These vellum leaves contain two passages from *The Temple of Glas*, ll. 98–142, and ll. 736–754 with 762–3, also two poems, one of which is a cento of lines from *The Temple* ingeniously fitted together, the other at first sight original, but actually a mosaic of small borrowings. The other scraps of poetry include a passage from the *Compleynt* (No. 78, above), and a tantalizing fragment from a lost poem on Sir Eger de Femyne. Of the printed versions, Berthelet's (?1530) is more important than the second Wynkyn de Worde which it resembles, since it has a short interpolation not found elsewhere, but containing a decisive anagram.

The numerous manuscripts and early prints attest, as Schick says (p. xiii), the popularity of the poem; in spite of some attractive passages it can hardly be thought to merit it as a whole. There is perhaps another reason for the many copies, that the poem was used as a quarry by lesser rhymesters, as by 'Lucas'. This obvious tinkering at it by others adds to the many puzzling circumstances of the poem. Sir John Paston demanded his copy in a hurry in 1461/2, when he was wooing Anne Haute; he probably wanted it, just as Slender wanted his 'Book of Songs and Sonnets', to woo another Mistress Anne. In addition, there are parallels with *The Kingis Quair*, and with the later *Court of Love*.

First it would be well to summarize the poem. *The Temple of Glas* starts as a gloomy inversion of the gay model set by the poetry of the Rose. It begins in December with 'greuous heuines', with depression and oppression, a deadly sleep, and a vision of a 'grisli dredful place'. Like the lover of the Rose, however, the poet long seeks an entry, finds a wicket, and goes in. In a temple he sees figures of true and famous lovers (many of them the Ladies of *The Legend of Good Women*) painted

---

[1] Stow corrects to 'Glas' in the title, and the contemporary Index has 'The Temple off Glasse'; but the running-titles are left as 'Bras'.

on the wall as offering their complaints to a painted Venus, 'fleting in
þe se'. The living figures that crowd the temple are unhappy lovers,
including those under enforced vows of chastity or marriage (a recurrent
theme is the Serpent of Jealousy), and Venus's statue is the centre of
their devotion. Among these is a lady, a suppliant. To her the statue
acts after the fashion of figures of the Blessed Virgin in legends, and
inclines meekly its head; it then pronounces a discourse of comfort for
her fidelity, with Griselde, Penelope and Dorigen as examples. The
corresponding description and complaint of the lover, the unhappy man,
is inordinately long and wordy, and ends with a lengthy prayer and
vows of fidelity. Venus turns her gaze on him, pronounces a long discourse, and urges full confession to the lady. Two of the most hesitant
and discouraged lovers in poetry at last come to an understanding, and
so enable Venus to link them in a golden chain, and, after a hundred and
fifty lines of homily, including the famous Statutes, to betroth them.
Song is raised in praise of Venus and Cupid, and wakens the dreamer.
In his grief at losing sight of the lady, he purposes to make a little
treatise in honour of women. He sends his 'litel rude boke' to his lady.

The poem is not only lengthy but also confused. One exasperated
early reader of MS. Bodleian 638 (perhaps an Astley) wrote after the
man's first complaint, 'hᶜ vsque nescio quis' (l. 847), and after his
second, 'who in all godly pity maye be' (l. 970). There are anomalies:
Venus is first painted, then a statue, then a speaking, moving goddess.
Confusion is partly due to imperfect cancels, to insertions and expansions.

Schick distinguished two states in *The Temple of Glas*. There are in
fact three states discernible in the manuscripts, traceable by changes in
two distinct passages which describe the lady: State α, which is found
in MSS. Tanner, Pepys, and Longleat; State β, which is found in the
related S and G; and State γ, which crisscrosses α and β, and is found
in Fairfax 16 and Bodleian 638.

In State α, the lady is compared with May, with the rose and the ruby
(l. 225); roses and lilies are mingled in her (276); she is clad in green and
white (299); and her embroidered device is 'De mieulx en mieulx'
(309–12). In the later passage, Venus crowns her with

> braunchis white & grene
> Of hawthorn . . .
> bowȝis . . . faire & swete (504–10),

which signify lasting unity (513). The lady replies to her lover, 'To do
ȝoure will de mieulx en mieulx magre' (530). Her name is not given.

In State *β*, the lady is still like May, the rose and the ruby, and still mingles rose and lily. But she is clad in black, red, and white, and her embroidered device is 'humblement magre'. Venus crowns her with roses white and red, refers explicitly to her name Margaret, and commends to her the fresh singleheartedness of the daisy (510–14). The lady's reply to her lover is 'humblement magre'. The conclusion of the poem has vanished, and in its place there is the *Compleynt*, explicitly to Margaret.

In State *γ*, the lady is clad in green and white and her motto is 'De mieulx en mieulx'; but in the later passage she is crowned with roses white and red, and her answer is 'humblement magre'. The name Margaret and the daisy are omitted.

That is to say, State *α* has a green and white and leafy background, with a commonplace motto (twice repeated). State *β* has a red and white and flower background of rose and daisy for a lady named Margaret, whose motto (twice repeated) is 'humblement magre', also a *Compleynt* to Margaret. But whereas State *γ* begins as does State *α* with green and white and 'de mieulx en mieulx', it later eliminates the leaves and changes to red and white and 'humblement magre' like State *β*, yet omits the Margaret-daisy reference. There was then to hand about 1450 a partially altered copy, which the owner, or the scribe, of Fairfax 16 got hold of, and which was transmitted to the allied but later MS. Bodleian 638.[1]

In addition to these three states, representing the chief stages of transmutation, there are alternative stanzas concerning the lady, some in F.B.G. and S, some in G and S only. There is the circumstance that in B alone certain lines have been corrected and the corrections erased. The mistakes made by Shirley in S (he turns 'Philologye' into 'Philosophie' (l. 130), and 'Parcas' into 'percaas' (l. 237), and makes nonsense at l. 119 of the Jove-Europa story), leave one wondering what other confusions he may have introduced into the text. Finally, one interpolation in Berthelet's print (c. 1530) points to the existence of yet another state, since it occurs in no other text, yet carries a decisive anagram.

It must be kept in mind that no existing manuscripts give us the original poem for Plesaunce, but only the Plesaunce poem as Roos adapted it for other purposes, and altered his anagrams or introduced fresh ones. His habit in his later long poems, of inserting a reminiscent anagram into a passage suitable by story or sentiment, sometimes makes

---

[1] For another interpretation of these revisions, see J. Norton Smith, 'Lydgate's Changes in the *Temple of Glas*', in *Med. Ævum*, 1958, XXVII, 166–72.

it difficult to use these anagrams for criteria in dating. This is so with *Reson and Sensuallyte*, of which there is in effect only one valid text. Here, however, through many differing manuscripts, it is possible to discern layers of modification. The first fifty lines of the poem introduce the nucleus of the Plesaunce circle: HOMFREI; AlIAn COBHAm; ANTI–ONA; –ISAB–Th BeWMONT, –Ar–OLF. The initials of the names of the unhappy Ladies (with that of Jason) give ELIs. PHel–P, PhilEP; AlIA–.; A–T–G, similarly to other early poems. But there are no double acrostic anagrams in this passage until near the end.

The story of Venus, Mars, and Vulcan (ll. 126–8) in no more than three lines yields a suggestive anagram: (C)O–HA(M); VAV. The story of the marriage of Mercury and Philology supplies another lady's name, (M)A. –TAnHOP, WILOW., not surprising, for the association of Maud Stanhope with Mercury is a constant in these poems, as in *Ragman Roll*, and *The Chance of the Dice*. Later anagrams here will be found to recur to these two names: to Elisabeth Cobham, who married Lord Strange of Knokyn in 1439; and to Maud Stanhope, who married Lord Willoughby, considerably her senior, before January 1448.

Nevertheless the Plesaunce names persist at first. The Lady described (ll. 247–97) gives E–ISABeTH BEW–O–T, BAR–OLF; ISMAnIA SCAL–S WHA–ISBOrO–H; AnT––O–A, and the 'devise' AI TOT FOrFAIT FOr–A–T. But at the end of the description, the lines occur in two forms (ll. 298–314/15). In MSS. G and S, or State β, the anagram gives a suggestion of the name Longueville: –OnG–EVI. FOrFAIT; the MSS. of State α yield E––SABETH ST–AnG. KNO., FAW–O, TOT FOrFA–T FOrFA–T. Berthelet's print interpolates four lines between ll. 314 and 315, which alone give FA–O––RG, and the whole passage gives a fuller version of the anagram of State α: E––SA–ETH COBHA., STRAnG, KnO.; FAW–OM––RG, TOT FOrFA–T FOrFA–T.

The Lady's Complaint to Venus, as in State α (ll. 321–70), introduces the second name: ELYSAB–Th CO––AM STRAn.; MAVD STAnHO. WI––OVG–BI; FAWCOM. The alternative passage on Jealousy in State β, introducing the Mars-Venus-Vulcan story (ll. 321–34 and stt. 3 a–d), eliminates Lady Willoughby's name and gives instead StRANG. FAW–O(M)B.; VAVASO. Venus's answer to the Lady (ll. 377–453) runs the anagrams of the names down through successive stanzas: stt. 9–11, MAWD STANHOP WI––OWBY TOT FOrFAIT; stt. 12–13, FAW–ONB–RG, (S)TRANG.; st. 14, FOrFAIT FOrFAYT; stt. 15–16, COBHAM; stt. 18–19, E––ISA–ETH; st. 17, FIS–OWIS. The additional stanza in MSS. G and S, F and B does not seem to affect the anagram. The Lady's thanks to Venus (ll. 461–502) repeats these names, with the omission of FisLowis, and the addition of Vavasour: (E)LISABETH CO–HAM ST–AnG; MAV. STANHO. WILOVBY; FAWCOM., VAVASO, TOT FOrF––T FOrF––T. The variant stanzas in MSS. G and S, F and B, however, have a Plesaunce anagram: PHILI(P), BeWMO–T BARDO–F. The garland passage (ll. 503–16, stt. 27–8) in State α with white and green and the hawthorn gives the names: –OBHA., STRAN. KNOKIn; FAW–O–Be.; TOT FOrFA–T FOrF–IT. States β and γ (MSS. G and S, F and B) convert st. 27 into VERNON in the caesural intitals chiefly, thereby nullifying the other anagram; this is done by knocking out the final K of st. 27, and inserting a caesural R with the suggestive word 'Roses'. Through the three stt. 27–9 the poet also strings his complete 'devise': AI TOT FOrFAIT FOrFAIT. With the description of the Knight (ll. 548–66) the anagram is still of Plesaunce: E–I–ABETH BeWMONT; FOrFAIT FOr–A–T. But his stanzaic complaint reverts unequivocally to the Fawcomberg theme (ll. 701–42, stt. 31–6): (EL)ISABeTH (C)OBHAM; FAW(C)OMBeRG; MAW. STANHO. WILOWBY; IAY TOT FOrFAIT FOr–AIT. His description of the lady (ll. 743–91, stt. 37–43) repeats this with some variation: E–ISAB–TH COBHAM STRAnG; FAW(C)OM––R.; MAWD STAnHO(P) WILO––H–Y; VAVASO. This anagram is run on a different system, not in successive stanzas; the anaphora of 'Hir' in st. 37 forces a similar concentration of letters in other stanzas, and the anagrams are widely diffused throughout, and have to be pieced together.

Venus's answer to the Knight repeats ELISAB–TH, FAW–O–BErG (ll. 883–96, stt. 57–8) and ST–ANGE (ll. 897–910, stt. 59–60). But the preceding stanzas in all texts yield LONG–VYL (stt. 52–3); and the turn of stt. 55–6 gives V–RNON, precisely at the hopeful sentiment:

> Beþe not astoneid of no wilfulnes,
> Ne nouȝt dispeired of þis dilacioun. (ll. 876–7)

The Knight's supplication to the Lady, thoroughly in Plesaunce style, has a Plesaunce anagram, E–ISA––TH, BeWMONT, AnTYGO., but it looks as if an attempt had been made to introduce Roos's later lady, –O–GEVI., V–RNO (ll. 970–97). The beautiful song to Venus, planet and goddess (ll. 1341–61), repeats the Cobham anagram: (E)L––A––TH CO–HA.; FA(V)–ONBe–G; TOT FOr–A–T. The conclusion of the poem falls into two parts: in all manuscripts ll. 1362–79 give COB–AM, ST–AnG, KnO–In; FIS–OWIS; FOrFAIT FOrFAIT; the remaining lines (1380–1403), lacking in MSS. G and S, introduce again Maud Stanhope and the poet's full 'devise' as final signature: MAV. STANHOP. WI–OV–BI, and AI TOT FOrFAIT FOrFAIT.

A tentative explanation for all these phenomena would run as follows.

First, Roos set out to write a dream story for the Plesaunce group, probably in 1438, a winter's tale, gloomier than *The Isle of Ladies*, but like it, starting off with islets or craggy rocks. While he was engaged on it, the marriage of one of the group, the Duchess's younger sister, Elisabeth Cobham, with Lord Strange of Knokyn was planned (1439), and Roos began to turn the story towards them; but the description of the Lady had already embodied the anagrams of Elisabeth Beaumont and Lady Scales. These he left, and began his Cobham-Strange anagrams in the further description of the Lady kneeling before Venus, as it appears in all texts except G and S. All this would be about 1439. In the later 1440s, further events happened, and the anagrams display them: before January 1448 Maud Stanhope had married Lord Willoughby; and at some time before Lord Strange's death in 1449, the Fawcomberg-Strange affair had taken place (cf. *Mars*, No. 73, above). Fawcomberg's double game has already been pointed out in *Anelida and Arcite* and in the *Legends*. The anagram in the Song to Venus, however, displays a sympathetic interest in it. The conclusion of the poem, lame and unimpressive, unites the two ladies, but omits the man's name. This brings the alterations to c. 1448–50. By March 1449 (if we may trust the probable date of the *Compleynt* that follows this poem in MSS. G and S), Roos had met Margaret Longueville, *née* Vernon, and two anagrams in MSS. G and S show her strong influence; in one he attempts imperfectly and unsuccessfully the difficult new name Longueville; in the other he converts the description of the hawthorn wreath to roses and the daisy exemplar, openly names Margaret, and, using the caesural letters only, hides in one stanza the name VERNO.; to get this he alters the consonants. He also converts the trite motto 'de mieulx en mieulx' into one where the second word 'magre' suggests Margaret. MSS. G and S are not the only manuscripts to exhibit this change to Roos's own personal emotions; rather skeletal forms of Margaret's surnames appear, in all the texts, in Venus's answer to the Knight, and in his supplication to the Lady.

From the incidence of the anagrams we must conclude that all the existing manuscripts cover the period c. 1438–c. 1450–2, that is, from before the Strange marriage till near the poet's marriage with Margaret Longueville. All show references to the Fawcomberg-Strange affair, and introduce Lady Willoughby's name (before 1448); all, by the anagrams, show signs of conversion to Margaret Longueville (Vernon), though only G and S display the changes fully, in flowers and mottoes as well as in anagrams. One piece of symbolism still remains unexplained, the hawthorn branches with the colours green and white. They may be the only sign left in the poem, in State α and partly in State γ, of a stage of alteration at about 1444–5, and of an attempt to fit the poem to Margaret of Anjou, a Valois bride (green and white), marrying Henry of the hawthorn, and thereby uniting the rose and the lily. But the anagrams give this no support.

The diffusion of the anagrams forces one to modify one of Schick's conclusions (pp. xxii, xxxii). MS. Gg. 4.7 can no longer be considered the oldest text of this poem, since it contains the full Margaret changes, and also the *Compleynt* to Margaret. This copy cannot be earlier than about 1449–50. The poem is, however, the last item in the manuscript, the Chaucerian part of which may well be older, and even go back to Duke Humphrey's ownership, as has been postulated by Manly. One must also defend Berthelet from Schick's charge (p. xlvii) of wanton interpolation, since the four lines that appear only in his print materially assist the Fawcomberg anagram.

The Temple of Glas has been so much worked over and pulled about that it is difficult to apply critical standards to it. It can hardly be considered a well-contrived whole; yet it has some beautiful parts, especially the fine song to Venus ('Fairest of sterres', ll. 1341 ff.), a ballade very close in expression to the prayer to Venus the planet of eve, which concludes *The Black Knight*. It has a truer singing note than Lydgate can achieve, and this in spite of its anagrams. Almost as striking are the stately and rich rhythms of the opening of the Knight's confession of love to the lady:

> Princes of iouþe, & flour of gentilesse,
> Ensaumple of vertue, ground of curtesie,[1]
> Of beaute rote, quene & eke maistres
> To al women hou þei shul hem gie.

One metrical usage is significant, the increasing run-on of stanzas which is a mark of Roos's practice; thus in the lover's complaint there is run-on in stt. 34–5–6, 38–9, 41–2–3, 50–1.

The already difficult problems of *The Temple of Glas* are further complicated by its relation on the one hand to *The Kingis Quair*, and on the other to *The Court of Love* of the sixteenth century. The first is the more easily dealt with. Now that Lydgate's authorship of *The Temple of Glas* is ruled out, and the poem is seen as basically a Plesaunce poem with later accretions, it is plain that *The Kingis Quair* is the earlier poem, and Roos the imitator. The *Quair*, for which I accept the royal

---

[1] These two first lines, with variants, are found as a fragment in a manuscript in Madrid. See Bukofzer, *Music and Letters*, XIX, 120.

authorship, must have been written well before James's death in February 1437; Roos may easily have seen the royal poem, written for Edmund Beaufort's elder sister, through his sister-in-law's Beaufort connexion. Or Duke Humphrey, who furthered James's release in 1424, may have put the *Quair* into Roos's hands for imitation in his Plesaunce days. Both James and Roos are indebted to Lydgate; parallels between all three writers are not surprising.

The Court of Love will be fully considered later (Chapter XII). Here a warning note on the statutes of Love must suffice for the present. There seems to be no connexion of authorship between the precepts of love in *The Temple of Glas* and the statutes of love in *The Court of Love*, both addressed to men, on the one hand, and the *Ten Commandments of Love*, which are enjoined on a woman (Robbins, *Secular Lyrics*, etc:, No. 177), on the other hand.

The conclusion of *The Temple of Glas* promises to write a little 'processe' in praise of women, a promise which would be impossible to Lydgate, whereas it is Roos's constant preoccupation.

No. 80. *Reson and Sensuallyte*, continued (see No. 61, above).

The later allusions in the anagrams in *Reson and Sensuallyte* still need to be considered; involving as they do Roos's friends of Queen Margaret's Household, and his courtship of Margaret Longueville, they fit in here. It will be seen that Roos inserts these anagrams throughout the poem; the one authoritative text precludes data or conjecture on the layers of writing, such as can be dimly discerned in *The Temple of Glas*. Margaret Longueville's name is often dovetailed into descriptions early in the poem, and other allusions of the 1440s appear in the central portion, the Garden of the Rose. It is not, however, till the Chess-Game that, together with the retrospective anagrams and sentiments of the Maiden's Pawns, allusions to Margaret Longueville begin to take on the guise of personal statements. But just at this interesting stage the poem breaks off (perhaps Roos had won the lady), and what was promising to develop almost into a private memoir is lost to us. It must be stressed that the last thousand lines or so of the already very free translation form practically an original poem; it gives us Roos's own knowledge (like his casual reference (l. 6279) to Aristotle's view of the influence of the rainbow on plant life), and his own opinions, as on the value of the prudent mean in everything (ll. 6338–52), or on widows re-marrying (ll. 6900–30) (a subject which by 1450 lay near his heart and in which the anagram is pointed).

Margaret the queen has an obeisance from Roos in the first part of the description of the Maiden's 'quene or the fers'; ll. 6595–611 give MA(R)–A(R)–T ANIOW in the line initials; but in the caesural initials Roos prepares for his next anagram by VER–O–. In the moralization of the Fers as womanly grace and mercy, the personal anagram celebrates not only his lady but also her parents: MA(RG)AReT LONGEVYLL, VerNON; RICHARD, BENEDI–TA. TOT FOrFAYT FOrFA–T (ll. 6617–82). Again he is a little disingenuous in the description of the Maiden's King; the opening lines (6839–64) give HENRY in line-initials, with AI FOrFAIT FOr–AI–; later appears an obvious MAR–A–ET with ISM(A)NYA; but in the last paragraph (6917–22) words, not initials, are insinuating his own Margaret's name: longe:wil: euer in oon:non. 'Ever in one' is a phrase which Roos becomes more addicted to in his later poems; the insertion of 'I' into '(e)ver-noon' would be just the symbolic play to delight him. So much for the two Margarets together.

The intrusion of Margaret Vernon or Longueville into Plesaunce anagrams begins at once in the opening lines, a Plesaunce braid: VerNON (ll. 1–22). In Nature's beauty (ll. 315 ff.) she is verNON, –ONGVEVI.; in Juno's beauty she appears in the line-initials only, V–RNON; FOrFAIT (ll. 1368–80); in Venus's beauty, she appears twice and emphatically, MARGARET VeRNON, LONGVIL (ll. 1554–76), and again (ve)RNON LON––– –IL (1581–98), with ISMANYA SCAlys, and the full 'devise', IAI TOT FOrFAIT FOrFAYT. In the Garden of the Rose, the poet is made free of the garden for as long as he does no 'vilenye' (ll. 5064–84); the anagram is –ERNON LONgVile; SCA––S; AnIS COKAIn; B. CHA––TO–; TOT FOrFAIT. Here, as again in lyrics in MS. Ff. 1.6, names of Margaret's sisters are associated with her, Agnes, wife of John Cokayn, and Benedicta, wife of Thomas Charlton. A little further on, Cupid's power to tame the proudest, and 'make hem to lowte Vn-to his subieccion', is rather pointedly addressed to MA––G––ET VE(R)NON, FOrFAIT (ll. 5278–94); just so in *The Isle of Ladies* had Love tamed the Amazonian queen. The Maiden's Fourth Pawn, Doulz Semblant, slips Margaret in towards the end as VAR(N)ON (ll. 6298–310). The Fifth Pawn, Port and Manere, associates her with the dead Lady Beaumont, and the living Lady Somerset: (MAR)GA. VERNON (ll. 6335 ff.). In the Maiden's Rooks, she is coupled with Lady Willoughby, Lady Scales, and Elisabeth FitzLowis: MA(R)–A(R)ET V–(R)NON (ll. 6717 ff.). In the Poet's Pawns, she has sole control of the Second Pawn, Syght: MA(R)–AR–T VEr. (ll. 6957–63). At the end of the Third Pawn, Doulz Penser, her name runs through the passage of surely personal confession on the 'deceyt of apparence' and the lover's straying by 'merours of fals plesaunce': MA(R)GA–ET LONG. It certainly looks as if Sir Richard had some difficulty in convincing his

Margaret that his devotion for Lady Beaumont was, like its object, dead.
These anagrams probably date from about 1449 to 1452.

After the 'quene or fers' Roos fittingly turns his anagrams to ladies
of her Household. The Maiden's Knights, Shame and Timidity, give
the names of ISMANIA SCALYS, WHA––S–BO–OVH; STAn–OW; BABThOrP;
with IAI TOT FOrFAIT FO–F–IT. (ll. 6683–716). Her Rooks provide a long
list: MAUD STANHO., WYLOUHBY; I–(M)AnYA WHAlISBORO.; –LISAB–TH
FISLOWIS; KATH. WHITTIn–HAM; with TOT FOrFAIT FOrFAIT (ll. 6717–77).
Her Awfyns give two ladies with full names: ELISAB–TH GrEY, FI–HWGH;
An. MOLYNS, WHAl–BOROV–H, HAMPD–N; also SCAl.; KATH. WHYTTIn–
HAM; BABThORP; with AY TOT FOrFA–T FOrFAYT (ll. 6775–818). These are
all people found in the Jewels Accounts and met in *The Chance of the
Dice* and *The Assembly of Ladies*. Katherine Whittingham must now
be the French lady, *née* Gatevyne. Lady Grey, *née* FitzHugh, was
widow of Sir Ralph Grey of Heaton; like Lady Scales and Margaret
Stanlow, she was a member of the Escort, and remained in the Queen's
Household. Ismania Scales's sister, Anne Moleyns, the second English
love of Charles d'Orléans, had married by November 26, 1442, Edmund
Hampden, one of the King's Squires. In these anagrams of the three
important chess pieces, Roos forms an unusually compact group of the
chief ladies of the queen's entourage, and of others, like Maud Stanhope, the second Lady Willoughby, and Lady Moleyns (who retained
her title), closely associated with it.

Two other references must be dated after 1450. Twice Antigone's
name is accompanied by her second married name, D'Amancier: in the
Sixth Pawn, Foresight, she appears among other imprudent ladies as
ANT. POW(I)S, DAMANS.; and in the Seventh Pawn, in the list of anti-
feminine monks, she and Eleanor Cobham are coupled, she as ANTIGONA
DAMANSI. The inference here must be that the Abbots Curteys and
Whethamstede, as well as Lydgate, were opposed to the 'sorceress' and
her daughter, for so Antigone must surely have been.

There are also here further references to the Fawcomberg-Strange
affair, fully illustrated in *The Compleynt of Mars*, and often alluded to in
the anagrams of *The Temple of Glas*. The first occurrence of it comes
in Diana's cautionary tale of Jason and the golden fleece (ll. 3521–82):
FAWCOMBE(R); E–ISA(B)ETH (C)O(B)HAM STRAn. KnOKIn; MAVD STAnHOPE
WIL–OWBI; IAI TOT FOrFAIT FOrFA(I)T. This is the only time here that,
as often in *The Temple of Glas*, *Anelida and Arcite*, and elsewhere,
Lady Willoughby's name is coupled with the lovers. Another of Diana's
warnings concerns 'beddes perilouse', especially the contrivance made by
Vulcan to entrap Mars and Venus, while the gods laughed them to scorn;

B B

the anagrams bring back the names of *The Compleynt of Mars*: AlYAnOR COBHAM (ll. 3760–70); E–ISAB–TH COBHAM, STRANGE; FAWCONBeR.; TAlBOT; with TOT FOrFAIT (ll. 3771–802). They are repeated with variations in the further description of the Siren's song and of Vulcan's bed (ll. 4127–55): FAW–OMBE.; ELISABeTH K–OKIn; VALLAn; with TOT FOrFAIT. Again they underlie the next passage, the fall of Icarus, very greatly enlarged from the brief French original of *Les Echecs* (ll. 4163–99): FAW–OM.; CO–HAM STRAN., KNO–IN; TAl–OT; with TOT FOrFAYT FOrFAIT. Roos points the moral, the middle way and the benefit of good counsel; it is an implicit judgment on the lovers and their presumptuous folly. So is the next occurrence, in the Sixth Pawn, where they appear among the imprudent lovers as E–ISAB–TH –OBHAM, FAWCOMB. (ll. 6375–432).

Lady Willoughby, the third party with Fawcomberg and Lady Strange, is mentioned twice again in the anagrams. In the description of the power of Mercury, god of eloquence (ll. 1685–99), comes MAUD STAnHOP, WI–OGHBI; and again in the 'shappe and . . . array' of Mercury (ll. 1709–33) 'Quik, lusty, fresh, and ryght plesant', she is joined with two other such ladies: MAV. STANHOP, W–LLO–GHB.; ISMAN–A; B–W–ONT. In the Maiden's Rooks, Doulz Regarde and Bialocoil (6717–74), she is associated with Margaret Vernon, Lady Scales, and others: MAUD STANHO., WYLOUHBY.

A glance at the dates connected with these people of the queen's court may help with an approximate dating of the continuation of the re-working of the poem. All must be later than 1445, the Anjou marriage. Lady Willoughby is first known as such in January 1448/9. Lady Scales and Lady Scroop (Curtesye) lived on from the Plesaunce period into the queen's time. Margaret Longueville's first appearance in the Jewels Accounts, probably as a newly-made widow, is September 1449–September 1450. Antigone's husband, Lord Powis, died in 1450, and she forthwith married her Frenchman, Jean D'Amancier. It looks as if the latter part of the poem was written about 1449–52. Where exactly any break and resumption took place is difficult to say, because of Roos's practice of insinuating Vernon-Longueville into the Plesaunce ana-grams. I would hazard the guess that it may have been in the midst of the Garden, before the entry of Déduit; quite certainly it preceded the Chess-play. The last section of the translation, much of it original, is much stronger, closer in writing, more authoritative in tone, more mature in its judgments. The poem has become for Roos a 'recherche du temps perdu'. He looks back on Plesaunce, and sees his part in it as a dry tree, 'made naked and bareyn' by a useless devotion; on Eleanor Cobham, and sees her, not as a sorceress, but as herself bewitched by her folly and imprudence and the greed of her underlings; on Lydgate and the two noted clerics, and revolts violently from their antifeminism. In his new circle, the queen's court, Lady Scales, still firm and steadfast, links the two periods of his life together; and for Margaret Vernon the dry tree of dead emotion springs again to life and hope. The poem has by 1450 become a mirror reflecting the past and the present of Roos's life.

No. 81*a*. 'O bewtie pereles': a dedication of a 'litill Boke', in two stanzas of rhyme royal with two stanzas of four short lines, of which the last is illegible (printed, Robbins, *Secular Lyrics*, pp. 206 and 288). I assume the first word of the fourth stanza to be 'Let'.

> *Incipit.* O Bewtie pereles, and right so womanhod.
> *Explicit.* Do that exchue | . . . ce.

The unique copy is in MS. Royal 19.A.iii, fol. 16 v. It follows directly after the original French of *La Belle Dame sans Merci*, the only English verse in a volume of French poetry, and the only vellum sheet in an untidy paper volume. I have already given reasons for thinking this volume to have been in Roos's possession, and this poem to have been another dedication to his translation of *La Belle Dame* (see above, Chapter III). It is addressed to a most goodly lady, with the request that it may be read over or 'rehersed' 'Vnto suche fayre þat do excile pite'; the poet pleads, 'Where bewtie is, of right þere is pities place'. In *Reson and Sensuallyte* we have seen Roos combining anagrams of his two Margarets, the queen and his lady, not always with frankness. Here he plays the same game: MARGA--T DAnIOW; (L)O---VI.; AI TOT FOrFA-T. It is easy to see that Roos would wish to replace his Plesaunce dedication by one to the queen. A shadowy indication of 'Longueville' shows the dedication to have been written after 1449.

No. 81*b*. A taut and tiny poem (four stanzas of four lines) is found in a later manuscript of Tudor minstrelsy.

> *Incipit.* I hard lately to a ladye.
> *Explicit.* and grante good wyll.
> I nyll, quoth she.

In MS. Ashmole 48, on fol. 18 v., it is copied twice, with 'Fynis, quoth G.F.' and then 'fynis quoth Christopher Curtis'. Wright printed it in *Songs and Ballads*, pp. 28–9 (Roxburghe Club, 77, 1860). To the lover's pleas, the lady 'dyd featly, Grant and denye' ('I wyll . . . I nyll') without relenting. The anagram runs MARGAReT; FOr–AIT.

No. 82. A poem at present accepted as written in the reign of Richard II, proves on examination to be a work of later than 1445, *The Cuckoo and the Nightingale*, a more distinctive and exactly descriptive title than 'The Boke of Cupid'. Bradshaw was the first to cast doubt on Chaucer's authorship; Skeat at first inclined to Hoccleve, against Furnivall's doubts. Then, discovering the colophon, 'Explicit Clanvowe', in MS. Ff. 1.6, Skeat claimed him as the author, writing for Queen Joan of Navarre. The realization that in 1392 Sir Thomas Clanvowe was *at Woodstock* given a pension on his marriage with Perrine Whetteney, a waiting-lady of Anne of Bohemia, seemed to clinch the matter. Clanvowe is accepted (as by C. E. Ward and Brusendorff) as the author under Richard II of this poem which is to end with a parliament of birds outside the royal palace of Woodstock.

There are some loose stones in this foundation. First, the colophon as a proof of authorship: Robbins's suggestion (*P.M.L.A.*, June 1954, LXIX, 630), which I would support, that the colophons and signatures in MS. Ff. 1.6 are not those of authors, but of copyists, weakens the authorship claim. Secondly, 'at Woodstock' in the document simply means that the court was there at the time of the grant; it has no bearing on the authorship of the poem. Sir Thomas Clanvowe came of a Hertfordshire family. Moreover, every king and queen visited Woodstock from time to time till its destruction in the seventeenth century. Thirdly, Brusendorff's identification of the queen mentioned with Anne of Bohemia, and his assumption of her patronage of a daisy-cult, based on the Prologue to *The Legend of Good Women*, are now nullified by Roos's authorship of the daisy portions of that prologue. Finally, the anagrams bring the whole unsafe structure down, for they show it to be a Fawcomberg-Strange-Stanhope poem, with side-compliments to Queen Margaret of Anjou, and to Margaret Longueville.

Before this is explored, however, another allied poem needs first to be considered, *A Seying of the Nightingale*, now ascribed to Lydgate.

No. 82*a*.

Incipit. In Iuygne whan Tytan was in þe Crabbes hed.

An unfinished poem of fifty-four stanzas of rhyme royal; printed by MacCracken, *Minor Poems*, pp. 221–34, and by Otto Glauning, E.E.T.S., 1900, E. Ser. 80.

It is found in three manuscripts: Trin. Coll., Camb., R.3.20 (Shirley's); Harleian 2251 (Shirley's and Stow's); and Add. 29729, Stow's own copy; all three name Lydgate, but the attribution in all three rests on Shirley only. The poem is in two disparate parts, and not even Schirmer, who analyses it more closely than anyone else, stresses sufficiently the change in theme, tone, style, and metrical usages.

The poem begins in the highest style of courtly poetry, with the poet listening in a valley on a summer's eve to the birds, and especially to the nightingale's call, 'ocy, ocy'. This he interprets as a plea to Venus and Cupid to slay all false lovers. Musing on this, he falls asleep among the dewy flowers (stt. 6–7), and has a vision. A messenger comes, announcing himself as from the true God, and deploring his misunderstanding of the song, which is sacred, not profane, and celebrates not Cupid but the Passion of Christ. By stanza 12 the poem has made a complete *volte-face*, and for another forty or so stanzas it continues in the most ardent language of Christian devotion. The change of theme is reflected in a change of style, from the elegant, smooth simplicity of the poetry of love ('I [hade] not herde suche song in dovne ner daale', or 'Vpon þe eve the sterres did appeere') to the heavy aureate style of Lydgate's religious poetry: 'Let hem devoyde frome þoblyuyoun' (st. 41). Most noticeable metrically is the run-on of stanzas, four times in stt. 1–14, but not again till stt. 50–52. The introduction is artistically clear, concise and economical in expression; after st. 12 or so, the poem overflows with emotion, but shows little sign of stringency or climax.

The anagrams help to explain the puzzle: Introduction, st. 2, the nightingale's song, STANHOPE; st. 4, mercilessness in love, ELYSA--TH; stt. 4–5, true lovers, IS-AN. SCA--S; st. 6, evening, MAV-; diffused, TOT FOrFAIT FOrFAIT. The Dream, st. 7, ANTIG.; st. 8, the message, IS-ANIA; FOrFAIT; st. 9, the nightingale and the thorn, B-W---T; stt. 9–10, love pure and free, wh-LISBOROV.; st. 11, the bird's ardour, PHI---; st. 12, AlIAN. Already in the Dream, the anagrams become less full; they peter out, and after st. 12 they cease, and the religious poem is then fully developed.

Can one explain it thus? One summer before the autumn of 1441, Sir Richard Roos began a dream poem on the nightingale. He may or may not have finished it. Lydgate, in touch with Humphrey of Gloucester, got hold of it, and either altered the end, or completed it in his own style, doubtless glad of the opportunity to allure readers to devotion by an attractive courtly opening. I think he began by tampering with stt. 7–12 (the Dream), where slight changes could invert the sense (e.g. in l. 52, 'not to lede' may replace an original 'now to lede'). The tampering involves whole lines and sentences in stt. 11 and 12, and wrecks the anagrams; and from then on Lydgate has it all his own way. One cannot say whether Roos knew of these depredations; in any case he would not wish to recover a poem now spoilt for courtly love. It does not occur in any of the manuscripts particularly associated with him.

To return now to *The Cuckoo and the Nightingale*. In the time of Queen Margaret, probably in the late 1440s, Roos sets out to write yet another poem against Fawcomberg, and in sympathy with Maud Stanhope. She had been the nightingale of the earlier (either abortive or pirated) Plesaunce poem; she will be so again, and set over against her is the mocking, faithless cuckoo, Fawcomberg.

No. 82*b*.   *Incipit.* The god of love, a! *benedicite*!

It is in quintains, and completed in 290 lines.

This is not a midsummer-eve dream poem, but a poem of a sleepless May dawn ('the thridde night of May', l. 55) when again the birds preen themselves (l. 76; cf. *A Seying*, l. 7), and sing for joy. Again the poet, lulled by the river's flow, drowses, 'Not al a-slepe, ne fully wakinge' (l. 88; cf. *La Belle Dame*, l. 1), and hears first the cuckoo's ill-omened note, and only afterwards the nightingale. He is able to understand their altercation on love and lovers. At last in anger he chases away the cynical cuckoo (l. 216), and the grateful nightingale tells him to practise daily in May the medicine of love: 'Go loke upon the fresshe dayesye'. She then tells the other birds of her grievance against the cuckoo, and they suggest a parliament to be held on the next St. Valentine's day at Woodstock, under the maple before the queen's window. The nightingale then flies into a hawthorn, and sings so loudly that the poet wakes.

The anagram keeps closely to the short stanzas with only a little overlapping, and with nice adjustment to the sense. Ll. 11–25, the power of love, MA–D STANHO.; ll. 26–35, FA–COMBeRG; ll. 36–47, the poet's susceptibility, –(L)ISAB–TH BeW(M)ONT, BAR.; ll. 51–5, IS–ANIA; ll. 59–65, the green and white (Valois colours) daisied glade, DAnIOW; ll. 73–80, STAn–O.; ll. 81–4, the river's melody, ThAME–, RI–H–on–; ll. 86–95, the cuckoo's unwelcome call, FA – – –MBER.; ll. 96–100, the nightingale's song, STAN.; ll. 101–5, IAQU–TTA; ll. 106–10, WIL–BI; ll. 111–15, STRANGE; ll. 116–26, the cuckoo's defiant answer, FAWC–MB.; S–A(N)HO.; ll. 131–5, AIIAn.; ll. 136–45, AIISABETH ST–AN.; ll. 146–63, the nightingale praises love's good effects, STAnHOP, WILLOW., SCALIS; ll. 164–85, the cuckoo enumerates love's evil effects, FAW– –NB–RG;

STAnH–P, MAUD; WHAlI–BOrO–H; FOrFAIT; ll. 186–95, the nightingale defends love's worthy votaries, IS–ANIA; –TANHO–E; FOrFAJT FOrFA–T; ll. 196–205, the cuckoo abuses Love as wilful, STANHO.; FOrFA–T FOrFA.; ll. 206–15, the nightingale appeals to Love, Be–MONT; STAn–O.; IS––An–A; ll. 216–25, the poet chases off the cuckoo, FAW––MB––(G); TOT F––FAIT; ll. 226–60, the nightingale's thanks, including, ll. 226–39, IAI TOT FOrFAIT FOrFAIT; ll. 239–47, the virtue of the daisy, (M)A–GA–ET LON.; STAnH.; ll. 244–56, FOrFAIT FOrFAIT. Ll. 261 ff., the other birds, TOT FOr–AIT; ll. 265–72, against the false cuckoo, FAW(C)O––E–G; ll. 278–85, the parliament at Woodstock, S(C)A–ES; STAn–up.; AnYOU; ll. 286–90, the nightingale's closing song, STAnLOW; diffused, TOT FOrFAIT FOrFA–T.

It is evident that the false cuckoo represents Lord Fawcomberg, and the nightingale with its idealistic arguments is the eloquent Maud Stanhope, Lady Willoughby. In the first clash between them, reference is made to Elisabeth Strange; other ladies named are Jacquetta of Luxemburg, Lady Rivers; Lady Scales; and by reminiscence of the 'old and unlusty' poet (l. 37), Lady Beaumont. Yet he is not so unlusty that he cannot woo Margaret Longueville, the daisy that can ease him of his pain (l. 245). The poet chases away the cuckoo with a stone from the brook which has suddenly taken the place of the river (l. 214). The scene is laid in the white and green and daisied glade of the Valois Queen Margaret DANIOW, beside the river Thames, apparently at Richmond (a rare locality in Roos's poems and anagrams), and is adjourned to her chamber-window at Woodstock. The maple of the final rendezvous was probably an actual tree;[1] but the hawthorn is the royal badge for the King's Knight; and in concluding, the poet compliments yet a third 'daisy', his old friend, Margaret Stanlow. The style of the poem is fresh and simple, not unlike that of *The Assembly of Ladies*, and possibly for the same reason. In no other poem does the poet scatter his 'devise' so profusely, why, I do not know.

Henry VI was often at Woodstock before his marriage, generally in August or September; later, only two visits are recorded, August 4, 1447, a little early, and August 6, 1458, much too late, for this Longueville poem.[2] Possibly the poet anticipated another visit there which did not come off; Queen Margaret was much preoccupied with Plesaunce. The

---

[1] I cannot find a heraldic maple as a relevant crest or badge. The nightingale's final song, 'Terme of [my] lyf, Love hath with-holde me', is reminiscent of Charles d'Orléans's *La Retenue d'Amours*. 'Terme de ma vie sans variance' was a motto of the Bowes family.

[2] Mabel Christie, *Henry VI*, pp. 383, 388.

poet repeats his earlier interpretation of 'ocy' (*The Seying*, stt. 3, 8–9) and ignores, if he ever knew, Lydgate's pietistic explanation.

Clanvowe, the copyist of the poem in the 'Roos scrapbook', still eludes me; no fifteenth-century Clanvowe has emerged. Dame Perrine Clanvowe's will of 1422 makes no mention of any kinsfolk of her husband. The only connecting link between Roos and a younger Clanvowe appears to be Ocle Pichard (Pychardsokell where Dame Perrine lived), their Herefordshire seat; it was also the home of the Pichards, and a Pichard betrayed the secret of *My Lady Dere* (see above, No. 44).

No. 83. *Poems for the Vernon family and others* in MS. Ff. 1.6.

References to the queen find no place in the Vernon lyrics in MS. Ff. 1.6, the manuscript which I have called 'the Roos scrapbook', and which probably came down through Mary Vernon, Margaret's niece (see above, Chapter III); some are mere fragments.

No. 83a. 'Euer yn one with my dew attendaunce' (fol. 153 v.): a single stanza of eight lines (abababab) (Printed, Robbins, *Secular Lyrics*, No. 166). It is a conventional verse, built up on clichés, perhaps on 'devises'; Roos can do much better, and has done so. The anagram gives MA––A–ET, For–AYT; and the opening phrase has been seen before to contain the name Ver–n–on.

No. 83b. 'Veryly | And truly | I schall nat fayne' (fol. 154): three twelve-syllable lines with internal rhyme (aabccb). Printed by Robbins, *P.M.L.A.*, LXIX, 639. This is a protestation of devotion and fidelity, a little more vigorous than the preceding, though as full of tags. The eighteen line-initials give MA––A––T VerN–N; it is possible that out of the residue can be obtained THY WIF, in imitation of a poem in the same manuscript ('I may well sygh') which contains ALYAn MA FAM– (see above, No. 41a).

No. 83c. 'What so men seyn' (fol. 56): four stanzas of eight short lines of four syllables (aaabaaab) (printed in *Reliquiae Antiquae*, I, 23, 1841; and by Robbins, *P.M.L.A.*, LXIX, 632). The poem attacks false and inconstant lovers:

> For euery daye
> They waite ther pray
> Wher-so they may
> and make butt game.
>
> *Incipit.* What so men seyn | Love is no peyn
> To them serteyn | butt varians,

Explicit. Hitt were pete | Butt they shold be
Be-gelid, parde | with-owtyn grase.

In *Reson and Sensuallyte*, Roos associated names of Margaret Vernon's
sisters with hers in anagrams. This poem seems to be addressed only
to Benedicta Charlton, and Anne Bradbourn but in very skeletal form,
BeNe–IT SH––LT.; An. B–A–B. The poem may have stopped short from
being a fully family chronicle, like the next two to be considered. This
kind of verse, like Touchstone's, can without effort be rhymed so 'eight
years together'.

No. 83*d*. 'Ffor to prevente' (fol. 143 v.–144): a poem of twenty stanzas
of three lines of four syllables (aab); or perhaps of ten stanzas of six lines
(aabccb) (printed by Robbins, *P.M.L.A.*, LXIX, 636–8).

Incipit. ffor to p[reu]ente
And After rep[e]nte } hyt were ffoly.

Explicit. In the weste
That goyth to reste } Euerry nyght

This is a much more interesting poem than most of the short pieces in
the manuscript. It is as rough as *How a Lover*, and as vigorous, with the
same taste for the archaic phrase ('the louesom lere'), and the unusual
word: 'And more orryaund | And pwere gloryaund | In bewte'. It
describes the laughing cheer of an incomparable star, which rose
against a sky of blue, and enchanted the lover with its orience. But
a wicked wind rises behind him and blows up a black cloud; he prays
for the cloud to disperse, that every night he may see 'The starre so
ffre | shynyn[g] bryith'. There may be a vague memory here of a
Canzone of Petrarch on Laura's death (Poem 325, ll. 61–76), especially

Fra tanti amici lumi
una nube lontana mi dispiacque.

The handwriting is thick and blotted, like that of an old person, and
some of the contractions are mishandled; the spelling is odd.

It is a surprise to find that the anagrams betray it as a Vernon 'braid'
of Margaret's brothers-in-law (see above, p. 73), and not, as one would
expect, a poem for her alone, with the phrase 'Euere in on' (l. 28):
MA––A–ET ROS; IOH. CO–AIn; THOMA– SHA––Ton; IOH. STAnLEI; IOH.
B–A–BO.; WIMBI–H. These are John Cockayn, Thomas Charlton, John
Stanley, John Bradbourn, husbands of Agnes, Benedicta, Elisabeth, and
Anne Vernon, together with Wimbish, a friend of Plesaunce days;
there is no 'devise'.

No. 83*e*. 'Welcome be ye my souereine' (fol. 135–6): a cycle of four
verse paragraphs (or separate poems) of twelve or thirteen octosyllabic

lines (except the third, which is decasyllabic) (printed *Nugae Poeticae*, 1844, pp. 68–9; and by Robbins, *P.M.L.A.*, LXIX, 634–5).

> *Incipits.* (1) Welcome be ye my souereine.
> (2) Come home, dere hert, your tarieng.
> (3) To you my Ioye and my wordly plesaunce.
> (4) There may areste me no pleasance.
> *Explicits.* (1) Gladnesse ye haue brought me a-gaine.
> (2) Depart frome me til your comyng.
> (3) Yet aske I mercy to be in pacience.
> (4) Lett him haue therof repentance.

The most remarkable thing about these verses is that they are the utterances of a woman: first, welcoming her man; then lamenting his absence; then confessing to a charge made by him in a letter, and seeking his forgiveness; and lastly reproaching him for not showing awareness of her woe. The flatness of style and lack of polish are such that one might suspect an unpractised versifier, possibly a woman. Against this personal view, and in favour of their being dramatic utterances, one must put the existence and scope of the long anagrams ending with the 'devise'. The first yields, MA–GA––T ROOS; I. STAN––Y; the second, IOH., AGN–S COKAYN and IOHAn B–ADB.; the third, BEN–D–TTA, E–ISAB–TH; the fourth, THOMAS CHARLTO., WIMBISH and IAI TOT FOrF–YT. Two of the married pairs are separated, Elisabeth from Sir John Stanley, Benedicta from Thomas Charlton. These two poems give the impression that Sir Richard's new relations had demanded proofs and examples of his skill in versifying to order with hidden puzzles; he was obliging, and did his best with probably rather uninspiring subjects, once successfully. The occasion would be either Roos's wedding, or some similar family gathering, and the place of writing probably Haddon Hall itself. Among the poems to Margaret Vernon's family is interposed one to Roos's own kin.

No. 83*f.* 'Alas, alas, and alas, why': a poem of six quatrains (aabb) (printed in Robbins, *Secular Lyrics*, No. 167).

> *Incipit.* Alas, alas, and Alas, why
> hath fortune done so crewelly.
> *Explicit.* Wyt-oute faynyng of my hert
> Thow I fele neuer soo grete smert.

The only manuscript is Ff. 1.6, fol. 137 v. The lover addresses his beloved, deplores their separation, and protests his fidelity. A clue is offered in the opening line, 'Alas why'; it is found in French as a personal motto in MS. Royal 17.D.vi, once the property of William

FitzAlan, Earl of Arundel (1438–87), a connexion of Roos on his mother's side. The flyleaf has been used as an *album amicorum* and among many signatures are found, close together, 'Alas porquey. Duddeley. Alianor Roos'. This is a cousin of Sir Richard, Eleanor, younger daughter of Sir Robert Roos of Hunmanby; by March 8, 1449, she had married Humphrey Dudley, a son of Sir John Sutton, and younger brother of John Sutton, first Lord Dudley.[1] In compliment, probably for the wedding, Roos quoted Humphrey's 'devise', and worked in their anagrams: HOMFrI SWTTON; AlIAnor ROOS, and his own AY TOT For–AIT. It is very natural to find this purely family poem only in 'the Roos scrapbook'.

IV. POEMS FOR ELEANOR COBHAM AND
ANTIGONE D'AMANCIER

Some dozen short poems, six of which are found only in 'the Roos scrapbook', MS. Ff. 1.6, by their anagrams give interesting proof that Sir Richard Roos went on writing poems for Eleanor Cobham after Duke Humphrey's death, in the last years of her life. The Duke died in February 1447; in January 1449/50 Antigone's husband, Henry Grey, Lord Powys, died, and his widow forthwith married Jean D'Amancier, Master of the Horse to Charles VII. In Letters of Legitimation taken out for her in France in 1451, she is described as natural daughter of Humphrey, Duke of Gloucester, and wife of Jean D'Amancier.[2] She then disappears from obvious English records. D'Amancier was often employed as an envoy in the 1450s: to Savoy (1452–3), to Bruges (1455), to Milan (1458), and finally to Venice, where he died in October 1459. Eleanor Cobham is believed to have died in 1454. Whether Antigone as again a widow returned to England, I do not know, possibly not, with civil war already threatening. On the other hand, the Yorkists favoured the Gloucester connexion and may have allowed her to return to some dower-house, or to live with her son Richard (who was killed in 1466) or with her married daughter Elizabeth Grey, Lady Kynaston.

Poems which contain in their anagrams forms of the name D'Amancier (Amansier, Amancy, Amansy) can therefore be dated fairly closely,

---

[1] *Cal. Close Rolls, 1447–54*, pp. 86–7; and see in Salt Soc., 1888, IX, 64–5. There were other marriage connexions with the Sutton-Dudleys of interest to Roos. Humphrey's nephew Oliver married Katherine, daughter of Lord Latimer and of Elisabeth Beauchamp; and Oliver's sister Margaret was the second wife of Sir George Longueville, father-in-law of Margaret Vernon-Roos (*loc. cit.*, pp. 71, 76).

[2] J. Balteau, art. in *Dict. de Biographie Française*, II, 1936.

c. 1450–4; unless indeed Antigone had been acquainted with her Frenchman for some time, possibly from the early years of the queen's coming to England. Conjecture as to how she may have met him can only point to the three French embassies on the surrender of Maine, in July to August 1445, in December 1446, and in February 1447, this last led by Dunois. It is possible that Jean D'Amancier was in attendance on the ambassadors, and that this led to his future promotion as envoy.

The poems in MS. Ff. 1.6 are here considered in the order of their occurrence in the manuscript. With the exception of the first, which is also met with elsewhere, and which is found early in the volume, the poems are in close proximity, though not in sequence, in the second half of the manuscript.

No. 84. *The Complaint of Venus:* a poem, or more probably a group of three independent *ballades* with an envoy, in all nine stanzas of eight decasyllabic lines (ababbccB), and one of ten lines (aabaabbaab). The rhyme-sounds are identical in all three stanzas of each *ballade*; therefore twenty-four lines run on three rhyme-sounds. The paragraphing of the Envoy suggests a triple movement, aab | aab | baa | b.

> *Incipit.* Ther nys so high comfort to my pleasaunce
> When that I am in any hevynesse.
> *Explicit.* To folowe word by word the curiosite
> Of Graunson, flour of hem that make in Fraunce.

The poem is found in seven manuscripts and two early editions: Ff. 1.6, Fairfax 16 (Lord Stanley's manuscript of 1450 onwards), Tanner 346 (Lord Greystoke's manuscript), Pepys 2006 (the Kyriel manuscript; the latter part, ll. 45–82 twice over), Arch. Selden B.24; Trin. Coll., Camb., R.3.20; and Ashmole 59. That is, two of its manuscripts contain also *La Belle Dame sans Merci*, three contain *The Black Knight*. MS. R.3.20, a Shirley and Wilmer manuscript, has none of Roos's longer poems, as has its companion, R.3.19, but it has two of his shorter pieces, 'All Virtues' and *Gentlewoman's Lament* (see above, Nos. 6 and 77). It has too Shirley's long and erroneous note on *The Compleynt of Mars*, and his consequent note on the Graunson *ballades*; MS. Ashmole 59, Shirley's volume of his old age (he died in 1456 so that the date fits), repeats the attribution to Chaucer and the reference to Graunson, but says nothing of the people concerned.

The early printed texts are those of Julian Notary who also printed *The Compleynt of Mars*, 1499–1502 (see above, No. 73), and of Thynne, whose 1532 edition of Chaucer contains several of Roos's pieces, and was called by Skeat a 'collection of Middle English poems'.

The Complaint of Venus was assigned to Chaucer by Shirley, who probably invented the title, to connect it with *The Compleynt of Mars*, a connexion not now accepted. It has ever since been included in the Chaucer canon, and assigned conjecturally to 1392. Skeat passed its grammar and rhymes as Chaucerian, even accepting 'aventure: honoure' (ll. 22-3), a rhyme not of regular Chaucerian usage. As the Envoy makes plain, it is a free translation and adaptation of three *ballades* from the French of Oton de Graunson.[1]

I suggest that the translation is by Sir Richard Roos, and that the anagrams show it to have been made with reference to the Gloucester family, possibly over a period of years. It has, especially in the first Ballade, the vocabulary adopted in the early Plesaunce period ('plesaunce, governaunce, aventure'). The reference to age in the Envoy seems to us absurd in a man of forty, but is not impossible in that century, when the biblical span of seventy was taken as allotted; at forty, life was half over, and a man on the downward slope.

The anagrams are repetitive in the three ballades, but in different forms of the names and 'devise', on the same method as in *The Compleynt of Mars*:

I. HOMF. PLAnT---(N)-T; AlIAn. C.; AnT. P-WIS, AMANSI.; TOT FOrF-IT FOrF-IT.

II. P(L)AnTA.; AlIAn. -OBHA-; AnT. -OWIS; JeAN AMANCI.

III. HO. P(L)ANT---NeT; COBHA-; ANT.; (Je)AN AMANSI.; TOT FOr---T. *Envoy.* AlIAn -OBHaM; (G)-OU-(E)ST.; TOT FOrF--T.

The anagrams are unusually clear, and leave little residue; but the interpretation of them is not so easy, and has to be related to the content. The first Ballade, very freely rendered from Graunson's No. 1, 'Il n'est confort qui tant de biens me face', is turned from praise of a lady to that of a perfect knight. The terms would well beseem the Duchess praising the Duke in the early 1430s; but the appearance of Antigone's two married names indicate the early 1450s. The poem is on a living man; it seems hardly conceivable that Eleanor Cobham by 1450 had not yet been told of Humphrey's death. Is it possible that it is Antigone's defensive description of her new love, as one worthy to wed a Plantagenet's daughter? The other two ballades are less difficult; the second, 'Now certis, Love, hit is right convenable' (cf. No. iv), is a conventional description of the effects of love and jealousy, and there is nothing to show for which sex it is spoken; the third, 'But certes, Love, I sey not in

---

[1] 'Les Cinq Balades Ensuivans', Nos. 1, 4 and 5. *Oton de Grandson, Sa Vie et ses Poésies*, by Arthur Piaget. Lausanne, 1941, pp. 209-13.

such wise' (cf. No. v), is a woman's protestation of love in spite of
Jealousy, and the sex has again been altered. In the second, Jealousy is
more stressed than in the French; thus the lines

> For subtil Jelosie, the deceyvable,
> Ful often tyme causeth desturbyng. (ll. 43–4)

are invented in the English. In the third the figure and effects of
Jealousy are lacking in the French original; thus there is no warrant
for the lines:

> No fors thogh Jelosye me turmente. (l. 53)
> And let the jelous putte it in assay. (l. 62)

The Envoy, found only in the English, is confined in reference to the
Duke and Duchess; Antigone is not mentioned in the anagram. The
complaint of the difficulty of rhyme in English has point for the ballades
since the translator, like his model, has strictly adhered to three identical
rhyme-sounds in the stanzas; but it is mock-modest for the Envoy,
since with a final unnecessary flourish the poet has run a ten-line stanza
on two rhymes only.

Some light on the whole is thrown by the textual differences in
Ballade I, which affect the anagram; they are such as to make another
S and An available in l. 8, at the expense of an unwanted For and P;
these are readings of Shirley in MS. Ashmole 59: 'Sith he is croppe and
roote of gentylesse' takes the place of the refrain-line, 'For every wight
preiseth his gentilesse'. Again in l. 22, the caesural initial is B in
MS. Ff. 1.6, and Pepys 2006 (Hand B only), but W in MS. Fairfax 16
and Tanner 346. The effect of the change in l. 8 would be to add An
and S necessary for Amansier; the variation in l. 22 is less significant,
though the B suggests that at one time the anagram ran c–bham, and
that Roos destroyed this to get am for amansi, leaving the h high and
dry.

The inference from all this may then be, that Roos, taking a hint but
little more from Graunson, wrote the first Ballade in high laudation of
the Duke as spoken by the Duchess, after Antigone's marriage in 1435
to 1436 to Lord Powis. Later, after 1450, Roos altered it slightly, to
include the second married name, tied it up with the original *envoy*
(inserting the 'excusacion' on his age), and with two other Graunson
ballades of the same group, adapted to stress the theme of jealousy, and
including the name of Jean d'Amancier. This indeed suggests that
Antigone had been in contact with him before her husband's death.

The remaining poems of this group, anonymous and unclaimed, do not trespass on the preserves of any other poet. Those in MS. Ff. 1.6 will be considered first.

No. 85*a*. 'My-self walkyng': a poem of three stanzas of seven octosyllabic lines (ababbcc); a lament for extreme misfortune, and loss of wealth and repute; printed in C. Brown, *Religious Lyrics of the Fifteenth Century*, No. 169, and in *Reliquiae Antiquae*, I, 26.

> *Incipit.* My-self walkyng all allone,
> ffull of thoght, of Ioy desperat.
> *Explicit.* Soo haue I lost my Countenaunce
> Of all the world to my plesance.
> (deleted: My hoole comfort & my plesaunce.)

The unique manuscript is MS. Ff. 1.6 (fol. 139); it is preceded by the phrase 'A god whene' (a suitable motto, not a name disguised) and by the drawing of a barrel and two fishes (luces), which looks like a rebus, and is probably that of Leweston, the copyist. The anagrams are: HOMFr–Y (line-initials), AlIAn (c)OBHAM (caesural initials), and, diffused, AnT. AMANS(I); TOT ForFAIT. The substituted line is reminiscent of Humphrey's motto 'Mon bien mondain'.

No. 85*b*. 'In ffull grett hevenesse': a lament in the first person against the 'rancoure off this wekyd wor[l]de' and the evil power of the world, the flesh, and the devil, in six stanzas of seven octosyllabic lines (ababbcc); printed in Brown, *Religious Lyrics*, etc., No. 173.

> *Incipit.* In ffull grett hevenesse myn hert ys pwyght.
> *Explicit.* Tho Comfort the trewth and all ffalshed deface.
> amen pure cherite.

The only manuscript is Ff. 1.6 (fol. 144 v.). There is no indication of the sex of the speaker, who is very bitter against false report. The curse pronounced on wicked tongues, 'The Skene ther-off a-wey to pell', is like Roos's on defamers of women in *Reson and Sensuallyte* (ll. 6498–500). The anagrams are: HOMFR(E)Y; ALIAn COBHAM; AnT. AMAN(CIER); STIWA.; IAY TOT ForFAIT ForFAIT. Sir John Stiward, one of Eleanor Cobham's Keepers, died in 1447/8.

No. 85*c*. 'O Cryste Jesu, mekely I pray to the': a poem in three stanzas of rhyme royal, an invocation of the Holy Name against perils from without and from within; printed in Brown, *Religious Lyrics*, etc., No. 125.

> *Incipit.* O Cryste Jesu, mekely I pray to the
> To lete thy name, wedyr y ryde or gone.

Explicit. That thow me saue from eternall schame
That haue full feght & hole truste in þi name.
Explicit.

The sole manuscript is Ff. 1.6 (fol. 146 v.). The chief metrical peculiarity is the very strong syntactical run-on between stanzas 1 and 2.
The expressions are more forcible than is usual in Roos's smooth poetry:
the power of the Name, impressed on the suppliant's forehead, is to
make all mortal foes 'stonde styll as eny stone', and to drive out of sight
the

> wicked spretus so oryble & blake
> That besy bene to wayte me day & nyghte;

a petition of peculiar poignancy for the repentant sorceress. The
speaker's sex is not indicated. The term 'wedyr y ryde or gone' may be
a mere cliché, or it may point to an impending journey.

The anagrams are interesting. The line-initials sufficiently indicate
two people: st. 1, (c)OB–AM; st. 2, AI–An; st. 3, –OMF. The caesural
initials fill these out, and bring out what has lain concealed, another
name, and the 'devise': HOMFr.; ALIAn COB–AM; AnTI. POWIS, DAMAnS;
TOT FOrFA–T.

No. 85*d*. 'Grettere Mater': 'a complaint for lack of mercy' in four
stanzas of eight decasyllabic lines (ababbcbC) with a variable refrain;
printed, MacCracken, *Lydgate's Minor Poems*, p. 381.

> *Incipit.* Grettere mater of dol and heuynesse
> Noe more cause haith no man to complayne
> *Explicit.* I nere but dede, pleynely, þis is no fable,
> Withoute recure, for lacke of mercy.

The sole manuscript is Ff. 1.6 (fol. 152 v.–153). The speaker languishes
in a quotidian fever, weeps 'Lyke Nyobe and Myrra' (this suggests a
woman), and invokes good Hope. By contrast with the last poem, this
is not a religious complaint but a secular appeal for mercy:

> Whate vayleth bewte which ys nat mercyabill?
> Whate vayleth a sterre when hit do nat schyne,
> Or grete poure that lyste nat to declyne
> His heres downe, to here pytusly
> Compleynt of nedy, whiche yn theyre payne
> Crye for recur, and there is no mercy. (st. 3)

The 'star' may be a reference to the Cobham arms; but stars play a
noticeable part in the poems of this manuscript. The comparison
(st. 4) to Achilles' sword, of which the edge was fatal, but the 'plate was
medycynabill', is new in Roos, I believe, but Niobe and Myrrha are

memories from *The Black Knight* (ll. 178–80), and from 'For lac of sighte', which is also in this manuscript. The anagrams, which are obscured by a smoke-screen of the letter w, run thus: HOMFR.; ALYAN. CO–HAM; ANTIG. POWiS, DAMANCI; TOT FOrFA–T.

No. 85*e*. 'This ys no lyf': a ballade of three stanzas of rhyme royal; Robbins divides into two poems, printing the first stanza only as No. 165 in *Secular Lyrics*, and the other two in *P.M.L.A.*, LXIX, 638; but the *Index*, No. 3613, includes all three stanzas. Only stt. 2 and 3 have a variable refrain.

> *Incipit.* This ys no lyf, alas, þat y do lede.
> *Explicit.* Alas your vnkyndeness þus haith my herte schente.

The only manuscript is Ff. 1.6 (fol. 153 r.–v.). The poem may well not be in its final state; some lines have twelve syllables, and the third stanza is incoherent. The ending is a repeated farewell to 'my lady', 'dyre herte', 'chef yn remembraunce'. The first and second stanzas have no explicit reference to love, but complain of a death in life, of heaviness and sorrow lacking comfort and remedy. The interwoven anagrams unite the three stanzas and cover only two names: st. 1, ALYAn.; AnT.; st. 2, CO–HAM; P–WYS; stt. 1 and 3, AMANCIE(R); diffused TVT FOrFAYT FOrFA–T. It seems then that Eleanor Cobham is saying farewell to Antigone, her 'ioy and rote of . . . plesaunce', as if she had accepted the French marriage as a 'fait accompli'.

No. 85*f*. The sense and purport of the next poem in MS. Ff. 1.6 (fol. 153 v., printed by Robbins, *P.M.L.A.*, LXIX, 638–9) have been concealed by misarrangement of its three rhyme royal stanzas. Its apparent *incipit* is 'Yit wulde I nat the causer faryd A-mysse'. Its actual *incipit* is, I believe, the apparent eighth line: 'Now ye that bathe in myrthe and pleasaunce'; that is, the apparent second and third stanzas shift up to be first and second, and the apparent first stanza drops to the third. The poem then progresses logically from an address to the fortunate, to a statement of separation as the immediate cause of woe, and finally to resigned acceptance. It emerges thus as an impressive and dignified lament by a woman of high place for a change from security to 'al disease', for a joyous 'auenture'. Many phrases suggest the Gloucester background, 'plesaunce', 'myn auenture', and the theme of worldly power; Gloucester's mottoes were 'Mon bien mondain', and 'In good aventure'. The unusual idea 'thrall' with 'subject' reminds us that Eleanor Cobham had been the wife of the king's highest subject; now

C C

she is reduced to thraldom. The lines are carefully shaped, with clear caesuras, much more so than in the preceding poem. The anagram yields: HOMF--Y; ALIAN.; ANTI-ON. DAMANSI.; IAY T-T FOr-AIT. Like the immediately preceding poem, it is a farewell to her who 'moste nedys departe', and an acceptance of the situation.

This closes the little series of d'Amancier poems in MS. Ff. 1.6; there are still some which have strayed into other manuscripts, another half-dozen.

No. 86a. *Alone Walking:* a 'Virelay' of five stanzas of eight four-syllable lines, rhyming aaabaaab, and with the stanza-rhymes linked, so that there are only six rhyme-sounds in the forty lines.

> *Incipit.* Alone walking
> In thought pleyning
> *Explicit.* Doth me avaunce,
> And thus an ende.

The only manuscript is Trinity College, Cambridge, R.3.19 (fol. 160), a Wilmer gift. The lyric was printed by Stow (1561), and again by Skeat (VII, No. xxv, p. 448). Skeat showed that its non-Chaucerian rhymes ruled it out as by Chaucer (*Chaucer Canon*, p. 122). He noticed the word 'ure' (destiny) as interesting; it occurs also in *The Black Knight* and *The Court of Love*.

The lines are too short for a double acrostic; the line-initials yield in anagram: -OMFr-Y; AlIAn. -OB-AM; AnTI-ON. DAMANCI-R; STIW-D; WIT-In---M; WIMBIS. There is no 'devise'.

This very personal lament (cf. No. 85a) seems to represent a memorial of the dead and the living. Sir John Stiward had died (1447-8) within about a year after the Duke; Sir Robert Whittingham, the elder, died in 1452, two years before Eleanor herself. The only survivor was Nicholas Wymbysh who lived on to old age (1461).

A lament, found in MS. Rawl. C.813 (*Anglia*, XXXI, pp. 354-6, No. 23), bids farewell in the terms of a lover to his lady.

No. 86b.

> *Incipit.* With woofull harte plungede yn dystresse.
> *Explicit.* for yll-wyll ys muche, we nede no more,
> That I haue yow fautyd, I am sorye therfore.

The poem is in eleven stanzas of rhyme royal; like the few other Roos poems in this Tudor collection, it is not highly polished. The writer laments the loss of 'all solace, all worldly plesure', and complains to the 'sweetheart' of the 'inward wound' of her indifference:

> And yn especyally now of late
> ye haue encresyd my peynes sore;
> I haue dyspleysyd yow some-whate
> in your mynde, I wotte nott wherfore. (st. 4)

A lasting separation is foreseen:

> farewell! I see that all thyng endes;
> farewell for euer, your companye. (st. 8)

The anagrams run: st. 1, AlYAn.; stt. 1–2, –OB.; WIMBIS; st. 3, HOMF–Y; stt. 3–4, ISMANY; stt. 4–6, WHA–Y–BO–O; st. 6, AMANCY; stt. 10–11, TOT FOrFAIT FOrFAYT. There may be still more names in stt. 7–11, but I cannot be sure of them. The anaphora on 'Farewell' in stt. 8–9 is not, I think, taken advantage of.

No. 86*c*. 'I see A Rybane': a poem of seven stanzas of eight lines on an octosyllabic basis (ababbcbC), with a varying refrain on 'better A-byde'; printed in Brown, *Religious Lyrics of the Fifteenth Century*, No. 183, under the title, *Counsels of Prudence and Patience*.

> *Incipit.*   ffor þe bettur a-byde.
> I see A Rybane Ryche and newe
> Wyth stones and perles Ryally pyght.
> *Explicit.* And brynge vs to þe blysse of heuene,
> ffor the better ther euer to A-byde.
>   Explicit.

The two manuscripts are MS. Cotton Caligula A.ii (fol. 67), and Advocates MS. 1.1.6. The anagrams run thus: stt. 1–2, GLOV–– ST–R; st. 3, HOMFRey; st. 4, ALIAn. –OBHA–.; elsewhere, ANTIGO. DA–ANSIER; BABTH.; WHITTInGHA–; STAFFOrD; IAY TOT FOrFAIT FOrFAIT. These names, taken together with the tenor of the poem, present an interesting situation. The verses are not in Roos's usual courtly style, but in one which at first recalls the *Pearl*, by the strong alliteration and accentual beat, and by the ornate and jewelled opening stanza. The poet describes a jewelled band, (an 'orfray') with a motto or 'Resoun', 'ffor þe bettur a-byde'; with proverbial sententiousness he counsels patience and forbearance. The last stanza gives the clue to the whole:

> I haue wyste mene in prysoun be caste,
> And lyve ther-in sex yere or seuene;
> And ʒyt be holpene owte at þe laste,
> ffor ofte mene mete at vn-sette steuene;
> Wyth freend & foo god makes euene.

This is a poem of advice to Eleanor Cobham, and its final encouragement is enhanced by the jewels of the ribbon, carefully chosen, as were those in *How a Lover*. Pearls were of avail for the eyes, and against weeping; royal rubies (I take this to be the meaning of 'Regalles Rubies'; 'c'est li sire des peres, . . . la gemme des gemmes'. Cf. *The Flour of Curtesye*, ll. 120–1) bring honour and grace to the wearer, and rejoicing wherever he may come; the celidony is healthful, brings fulfilment of wishes, and is of avail against royal anger:

> Cuntre ire de prinze e de reis
> Dune force, aie e defeis.

Above all the sapphire can set a prisoner free, breaking strong bonds; if the four corners and the door of the prison are touched with it, the door will open. Moreover, it brings men into accord with each other.[1]

This pretty piece is then not a poem merely of general moral advice, it is a jewel of comfort sent to Eleanor Cobham, begging her not to be rash, but to possess her soul in patience. Unlike several of this group of poems, its reference is not confined to Eleanor and Antigone, but brings in the names of former friends now at court, Babthorpe and Whittingham, and above all Stafford, who must be Humphrey, Earl of Stafford, son of her old friend, Anne of Woodstock. This is to assure her that she is not forgotten; the hidden meaning of the precious stones may even imply that she may look forward to freedom. It is possible (though not documented) that after Gloucester's death, some felt that Eleanor's power to do harm was gone, and that the royal mercy might be extended. 'Sex yere or seuene' of imprisonment would bring us only to 1448 as an upward limit; it must have been nearer nine or ten years, for a poem of 1450 onwards; the understatement is imposed by the rhyme. It seems as if Roos, exchanging his accustomed elegance for this lilting old-fashioned style, hoped to get the poem through to her to comfort and yet to restrain.

This hope of release is hinted at obscurely in a poem to be found, with music, in a Tudor manuscript (Add. 31922, fol. 116 v.).

No. 86*d*.

Incipit. My thought oppressed, my mynd in trouble.

A lament of four stanzas of rhyme royal, with repetitive decoration in stanzas 2 and 4. The first stanza runs on an anaphora of 'My' for five

---

[1] *Anglo-Norman Lapidaries*, ed. Studer and Evans, Paris, 1924. See especially pp. 120, 140 (sapphire); p. 44 (celidony); p. 126 (ruby); p. 108 (pearl).

lines; the initials of the next words, T B I L Ye, can form LIB--TYe. The rest of the anagram yields: stt. 1–2, –OBHAM; stt. 2–4, ANTI–ON. POWIS, AMANSIER; stt. 3–4, HOMFRI; TOT FOrF–YT. The Duke's motto, 'good aventure', repeated in the last stanza, recalls him also:

> right suere to haue no good aventure
> no good aventure in me to haue place.

A shorter poem, also set to music, is preserved in Royal Appendix, 58, fol. 18 v. to 19 v.

No. 86*e*.

Incipit. Thofe I doo syng, my hert dothe wepe.

A lament of heaviness and remediless wrong in two stanzas of rhyme royal. The consonantal anagram, for which only two vowel-initials are provided, gives: C–BH–M; D–M–NSI–R; B–BTh.; TOT FOr--YT. The poem may have been shortened by the composer.[1]

No. 86*f*.

The last d'Amancier poem to be dealt with here (but see also Chapter XII) turns up in the little cluster of lyrics in the alchemical manuscript, Ashmole 176 (fol. 100); catalogued as two poems (Nos. 13 and 14), it is actually No. 11. It is printed here in full as two octosyllabic quatrains (abab):

> Alas to who*m* should I co*m*playne
> or shewe my wofull heavynes
> syth fortune hathe me in disdeyne,
> and am exyled remedylesse.
>
> Adewe adewe my hartes lust
> adewe my ioye and my solace
> with double sorowes co*m*playne I must
> vntyll I dye alas alas.

Even on this very restricted range of letters, the anagram gives: Al–An. CO–HA–; AMAnSI–R. The names suit the theme, leave-taking and complaint for exile; to Eleanor Cobham of Plesaunce, the Isle of Man must have seemed as far as Ultima Thule.

The wealth of personal allusions in poems treated of in this and the preceding chapters shows how central was Sir Richard Roos's position in the Lancastrian court and society of his time. He hears everything,

---

[1] For knowledge of these two poems I am indebted to Mr. P. J. Frankis.

knows about everyone, not unlike John Chamberlain, or Horace Walpole, or Crabb Robinson later, with this difference, that Roos is also a poet, and for diaries and letters he writes in discreet, anagrammatic verse. The changes affecting the Gloucester family he would of course know, and he writes with readiness to help the imprisoned Eleanor, and Antigone who deserts England for France. The family history of the Beauforts, past and present, he knows intimately.

Of lesser members of the Plesaunce circle, such as Elisabeth Cobham and Maud Stanhope, he has sympathetic knowledge. The troubler of their peace, Lord Fawcomberg, is treated at first with some lenience in the high tradition (as Mars or Arcite), but with increasing asperity, as the satires will show. Some who passed on from Plesaunce to be pillars of the queen's court, Lady Scales, Margaret Stanlow, Humphrey, Earl of Stafford, Duke of Buckingham (Anne of Woodstock's son), retain his constant love and respect. Through Lady Scales, and through old acquaintance with Jacquetta of Bedford, Roos comes into touch with young Anthony Wydville, a connexion helpful later.

Roos's wooing of Margaret Longueville, a Vernon of Haddon Hall, brings him into the rather independent group of gentry in south Derbyshire. For her family he writes a few poems, but they seem to remain on the circumference of his life. He takes Margaret with him to his true centre, the court. Just as he had made his niece Eleanor Roos the naïve narrator of *The Assembly of Ladies*, so he gives to his wife a place in his poetry as the intelligent observer in *The Flower and the Leaf*.

CHAPTER X

Satirical Verse

S IR RICHARD ROOS produced in his early and his later periods what may be called community satire. In *Ragman Roll* and in *The Chance of the Dice*, the sarcasm, though sharp enough at times, is subdued to the needs of a social merry-making, where not all the participants are pilloried. But there are other opportunities, and the forger of a weapon can seldom resist using it to display his skill. We can, I believe, find Roos writing satirical ballades and verse-letters, which seem at first to come from the same corner of his brain as the unflattering characters of the two verse-games, but which develop into bitter and venomous invective against Barbelina Herberquyne and Lord Fawcomberg. He is writing at first for the Plesaunce group.

No. 87. *Balade Against Woman Unconstant* (Stow's title): a ballade of three stanzas of rhyme royal, with no Envoy, but with a refrain.

> *Incipit.* Madame, for your newefangelnesse
> Many a servaunt have ye put out of grace.
> *Explicit* (with refrain).
> Al light for somer, ye woot wel what I mene,
> In stede of blew, thus may ye were al grene.

There is no 'signature'. The poem occurs in three manuscripts: Fairfax 16 (the best text), Harleian 7578, and Cotton Cleopatra D.vii from which Stow printed it as Chaucer's. There is no manuscript attribution to Chaucer, and it is classed as doubtful by Pollard and Robinson; Skeat accepted it; Furnivall and Brusendorff (p. 441) rejected it outright.

The refrain, which, if not proverbial, yet expresses a commonplace of *amour courtois*, is also found in a *balade* of similar purport by Machaut (see Robinson, p. 981); we know that Roos used Machaut's *Dit dou*

Lyon in two of his narrative poems. In Deschamps' lyrics Roos would find models for 'Injures contre une femme':

> Perverse en cuer, de semblant tricheresse,
> Douce en parler, en oeuvre venimeuse
> (S.A.T.F., V, 214, No. 975; cf. Nos. 318–19, 777, 804).

Similar attacks on inconstant women are made in *Ragman Roll*, on 'womane stabill as the mone' in a cruel and gross stanza (15), or on one whose

> gyse ys for to holde men in hande
> And with your eye fede her blyndenesse (25).

In *The Chance of the Dice*, with different application, the weathercock has already come to the writer's mind. There too are portraits of inconstants, both men (st. 5, 'There Jason falseth oon ye falsen twoo') and women (stt. 27, 41); finally

> Creseyde is here in worde, bothe thought and dede . . .
> ffor tymes moo than peyntour chaungeth hewe
> Ye leue youre olde and taken newe and newe (55).

Delilah is not mentioned in the games. Wily Candace, who is only once mentioned by Chaucer, and then probably in error (*Parl. of Foules*, l. 288) would be familiar to a reader of the alliterative *Alexander*, Candace who tires her head and entices Alexander into the room turned round by twenty elephants:

> Loo now ʒe here withouten hiʒt in-to my handis sesed,
> Bot in a womans ward for all þi wale dedis (l. 5313)

The anagram yields BEWMONT; ISMA–Y SCAl–S, WH– – – –B–RY; TOT FORFAIT. One must assume that the poet is arraigning Elisabeth Phelip, now Lady Beaumont, before his friend and confidante, Lady Scales.

No. 88. *A Balade Pleasaunte*: a poem of seven stanzas of rhyme royal. Printed by Stow, and by Chalmers (I, 563–4).

> *Incipit.* I haue a lady where so she bee
> That seldome is she soueraine of my thought
> *Explicit.* For were she well, of me I did no cure.
> Explicit the discriuing of a faire lady (Stow).

The only manuscript is Trin. Coll., Camb., R.3.19. Stow's inclusion of the poem in his Chaucer volume was at once attacked by Francis Thynne; and its position was again assailed by Tyrwhitt. Skeat's comment on the date is erroneous and misleading (*Canon*, p. 123); the writer does not say (st. 6) that *he* was fifteen years old at the wedding of Queen Jane, but that *the lady* was so:

> Is it not joy that such one of her age . . .
> Should in her werke be so sadde and sage
> That of the wedding sawe all the noblesse
> Of queene Iane, and was tho as I gesse
> But of the age of yeeres ten and fiue.

The poem is a description of the appearance and disposition of an elderly lady, *per contrarium*; she is fair, but yet no angel; she has every comeliness, but yet she is short, beetle-browed, and stumpy-fingered, and 'Her skin is smooth as any oxes tong'. She has the inversion of all the virtues; busy-idle, as harmless as an ape, and as meek as a hornet. It is the style that Roos will develop mordantly later. Even here it seems unkind of an ageing woman, and one's distaste is turned to dismay by the line initials anagram: An STAFFOr. BOWSHIR WO--ST.; IAI T-T FOrFAIT FOr-AIT. Can this portrait really paint the same elderly lady whom Roos praised highly in *The Isle of Ladies*? But when the caesural acrostic letters are added, the sting is drawn; the whole displays the names of four more ladies of the Plesaunce group, thus reducing the apparent slander to a merry flyting: AnN STAFFOr. BOWSHIR WOO-STO.; AnTIG.; ISMANIA S-AL-S; WHITT.; STAn-OW; IAI TOT FOrFAIT FOr-AIT. We have had evidence in the history of Richard Roos, Esquire, of the lengths to which a coterie's practical joke could be taken. The reference to the wedding of Joan of Navarre with Henry IV, February 1403, probably recalls some of the old lady's reminiscences; it was in July of the same year that her second husband, Edmund, Earl of Stafford, died at the battle of Shrewsbury. Actually Anne of Woodstock, born c. 1382, was fully twenty in 1403, so that the reckoning 'But of the age of yeeres ten and fiue' is a masterly and mocking understatement (G.E.C., V, 178). Her death in October 1438 gives a downward date for the poem.

A similar short poem of inverted assertions proves to be a stone thrown in jest into Lady Scales's garden.

No. 89.

Incipit. Welcom be ye when ye go

It is in two stanzas of eight lines, and occurs among songs with music in MS. Arch. Selden B.26; it is printed in *Early English Lyrics*, No. 125. The anagram runs: st. 1, IS-ANIA; st. 2, WHA-ISB.; stt. 1-2, TOT FOrFAIT.

A complaint of an unsuccessful lover, written in a humorous satirical vein, is addressed to two of Roos's men friends, and aimed at Disdain and Daunger in the ladies of Plesaunce.

No. 90. 'The Servant of Cupyde Forsaken': a poem of nine eight-line stanzas of octosyllabic lines (ababbcbC) with a varying refrain, and including an Envoy addressed to all women. Printed by MacCracken, *Minor Poems of Lydgate*, II, 427–9.

> *Incipit.* Ful longe I haue a seruant be.
> *Explicit.* Whos galle ay newe doþe infect
> þe sugre of men in euery place.

It is known in only one manuscript, Shirley's own, MS. Add. 16165, which calls it 'Complaynt Lydegate', with a marginal comment to the Envoy, 'Be stille daun Johan, suche is youre fortune'. The monk's biographers have been misled by the poem into very natural, but now untenable, conclusions on his mis-spent youth.

The anagrams run as follows:

Stt. 1–2, AlIan. COB–AM; ISMAnIA SCA–ES; ForF–IT.
Stt. 3–4, E–ISA––Th B–WMONT; AnTIGO–A.
Stt. 4–5, ForFAIT. Stt. 4–6, MA–D –TANHOP.
Stt. 6–7, I–MAnIA SCAL.; ForFAIT.
St. 7, AlIAN.; AnTIGO–A. St. 8, MAVD; (CH)AW––Th.
St. 9, Envoy, WIM–YS; WhITT.

The omission of the name of Anne of Woodstock may point to a date after October 1438.

The repetition of Eleanor Cobham's name in st. 7, and the coupling there with Antigone, seem to fit the distinction drawn between 'some fer ronne in age' and the young, 'ful wylde and rage'. The poet's range in the poem is like Sheridan's from the maiden of fifteen to the widow of fifty, or like Donne's, 'both fair and brown', but with a more rueful tone. Roos's self-mockery comes out in his slangy expressions: 'I blewe alwey the bukkes horne'; or

> And þus I pleyde Iacke þe Haare,
> And gane to hoppe a newe trace,
> And sange 'Go, farewell, feldfare'.

His conclusion, 'I may singe þe Chaunteplure', refers of course to the elegiac songs, like parts of the funeral service; but there may be a hint of recent association with Charles d'Orléans, whose mother, Valentine of Milan, adopted as a badge of grief the 'Chauntepleure' in its other meaning, a watering-pot.

Another Plesaunce squib is a ballade in four stanzas of rhyme royal against the false seeming of maidens and wives.

No. 91.

> *Incipit.* Of their nature they greatly them delite
> With holy face feined for the nones.
> *Explicit.* Written in the lusty season of May.

The only manuscript is Trin. Coll., Camb., R.3.19; it was printed by Stow, and by Chalmers (I, 560). The anagram runs: st. 1, BeWMO–T; stt. 1–2, –LISABeTh; st. 2, AlIAN.; stt. 2–4, –OBHAM; st. 3, BAr–O–F; stt. 4–5, MAV. STANH––E. After a good opening stanza on hypocrites, the poem falls off sadly, but it has several of Roos's expressions: 'reliques' with the second sense of 'lovers'; 'exiled'; 'do the besie cure'; 'he should be shent'. The extreme roughness of the metre (ll. 19–21 are of 14, 8, and 10 syllables respectively) may point to an unpolished effort.

No. 92. *In Praise of Women:* a poem of twenty-five stanzas of rhyme royal (printed by Thynne and Urry (pp. 456–8), and in Chalmers, I, 344–5).

> *Incipit.* Al tho [that] list of women evill to speak
> And sain of hem worse than they deserve.
> *Explicit.* There as she and all good women shal be in fere
> In Heauen aboue, among the angels clere.

The only manuscript is the Bannatyne MS. (fol. 275), written in 1568, and printed for the Hunterian Club (1873, p. 799) and by Ritchie for the Scottish Text Society (n.s. XXVI, 64–70). Skeat affirms the poem to be 'probably by Lydgate', and suggests that it is the poem promised at the end of *The Temple of Glas*. That may well be. MacCracken does not admit it as Lydgate's. It is in Roos's smooth courtly style, and has the routh: trouth: slouth rhyme in four stanzas.

The poem is repetitive and shapeless, and possibly somewhat disordered; as it stands, it can be divided into five sections, alternating praise of women's virtues, and exposure of the wiles of false deceiving men. The anagrams are strung along through the stanzas in pairs or small groups, and sometimes suit the subject of the stanzas; thus the first section gives women's names, but the last a man's only.

(1) stt. 1–4. Women are the cause of knighthood and nurture and of all worthiness.

(2) stt. 5–11. Men use many tricks to beguile 'these innocent creatures', and having succeeded, allow them to be defamed.

(3) stt. 12–15. Yet women are truer than men, and it is they who suffer enticement.

(4) stt. 16–19. Men appeal to women's pity with 'a painted processe'.

(5) stt. 20–5. Women are full of ruth and goodness, and should be reverenced because of the Blessed Virgin.

The anagrams run as follows: stt. 1–4, CO–HAM, AlIAn., E–ISA–ETh, TOT FOrFAIT; stt. 3–6, FAW–OMB.; 5–6, ST–ANGE; 6, STAN–OP; 8, willYAM, 8–10, FAW–OMB; 8–10 ISMAnYA SCALiS; 11–12, STANHO.; 12–14, WILL–BI; COBHAM; 14, FAWCO–B.; 15–16, STANHOP; FOrFAYT; 17–19, NeVILe; 18–19, STAnHOP; 20, FA– – –B–RG; 21–3, WIL–IA. N–VILe FAW– – –Be–G; 24–5, TOT FOrFAIT FOr–AIT.

It would be possible to fill out some missing letters from non-adjacent stanzas, but it seems preferable to leave the names as they stand, with the signature 'devise' at the beginning and at the end, and again in short form in the middle.

This trio, Lord Fawcomberg, Elisabeth Cobham, Lady Strange, and Maud Stanhope, Lady Willoughby, we have already found in association. They are here accompanied by complimentary references to Elisabeth's sister, the Duchess of Gloucester, who has elsewhere been called 'Auctour of norture', and to Lady Scales. There is no reason, however, to think that their names should be added to the roll of those whom Lord Fawcomberg had deceived. The theme of the poem, a protest against deception followed by betrayal, looks as if he not only kissed and rode away, but also told, thus violating the second statute of courtly love: 'Secretly to kepe Councell of love, . . . It may not sown in every wightes ere' (*Court of Love*, 309). But the tone is one of expostulation, no more, and it is not till Fawcomberg stoops to more ignoble game that Roos sharpens his arrows.

These few poems can well be called 'toothless satires', half-playful snapping and growling as of a young animal; in those still to come, attacks on a man and a woman, the poet shows his fangs in anger and disdain, even in scurrility and obscenity. One must think that it is the woman who chiefly rouses his disgust, since he has already treated the man with some tolerance. It is again William Neville, Lord Fawcomberg; and again, as in *The Compleynt of Mars*,[1] the first clue is the angle-hook, the Fawcomberg badge, with the fishing metaphor.

No. 93. *Balade of a Reeve*, Versions A and B: a coarsely satiric balade of

[1] Brusendorff noted these correspondences (p. 283 and note).

three stanzas of rhyme royal, with refrain; printed in parallel columns by Brusendorff, pp. 280–1.

> *Incipit.* Hit is no right alle oþer lustes to leese
> This monethe of *May* for missyng of on cas.
> *Explicit.* þus holde I bett þan labour as a Reve. (A version)

There are two manuscripts: Add. 16165, fol. 244 r.–v., Shirley's manuscript, with the running title, 'Balade by Chaucer'; and Harleian 7578, fol. 15 r.–v., which Brusendorff considers to be 'a very corrupt and careless copy of a text like Shirley's' yet with some better readings. The anagrams run: Version A, FAl–OMB–R.; BARBAlINA HARBA–CY.; IAY TOT FOr–AIT; the residue consists mostly of the letter T. Version B, FA–OMB.; BA(R)BALInA HA(R)BARCI.; IAI TOT FOr–AIT; (R.R.). Both versions contain unimpaired the allusion of the third stanza:

> If I hade leve to hunt in euery chace
> Or fisshen and so myn angle leese
> That *Barbell* had swolowed boþe hooke and lace.

Barbelina Herberquyne, Queen Margaret's 'Almain' attendant, naturalized together with the French ladies in 1449,[1] had been included in the anagrams of two early poems of compliment to the queen (see above, Nos. 64 and 68). In *The Chance of the Dice* later she is scornfully dismissed as boisterous and indiscreet (st. 13). The coupling of her name with that of Lord Fawcomberg in some of the *Legends*, and in this group of poems, indicates Roos's belief in an intrigue between them. The ambiguous phrase here, 'an esy pas In lowe cuntrey ther as hit may not greve', probably glances at her 'Almain' origin.

A poem of the same order as this last is addressed to one 'Burgeys'.

No. 94.

> *Incipit.* Burgeys, thou haste so blowen atte the cole
> That alle thy rode is from thine face agoon.

The only known manuscript is Harleian 7578, fol. 15 v., where, after the 'Balade of a Reve', it is tacked on to the 'Complaint to my Lodesterre' from which Skeat rightly separated it (see below, No. 101*b*); that is in rhyme royal, this in seven eight-line stanzas. It is extremely coarse, and has only recently found an editor (R. H. Bowers in *Mod. Lang. Notes*, June 1955, LXX, 396–8). It addresses with satiric mock-sympathy a 'maistre reveloure', a man suffering the effects of 'excesse of venerye'. The anagram runs thus: stt. 1–2, MA–D STANHOP; st. 3, BA–Be–INA; TOT

---

[1] *Cal. Pat. Rolls, 1446–52*, p. 240.

FORFAIT FOR--IT; stt. 3-4, HE-BE--In; st. 4, WhA-YSBO-O.; st. 5, STAN-O.; TOT FORFAIT; st. 6, FAW-ONB.; STRAn.; st. 7, FAW---B.; STAN.; FOR-AIT.

The allusion to a lodging 'atte the stronde' almost certainly implies the street in London. The man's ghastly resemblance to 'oon of the thre dede kinges' must allude to the well-known 'Lai des Trois Morts et des Trois Vifs' where three noblemen meet three skeletons, and find they are themselves. It is the basic idea of the Danse Macabre which was depicted on the wall of the cemetery of the Innocents in Paris, where Roos and Fawcomberg might well have seen it. The six figures of the *Lai* were once painted on the west wall of the chapel at Haddon Hall, where Sir Richard had special opportunities for observing them; now only 'Les trois morts' remain.[1]

The name Burgeys is difficult to explain; may it be a familiar shortening, perhaps by way of disguise, of the name Fawcom-berg(e)? The writer says that he himself was one of the company that heard the man's vows of repentance.

No. 95. 'Loke wel aboute': a balade of six or seven stanzas of rhyme royal in variable order, with refrain. Printed by Stow, Chalmers, Skeat (*Chaucer*, VII, No. xiv) as 'Warning Men to Beware Deceitful Women', and by Robbins (*Secular Lyrics* etc., pp. 224, 290) as 'Scorn of Women'.

> *Incipit.* Loke wel aboute, ye that lovers be,
> Lat nat your lustes lede you to dotage.
> *Explicit.* They coud nat wryte wommanes traitory;
> Bewar therfore; the blinde et many a fly.

There are four manuscripts, Trin. Coll., Camb., R.3.19 (a Shirley manuscript), and O.9.38; Harleian 2251; and MS. 1306, Engl. Coll. at Rome, a manuscript of Lydgate's poems (R. A. Klinefelter, *Mod. Lang. Quart.*, 1953, XIV, 3-6). The last stanza, on parchment and ink, appears adapted in *The Remedy of Love*: 'Yf all the yearth were parchment scribable' (ll. 239-45; Chalmers, I, 540); in this 'Tudor poem' (*testè* Skeat), it is still used to enforce the same theme. From Thynne's *Chaucer*, this stanza was transferred to the 'Devonshire Manuscript', Brit. Mus., Add. 17492, and by the substitution of two complimentary nouns turned to the praise of women (see *R.E.G.*, 1956, N.S. VII, 55-6; also R. Harrier, *ib.*, 1960, XI, 54). Some user of MS. R.3.19, but not probably Shirley himself, put 'Chaucer' in the margin. Tyrwhitt and Skeat ascribed the poem to Lydgate; MacCracken, though doubtful,

---

[1] An excellent cut of this subject is in Wynkyn de Worde's edition of *The Contemplacyon of Synners* (1499), sig. F. ij v. The six figures meet beneath a crucifix at a cross-roads.

inclines to think it spurious (*Minor Poems*, p. xlix). The phrase that gives him pause, 'laughe and love nat', is certainly one quoted by Roos as if Lydgate's (see above, No. 64), and is not found in Lydgate's undoubted works. MacCracken's unconscious tribute to Roos is welcome; the poem is 'much more biting and forcibly effective than any of Lydgate's satire'. The anagrams explain this; they yield from six stanzas: WIL–YAM FAW–OMBe.; BA–B–LYN HE–Be–CIN; ELYSABeTH –OBHAM; SAl–SBV–; TOT ForFA–T ForFA–T; the extra stanza gives STAn–O–E, WILBe. This coupling of Barbelina with Maud Stanhope, and with Elisabeth Cobham (Anelida, and the Venus of *The Compleynt of Mars*), may hint that Fawcomberg was not off with the old loves before he was on with the new; but the tenor of the poem is treachery in women, and one cannot doubt that Barbelina is aimed at. The Lord Salisbury of the 1450s is Sir Richard Neville, husband of Alice Montague, father of Warwick the Kingmaker, and eldest brother of Fawcomberg. The final proverbial phrase, 'The blinde et many a fly', seems to connect the poem with the four stanzas, also in MS. R.3.19, beginning 'Of their nature they greatly them delite' (No. 91 above) and it might be tempting to see the two poems as one whole. But the anagrams are against this, since they are for Plesaunce in No. 91. Roos has elsewhere picked up an effective phrase, and put it again to use.

No. 96. 'O mossie quince': a poem of four stanzas of rhyme royal of which three stanzas were printed by Stow and Chalmers; a fourth stanza occurs as the second stanza in the only known manuscript, Trin. Coll., Camb., R.3.19, and is printed by Skeat (*Chaucer Canon*, p. 124). There is little logical sequence in this pungently unpleasant poem, whether with or without the fourth stanza. The poet feigns to commiserate with this 'louely leud maistres' over her ugliness in age, as she withers like an overripe fruit, a 'mellow costard'. The anagram is helped out by the extra stanza, especially with the 'devise'. It is carefully contrived: the line initials give nothing away; but the double acrostic anagram reveals FAWCOMB––G; DAMe BarBELY. HE–B––CUY.; IAY TOT For–AYT. The allusion to St. Barbary is one hint at the Christian name, and the address as a 'quince' suggests the end of the surname.

The next two anti-Barbelina poems to be considered here occur in MS. Ashmole 176, Tudor copies in an alchemical manuscript; a date indication in one verse makes one put them late:

> This vij yeares and some deale more
> wth her I dyd take payne

and cannot say but she therefore
rewarded me agayne.
but nowe I am forsaken
another she hathe taken.

Lord Fawcomberg's period of imprisonment in France ran from May 16, 1449, to some time probably in 1452, possibly to mid-1455 (Ramsay, II, 93; G.E.C., V, 282 (h)). The connexion with the waiting lady may have begun before 1449, or more probably after 1452. In either case, these poems must be dated in the 1450s.

No. 97*a*. 'My Ladye hathe forsaken me': copied (fol. 98) as a poem of six stanzas of four long lines (aabc) with varying refrain, but actually each stanza has a quatrain (8.6.8.6., a.b.a.b.) followed by two couplets of six syllables (ccdd). The poem is not printed, as far as I know, and is not included in the *Middle English Index*.

> *Incipit.* My Ladye hathe forsaken me
> that longe hathe ben her man.
> *Explicit.* thus he that lackethe strengthe
> she lettethe hym slyp at lengthe.

The anagram gives: WILLIAM, LD. FAW–OMB.; BARBALIn HARBA––VIn; FOrFAYT; SALISB––Y. It is difficult to know whether Lord Salisbury is cited here (and in the second poem) as the supplanting favourite, or the supplanted, or invoked merely as Fawcomberg's eldest brother. A certain amount of anti-Yorkist animus may be surmised, since he was the leading follower of his brother-in-law, the Duke of York.

No. 97*b*. 'I can be wanton': a poem of six stanzas, written as if of two long lines, actually of octosyllabic quatrains with alternate rhymes; the phrase 'crye howe' is recurrent in various combinations, though not as a refrain. The only manuscript, as far as I know, is Ashmole 176, fol. 98 v.; unprinted and not in the *Index*.

> *Incipit.* I can be wanto*n* and yf I wyll
> but yf youe touche me I wyll crye howe
> I can be merye and thinke no evell
> but yet beware, one cometh, I trowe.
> *Explicit.* and I wilbe styll and crye howe no more.
>   finis.

This poem of mock-modesty is written in a more vulgar style even than the preceding; both employ homely proverbial phrases, there, 'Ye knowe that newe brome swepeth cleane', and here, 'not for my mothers blacke cow'. The anagram is less full than in the preceding poem, but

still clear enough: FAW–OMB. BARBA–In YA–BA–KIn; SA–I–BW–Y; FOrFAIT
FOr–AIT.

No. 98. *The Hood of Green:* a poem of twenty-one eight-lined stanzas
(ababbcbc), with varying refrain. Printed by J. O. Halliwell for the
Percy Society from the only known manuscript, Harleian 2255 (fol.
153–6), in *A Selection from the Minor Poems of Dan John Lydgate*,
(Percy Soc.) IV, 199–205. MacCracken (*Minor Poems*, p. xxxi) 'cannot
believe that Lydgate ever sank to [its] abominable filth'. Lydgate's
admirers will be glad to find other fifteenth-century shoulders to shift
it to.

> *Incipit.* My fayr lady, so fressh of hewe
> Good thryft come to your goodly face.
> *Explicit.* And that the cokkow me awake
> To looke upon your hood of green.
> Explicit quod Lydgate.

At first sight the anagrams appear impossible to be sorted out, and the
repeated letters as wildly confused in their scattered repetition as those
swept up by the French gardeners. Gradually one sees that the method
is again that of stringing the names down stanzas in small groups, with
some overlap, as in many poems. Again too, it would be possible to
fill out the names by picking letters at random from the residue; but it
seems preferable to keep to the run of the stanzas: st. 1, FAW–OMB––G;
1–2, SALIS–W–Y; 1–3, TOT FOrFAIT FOrFAIT; 4 and 6–7, BAr–Al–N HARBE–
–CYN; 8–9, FAWCOMB.; FOrFAIT (st. 8 has a comparison with two fish,
but neither is a barbel); 9–10, SAL–SBU., N–U–LL; 11–13, FAW–OMB––G,
BA–BA–INA HA–B–––––IN; 12–14, FAW–OMB.; 14–15, FAW–OMB––G;
15–17, SAlISBWRI; 16–19, NEUIL; 16–18, BARBA–INA HAr.; 18, FOrFAIT;
19–21, FAWCOM.; 17–20, BAr–ALIN HA–––CUYN; 21, TOT FOrFAIT.

The satirical description of a woman, often by contraries, is a known
type of verse, to which Hoccleve and others contributed. Roos has already
tried a modified form in the *Balade Pleasaunt*, and, also for Barbelina,
in 'O mossie quince'. Neither poem fully prepares us for the savagery
of this poem's onslaught. The method is to invert the medieval
catalogue of feminine traits of beauty; if phrases of courtly poetry are
used, it is *per contrarium*: 'This fair floure of womanheed' (st. 6); 'This
sovereyn lady moost enteer' (st. 15). The alliterative freedom and the
speed of the verse remind the reader of *How a Lover*, and phrases and
images from that poem (and others) recur: 'Rympled liche a nunnys
veylle' (st. 7), 'so wrymplyd as a mase' (st. 17), and the St. Valentine
echo 'Tyl every foul chesyth hys make' (st. 21). The flow of comparisons

D D

is as full as that in 'As ofte as syghes'. One image has its equivalent in *The Chance of the Dice*: the weathercock of St. Andrew Undershaft's (st. 9) is paralleled here (st. 10): the woman's elephantine limbs are as solid as if

> The greet clocher up for to bere,
> A belfrey for the bodyfaunt.

The great 'clocher' of Westminster was a landmark to all Londoners. Other parallels come from one interested in the craft of writing; her rough skin would be 'A froward velym upon to wryt' (st. 20), and in heraldry:

> Hire cote armure is duskyd reed
> With a boordure as blak as sabyl (st. 18)

The first dozen or so stanzas, for all their extreme coarseness, can be humorous and even witty, revealing the associative powers of the true humourist; in eight words the writer cuts out the silhouette of a stout, waddling woman: 'She is no bot, she is a barge' (st. 5). But as the poem proceeds, it justifies MacCracken's strictures on its obscenity, and for all its vigour, the humour turns to truculence, and the wit is lost in the sickening torrent of invective. Raw hatred and loathing consume the poet. It is a relief to turn from this to a pair of verse-letters, indecorous enough, but one at least of which retains some semblance of literary standards.

Two verse-letters occur in one manuscript only, the one obviously the response to the other, both exercises in abuse.

No. 99*a* 'To my trew loue and able': a poem of five stanzas of rhyme royal, with three short lines of address (aab) and a concluding short couplet. The only manuscript is Rawlinson poet. 36. (fol. 3 v.); printed by Robbins (*Secular Lyrics*, No. 208).

> *Incipit.*   To my trew loue and able—
>   As the wedyr cok he is stable—
>   Thys letter to hym be deliueryd.
>   Vnto you, most froward, þis lettre I write.
> *Explicit.*   Youre swete loue wyth blody naylys,
>   Whyche fedyth mo lyce than quaylys.

The letter purports to be by a reproachful woman. The anagram, not handled with Roos's usual easy unobtrusiveness, indicates: WI--IAM FAWCOMBE-(G); BARBALIn HA–BE–KUY.; SA–IS–W–Y; FOrFAIT.

The poem begins with the inverted method of apparent compliment:

> The Goodlynesse of your persone is esye to endyte . . .
> Most fresch of contenaunce, euyn as an Oule.

The writer describes in detail the victim's features, his ill-shapen body, his awkward legs and shambling gait; they would defeat the skill of 'alle the peyntours in a land togedyr'. The fifth and last stanza condoles with his unfortunate mistress in terms increasingly gross, culminating in a disgusting farewell. The poem is deliberately crude in handling, rough in versification, its images wildly abusive rather than pointed and precise; Roos seems to be writing dramatically, contriving such a letter as Barbelina would write. The answering letter shows much greater skill and discrimination, and maintains a tone of suavity, superiority, and disdain.

No. 99*b*. 'To you, dere herte, variant and mutable': a verse-letter in eight stanzas of rhyme royal, with a couplet for address, and a farewell octosyllabic couplet; printed by Robbins (*Secular Lyrics*, No. 209).

> *Incipit.*   To you dere herte variant and mutable
> Lyke to Carybdis whych is vnstable.
> O fresch floure most plesant of pryse
> *Explicit.*   Youre owne loue trusty and trewe
> You haue forsake cause of a newe.

There is no 'signature', but the 'devise' appears. The anagrams run: WILLIA(M) NEVIL FAWCOMB–RG (stt. 1–3); BA–BALIn (3–4); SAl–SBW–Y (4–5); HAR(BE)KUYN (6); SAlYS–V–Y (6–8); AY TOT FOrFAIT FOr–AYT (8 and diffused). Attribution to Roos is based on these, and on the similarity of the style, not only to his general effect, but also to the method and the pungent comparisons of the satiric portraits of the two games; on the reference to Caribdis, such as Roos used already in *How a Lover*; and especially on the reference to a 'water-bowge'. The comparison in stanza 3 of the hanging breasts of a woman with a water-bouget could only come from one to whom the stylized outlines of this heraldic design were of daily familiarity, and its aptness is shown by reference to woodcuts of the period.[1]

The only known manuscript of these two letters is Rawlinson poet. 36.1, a curiously mixed volume of religious and secular poetry. After these poems, which are written in a small precise hand, come four short love poems in a large, heavy, angular hand, with a similar signature, 'q*uod* Jon S. Amant'. They are curiously like Roos's style in choice of words, but so lumbering in rhythm as to suggest an extremely clumsy novice; the writer confesses his inaptitude with 'papir nor yng'. No John St. Amand appears in the lists of the Household, but Sir William

---

[1] E.g. in the German version (printed 1472) of Jacobus de Theramo Palladinus, *Consolatio Peccatorum seu Processus Belial*, the thirteenth woodcut on the Judgment of Solomon (Bodl. Lib. Auct. VI, Q. IV, 42).

Beauchamp of Powick, who in 1433 was a King's Carver together with Sir Robert Roos, married Elizabeth Braybrooke and became Lord St. Amand *jure uxoris*. Her mother was a Raleigh, as was the mother of Ismania, Lady Scales. In the reformed Household of 1453, Lord St. Amand was one of those retained about the king's person. The manuscript, obviously a private collection, probably had the Household in its background.

In this answer to the 'letter of derision', the poet takes a high critical tone:

> The ynglysch of Chaucere was nat in youre mynd,
> Ne tullyus termys wyth so gret elloquence,
> But ye as vncurtes and Crabbed of kynde
> Rolled hem on a hepe it semyth by the sentence. (st. 2)

He bids the writer construe the glose, and proceeds to answer the items, feature by feature, in terms equally unflattering but wittier, like the suggestion that the 'camusyd nose' with its broad nostrils would be

> Vnto the chyrch a noble Instrument
> To quenche tapers brennyng afore the roode.

The lady's 'nyce aray' is derided, especially the 'dagged hood leyd on pancake wyse'; and her dancing ('As a wylde goos kepyng your contenaunce') is mocked as mercilessly as in the characters of *Ragman Roll*, st. 9, and *The Chance of the Dice*, st. 7. Finally, as if she was a hen, he wishes her 'the pyp and the pose', and with savage sarcasm consigns her to an unconventional resting-place in paradise.

These satiric poems form, with all their ugliness, a not unwelcome complement, even a corrective, to Sir Richard Roos's conventional and idealistic poetry. There is a robuster fibre in him than one might expect from the poet of the *Isle of Ladies*, and an eye which delights in gargoyles and grotesques. Just so was Keats to describe his 'Duchess of Dunghill'. The poems show the tradition of the 'flyting' to be alive in England, as it was then in Scotland, and is still in India in spoken form. In France also, Deschamps had shown his equal mastery of poems of praise and of abuse, and in very similar terms. Ross's sardonic humour everywhere finds full vent in antitheses and contradictions; and the tartness of his strictures on his opponent's bad writing reveals his own literary standards.

CHAPTER XI

The Last Years

DOCUMENTARY proof of Sir Richard Roos's imprisonment in the 1460s or 1470s has yet to be found; but it is difficult to think of any other explanation for the complete absence of documentary mention for twenty years of a King's Knight, whose family was so closely identified with the queen's struggle. Sir Thomas Malory's imprisonment, long assumed, has now been proved, and found not incompatible with the writing of *Le Morte Darthur*. Similarly we have, I believe, a poem of some length from Sir Richard in prison in Windsor Castle (as the anagram conveys), but written in a partly disguised form, and for an express purpose.

No. 100. 'The Prisoner to Vere': a poem of twenty-six stanzas, comprising an introduction of nine eight-line stanzas, fifteen stanzas on 'Veer' in rhyme royal, a concluding stanza of eight lines (st. 25), and an Envoy in rhyme royal to the 'lytell Balade'. Printed by Todd in his *Illustrations . . . of Gower and Chaucer*, 1810, No. 6; and by E. F. Piper (from Todd's text) in *Philological Quarterly*, 1926, V, 331–5.

> *Incipit.*   Halfe in A dede sclepe not fully revyued
>   Rudely my sylfe As I lay a lone.
> *Explicit.* Sey that thow were made in A prysone colde
>   Thy makyr standyng in dyssese and greuaunce
>   Which cawsed hym the so symply to avaunce.

There is no obvious 'signature', though in st. 6 the present tense 'I Aryse' in a sequence of preterites suggests that there was a deliberate avoidance here of the 'signature', marked enough to attract attention. The anagrams of the opening stanzas, however, contain the 'signature' phrase and the 'devise' (I read from the MS. facsimile).

The poem is found only in the initial flyleaves of the Ellesmere manuscript of *The Canterbury Tales*. As a marginal motto beside the

Envoy, is written 'ffortune be ffrendely'; between stt. 25 and 26 in the margin stands 'p*er* Rotheley', in the same hand as the text. The poem has therefore been assigned to an unknown poet of this name. This assumption may also have been made by a reader, possibly of the sixteenth century, who wrote in a small upright italic hand, beside the line 'So he put hys enemyes to vtter confusyoun' (176), the comment, 'confusyon ER of your working'. E.R. may allude to Rotheley, or it may not; it may be a Lancastrian outburst against 'Edwardus Rex'. Rotheley is both a place-name and a surname. The place is in East Leicestershire, but not particularly near Belvoir Castle; there does not seem to have been a manorial family there. Rothleys (William and Roger) are found in Dartford, Kent, in the reigns of Henry VI and Edward IV;[1] a William Rotheley is a London goldsmith in 1453;[2] a William Rotheley attests the ownership by a cleric of a devotional manuscript (Laud 108. Misc.). A John Rotheley went to France in the retinue of 'Edmund marquis of suffolk' in 1447/8; whether this refers to William De la Pole (more likely), or to Edmund Beaufort, this Rotheley comes the nearest to any connexion with Oxford's associates.[3] But here 'Rotheley' is, I believe, a ghost-name, made up by the copyist from a misreading of two contractions, perhaps run together for concealment: 'Ro.che'ler'. No two letters are more easily confused than c and t; and various contractions of 'chevalier' are found, e.g. 'Chel'r'; or 'chir̄' on Sir Richard Tunstall's Garter stall-plate (No. 88). Sir Richard Roos signs the flyleaf of his 'grete book' in full with 'A moy Richard Roos chevalier'. Rotheley then may conceal the real name of the writer.

The poet uses other means within the poem of drawing attention to himself. The first line is a formula similar to the opening line of *La Belle Dame sans Merci*, which runs 'Half in a dreme, not fully wel awaked'; here it becomes 'Halfe in A dede sclepe, not fully revyued'; this is almost as effective and revelatory as a signature. One may indulge in a fantasy by way of illustration, and, disregarding chronology, imagine the poet Gray captured by bandits on an Italian tour. If his friends had received an unsigned and apparently harmless descriptive note, which nevertheless incorporated, even in garbled form, the line 'The curfew tolls the knell of parting day', would they not have been sure of the writer? So here the suggestion of the first line of Roos's well-known poem is tantamount to a signature. There are also for us the hallmarks of Roos's style, and many confirmatory signs and tokens: the routh-trouth

---

[1] *Cal. Close Rolls, 1461–8*, p. 408.   [2] *Ib., 1447–54*, p. 439.
[3] Dep. Keeper of the Publ. Records, *48th Report*, p. 376.

rhyme (st. 16), the April showers and May flowers couplet (st. 12 and cf. 15), the favourite epithet, 'demure', the word 'noxiall' (by night) as in 'The Flower of Womanhood', st. 3 (see No. 49, above), the Chaucerian exclamation, 'Ey benedicitee', as in *The Isle of Ladies* and *The Assembly*, the locution 'Owte excepte' which Charles d'Orléans used (*Love's Renewal*, l. 5096); and above all, the syllabic variation of the lines in this rough-hewn verse.

The address to Vere and the story of the celestial apparition of the silver star which sprang into his ancestor's shield as 'A .v. poynte mollet', all this gives a downward date for the poem, April 14, 1471, the battle of Barnet. After that day's disastrous confusion in the mist between the silver star of Vere and the blazing sun of York, there could be no further appeal to this Vere legend; no longer could the mollet 'Resplende ouer euery Region'. This poem—one poem, not two as has been thought—has been dismissed as merely a flattering tribute to the House of Vere; it is much more than that. It has the function of a fiery cross. It is a call to action, sounding as a plaintive or a pastoral pipe. The burden is 'awake, arise'. Vere is appealed to as Brutus is by Cassius; the poem is to the same purport as the 'bill' thrown in at Brutus's window, 'Brutus, thou sleeps't; awake and see thyself';

> Who than ys so precyous or may do more
> Than lusty Veer?

The cleverness of the disguise of this verse-letter urging to an active renewal of Lancastrian allegiance is in itself proof of the need for secrecy and caution. The poem begins as a dream, a repeated voice, 'Sclepe thow no more', and again, 'Awake and aryse'. The perturbed dreamer prays to the Trinity for protection and guidance. The change from this portentous opening is pointed by a Latin heading: *Incepcio materie cum p(ro)prietatibus Veeris etc.* Now the poem disarmingly turns to praise of the merry spring, when trees and plants flourish and birds and beasts rejoice and men with them. Lusty Vere is compared with the boar that 'walkyth Joyyng whettyng his tuskes' (st. 14), a vigorous boar, 'styffe in tryeuth'. Then is slipped in the Lancastrian propaganda:

> And to the lyons obeysaunt in all howrys
> Redy w^t hys power to helpe in all stowrys
> The lyon hys lorde wher he standyth in dystresse
> Hys natyff Attendaunt on the lyonnesse (st. 15).

This blue boar is now foremost in the land:

> Wherffor now of all England he hathe avauntage,
> Owte excepte the Blode Ryall the moste trwyste lynage (st. 18).

From the blue boar, the Vere badge, the poet turns to the arms of Vere, and blazons them correctly. He tells the legend of the star, how under divine guidance a crusader Vere saved his king 'in the land off hethynes' by the light of a miraculous meteor. The poet prays that once again the mollet may shine

> Worthely and knyghtely As a lorde off Renown
> And for the encrece off thy lyght that y^t ffall not derke (st. 25).

In the Envoy the poet sends forth his 'Balade ffull Rude of composicioun' with the warnng 'nothynge to[o] bolde'; and states that he is in prison. There have been earlier hints at this in the poem, in the formal prayer to Christ Who made 'vs ffre where Affore we were thrall' (st. 7), in the petition to be preserved 'from all errowre' in this matter, and, *per antifrasim*, in the wry allusion to dreams coming from 'robuste metes' and repletion.

John Vere, 12th Earl of Oxford, has been suggested as the recipient. More likely is his second son, John, the 13th Earl,[1] who came to terms at first with Edward IV, and in 1465 was Queen Elizabeth's Chamberlain. But in 1468 he came under suspicion, and was in the Tower. Pardoned in 1469, he escaped to join his brother-in-law, the Kingmaker, and then stayed with him and Margaret of Anjou, and took a prominent part in the Re-adoption. The period of the poem is probably 1468-9 as will be argued later. Oxford's defence of St. Michael's Mount, his capture, and long imprisonment in the castle of Hammes, filled up the 1470s. When Sir Richard Roos in 1482 bequeathed 'a Tablett of Ivorie wrought with Imagery' to the Countess of Oxford, then at a low ebb of her fortunes, was it from compunction at having urged her husband to action?

The poem is not to be judged by high critical standards, because (although the craftsmanship is very fair) it was not conceived as an imaginative creation. It is an urgent message, written by a man some thirty years older than the young earl, a member of a family strongly Lancastrian, of which the head had been executed, and one younger member had gone over the sea to help the 'lionnesse'. The writer has no influence (st. 8), yet he writes without subservience, recalling Vere's ancient lineage and allegiance. The story commemorated in the Vere arms had a counterpart in Roos's own arms of the water-bougets, in a similar crusading legend of the Trusbuts, on the distaff side of his family. Vere and he had a mutual ancestor in Bartholomew de Badles-

---

[1] Todd, supposing the poem to be Chaucer's, identified Vere as Robert, 9th Earl of Oxford. Piper rightly attaches the poem to the 13th Earl, but mistakenly identifies the boar with Richard III.

mere; and Roos on his seal quarters the Badlesmere arms; naturally he writes as an equal. Only a man of Roos's background could so address the earl and invoke the valour of his ancestors; such remonstrance is not for an unknown Rotheley. The disguise is cleverly contrived, a vision and a prayer, to be dismissed by any suspicious reader as harmless piety. The beginning of the Vere portion is to a casual eye like the Ver passage in Lydgate's *Testament*, stt. 37–45 (ed. MacCracken, I, 339 ff.), and 'tarrage' (st. 11) is one of Lydgate's words for tang or savour. Long before the point is reached, any censoring reader would probably have dismissed it as innocuous, old-fashioned versifying. Indeed, Roos may have been making a deliberate attempt to imitate the propagandist 'prophecies' that ran from mouth to mouth among the people, such as this on Oxford and Warwick:

> Ye blew bore and ye mullet through England shall ryde,
> troy(towne) shall tremble and quak
> for feare of a child with chapled yt in will glide.
> ye mullet in troy 138 dayes shall mak.
> then shall a beare yt long hath byne tyd at a stak
> hath bine caus of much debat
> shallbe caus of vnitye;

and so on through the antelope of Egremont and others, the whole not far removed from Hotspur's 'skimble-skamble stuff'.[1]

The poem is full of double acrostic anagrams, political in reference, and the inference is that Oxford, or someone with him, was conversant with the method sufficiently to 'de-code', and to realize variations in the working. Sometimes a brief message is conveyed, like that of the Envoy that the writer is at Windsor. There are many names, strung down the stanzas, and they seem to be names of influential or useful Lancastrians. One can but smile at Roos's ingenuous-ingenious use of his material, suiting as always the names to the theme; here the two stanzas of the Prayer are suitably used for the names of two clerics, John Morton the future archbishop, and Rauff Makerell, who both were included in the Act of Attainder of 1461.[2] But mostly he is ingenious, with some new tricks. Many names in the line-initials only are fairly obvious, e.g. Talbot from BTTLTAF (st. 21) or Stanley from TNELSTA (st. 23); generally these obvious names are of lesser Lancastrians, but sometimes as with these two they are Yorkists. The more important names, Warwick, Clarence and others, lie in a deeper layer in the double

[1] MS. Rawl. D.1062, fol. 95 and 96 v.–97 (with a table of the badges or 'emblems').
[2] *Rot. Parl.*, V, 477B.

anagrams; so does the message, which, slight in early stanzas, becomes more important at the end. There are then two methods here: an acrostic anagram of the line-initials only or of the caesural initials only; and also the double acrostic anagram, using the same initial letters again. Compared with less urgent anagrams, there is here little residue, and few letters of frequency (T.W.Y.). Almost all the letters are needed, e.g. the one Q in st. 20, and there are many more internal capitals than usual. I read the anagrams as follows, but it is only too possible that some of the message has eluded scrutiny.

Stt. 1–4, the first Voice: ORMON–; SOME–S–T, BeWForT; WhITTInGHAM; DAWSO–; IS–AnIA SCAlIS; IAI T–T FO–FAIT; I ROOS Anon.

Stt. 5–6, the Voice again: BATTE––BY; HAMPTON; HUnGreF.

Stt. 7–9, the prisoner's prayer: VER; MORTO–; MAK.; ROOS; (R–B–RT) wh–TT–––AM; AWAY AFTR. TOW. BAT.; wIth Me In AMBVSH.

Stt. 10–13, Springtime: ION. COn.; HAWT; FISWAT.; AT Fer–brEG; M–SSAG. JOIN WA–WIC. FO––OW AFT. IN HAST.

Stt. 14–17, Vere as the Boar: BATH; H––BART; Th. SAn–T–OW; FI–HEW; SOTTON; B–WMONT. HAYFor. JAS. TVDO–; C–(ARe)NS; WEls.

Stt. 18–20, the Blue Boar: THO. NEVIL, BASTA. FAWCO–Be.; C–ARENs; AlBA.

Stt. 21–5, the Vere Mollet: TALB–T; PIGOT; DACRe; CHeIN––; STAN–LE.; TVDO.; WHyTT––HAM; C–W(R)T(E)NA.; BATTL. AT HeSHAM; QUEn, PrInC. EDWA(R)D GOn TO FR(AUnce) TO LOVIS; HeN. PLAnTA. TAn AT WAD––GTO. B(RO)GHT TO TOW(Re); WATCH FO(R) WA(R)––C, C–A–(Ens) (BO)TH.

St. 26, Envoy: In Pr–S–N AT WInSO(R).

The introductory stanzas present the writer's signature in three ways: the first-line quotation; the 'devise', and the 'signature' phrase found in the anagrams. They also give the names of his Beaufort connexion, now Edmund Beaufort II, whom the Lancastrians called Earl of Somerset; and of prominent Lancastrians, John Butler, sixth Earl of Ormond; Lord Hungerford; Dawson, probably the Master of the Ordnance (Devon, *Issues*, II, 444–5); Battersby is a name in the queen's Household in 1453; Hampton is probably for the faithful Edmund Hampden. The Prayer addresses Vere with very little disguise, and starts a message, probably meant further to establish the writer's identity and credentials. It is fact that Morton and Lord Roos got away after the battle of Towton in 1461; Sir Richard and his friend Robert Whittingham may well have been taken in an ambush; the place is not given till later, in st. 12 by the backward syllabic method: AT Fer–brEG., i.e. Ferrybridge, that minor engagement which immediately preceded

Towton. Then, with the flourish of a Latin heading, the *materia*, the real gist, is introduced, the message: to follow after and join Warwick in haste. The stress on the spring, most profitable of seasons, making men courageous, active and lusty, implies preparation for a spring campaign. The line-initials give the names of Lancastrian adherents, as of John Conyers of Hornby, or Beckington, Bishop of Bath; less obvious are the great men, Clarence, Jasper Tudor, and Lord Welles. The stanzas (18–20) elaborating on the Blue Boar repeat Clarence, and seem to indicate St. Albans; the obvious name is that of Thomas Neville, Bastard Fawcomberg, who, unlike his father, faithfully followed Henry VI. The message has not run clear; there may be more there. In the last stanzas it rises plainly to view in the double anagrams. Most of it narrates events after Hexham of 1464; the flight of the queen and the prince to France to seek the king's help; the capture of King Henry at Waddington Hall near Clitheroe and his imprisonment in the Tower. Then it comes down to the later period, that of 1468 onwards, which was marked by the open alliance of Warwick and Clarence, first by a marriage tie, and then by their joint manifesto of July 1469. This was followed by the Neville rising in the North, stopped by the Yorkist victory of Edgecote later in the same month; early in the next year (February 1470), the unsuccessful Lincolnshire rebellion was punished by the execution of Lord Welles and his heir. All this testifies to the activities of Warwick, and of Clarence. These seem undoubtedly to be the risings to which the poem points;[1] but to place it more precisely in date than between Hexham (May 14, 1464) and the execution of Lord Welles in March 1470 is difficult. Neither can one be very precise about Lord Oxford's movements. He was sent to the Tower on suspicion of Lancastrian sympathies in November 1468, but was pardoned in April 1469, whereupon he joined the Kingmaker and Clarence. Was this poem sent to him before 1468 or in 1469? Sir Richard's own state is equally conjectural. He may have been among the many Lancastrian knights arrested in 1468 (Ramsay, II, 335), and have escaped execution, continuing in prison till the Re-adeption of September 1470. Before his capture, he may well have been entrusted with the task of persuading Lord Oxford; unable to act in person, he set his wits to work to get a message through:—to expect both Warwick and Clarence with the Lancastrian stalwarts in the spring, and to join them in all haste. Finally, he tells his friends where he is, at Windsor.

The prison-poem to Vere was a last desperate personal effort by Sir

---

[1] The clearest account of all this is to be read in Ramsay, *Lancaster and York*, Vol. II, chapters 22–4; there will be found almost all the names given in the anagrams, e.g. Sir Roger Pigot, p. 343.

Richard Roos in the 1460s to rouse a lapsed Lancastrian to the aid of his king. The Re-adeption of Henry VI in 1470-71 was as brief as it was disastrous to the royal family, to Vere, to Warwick the Kingmaker, and ultimately even to 'false, fleeting, perjured Clarence'. After the crushing defeat at Tewkesbury, the Lancastrian party disintegrated; if Richard, Duke of Gloucester, had been other than he was, it might never have regained cohesion and power. The enormous pardon-roll of 1472, and those of the following years, show the Lancastrians' acceptance of fate; even such a woman as Margaret Wentworth, dowager Lady Roos, whose adored son Philip had been executed with Thomas Lord Roos nearly a decade earlier, and who must have execrated Edward IV, sought pardon with her grandson heir.

For some more pliable souls there was already in being a precarious way back to court favour, 'as on the unsteadfast footing of a spear', provided since 1464 by the mésalliance of Edward with Elizabeth Wydville, Lancastrian by marriage and by birth, widow of Lord Ferrers of Groby, and daughter of Jacquetta of Luxembourg. The Wydville party, or faction, Lancastrians pardoned and promoted, had driven a spearhead into the ranks of the king's genuine Yorkist supporters. After the execution by Warwick in 1469 of Lord Rivers, the queen's father, the point of that spear was her brother, Anthony Wydville, Lord Scales, Earl Rivers. His political course did not run straight, since Edward conceived a dislike and distrust of him, probably stimulated by Richard of Gloucester, but his position as Governor to the Prince of Wales kept him important; it ultimately led to his death under Richard III. Attached to him in the 1470s was his cousin, Richard Haute, son of a former lord mayor of London, and of Anthony's aunt, Joan Wydville. Haute followed his cousin up the ways of court advancement, through tourneys and special missions, finally into the royal Household of the little Princes, and at the last preceded him to the block. It was through Wydville interest, we may be sure, that Richard Haute, on marrying Eleanor Proute, *née* Roos, gained in 1474 two Roos manors in Yorkshire. There are thus quadruple links here, Anthony Wydville, and his cousin, Richard Haute, and the elder knight, Sir Richard Roos, and his niece, Eleanor. If Roos went to anyone for patronage and help, it might well be to this man of letters, son-in-law of Ismania Scales, for whose marriage-project Roos had written the 'Legend of Ypermystre' (*q.v.*), and also two complimentary Valentines, now found together in one manuscript, and printed only by Skeat (*Chaucer*, IV, xxvii-xxx), who attributes both to one author and to the same occasion.

No. 101*a*. 'Al hoolly youres': a Valentine poem of four eight-line stanzas, decasyllabic (ababbcbc). Skeat entitled it 'Complaint to my Mortal Foe' (l. 26) (*Chaucer*, IV, xxvii).

> *Incipit.* Al hoolly youres, withouten otheres part,
>   Wherefore? Ywis that I ne can ne may . . .
> *Explicit.* Sith I am youres til deth my herte wol kerue
>   On me your man now mercy have and routhe.

The only manuscript is Harleian 7578, a miscellaneous collection, which also contains other poems claimed here for Roos, such as *The Deth of Pyte*, and the *Reeve*.

The anagram gives: Th–MAS, ISMANIA SCAlES; ISAB. BOVRC–––R; AnThONY WIDVI.; TOT F––FAYT. The Wydville connexion is prepared for by the three opening words, which translate 'A vous Entier,' the Bedford motto of Anthony's mother, Jacquetta of Luxembourg. Anthony's own motto, 'Nulle la vault', is not used in the poems; he may not have assumed it till the actual wedding. Elisabeth, the only child and heir of Thomas, Lord Scales, married first Sir Henry Bourchier, a grandson of Anne of Woodstock. He died about 1458; and in 1460/1 she married Sir Anthony Wydville. She was aged twenty-four and upwards at the time of her father's murder by the Yorkist Londoners in July 1460.[1] At the time these two poems were written, before March 1461, Lord Scales was presumably still alive. The style is noticeably Roos's; his 'routhe: trouthe' and 'sterve: kerve: (swerve)' rhymes occur in both poems. Skeat's parallels with lyrics are drawn from poems now claimed for Roos, and others could be pointed out.

No. 101*b*. 'Of gretter cause': a poem of seven stanzas of rhyme royal. Skeat's title (*Chaucer*, IV, xxix) was 'Complaint to my Lode-Sterre' (l. 12).

> *Incipit.* Of gretter cause may no wight him compleyne
>   Than I, for love hath me sette in swiche caas.
> *Explicit.* For yitte wiste I neuere none of my lyfe,
>   So litel hony in so fayre hiue.

The anagrams are in substance the same: THOMA., ISMANIA S–AL–S; ISAB. BORSHIR; ANTHONY WID.; TOT FOrFA–T FOrFA–T. This poem is more vigorous, even a little rebellious in tone; the lover might, in absence,

> vnteye my reyne
> And for the tyme drawe into a-nothre cheyne.

---

[1] G.E.C., *Complete Peerage*, XI, 507; cf. *Her. & Geneal.*, VIII, 439.

Another wedding poem for the Wydville-Scales marriage of 1460/1 has added interest in its metre, and in its later attribution.

No. 101*c*.

> Myne hert is set vppon a lusty pynne
> I pray to venus of good continuaunce.

It is a joyous paean in seven stanzas of rhyme royal, found only in MS. Rawlinson C. 86, fol. 55 v., and printed by R. Cords in *Archiv*, CXXXV, 302. Metrically it is ambitious and complex, a sort of *sestina*. The first stanza provides in order the first lines of the succeeding stanzas; and in each stanza the last line repeats the first. The attribution, 'ffinis quod Quene Elyzabeth', has been interpreted as Elizabeth of York, wife of Henry VII. The anagrams indicate that the transmitter (not the author) of the poem was more probably her mother, Elizabeth Wydville. With well-marked caesuras they give clearly a complete wedding group: stt. 1–2, AnTHONI WIDVI.; ISMANI; stt. 3–4, --ISABeTH BOWSHI.; WIDVI.; stt. 5–6, ISMAnIA; THOMAS; STAFForD; diffused, TOT ForFA–T ForFA–T. Elisabeth Scales is the bride, 'ful famous & borne of nobil kyn'; their names are given, Thomas and Ismania, i.e. Lord and Lady Scales. The Stafford is probably the Lord Stafford of the day, whether Humphrey or Henry depends on the month of the wedding, now uncertain. He was of the first family of Anne of Woodstock, whereas Elisabeth's first husband, Sir Henry Bourchier, was of the second family. It is more likely that the poem was kept (as a modern girl would keep a wedding-photograph) by Anthony Wydville's sister than by his yet unborn niece.

Elisabeth Bourchier, Lady Scales in her own right, died in September 1473, and Anthony Wydville, though childless, remained unmarried for some years. A poem which has long been attributed to Wydville, Lord Rivers, facing execution in 1483 under Richard III, is shown by the anagram to have been the work of Roos, and to have been originally a lament for Rivers's first wife.

No. 101*d*. 'Anthony Wydville's Lament': a poem of five stanzas of eight lines (aaabaaab) with the final rhyme linked to the next stanza. Berdan (*Early Tudor Poetry*, p. 150) calls it 'an example of dispondeus trimembris with iambic differentia'. Printed in Arber's *Dunbar Anthology*, 180.

> *Incipit.* Somewhat musing, | And more mourning
> *Explicit.* But she (i.e. Fortune) it meant | Such is her won.

The only manuscript is Add. 5465, a 'Fayrfax MS.' of music, the compilation of Robert Fayrfax of the Chapel Royal under Henry VIII. He was probably a member of the great Yorkshire family with whom the last Roos sisters married; the manuscript was owned in 1618 by Charles Fairfax, the antiquary, of that descent. One of the composers of the collection of lyrics set to music is Edmund Turges; he may have been a descendant of John Turges, Queen Margaret's harper, whom Roos praised in *The Chance of the Dice*.

The anagram of stt. 1–4 runs: ANThON. WI., RI.; –LISAB–Th S–Al–S. TOT FOFFA. The line-initials of st. 5 do not add to the anagram, or form a fresh name; and it is very possible that Rivers, waiting for his death at Pomfret in June 1483, added a stanza to Roos's sympathetic poem on the death of Elisabeth, Lady Scales and Rivers in September 1473. Or he may have substituted a stanza, and thus broken letters off the original anagram. This would account for the idea that the whole poem was Rivers's swan-song. There are other examples of this kind of adapting (see Chapter XII).

A fifth poem is written 'high and disposedly', in terms fit for a brilliant marriage-project.

No. 101*e*. 'Honour and Ioy': a poem of five stanzas of rhyme royal. Robbins entitles it 'A Letter to His Heart's Sovereign' (*Secular Lyrics*, No. 191). It is found in Trinity Coll., Camb., MS. R.3.19 (fol. 159 v.).

> *Incipit.* Honour and Ioy, helth and prosperyte,
> Be vnto yow, my hartys souuerayn.
> *Explicit.* That, truly and god, ther ys no remedy,
> Without your comfort, but mercylese to dy.

The arrangement of part of the anagrams is unusual. 'Forfait' is tangled in the caesural initials of ll. 3–7 of st. 1; 'Anthony' similarly but more obviously in the line-initials of st. 3. The whole gives: st. 1, FOYFAIT; st. 2, AY TOT; st. 3, ANTHONY; stt. 3–4, WYDVI.; stt. 3–5, MA––––ET STVA–D, SCOTLAND. There is a rather large residue. The reference to Margaret Stuart is supported by the pointed allusion to a pearl, the only jewel named: 'There ys no gold, perle, nor precious stone' (l. 12), and by the farewell address, 'Now constant gemme, myn hoole comfort, | I take my leue oonly at your good grace.' It gives an added suggestion of international amity to the line, 'So that betwene shalbe no stryfe' (l. 25). The phraseology throughout is courtly and stately, using the terms common to love and to royal forms.

After four years of widowerhood, Rivers was proposed in 1477 as a match for the young Duchess of Burgundy; but Clarence was also a

candidate, and Edward IV cut the knot by supporting a third party,
Maximilian of Austria (Ramsay, II, 419–20). The next attempt went
much further, the marriage of the Lady Margaret, sister of James III,
being authorized by the Scottish parliament in June 1478, and the
money voted in March 1479. In late August, Edward signed the safe-
conduct for her coming into England, with the purpose of marriage
before November 1. But the whole project fell through (*ib.*, II, 437).
The poem can be assigned to the years 1478–9, probably more narrowly
to the autumn of 1479, as a letter intended to greet the Scottish princess
on that southward journey which she never undertook. It is interesting
for us to realize that Roos's powers of writing elegant and courtly verse
are undimmed as he approaches the age of seventy.

We are also prepared by these poems concerned with Anthony
Wydville, now Lord Rivers, for Roos's adopting him as his patron, and
identifying himself with the interests of the Wydville party in *The
Romaunt of the Rose*, to which he returned after a lapse of some thirty
years, as its hidden allusions show.

No. 102. *The Romaunt of the Rose*, Fragment C.

Incipit.   Whanne Love hadde told hem his entente
        The baronage to councel wente (ll. 5811–2; French, ll. 10681–2)
Explicit. To reden in Divinite
        And longe have red . . . (MS. ll. 7691–2; French, ll. 12352–3)
        And you shal have absolucion (Thynne, 1532, l. 7696)

After a gap of nearly five thousand omitted lines, the translator picks
up, and covers nearly two thousand lines, then ends abruptly, leaving
over nine thousand lines still to be done.

The fragment is not 'signed' with Roos's former phrase; but the
first sixty lines contain a new proper-name cryptogram, worked out of
different material on the easy consonantal method that Roos had found
feasible, even in translation, in Fragment A. The names, in the opening
section, of the attackers and defenders of the tower of Jelousie, have
undergone some changes; Bialacoil now becomes the easier-rhymed
Fair-Welcomyng; some are awkwardly and cumbrously translated, as
Wel-Heelynge for Bien Celer. There is no capitalization here in the
unique manuscript, but there is in Thynne's edition of 1532; as we have
seen, Thynne seems to have had access to Roos material. The names
as in Thynne are Love (twice), Richesse (thrice), Fals-Semblant, Absti-
naunce, Wikkid-Tunge, Normans, Curtesie, Largesse, Fair-Welcomyng,
Delit, Wel-Heelynge, Shame, Drede, Hardynesse, Sikernesse, Fraunchise, Pite, Daunger, Venus (ll. 5811–70). This gives the twenty-five

initials L.L.R.R.R.F.S.A.W.T.N.C.L.F.W.D.W.H.S.D.H.S.F.P.D.V. These can be read as follows: R–CH–RD H–WT; AN. W–DV–LL; F–SL–W–S; S(T)–FF–RD; one letter, P, is left unused. If one were to use letters again (and there need be no rules in this game), one could also read R––S, R–V–RS, SC–L–S, D–RS–T, the first a 'signature', the two next reinforcing the name of Anthony Wydville, the last (Dorset) the title in April 1475, of the queen's eldest son, Thomas Grey. The third and fourth names need some comment. Sir Henry Lewis or Fitzlewis (Fislewis) of Horndon, Essex, was a Lancastrian, who, after following Margaret of Anjou to Tours, submitted to Edward IV with Henry, Duke of Somerset, and others, when they yielded Dunstanborough Castle in 1463. He obtained his pardon in 1469–70;[1] nevertheless he was made 'ruler and governor' of King Henry's Household at the Re-adeption in 1470,[2] and what saved him from Yorkist vengeance I do not know. He survived to die quietly in May 1480, predeceasing Sir Richard Roos.

As we have seen, Wydville's two ambitious marriage projects came to nothing; within fourteen months of the Scottish negotiations, by October 1480, he married Mary, youthful daughter and heiress of Sir Henry Fitzlewis and of Elizabeth Beaufort, the daughter of Edmund, Duke of Somerset, and of Eleanor Beauchamp, dowager Lady Roos. Henry Stafford, grandson of that Duke and Duchess of Buckingham who had been favoured by Margaret of Anjou, was a first cousin of Mary Fitzlewis, since his mother also was a Beaufort girl, Margaret. It will be remembered that a third sister, Anne Beaufort, had married William Paston, friend of Richard Roos, Esquire. Henry Stafford, second Duke of Buckingham, had taken part in the queen's coronation, and in 1466 had married her younger sister Catherine; he was made a K.G. in 1474. He is known to history and to readers of Shakespeare as the creature for a brief period of Richard III; he helped him to arrest Rivers and Haute in 1483. Soon he too revolted, and himself became a victim.

The chain of letters in the proper names is thus seen to be a braid of names in the Wydville party as it touched Sir Richard Roos's later interests: Fitzlewis, husband of his Beaufort sister-in-law's daughter; Stafford, son of another such daughter; Haute, his nephew by marriage; and through Haute, and through old associations, the most influential person, the queen's brother, Anthony Wydville. This cryptogram supports the assigning of Fragment C to Sir Richard Roos; and it enables a date within a decade or less. There is no reason to connect

---

[1] Pardon Roll., 8–9 Edw. IV, C. 67, 46, memb. 30.
[2] For Fitzlewis, see Scofield, *Edward IV*, I, 156, 252, 265, 542; and for the family, H. L. Elliot in *Essex Arch. Soc.*, New ser., VI, 37.

E E

him with Richard Haute till the latter's marriage before July 1474. In that same July 1474 there was a family occasion which must have brought together several of the clan, the baptism of Margaret, little daughter of William Paston and of Anne Beaufort. The godparents were Henry Stafford, Duke of Buckingham, Anne Paston's nephew; Margaret, Duchess of Somerset, Edmund Beaufort's sister-in-law, and the dedicatee of two of the *Legends*, now an aged lady; and 'Anne, Countess of Beaumont', presumably Joanna, second wife of William, Viscount Beaumont, who was the son of Sir Richard's 'Lady Bounte', Elizabeth Phelip.[1] It is possible that Sir Richard and Dame Margaret Roos were there too, and the Haute couple, since Sir John Paston was still courting Anne Haute, Richard Haute's sister. About 1474 is therefore a *terminus a quo*; Wydville's marriage to Mary Fitzlewis late in 1480 can hardly be the *terminus ad quem*, since the satire of Jean de Meun is not suitable for wedding compliments. The anagrams have something to contribute to the dating, and must now be examined.

The identifications of the name-initial cryptogram are confirmed in general by the results of the usual double acrostic anagrams. That same passage, the introduction (ll. 5811–76), yields: ANTHONY WID., S–Al–S, NUSELS; HO–F––Y STAFFOrD; MA–GA––T, E–I–ABETH, BeAUFOrT; AN PASTON; HAWT; FIS–OWIS; BO–HI––; HA–BA–T, DOUNST.; AI TOT FOrFAIT FOrFAIT. Both Anthony Wydville's titles, Scales and Nusels (Newcells, Nucelles, etc.), were borne in right of his wife. Stafford, Haute, and Fitzlewis have already been noted; and here are added the three Beaufort sisters, Elizabeth Fitzlewis, Margaret Stafford, wife of Humphrey Stafford who had been killed in 1455 at St. Albans (later she married Sir Richard Darell), and Anne Paston. One would like to think that the Bourchier of the anagram is the future translator, Lord Berners; but in this group it is more probably his elder brother, the heir of the Earl of Essex, Sir William Bourchier, who by 1467 had married Anne Wydville. The Herbert (Harbart) who appears here is William Herbert, Earl of Pembroke, later the Earl of Huntingdon, who owed Sir Richard Roos a debt of £15 in 1482; in 1466 he had married Mary Wydville, and had been created Lord Dounster (Ramsay, II, 321). This anagram then, like the cryptogram, forms a 'braid' of Wydville's brothers-in-law, his nephew, and three of the Beaufort daughters with some of their men, Fitzlewis and Stafford. This is the new set, the younger generation, into which Sir Richard Roos has made his way, by dint of old friendships, and ties of kindred both old and new.

The anagrams continue through the translation. Love expresses his

---

[1] *Paston Letters*, ed. J. Gairdner, 1875, III, pp. xxxvi–xxxvii.

fidelity to his mother, Venus; shifting slightly to suit the theme, the anagrams run: ANThONY WID., S–A–YS; ISMAnIA; –LISAB–Th; BEA–M–NT; AN PAST–N; FOrFAIT. Here Roos salutes Wydville, and his first marriage connexions, Lady Scales and Elisabeth Scales; the name Elisabeth recalls Roos's own first 'Lady', and he includes Beaumont, and as a younger votary of Venus, Anne Paston, *née* Beaufort.

The substance of Jean de Meun's satire is little fitted to compliment; the anagrams accordingly take a very different turn, to explain which one must recall the fate of Eleanor Cobham and her necromantic associates, which Roos had already commented on in the earlier *Romaunt* (A), and in *Reson and Sensuallyte*. 'Charges of sorcery, like charges of heresy, always left a mark', says Ramsay, and Roos was to observe history repeating itself with permutations in the 1470s. The Duke of Clarence's wife Isabel (*née* Neville) died after childbirth in December, 1476; he charged one of her attendants, Ankarette Twynyhoo, a widow, with poison or bewitching, and had her executed forthwith with only a shadow of legality. Another charge, of poisoning the infant, was preferred against Sir Roger Tocotes and John Thuresby, and the latter suffered. The Court party, probably seeing in all this a covert threat to Queen Elizabeth Wydville, countercharged Clarence's follower with sorcery; as Ramsay remarks, they found another Oxford man, John Stacy, to play the part of Roger Oonly or Bolingbroke—another necromancer and astronomer. He under torture involved Thomas Burdet, one of Clarence's familiars, who had spoken rashly against King Edward; a Thomas Blake was also included in the indictment of May 12, 1477. Roos could not fail to be conscious of the parallels with the events of 1441; again a woman and two men (for Blake was pardoned) were accused of poisoning, sorcery, treason, and seditious prophecy ('the letter G'), the object of the accusation being to pull down their employers from power and high place. It is not then surprising that, just as Roos had pilloried Roger Bolingbroke, Southwell, and Margery Jourdain as Avarice and Envy in the first part of *The Romaunt*, so now he uses the long portrait of Abstinence-Streyned (ll. 7364–405) to name these unfortunate underlings who were sacrificed by Clarence and by the Court party to their intrigues: AnCAReTT TWINIHOO; IOHAN STASI.; THO–AS BU–DET; THO–AS B–A–E; –OGET TO–OT–S; FOrFA–T FOr(F)A–T. In the brief sketch of Fals-Semblant (ll. 7406–20) who had

> Don on the cope of a frer
> With chere symple and ful pytous,

but who had 'of Treason a potente' we find (G)ODA–D; FOrFAIT; Dr. William Goddard, a Minorite, was brought by Clarence before the Privy

Council to testify that the condemned men maintained their innocence to the last. Clarence sealed his own doom by his continued recalcitrance; within a year he had died in the Tower, probably on February 18, 1478. Two days later, the king had 'rendered void' the judgment on the dead Ankarette, on the petition of her kinsman Roger Twynyhoo.[1]

These references are clear pointers to the date of the translation. 1474 is still the upward date, the Haute-Roos marriage; the events of 1477 are fresh in men's minds, but the death of Clarence and the rehabilitation of his victim could hardly yet have taken place. This part of the translation must therefore date between May 1477 and February 1478. There is no reference to the Wydville-Fitzlewis marriage of late 1480. When and why the translation was broken off abruptly we can only conjecture; Sir Richard died in March 1481/2.

Why it was undertaken is more understandable. The resumption had been the outcome of Roos's new marriage connexion with the Wydville clan. He may have been encouraged to start again by Wydville himself, who, after the execution of Tiptoft, was the chief patron and practiser of letters in the country. He was the inevitable person for Sir Richard Roos, Lancastrian poet, to turn to in these days of his fallen fortunes; the Haute marriage of his niece would put the chain of association into his hand.

That connexion, and perhaps appeal, may explain a feature of Fragment C which has puzzled critics, and which seemed to indicate a very different translator from the light-hearted craftsman of Fragment A. The pious moralizings added to C have always appeared incongruous, and they especially surprise in this soldier-poet. In *The Isle of Ladies*, he had objected to such intrusions in poetry:

> For counsell cordes not well in ryme . . .
> Wherefore hereof more mencyon
> Make I not now ne longe sermone.
> To ryme a counsell I refuce (ll. 1252–66).

Already at the end of Fragment B we have had such additions as advice to youth to amend his follies (ll. 3239–43), and precepts on marriage (ll. 4821–5), suitable enough from a man no longer in his first youth; the interpolation on the man of lowly birth ennobled by gentle deeds is in accordance with the high doctrine of chivalry (ll. 2187–98).

---

[1] For these events, see Ramsay, *Lancaster and York*, II, 419–22, and *3rd Report of the D.K. of the Public Records*, App. ii, 213. It should be noted that Anthony Wydville was one of the commissioners to try Burdet, Stacy, and Blake.

In Fragment C, with its more ecclesiastical background, the interpolations take on an air of formal, even conventional piety:

> Abit ne makith neithir monk ne frere,
> *But clene lyf and devocioun*
> *Makith gode men of religioun* (ll. 6192–4);

and there is the hagiological interjection on the eleven thousand virgins,

> Whanne they resseyved martirdom,
> *And wonnen hevene unto her hom* (l. 6251).

St. Paul is viewed retrospectively as one that *'loved al hooly chirche'* (l. 6661). All these give the impression that they are aimed at some one; they are not the expression of the natural taste of this poet, who has always brisked up when military operations are being described. They are in tune with the Anthony Wydville who, after the vicissitudes of favour and danger in 1469–72, his 'grete tribulacion and aduersite', seems to have experienced almost a religious conversion, if we accept the expressions of his Prologue to the *Dictes* of 1477, or of Caxton's Epilogue to the *Cordyale* of 1479. It is of course possible that Sir Richard also was preparing to 'faire son âme'.

The chief stylistic arguments for 'Fragment C' being also translated by Sir Richard Roos, despite obvious differences of tone from A and B, are precisely the same two points as before, the use of distinctive words, some found in MS. Ashmole 44, and the particularizing of general military terms (see above, No. 60). Thus 'hauteyn', a word not common in Chaucer, and not to be found in the poems of the Roos *corpus* that are in Skeat, Volume VII, but occurring once in *The Temple of Glas* (l. 323), in *Reson and Sensuallyte* (l. 5287), and in Fragment B (l. 3739), is noticeable in C; 'ful hauteynly' (l. 5820), and 'cruel and hauteyn' (l. 6101) where the word is added for the rhyme, and perhaps also for its suggestion by sound of (Richard) Haute. On the other hand, the word 'trufle', a Chaucerian term, found in the French, and in *Alexander* (l. 1894), is replaced in C, l. 7517, by the word 'jape'. 'Jape' is of course a Chaucerian word, but it is obviously a word that had lived on to be the current slang of the young men of the fifteenth century, of Roos in *The Assembly of Ladies* (l. 348, 'Is it [a] jape, or say ye sooth? quod she'), and of Charles d'Orléans in his English poems. The use of the native word 'salowe' early in Fragment A (l. 355), and the more striking insertion of it in C of the pale horse of the *Apocalypse*, 'that *salowe* hors *of hewe*' (l. 7390), are strong links binding the two fragments together. These are the first citations of the word in Middle English;

there are none from undoubted Chaucer, from Lydgate, or from the body of fifteenth-century poetry.

The particularizing of military terms is found in Fragment C in the jesting reference by Fals-Semblant to the tower of Richesse:

> Nought rought I whethir of ston, or tree
> *Or erthe, or turves though it be,*
> Though it were of *no vounde ston,*
> Wrought with squyre and *scantilon* (C, ll. 7061–4).

Roos had seen defensive earthworks in Normandy; and in Plesaunce he had seen Duke Humphrey's Tower in building, and may have heard the Kentish mason talk of 'vounde stone', and of his mason's rule, his scantilon; and he inserts the words. Sometimes the added word may be partly a memory from the *Alexander* manuscript; Richesse is to arm herself 'With swerd *or sparth* or gysarme' (C, l. 5978). There are two occurrences in the *Alexander* of the Norse word 'sparth', a battle-axe. Again, at C, l. 6279, the vague word 'perriere', though it was an easy rhyme, is replaced by 'trepeget', perhaps from practical knowledge, perhaps from a memory of Sir Balaan assaulting Alexander's siege-works at Tyre 'With traumes & with tribochetis' (l. 1296). Practical experience enabled the translator to replace a vulgar imprecation on the Norman soldiers by a precise descriptive phrase, 'full of janglyng' (C, l. 5852).

The closer, firmer texture of Jean de Meun's writing may be partly responsible for the more solid and less fluently attractive verse of Fragment C. There is much less interpolation of tags, clichés, and words for the rhyme. 'Fyve and fifty *ferther ne neer*' (l. 7098) is not typical of Fragment C; the additions are few, and most have some point, as that on flaying a wolf, 'bak and side' (l. 7314), which is a huntsman's added detail. Finally, the Roos of the satiric portraits is seen again here, in this clear-cut, hard style, and in the capacity for enlarging on the pictures of beggars and hypocrites. The vigorous and often ugly realism of many words and expressions, as in the defence of Fals-Semblant (ll. 7254 ff.), or the disguise of Dame Abstinence (ll. 7360 ff.), is not beyond the reach of the writer of the two game-poems, and the attacks on Barbelina (see above, Chapter X). The English can at times be more racy and salty than the French, even when inaccurate:

> . . . beggers with these hodes wide,
> With sleighe and pale faces lene
> And greye clothis not full clene,
> But fretted full of tatarwagges,
> And highe shoos, knopped with dagges,

That frouncen lyke a quaile pipe,
Or botis rivelyng as a gype
(ll. 7254–60; *Le Roman*, ll. 938–43).

The translator knows *Le Roman de Renard*, but does not seem to expect his readers to do so, seeing that he translates 'dame Belin', and 'Sire Isengrin' as the wether and the wolf, and 'daunz Tiberz' as 'Gibbe oure cat' (*The Romaunt*, ll. 6259–60; 6204). Duke Humphrey's copy of *Le Roman de Renard* is still extant (Vickers, p. 415); Caxton's translation of the work was finished early in June 1481, and the book was probably out in time for Roos to see it before his death in March 1482.

Among the very numerous extant manuscripts of the original *Roman de la Rose*, it would be improbable that the actual manuscript(s) used by Roos could be distinguished with certainty. Yet some relation of the English version to the groups of French manuscripts classified by Langlois[1] has been discerned. Group L is said to lie behind the first part (Robinson, *Chaucer*, p. 1043); this I would confirm and add that some approach to the search may be made, not only through the text, but through the ownership of volumes. Thus in Group L, there is one significant manuscript (Ly in Langlois, pp. 240, 14), British Museum MS., Royal 19.B.13. This manuscript was bought from the executors of Sir Richard Stury (friend of Chaucer and Froissart) by Thomas of Woodstock, Duke of Gloucester. Stury died in 1395 or 1396, Gloucester in September 1397. The manuscript was therefore in the possession of the Duke for only a few months. How it got among the royal books is not known but it is conjecturable. Richard II would impound the possessions of the Duke, just as Henry VI later did those of Duke Humphrey. From the royal books, it was probably conveyed to the library of the next following Duke of Gloucester, the most literary in taste of the sons of Henry IV. Very probably Sir Richard Roos saw it at Plesaunce, and then later had access to it again in the royal library.

The class of French manuscripts thought to underlie Fragment C is group F; on this I have nothing to add, except the warning that not all the existing manuscripts were classified by Langlois. Such an unclassified manuscript in the Bibliothèque Nationale was owned by 1485 by Louis de Bruges, seigneur de la Gruthuyse (Langlois, pp. 13–15), whom Edward IV created Earl of Winchester in 1472. Gruthuyse procured later for the king some of his finest manuscripts, and was himself a noted collector. Anthony Wydville gave him a copy of Christine de Pisan (Harleian 4431), which had been his mother Jacquetta's. This

---

[1] Ernest Langlois, *Les Manuscrits du Roman de la Rose, Description et classement*. Paris, 1910.

manuscript of *Le Roman* contains on the end flyleaf inscriptions in English hands, including the name 'Le Bourgchier' with the motto 'loyaument et liement', and a signature, 'Galfridus Varyn'. Paulin Paris[1] rightly says that this is not necessarily the scribe. Obviously the manuscript was at one time either in England, or in English hands. The names Bourgchier and Waryn on the same flyleaf naturally recall that branch of the Bourchier family which *jure uxoris* became the Lords Fitzwaryn; Fulc Bourchier, fourth Lord Fitzwaryn (in right of his mother), died in 1479. There was a FitzLewis marriage connexion in the Fitzwaryn family early in the fifteenth century.[2] The Bourchier clan always held a moderate course politically, and the marriages of the sons of Henry Bourchier, the Yorkist Earl of Essex, reveal their ties with the Wydville party, Sir William with Anne Wydville, the queen's sister, Sir Henry with a daughter of Lord Scales, Sir John with a niece of Lord Ferrers of Groby. The most literary member of the Bourchier clan, John, Lord Berners, was made a K.B. in 1477–8. The Bourchiers in fact were quite possibly among the acquaintance of anyone who, like Sir Richard Roos, was on the outskirts of the Wydville party.

There are also possibilities of indebtedness to manuscripts no longer traced. A copy of Jean de Meun's *Roman de la Rose* was given by Charles VI to the Earl of Salisbury in 1411 (Langlois, p. 200); this is Thomas Montacute, ninth Earl. By 1424 he had married Alice, *née* Chaucer, whose first husband had been Sir John Phelip, and who later became Duchess of Suffolk; she ended as a Yorkist, and died in 1475. Altogether one may assume that, even if Sir Richard Roos did not himself possess a copy of the French, there was probably more than one manuscript which he could get access to or borrow.

In this detailed examination of poems which can be viewed as composing the *corpus* of Roos's poetry, we have been expanding the known circumstances of Sir Richard's life, following him from one group of associates to another. We have passed from the Plesaunce group to the Beauforts, from Queen Margaret's court to Margaret Vernon, from the revels of the Household to the prison appeal to Vere, and finally to the growing Wydville party, with its many tendrils still clinging to such old Lancastrian families as Stafford, Beauchamp, Beaufort, and Fitzlewis, and, through Haute, even to Roos's own family. Sir Richard has scattered throughout his poems cryptic allusions (badges, devices, anagrams) to the actors of his personal drama, like a 'hare' laying a trail;

---

[1] *Manuscrits françois de la Bibliothèque du Roi*, VI, 274–5.
[2] G.E.C., V, 507.

but yet with no thought for posterity's knowledge or ignorance, but merely with the desire to interest the coterie of the moment. All this is not literary mystification, but simply compliance with the fashion of the times, the amusement of the group, and his own ingenious impulses.

That Roos, and not another, not Lydgate, nor George Ashby, nor 'Picard', nor John St. Amand, is the writer of these poems, is a strong assumption, since these allusions reach out and draw into one circle men and women connected with his family and with historical groups. The double link is doubly convincing. Sir Richard is seen as the weaver of a tapestry spun from point to point of Lancastrian history. The strong threads of the warp are the historical persons, the Duke and Duchess of Gloucester, the Duke of Somerset, Margaret of Anjou, 'starry Vere', and Anthony Wydville. The cross threads are drawn through the lives of his private friends, Elisabeth Beaumont, Antigone, Lady Scales, Margaret Stanlow, Margaret Vernon and her family, and Eleanor Haute. What other man but Sir Richard Roos could weave this woof into this warp, to produce this particular and complex pattern?

CHAPTER XII

The Tudor Aftermath

SIR RICHARD ROOS died in 1482 without any apparent care for his manuscript remains, or for his fame. One might well expect to say, 'And there an end'. It is disconcerting to find him rise again in Tudor manuscripts, 'with mutilations manifold', and like another Banquo, push others from their stools. Despite his 'nonchaloir', he appears to hold a lien not only on the past and present, but also on the future.

We have seen already how one unknown Tudor copyist gathered a little sheaf of his short poems, a sheaf which was ultimately raked in by Ashmole's powerful scoop, and bound up incongruously in MS. Ashmole 176 among astrological notes. Another Tudor collector has a little cluster of Roos's lyrics at the centre of his very varied assortment of early sixteenth-century work—MS. Rawlinson C.813. Again, an unknown poetaster, fired by reading Thynne's Chaucerian miscellany of 1532, and having somehow access to poems by Roos not in general circulation, takes them over, and under the name of Philogenet produces a fresh patchwork, *The Court of Love*. Finally a poet, with yet other Roos manuscripts coming to hand, copies, alters, modernizes, seems to appropriate them, and certainly has them ascribed to him. Greatness is thrust upon him, he perhaps unknowing all the while. Similar ascriptions to his poetic yoke-fellow, and to 'Uncertain Authors' in the first Tudor miscellany of lyrics, present themselves. These phenomena characterize the Tudor aftermath. The lyrics in the two Tudor collections have already been seen. There remain the poems of 'Philogenet', of 'Wyatt', of 'Surrey', and of 'anonymous poets' in Tottel's Miscellany.

I. THE COURT OF LOVE

The Court of Love presents a very complex problem. I shall try to show that, as I believe, it contains embedded in it the remains of poems, one similar to *The Temple of Glas*, written by Sir Richard Roos, which the unknown poet Philogenet treated as freely as I surmise that Roos treated Chaucer's *Legends*.[1]

The supposition that Philogenet had been able to get hold of poems or drafts by Roos can best be supported by finding whom he was writing for. *The Court of Love*, as Skeat showed (*Chaucer*, VII, pp. lxxii–lxxx), is in part (though not as much as he thought) a pastiche of fifteenth-century courtly style, and was probably put together under the influence of Thynne's edition of Chaucer of 1532. It is not surprising, therefore, that it is not a straightforward Lancastrian poem; the reference to 'the fawcon, our own hartis welth' (l. 1363), with its homage to the Falcon of York, would be impossible in a Lancastrian poet. On the other hand, it is accompanied (l. 1354) by a reference to 'a temple shapen hawthorn-wise', and to boughs of hawthorn (l. 1433) One may well ask why there should be either Yorkist or Lancastrian emblems in a poem assigned to the 1530s, rightly, I believe, as it now stands. The first clue lies in the interpretation of the poet's name, Philogenet. This does not probably bear Skeat's translation, 'Dearborn, Loveborn', as a surname. The compound '-genet' was already familiar to English ears; and it is more likely that the poet was proclaiming himself to be a lover of the broom, to be of Plantagenet allegiance. Only one lady carried on the legitimate Plantagenet name in 1530, and that was Lady Margaret Pole, daughter of George, Duke of Clarence, and of Isabel Neville (daughter of the Kingmaker), wife of Sir Richard Pole of Medmenham, a second cousin of Henry VII. Created Countess of Salisbury by Henry VIII in 1513, she was executed for treason by him in 1541. She was a grand-daughter of the Falcon, Richard, Duke of York.[2]

This identification of Philogenet's patroness is borne out by allusions in the poem. Sir Richard Pole's stepmother survived his father Geoffrey Pole by many years; her maiden name was Bona Danvers. The 'little Philobone', the queen's chamberer of the poem, may well be inspired by some young kinswoman or namesake of Bona Pole, received into the Countess's household.

The Countess was governess to Princess Mary Tudor from May 1520 to October 1533; hence the introduction of the 'gold' in the little battle of flowers that closes the poem, for the marigold was the princess's emblem:

> Eke eche at other threw the floures bright,
> The prymerose, the violet, the gold. (ll. 1436–7)

[1] For similar maltreatment, see the anonymous plagiarism, part précis, part paraphrase, in 123 quatrains, of Alain Chartier's *Débat des deux Fortunés d'Amour* (310 quatrains), printed in *Le Jardin de Plaisance*, ed. Droz and Piaget, II, 267–71.   [2] G.E.C., *Complete Peerage*, XI, 399–401.

Violet and viola or wild pansy are little distinguished in early flower naming, and the pansy was the emblem of this family of Pole. One of the damning charges brought against the Countess in 1538 was that she had had embroidered a tunic with the royal arms within a wreath of pansies and marigolds, as if to signify an alliance between a Plantagenet-Pole and the Tudor princess.

The Lancastrian hawthorn (ll. 1354 and 1433) is no longer surprising in this Plantagenet poem, since the two Henry Tudors adopted the hawthorn in another and bolder form than the modest hawthorn buds of Henry VI, a fruited bush (symbol of attainment), 'ensigned' with the royal crown, possibly in allusion to the legend of Bosworth Field. This was still the device of Henry VIII at the Field of the Cloth of Gold.[1] The stress on the red and white daisy of Queen Alceste (ll. 101–5), though originally meant for other Margarets, is suitable to the Countess's name.

So much for the allusions on the surface of this production of the 1530s. But there are many undercurrents. If one is to seek channels how 'Philogenet . . . of Cambrige, clerk', adherent of Margaret Pole, *née* Plantagenet, could get hold of a poem or poems, possibly an unfinished draft, by Sir Richard Roos, the answer seems to be, through the Beauforts. On either side of the Pole family, the tracks lead back there. Sir Richard Pole's mother, Edith St. John, was a stepdaughter of John Beaufort, Duke of Somerset (d. 1444), elder brother, and predecessor in the title, of Edmund Beaufort, Count of Mortain.[2] She was therefore a niece of the half-blood of Edmund Beaufort. Edith's mother Margaret (*née* Beauchamp), as dowager Duchess of Somerset, must have kept in touch with her brother-in-law's children, for as late as July 1474 we have found her acting as godmother to the infant daughter of Anne Paston, *née* Beaufort, third daughter of Duke Edmund, and of Eleanor, *née* Beauchamp. In her own family, on the distaff side, Lady Margaret Pole, *née* Plantagenet, was grand-daughter of the Kingmaker and of Anne Beauchamp, younger step-sister of that same Eleanor Beauchamp, the wife successively of Thomas, Lord Roos, and of Edmund Beaufort. Moreover, her daughter Ursula Pole married Henry Stafford, great grandson of Margaret Beaufort, daughter of that same Edmund and Eleanor. This Beaufort channel of transmission is supported by Beaufort anagrams in the poem.

There is also another but less likely channel of acquaintanceship. Bona Pole, *née* Danvers, was a younger stepsister of Agnes Danvers,

---

[1] Bury Palliser, *Historical Devices*, etc., p. 376.
[2] Arthur H. Plaisted, *Medmenham*, 1925, p. 69.

who after 1461 was the second wife of Sir John Wenlok.[1] Wenlok, as
chamberlain of Margaret of Anjou, was certainly known to Sir Richard
Roos; indeed, they had been sent on a small mission together in the
summer of 1451 (see above, p. 70), a date not far from Roos's marriage,
and, as will be seen, from the writing of the basic poem here.

No. 103. *The Court of Love:* a narrative poem of 1442 lines of rhyme
royal, printed by Stow in 1561, and by Skeat (*Chaucer,* VII, No. xxiv).

> *Incipit.* With timerous hert and trembling hand of drede.
> *Explicit.* And Venus yet I thanke I am alyve.

The poet-hero, who gives his name as Philogenet (l. 912), having
resisted Love, receives a summons to his court. There he is helped by
an old acquaintance, Philobone. He confesses his fault, is bidden to
love, and is instructed in the Statutes. He then joins the suppliants to
Venus, and vows to serve her; indeed, he already loves a lady seen in a
vision. Philobone leads him to the lady, Rosiall, and the poet describes
her in rapturous detail. At her discouraging reception he swoons; she
then proves kinder. Philobone takes him over the court, to see its
throngs of unfortunate lovers, and its allegorical inhabitants. (Some
portion here is lost.) Pity, whose shrine Philogenet had seen, rises from
the dead to reconcile Rosiall to her lover. He stays till May, when the
birds sing their mattins, and takes part in May's flowery celebrations.

Just as there are unexplained anomalies in the handling of *The
Temple of Glas*, where Venus is first a painting, then a statue, then a
living goddess, so here there are some confusions. At the beginning, the
poet is eighteen years old, and has to ask his way to the Court (ll. 43,
58); but when at the Court, he is old and 'fer y-stope in yeres', and avers
that he has been a hundred times at Love's gate (ll. 280-3). Again,
there are two descriptions of unhappy lovers, very different in scope and
style. The likenesses to *The Temple of Glas* were pointed out by Schick
(p. cxxix) in detail. Skeat supplemented them by parallels with Chaucer,
with *The Romaunt of the Rose*, with *La Belle Dame sans Merci*, the four
long fifteenth-century poems, and other poems such as *Anelida*, which
I now assign to Roos, and *The Birds' Praise of Love*. I would add very
strong likeness to parts of *How a Lover*. Of these poems, all but these
last two were in print in Thynne's edition of 1532. And one should
note that the unique manuscript of *The Court of Love* is MS. Trin.
Coll., Camb., R.3.19, which also contains, *inter alia*, *La Belle Dame*, *The
Black Knight*, and *The Assembly of Ladies*.

[1] F. N. MacNamara, *Memorials of the Danvers Family,* 1895, pp. 144-5.

The anagrams of this composite poem cannot be expected to follow a clear course; some verses and passages have been tampered with. Their range proves to be wide, from Beaumont allusions of before 1441, to the time of the Anjou marriage, to the Fawcomberg-Strange affair of before 1449, to Margaret Longueville, c. 1450, and to Beaufort anagrams of the mid-1450s. Nevertheless they are perhaps more useful in this than in any other poem, since they help to isolate Roos's poem from the accretions of Philogenet. They also show Roos using up older material, and continuing certain old themes in new verses. Finally, the Beaufort anagrams, datable 1454–5, give a downward limit of date for the main theme of the original poem, and support what has been said of Beaufort connexions and transmission. The anagrams run as follows:

Ll. 1–42, Dedication of the 'flour of port in womanhede': ELISAB–Th B–AUMONT; CATh. WhITT.; MAUD STAN–OP.; ISMANIA S(C)A(L)IS; TOT FOrFAIT FOrFA–T. The eloquent Maud Stanhope's name is to be found, typically, in stt. 3–4, which appeal to Calliope, Minerva, and Melpomene for sugar-drops from Helicon.

Ll. 83–96, the story of Mars and Venus discovered by Phoebus: FAW–O(M)B.; STRANG–; –U(L)PIP.; TOT FOrF–IT. The truncated form of Lady Strange's mother's name, Culpeper, may be due to later alteration. These stanzas are thus a personal, as well as a literary allusion.

Ll. 133–55, the poet watches the queen of love, Alceste of the daisy: MA–GA(Re)T DANIOW; VerNON, (L)ON.; ISMANYA S(C)A–IS. Roos here includes his wife, and Lady Scales, the earlier Alceste, with the queen.

Ll. 225–38, Dido, Æneas and Anelida in the temple-windows: H(En). (CAr)D. B–W–O–T; FAW(C)OM.; STAn–OP.

Ll. 309–15, the second Statute, on keeping counsel in love: I–MANIA SCAlE.

Ll. 624–93, the poet's prayer to the queen, on his devotion to the dream-lady: MAR–A––T LON–VIL; B–AVFOrT; HOMFRI STAFFOrd, B––IN–HAM; ALYAN. SOM–RSeT; MARGAR–T; B–AUCHAMP; EDMuND; FOrFAIT. These names run straight down the stanzas, and need some rearrangement. Longueville is mainly in the caesural letters of the first two stanzas.

Ll. 694–721, the shrine of Pity: E–ISA––TH PHI–IP, B–W–ONT; ANTI–ONA; IS–ANIA SCAlIS; IAI TOT FOrFAIT FOrFAIT.

Ll. 778–834, a formal description of the beauty of Rosiall: STAFFOr–, HOMFr., BU(C)IN–HA–; BeWFOrT, MARGA––T; –LISABeTH; (J)OAN.; AlIAn., (ED)MuND SOM–(R)S–T; ANNe NeUILL.

Ll. 848–89, the poet's plea to Rosiall: STAFFor., BuCIN–HAM, HOMFrI; ANN. NeVI(L); MARGA––T B–WForT; AlIAn.; EDMUn. SOM––S–T; ELISA––Th.

Ll. 1030–57, on Despair and Hope: AlYAn. C–BHAM; E(L)ISAb–Th BA–D––F, BeWM––T; YSMAn–A.

Ll. 1058–78, debate between Lust and Delyt: STAnHO., Wi(LL)O–HBY; N–VIL, FA––O–B.

Ll. 1191–7, Dissemble: DAUN–.

Ll. 1198–121, Shamefastness: ELISAB–Th SOM–R––T; IOAN H–WTH; ForFA–T.

Ll. 1219–53, and ll. 1177–91, in that order, Avaunter or Boaster: FAWCOM(BurG); ST–AN–(E), ELI–AB–TH COBHA–; STANHOP; WIL(L)O–HBI; ForFAIT ForFAIT; HARBe–QuYN.

L. 1282–95, the central stanzas on Prevy Thought: AlIAN. COBHAM; ISMAnIA SCA–Is.

Ll. 1317–51, the revival of Pity: MA DAM. MARGAR–T (L)O–GU––I–., AY TOT ForFAYT ForFAIT.

Ll. 1352–42, the Birds' Mattins: ISAB–AV, YOLAnD, DANYOW, MARGAReT; BeAT–IC. TALBOT; JAC–TTA B–DFor.; IS(M)AnIA SCAL–S; AlIAN. SO.; WH–TT–NGHA.; STAnHOP. (The only bird which seems adapted to the anagram is the true turtle-dove for Ismania Scales.)

Ll. 1436–42: SOME–S–T, BeW.

From these multifarious names, some pattern is found to emerge. It seems clear that the occasion of the Rosiall descriptions was the marriage of Margaret Beaufort, daughter of Edmund and Eleanor Beaufort, Duke and Duchess of Somerset, with Humphrey Stafford, son and heir of Humphrey, Duke of Buckingham, and so grandson of Roos's old friend, Anne of Woodstock. Fortunately this event can be dated fairly closely: Henry Stafford, their son, and the future favourite of Richard III, was born posthumously on September 4, 1455, some four months after the young father was killed, like his father-in-law, at the first battle of St. Albans, in May 1455. The wedding was probably late in 1454. These portions of the poem therefore date from 1454–5; the names suggest wedding groups. Beauchamp in the first such group (ll. 673 ff.) was the maiden name of Eleanor Beaufort, the bride's mother; Anne Neville (c. l. 820) was the mother of the bridegroom. Elisabeth Beaufort and Joan Howth were the bride's sisters (see above, No. 72), and they are celebrated again separately as Shamefastness. Built in around this central structure are allusions covering more than a decade. The earliest, dating from before 1441, are those to Elisabeth Beaumont and her friends. The recalling of Roos's own poem *The*

Deth of Pyte gives her maiden name, Elisabeth Phelip, and couples Antigone with her (ll. 624–721). Again, 'Dispair and Hope' (ll. 1030–57) revives the theme of his double poem on Hope, and repeats the 'Plesaunce braid', including Eleanor Cobham; so too Prevy Thought (ll. 1282–95). The next anagram in time is the long list of the Angevin royalties and of the Escort of early 1445; 'The Birds' Mattins' and 'The Birds' Praise of Love' (see above, No. 68) are indeed closely allied. That Yorkist phrase on the falcon may be conjectured to be due to Philogenet, gained by easy substitution for another bird, possibly, after the kingly eagle (for Henry VI), the 'royal swan' for Duke Humphrey, who used the Bohun swan as badge. The identity of the queen's name, of the Beaufort bride's name, and of his wife's name, gives Roos the chance to fold in discreetly the names Longueville and Vernon, even into the description of the queen of love (ll. 133–55), and into the first wedding-list (ll. 624–39). His own wedding day was not far behind him, and it is pretty to find the resurrection of Pity associated with the name of his lady, Margaret Longueville (ll. 1324–44). A reminder that *The Chance of the Dice* is not far off in time comes in Dissemble, for John Daunt is one of the two dissemblers of the game-poem (*Dice*, st. 19). Finally the recent misdemeanours of Lord Fawcomberg are recalled, very openly in the allusion (ll. 82–91) to *The Compleynt of Mars* (No. 73) and in the Don Juan-like portrait of Avaunter, which includes his two victims, Lady Strange, and Lady Willoughby, and also, if my re-ordering of the stanzas is accepted, Barbelina Herberquyne, whose affair must have already begun. It is amusing to observe how Maud Willoughby stands up to the deceiver, and uses her eloquent tongue in the debate between Lust and Delyt (ll. 1058–78), only to be brushed aside contemptuously at the last: 'Now stint, quoth Lust, thow spekest not worth a pin'. May this be a sample of Fawcomberg's methods in argument?

It is not so difficult to demonstrate and identify the anagrams as to interpret their place in the completed work, and to discover how the poem that we now have, a piece of patchwork, was produced. Had Roos already fitted together various independent poems of his own, to produce, perhaps in a hurry, a compliment for the Beaufort-Stafford wedding? Or had Philogenet got hold of another 'Roos scrapbook', and used its diverse poems as jigsaw pieces, rewriting and altering as he went, unaware of the diverse anagrams. Either is possible—or both together. Certainly some passages yielding the older anagrams are like detachable *ballades* of three stanzas, such as Dispair and Hope, or the double *ballade* which forms the very independent introduction; so too is Lust and Delyt of later date. But there are more queries yet. Must we limit Roos's work within the range of the anagrams, or may we look for his hand beyond them? May we accept Roos even in parts which show the false concords that Skeat exposed, and ascribe these to over-working by Philogenet, even occasionally (e.g. l. 347, 'helden') to errors of a copyist or printer? In short, can we with any precision trace the dovetailing of the work of the two writers? Contamination is clear in places, as in the intrusion of Philobone at Pity's shrine, and above all in the last two stanzas. Here, as we have seen, the anagram is for Somerset; and the blue and white garlands display the Beaufort azure and argent. But we have also seen that the violet and the gold together (and Roos never elsewhere mentions the marigold) are Pole-Plantagenet Tudor symbols.

In general one may surmise that Roos set out to write a poem, independent of *The Temple of Glas* but on comparable lines, though in a more cheerful vein, with the similar idea of a temple or court of Love thronged with suppliant lovers, and of the instruction in the Statutes of Love. This poem will be more modern and more courtly in its presenta-tion of *amour courtois*; thus his Statutes, much expanded, enunciate, not Lydgatian morality, but the morality of the devout lover. To these statutes Philogenet, who is of a very different temper from Roos, adds a cynical twist, with realistic and even objectionable additions. Indeed the distinction between Roos and Philogenet is seen most clearly in the Statutes of Love. The first ten and the twelfth express the full and absolute devotion of *amour courtois*, the second being directed to Roos's confidante, Lady Scales. The phrases 'exyling slaunder' (l. 313) and 'exylen all pite' (l. 336) are reminiscent of the second envoy to *La Belle Dame* (No. 81 above); the phrase 'my lady dere' is constant in Roos, and so are the rhymes in -aunce and -ayne (cf. ll. 372–6). The first stanza of Statute 14 is reminiscent of one theme of *The Isle of Ladies*. The other Statutes 11, 13, and 15–17 are expressive of gallantry rather than of devotion, and tend to lapse into vulgarity (11) and indelicacy (16–17). Statutes 18–20 come directly from *Le Roman de la Rose*.

The description of the dream-lady in the prayer to the queen is entirely in Roos's line of sentiment, and in his smoothest manner, with his 'routh: trouth: slouth' rhyme (ll. 646–9), his frequent repetition of 'plesaunce' (ll. 655, 669, as rhymes; 695), his linking of stanzas, and use of such words as 'fresh, demure, ure' (i.e. destiny, l. 634; cf. *Black Knight*, 151, 302, 482). Moreover, this passage ends with a stanza con-taining the 'extended signature':

> I gave anon hir image fressh bewtie;
> 'Heil to that figure sweet! and heil to thee,
> Cupide,' quod I and rose and yede my way. (690–2)

This leads directly to the shrine of Pity, with its linked stanzas, and its 'womanhede: dede' rhyme (713-14). Already, however, Philogenet has turned to his guide, Philobone (699), and he then takes charge for some sixty lines. If *The Deth of Pyte* is accepted as Roos's, and as a Lady Bounte poem, the whole invention here of Pity's rich shrine, with its anagram for the same lady, and especially of her resurrection, touchingly dedicated to Margaret Longueville, shows him continuing to compose on a theme of his improvising.

The poet's bill to Rosiall (ll. 841 ff.) has many marks of Roos's style, 'persant (849), ure (862), memorial' (876, cf. *The Flower of Womanhood*, l. 23, No. 49 above); the 'plesaunce' rhyme (ll. 884-6); the Northern inflexion, 'me thinkes' (874); the reference to himself in the guise of Troilus (872, cf. *The Flower of Womanhood*, l. 38), and to Antony; and the phrase 'And all your man, y-wis, my lady dere' (851) contracts into one line the concluding couplet of the *Compleynt* to Margaret.

The lover's protest to Rosiall, and his swoon, with its stress on her ruthlessness and his truth, its 'plesaunce: suffisaunce' rhyme (ll. 991-2), its phrase 'wan as assh[es] pale' (l. 996; cf. 'Lych as asshis dede, pale of hewe', *Compleynt*, l. 27), its rhetorical repetitions and antitheses, is in Roos's 'peyntede style', on a theme from *The Isle of Ladies*, together with the more ornate methods of a full-dress poem like *The Black Knight*.

It will be found that in these passages, which by reason of anagrams, sentiment, and style I have assigned to Roos, there appear none of those grammatical solecisms and pseudo-archaisms to which Skeat drew attention. The only exception is in l. 81, 'That may the castell maken for to shene', where 'shene' appears as a verb. I suspect that Roos may have written 'maken fair and shene'; it is one of his favourite epithets, especially as a rhyme. On the other hand, the one northern inflexion ('me thinkes', l. 874) is in a Roos passage.

The many parallels with those of Roos's poems which were printed by Thynne should not be too much stressed as proof of Roos's part in *The Court of Love*, since it is probable, as Skeat suggested, that Philogenet was stimulated to write by the appearance of the volume of 1532. There are, however, two important poems not in Thynne's collection, to which there is great affinity here, *How a Lover Prayseth hys Lady*, and *The Birds' Praise of Love*. The only known manuscript of the former is Fairfax 16, and of the latter Gg. 4.27, both significant for Roos. It should perhaps be noted here that at l. 582, in a passage which I take to be by Philogenet, Skeat points out a parallel word and spelling with an interpolated stanza of *The Temple of Glas* (st. 25*b*), which is

found only in four manuscripts, two of which are Gg. 4.27 (State β) and
Fairfax 16 (State γ).

To consider first *How a Lover* (No. 1 above). The six-stanza proem
of *The Court of Love* runs on the same lines (though with greater art)
as that passage in the early poem where the poet appeals to the rhetoricians and to the Muses:

> Cum on tulius with sum of thy flouris
> Englesshe geffrey with al thy colourys
> That wrote so wel to pope Innocent (ll. 216–19);

> Virgil, barnard, Austyn and varro (l. 225);

> They konwe me not, my al ys yn veyne
> ffare wel ye musez al of thryes thre
> And namly vrania and caliope
> I haue slept out of the hul of parnaso
> Elycona vn to Thymus the hul ys go
> ffro me dulle asse (ll. 227–32).

In *The Court of Love*, there is greater selection and a more sophisticated
tone:

> The blosmes fresshe of Tullius garden soote
> Present thaim not, my mater for to borne:
> Poemes of Virgil taken here no rote,
> Ne crafte of Galfrid may not here sojorne.
> Why nam I cunning? O wel may I morne (ll. 8–12).

> Calliope, thou sister wise and sly,
> And thou Minerva guyde me with thy grace,
> That language rude my mater not deface.

> Thy suger-dropes swete of Elicon
> Distill in me, thou gentle Muse I pray,
> And thee Melpomene I calle anon (ll. 19–24).

Later, in a Statute written, or worked over, by Philogenet occurs the
phrase, 'lych a dulled ass'. A minor point in the proem leads to an
attractive and perhaps significant coincidence; the word 'metriciens'
had to Skeat 'a remarkably late air'. But Trevisa used it early in his
translation of the *Polychronicon*, which he undertook at the behest of
Thomas, Lord Berkeley, father of Elizabeth Berkeley who married Sir
Richard Beauchamp, Earl of Warwick, and whose daughter Eleanor
married Sir Richard Roos's elder brother. And it was for Richard
Beauchamp that was made the splendid manuscript of Trevisa's work,
now MS. Add. 24194.

The next passage in *The Court of Love* that runs very close to *How*

a Lover, ll. 248 ff., is the description of the lady's beauty; it runs even
closer to the original of both in Geoffrey de Vinsauf, *Poetria Nova*.[1]
In the earlier poem, the borrowing is freely adapted and expanded; in
the later, it is almost a straight translation. Comparison with the original
enables one to clear up some points that puzzled the editor:

> With lovelich browes, flawe, of colour pure (l. 782).

Skeat suggested 'flawe' as a northern form from *flavus*, or yellowish;
but Geoffrey's golden-haired lady had eyebrows as dark as the
bramble or whortleberry:

> vaccinia nigra coæquet
> Forma supercilii (*Poetria Nova*, ll. 565–6).

'Flawe' is then a misreading for 'slawe', a form of sloe; the usual
southern form occurs in *The Romaunt of the Rose*, l. 928, 'blak as bery or
ony slo'.

At l. 787, Skeat thought the comparison of the lady's nose to the
milky way was 'surely . . . quite unique'; but Geoffrey continues:

> Geminos intersecet arcus
> Lactea forma viæ; castiget regula nasi
> Ductum (ll. 566–8).

Here the milky way is the white skin between the eyebrows; the English
poet has misread his original. The eyes like the smaragde or like stars
come from

> Luce smaragdina, vel sideris instar ocelli (l. 570).

The conceit of the pregnant lips, already noted in *How a Lover* (No. 1),
is repeated here; the four lines added from Maximinian sound more like
Philogenet's vein. The unusual phrase 'sharply slender' (l. 804) is a
shot at 'astrictus zonae' (l. 593). The references to Jupiter's loves
(ll. 820–6) which Skeat took as a proof that the author had read
Metamorphoses VI, are all to be found in Geoffrey de Vinsauf.

There are three reasons, in addition to the anagrams, why I take this
passage of translation to be almost entirely Roos's: first, we know his
tendency to make two drafts, and here we have a free working in early
'doggerel', and a strict translation in the more artistic rhyme royal.
Then the general style is his, the rhymes 'hede: womanhede; governaunce: plesaunce'. Thirdly, the modest withdrawal, following Geoffrey's example:

> I hold my pees of other thinges hid:—
> Here shall my soul, and not my tong, bewray (806–7);

---

[1] Ed. E. Faral, *Les Arts Poétiques du XIIe et du XIIIe Siècle*, Paris, 1923,
pp. 197 ff.

Taceo de partibus infra:
Aptius hic loquitur animus quam lingua (594-5).

This injunction is obeyed also in *How a Lover* (435), though with greater freedom of expression.

One of the most interesting parts of the poem is the conclusion, 'The Birds' Mattins'. It is a much better poem than 'The Birds' Praise of Love' (No. 68, above); the anagrams prove both to have been written for the Angevin royal ladies. There is a general likeness to Roos's work, though it is free and original in details of metre. Vocabulary is more indicative: 'hertly' is a compound popular with Roos, and 'amoryly', which Skeat rejected (1382), is like the 'folily' of *La Belle Dame* (490, 522, 533; cf. 'notorily' in *Paston Letters*, No. 263, *ad fin*). In both, the goldfinch is called fresh and gay. The main difference between the two Bird-poems is that the simpler one is not a parody of a religious service, whereas this is. In that, it is reminiscent of *The Lover's Mass*, and since all these three poems were written in the spring of 1445, it may well have led up to *The Lover's Mass*, and been the companion poem for the queen. The only manuscript of the simpler 'Birds' Praise of Love' is Gg. 4.27, which also contains *The Temple of Glas* (State β) with the *Compleynt*, and also Chaucer's *The Parlement of Foules*. It is just possible that Philogenet not only had access to some form of *The Temple of Glas* (probably a print), but also to MS. Gg. 4.27, and to MS. Fairfax 16. But no connexion of these two manuscripts with the Beauforts is so far known. The possibility can at present be neither asserted nor excluded; but the run of the Beaufort anagrams makes it seem almost certain that, in the poem by Roos to which Philogenet had access, the translation from Vinsauf was already in place. 'The Birds' Mattins', with its anagrams of a decade earlier, may possibly have been put in by Roos; I think it more likely that Philogenet found it as an independent poem and tacked it on.

The most powerful passage in the whole poem is the second description of the wretched lovers, with that of the allegorical persons. Envy who 'rokketh in the corner yond, And sitteth dirk' (1255-6) reminds us of Roos's added line in *The Romaunt of the Rose* (1906), 'Rokyng for wo right wondir narwe'. The picture of Prevy Thought (1268 ff.), whose imagining takes him swiftly over the world, is like the lover's thought in *The Isle of Ladies* (ll. 1377-86, 1589-92), or the praise of thought as superior to sight in 'Cassamus roos'; and the occurrence of Secret Pense in *The Parlement of Cupid*, a mental state masquerading as a place, makes it unnecessary to follow Skeat and wish to alter to Sweet Thought. Vignettes like those of Dissemble, Shamefastness, and Avaunter (1191-1253) are allied to the portraits in the satirical poems;

indeed Dissemble portrays an identical member of the Household. Were it not for the anagrams, and for our knowledge of Roos's not inconsiderable powers as a satirist, we might have been inclined to give only the idealistic passages to Roos, and all the harsher to Philogenet, but this we may not do. One can, however, suggest that to Philogenet, *Amour Courtois* has become a game. Indeed, his attitude to women is much like that of a hero of Restoration Comedy; his Philobone is a little pert, his Rosiall faintly ill-bred, as Roos's women are not. Philogenet has the realism of the robuster early Tudor period.

To sum up:—*The Court of Love* is almost entirely the work of Sir Richard Roos, but with interpolations by 'Philogenet', an unknown poet of about 1532, a self-confessed adherent of the Plantagenet-Pole family. The basic poem was written in celebration of the marriage in 1454/5 of Humphrey Stafford and of Margaret Beaufort, daughter of Edmund and Eleanor; and it was probably through Beaufort channels that 'Philogenet' acquired Roos material. Other anagrams in the poem refer contemporaneously to the Plesaunce period, to the royal marriage, to Margaret Vernon, and to the Fawcomberg scandals. Some of these occur in detachable passages; and it is not clear whether the knitting up of the whole is partially Roos's doing, or entirely 'Philogenet's'.

II. THE 'WYATT', 'SURREY', AND TOTTEL POEMS

(*a*) INTRODUCTORY

It is one thing to ask the reader to review, perhaps unwillingly, the claims of Roos to poems hitherto assigned to Lydgate, even to Chaucer; it is quite another to lay before him a more sweeping and subversive claim: that all but a few of the lyrics and shorter poems now attributed to Sir Thomas Wyatt, including those for which he has been most praised, are basically or entirely the work of Sir Richard Roos, and are therefore about a century older than their assumed date. In addition, I would claim for Roos the poems doubtfully assigned to Wyatt by Professor Kenneth Muir, about half the short poems ascribed to Surrey, and some two dozen from among Tottel's group of 'Uncertain Authors',[1] and *The Courte of Venus*, and from the 'Harington' or 'Arundel' anthologies. The argument for this statement rests mainly on the single or double acrostic anagrams contained in these poems, chiefly identical

---

[1] K. Muir, *Collected Poems of Sir Thomas Wyatt*, 1949; *Tottel's Miscellany*, ed. Hyder Rollins; the poem numbers of these two editions are adopted here for reference.

with those already familiar, but with some interesting new variations; also on parallels of thought and phrasing, and correspondences with the poet's known interests and preoccupations. As the poems are examined here, it will be found that light is thrown on the admittedly very unequal imitations of Petrarch. Some of the minor Wyatt puzzles take on a fresh aspect; new problems also arise.

The anagrams are so wide in range that it will be found that, with one important exception, each chapter of this study can be enlarged with fresh examples. Each period of Roos's interest is represented, and there are some fresh developments within the group. The Plesaunce coterie (Chapter V) is amply illustrated; the poems to Lady Beaumont are greatly increased by similar protestations and reproaches; poems justifying the poet's grief and resentment are again addressed to his chief confidantes, especially Lady Scales; and there are several Plesaunce 'braids'. The solitary dedication of a poetic work (Muir, 142) can be attached to autobiographical poems to be found in Tottel. Sir Richard's other interests of the early period (Chapter VI) are served by two poems for the Bedfords (Muir, 8, 115) and by one for his sister-in-law, Eleanor Beaufort, *née* Beauchamp (Muir, 176). The translation of this early Plesaunce period (Chapter VII) now covers also lyrics; it embraces the Petrarchan sonnets and imitations, and a few *canzoni*, and includes fragments from Latin writers, Ovid, Seneca, and Boethius. As for French, the influence of Charles d'Orléans is discernible in some lyrics; an antiphonal dialogue, a debate between a lover and his lady, is a miniature of *La Belle Dame sans Merci*, and like it, is addressed to the family at Plesaunce (No. 198). The break in the chain of Roos anagrams comes in his later period (Chapter VIII); there is no lyric here for the king or queen. Yet of personal poems of this period (Chapter IX) there are some interesting examples; of two love-poems for his future wife one (Tottel, 278) reads like a companion poem to the octosyllabic *Compleynt* (No. 78, above). Maud Stanhope the well-spoken, already known at Plesaunce, has played a leading if rather enigmatic part in the poetry of the 1440s and 1450s; here her two later marriages are celebrated (Muir, 41, 85). Lord Fawcomberg's 'Strange' escapade is again referred to in two poems, one a sonnet on the metamorphoses of Phoebus and Jove (Tottel, 241). Of satires there are a few more; a verse-letter, humorous rather than virulent, is so because addressed to Lady Beaumont and her friends; but two poems for Barbelina (Muir, 35, 170) are again written with a pen dipped in gall (Chapter X). The work of Roos's last twenty years (Chapter XI) has now the addition of a poem of c. 1461 for Anthony Wydville, and another, of 1464, for his sister Margaret (Muir,

109, 104). A tiny prison lament (Muir, 168) and two such from 'Surrey' confirm Windsor as the place of Roos's captivity. A solitary poem to Humphrey Stafford (Muir, 193) invites comparison with the praise of Buckingham in *The Dice*, st. 34. Above all, a considerable number of poems, some even more poignant and revealing than those already seen, concern Eleanor Cobham and Antigone D'Amancier (Chapter IX).

There will be two immediate objections to acceptance of this claim and interpretation—the question of the manuscripts with Wyatt's signatures and other symbols; and the question of translations, some apparently from writers contemporary with Sir Thomas. Surrey's authorship has not even these lines of defence; his claims rest on slight support.

The two chief manuscripts for Wyatt (I quote from Professor Muir's edition as authoritative) are Egerton MS. 2711, 'by far the most important' as containing 101 short poems, 'some of them in Wyatt's own hand, and others corrected by him' (p. 255), and therefore called Wyatt's own or personal manuscript; and the 'Devonshire' manuscript, Add. 17492, an anthology of Wyatt's and other poems, which was at one time in the hands of Henry Howard the poet, Henry Fitzroy and his wife Mary Howard (the young Duke and Duchess of Richmond), Mary Shelton the maid of honour, and Lady Margaret Douglas— in short, a court album of about 1529–37. Professor Muir makes no allusion to these connexions of the Devonshire manuscript; but presumably he tacitly accepts, as do others, Miss Foxwell's identifications in her edition (Vol. II, Appendix C). In addition, the Arundel manuscript, only recently rediscovered,[1] but of which the copy in MS. Add. 28635 has long been known, originated in the Harington-Markham group, and remained in the hands of the Haringtons, from whom in the eighteenth century came *Nugae Poeticae*.

The first need, as with *The Court of Love*, is to seek channels of transmission of Roos's poems to these later circles. The extreme scarcity of Beaufort anagrams makes very unlikely a Beaufort background, such as was clear for *The Court of Love*. There are, however, at least two other such channels. The first can be traced through Maud Stanhope, Lady Willoughby, the second through Wyatt's mistress, Elizabeth Darell.

There are two intimate Stanhope poems (as well as several which include Maud's name) in the Egerton and Devonshire manuscripts: one (Devonshire) celebrates in anagrams Maud's second marriage before 1456 to Sir Thomas Neville; the other (Egerton) her third marriage in

---

[1] Ruth Hughey, 'The Harington Manuscript at Arundel Castle and Related Documents', *Library*, 1935, Fourth Ser., XV, 388–444.

1461 to Sir Gervaise Clifton. Maud had no children, but her brother, Sir Richard Stanhope, who married a Markham girl, had a great grandson, Edward, whose wife Alicia (Alice Flye) was an *ancilla* of Mary, Duchess of Richmond. His more famous cousin and namesake, Sir Edward Stanhope (father-in-law of the Protector, Edward Seymour), married a Clifton girl, daughter of a later Gervaise Clifton. Poems collected by Maud Stanhope, whom Roos had known since the early days at Plesaunce, might well come down into the hands of a young Mistress Alice Stanhope (*née* Flye), and be shown to her patrons, the Richmonds. More than one of Roos's dedicatees died childless, like himself; Maud Stanhope and Anthony Wydville are examples. We must be prepared for manuscripts of Roos's poetry to descend in collateral lines, and for the probability that there were copies of Roos's poems, singly or in clusters, in the possession of remote descendants of the original dedicatees. They would be likely to persist in the hands of those Lancastrian families that, by a long tradition, continued to be the reservoir for court service. There had been a deflection during the Yorkist reigns; but under the Tudors, the Lancastrian families re-appear, sadly depleted, but reviving by marriages with newer blood. To read in Hall the names of the courtiers and jousters is to realize this continuity by the recurrence of fifteenth-century names and Lancastrian mottoes. Princess Elizabeth Tudor's waiting-ladies at one time included, with Isabella Markham, a Saintloe, a Willoughby, and a Grey.

The Elizabeth Darell channel runs even nearer both to Roos and to Wyatt, and also cuts across the Richmond circle. Elizabeth Darell was the daughter of Sir Edward Darell of Littlecote, Wiltshire, of a well-known family. Her father was vice-chamberlain, and she herself a waiting-lady, to Catherine of Aragon. Her connexion with Wyatt was long, and she outlived him, she and her sons being provided for in his will. Her grandmother was Joan Haute, cousin of Anthony Wydville, and sister of that Sir Richard Haute who was the third husband of Eleanor Roos. Her great-uncle, Sir Richard Darell, was the second husband of Margaret Beaufort, daughter of Edmund and Eleanor of Somerset, and the Lady Rosiall of *The Court of Love*. Elizabeth's father, Sir Edward Darell, married thrice, and his third wife was Alice Flye, widow of Edward Stanhope. An elder cousin, another Elizabeth Darell, had married John Seymour of Wolf Hall. Elizabeth Darell's roots therefore go back to touch kinsfolk and friends of Roos; her contemporary connexions bring her into the Stanhope and Seymour circles.[1]

---

[1] E. K. Chambers, *Sir Thomas Wyatt*, etc., pp. 141–4; and C. E. Long in *Wilts. Archaeol. Magazine*, 1858, IV, 226–7.

Her great-nephew, 'Wild Will Darell', was to write a 'Knavery' on the building of the great Thynne palace at Longleat, where two important Roos manuscripts were soon to lie.[1] She too, through her grandmother, or her great-aunt by marriage, might have seen, or handled, or even possessed a volume of Roos's poems.

There is also a third thread of connexion. Henry Parker, Lord Morley (c. 1476–1556), courtier, man of letters, and translator of Boccaccio and Petrarch, had connexions with the group whose names appear in the Devonshire manuscript. His daughter Jane had married George Boleyn, Viscount Rochford, Surrey's cousin; another daughter, marrying Sir John Shelton, was the mother of Mary Shelton, the maid of honour. Henry Parker's own mother was that Alice Parker, *née* Lovell, Sir Richard Roos's great-niece, to whom in his will (1482) he left a book of prayers. After Sir William Parker's death she married Sir Edward Howard, uncle of the poet, whom, however, he never knew. Henry Parker was, in youth, brought up in the household of the Lady Margaret.[2]

The crucial question from all this is, what of Sir Thomas Wyatt and his repute? To dismiss him as a fraudulant plagiarist is too facile, and would be unjust. The Tudor conception of plagiarism was not ours; 'all literature was considered common heritage, and any poet's right to borrow was estimated solely by what he made of it.'[3] The attitude to older literary material, especially if anonymous, was little different from that to more substantial possessions, clothes, or furnishings; they were all movables, 'meubles', within the owner's absolute power, to be freely adapted to present needs. The habit of making excerpts or centos from long poems is amply illustrated in the manuscript collections of the fifteenth to sixteenth centuries; in MS. Sloane 1212 from *The Temple of Glas*; in MS. Rawl. C.813 from Hawes' poems;[4] and in Caius Coll. MS. 176 from Gower's *Confessio Amantis*. None of these productions bears any reference to its source, and some are certainly presented as original poems. It has only lately been realized that a dozen poems at the end of the Devonshire manuscript are not sixteenth-century lyrics, but excerpts from earlier poems, from *La Belle Dame sans Merci*, *Anelida and Arcite*, *Troilus and Criseyde*, and *The Letter of Cupid*. A poem (No. 14) hitherto attributed to Lord Thomas Howard, is an assembled work, made up out

---

[1] Daphne Bath, *Longleat*, etc., pr. pr. 1953, p. 13.

[2] *Lives from Boccaccio*, transl. by Henry Parker, Lord Morley, ed. H. G. Wright, 1943, E.E.T.S., No. 214. Introduction.

[3] W. B. C. Watkins, *ELH*, 1944, XI, 265.

[4] See *Pastime of Pleasure*, E.E.T.S., O.S., No. 173, ed. W. E. Mead, p. xxxviii, Note 1.

of stanzas from *Troilus and Criseyde*, Book IV. The last collector of the manuscript therefore, with access also to Thynne's *Chaucer* of 1532, made no distinction between original and borrowed poems.[1] In whatever way Wyatt got hold of Roos's lyrics, whether through Elizabeth Darell, or through the Stanhopes, or through Mary Shelton, he would see no obstacle to making this anonymous matter serve his turn. His autograph correcting of many of the poems in the Egerton MS. must be viewed in a new light. He was not polishing his own verse, but modernizing old-fashioned stuff, bringing it up to date, and into line with the taste of his time, and especially altering it to fit the instrumental music of his day, a *desideratum* at the court of Henry VIII. It is doubtful that these young people knew whose the poems originally were, very doubtful that the secret of the double anagram had been preserved. It is possible that the girls who wrote their comments in the Devonshire manuscript were aware of Wyatt's doings, probable that they would think nothing of it. But Wyatt died suddenly in his prime; and his legend grew up and was handed on by Leland, and Surrey (who never, however, explicitly credits him with lyric-writing), and Tottel (who even alters a poem to fit the growing Wyatt-Anne Boleyn myth), and Puttenham (see *Wyatt*, ed. Muir, pp. xxxiii-xxxvi). The evidence of the Egerton MS. is that Wyatt wrote out, or had copied, lyrics which pleased him, or attracted him by their similarity in sentiment and theme to his own experience. I believe that in some he added or inserted lines and even stanzas, traceable where the anagram ceases to work. He may sometimes have added those short refrains, so effective for lute-music, and much in the taste of his day.

To get at, or nearer to, the Roos original, Wyatt's corrections have to be disregarded; fortunately Professor Muir's detailed textual notes make this possible. Thus No. 99, 'What rage is this' (also reproduced in facsimile), yields by 'Old Egerton' (OE) a slightly different and more coherent anagram than that of Wyatt's version. Both, however, furnish the important name, D'Amancier; and in general the stylistic correction often leaves the anagrams undisturbed. Still, the whole anagram might be clearer, and better arranged; and it is probable that even 'Old Egerton' is at one remove (or indeed *x* removes) from the original poem.

The 'Wyatt signatures' (on which Professor Muir makes only one correction, p. 256) are various in form: 'W.'; 'Tho'. (often beside the middle of a poem in the margin); 'Wyat' seen at the foot of some rondeaus

[1] E. Seaton, 'The Devonshire Manuscript and its Medieval Fragments', *R.E.S.*, 1956, New Ser., VII, 55–6. See also Richard Harrier, 'A Printed Source for Dev. MS. 17492', *ib.*, 1960, N.S. XI, 54.

and sonnets; 'T.V.' interlaced after autograph poems; 'ffynys qd Wyatt' (Nos. 110, 111, 115); 'fynys'. In the Devonshire manuscript, the earlier groups are seldom signed, though signatures or names of other authors are given; and the later group has not T.V. as Miss Foxwell thought, but F.S. which *may* stand for Finis. To our ideas, it is difficult to equate the more explicit of these with anything but a claim to authorship, or at least an ascription. Yet in MS. Camb. U.L., Ff. 1.6, we have seen several personal poems by Roos with other names, mottoes, and symbols appended, and have been forced to conclude that these denoted friendly copyists (and see No. 83*f*). One may assume that something of the same kind is happening here, with, added, the possibility that the name indicates the bringer of the poem to the knowledge of the group. Thus John Harington ascribes a 'Wyatt' poem ('Now all of chaunge Must be my songe', No. 158) to 'Smithe of Camden' (Hughey, *loc. cit.*, 430); yet its anagram runs, BeAUMONT, BArDO.; YSMANIA SC–L–S; whITT.; WYMBYSH; AI TOT FOr–AIT. It certainly looks as if Wyatt was copying out, adapting, modernizing, and tidying stylistically such poems as he approved, or as struck home to him. Several uncorrected poems are also unsigned, e.g. Nos. 62 and 78, both 'D'Amancier' poems. In certain longer poems the anagram ceases altogether for a run of lines or stanzas, and here it is legitimate to postulate a grafting-in by Wyatt on the original poem; such grafts are Nos. 66, stt. 4–7, and 84, stt. 7–11, again both 'D'Amancier' poems. Wyatt's admirers will be pleased to recover for him here some fine stanzas.

Miss Hughey (p. 427) defined the textual 'puzzle set' as 'Wyatt's manuscript, Grimald's corrections, other people's corrections, Harington's anthology, Tottel's *Miscellany*'. One must preface this with Roos's originals, and *x* copies o íthem, before they reach Wyatt and Wyatt's corrections; nothing of the Devonshire manuscript can be thought to be in Roos's own hand. 'A big problem' indeed.

Yet in certain ways some existing problems are simplified. From the eighteenth century and Warton downwards, Wyatt has puzzled critics by his contrary powers and effects; unequal and harsh in expression, deficient in taste, irregular in metre, lacking in emotion and sense of beauty; yet occasionally expressing fiery passion in a felicitous 'union of strength and grace'. Professor C. S. Lewis has unwittingly got very near the truth: 'if . . . Wyatt were not known to be the author, no one would dream of classifying the poem as anything but late medieval (No. 8, "Myne olde dere En'mye", from Petrarch). . . . some medieval habits hang about him . . . a man who was escaping from the late medieval swamp'; then the summary praise: 'his best pieces are very remarkable

work indeed.'[1] These discrepancies are not surprising in verse originally written between c. 1430 and 1460, but now subjected to renaissance
standards in criticism. Unevenness of tone and metre are understandable in a writer whom we have seen steadily training himself during
these decades away from doggerel to the smooth syllabic stanzas of *The
Flower and the Leaf*. And the un-Petrarchan flavour of many of the
translations from that poet is no surprise in a writer more conversant
with the French styles of Eustache Deschamps and Charles d'Orléans.

These fresh aspects will cast a clearer light on the many anomalies
of the sonnets. We have seen that a protégé of Humphrey of Gloucester
was certain to be in contact with learned and intelligent Italians. Roos's
acquaintance with the tongue would as likely be acquired aurally as by
close study. He was probably picking it up *viva voce*, and, as Milton
was to suggest, 'at any odd hour'. This would account for lapses from
accuracy in the earlier sonnets; it suggests too why first lines or first
quatrains are closely rendered, to be followed by a very free or even
original ending. Sonnet 20 (Muir, No. 47), 'The lyvely sperkes that
issue from those Iyes', has nothing of Petrarch but that line: 'Vive
faville uscian de' duo bei lumi', which might well linger in the ear of a
poet listening with the Duke and Duchess as they were read to by the
Italian secretary of the day. The sparks 'perst' (not, surely, 'prest') his
heart with pleasure; and he writes a sonnet of his own on the lightnings
from the eyes of his Elisabeth, and includes the names of his patrons:
HOM.; COBHAM; ANT.; E–ISA––Th P.; WiTT.; TOT For–A––. And here
comes one explanation for the awkwardness of some of these early
sonnets; not only is the translator grappling with a new language, and
a new verse-form (in which Chaucer gave no help), he is also working
into the fabric his usual anagrams. Any two of these difficulties would
daunt most versifiers; the third might well break the poem's back. At
least we have in this early date the explanation of those inflexional
rhymes that make, e.g. Sonnet 2 (Muir, No. 4), 'The longe love, that in
my thought doeth harbar', so difficult to read as Tudor poetry. The poet
of the 1430s is merely continuing at first his usual French-trained
methods and accentuation.[2]

The anagrams increased the poet's pains; they can lighten ours. Of
the thirty-one sonnets in the Foxwell and Muir editions and four to be
found among Tottel's 'Uncertain Authors', four are written for Eleanor
Cobham and Antigone D'Amancier (Muir, Nos. 30, 160, 175, 184). All
the rest must be dated before that guillotine date of Plesaunce, 1441.

[1] *Engl. Lit. in the Sixteenth Century*, pp. 223, 224–5, 230.
[2] See, however, P. Thomson in *R.E.S.*, 1959, N.S. X, 225–33.

Sonnets 1–3 (Muir, 3, 4 and 7), and Tottel, 173, 179, are to Elisabeth Bardolf, without her married name, and are possibly of the earlier 1430s; all other sonnets which include her name address her as 'Beaumont'. Within that group of some thirty Plesaunce sonnets, we shall find every variety of skill, both in translation and also in original verse: in translation, from the stiffness and literal accuracy of 'The longe love' (No. 4) to the precision, force and ease of 'The piller pearisht is whearto I lent' (No. 173); and in original verse from the bare conversational simplicity of 'Eche man me telleth I chaunge moost my devise' (No. 10), to the dignity and beauty of the two sonnets in Tottel (Nos. 218–19) on Petrarch and his Laura; Laura, who is outshone by Elisabeth Beaumont, and perhaps by Ismania, or so says TOT FORFAIT.

With the Sonnets, then, some difficulties are smoothed out. This is not always so with poems which have been called translations from authors of the late fifteenth or early sixteenth centuries, and which yet appear to contain anagrams. In some of these poems, close scrutiny shows that the term translation has been too loosely used. Thus the sonnet 'I abide and abide and better abide' (No 160) has been traced by Miss Foxwell to Serafino (fl. 1490) and she appends the 'original' (Vol. II, 203). It is impossible to share her conviction; 'Lasso oimè' is a poem of some thirty lines with refrains; certainly the refrain hammers on the phrases, 'gli è gran tempo', 'io ho bon tempo', but there is no other similarity in theme or expression. One is reminded of Dr. Johnson on 'Go before, I'll follow'. Moreover, not only has the sonnet a clear D'Amancier anagram, but it is the obvious answer to the poem, 'ffor þe bettur a-byde' (No. 86c, above); it omits reference to the significant jewels, otherwise it is a straight retort of exasperated impatience. Elsewhere, a source has been too hastily asserted where it is permissible to see only the expression of 'common form' in courtly poetry; thus the stolen kiss was a theme of Charles d'Orléans well before it was picked up by Serafino.

Again, historians of literature are faced with the light-hearted ascriptions and the omnivorous nature of sixteenth- and seventeenth-century editors and anthologists; thus much of Stow's *Chaucer* is now jettisoned, and much of André Du Chesne's 1617 edition of Alain Chartier. The French basis of 'Ye old mule' was certainly available in print by 1529; but its modern editor puts it further back among poems of the Lyons group in the fifteenth century; the English appears to be very aptly a satire on Barbelina (c. 1450). Or a poem has been traced to a French contemporary of Wyatt, as Sonnet 19 to St. Gelais, but later is found to go back to an Italian author, here doubtfully Sannazaro (1458–

1530); the 1531 and 1533 editions of Sannazaro may justifiably be regarded with caution (Berdan, *Early Tudor Poetry*, 451–2). There is so much flotsam and jetsam of lyric poetry adrift across the Continent in these centuries that it is rash to exclude the possibility of a French lyric having its basis far back in Italian, and *vice versa*. Thus, Serafino was at the court of Milan in the 1490s, only some thirty years after Milan and Asti had been torn by the usurping Sforza from the suzerainty of Orléans; Charles's Italian secretary, Antonio Astesano, was the collector (1450–53) of one of the important manuscripts of the Duke's poems. There are possibilities here of transmission of poetic ideas, as the stolen kiss, or the strayed heart. Charles, constantly externalizing and apostrophizing his heart, is only developing what Miss Foxwell rightly calls (II, 17) a long tradition from Provençal poetry, continued by Chrétien de Troyes.[1]

Thus to assert that a 'Wyatt' lyric, with foreign analogues in sixteenth-century editions and collections, cannot go further back than that century, is dangerously dogmatic; the history of every such poem calls for close scrutiny, and there are not many on which absolute certainty is possible. A few (very few) poems appear to cover significant anagrams, yet have not been traced further back than a date later than Roos. Such is 'Vulcane bygat me' (Muir, 100), where the Latin epigram of Pandulpho (fl. 1500) appears to be the *terminus a quo*; but since the anagram on Strange of Knokyn is clear and relevant, one must assume the possibility of an earlier source, not yet found. An even bolder suggestion is possible, not now proved, but proof may well be found some day. There are some dozen lyrics in the 'Wyatt' manuscripts which have been traced to Serafino as source. Two of these (Muir, 160 and 118) can be ruled out at once; the likeness is 'common form' merely. Two go back to a common source in Petrarch (Muir, 22, 134). Others are indeed verbally close, but it is curious that the vigorous idiomatic phrasing is in the English, and the blurred vagueness in the Italian:

> For I have sene a shippe into haven fall
>   After the storme hath broke boeth mast and shrowd.
>   (Muir, 60)
> Chi ho' visto nave ritornarsi in porto,
> Dapoi che rotte ha in mai tutte soe vele (Foxwell, II, 215).

The small textual crux of 'thretning' or 'threning' in Muir, 48, is relevant here. 'What nedeth these threning wordes' is the reading of the Egerton MS.; Tottel and the Arundel MS. read 'threatnyng', and later editors emend to 'thretning', supported by Serafino's 'A che minacci'.

[1] *Cligès*, 2817–54; 4503–25; 5180–91.

But 'threning' is possible, especially to a poet with a love of the occasional lofty word, and familiar with the *Threnes* of Jeremiah; as the *durior lectio* it should command some respect. Here again the English has a more unusual word, Serafino an obvious and conventional reading. Finally, what is one to conclude from the epigram called by Tottel 'The louer compareth his hart to the ouercharged gonne' (Muir, 61) which in Old Egerton by its anagram refers to King James II of Scotland? Again all the vigour is in the English, all the flatness in Serafino:

> Cracketh in sonder, and in the ayer doeth rore
> The shevered peces (Muir, 61);

> Se stessa rompe et poco offende el resto (Foxwell, II, 216).

The conclusion is forced on us that the English sounds like the original verse, the Italian like the translation. We know something of the flow of manuscripts from the Continent into England, very little of the reverse traffic. But with the coming and going of ambassadors and travellers, like Anthony Wydville, or like Jean D'Amancier with his English wife Antigone, the possibility of English manuscripts, or poems copied from them, being left in foreign hands cannot be ruled out.[1]

(b) AUTOBIOGRAPHICAL POEMS

These preliminary and general considerations must be justified by a detailed examination of the greater part of the poems concerned, and first of those of Wyatt. The poems will be grouped first according to their application to Roos's earlier life and concerns (see above, Chapters V–VI); then according to certain types of lyric, Sonnets, Epigrams, and Rondeaux; finally according to the light thrown on his later personal connexions especially with Margaret Vernon, Maud Willoughby (*née* Stanhope), Anthony Wydville, and above all, Antigone D'Amancier (see above, Chapters VIII–XI).

A poem in the Devonshire manuscript, of unusual interest among the many Plesaunce poems, is 'Lament my losse, my labor, and my payne' (Muir, No. 142), 'a rather dull complaint of mis-spent youth', in Miss Foxwell's judgment (II, 163); Sir Edmund Chambers saw in it an 'Envoi' and a sign that 'Wyatt' meant to publish his poems. The poet announces his intention of telling his love-story as a cautionary tale; some readers may wonder why he writes so plainly, especially when it is

---

[1] Serafino visited Milan in the 1490s when the English envoy, Robert Sherburn, later Bishop of Chichester, was there, but I can find no connexion between this (? Hampshire) Sherburn, and the Norfolk Sharneborns of the Household of Queen Margaret.

agony to recall his experiences. He begs the reader to take the work in good part, and accept his purpose:

> To tell men howe in youthe I ded assaye
> What love ded mene and nowe I yt repente,
> That musing me my frendes might well be ware.

Sergio Baldi[1] shows that the impulse to the poem comes from Petrarch's 'Voi ch'ascoltate in rime sparse', very suitably, since that is Petrarch's introductory sonnet. Only the first stanza is much indebted.

The anagram reads: st. 1, HOMFr.; 1–2, AlYAn; B–WMO–T; ISMAnY; 1–3, SkALYS; 2–3, P–ILYP; 3–4, R(R); 4, STAn–OW.

Such a poem of autobiography exists; it is to be found among the poems by 'Uncertain Authors' in Tottel's *Miscellany*:

> Sythe singyng gladdeth oft the hartes
> Of them that fele the panges of loue (Rollins, No. 185).

It has recently been discriminatingly commended as 'a very gem of this transitional art, the disarming tenderness of the Middle Ages in . . . sober quatrains'. [2] It has been traced to Petrarch's canzone, 'Nel dolce tempo', but it substitutes autobiography for the Petrarchan triple metamorphosis of the lover; Roos is not at all mystical, and seldom extravagant in love. It ranges further, however, than the book *In Vita di Laura*; the theme very naturally leads the poet in the latter part of the poem to an early lyric of *In Morte*, No. 268, a canzone (No. 22) which immediately precedes the sonnet 'Rotta è l'alta colonna', the basis of a Beaumont sonnet. This canzone gives the lines 'he brought to nought My pleasantnesse for euermore' (l. 272) from 'ogni dolcezza de mia vita è tolta', and the Nashe-like line 'And earth dothe hide her pleasant face' (l. 284) from 'terra è fatto il suo bel viso' (l. 34). The long anagram is interwoven repetitively down through the whole poem, beginning thus: stt. 1–2, ISMAnYA; 2–3, HOM.; 1–3, –EW–VNT; 5–6, AnT–G.; 6, AlIAn.; 4–7, MAVD; 7–9, WILOW.; 7–8, HOMFr.; 10, ISM–NI; 11, COB.; 11–12, AI TOT ForFAIT. I omit stt. 13–54, which continue similarly, and resume at st. 55 (l. 217): stt. 55–7, POWYS; 57–8, MAVD; 58–61, STAnHOP; 61–3, ForFA–T ForFA–T; 64–5, WIL(LO)B; BE–MO–T; 65–6, AlIAn.; 68, HOMF–I; 69–70, TOT ForFA–T; 72, MAVD; 73, WiMB–SH; 73–4, ForFAIT; 74, ISMANIA. This covers the climax of the lady's death, and the finest part of the poem, the threnody:

> For by this cursed deadly stroke,
> My blisse is lost, and I forlore:
> And no help may the losse reuoke:
> For lost it is for euermore. . . .

---

[1] *La Poesia di Sir Thomas Wyatt* (etc.), Florence, 1953.
[2] C. S. Lewis, *Engl. Lit. in the Sixteenth Century*, p. 238.

The loke which did my life vpholde:
And all my sorowes did confounde:
With which more blisse then may be tolde:
Alas, now lieth it vnder ground (ll. 277–89).

The definite references to the passage of time, though of great interest, are not as clear as they seem. The first thirteen stanzas narrate
the poet's carefree, heart-whole youth, 'ny twenty yeres' (st. 3), that is
till about 1430. Then, as in *The Romaunt of the Rose*, Love wounds him,
and the dart remains in his side, and he cannot 'wring it out again'. That
was 'nye three yere ago' (st. 17). In silence he endures the pangs of
unrequited love for 'a yere and more' (st. 36). Then a desperate appeal
to the Lady brings him to bliss, and he continues in joy till three weeks
ago ('Not fully twenty dayes ago', st. 56). Death then comes by stealth,
and robs him of his joyfulness (st. 68). This date we know with some
certainty; Lady Beaumont died in the summer or early autumn of 1441.
But the period between about 1430 and 1441 is not fully covered by
three years of courtship with barely two years of happiness. This would
begin the courtship at 1436, too late a date as we know from the many
Phelip-Bardolf poems. Either some stanzas have been lost, or we are up
against the many mistakes possible with numbers. Roos would almost
certainly write his numbers as numerals, 'iij yere ago'. We have seen
(No. 27, above) how easily a numeral may be dropped, altered or overwritten. If Roos originally wrote, 'Yet was it nye viij yere ago', we
should be in 1433, a date which fits well. If a manuscript of the poem
should ever turn up, we could probably resolve these difficulties; at
present the evidence remains that Roos wrote the poem in the middle of
1441, within three weeks of the death of 'Lady Bounte'; he is preparing
for his 'month's mind'.

Two other poems of Tottel's 'Uncertain Authors' seem to be closely
allied with this poem of 1441, No. 198, 'In sekyng rest vnrest I finde',
and No. 175, 'To this my song geue eare who list'. 'In sekyng rest' is in
the same metre as 'Sythe singyng', the octosyllabic quatrain; in fourteen
stanzas the poet laments the day when were taken from him his 'free
choyse and quiet minde'. He had been like the bird on the briar,
preening herself in ignorance of the fowler's net, or like the boat sailing
at will on calm streams; then he set his course by 'a goodly starre', but
his tackle has failed. He blames Fortune for the loss of his joyful mind.
In the description (st. 12) of the storm and shipwreck there are affinities
with Petrarch's 'Lasso, Amor mi transporta' (235). This poem, still
referring to Lady Beaumont, is addressed to his four chief women
friends: stt. 1–4, MAVD STANH., WILL–WBI; stt. 6–7, ANTI. POWIS; MAVD;

stt. 7–9, E–ISAB–TH; stt. 9–10, STAn–OW; TOT ForF–IT; stt. 11–12, ISMAnI; stt. 13–14, –AVMONT. Later tampering would seem to be evidenced by the phrase, 'my compasse brake'; the corresponding Italian word is 'governo', rudder.

'To this my song geue eare who list' (No. 175) is in a different metre, the six-line stanza; but the theme is the same, youthful liberty lost when Cupid, seeing his scornful will, lies in wait for him; now he lies fast bound; let others beware. There are several parallels with Roos's poems: Cupid's anger at his 'spitefull vse' is like that of the god in *The Court of Love*, and derives from *Le Roman de la Rose*. The stanza describing the lady resembles those of the game poems describing the non-pareil:

> Such one, as nature neuer made,
> I dare well say saue she alone. . . .
> Such one she is, I know it right,
> Her nature made to shew her might.

The bemused poet is 'as a man euen in a maze', and begins to 'stare, and gaze'. The anagrams give a full 'Plesaunce braid': stt. 1–2, AlIAn.; AnTIGON; st. 3, ISMAnIA; stt. 3–4, HOMFrI; stt. 4–5, whITT.; stt. 5–6, MAV. STAnHO.; st. 7, S(c)A–IS; stt. 7–8 and 10, STAn–OW; E–ISAB–TH; stt. 8–10, BeWMO–T; stt. 9–10, BA–DOLF; st. 9, WIMBI; st. 10, BA–Th. st. 5, For–AIT.

The same theme is resumed, but with a lighter and freer handling of the six-line stanza, in Tottel, No. 223, 'In fredome was my fantasie | Abhorryng bondage of the minde'; here with a debonair and cavalier tone, the poet willingly accepts his thraldom, confident of the lady's ultimate relenting. The caesuras in this strongly-marked rhythm are very clear, and the poem is again to his friends: st. 1, B–WMONT; stt. 1–2, STANH.; stt. 2–3, ISMAnI; stt. 2 and 5, TOT ForFAIT ForFAIT; st. 3, S–AlIS; stt. 3–4, WILOBI; stt. 4–5, E–ISABETH.

Unfortunately Roos cannot always transmute his feelings into lightness and grace. 'If euer wofull man might moue your hartes to ruthe' (Tottel 168) is a long and tedious poem of seventy lines, the poet's appeal to ladies to acknowledge him as a true lover. Its anagram runs: ll. 1–10, HOMF–I; An–IGONA; ll. 1–11, ISMANIA.; ll. 10–20, (c)OBHAM; ForFA–T; ll. 1–30, SCA–IS, WHA–Y–BOr; ll. 31–51, ––ISAB–TH B–WMONT; whYTT.; ll. 35 ff., MAVD STANHO.; ll. 61–70, TOT ForFAYT. The poem gathers up rather dully a number of familiar themes and devices: the 'ruth: truth' rhyme; the inability to add 'colours'; the lady as a nonpareil except for her lack of pity; the lover's dumbness in her presence, his constancy in absence. One line lightens the whole:

For, where she comes, she shewes her self as sonne among the starres.

These linked poems of confessional autobiography are a rare phenomenon in later medieval poetry—at least in England. They are a valuable addition to the late medieval repertory of 'kinds'. Here they have
led us away from the 'Wyatt' manuscripts into the later Tottel's *Miscellany*. To return to the manuscripts.

(c) POEMS FOR PLESAUNCE

Of the 101 poems in the Egerton manuscript, three-quarters have
anagrams for the people of the Plesaunce period, in various groupings.
When Antigone appears in these groups, she is twice given the name of
Powys (Muir, 61, 81), so that these poems date from after 1435/6. But
no conclusions on the original composition of the manuscript collection
can be drawn, since many D'Amancier poems have preceded them.
These Plesaunce poems include the Sonnets, Rondeaux, and Epigrams
of the Egerton manuscript, except one in each category. Of the remaining quarter, the largest group (18) is for Antigone D'Amancier (1450–4).
Four poems show no anagrams, and I do not assign them to Roos (Muir
34, 39, 40, 80). The remaining few poems are of the later period,
c. 1450–61; of these, two celebrate Maud Stanhope's later marriages in
1453 and 1461. This intimate circumstance makes one suspect Stanhope
provenance for the Egerton manuscript.

Of the sixty-six poems only in the Devonshire manuscript, all except
about half a dozen are addressed to the people at Plesaunce. Of these
excepted poems, two only are for Antigone D'Amancier, one for the
Bedfords, and one for Talbot. One poem (Muir, 105), unusually
addressed to two men—friends of long standing—might be of the earlier
or the later period. The only poem involving Maud Stanhope is, I
believe, a jest against her (Muir, 166). I see no clear indication here of
the background of the manuscript, whether Stanhope, Darell, or Parker.
The prevalence, however, of Plesaunce poems, and of poems intimately
connected with Antigone, which must surely have followed her to
France, raises the conjecture whether collections of hers were ultimately
the basis of these manuscripts, with their poems not found in general
fifteenth-century circulation. If her movements as again a widow after
1459 could be traced, an earlier means of transmission for these manuscripts might be arrived at. Of the 130 or so poems of Plesaunce connexion in the two chief manuscripts, and the few in Tottel only, in
The Courte of Venus, and in stray manuscripts, I propose to deal fully
with the Sonnets, Rondeaux and Epigrams because of the interest of
their verse-forms, and with all poems closely dependent on the Italian,

also with the most interesting of the poems for Antigone D'Amancier. Of the rest, I shall comment in detail on a selection, interesting for one reason or another, and shall relegate the remainder, with their anagrams, to an appendix. It must be borne in mind that the Devonshire copies show no corrections; there is no 'Old Devonshire' text which is a stage nearer to the original poem.

There are about a score or so of 'Plesaunce braids', introducing the Duke and Duchess of Gloucester. Some of these are lengthy and ambitious literary efforts, such as *Jopas Song* (Muir, No. 101) or the translations of Petrarch's 4th and 28th Canzoni (Muir, 96 and 8), and are part of the experimentalism of that literary centre, which the Duke stimulated.

Jopas Song, longish, but a fragment, probably through loss of leaves since it is the last poem in the Egerton manuscript (Muir, 101), is in Wyatt's own hand, with many corrections, but without a signature. It is a pedestrian poem, a verse description of the Ptolemaic universe (possibly a translation), prefaced by Virgil's lines on the song of Iopas at Dido's feast. The corrections show Wyatt working over the style, but for the poem more nearly as Roos left it, we must go to the uncorrected readings of 'Old Egerton'. Its anagrams yield: ll. 1–11, wh(AL)I–BOrO; 12–16, IS–AnIA; 17–24, BArDO–F; 25–34, skALe–, IS–An.; 35–40, BeW–OnT; 40–6, AlIAn., AnTI.; 47–56, (M)A–D (S)TAnH–P; 55–end, AlIAn.; E–ISABeTH Be–(M)ONT, BArDO–F. Maud Stanhope's name occurs as elsewhere at the mention of Mercury; there is no sign of her married name.

The much finer and more interesting poem in the same measure, 'So feble is the threde' (Muir, No. 96), is so partly because it is translated from Petrarch; to him it owes its weightier matter, and the inspiration of its vivid phrases. The Envoy, though with Petrarch's opening line, leaves him at once for more intimate expressions. Like *Jopas Song*, it is in Wyatt's hand in the Egerton manuscript, much corrected; and again Old Egerton must be considered. The anagrams run with much overlapping through the long stanzas, and there is a large residue, chiefly of letters of frequency, T and W: HOMFrI; AlIAn. –OBHAM; E–ISAB––Th. BARDOLF, B–WMONT; ISMAnIA skAl–s; AnT. POWIS; MAUD STAn.; STIWA–D; STAn–OW; WhITTIn–AM; WIMBIS; BABThOR.; IAI TOT FOrfAIT FOrfAIT, FOrfAIT. The name Powis dates the poem 1436 and onwards; and the absence of Anne of Woodstock from the long list suggests a date after October 1438. The title reference to Spain may mean that Wyatt was there when working over his version. A long Plesaunce 'braid' of similar date, 1436–8, is found in the Devonshire manuscript in a rather curious poem which reads like an awkward translation, 'Payne of all payne, the most grevous paine' (Muir, 141). Neither Nott nor Miss Foxwell (II, 162) attributed it to Wyatt. The stanza looks like rhyme royal, but the line lengths vary from 7, 8, 9, 10 to occasionally 11 or 12 syllables. The 'curious jog' that Miss Foxwell noted may be due to experimentation in trisyllabic feet in some lines, e.g. amphibrachs in 'Recorde of Therence in his commedis poeticall' (l. 24). This reference recalls that a copy of Terence was among the books given by Duke Humphrey to Oxford in 1443.[1] The next stanza is devoted to the fate of Lucrece; the final address to Venus to help all true lovers is in the due form of several of Roos's love-poems. The anagrams run thus: st. 1, HOMFRY; st. 2, ALYAN. COBHAM; st. 3, ANT. POWYS; st. 4, An. WODSTO.; st. 5, BARDOL., BeAUMONT; st. 6, ISMANIA SCAL–S; st. 7, STAnH–P; st. 8, KATh. WiTT.; st. 9, STANLOW; st. 10, STYWA(R).; st. 11, Tot FOrFAIT.

Occasionally a poem may celebrate a temporary loosing of the bonds of thraldom in love. 'Ffarewell, the rayn of crueltie' (Muir, No. 11, four quatrains in monorhyme) is addressed to Lady Scales (YSM. SC.) with regard to Lady Beaumont (ELISA––TH –ARDO–F). The poet (TOT FOrF–IT) has dearly bought his liberty, and now lives in 'ioyful pain'. The sentiment is similar to that of Rondeau 3 (Muir, No. 15), and so are the anagrams.

Two enigmatic poems, rightly held among the chief beauties of 'Wyatt's' lyrics, have Beaumont-Scales anagrams: 'They fle from me', and 'There was never nothing more me payned' (Muir, Nos. 37–8). The first has many variants, and Tottel tried to iron out some of the attractive metrical hesitances of the manuscripts' lines. The anagrams of 'Old Egerton' yield: st. 1, BeW–O–T; AnTIG; BABTh.; stt. 1–2, BA–D.; S–A–IS; st. 2, whITT.; st. 3, IS–AnIA; TOt–––FAIT. The Devonshire manuscript has several variants, one of which (B for G in st. 1) cuts down the name Antigone; by introducing 'for' into l. 15 it enables the completing of the 'devise'; Tottel's version, by starting l. 3 with 'Once', fills out the name B–W–OnT. 'There was never nothing more me payned' is known only from the Egerton manuscript; it is written in eight and six with a short refrain which may have been added. It gives BeWMONT; ISMAn. SCAlYS, WHAl–SB–––VH. The scene described in st. 2 of the first poem has a parallel in the third temptation of Sir Gawayn by the Green Knight's lady, and it will have many imitations; the emotional tension of the second has no predecessor in English poetry, and one can only look forward to Meredith's *Modern Love* for this sense of 'tragic hints', and of 'cravings for the buried day'.

'Suffryng in sorow in hope to attayn' (Muir, 107) poses a problem,

---

[1] Anstey, *Epist. Acad. Oxon.*, I, 236.

since the stanza initials give SHELTUN, but the double acrostic anagram gives: ELISA–ETH BARD. (B)–AUMONT; CATH WHITT.; IS–ANIA S–A–ES, WHA––S–ORO.; STAN––W; AI TOT FOT–AIT; (R.R.). The poem is known only in the Devonshire MS. and there are no corrections, no Wyatt signature. The maid-of-honour Mary Shelton's name is written on the page, while Margaret Howard writes beside the poem: 'Yt ys not h[?ir]' (see Foxwell, I, 258). I think it probable that the stanzas were not originally in this order and that some reader among the Tudor owners, seeing the coincidence of the stanza-initials, rearranged the seven self-contained stanzas. The change of pronoun from first to third person in the refrain is perhaps indicative; and stanzas 4 and 5, which change from personal complaint to general reflections, should probably close the poem. If so the stanza-initials originally ran SHEUNLT, and had no significance for Roos, whom I have not found using this method of indicating a name.

What Tillyard calls 'the delicate yet passionate pleading' of 'And wylt thow leve me thus?' (Muir, 113) covers even with the single anagram of its short lines the names HeLISAB–Th (B)–––ONT; AnT. The line 'Never for to Depart' and the appeal to Pity are particularly in Roos's manner. Yet the poem ends with 'Fynys qd.W.'

'Syns loue ys suche' (Muir, 125) shows in its four eight-line stanzas a careful handling of the anagram. The line-initials give: YSMANIA SC––S; MA–GA––T STANLOW; T–T FOTFAIT FOT–AIT. The theme is 'freedom at last' and only in the caesural initials does the significant name emerge: E–ISABeTH BeWMONT BA––O. It is a grave and weighty poem on the poet's 'yeres of rekles youthe' when folly framed his thought amiss. A poem of similar sentiments and also addressed to Scales and Stanlow is 'Now must I lerne to lyue at rest' (Muir, 129): ISMANIA SC–––S; STAN––W; B–WM–NT; B–BThO.; TOT FOT–AIT; (R.R.). The 'beautiful and solemn love-litany' (Tillyard's praise) of 'Fforget not yet the tryde entent' (Muir, 130) is written for ISMANY alone by TOT FOTF–YT; whereas 'Blame not my lute' (Muir, 132) had a larger audience prior to 1438: BeWMO–T, BA–DO; WH–TT.; BABTH.; An STA–FOTD; YSMAn–A; STAn––W; TOT FOTFA–T FOTFA–T. A different tone, of impatience and dissatisfaction, informs 'Me list no more to sing' (Muir, 138). It is the companion poem of 'Sins you will nedes that I shall sing' (Muir, 137). There the poet had forced his 'brokin lute, vntunid stringes' to sing for his friends: SCA––S ISMAnI; B–AUMONT, BA–DO; C–Th. WhITT.; STYW––D; TOT FOT––YT. But there has been criticism of his efforts, as the second poem shows:

> For what I song or spake
> Men dede my songis mistake.

> My songes ware to defuse,
> Theye made folke to muse.

It probably came from a higher quarter, since the anagram runs:
HOMF–Y; ALYAn.; ANT.; ––AUM–NT; STYW––D; WIM–IS.; WITT.; Tot
FOr–AYT.

'A! my herte, a! what aileth the' (Muir, 150) uses the same refrain
as governs a poem in the little Tudor collection, MS. Ashmole 176
(No. 17*a*, above). Both display Beaumont anagrams with variations,
Ashmole's being the more complete. By contrast the Devonshire MS.
anagrams are scrappy: B–WMO–T; ISMAnIA; AlIAn.; WhITT.; MAV.; TOT
F–––A–T. It is possible that the poem has been cut down.

A poem which certainly sounds at first like a translation was traced by
G. F. Nott to Serafino's 'strambotto', 'L'aer che sente el mesto e gran
clamore' (Foxwell, II, 218). It is 'Resound my voyse, ye wodes that
here me plain' (Muir, 22). But any likeness to Serafino does not extend
beyond the first stanza, hardly beyond the first two lines; there are no
rivers in the 'strambotto', and one line, 'Par che ne treme in arbore ogni
foglia', is the precise opposite of 'The hugy okes haue rored in the
winde' (Tottel's reading, No. 59), a line which conveys a sou'wester with
a Housman-like force. Petrarch was one of Serafino's chief models, and
much closer to the English is Petrarch's Sonnet 260 (*In Morte*, 301):

> Valle, che de' lamenti miei se' piena,
> fiume, che spesso del mio pianger cresci . . .
> colle, che mi piacesti, or mi rincresci, etc.

There is also a similar passage in *Trionfo d'Amore*, iii, 112–20. The
anagram is addressed to ALYAn. CO–HAM in complaint against E–ISAB–TH
BEWMO–T, BARDO., and is signed TOT FOrF––T.

Two companion poems in short lines (44464446), 'Longre to muse |
On this refuse', and 'Love doth againe | Put me to payne' (Muir, 155
and 156), have single anagrams which involve the maiden names of Lady
Beaumont; they may have been written, the one before, the other after
her marriage. 'Longre to muse' gives: AlIAN. COBHA.; –LISAB–TH
PHYLI., BAR.; Wh–TT.; SCAl–S; TOT FOrFAYT FOr–A–T. 'Love doth againe'
has: MA DAM PHYL., BA–D., B–WMOnT; (Al)IAn. –OBHAM; HOMF.; AnT.;
STYWA–D; WITT–N–HaM; AI TOT FOrFAIT FOr–AYT. Another poem (Muir,
134) based on Petrarch, and addressed chiefly to Lady Beaumont and
her gentlewoman, is the aggressive 'Perdye I saide yt not | Nor never
thought to do'. It is a very free rendering of Petrarch's Canzone 19
(*In Vita*, 206) 'S'i' 'l dissi mai, ch'i' vegna in odio a quella' (Foxwell, II,
168); Petrarch's six long nine-line stanzas and a concluding five-line

stanza afford the framework: 'S'i' 'l dissi' . . . Ma, s'io no 'l dissi . . .
I'no 'l dissi già mai'. Roos's six eight-line stanzas of short lines turn the
despairing adjurations to the 'happy impetus' (Tillyard's praise) of
indignant denial. He keeps an image here and there, e.g., the appeal to
the stars (st. 3; cf. Petrarch, l. 5); but his adaptation works away from
the original; thus the reference to the Trojan war (st. 3) replaces
Petrarch's to Israel's exodus out of Egypt (ll. 26-7). At the end Roos
returns to Petrarch:

> For Rachell have I seruid
> (For Lya carid I neuer).

Compare 'Per Rachel ho servito e non per Lia', etc. Roos declines,
however, Petrarch's bold flight to heaven in Elijah's fiery chariot. The
poem gives striking proof of Roos's power of independent treatment of
a given theme. The single anagrams yield: ELISAB–Th P., B–WMONT;
CATh. WiTT– – –AM; STYWA–D; WYM–Y.; AY Tot ForFAIT For–AYT (R.R).
The similarly vigorous defiance of 'I am as I am and so wil I be' (Muir,
167), with its rocking rhythm breaking the decasyllabic line, is again
addressed to Roos's friendly critics, but without mention of the cause of
the trouble: IS–ANIA; AnTIG.; STAnHOP, WIlL–WBY; B–IDJIT BAB.; IAI TOT
ForFAIT ForFAIT. A name rare in the anagrams occurs here (and in No.
114, see appendix to this chapter), Bridget Babthorpe, *née* Pilkington,
the second wife of Sir Robert Babthorpe (died 1436), and stepmother of
Roos's friend, Ralph.

The gay song 'A Robyn, Joly Robyn' (Muir, 55) is a debate between
men on the 'doublenes' or otherwise of women. The lines are brief,
yet the double anagram is used to give the names of three Plesaunce
ladies, and of two men, with the poet's 'devise': ISMANIA SCALiS; MAVD;
WiMBIS; BABTho.; AnTI–ONA; TOT For–AIT. The variants of the refrain
in the Devonshire manuscript hardly affect the anagram, but the fourth
stanza, lacking in Egerton, helps the 'devise'. Set to unexpectedly
delicate and plaintive music by Cornish, it found its way into *Twelfth
Night*. It is to the same two men (BABTh.; WYMBY.; Tot – – –FAIT) that
two angry stanzas are addressed: 'To wette yowr Iye withouten teare'
(Muir, 105). In blunt colloquial phrases they attack feigned tears and
sickness, 'prating and flattering', in short, all the wiles of women.

Eleanor Cobham was occasionally the chief object of Roos's earlier
poems. In the Devonshire manuscript, there is one such poem, 'Ffarewell all my wellfare' (Muir, 108). In its anagrams, the complete
absence of I and Y is noticeable and probably intentional; they yield:
HOMF(R).; Al–An C–BHAm; ANT.; Tot ForFA–T For–A–T. A woman is

speaking in complaint of her ill-fortune and helplessness ('There ys no shyffte to helpe me now'), and against a faithless man who has left her alone 'To suffer sorow and shame'; yet all her intent was to 'ease hys payn'. The language of a forsaken woman is here skilfully adapted to this situation in which the Duke seemed powerless to save his wife. The poem does not, however, hint at imprisonment, and one may guess that, like her *Complaint against Fortune* (No. 42*b*, above), it was written in the midst of the proceedings of 1441.

(*d*) SONNETS, EPIGRAMS AND RONDEAUX

The Sonnets, nearly all of the Plesaunce period, are considered here together, because of their special interest in literary history. The first three, all translated from Petrarch, form a tiny group addressed to Elisabeth Phelip: 'Caesar, when that the traytor of Egipt' (Muir, No. 3); 'The longe love' (No. 4); and 'Who so list to hount' (No. 7). No. 3 yields the anagram, (E)–ISAB–TH P(H)IL. BA–DO.; ANT.; CATh. whIT.; FOR. No. 4 gives: E–ISABeTh P. BA–D–L.; S–A–S; WiTT.; TOT FOr–A. No. 7: ELISAB–Th, –HelI–, BA–D.; CATh. whIT.; WYM–I–H; FOr–I–. These three may then be the earliest in time. In the first, it is not Caesar and Hannibal who are relevant to the translator's situation, but the reflections of the sestet on the covering of sadness under a show of mirth. 'The longe love' is a painstaking exercise in translation, the only freedom coming in l. 9 where (perhaps by misunderstanding) Roos lights on a charming ambiguity, whereby Love, affrighted by the lady's firmness (or Daunger), flees 'vnto the hertes forrest' as if to some 'Forêt de Longue Attente'. Roos is expressing Italian sentiment in the terms of French poetry more familiar to him. In No. 7, only the beginning and the end of the beautiful poem, 'Una candida cerva', are kept to, and the whole is turned into a hunting poem, quite alien from Petrarch's painterly vision of the solitary lover. Roos can use Petrarch's 'Cesar's I ame' without 'arrière-pensée', since the English 'Caesar' was then only in his early teens; but he seems to be accepting that the lady is meant for another.

When Roos begins his sonnets to Lady Beaumont, a certain hardening of feeling is felt. In Sonnet 4, 'Was I never yet of your love greved' (Muir, No. 9), he inserts the negative into Petrarch's death-wishing lines: 'I will *not* yet in my grave be buried'. The anagram gives: --ISAB–Th B–WMONT, P–Y–I.; WYM; TOT ---FAY. IS–ANYA. Sonnet 5, 'Eche man me telleth I chaunge moost my devise' (No. 10), has a fresh meaning for the reader who has watched Roos dealing with 'devises'.

The anagram runs: A MOY Li MYE–S (Devonshire MS.); or A MOY
––MYEVS (Egerton MS.); AY TOT FOr–AYT; C–B–AM; BABTh. The first
'devise', 'A moi le mieux', is that found with Roos's signature in MS.
Add. 30864; the second is the 'devise' of all his poetry. Babthorpe,
probably Ralph, is his friend. The Duchess's name is supported by
phrases ('after oon rate', 'alwaies oon') reminiscent of her motto, 'al
en un'. The whole sonnet seems to indicate some re-assertion of
allegiance, or some crisis in Roos's hopes as a lover. Sonnet 6, 'Yf
amours faith, an hert vnfayned' (No. 12), shows Roos not only keeping
strictly close to Petrarch, but also manipulating the anagram. The line-
initials are concealed by the repeated 'Yf' of the anaphora. Disregard
'Yf', and what looks at first like an unconvincing and sketchy anagram
works out almost in full: ELISA––TH B–WMONT; SCA–Y.

The original Sonnet 7, 'Ffarewell Love and all thy lawes for ever'
(No. 13 and p. 260), needs to be disengaged from the alterations in Egerton manuscript. The version in the Devonshire manuscript is, I believe,
Roos's, unchanged, and when quoted it presents an illuminating contrast with Wyatt's version, in vigorous phrasing and rhythm:

> Nowe fare well Love and thy lawes for ever:
> Thy bayted hokis shall tangill me no more
> To[o] sore a profe hath called me from thy lore
> To surer welthe my wyttes to endevor
> In blynde error whylist I did persever
> Thy sherpe repulse that prycketh so sore
> Hath taught me to sett in tryfels no store
> But scapt forth, for libertie is lever.
> Therefore farewell: goo trouble yonger hertes
> And in me clayme no more authoritie,
> With idill youth goo vse thy propertie
> And therupon go spend thy brittil dertes
> For hetherto I have lost all my tyme
> Me liste no longer rotten boughes to clymbe. (Muir, p. 260)

The anagram is clearer here: I–MANIA SCA.; M–RG. ST–N(LO)W; WITT.;
TOT FOrF––T. Roos is addressing his confidantes in a tone of grave and
mature resolution; much later, in *Reson and Sensuallyte* (6938–41) he
will look back on this unavailing love as 'a drye tre, Without lefe, fruyt,
or flours, . . . naked and bareyn'. Consolatory recourse to Seneca and
Plato, as in the Egerton manuscript, is not impossible in a Gloucester's
man; but it may be Wyatt's addition.

Sonnet 8, 'My hert I gave the, not to do it payn' (No. 14), is closely
translated from sixteen lines of Serafino; its anagram is sketchy and unconvincing, and it cannot be claimed for Roos.

The original sonnet, 'There was never ffile' (No. 16), expresses to the same two ladies as Sonnet 7 and to Antigone his resentment, and regrets his 'lytyll perseyvyng and tyme myspent'. This is a reading of the Devonshire manuscript, which again yields the clearer anagram: AnTIG.; ISMAnIA; STAn–OW; BA(R).; BAB.; FOrFA–T. The lines show a constant shift to a trimeter movement.

The next three sonnets (10–12) are close to their Petrarchan originals, yet firmly handled. The first two, 'Som fowles there be' (No. 24) and 'Bicause I have the still kept fro lyes and blame' (No. 25), bring in Eleanor Cobham and Antigone: AlIAN.; AnT.; B–AMONT, –ARD.; STAnHO.; FOrFAI. (24); AlIAn.; AnT.; B–AUMO–T; TOT FOrFAIT (25). Sonnet 12, 'I fynde no peace and all my warr is done' (No. 26), addresses its antithetic complaints to his two confidantes: IS–ANIA; –TANL–W.

The original Sonnet 13, 'Though I my self be bridilled of my mynde' (No. 27), is a fine expression of the theme of the burning heart (cf. René d'Anjou's emblem) devoted and ready

> At all howres; still vnder the defence
> Of tyme, trouth, and love.

This is again meant for his lady and his two friends: BeW–O–T; ISMAn. SC– – –S; STA– –OW; WhITT.

The next two sonnets, 14 and 15 (Nos. 28, 29), are clearly from Petrarch, and are written for the same group. The now popular sonnet, 'My galy charged with forgetfulnes', for all its metrical roughness has been praised as 'the production of an energetic mind'. It is probable that the admired line 'The starres be hid that led me to this pain' is Roos's, since the only correction in Egerton manuscript is that of 'wretched' (obviously miscopied) to 'wrethed' for 'attorto'. The anagrams in their sketchiness betray the translator's difficulty: –ARDO.; AnT–G.; I–MAn–A; STAnLOW; –T–WARD; WiTT.; (R.R.). Sonnet 15, 'Auysing the bright bemes of these fayer Iyes' (No. 29), sounds like an early attempt at translation, before the translator had learnt to avoid inflexional rhymes. The anagrams are for B–W–OnT BA– –O–F; CATH. whITT.; STIWA. Sonnets 16 and 22, with 30 and 31 (Muir, 30, 160, 184, 175), all with D'Amancier anagrams, will be considered later. Sonnet 17, 'Love and fortune and my mynde, remembre' (No. 31), is faulty in translation and metre, and in spite of the anagram one doubts that it could have been meant for the Duchess's eyes in this form: ALIAn.; ELYSAB–Th BeWMO–T, BArDOL.; FOrFAIT. The unusual completeness of the anagram suggests that the lady's name was the poet's chief consideration here. Sonnet 18, 'How oft have I, my dere and cruell foo' (No. 32), in spite of its ultra 'conceited' original in Petrarch, is better managed, with firm forcible lines, culminating in the free translation of the final antithetic line: 'And yours the losse and myn the dedly pain'. The anagrams, as in the next three sonnets, prepare us for the Duke's critical eye on it: HOMFrEY; ALIAn.; ANTIG.; PHY–I., B––D.; ToT For––I. Sonnet 19, 'Like to these vnmesurable montayns' (No. 33), comes from an antithetic sonnet 'Simile a questi smisurati monti', once attributed to Sannazaro, but now called (by Berdan) only doubtfully his. The unfortunate line, 'Cattell in theim, and in me love is fed', is not entirely the poet's fault; the development of the language has betrayed him, leaving 'herds' as a poetic word, but consigning 'cattle' to the market-place. The anagram runs: HOM.; COBHA.; AnTIG.; P–ILi–; SCA––S; For–A–T. 'The lyvely sperkes that issue from those Iyes' (Sonnet 20, No. 47) shows Roos flaring up into an original sonnet from the mere spark of a Petrarchan first line, 'Vive faville uscian de'duo bei lumi'. The anagrams reveal his audience: HOM.; COBHAM; ANT.; E–ISA––Th P.; WiTT.; ToT For–A. In Sonnet 21, 'Suche vayn thought as wonted to myslede me' (No. 56), he reverts to following Petrarch closely, except in the eighth line. The anagrams are ALYAn COB––M; AnT.; B––UM––T; whITT.; WIMBISS.

The original Sonnet 23, 'Dyvers dothe vse as I have hard and kno' (No. 145), expresses indifference; the neglected suitor throws the blame back on the inconstant mistress; the anagrams show that this sonnet is addressed only to the lady with her companion: B–W––NT BA–DOL.; CATH. whITT. Similarly the uncorrected Sonnet 24, 'Mye love toke skorne my servise to retaine' (No. 153), is a smoothly written and private complaint to his friends: ISMAn. SCAl–S; M. STA–––W; B–WM. BA–D.; WHYT.; TOT For. Sonnet 25, 'To Rayle or geste ye kno I vse yt not' (No. 139), hammering on the negative word as rhyme, is a vigorous protest to ALYAn.; AnTI.; –LISAB–Th B––MO–T, signed ToT For–AIT.

Sonnet 26, 'Vnstable dreme' (No. 79), has been derived from a *strambotto* of Filosseno (Foxwell, II, 205); the general idea of a lover's happy dream is common to both, no more.[1] The English sonnet seems to have been written on board ship, 'this tossing mew' (Tottel reads 'seas' for 'mew'), and 'My body in tempest'; there is no ship in Filosseno. The anagram justifies a connexion with the greater poem on a lover's dream, 'They fle from me': PHIL., BeAUMO–T, BARD–L; –OB–AM; whITT.

Sonnet 27, 'You that in love finde lucke and habundance' (No. 92), has been called a Chaucerian imitation, referring to the month of May,

---

[1] Cf. P. J. Frankis, 'The Erotic Dream in Med. Engl. Lyrics', in *Neuphilolog Mitteilungen* (1956), LVII, 228–37.

fateful in Wyatt's life. But since the anagram runs HOMFR–Y; ALIAn.; AnT.; –ArDOL.; WHIT.; STI–ArD, it is probable that it reflects some complaint uttered by the Duke, for whose war policy May in many years had brought bad fortune, from May 1429, when Orleans fell to Joan of Arc, and onwards. In May 1432 he and Cardinal Beaufort were in conflict; he broke away from the unsuccessful conference in France in May 1433; and in May 1434 his proposals for the conduct of the war were rejected by the Council. In May 1435 the French successes against Lord Arundel resulted in the capture and death of that great leader, and they were continued till May 1436. Then, in that summer, Fortune smiled again at the siege of Calais, which Roos celebrated in *Anelida and Arcite*. As for the one crux in the sonnet, it is deplorable to have to destroy the image of a mysterious astrologer conjured up by the doubtful name Sephame (Muir),[1] or Sephanes (Foxwell, I, p. 39), or Sephances (Arundel MS.); he was after all a guesser, not an expert: 'He gest, I prove, of that the veritie'. I fear that the name may be a later misreading of Popham; Sir John Popham was Treasurer of the Household in 1438 (*Cal. Pat. Rolls*, 1436–41, pp. 134, 139, 168). The sonnet is in the spirit and style of Charles d'Orléans, especially of those French poems translated about 1438 to 1440 into English; such are 'This dyane day, the first in moneth of may', or 'The secund day of fayre fresshe lusty may' (ed. Steele, pp. 63, 77).

A similar change to a politico-personal application may be seen in Sonnet 28 (No. 95), 'If waker care, if sodayne pale Coulor'. The opening is suggested by Petrarch, but the rest is highly original. The crux lies in ll. 6–10, with the puzzling l. 8 of Old Egerton: 'Her that ded set our country in a rore', altered by Wyatt to 'Brunet, that set my welth in such a rore'. He may have taken the name from the lines following:

> Th'unfayned chere of Phillis hath the place
> That Brunet had: she hath and ever shal.

This has been read as a clear reference to Anne Boleyn; and Phillis is then Mary, Duchess of Richmond (Foxwell, II, 52). We have seen, however, that Phillis is one of Roos's names for Elisabeth Beaumont, playing on Phelip, Hypsifile, and Phyllis and Demophoon (see above, Nos. 5 and 10). Phillis is then more easily identified for Roos than for Wyatt. But what of the troubler of the peace, Brunet, whose name seems to have been in the original? Only one woman of Roos's circle could have been said to set the country in an uproar, and that was the 'sorceress', Eleanor Cobham, against whose hold on Humphrey the

---

[1] There was, however, an Edward Sepham of Oxford (1528–30; d. 1554), a cleric, and a contemporary of Wyatt (W. H. Wiatt, *N. & Q.*, June 7, 1952).

very market-women of London raised a public protest. Whether the Italian-sounding Brunet was an apt name for her we do not know, since no detailed description of her exists; but the miniature of her with the Duke (reproduced by Vickers, p. 206) certainly does not display the conventional golden hair. The anagram runs: BEWMO–T; ISM–NI S(C)–––S; ST–NHOP; WIMBIS; TOT FOF–I–. It is a difficult anagram, since it lacks the letter A; was the poet deliberately keeping all appearance of ALIAN. out of a poem not intended for the family at Plesaunce? Sonnet 29 (No. 173), 'The piller pearisht is whearto I lent', a free translation from a political Petrarchan sonnet, has been assigned a political significance for Wyatt with Thomas Cromwell, executed July 28, 1540 (Foxwell, II, 53). Roos's anagram is purely personal: ISMAn.; B(E)WMONT, BA–DO.; TOT FOrF––T; rather unexpectedly, for the poem could easily be read as referring to the disastrous events of 1441.

These sonnets, all written within the decade 1431–41, put back the history of the sonnet form in England by nearly a century from the accredited date. Their forms and rhyme-schemes are of extreme interest, even more so at this earlier period. One can watch Roos's growing facility in handling this new form. At first he keeps the division into octet and sestet, and the five rhymes, these always with a concluding couplet. It is not till Sonnet 8 ('My hert I gave thee') that he extends to six rhymes. In Sonnet 25, the insistent rhyme word 'not' forces him to reduce the rhymes to four, with a final couplet. The original May morning sonnet cuts down even further to three rhymes; and the sestet is turned into a quatrain and couplet in its rhymes, though not in its sentence structure. The later D'Amancier sonnets, written c. 1450–4, will prove to be much freer in structure, with occasionally the alternate quatrain instead of the enclosed (e.g. Sonnet 30, No. 184).

The greater number of the thirty-one Epigrams, grouped together by Miss Foxwell, but actually, like the Sonnets, scattered through the two chief manuscripts, yield similar Roos anagrams, and these sometimes help to elucidate the poems. Her first three Epigrams (Muir, Nos. 42, 54, 44) originally, I believe, formed one Ballade, and should be re-arranged as 54, 42, 44. Nos. 1 and 2, 'Who hath herd' and 'She sat and sowde', are both on a lady ill-wishing the poet as she sews. The three make a coherent story if they are re-assembled thus: I. 'She sat and sowde'; II, 'Who hath herd'; and III, 'Alas, madame', with its climax of the stolen kiss restored; 'The angry lady sitting and sewing wishes my heart were in her sampler, but pricks her own finger instead (No. 54); who ever heard of such misprision as to take her finger for my heart? (42) And all this pother for a stolen kiss! Let me then repay it with interest' (44). This is exactly the impertinent climax that Charles d'Orléans works up to in his English poem of mock-confession on the same theme, 'My gostly fadir, y me confesse'—'y restore it shalle dowtles' (Steele, *Engl. Poems*, p. 133). The three stanzas are corrected in the Egerton manuscript. In 'Who hath herd' (42), the corrections do not affect the anagram, and Old Egerton and Devonshire agree. In 'She sat and sowde' (54), and in 'Alas, madame' (44), whole lines are changed, and the anagram is affected, but not beyond recognition. The Old Egerton anagrams give: 'She sat and sowde', AnTIG.; STIWA–D; 'Who hath herd', STAnHO.; FOrFA–T.; ST–WAR–; 'Alas, madame', AlYAn.; ST––HO.; TOT FOrF–IT; R. The overlapping of names from verse to verse is constantly Roos's method, and here serves to tie the stanzas together; exactly how the four personages were involved in the episode remains the poet's secret.

Epigram 4 (Muir, 46), 'The wandering gadlyng in the sommer tyde', has been traced to two passages in *Orlando Furioso*; the 'timida pastorella' (i, 11) is not at all close; that in xxxix, 32, is more so: 'Much like to him that waking new, doth chance | On poisond serpent tred'. If it is originally by Roos, the serpent simile probably goes back to its basis in *Æneid*, II, 378–81. The anagram appears to be STIWA.; TOT; Sir John Stiward had also appeared in the stolen kiss sequence. The application to Jealousy surprising the lovers is original.

Epigram 5 (Muir, 48), 'What nedeth these thre(t)ning wordes?', on the stealing of a lady's glove, has a close parallel in a *strambotto* of Serafino, 'A che minacci'. Nevertheless the anagram is full and clear: ALIAn.; MaWD STAN–O. (see above, pp. 463–4).

Epigram 6 (Muir, 49), 'Ryght true it is, and said full yore agoo', is against false and hypocritical friends. The anagram yields: AlYAn.; ST––H.; T–T FOrF–YT; R. It is not a distinguished verse; and the subject is discussed with more vivacity in the verse-letter, No. 152. Epigram 7 (Muir, 50), 'What wourde is that that chaungeth not', was altered by Tottel to fit the Wyatt-Anne Boleyn legend. The third line, 'It is myn aunswer, god it wot' (Egerton), appears in him as 'It is mine Anna', etc. The anagram gives: AlIAn.; AnTIGO.; whYT.; the lady of whom Roos would complain to them would be his Elisabeth, and P(h)ilip is nearly as much a palindrome as Anna. The second line, 'Though it be tourned and made in twain', is a good definition of Eustache Deschamps' method of syllabic division and reversal (see above, Chapter III, II). The riddling Epigram 8 (Muir, 174), 'A Ladye gave me a gyfte she had not', gives the anagram, AlIAn.; IS–AnIA SCAlIS; FOr–AI.

In Epigram 9 (Muir, 59), 'Some tyme I fled the fyre that me brent', the phrase 'From Dovor to Calais' has been taken to allude to the known travels of Wyatt. He has certainly altered the 'by hilles and dales' of Old Egerton and Tottel into 'by water and by wynd', which merely re-inforces 'By see'. It is possible that at some earlier stage he substituted Dover and Calais for other places; but 'Do.' is used in the anagram, and Roos must have crossed between these ports. The anagram of Old Egerton yields: –LISAB–Th BA–(DO)–F; ANT.; Tottel's other variants affect the caesural initials, and add WIM––S. Epigram 17 (Muir, 81) offers a similar problem, with its final line 'At Mountzon thus I restles rest in Spayne', which naturally has been applied (Foxwell, II, 69) to Wyatt's stay at Barbastra near Mountzon on his embassy of 1537. I know of no documentary evidence of Roos ever being in Spain; there is one casual reference in an early poem, *How a Lover*, which suggests personal knowledge: he approves the lady's pretty finger-nails, 'not peyntyd as in spayne'; but this is susceptible of other explanations. The Epigram begins as a free translation from the opening of Petrarch's Sonnet 103, 'Vinse Anibàl e non seppe usar poi'. The anagram gives: B––[M]ONT; IS–AnIA SC.; the M is due to a variant in Tottel, l. 5. Epigram 18 (Muir, 88), 'I lede a liff vnpleasant', has also been related rather arbitrarily to Wyatt's Spanish sojourn, and interpreted politically. But its anagram reads: PHILIP; SCA––S; wh–T; TOT.; this seems to point to an early poem. Epigram 19 (Muir, 94) is similarly interpreted by Miss Foxwell, 'From thes hye hilles' (viz. the Pyrenees), and a parallel is asserted with *Orlando Furioso*, xxxvii, 110. This, however, says precisely the opposite: Ariosto's torrent rushes down, to diminish in the valley to a fordable brook; the English rill gathers force till 'at the fote it ragith ouer all'; even so fares love. Nearer than this is Petrarch's sonnet to the Rhône (*Vita*, No. 208) 'Rapido fiume, che d'alpestra vena, rodendo intorno . . . il tuo corso non frena' etc. Petrarch's contrast between 'nibbling' and an unbridled, unwearied flow is parallel to the English between 'trilling' and 'raging'. The poem is in Wyatt's own handwriting, and the last couplet is much altered; in Old Egerton it sounds more like an older style:

> His rayne is rage, then botyth no deny,
> The first estew is only remedy.

The anagram of Old Egerton is very sketchy: ––ISA––TH ––W–O–T; WI––IS. Epigram 20 (Muir, 97), 'Tagus, fare well', is also in Wyatt's handwriting. Its seventh line shows in Old Egerton a probably prior correction with an imperfect cancel: 'My Kyng, my Contry, for whome

H H

only alone I lyve'; the first half does not affect the anagram, and may have been Wyatt's substitution for some reference more in keeping in a love poem. The anagram of Old Egerton is: (B)–WMO–T; AnT–G.; TOT FORF--T. The reference to Brutus, founder of London, has no parallel in Wyatt; but we have found Roos more than once calling London 'New Troy', and himself Troilus. The inspiration of the poem is a phrase from Boethius, possibly from Chaucer's version (Foxwell, II, 71).

In dealing with these 'Spanish' epigrams, we have passed over Epigrams 10–16. Epigrams 10 and 11 (Muir, 60, 61) are very close to *strambotte* by Serafino; nevertheless the anagram of No. 60, 'He is not ded', etc., in Old Egerton and the Devonshire manuscript is AlIAn.; TOT FOR–A–T. That of Epigram 11 (Muir, 61), 'The furyous gonne in his rajing yre', is even more significant. Old Egerton gives IAyMyS II, SC–TLAn. It compares a heart broken by the force of flaming desire with an overcharged and exploding gun. James II of Scotland, nephew of Edmund Beaufort, met his death thus before Roxburgh Castle on August 3, 1460, on the discharge of a bombard. He had just renewed war with England in the Lancastrian interest and his death was a blow to Queen Margaret. Old Egerton readings are 'canon', and then 'bombard'. Epigram 12 (Muir, 64), 'Th'Enmy of liff', is 'derived from St. Gelais', probably himself borrowing from earlier Italian. Its anagram appears to be WiTT--HAM; ST–WA–D. Epigram 13 (Muir, 68), 'Nature that gave the bee so feet a grace', on the lover who from a kiss can suck both honey and poison, is a straightforward expression of a love-conceit. Its anagram gives --IS–B–TH B–W–ONT. Epigram 14 (Muir, 75), 'Desire, alas, my master and my foo', is both written and heavily corrected in Wyatt's own hand, and the version in the Devonshire manuscript shows many variants. The anagrams are substantially the same, but Old Egerton's is the clearer: E–ISA--Th B–WM–NT; ANT.; FOR. The suggested likeness to a ten-line poem by Maurice Scève is not at all close. Epigram 15 (Muir, 76), 'Venemus thornes that ar so sharp and kene', closely parallel to Serafino's 'Ogni pungenta e venenosa spina', is in Wyatt's own hand in Egerton, and yields a rather fragmentary anagram: AlIAn.; ISMAnI.; M–V– ST----P; F--F–I–. Devonshire, with considerable variation, yields: ISMAn. SC--IS; MAVD; F--F–IT. Tottel's further differences, though small, produce a different anagram: E–ISABeTh PHI–IP; MAV.; F-----T. The theme is like that of the bee epigram, poison and solace from the one source. The matter of Epigram 16 (Muir, 80), Josephus's story from the horrors of the siege of Jerusalem ('In dowtfull brest'), is far from Roos's usual theme and even his style; yet the anagram is ISMAnY; ST–WAR.; FOr–––T. I cannot explain its application.

Epigram 21 (Muir, 98), 'Off purpos Love chase first for to be blynd', is a paradox of compliment. It is in Wyatt's handwriting. The three lines (2, 4, and 6) that he alters were earlier both simpler and looser in style, and they help to give a slightly more coherent anagram in Old Egerton: A(L)YAn. COBHA.; AnT.; FOr–AI.

Epigram 22 (Muir, 100) will be considered later; it is the last of those in the Egerton manuscript. The two next that are in the Devonshire manuscript (Muir, 133 and 135) have no anagrams for Eleanor Cobham, but are only for another member of the Plesaunce group, Anne of Woodstock. Epigrams 25 and 26 (Muir, 179, 191) are found in Tottel only, the latter from Ausonius, and run on very restricted sets of letters; I can trace no anagrams in them.

Epigram 27 (Muir, 127), 'My loue ys lyke vnto th'eternall fyre', is in Devonshire MS. only, and gives: B–WMO–T; YSMAn.; TOT. Epigram 29 (Muir, 171), the charming octave, 'A face that shuld content me wonders well', is meant for Roos's two confidantes and comforters, Lady Scales and Margaret Stanlow: S–Al–S, W–A––SB.; STAn–[O]w (the O is only found in Tottel). The poem appears also in MS. Add. 36529, a Harington manuscript. Epigrams 30 and 31, like 22, will be examined later.

The Epigrams are all in the characteristic Italian form, the *ottava rima* (abababcc), as are the *strambotte* of Serafino; Roos's usual eight-line stanza was that of the French *Balade* (ababbcbc). We have seen him turning rhyme-royal to octosyllabic verse (see above, No. 19); we find him making a similar shortening in one of the three octaves or epigrams among Tottel's 'Uncertain Authors'. Tottel, No. 229, 'Suche grene to me as you haue sent', is entitled by Tottel, 'Of a Rosemary braunche sente', though the plant is not named in the poem. It is on the rhyme-scheme of *ottava rima*, but in octosyllables. The lady who sent him this token of remembrance is IS–AnYA S–Al–S; FOr–A–T. Tottel, No. 230, 'As I haue bene so will I euer be', a protestation of rock-like constancy, is addressed to B–AV–ONT; STANH.; and No. 231, 'The golden apple that the Troyan boy', on an apple received from his love, gives, ––WMO–T; WhITT. One must remember that in these three epigrams, known nowhere else, one is at the mercy of Tottel's smoothing-iron.

The Rondeaux make a usefully compact little group of nine poems; it is a form favoured by Charles d'Orléans. According to the anagrams, all but one were written in the Plesaunce period. Rondeau 1 (Muir, 1), 'Behold, love', is a fairly free adaptation from Petrarch's Madrigal, 'Or vedi, Amor'. Although expanded from nine to thirteen lines, it loses the charming picture in the original of the girl sitting barefooted and with flowing hair among the flowers and grasses, a southern idyll unsuited to the Thames estuary. The anagram gives BeWMO–T; AnTIG.; BABTh.; WhITT.; R.R., TOT. Rondeau 2 (Muir, 2), 'What vaileth trouth', apparently original, gives B–W–ONT, BARD–LF; WhITT; IS–An–A; TOT. The phrase 'What vaileth' is frequent in the poems of these manuscripts and of MS. Ff. 1.6. The third Rondeau (Muir 15), 'Ffor to love her for her lokes lovely', gives BAR––L.; ISMAnY; TOT FOrFAIT FOrF–IT. It is signed 'Wyatt' in the margin. The unusual spelling of 'truth' as 'trought' (Egerton) is found in MS. Ff. 1.6, and also in Sir John Paston's letters.

Rondeau 4 (Muir, 17), 'Helpe me to seke for I lost it there', begging for the return of the lover's heart, is a link in the chain of conceits that run from Chrétien de Troyes and Charles d'Orléans, and then through Marot to Sidney and Sir John Davies. The line-initials give AlIAn –OBHA.; FOrF––T; the caesural initials add YSMANIA, and fill out the devise to AI FOrFAIT. Rondeau 5 (Muir, 18), 'Yf it be so that I forsake the', gives: BAR–––F; ANTIG.; YS–AnIA; BABTh. It is derived by Miss Foxwell from Serafino, and from Marot's 'S'il est ainsy' (II, 18–22).

Rondeau 6 (Muir, 19), 'Thou hast no faith of him that [eke] hath none', exists in two versions; that in the Devonshire manuscript has an extra syllable in many lines, and these rather heavy regular decasyllabics are, I believe, the earlier version. Wyatt may in the Egerton manuscript have shortened and lightened the lines, and possibly added the refrains. There is little difference, however, in the caesuras, and in both versions the anagrams with very slight variations give: E–ISAB–Th B–W–ONT; ANTI.; WHYTT.; TOT FOrF–IT. The seventh Rondeau (Muir, 20), 'Goo, burnyng sighes', takes its first four lines from Petrarch's Sonnet 120, 'Ite, caldi sospiri, al freddo core'; the remainder diverges, and forces the conceit tastelessly. The anagram gives: AlIAn.; AnTIG.; BeAUM.; WhITT.; T–T FOrFAIT. The eighth Rondeau (Muir, 35) was written for another set of people. But Rondeau 9 (Muir, 45), 'What no, perdy, ye may be sure', is again for BeWM––T; YSMAN. SC.; WhITT.; W–*B–S; TOT FOr. The anagram has perhaps been sacrificed to elegance, for this poem on three rhymes is smooth and polished in Roos's best style. In all these rondeaux, the letters of the two half-line refrains are not needed for the anagrams; they may have been added later for musical setting.

(e) POEMS FOR JACQUETTA OF BEDFORD, ANNE OF WOODSTOCK AND ELEANOR BEAUCHAMP

Roos had occasionally included Jacquetta, Duchess of Bedford, in the Plesaunce group, and in one ornate poem, 'Exemplye sendynge to you, rowte of gentylnes', he had celebrated the Duke and the Duchess, bringing in the Duke's famous emblem, the root, and the name of his house in Rouen, Joyeux Repos (see above, No. 56a). It was perhaps this last idea that induced him to apply humorously to the Bedfords Petrarch's Sonnet, 'O cameretta' (*In Vita*, Sonnet 198), an apostrophe to his bedchamber and his bed. 'The restfull place, Revyver of my smarte' (Muir, No. 115) is a very free adaptation of the Italian, expanded to three stanzas of rhyme royal; it has for anagram: st. 1, IAQU–TTA Be–For–; stt. 1–2, ENTI–ReM––T V–STRe (i.e. 'entièrement vostre', a paraphrase of the Duke's motto 'A vous entier' (cf. *Assembly of Ladies*, 616); st. 3, I–MANIA; diffused, whYTTInHAM, this last probably for Sir Robert Whyttingham, who was the Duke's executor later. The acrostic is very obvious, even in the line-initials, as if for unaccustomed eyes. The refrain, on the bed sprinkled with tears, may even give a clumsy pun in st. 2, 'my *bed for* to forsake'. In the Devonshire Manuscript, the poem is followed by 'ffynys qd. Wyatt'.

Another, but a long, translation from Petrarch, by addressing Jacquetta of Bedford in the first and last stanzas, distinguishes her from the full Plesaunce group as the chief dedicatee. 'Myne olde dere En'mye, my froward master' (Muir, 8), in twenty-one stanzas of rhyme royal, translates closely, though with some interpolations, Petrarch's Canzone 28 (*In Morte*, 360), 'Quell' antiquo mio dolce empio Signore', in ten stanzas of fifteen lines with a seven-line conclusion. Petrarch arraigns Love before the tribunal of Reason, the queen of the soul. Love defends himself. The lover's final charge is of his lady's death; Love denies his responsibility. Reason, when challenged, defers her verdict. The alterations are thoroughly in Roos's style. His stanza 15, on the devout lover's lessons learnt in the school of love, is an interpolation between ll. 104 and 105 of the Italian; this original stanza yields E–ISA––Th PHIlI. In the list of Worthies he inserts (st. 13) Homer's Achilles and Scipio Africanus, but cuts out Lucrece. His omission (st. 9) of the charge that Love uses potions and charms may have been a cautious withdrawal from Eleanor Cobham's dangerous ground. Some interpolations are those of the active man as against the clerk; Love in youth took him from the art that 'maketh a clattering knyght' (st. 11; cf. Petrarch, l. 81); the foolish lover 'stryveth with the bit | Which may ruell him' (st. 18; cf. Petrarch, ll. 132–3). For a long simile on an advocate, he substitutes the fable of the ungrateful serpent (st. 16). He thus treats Petrarch's images freely, changing also the yoke of love to its whetstone (st. 5). His most puzzling translation is Love's answer to the despairing cry of the bereaved lover: 'Not I, quod he, but price, that is well worthy' (st. 20) for 'Io no, ma Chi per sè la volse' (l. 150); there may be a scribal error (possibly for prince). The anagrams run thus: st. 1, IAQueTTA; stt. 1–2, I–(M)AnIA SCA–.; BA–THO.; 2–3, STAnHOP.; 4, HOMFrI; 5–6, AlIAn. CO––AM; ANT–G.; chAWOrTH; 8–9, B–WMONT; 9, STAnHO.; 10–11, FOrFAJT; 11–12, E(L)I–A––TH; 13–14, SCA–I–; BA(R)DO.; 15–16, E–ISA––Th PHIlI.; 16–17, IS–ANIA; 18, B–WMONT; 19, COBHAM; 20–1, IAQU–TTA B–DFOrD.

Roos had made avowal by anagram of his liking for the sympathetic elderly lady, Anne of Woodstock. In the Devonshire manuscript, a few more poems signalize her, and must precede October 1438: two Epigrams, 'All yn thi sight my lif doth hole depende' (Muir, 133), and 'The fructe of all the seruise that I serue' (Muir, 135); also 'It was my choyse, yt was no chaunce' (Muir, 121), and 'What shulde I saye' (Muir, 143).

Epigram 23 (Muir, 133) is a conventional love-poem, and is addressed to ISMAn.; STAF–FOrD W–––STO. Tottel's variants in the final lines slightly diminish the anagram. Epigram 24 (Muir, 135) is in the Devonshire manuscript only, and has a similar anagram to No. 23: YS–AN.; An STAFFOrD; FOr–AIT. The classical allusion (here to Tantalus), noted by Miss Foxwell (II, 74) as rare in Wyatt, is common in Roos, in a limited range, since he has the Middle Ages' 'unspoiled appetite for myth'.

The third poem (Muir, 121), with its stanzas linked by repeated phrases, 'What vaylyth Right', 'Yt lastyth nott', has a full anagram and devise: –LISAB–TH PHYL., B–AUM–NT; An STAFFOr., WO–DSTO.; WYMBIS; AY TOT FOrFAYT FOrFAYT. In the poem (Muir, 143)

> What shulde I saye
> Sins faithe is dede,
> And truthe awaye
> From you ys fled,

sharp thrusts of reproach are directed against B–W–(O)NT, together with CATh. WhIT.; BAB.; S–AFF.; AY FO–FAY. The name Stafford is probably meant for Anne of Woodstock, Lady Bourchier, and it has a particular interest here. On the end flyleaf of MS. Ashmole 39 occurs (as has not been noted) a variant of these first four lines:

> What shuld I say sith faith is ded
> And truth is exiled in whomanhede

This is a Bourchier manuscript, and above these lines occur the signatures, Isabell Bourgchier, Anne Bourgchier (three times), and Thomas Bourchier. At the foot of the page is written neatly and very small an eight-line stanza, 'O ye women wyche be enclyned', ending 'A myghty scheld of douvbleness'. This is the Envoy of 'Doubleness' or 'This worlde is ful of variaunce' printed now as Lydgate's (MacCracken, p. 438) but claimed above for Roos (see No. 48). The Bourchier names may be thus identified: Thomas Bourchier, consecrated Bishop of Worcester in 1435, and later Archbishop of Canterbury (the manuscript is a history of the Blessed Virgin); his mother Anne of Woodstock (d. 1438); and his sister-in-law, Isabel, daughter of Richard of Cambridge, and grand-daughter of Lady Beatrice Roos, who in 1435 married Henry Bourchier, Earl of Essex. The interspersing of these Bourchier names with scraps of two poems, one a Plesaunce poem, and the other with double or ambivalent anagrams for Plesaunce or for Warwick Castle, is significant for Roos's authorship in the mid-1430s. And for the transmission of the poem one may note that Protector Seymour's wife was Ann Stanhope of Sudbury, Suffolk; her mother was Elizabeth Bourchier, a great grand-daughter of Anne of Woodstock.

Eleanor Beaufort, *née* Beauchamp, with her ambitious husband Edmund Beaufort, is given a classical warning against court favour. 'Stond who so list vpon the Slipper toppe | Of courtes estates' (Muir, No. 176) is a ten-line translation from the thirteen concluding lines of a Senecan chorus (*Thyestes*, Acts II–III). Roos had access to the drama of Seneca in Duke Humphrey's library (Vickers, p. 412). The poem exists in two versions with considerable variation. That in the Arundel MS. begins correctly with 'toppe' for *culmine*, but with a puzzling rendering in the eighth line. Tottel's version (No. 118) inserts an allusion to Fortune by translating *culmine* as 'whele' with consequent change of rhymes; but his line 8 is much nearer the Latin. Both versions lose the point of the last line, 'Ignotus moritur sibi', and blur it with a vague expansion, 'Doth dye vnknowen, dazed with dreadfull face'. Jasper Heywood will get it better: 'Departeth yet unto him selfe unknowne'; and Marvell in his version, 'Climb, at Court, for me, that will', shows still greater complexity and insight. The anagram is clear in both forms: the Arundel MS. yields A–IAn. B–AUS–A–; –D–UnD ––WForT; Tottel has it more fully: ALIAn. B–AUSHA–; –DMUnD B––ForT.

The poems considered hitherto are of the Plesaunce period which closed in 1441 (see Chapters V–VIII); now come those written by the King's Knight (see Chapters VII–XI).

(*f*) D'AMANCIER POEMS

Next to the autobiographical poems, which, for the study of the fifteenth century, have an interest second only to the exclusively self-centred poetry of Charles d'Orléans, the most instructive group of anagrams in the Devonshire and Egerton manuscripts is that which covers the names of Eleanor Cobham and D'Amancier (see above, Chapter IX, IV). We have seen that Roos resumed his interest in Eleanor after the marriage in 1450 of the newly-widowed Antigone, Lady Powys, to Jean D'Amancier, servant of Charles VII. These poems again reflect Eleanor's misery and despair at the desertion of her, as it seemed, by her daughter, and her hopelessness of freedom. Nevertheless a message conveyed in one poem shows that a rescue was planned; and another appears to serve as a direct answer to a poem already known. Not all the poems will be noticed here, but only those of most interest.[1] This revival in 1450 of the sonnet-form, and of Petrarchan translation, is not surprising when we remember that the form was first practised by Roos for the Plesaunce group.

Sonnet 16 (Muir, 30):

> Ever myn happe is slack and slo in commyng,
>   Desir encresing, myn hope vncertain.

translates closely Petrarch's 'Mie venture al venir son tarde e pigre' (*In Vita*, 57), but adapting 'Eufrate e Tigre' to 'The Tamys'. The double anagram of the uncorrected text, Old Egerton, gives ALIAn.; ANT. DAMAnSIE.; HOMF. STAF--O. The last name probably stands for Anne of Woodstock's son, Humphrey Stafford, first Duke of Buckingham. The short-lined poem, 'What deth is worse then this' (Muir, 63), which laments a death in life, yields with its single anagram: Al. -OBHAM; AMA-S.; WIM.; TOT FOrFA-AIT. The uncorrected form of line 3, 'My worldly joye and my blys', is reminiscent of the Duke of Gloucester's motto, 'Mon bien mondain'.

A poem particularly interesting for all reasons is 'My lute awake!' (Muir, 66); and admirers of Wyatt will be relieved that half of it, and that the best half, may be saved for him. Stanzas 1–3 and 8 yield anagrams thus: stt. 1–2, ALIAN.; stt. 3 and 8, C-BHAM; stt. 2–3, ANT. POWIS, AMANS--R; diffused, T-T FOrFA-T FOrFA-T. But in stt. 4–7 there is no anagram, and it is here that there comes the theme of retribution,

---

[1] The full list of D'Amancier poems is as follows: MS. Egerton, Muir, Nos. 30, 53, 57, 58, 62, 63, 65–7, 70, 72, 74, 77–8, 83–4, 89, 91, 99; Devonshire MS., Muir, Nos. 140, 160–1; other sources, 172, 175, 184–5; also 'doubtful poems' 216, 222–3, 225, 228.

and the echo of Villon ('Perchaunce the lye wethered and old'), Villon who was hardly likely to be quoted in England before 1454. On the other hand, the sea image of st. 3 is natural for a prisoner in Peel Castle:

> The Rokkes do not so cruelly
> Repulse the waves continuelly,
> As she my suyte and affection.

The poem was deservedly popular; it is also found in the Devonshire MS., in Tottel, in *The Courte of Venus*, and in Harington's *Nugae Antiquae* (II, 252), where it is attributed to the Earl of Rochford, presumably the father or the brother of Anne Boleyn, beheaded with her. It is a clear case of a short lyric by Roos, cleft for a shoot to be grafted in, almost certainly by Sir Thomas Wyatt. A similar grafting can be seen in 'All hevy myndes' (Muir, 84), where stt. 7–11 carry no anagram, and have almost the air of an independent poem, 'Where is my thoght?'; certainly they add beauty to the poem. Of stt. 1–6 and 12–15 the anagram reads: AlIAn. –OBHAM; HOMF–I; ANT. DAMAnS.; W–LOUH.; TOT FOr–AIT FOr–AIT.

Next to the lute lyric in the Egerton MS. comes a despairing plea for life and liberty: 'If chaunce assynd | Were to my mynde' (Muir, 67); it is signed 'Tho' and might well appeal to Wyatt as fitting his own situation. Its single anagrams are: AlIAn. –OB–AM; AnTIGO. AMAN.; –AWD WILLOBY; TOT FOrFAIT FOr–A–T, again introducing Lady Willoughby's name. 'Lyke as the Swanne towardis her dethe' (Muir, 70) has been attributed to sources in Filosseno and Serafino. It is a common poetic notion, and we have seen Roos interpolating it into *Reson and Sensuallyte*, with special reference to the Bohun swan, one of Duke Humphrey's badges. The anagram here is: HOMF–Y; AlIAn COB–AM; Ant. DAMAnSI. A political allusion to Wyatt's dependence on Cromwell and his fear of Bonner has been read into 'Most wretched hart most myserable' (Muir, 91); but the anagram is full and clear: AlYAn. –OBHAM; AnTIGO. DAMAnS.; MAUD STANHO. WI––UHBY; AI T–T FOrFAIT FOrFAIT.

The poem of 'powerful and gloomy feeling' (Tillyard) 'What rage is this? What furour of what kynd?' (Muir, 99) is a very interesting example of Roos's original poem, in Wyatt's own handwriting and overlaid by his copious alteration of words and rhymes, as can be seen in Muir's facsimile (p. 84). Only from Old Egerton can the anagram be obtained: CO–HAM; ANTIGO. DAM–NS––R; S––LYS; TOT F. Even so it is fragmentary, and it is possible that Wyatt did not copy the whole poem, but only such stanzas as he applied to himself. Both versions are violent in tone, but Wyatt has polished somewhat while adapting.

The Devonshire MS. has its three D'Amancier poems near the end, with two in sequence, almost as if the collectors had acquired a fresh manuscript source. 'The Joye so short, alas, the paine so nere' (Muir, 140), with its Chaucerian first line, is a mournful poem of parting. The reader's natural assumption is of two lovers: but the anagram yields ALYA. COB.; AnTI. POWYS, DA–ANCYeR; WHALYSBrOU; FOrFAYT. It is well concealed, lying deep in the poem beneath the layer of line-initials, the anaphora of T and W. It is unusual for an anagram to unite the names Powys and D'Amancier, and one might infer a poem of 1450, soon after the actual departure of Antigone for France. The most interesting is the irregular sonnet 'I abide and abide and better abide' (Muir, 160), an impatient and colloquial rejection of intended comfort. It appears to be the prisoner's answer to the poem of good counsel 'ffor þe bettur a-byde' ('I see A Rybane Ryche and newe', see above, No. 86c). The speaker here brushes aside the promise that never issues in performance: 'Thus do I abide I wott allwaye, | Nother obtayning nor yet denied'. In spite of the hasty air, the anagram is very careful; the essential names are visible in the line-initials; the caesural initials merely fill them out, then indicate one more (Stiward), and give the 'devise': ALIAN.; ANT. AMAnS.; STI–A.; AY TOT FOr–AIT. The locution with 'better', meaning to repeat or continue an action, can still be heard on the lips of Yorkshire folk: 'I wrote and better wrote, but no answer'. The likeness to Serafino that Miss Foxwell found in the sonnet is hardly discernible.

Other sources, manuscript and printed, yield a few D'Amancier poems. 'Like as the byrde in the cage enclosed' (Muir, 172) seems to Professor C. S. Lewis not only medieval but also bad (*Engl. Lit. in the Sixteenth Century*, p. 223). Read as an amatory conceit, it may indeed be felt as frigid; realized as an actual alternative facing a woman in prison, it has poignancy: 'By losse of liefe libertye, or liefe by preson'. The piteous thinking swings from the one extreme to the other ('deathe were deliueraunce and liefe lengthe off payne'), like a bird dashing against its bars. The anagram (in MS. 168, Corpus Christi Coll., Camb.) runs: ALIAn COB––M; AnT. AMANSI–R; WHYTT.; B–BTHO.; B–WMO–T; WYLO–BY; STYW.; WIMBIS.; TOT FOr––YT. Tottel's version (271) gives the slight variants, ALIAn –OBH–M; Ant. DAMAnSI–R. The poem should probably be read together with the anagram and secret message of 'During of payne and greuous smart' (Muir, 225). Here Roos is doing what he will later do much more ambitiously in the prison poem to Vere (No. 100 above), conveying a message. We have already seen

him using an anaphora of 'My' to insinuate the word 'Liberty' into a
D'Amancier poem (see No. 86*d* above). Here he uses an anaphora of
T in stt. 2 and 3 to disguise the whole anagram, and to sink the message
below the surface, to avoid a Keeper's scrutiny;[1] next to the T's are the
letters S.T.L.C.P.C, which are essential to the message. The whole
anagram, then, runs thus: st. 1, A--An. CO-HA.; stt. 2-3, P--L CAST.;
st. 4, WAL.; stt 3-4, AWA-T; stt. 5-6, BOT AT S. SWIThyN. It looks as if
there was planned a rescue by boat from the walls of Peel Castle, in
the middle of July. The absence of names, other than Eleanor's name
very sketchily, makes it impossible to be sure of the period; but if
taken together with the poems of patience and impatience (cf. 'I abide
and tarrye the tyde', Muir, 160), it suggests the four years of the
D'Amancier appeals, 1450-4. Probably the idea was to escape to her
daughter's French home. The single stanza of translation from Ovid's
Ex Ponto, 'When ffortune gave good wynde vnto my saile' (Muir, 222),
with the anagram AL-AN; AN-IG. AMAn(s)., may reveal the fate of the
attempt; 'a pirrye rose' and 'blew my frendes and me a sonder', and
'my Shypp was all to shaken'. The possibility of a journey by water
may also underlie the D'Amancier poem, 'Though this the port and I
thy seruaunt true' (Muir, 78), an appeal for help to Citherea; 'Remembre
thou me, en vogant la galere'. The anagram runs: AlIAN. COBHAM;
AnTIG. POWIS DAMAnCIER; BABTh.; WiMBYSH; FOrFAIT FOrF--T. We may
conjecture that Citherea stood for Antigone, 'By sees and hilles elonged'
—from the suppliant's sight:

> Withoute thyn ayde, assuraunce is there none.
> The ferme faith that in the water fleteth
> Succor thou therefor: in the it is alone.

The four 'Wyatt' sonnets that have D'Amancier anagrams are an
interesting sign of Roos's revival of this Plesaunce novelty for the former
lady of Plesaunce. As well as the two just mentioned, there are also
two original sonnets, both in Tottel only as Wyatt's. 'Such is the course
that natures kinde hath wrought' (Muir, 184; Tottel, 84) is a plea for
generous treatment:

> Ainst chainde prisoners what nede defence be sought?
> The fierce lyon will hurt no yelden thinges.
> Why shoulde such spite be nursed then in thy thought?

Its anagram is: AnT. DAMANS.; COB.; STIWAR.; Wh--TT.; TOT FOrFA-T. The

---

[1] For a brief contemporary example of an acrostic set within the line after an
anaphora (LOVE, after 'Hit is' or 'Hit'), see Furnivall, *Pol. and Rel. Lyrics*, p. 260,
E.E.T.S., No. 15. It is not an anagram, as said in the *Middle English Index*,
No. 1634.

double sonnet, 'The flamyng sighes that boile within my brest' (Muir, 175; Tottel, 101), has no sign of being tampered with; nevertheless I suspect that the two ten-line stanzas have been later turned into sonnets by prefacing four lines to each. These quatrains are not essential to the sense and syntax, and not necessary to the anagram. Out of the remaining twenty lines come the names: HO–FrI; ALIAn COBHAM; AnT. DAMAnSI; WhITT.; TOT FOrFAIT.

A disillusioned poem with a mournful burden, on the dangers and disappointments of 'happy hap', is 'To my meshap alas I ffynd' (Muir, No. 216). It is found in the Devonshire MS. (Item XLII); in Tottel among 'Uncertain Authors' (without the refrain, 'So offten warnd'); and in MS. Ashmole 48 with a sixth stanza which rounds out the anagram. That of the Devonshire MS. runs thus: AlYAn. COB–Am; MAVD STANH.; DAMAnSIER; ISMAn. SC– – –S; BABTHO.; WYMB–S; TOT FOrF– –T. Tottel's variants make only slight differences in the spelling of the names; the sixth stanza in MS. Ashmole 48 adds: AlIAN., FOrFA–T. The circumstance that the stanza initials, TAWIT(H), can be anagrammatized as 'Wiatt' has led to the suggestion of his authorship, or, more recently, of dedication to him by Francis Bryan.[1] Probably the occurrence of these letters is fortuitous. Muir classes the poem as 'doubtful'. But there can be little doubt that its writer also wrote the Plesaunce poem, 'Suche happe as I ame happed in' (Muir, No. 36), with its similar play on the word 'hap' (see Appendix to chapter). Their close relation is shown by the identity of one line in the two poems: 'A new kynde of vnhappenes' (Muir, 36, l. 5) and 'No new kynd of vnhappinesse' (Muir, 216, l. 12). In the D'Amancier poem Roos has picked up a line and theme of the earlier Plesaunce poem to enforce the lament of one who has found the gifts of fortune turn to bitterness, joy to dolour, mirth to mischance.

In the lyrics attributed to Surrey by Tottel, some known only through him, there is a little group of D'Amancier poems. The first, 'When ragyng loue with extreme payne' (Tottel, 16; Padelford, 13), is a poem on Helen and the wars of Troy as an example of long suffering. The stanza initials form WIATT, yet Hyder Rollins does not attribute it to him. The anagrams give: stt. 1–2, AnTi(G)O. DAMAnSI.; st. 3, Al–An. –OBHAM; stt. 3–4, STAn(H)O.; stt. 4–5, TOT FOrFA–T; ROS (this last unusual).

The next poem, 'O happy dames, that may embrace' (Tottel, 17; Padelford, 21), has been traced to Serafino, but it goes further back to Ovid's *Heroides*, to a part of the letter of Phillis which had not been used in *The Legend of Good Women*. It is found also in the Devonshire manuscript, in the hand of Mary Shelton, and in *Nugae Antiquae* it is

---

[1] A. S. Dalby in *Studies in Philology*, July 1950, XLVII, 485.

ascribed to John Harington. (I, 187). Its anagrams give: stt. 1–2, AnTIG.; st. 2, HOMFRI; st. 3, whiTT.; stt. 4–5, AliAn. –OBHAM; st. 6, DAMANS.

The chess poem, 'Although I had a check' (Tottel only, 21; Padelford, 12), has the single anagram, AliAn.; DAMANSY; AI TOT FOrFA–T FOrFAYT. It is probable that a warning about the attempted rescue is intended within the chess-metaphor, and that Roos is speaking for himself, as the full 'devise' shows: 'I have had a check, but I have found another expedient (a "neck" or nick, a move), to drive away the knight's men. I will use *my* power as a knight; so stand stoutly, and take good heed; I will try again.'

The poem, 'The stormes are past, these cloudes are ouerblowne' (Tottel only, 34; Padelford, 37), was said by Surrey's son to be his father's last poem (1546/7), a prison poem. Against this statement must be set the more hopeful tone of the lines:

> Danger well past remembred workes delight:
> Of lingring doutes such hope is sprong pardie,
> That nought I finde displeasaunt in my sight.

The anagram runs: ll. 1–10, AnTIG. DA–ANSIR; ll. 10–14, –OBHa. The poem has seventeen lines, and line 8 is obviously lacking; possibly it would have supplied the missing letters C and M. The last four lines do not help the anagram, and it looks as if the poem had originally been a sonnet to which Surrey tacked on the last four lines, which are indeed applicable to him and to his fighting for his country. In this sense his son's statement may be justified, that Surrey appropriated to himself the poem and its sentiments.

In the last poem of this quintet, similar changes may be guessed at: 'The fansy, which that I haue serued long' (Tottel only, 36; Padelford, 9), a three-rhyme sonnet, with the anagram: DAMAnSI.; AliAN. –OBHA–. The reference to being 'amiddes the hylles, in base Bullayn' has naturally been taken to refer to Surrey's share in the siege of Boulogne and Montreuil in 1545–6. The rhyme in -ayne is necessary to the sestet; if the speaker is Antigone D'Amancier, the original reading may well and more naturally have been 'base Almayn'. It will be seen that the sonnet may be read as an autobiographical justification of her second marriage, with its flight from the throng of her former associates, and its recourse to her guide who brought her out of the way wherein she wandered in error. Jean D'Amancier was sent on various missions in the years after his marriage, and may well have been in Low Germany.

Among Tottel's poems by 'Uncertain Authors', one more D'Amancier poem is to be found, moving in its effect; it is 'Walkyng the pathe of pensiue thought' (Tottel, 252), where the despairing prisoner calls on liberty and repeats 'ioye shall I neuer'. The anagram ANTIGO. DAMANCI–R is very obvious in stt. 3–4; stt. 4–6 give AlIAN. COBHAM; and diffused are SCALIS, B–WMONT, and HVNGReFORD. The naming of presumably Viscount Beaumont (or possibly of his second wife Katharine Neville), and of Robert Lord Hungerford, or possibly of his cousin and namesake, Lord Moleyns, husband of the Moleyns heiress, Eleanor, is rare in these poems.

These D'Amancier poems in the 'Tudor' manuscript collections again warn us to read poems apparently in the love-convention with a wary eye. The well-worn terms may have other or wider application and an apparently fantastic and trite notion (so Tillyard dismisses a death-in-life poem, Muir, 63) may have the urgency of a prisoner's experience, to account for the admitted 'high quality' of the verse. Roos here has extended the range of a narrow poetic style. He is writing with sympathetic insight of a political prisoner, of her appeal to her daughter, and of her despair and desolation at that daughter's marriage acros the Channel. Roos seems to have acted as intermediary in a correspondence carried on in the guise of harmless poems; chiefly they were reproaches from Eleanor Cobham, but some bore messages to her of hope and comfort, even of practical plans for rescue.

(g) TALBOT AND STANHOPE POEMS

Poems by Roos for the great Talbot (as distinct from complimentary references in long poems) seem to be rare; there is one in MS. Ff. 1.6, a woman's lament for absence, 'My woofull hert thus clad in payn' (see above, No. 55*d*); here in the Devonshire manuscript is one which might well be a bluff, reassuring answer; 'Sum tyme I syghe, sumtyme I syng' (Muir, No. 117). Its mainly consonantal anagram is sketchy but fairly straightforward: I–HAn TAl––T SHR–WS–––Y WAT––FOr. The last stanza's 'Whyle lyff dothe last . . . neuer to change' glances obliquely at his wife's 'raison', 'Tyll deth departe', and also at her sister's 'Never new'. The blunt soldierly tone is not Roos's usual mode; he is writing dramatically. The poem must be dated between the Waterford creation in 1446, and Talbot's death in 1453.

Only a few 'Wyatt' poems isolate Maud Stanhope from the Plesaunce circle, but all those are interesting, especially since one suspects Stanhope connexions in the background of the chief manuscripts. The earliest in time would seem to be one in MS. Add. 36529, a Harington manuscript, from which it is printed in *Nugae Antiquae* (I, 194): 'Playn ye, myn eyes, accompany my hart' (Muir, 220, a 'doubtful' poem). It looks like an imperfect sonnet, lacking ll. 7 and 8. The anagram is STAnH-P., WYLLOWBY; BABTh.; TOT For-AI-. Two more poems can be approximately dated by their inclusion of the names of Maud's second and third husbands. 'Ye know my herte, my ladye dere' (Muir, No. 41), found mutilated in the Egerton manuscript, is fortunately complete in the Devonshire; it is an elaborate address to the lady from her faithful and patient lover. Roos must have written this for Sir Thomas Neville; and perhaps for his inexpert benefit the names are sufficiently clear in the line-initials, and are merely filled out by the caesural initials: MAUD STAnHo., WIL---HBY; THOMAS, SAlISB-RY; AI TOT FOrFAYT FOrFAYT. Lord Willoughby died in 1452, and in the following year his widow had licence to marry Sir Thomas Neville, son of Richard, Earl of Salisbury, and, ironically, nephew of Lord Fawcomberg; their signatures are found together in a copy of *The Canterbury Tales*, MS. Sloane 1685 (Manly and Rickert, *Cant. Tales*, I, 507-9).

In the next poem, 'To seke eche where, where man doeth lyve' (Muir, 85), only in Egerton MS., cannot have been written till some eight years later, when Maud Stanhope, again a widow by Sir Thomas's death on the Yorkist side at Wakefield in December 1460, was granted a licence to marry Sir Gervaise Clifton, August 10, 1461 (*Test. Ebor.*, III, 336). Gervaise Clifton, Treasurer of Humphrey of Gloucester, must have known Maud Stanhope as a girl at Plesaunce; later he was treasurer of Calais; he was executed after Tewkesbury in 1471. Maud, who had no children, outlived him (and Sir Richard Roos), dying in 1497 (*Inq. Post Mortem, Henry VII*, II, Nos. 12-14). The anagram runs: G. CLIFTO-; MAUD STAn-OP.; WILL-UGBI; N--ILL; TOT FOrFAIT. For Sir Thomas Neville, Sir Richard in the leisured time of peace had evolved 'an intricate stanza', which, as Tillyard says, was made to express 'a fine range of tone'. Even in the early months of the war, he writes for Clifton this rich lyric, a variation on the theme of his earlier 'Iuellis pricious cane y none fynde to sell':

> I cannot gyve browches nor Ringes,
> Thes goldsmythes work and goodly thinges,
> Piery nor perle oryente and clere.

The references to France ('Ffraunce would I gyve if myn it were') are apt for one of the guardians of England's last foothold across the Channel.

The poet has twice honoured his old friend Maud, and he does not forbear in these manuscripts to allude to the unfortunate Fawcomberg *imbroglio.* There still remains Maud the fluent arguer, whom Roos had introduced (by anagram) into *The Court of Love* as Delyt in a debate with Lust (Fawcomberg). Now he will mock her gently by parody in the poem (Muir, No. 166)

> Deme as ye list vppon goode cause
> I maye and think of this or that.

with the refrain,

> I wolde yt ware not as I think,
> I wolde I thought yt ware not.

This is not Roos's usual style, but surely a skit of Maud's manner of choplogical circular argumentation, which irresistibly recalls the verses read as 'evidence' before the King of Hearts:

> If I or she should chance to be
> Involved in this affair etc.

The well-spoken Maud Stanhope, like other well-spoken women, could on occasion be slightly ridiculous. Again the anagram includes her Neville name (after 1453), and again involves, why I do not know, Babthorp: MAVD STAn–OP, WILOU––BY, N–VIL; ISMA–Y; B––BThO.; TOT FOrFAIT.

(*h*) POEMS AGAINST FAWCOMBERG AND BARBELINA

Fawcomberg's *affaires* (see above, Chapter IX) govern a poem interesting by its virtuosity of form, and by the balancing of the sentiment in debate. It is the triple poem 'Lo, what it is to love!' (Muir, No. 87, Egerton MS., not corrected), where in the three parts, each stanza exactly balances and answers its corresponding number in the other two sections, e.g. st. 2, 'Ffle alwaye from the snare'; 'Ffle not so much the snare'; 'Ye graunt it is a snare'. The metaphor from 'chaunce on the dise' runs through all the third stanzas; the argument of the whole is, can one indeed love and be wise? The first section is against it, with moral warnings of long repentance for short delight; the second section, 'Leve thus to slaunder love!', defends love as 'a plaisaunt fire, Kyndeled by true desire'; the third section sums up, not without some ambiguity: 'Who most doeth slaunder love | The dede must alwaye prove', but is sure that 'To love and to be wise | It were a straunge devise' (the epithet is significant, as is the repetition of 'plaisaunt'). The stress is on folly, as it is with the imprudent lovers of the Sixth Pawn in *Reson and Sensuallyte* (ll. 6375–432). This classical tag on love and wisdom as incompatible, though best known from Plutarch's 'Life of Agesilaus'

(North's Transl., p. 617), need not surprise us here. Plutarch, in the Latin translations of the Italian humanists, was one of the authors most admired by Duke Humphrey, and by his friend, Abbot Whetham-stede.[1] The anagrams of the sections are conducted much as were those of the allegorical *Compleynt of Mars*; the final or sixth stanzas, repeating the first stanzas, are not brought into the anagrams:

Part I: FAWKOM.; STRAN.; MAV. STAN., WiLLOW.; TOT FOrFA–T.

Part II: –LISABeTH ST–AN., KnOKyn; FAWCO–B.; STAn., W–LLO.; SCAL–S; TOT FOrFA–T.

Part III: WILLOWBY, STAN–OP; –OB–AM, STrAn.; TOT FOrFAYT FOr––YT.

This poem, for which no source has been suggested, seems to carry a clear reference to Fawcomberg, Lady Strange of Knokyn, and Maud Stanhope, now Lady Willoughby. Epigram 22 (Muir, No. 100) is more puzzling, 'Vulcane bygat me; Mynerua me taught'. It has been traced no further back than to a Latin riddle on a cannon by Pandulpho (fl. c. 1500), to which two lines have been added, but the original poem must have been earlier still. Egerton MS. differs slightly but signifi-cantly from the Harleian MS. 78, and Tottel agrees with it; the anagram reads: –T–AnGe, KnOCIN; MAV. Harleian MS. loses the 'Kn' in the added seventh line, but gets the name ST–AnGe more fully. The theme of the poem has no reference to the Fawcomberg story; but an opening line which couples Vulcan with Minerva, and a riddle on a modern engine of Mars, would be a sufficient temptation to introduce Lord Strange and Maud Stanhope.

A sonnet of somewhat irregular structure among Tottel's 'Uncertain Authors', 'For loue Appollo (his Godhead set aside)' (No. 241), tells stories from Ovid's *Metamorphoses*, culminating in Jove courting Europa as 'A milde white bull'. The anagram proves this last to be the satiric point of the poem (cf. *The Compleynt of Mars*): (E)LeSA––TH ST–AnG.; FAW.; VA–––SO.; STAnH. There is no 'devise'. Rollins finds the source in Seneca's *Hippolytus*. It is interesting to find the sonnet form applied to satire, and with metrical freedom, the sense being broken after the seventh line.

Another poem on the Europa story proves to have the same hidden theme, 'Not like a God came Iupiter to woo' (Tottel, No. 281), a poem in heroic couplets. The anagram of ll. 1–11 reads, with very little residue: ST–AN(G)E; STANH(O)–(E); FAWCOMB(E). The second half of the poem appears to carry no anagram, and may be a later addition.

To add to the chapter on Satire (Chapter X) there is a verse-letter,

---

[1] Weiss, *Humanism in England*, etc., pp. 34, 36, 51, 64.

and a few squibs against Barbelina Herberquyne. The still novel verse-form, the satirical letter, is an interesting early venture of Roos's, of the full Plesaunce period, as the anagrams show. 'Greting to you bothe yn hertye wyse' (Muir, No. 152) is found in the Devonshire MS. only. The style is determinedly rough and plain. The writer feigns at first to be unknown, and therefore bold to speak his thoughts; but at the end he admits 'ye kno him full well'. He advises against false friends, and even 'frendes reconsilide', and supports his themes with approved commonplaces. The farewell stanza is contradictory: he is wandering, landless, hopeless, lifeless; yet 'The twentie daye of marche he wrote yt yn his house'. The year must be before mid-1441. The anagram runs: ELI–ABeTH BA–DO–F, BeWMONT; AnTYG.; ISMANYA SCA–E; WHYTTY-n–HAM; BABTh. (twice); IAY TOT FOrFAYT FOrFAIT. The inclusion of (Katherine) Whittingham's name may explain the farewell to 'the kat and the mowse'; there are other signs that she was in some sort a duenna to Lady Beaumont. The satire is general and admonitory, not personal or pointed.

For Barbelina a very different tone is adopted. Rondeau 8, 'Ye old mule, that thinck yourself so fayre' (Muir, No. 35), is in the usual terms of abusive contempt for BA–BeLYN; F–W–O–B.; wHYTT.; TOT FOrF–YT. If Whittingham here is for a woman it must be for the former Catherine Gatevyne. A French rondeau, 'Vielle mulle du temps passé | Vostre visaige est effacé', gives the start, but is soon deserted, since this waiting gentlewoman cannot be consigned to her old kitchen. The second line, 'Leve of with craft your beautie to repaire', is like the end of the original poem, 'Ne farder museau, ni poectrine'. The English poem is more unified, and keeps to the stable metaphor ('Kappurs' may be a misreading of 'kappuls').[1] The French poem is found in an anthology collected by Pierre Sala of Lyons who died c. 1529, but it is not his, and G. A. Parry has suggested an older Italian original.[2]

Epigram 30, 'Luckes, my faire falcon' (Muir, No. 170), a rather enigmatic poem which is a favourite with Wyatt's admirers, has the anagram BA–BALIn H., and there are possible traces of William Neville for Fawcomberg (– –ILL. – – –YL). It is not found in either the Egerton MS. or the Devonshire, but only in the Harington manuscript, Add. 36529, and in Tottel. The reference to lice is reminiscent of the farewell of the Barbelina verse-letter (see above, No. 99a). Tottel spells the name Lux; and it is possible that a source might be found among fifteenth-century French lyrics made for Jehanne de Lux or Lus, or for Isabeau

---

[1] I am indebted to Professor R. M. Wilson for this suggestion.
[2] *Mod. Lang. Rev.*, 1925, XX, 461–2.

Faucon, the latter in the *Livre du Faulcon des Dames* (see *Le Jardin de Plaisance*, II, Nos. 414–15 and 573–7).

(*i*) POEMS TO MARGARET ROOS

It is obvious that Roos was not obliged to confine his anagrammatic ingenuity to the pattern established in his usual practice, and in that of Chaucer and Charles d'Orléans. If he wanted to contrive a more complex cypher, there were many possibilities. One was practised later by Erasmus, in a Latin epigram in which two more letters in each line were used, the final letters of each hemistich; thus the line, *Impotenti amoris oestrO* | *Haec beata percitA*, begins the name IOHAnnes.[1] I have not found Roos practising this variation, suited rather to the inflexional Latin. But an easier pattern, using three letters in each line, adds to the line-initial and the caesural initial, the initial of the word immediately preceding the caesura; and this Roos seems to be adopting (or inventing) in a poem meant for Margaret Longueville. 'In eternum I was ons determed' (Muir, 71, Egerton MS.) explains that the poet had indeed once before thought to love for ever, but had built on sand. That devotion is now cast out of his heart: 'Nowe in the place another thought doeth rest'.

The anagram letters are these:

	(1)			(2)			(3)		
Line-initials.	In	For	Th	For	An	For	To	V	To
Pre-caesural.	E	LO	H	F	LO	Th	DO	Le	S
Post-caesural.	I	A	I	Th	TO	I	I	An	An
	(4)			(5)			(6)		
	W	Th	W	I	Th	For	In	Th	No
	R	Th	A	Long	B	H	E	F	P
	I	M	TO	O	Is	Th	Th	D	An

The line-initials (with one borrowing) give TOT FORFAIT FORF–IT; the post-caesural initials (with two borrowed) give MAR–A–ET; but the pre-caesural initials (with some borrowed) give (forwards) ELISA––TH, and (backwards) BA–DOLF, and PH., also LONGVILE. From the residue comes IS–ANI–. That is to say, from the ordinary pattern can be read the poet's 'devise' and (sketchily) the lady's Christian name; but to get her surname, one must bring in the unusual pre-caesural initials, and then one finds also the name of the poet's former love. Lady Scales hovers over the whole.

Another love-poem to Margaret is found among Tottel's 'Uncertain Authors' of the second edition, 'The Sunne when he hath spred his

---

[1] Hoyt Hudson, *The Epigram in the English Renaissance*, p. 28.

raies' (Tottel, 278). Rollins discredits Turbervile's ascription to Surrey as a 'loose statement . . . not worth taking seriously'; and Padelford did not include it in his edition of Surrey. Yet it is a charming thing, presenting a Lucretian view of nature in the guise of a 'pleasant land of counterpane', and achieving one couplet which lingered in Milton's memory:

> Then louers walke and tell their tale,
> Both of their blisse and of their bale. (35–6)

The rapid buoyant movement recalls the 'Compleynt' on the parting in March (see above, No. 78), and probably dates from later in the same season, a more ambitious and leisurely effort. The lover's complaint of his woe is reinforced by a doleful man, a Job's comforter (ll. 133–72). Fortunately Hope, 'A stedfast frende, a counsellour', encourages him with assurance of the lady's regard; the poet believes him, gives thanks to Love, and makes his final vows to the lady. In this long poem of nearly 300 lines, the anagrams are strung out at intervals: ll. 3–14, the joy of spring, –ARGAr–T, TOT ForFA–T; ll. 55–69, the lover's absence, MA–(G)AreT; ISMAN.; ForFAIT; ll. 90–107, the lover's torment, MA–GA., LON.; TOT ForFAIT; ll. 146–50, the doleful man, BABThor.; ll. 233–5, Hope's reassurance, ForFAIT; ll. 278–88, the final vows, MAR–AReT LOn–VILL. The poem thus proves to be a companion poem to the *Compleynt*, and recalls the Hope poem of the Plesaunce period. Its date must be about 1449 or 1450; there is no manuscript known.

Two later prison poems, attributed by Tottel to Surrey and accepted as his, prove to be addressed to Margaret Roos, the sonnet, 'When Windsor walles' (Tottel, 11; Padelford, 30), and 'So cruell prison' (Tottel, 15; Padelford 31). It will be remembered that the long prison poem addressed to Vere ended with the anagram of Roos's whereabouts: In PR–S–N AT WInso(R) (see above, No. 100). The sonnet is found both in Tottel and in the Harington MS., Add. 36529, with some variants. The manuscript yields: MAR–––ET (ver); –sMAn.; Tottel's version gives: MA–––ReT (VER); ISMAn. The longer poem in alternate rhyme, 'So cruell prison how coulde betide, alas, | As proude Windsor?', is a more complex matter. It carries an anagram only in the first and last parts, thus: ll. 1–10, MA––AReT LONG(U)I.; and ll. 41–50, MA–GAReT, ll. 45–50, VERe. The version in MS. Add. 36529 has only one significant change, 'unto' for 'into', but this supplies an additional U for Longueville. The VERe of the end may be the beginning of Vernon; but since the lines ask for some news of his 'noble fere' (the sound is suggestive), and since the 'Rothley' poem was to Vere, they are more likely to concern Oxford than Margaret Vernon. What of the intervening lines (ll. 13–40), without any obvious anagram? These may have been Surrey's addition, enlarging on the theme of courtly activities; on the other hand, the 'palme play' is found also in a poem for Eleanor Cobham (No. 42*a*), and the language is very much that of Roos ('ruthe: youth; holtes'). I know no documentary evidence that Sir Richard Roos could claim 'With a kinges sonne my childishe yeres did passe', but it is perfectly possible that he was for some time at court as page and older companion to little Henry VI.

Yet a fourth poem which points to Windsor is the epigram, 'Syghes ar my foode, drynke are my teares' (Muir, 168; Tottel, 116), with the double anagram, –INDSUR; ISMa–IA SC– – –S. For this MS. Harleian 78 has the better text; Tottel's variants do not help. Both texts have the concluding address to 'Brian'; but these last two lines are not needed for the anagram, and may be an addition.

(*j*) ANTHONY WYDVILLE

We have seen that Roos wrote poems for Anthony Wydville at various periods. Two more Wydville poems are found in the Devonshire Manuscript, the earlier of 1460–1, the other of 1464. 'The hart and servys to yow profferd' (Muir, 109), a request for good will and love to be graciously received, gives the anagram: AnThO–Y WYD–IL; E–ISAB–Th SCALy–; STANHOP; R.R.; TOT FOrFAIT FOrFA–T. This is another poem for the marriage of the young Wydville with Ismania's daughter, the Scales heiress (cf. above 'Hypermnestra', and Nos. 101*a*, *b*). The other poem has (unusually) a single acrostic anagram only, 'At last withdrawe yowre cruelltie' (Muir, 104), a more ornate and 'conceited' poem on the burning flames and quenching tears of love. The most obvious name in it indicates Mawtravers (st. 3), and the whole anagram runs: AnThONY WID.; MAR. WID.; THOMAS MAWT.; TOT FOrFAIT. In October 1464 Thomas FitzAlan, Lord Mawtravers, heir of Arundel, and a descendant of Roos's grandmother, was betrothed to Anthony's (and the queen's) sister Margaret, second daughter of Jacquetta Wydville; the marriage was not celebrated till the next year or even later. This was during that pause of Lancastrian exhaustion after the defeat at Hexham in May 1464 (when Lord Roos was executed), which Edward IV filled up by announcing his secret marriage in September to a Lancastrian bride. The Wydville-Mawtravers betrothal was the first of that succession of alliances which consolidated the Wydville party at the court. Roos's kinship with the Mawtravers-Arundel family, his former friendship with Jacquetta Wydville and with the Scales ladies, might give him excuse for a compliment to the rising Wydville family. It seems as if in 1464 he was free to write a poem of compliment; but the forced and exaggerated style may betray some unease. The poem has a particular difficulty as to its model. Rudolf Gottfried[1] has traced it to Pietro Bembo's 'Voi mi poneste in foco', in his collection the *Asolani* (Venice, 1505), and has characterized the English 'translation' as less witty, because heavier and more serious. There are certainly many similarities of paradoxical expression (and several differences) between stanzas two to four of the four seven-line stanzas of Bembo's poem addressed to Love, and the four nine-line stanzas of 'At last withdrawe yowre cruelltie' addressed to the Lady. The two first stanzas have little resemblance; the 'fire' of Bembo's opening line does not occur till st. 2 of the English. But we have seen in many of these poems strong affinities with Petrarch's collection, and here one may compare with Poem 55 (*Ballata* 3), 'Quel foco ch'i 'pensai che fosse spento', and slightly with Poem 48, the sonnet, 'Se mai foco per foco non si spense'. Poem 55 especially runs on a similar paradox of contraries; the fire of love should be quenched by the rain of tears, but 'pare a me che cresca' ('Then doithe the flame encresse'). There is a precise verbal parallel in the line, 'And make myn eys expresse' (the verb in its literal sense), and Petrarch's 'il duol per gli occhi si distille'. The most striking parallelism between the English poem and Bembo's lies in the idea 'No man alyve nor I | Of doble dethe can dy'. These, the concluding lines only, are parallel with the last lines of stt. 1 and 4 in Bembo: 'Che di due morti i non posso morire', and 'Tenersi in uita un huom con doppia morte'. The idea of dying more than once is proverbial, and is often expressed by Shakespeare.

In view of the unusually clear single anagram which cannot be ignored, one should perhaps consider the curious thread of association that runs in the background of the two poems. Zeno de Castiglione, Bishop of Bayeux, was a friend of Humphrey of Gloucester, and was in England in 1440-1, just before the break-up of the Plesaunce circle. His kinsman, Girolamo da Castiglione, orator and physician, was the friend and correspondent in 1456 of the English humanist, John Free. Free was secretary in Padua to John Tiptoft, Earl of Worcester, during his prolonged stay in Italy, 1458-61, Tiptoft, brother-in-law of Lord Roos, Sir Richard's nephew. Free died in 1465, the year after the poem was written according to its Wydville anagram, time enough for Free to communicate it to an Italian friend. Anthony Wydville himself was in Italy in 1476, at a time when he seems to have been renewing contact with Sir Richard Roos. Bembo (b. 1470) was then a child, and Bembo's

[1] 'Sir Thomas Wyatt and Pietro Bembo' in *N. & Q.*, 1954, 199, pp. 278-80.

future associate, Baldassare Castiglione of *The Courtier*, was not yet born. With this Italo-English circumambience, one cannot exclude the chance that Bembo, in his early manhood before 1505, might have met this poem by Roos, through the English contacts of the great Castiglione clan. Baldassare himself was later to come to England as an envoy; and later still Bembo was to be the friend in Italy of Cardinal Pole (cf. No. 103, above). Much is known, through Count Roberto Weiss and Rosamond Mitchell, of the humanist preoccupations of these men, especially Free and Tiptoft; but little or nothing is said of their casual interest in vernacular 'society' poetry, and its possible exchange. A favourite humanist amusement was the translation into various languages of short poems, epigrams, 'jeux d'esprit', and the like. A Latin rendering by an Englishman of the Roos-Wydville poem may have been intermediate here between the English original and a not very close Italian counterpart.

(k) TOTTEL'S 'WYATT' POEMS

A few of the 'Wyatt' poems found only in Tottel have been noted already where they seemed to fit in, such as the autobiographical poems. Roos anagrams appear in all sections of Tottel's *Miscellany*, in poems attributed to Surrey, to Wyatt, and to Uncertain Authors, and raise the questions, what further manuscripts did Tottel gain access to, and from what sources? The nature and scope of the anagrams may be some help to our conjecture.

The first poem of this category, 'Accused though I be without desert' (Tottel, 74; Muir, 178), contains a straight initial acrostic, which has escaped editorial notice; ll. 5–12 give STANHOPE. If this name is left intact, the rest of the double anagram gives BeWMO–T; AI FOR–AIT. Rollins suggests that an original sonnet has been cut short to twelve lines. If so, tampering may have extended also to the line-initial acrostic, which may then be meant to refer to a Tudor member of the family. The line-initials of ll. 1–4 are ASIF, possibly intended for A. FIS. Alice Fitz-Stanhope would be Alice, daughter of Alice Flye and Sir Edward Stanhope; Maud has been ousted by a sixteenth-century girl of her family.

The poem, 'Passe forth, my wonted cryes' (Tottel, 77; Muir, 180), reminiscent at first of Petrarch's 'Ite, caldi sospiri' (though less so than Muir, 20), yields from line-initials only, and from a restricted range of letters: PHI.; BA–D.; WIT.; YSMAn–A S–A––S, whA––S.; MA. STAn––w. Similarly the next poem, 'Your lokes so often cast' (Tottel, 78; Muir,

181), gives: AlYAn.; AnT.; BA–D–LF, B–WM–NT; WITTIn.; WY––YS; TOT ForFAYT For––YT.

'Synce loue wyll nedes that I shall loue' (Tottel, 107; Muir, 187), a smooth poem of six six-line stanzas, gives evidence of a careful working of the anagram. The name of 'Lady Bounte' and the 'devise' are hidden in the caesural initials: PHI–IP, BeAUMONT; TOT ForFAYT. From the line-initials (with the help of four caesural initials) come the names of the poet's confidantes in this profession of patient service: ISMAnYA S–A––S; STAn–OW, WYTTIn.; WYMBISH, and again AY TOT For–AYT. Another poem, 'For want of will, in wo I playne' (Tottel, 80; Muir, 182), shows similar differentiation. The caesural initials contain: BeWMO–T; WHYT.; STYWA–D; the line-initials yield: ISMANIA WHAL––BURY; –TAnLOW; AI ForFAIT; R.R. But the succeeding poem in eight-line stanzas, 'If euer man might him auaunt' (Tottel, 81; Muir, 183), does just the reverse. The names of the Lady, and of the ladies of Plesaunce, are in the line-initials, with some added letters, and the confidante's name is tucked away in the caesural initials: ELISA–ETH B–WMO–T; AlIAN.; AnTI.; STYWArD; and then also ISMAnIA S–Al–S; WHITT. It is difficult to avoid the conclusion that these poems, with their similar anagrams similarly treated, probably come from a group of poems in a single manuscript, in spite of their dispersal in Tottel.

The poem, 'Mystrustfull mindes be moued' (Tottel, 108; Muir, 188), is interpreted politically for Wyatt by Rollins; yet Tottel's title, 'The lover suspected blameth yll tonges', is justified by the double anagram (rare in six-syllable lines): E–ISAB–Th BeWMO–T; ISM,; A–TIG.; TOT. The poem may have been curtailed.

A very interesting poem, 'It burneth yet, alas, my hartes desire' (Tottel, 109; Muir, 189), a line-by-line dialogue between the lover and the lady, is a miniature of *La Belle Dame sans Merci*, but without pre-amble or setting, and with a lady who at last relents: 'Thou wilt nedes so; be it so, but then be trew'. With this parallel we are not sur-prised to find the anagram to be a 'Plesaunce braid': HOMFr.; AlIAN.; ANTI(G).; –LISAB–Th BA–D., BeWMONT; WITT.; STYWA––; WIM––SS; AI TOT FO–AIT. Two other poems found only in Tottel have similar ana-grams for the Gloucester family, Tottel, 113 and 270. 'I see that chance hath chosen me' (Muir, 190) is rightly headed 'The louer complayneth his estate'; it is not the lady of whom the poet complains, but rather of 'them, to whom I sue and serue, And other haue, that I deserue'. There have been other Plesaunce poems in this vein (see above, Nos. 15 (xiii), 40). Accordingly the anagram gives: HOM.; AlIAn. –OB–AM; AnTIG.; STYWA.; AI TOT For–AIT. Was Sir John Styward one of those 'other' of the refrain? The translation from Boethius (a conflation of three *Metra* in Book III which Rollins would trace back to Chaucer's rendering), 'If thou wilt mighty be, flee from the rage' (Tottel, 270; Muir, 195), gives a similar anagram with little residue: HOMF–EY; AlYAN. CO–HAM; ANT.; E–ISA––Th. STAN.; AI FOrFAIT. Dr. Tillyard has praised the 'weight and solemnity', even the 'positive grandeur' of the poem: it is indeed a remarkable piece of work, even more so in 1440 than in 1540. Its pointed counsels are only too apt to the idealistic but weak-willed Humphrey of Gloucester.

One poem of the 'Tottel only' group belongs to the later poems of after 1450, 'Suffised not, madame, that you did teare' (Tottel, 105; Muir, 185). The anagram shows AlYAn. COB––M (very clear), and –MAnS–R. There is a fairly large residue. It is obvious that the poem is not finished; it ends in the middle of a sentence, 'this shalt thou gain thereby . . .' But what is gained? The twelve lines (three enclosed quatrains) need a final couplet to make a sonnet; these two lines would probably have made the necessary statement, and completed D'Amancier.

(*l*) THE COURTE OF VENUS

Sir Edmund Chambers, convinced by the 'Envoi', 'Lament my losse' (Muir, 142), that 'Wyatt' meant to publish some of his poems, reproduced the poems of the printed anthology, *The Courte of Venus*, now extant only in undated fragments.[1] Of the fifteen anonymous poems (one a fragment), ten were included (some as doubtful) in Professor Muir's edition, and have already been dealt with as containing Roos's anagrams (Muir, 43, 52, 66, 103, 177, 224–8). The remaining four complete poems, including the opening poem or Prologue which gives its name to the collection, also contain anagrams.

(*a*) *The Prologue.* Fifteen stanzas of rhyme royal (Chambers, p. 211).

Incipit. In the moneth of may when the new tender grene.
Explicit. Out of their payne they should be lettin gone.

The poet, walking in a wood to ease his care, follows a distant hunt till he is weary, when he rests and laments his bondage to Venus (stt. 1–3). Genius visits him, sent by Venus to hear his complaint, and tells him to write it as a 'bill' and present it at the forthcoming parliament of Venus (4–10). Pressed by the poet, Genius tells some of the probable acts and effects of the court, especially against Diana (11–13). On his departure, the poet promises to describe the court, but for the present provides the reader with complaints of sorrowful lovers.

[1] *Sir Thomas Wyatt*, etc., 1933, pp. 110–18, 207–28. Also ed. by R. A. Fraser, Duke U.P., 1955.

It is probable that st. 12 should follow st. 8, as both are referring to Mercury; this also brings together the two references to Diana (stt. 11 and 13). The anagrams then run more smoothly, with the almost inevitable appearance of Maud Stanhope under Mercury. They are of the Plesaunce period; the repetition of the name Phelip may point to work early in the 1430s. The anagrams run thus: stt. 1–3, Introductory: PHI–I.; BeWMO–T; ISMAnIA; STAn–OW; IAI TOT ForFAIT. Stt. 4–6, Genius: PHI–I.; B–WMO–T; COB–A.; AnTIG.; WI–ISS; AI TOT For–AIT; WhITTI. Stt. 7, 8, 12 and 9–10, the court called: HOMFR; AlIAn. C–BHAM; STAnHO(P); S(C)A–IS WHA––SBORo(V).; TOT ForFA–T; stt. 11 and 13, the acts of the court: B–W––NT; –AVD STAN(H)O.; For(F)AI.; stt. 14–15, conclusion: BeWMO–T, BARDO.; IAI TOT ForFAIT.

The printed text seems to be corrupt in places: 'the roote of the heart' should surely be 'the morte of the hart' (l. 10); for 'surmount the parlyament' (l. 51) read 'summon', etc.; for 'inconueniently' read 'incontinently' (l. 88), etc. The poem is stiff in expression, especially compared with *The Parlement of Cupid* of 1445, but it is full of references and touches which recur in Roos's work, in *The Eye and the Heart*, *The Assembly of Ladies*, and *The Court of Love*. The concluding allusion to St. Uncumber has no parallel in Roos's work.

(*b*) Poem V (Chambers, p. 219): 'Fortune what ayleth the' in five six-line stanzas, has two phrases already familiar in Roos's poems. 'Adew farewel this nights rest' (l. 6) is paralleled in one of the poems in MS. Ashmole 176 (No. 51*a* above); and 'in mortal payne' generally heralds a Beaufort or a Beauchamp. So it does here, though not probably as the chief figure. The anagram, intertwined through the stanzas, runs thus: ForFAYT; MA–GA. (Ve)–NON Long.; B–WSHAM. This coupling is very rare in Roos's poems.

(*c*) Poem VI (Chambers, p. 220): 'I may by no meanes surmyse', the lament of a tormented lover, should have five eight-line stanzas, but half a stanza is missing, as also l. 5 of the last verse. The lost half stanza is not where an 'etc.' indicates it, at the end of st. 3, but at the end of st. 2, as the rhyme-scheme shows (ababacac); stanza 3 is complete. Its anagram yields familiar names thus: AnTYGO.; B––MONT; TOT ForFAIT; SCALe.; I––AnIA.

(*d*) Poem IX (Chambers, p. 223): 'Now must I lern to faine', in six eight-line stanzas with a variable refrain, 'Alas she was not so', contrasts the lover's fidelity with the lady's feigned faith. The single anagram runs: AlIAn. COBHAM; B–WMONT, BA–D.; S–Al–S; AI TOT ForFA–T.

Of the poems of *The Courte of Venus*, three are also found in the Egerton manuscript, and six in the Devonshire manuscript; it also contains four Roos poems not known elsewhere. The anagrams show the majority of these poems to be of Plesaunce origin, with frequent inclusion of Antigone and Maud Stanhope. But three poems date from 1450–4, being D'Amancier poems, one (not found elsewhere) containing the message about Peel Castle. Yet one more poem, not known elsewhere, is addressed to Roos's future wife. It is plain that, whatever the sources of this printed anthology, they went beyond the two chief manuscript collections, and beyond Tottel's range.

(m) TOTTEL'S 'SURREY' POEMS

The authenticity of Surrey's short poems rests chiefly on Tottel, with forty poems, and on the Harington manuscript, Add. 36529, with twenty-eight. Padelford (p. 219) considers the manuscript much more authentic than Tottel in text, but Tottel has several poems not found elsewhere. In addition there are stray poems, all overlapping, attributed to Surrey in the Egerton and Devonshire and other manuscripts, and especially eighteen in MS. Add. 28635, which Miss Hughey[1] has shown to be a copy of the Arundel MS., another Harington possession.

Of the forty-seven short poems printed as Surrey's by Padelford, I find twenty with Roos anagrams. Of these, seven, which are either prison poems to his wife, or D'Amancier poems, have already been signalized; the remaining thirteen must now be dealt with. They are all poems of the Plesaunce period, with varying combinations of names.

Two poems start with the Duke and Duchess. The melancholy auto-biographical poem in alternate quatrains, 'When youth had led me halfe the race' (Tottel, 3; Padelford, 15; Add. 36529), is allied in metre and tone to the long autobiography, 'Sythe singyng gladdeth oft the hartes' (Tottel, 185). Its anagram runs: st. 1, HOMFrI; st. 2, CO–HAM; stt. 7–8, ISMAn. S(C)AL.; stt. 6–8, (C)OBHAM; TOT F--F--T. Stanzas 3 and 4, which appear not to have an anagram, make better sense if placed at the end of the poem, leaving stt. 2 and 5 to develop the metaphor of the greedy eye. They also then fill out the 'devise' to TOT ForFAIT.

'If care do cause men cry' (Tottel, 265; Padelford, 28; MS. Ashmole 176, poem 1) consists of some sixty lines in 'poulter's meaure' (or 6 6 8 6) in praise of the lady, and in alternations of despair and hope. The first twenty lines, a moralizing introduction, give HOMFrI; AlIAN COBHAM; ISMANIA; ll. 20–40, a meditation on the lady's beauty, S–ALeS WHAlIS-B–R–H; WIM–I–H; ll. 40 to the end, E–ISAB–Th BA–DO–F; TOT ForFAIT. I have followed the version in MS. Ashmole 176, fol. 97–97 v., but its

---

[1] 'The Harington Manuscript', etc., *Library*, March 1935, XV, 405.

many small variants do not materially affect the anagram, not even in the complete re-working of the last ten lines. Tottel's lines 51–4 on fortune are in different order (53, 54, 51, 52), and his lines 55–60 are replaced by four lines in the manuscript:

> What meanest thow my fortune, thus fast fro me to flee
> alas thowe art importunate to work thus cruelly
> Thye crafte contynewally dothe cause me call and crye
> woe worthe the tyme that I to love my selfe dyd first apply.

The lover in the manuscript does not yield to a despairing death-wish, as Tottel's does.[1]

The smooth and very skilful poem, 'The sonne hath twise brought furth his tender grene' (Tottel, 1; Padelford, 11; also MS. Add. 36529), stands out in Roos's work as a long and striking experiment in *terza rima* (55 lines). It is full of Petrarchan echoes, as Padelford points out, and is an extended conceit on time and emotion, inextricably interwoven: the seasons (two springs, two autumns), heat and cold, fire and ice, day and night, light and darkness, stars and sun, life and death—it is like a fugue. Yet another hidden theme lies in the anagram: ll. 1–10, BeWMOnT; ll. 1–20, –LISAB–Th; AlIAN.; ll. 21–30, ISMAnIA; ll. 31–40, SCALe.; TOT FOrFAIT; ll. 41–55, WhALISBOROVH; ll. 50–5, ISMAnIA.

It comes as a surprise to find that the other version of Petrarch's Sonnet 109, 'Amor, che nel penser mio vive e regna', is also by Roos. It has been a commonplace of criticism to contrast Wyatt's clumsy double rhymes and rhymed inflexions in 'The longe love, that in my thought doeth harbar' (Muir, 4) with the firm masculine rhymes and polished lines of Surrey's 'Loue, that liueth, and reigneth in my thought' (Tottel, 6). But we have seen Roos more than once re-writing a poem, or composing two poems on one theme. Here the progress in technique is all his own; and he addresses the version differently, to his confidantes, the Duchess and Lady Scales, as the anagrams show: line-initials, AlYAN COBH–M; caesural initials, SCAL–S; in both, FOr–A–T. These are taken from the version in the Harington manuscript, 'Love that doth raine and liue within my thought', which Padelford prints (4) and which the anagrams seem to show to be nearer to the original translation.

Another sonnet, 'Brittle beautie, that nature made so fraile' (Tottel, 9; Padelford, 7), in the imperfect copy of the Harington manuscript, Add. 28635, is signed 'L. Vawse' and this Rollins accepts, while Padelford doubts Surrey's authorship. The anagram gives E–ISA–ETH BA–DO–F; TOT F–––AIT. The deliberate commonplaceness (after the ideal opening)

---

[1] Padelford does not refer to this manuscript version; Rollins does (II, 313) but without notice of the differing conclusions.

of 'two peason' and 'an eeles taile' is indeed like 'Lydgate's' or rather Roos's, 'Beware of Doublenesse', ll. 49–51 (No. 48 above).

'Alas, so all thinges nowe doe holde their peace' (Tottel, 10; Padelford, 1) is a sonnet in which the English adapter is generally allowed to have improved on Petrarch's Sonnet 131, 'Or che'l ciel e la terra e 'l vento tace'. The poet has set the beauty of his words and thoughts above the needs of the anagram, which is sketchy and ill-managed: Al–AN. –OBH–M; IS. SCal.; TOT For–––T. In another Petrarchan sonnet, 'Set me wheras the sunne doth parche the grene' (Tottel, 12; Padelford, 6; Add. 36529), from 'Pommi ove 'l sole' etc., Lady Scales reigns alone, whether in the Tottel or the Harington version: Tottel, IS–AnI. SCAlIS, whAlIS–oro; MS. Add. 36529, ISMAnY SCAlIS wh––IS–orow. There are more differences in the Plesaunce anagrams of the Petrarchan *Ballata* I (*Vita* 11), freely translated as a sonnet; 'I neuer saw emy Ladye laye apart Her cornet blacke' (Tottel, 13; Padelford, 3). Tottel gives: ISMAnY SC.; ––TIG.; B–WMO.; whITT; MS. Add. 36529 yields: ISM. SCAlY.; B–W–O–T; whITT. The translation of 'velo' as 'cornet' suggests the horned head-dress with pendent veil of a fifteenth-century lady rather than the Tudor 'gable' bonnet.

Tottel's title for the original sonnet, 'The golden gift that nature did thee geue' (Tottel, 14; Padelford, 8), is 'Request to his loue to ioyne bountie with beautie'; it is so closely in accord with Roos's presentation of his Lady Bounte that it is no surprise to find her monopolizing the obvious and concentrated anagram: B–WMONT, BArD–LF. One even wonders whether Tottel had some warrant in his source for his title. The change of 'Ladie' to 'Garret' (Gerald) in the second and fourth editions of Tottel seems now to be an editorial attempt to foster the Surrey-Geraldine myth, of the same order as the change of 'aunswer' to 'Anna' to foster the Wyatt-Anne Boleyn legend.

The poem 'O lothsome place where I | Haue sene and herd my dere' (Tottel, 23; Padelford, 16) is a meditation on the unhappy associations of a place of lost delight. Troilus, sadly viewing Criseyde's former haunts in Troy, is the model for this theme, rare in medieval poetry. The single anagram yields: stt. 1–2, E–ISAB–TH BeW–O.; stt. 1–3, WHITT.; st. 3, BABTh.; st. 5, COB.; some stanzas may be lost. 'As oft as I behold and se' (Tottel, 24; Padelford, 14) is a poem found in varying forms and number of stanzas; Tottel's six stanzas form a fairly coherent poem; the nine stanzas of MS. Add. 36529 (printed by Padelford), introducing spider, fly, and horse comparisons, are probably out of order—st. 3 should precede st. 8, and stt. 6 and 7 would be better if transposed. Tottel's version gives stt. 1–3, ISMAn–A SCAlIS, whA–ISB.; stt. 4–6, TOT

FOFFAIT FOFFAIT. The range of letters is restricted. The longer poem in the Harington manuscript yields: stt. 1–6, IS–AnIA SCALIS, whAlISB.; BeWM–NT; stt. 8–9, MA–D STAnHO.; stt. 6–9, TOT FOFFAIT FOFFAIT. A similar poem in MS. Harleian 78, 'Lyke as the wynde' (Muir, 169), is printed as Wyatt's (see Rollins, *Tottel*, II, 147–9), yet has a Beaumont anagram. 'Syns fortunes wrath enuieth the welth' (Tottel, 262; Padelford, 19), with its contrast between Boreas's frozen realm and the fervid sunshine of the lover's journey, has naturally been referred to Surrey's part in the Scottish campaign of 1542, though no explanation is offered of the poet's southward voyage. In what is at present known of Roos's life, it cannot be precisely placed, but the anagram is pre-1441; ELeSAB–TH B–WMO–T; MA–D STANHO.; YSMAn. S–Al–S.

It is rare to find Eleanor Beauchamp coupled with Elisabeth Phelip, but there is a pointer within the poem to prepare the reader. 'Geue place, ye louers, here before' (Tottel, 20; Padelford, 18) praises in vigorously racing stanzas a nonpareil of Nature's handiwork, an idea common in Roos. The lady is as true as was Penelope the fair, and Penelope elsewhere is used for Roos's sister-in-law (see above, No. 45). The anagrams run straight through: PHI(L)Y(P); ISMAnIA; AnTIG.; AlIAN. B–WSHA. SOM––set; TOT FOFFA–T.

(n) TOTTEL'S 'UNCERTAIN AUTHORS'

Not only in Tottel's 'Wyatt' and 'Surrey' poems does one find tell-tale anagrams, but also in many others which he was content to leave as poems of 'Uncertain Authors'. We have seen a few of these already as 'Epigrams', tiny posies for Elisabeth, Ismania, and Maud. There are yet others.

The original sonnet (in Shakespearean form), 'Lyke as the lark within the marlians foote' (Tottel, 173), gives: AlIAN.; BARD–LF; YSMAnYA; W–TT; M––D STAn.; WIM––S. This sets it well within the Plesaunce group. The two fine sonnets on Petrarch and his Laura (Tottell, 218–19) are an accession to the tributes to Lady Beaumont. The first of the pair praises Petrarch, 'hed and prince of poets all', and his only paragon Laura, a nonpareil. Nevertheless the anagram insinuates a comparison: P–ILI(P); BAR–O–F; B–W–ONT; FOFFA–T. The companion sonnet keeps Petrarch in his unattainable seat, but has found Laura's rival, and names her fully in: E(L)ISA––TH B–W–ONT; IS(M)An.; TOT FOFFAIT. The unusual rhyme scheme that Rollins notes is in accord with Roos's frequent practice of the enclosed quatrain. The second sonnet is also found in the Harington manuscript, Add. 28635.

Another 'Shakespearean' sonnet, 'Though in the waxe a perfect picture made' (Tottel, 233), celebrates the constant heart, greater than all others as marble and diamond are greater than even perfectly fashioned wax; it names: ELISAB–TH BeW–O–T. A curious moralizing sonnet, 'The Cowerd oft whom deinty viandes fed' (Tottel, 232), shows a new variation in the handling by quatrains of the subject and the anagrams. The theme is the beginner's luck of the undeserving, contrasted with the ill-fortune of the man of experience even though of 'trouth and manly hart'; the separate quatrains are thumbnail sketches of the coward, the sea-adventurer, and the nonchalant knight who scorns love. The three anagrams are: (C)OBHA–; WhITT; I–May(N)IA; I do not know their relevance to the subjects of the three quatrains.

A long poem in six-line stanzas, 'I read how Troylus serued in Troy' (Tottel, 237), is on the faithful love of Troilus, and we remember that more than once Sir Richard Roos has compared himself with Troilus, 'new Troilus' (see above, Nos. 49, 71). The long 'Plesaunce braid' of anagrams is woven down the stanzas among a scattering of extra letters (not the letters of frequency) in a way that is used again in *The Hood of Green*: st. 1, IS–An–A WhA––S–––H; stt. 2–3, AlIAn –OBHAM; stt. 3–4, ELISAB–TH; stt. 5–6, BEWMONT; st. 6, S–ALiS; stt. 6–8, STANHO.; stt. 7–8, (Ph)E–I(P); stt. 9–10, An STAFFOr.; st. 11, TOT FOrFAIT; stt. 11–12, BARD.; stt. 12–14, ISMAnYA; stt. 13–14, AnTY(G). The inclusion of Anne of Woodstock's name dates the poem before her death in October 1438.[1]

'Lyke the Phenix, a bride most rare in sight', a poem of twenty-seven lines on three rhymes (Tottel, 260), gives a repetitive anagram: ll. 1–11, ELISA––TH —W–ONT, FOrFAIT; ll. 12–27, E–ISA––TH B–WMO–T; (Phe)LI(P); TOT FOrFAIT. Its first lines rest on Petrarch; but the rest of the poem is a handling in miniature of the description of the lady borrowed from Geoffrey de Vinsauf, and twice given at large by Roos in *How a Lover* and *The Court of Love*. Here it follows the same course in brief, down to the modest withdrawal, 'What shall I say for that is not in sight?', and has the same praise of Nature for creating a nonpareil as we have had in *The Chance of the Dice*, st. 28. In one line, 'Her glistryng lightes the darkenesse of the night', Roos is a link in the chain that runs from the Duchess Blanche to Sir Guyon, to Juliet, and to the 'radiant light' of Virtue in *Comus*. Another Phoenix poem, slighter in tone, and longer, possibly through adaptation, is 'Geue place you Ladies and be gon' (Tottel, 199), in fourteen four-line stanzas. The first nine stanzas yield a clear anagram: stt. 1–2, ANTIG.; stt. 1–3,

[1] A similar ballad in MS. Add. 28635, 'Whan Cressyde came from Troye' (Rollins, II, 294), has no anagram.

E–ISAB–TH; stt. 5–7, (phe)LI(P); stt. 7–9, CO(B)H–M, ALIAN; but the moralizing stanzas 10–14 are probably added or tampered with (there are signs of FORFAIT at the end), possibly by John Heywood for Mary Tudor as William Forrest said in his copy (Harleian 1703, fol. 108–9). St. 9 in praise of the lady's abstinence from 'Bacchus feast' is not impossible in the Roos of *Ragman Roll* (st. 7), deriding Eleanor Cobham's waiting woman who ran from church to 'the temple of Bachus the taverne'. The comparison with Penelope has special application for Roos; and 'rosiall' reminds us of *The Court of Love*. The same favourite image as in the preceding poem (260) has again achieved perfection in this minor kind:

> Her beauty twinkleth like a starre
> Within the frosty night.

A sonnet as violent and turgid in style as this last poem was light is 'The restlesse rage of depe deuouryng hell' (Tottel, 179), a gruesome alliterative comparison of the lover's pains to the torments of Tantalus, Prometheus, and Sisyphus in 'Plutoes den' (cf. 'Wyatt', Epigram 24; Muir, No. 135). The anagram is clear but incomplete, and the poem may have been modified: (P)HE–I(P), E––SA––TH, ––WMO–T. Two stanzas (Tottel, 228) perhaps form an intended epigram on a riding metaphor, possibly are part of a longer poem: 'Lyke as the brake within the riders hande'. It yields: ELISAB–Th; ISMAN–A, with perhaps a suggestion of other names.

For two well-known poems which Tottel left as 'uncertain', Nos. 211 and 212, tradition soon established the attribution. Gascoigne was the first to call *Thassault of Cupide* the 'L. Vaux his dittie' (Rollins, II, 284); this may mean no more than that Vaux brought it to light and put it into circulation. Puttenham in 1590 ascribed it to Lord Nicholas Vaux; Percy in the *Reliques* suggested his son Thomas. Thomas, who certainly wrote some very heavy verses in *The Paradise of Dainty Devices*, has acquired the name of 'the poet' largely on the strength of these two poems. Yet the anagrams are, the one of Plesaunce, and the other, a unique phenomenon, of Roos's home-circle in his last days.

It is not beyond possibility that Lord Vaux should possess a poem or two by Sir Richard Roos. Sir William Vaux, an undistinguished but devoted Lancastrian, was killed at Tewkesbury. His wife Dame Katherine, *née* Penis(t)on(e), is better known than her husband because of her faithful attendance on Queen Margaret in those last days, and in imprisonment.[1] Her son Nicholas was brought up by the Lady Mar-

---

[1] She was from Provence, as is shown by her letters of indenization of Dec. 22, 1456 (*Cal. Pat. Rolls, 1452–61*, p. 342); she is styled 'wife of William Vaux the

garet Beaufort, and married first Elizabeth Fitzhugh, and then one of the Lancastrian Greens of Greens Norton. Made Lord Vaux of Harowden by Henry VIII, he died in 1523. Thomas Vaux, 'the poet', his son and heir by Anne Green, married Elizabeth Cheney. Katherine Vaux, his grandmother, might well have copies of a few poems by Sir Richard Roos; but I know no explanation of Vaux possessing one from Sir Richard's last days. The two 'Vaux' poems are *Thassault of Cupide*, and the more famous, *The Aged Louer renounceth Loue* (Tottel, No. 211; and No. 212 joined with No. 297).

'When Cupide scaled first the fort' (211), an allegory of love's siege, in fourteen octosyllabic quatrains, has been recently described as 'an erotic *psychomachia* which is perfectly medieval' (C. S. Lewis, *Engl. Lit. in the Sixteenth Century*, p. 237). The anagrams show it as a Plesaunce poem of before 1441: stt. 1–2, –A–DOLF; stt. 2–3, AlIAn.; stt. 2–5, KATH. WHITT.; stt. 5–6, E–ISAB–TH; stt. 7–8, BeAV–O–T; st. 10, AnTIG.; st. 11, WiMBISH; stt. 13–14, WHAlIS–OrO–H; diffused, TOT For–AIT. The poem may well have been tampered with, or deliberately altered, and I would suggest that the probable adapter was not Lord Vaux, but John Harington the elder, who wooed and married Isabella Markham. The prisoner's final address to the lady hints at this name, 'And sith that I haue ben the *marke*'; and Cupid's livery colours are 'siluer and sable', 'colours like to white and blacke'; these are not the colours of Lord Vaux or of his wife's family, the Cheneys; but they are the Harington colours, 'Sable, a knot argent'.[1] Cupid's arms, on the other hand, 'pearced harts with teares besprent', suggest a 'Pas d'Armes' devised by René d'Anjou.

'I lothe that I did loue' has early manuscript ascription to 'the Lord Vaws in time of the noble queene Marye' in MS. Ashmole 48 (mid-sixteenth century), and in Harleian 1703, copied by William Forrest, priest, under the same queen. But the anagrams belie the attribution: stt. 2, 4, and 5, MArGA––T LOn.; stt. 7–8, TOT ForFA–T; stt. 9–10, MA. –ErnO–; stt. 11–12, TALB–T; stt. 11 and 13, TOT ForFA–T; stt. 13–14, HAWT. In spite of imperfect anagrams, the allusions to Margaret Longueville, Mary Vernon, a Talbot, and a Haute are clear enough. They can, however, be made clearer by reference to poem No. 297, 'Vaine is the fleting welth' in five quatrains, in the same stanza, with the same heavy rhythm, and on the same theme of age and time. This

younger, esquire, born in the county of Provence'. Her name (unmarried) occurs in all five extant Jewels Accounts of Queen Margaret, and in the list of the queen's attendants in 1452–3 (see No. 70, above).

[1] C. A. Markham, *Hist. of the Markhams*, I, 41.

supplies to the anagram the most important missing letters: and the names in the two poems joined read: MArGA--T LOn.; MA. VErnO.; TALBOT; A-IAn. HAWT; HE-B--D; and yet another ForF--T. Of these, three are the ladies in immediate contact with Roos at the time that he made his will, his wife, her niece, Mary Vernon, and his own niece, Eleanor Haute. The Talbot lady is almost certainly Margaret Herbert, widow of Thomas Talbot, second Viscount Lisle (d. 1469–70), grandson of Roos's old leader, the great Talbot. She was a sister of that Earl of Huntingdon who owed Sir Richard £15 at the latter's death; through her mother, Anne Devereux, she was a kinswoman of the Longuevilles. This poem (and we see now that Nos. 212 and 297 are parts of the one poem, 297 probably the conclusion) is a true product of the 'danse macabre'; Sir Richard Roos tells his nearest and dearest, his kinswomen and friends, that desire has failed, and that soon he goes to his long home. The words are so universal and yet so homely that the old poet's lines were taken to the hearts of his compatriots. The stanzas on Helen's death and dissolution (297) were crystallized by Nashe into one immortal line; and the words of 'I lothe that I did loue', first balladed in broadsides, and after a century and more, sung by snatches on the stage of the Globe Theatre, were incorporated into the greatest English drama.

Looking back to the beginning of this section, and to the three suggested channels of transmission of Roos material to the Tudor reader, one may now venture to express a preference. I consider that the connecting link was most probably Maud Stanhope, Lady Willoughby-Neville-Clifton, who knew Roos at Plesaunce, and again at the royal court; who is mentioned in anagrams of the D'Amancier poems as if she were active on Eleanor Cobham's behalf; who was involved in Fawcomberg's 'affaires', and whose two later marriages are celebrated by Roos in two poems in the Egerton manuscript. The range of intimate poems here covers almost all Roos's poetic life. After her death in 1497, fifteen years after Roos's, the poems may have lain disregarded for some decades. But when her collateral descendants, the Stanhopes, Cliftons, and especially the Seymours, rose to prominence at court, the poems might well be brought again to the light, and be handed round for appreciation and for use as songs under a music-loving king. While one need not rule out altogether Elizabeth Darell or Lord Morley as channels, yet the material they might have access to would not probably be so wide in scope. These poems, whether in manuscripts or in Tottel, or *The Courte of Venus*, are as intimate as any which we have by Roos, even more so. All are unique copies, except for some overlapping between these Tudor documents. None had been put into circulation in the fifteenth century; in that they resemble Roos's other most self-revelatory poem, *Reson and Sensuallyte*, and his long message poem, *The Prisoner to Vere*.

In concluding this analysis (disquieting to many) of lyrics by 'Wyatt', 'Surrey', and 'Uncertain Authors' dissolving into Roos's work, I would select half a dozen poems (among many others) which seem to me to lay the onus of disproof on objectors to my attribution to Roos. They are: the sonnet, 'Eche man me telleth I chaunge moost my devise' (Muir, 10), with its anagram of Roos's two 'devises'; 'The restfull place' (Muir, 115), with its punning references to the Bedfords and their house; 'Ye old mule' (Muir, 35), who is Barbelina; the epigram on the exploding gun (Muir, 61), with its anagram giving an identifying reference to James II of Scotland who perished thus; and among the Cobham-D'Amancier poems especially 'I abide and abide' (Muir, 160), with its direct answering of a poem outside these manuscripts; and 'During of payne and greuous smart' (Muir, 225), with its message of the boat waiting at Peel Castle. In these the anagram is joined with an apposite poem, and with circumstances peculiar either to Roos himself (the 'devises', or his disgust of Barbelina); or to famous Lancastrians (the Bedfords); or to the fate of Eleanor Cobham; or to an event of extreme import to the Lancastrian cause, the sudden death of Queen Margaret's Scottish ally, the son of Joan Beaufort. This is more than mere coincidence; and the implications for the collections of poems are plain. When all these poems are dovetailed to fit into the periods of Roos's life, and read among his other poems, they settle down easily into their places.

It is hard, even painful, to clear our minds of the idea that we have inherited of the personality of Surrey and Wyatt as men and poets, not only as soldiers or diplomats. It has been built up out of the lyrics themselves. Yet the characteristics, the courtly smoothness or the aristocratic hauteur of Surrey, the dramatic quality of Wyatt (C. S. Lewis, Tillyard, Muir), his 'individual energy' (Courthope), his language 'direct, familiar, and unadorned' (Padelford), his 'astonishing variety of stanza forms' (Muir)—all these are equally applicable to Roos.

APPENDIX

PLESAUNCE POEMS NOT CONSIDERED IN DETAIL

Egerton Manuscript

Muir, 5. Alas the greiff. Anagrams: AlIAn. COBHA.; AnT. POWYS; B—WMONT, BARDOLF; WITTIn.; AI ToT For—AIT.

Muir, 6. But sethens you it asaye. AlIAn C—BHAM; HelISAB—TH BEWMO—T.

Muir, 21. It may be good. B—WMONT; AlIAn.; IAI ToT ForfAIT ForfAIT.

Muir, 23. In faith I wot not. ISMAnIA SCA——S, WH————B—R.; STAnLoW; ToT ForfAIT.

Muir, 34. Madame, withouten etc. No anagram. ? not by Roos.

Muir, 36. Such happe as I. HOMFR.; ALIAN.; —LISAB—TH B—AUM—NT BAR—O; SCA——S; WIM—ISH; WHITT.; AI ToT ForfAIT For—AIT.

Muir, 39. Patience though I. ⎫
Muir, 40. Paciens for my devise. ⎬ No anagrams. ? not by Roos.

Muir, 43. If fansy would favor. ElISAB—Th B—WMO—T; whITT.; AY ToT ForfAIT For—AIT.

Muir, 51. At moost myschief. PHI. BAR——LF; CATH. whITT.; ISM—N. SCAl—S; AI ToT ForfAIT ForfA—T.

Muir, 52. Marvaill no more. AlIAn. COBHAM; HOMF.; ANT.; PHI——P BA—D.; ToT ForfAIT. (single)

Muir, 69. I have sought. AlIAn. COBHA—; BEW—ONT; KATh. whITT.; B—BTho.; WY—BY——; ToT Forf—YT. ROS.

Muir, 73. Hevyn and erth. AlIAn. C—BHAM; AnT. POWY—; BeWMONT BA—D.; CATH.; ISMAnIA SCAl—S; WIM—SH; IAI ToT ForfAIT ForfAIT.

Muir, 82. Processe of tyme. E—ISAB—TH BEWM—NT BARD.; AnT. POWIS; SCAl—S; ToT ForfAIT For—A—T.

Muir, 86. O goodely hand. ALiAn. CO——AM; AnT—GON.; E—ISA—ET. —ARDO.; ForF——T.

Muir, 90. Th'answere that. ALIAN. —OBH.; ANT.; BeWMONT; whITT.; ISMANI; STYW.; ToT ForF——T.

Muir, 93. And if an Iye. AlIAn. COBHAM; AnTIGO.; —LISAB—Th BeWMONT BA—DO—F; CATh. whITT.; BABTHO.; ToT ForF—IT ForF——T.

Devonshire Manuscript

Muir, 102. Take hede be tyme. AlYAn. COB.; AnTI—ON. —OWYS; ToT ForFA(I)T.

Muir, 103. My pen, take payn. AlIAn.; AnT. POWYS; B—WMONT BAR.; whITT.; ANN STAFFor.; ISMANYA; W—MB; AY ToT For—A—T.

Muir, 106. I lovve lovyd. AlIAn.; AnTIGO.; An STA.; B—AUMO—T; whITT.; IS. S—A——S; STAn—O.

Muir, 110. What menythe thys? AlIAn. COB—AM; B—WM—NT; WIMBI.; STYWA.; ToT ForFAIT ForFAIT; (R.R.)

Muir, 111. Ys yt possyble? ALIAN. C–B–A–.; AnT.; YS–AnY S–A–YS; WHITT.; STYWA(R).; (W)Y–YSS; IAI TOT ForFAIT.

Muir, 112. Alas poore man. HOMF(R)Y; ALIAN.; WIM–I–H; STIWA(R)D; WHITT.; IAI TOT F– – –AIT.

Muir, 114. That tyme that myrthe. ALIAN.; BEWMONT; ISMANIA S.; BRIDJIT BABThO.; –ATHERIn WHITTInHAM; STYWA–D; AI TOT For–AIT.

Muir, 116. As power and wytt. (Al)YAn.; HOMF(Re).; AnTIGO.; (E)–ISAB–Th B–WMONT BA(R)DO.; WYMBYS; JAY TOT – – –FAIT. (See Greene, *Carols*, no. 468.)

Muir, 118. Pacyence of all my smart. st. 1, P– – –YP; 2, P– –IP; 3, P– – –IP; B–WMO–T; YSMAn.; WHITT.; BABThOR; WIMBIS; TOT ForFAYT For–AIT.

Muir, 119. In faythe methynkes. IS– –NI S–A– –S WH– – –SBO(R); ForF–IT ForF–YT. (fragment only).

Muir, 120. The knott whych ffyrst. ALIAN. COB–AM; ELISAB–Th BeAUMONT BARDOL.; WHITTI– – –AM; BABThOR.; WIMBY–H; ROOS; IAI TOT ForFAIT.

Muir, 122. So vnwarely was never. E–ISAB–TH BeAUMONT BA–DO.; WHITT.; STIW.; AI TOT ForFAYT For–AIT.

Muir, 123. Howe shulde I. HOM.; ALIAN.; ANTI.; ELISAB. BeAUM–NT. WIM– –SH. AI T–T ForFAIT For–AIT. (single)

Muir, 124. Full well yt. B–W–ONT; WHITT.; BABTHO.; AI TOT ForFAIT (single)

Muir, 126. Lo, how I seke. B–WMO–T BAR–O.; ISMANIA S–Al–S; STANLO.; TOT ForFAIT.

Muir, 128. Syns so ye please. B–WMO–T; ISMANIA S–A– –S; TOT For–A–T.

Muir, 131. O myserable sorow. (Fragment; probably Roos's.)

Muir, 136. Yf with complaint. ISMANYA SCAlYS; B– –M– –T; For– –IT.

Muir, 144. Gyve place all ye. GLOUST–R; AlYAn. COB.; AnN WOOD.; ISMANIA SCAlES WHAL– –B.

Muir, 146. The losse is small. (Fragment of four lines.)

Muir, 147. Spight hathe no powre. AlYAn.; AnTI.; P–YL.; YSMANYA S–A– –S; STAN–O.; BABTh.; STYWA–D.

Muir, 148. Grudge on who liste. AlYAN.; AnTIG.; BeWMOnT BA–DO.; ISMANYA; BABTh.; IAI TOT For–AIT.

Muir, 149. FFortune dothe frowne. (Fragment of four lines.)

Muir, 151. Hate whome ye list. B–W. BA–DOLF; ForFAIT ForF–IT.

Muir, 154. Tanglid I was. stt. 1–2, AlYAn. COBH.; 2–3, E–ISAB–TH; 3–4, B–WMONT; 5–6, B–BThO.; WHITT.; TOT ForFAIT ForFAYT.

Muir, 157. Wyth seruing still. ELI–A– –Th B–W–O–T; WiT.; AI TOT For– – – –; (single)

Muir, 158. Now all of chaunge. BeAUMONT BArDO.; WHITT.; YSMANI SCA– –S; WYMBYSH; AI TOT For–AIT.

Muir, 159. Dryven bye desire. One stanza. No anagram.

Muir, 162. Patiens, for I have wrong. One stanza. ? anagram.

Muir, 163. Whan that I call. E–ISAB–Th B–WMONT BA–DO–F; WITT.; ISMAnIA; STA– –OW; WY–BYSh; IAY TOT ForFAYT ForF–IT.

Muir, 164. To make an ende. EB—ISATH B–WMONT BA–DO.; CATh. whITT.; ST–W––D; TOT ForF–YT ForF––T.

Muir, 165. Wyll ye se. ALYAn. COB–AM; WYTT.; ST–WA(R).; T–T ForFAIT. (R.R.).

Minor Manuscripts

Muir, 169. Lyke as the wynde. ALIAn. CO––AM; AnT.; ELISA–ETh B–WMO–T BA–DOLF; whITT–––AM; STIWA–D; W–M––S; TOT ForFA–T.

Printed Books

Muir, 177. Dysdaine me not. BARD. BeWMONT; STIW–RD; TOT ForF––T ForF––T.

Muir, 186. When first mine eyes. No anagram. ? not Roos's.

Muir, 192. Throughout the world. (fragment.) BABTh.; –––FAIT.

Muir, 193. In court to serve. HO. STAFFO–D; IAI TO–.

Muir, 194. Speake thou and spede. ST–WA––; whIT.; ForF. (Six lines.)

Doubtful Poems

Muir, 214. Thye promese was. BeWM–NT, ––ISaB–Th; Y–MAnIA; BABTh.

Muir, 215. I se the change. –LISAB–TH PHILI–, BeWMONT; IAI TOT ForFAIT ForFAY–; IS–ANIA S–A–IS; BARDO.

Muir, 217. Hartte aprest. ISMAnYA S–A–YS; WHYTT.

Muir, 218. I will and yet. AlIAn.; BeWMONT, BARD.; ISMAn–A S–A–YS; WHITT.; WYMBIS.

Muir, 219. Vnder this stone. Not Roos's.

Muir, 221. I see my plaint. YsMAnIA; WYMBISH.

Muir, 224. To whom should I sue. STANHO. WILOW.; whITTI––HAM; IAI TOT For–AIT.

Muir, 226. Loue whom you lyst. ALIAn.; BA–DO, B–W–O–T; IAI TOT ForFAYT ForFAIT.

Muir, 227. Shal she neuer. E–ISA. ––WMONT; ISMAnY S–AlIs; ANTIGO.; WYM.

Muir, 229. But Lorde how straunge. ? no anagram. Not Roos's.

D'AMANCIER POEMS NOT CONSIDERED IN DETAIL

Egerton Manuscript

Muir, 53. Where shall I have. AlIAn. COBHaM; AnTI(G). DaMAnCIE; STYWA–D; BABTH.; WHITTI––HaM; WIMBYSSH; TOT ForFAIT ForFAIT.

Muir, 57. Tho I cannot. (Old Egerton). IsMAnY; ––BHaM; AnTYG. DAM–NSYe(R); TOT ForF–YT.

Muir, 58. To wisshe and want. AlIAn. COB.; AnT POWYS DAMANSIE; STYW––D; whITT.; WIMBISS; TOT ForFAIT ForFAIT.

Muir, 62. My hope, Alas. ALIAn COBHAM; AnT. P–WIS DAMANSI–R; ISMAN.; STYWA–D; WIMB–SH; AY TOT ForFAIT.

Muir, 65. Ons as me thought. HOMF. –OBHAM; ANT. AMANSI–R; wHITT; TOT FOrFAIT.

Muir, 72. Syns ye delite. AnTIGOnA DAMAns.; STAn–OW; TOT FOrFA–T FOrFA–T.

Muir, 74. Comfort thy self. Ant. DAMAnsIER POWIS (caesural only); AlIAn. CO.; wHITT.; TOT FOrFA–T FOr–A–T.

Muir, 77. To cause accord. AlIAn.; AnTI–ONA DA–AnsIE; WHITT.; IAY TOT.

Muir, 83. After great stormes. HOMFrY; ALYAn. CO–HAM; AnT. AMANSI; WH–TT; TOT FOrF–IT.

Muir, 89. Yf in the world. AlYAn.; AnT. AMAn–IER. T–T FOrFAY.

Devonshire Manuscript

Muir, 161. Absens absenting. HOMF–Y; AlIAn.; AnTI. DAMANCIE; YSMAN.; WIM––SH; AY FOr–AIT.

Doubtful Poems

Muir, 223. What thing is that. AlIAn.; AnTI. AMANCI–R (P)OWYS; WILOHBI.

Muir, 228. Dryuen by dissyr. ANTI. DaMANCI; ISMANIA; COB–A.

NOTE

Professor Kenneth Muir has been kind enough to keep me apprised of his work on the Dublin MS. of these and other poems (once owned by Sir George Blage), his edition of which is immediately forthcoming. From the few poems already printed, it seems that similar phenomena to those of the known MSS. are present, and similar problems will arise. One amendment may at once be made above (p. 503, and see p. 487); Muir No. 178, with its initial acrostic for Stanhope, may now be read as ANN(E) STANHOPE.

CHAPTER XIII

Conclusion

SIR RICHARD ROOS, fighter in France, frequenter of Plesaunce, King's Knight, member of the queen's Escort, is thus far a typical minor Lancastrian figure. In addition he was a copious translator, and a composer of *poèmes d'occasion*, of love poetry and *balades*, and of light verse down to satiric or laudatory stanzas for a court revel. He is perhaps the nearest to a troubadour poet that we have in our literature. Had he lived in the twelfth century, he might have conformed to that wandering type. As an Englishman of the fifteenth century, when England's domains abroad were narrowing and diminishing to the pin-points of Calais and the Channel Islands, he is stationary, under one dynasty of the English allegiance, yet deeply influenced by the 'douce style' of 'that sweet enmie Fraunce'. In him, more than in any other English courtly poet, history and literature merge. Not that he writes on historical themes. He never mentions Joan of Arc, the death of Talbot, or the loss of France. But he writes from within the scene that he depicts; sometimes in the camp, with the array and embarkation of an army, or the triumphant return of an expeditionary force, or the burial of a prince (had he seen the pompous obsequies of Bedford at Rouen?), or the defence of a castle, or the doings of archer and armourer as seen by a knight moving among them; sometimes in the court, the joust, the Maying, the ladies' assembly, the all-licensed revel. Even Chaucer himself, page of Lionel of Clarence, and later brother-in-law of John of Gaunt, could not move about the court with this assurance of belonging in it, for he was not 'to the manner born', but probably kept his hold there by his poetry. Sir Richard had the *entrée* as one of the privileged, and lived their life of knightly sports and pleasures, of which his poetry is a by-product:

> I se huntynge, I se hornes blow,
> Houndes renne, the dere drawe a-down,

And atte her triste bewes set a-rowe . . .
The hert y-chaced. . . .

I here folkes talke of stories,
Of princes noble and worthi conquerours,
Of chiualrye, of conqueste of victories,
Songes, dites y-made of paramours.
                    (*For lac of sighte*, stt. 3, 5.)

Roos has then a background of fighting, courtly life, and pageantry in England and Normandy as rich and varied as any medieval man could wish, presenting a brilliant banquet for the senses. He also had the advantage, inestimable for a young poet, of access to some of the best collections of books in this country, and perhaps in France. Hence we are able to answer with unusual certainty the questions, what books did he chiefly read, and how did he get at them? Obviously he read, admired, and imitated Chaucer,

that was, withoute wene,
Fairest in our tonge, as the laurer grene.
                    (*Flour of Curtesye*, 237–8)

Naturally, and not only for economic reasons, he shows most familiarity with the courtly poems, *The Boke of the Duchesse*, *The Parlement of Foules*, the romantic 'Tales' of the Knight and the Franklin, and above all, *Troilus and Criseyde*. He uses Chaucerian phrases, and emulates the metrical variety and tone so well that some of his poems have long been accepted as his predecessor's. He recognizes Chaucer's greatness, and in his own 'unconning' is truly humble on the short-comings even of his 'peyntede style':

We may assaye for to counterfete
His gaye style, but it wil not be.
                    (*Ib.*, 239–40)

and his translation is

ful destitute
Of eloquence, of metre, and of coloures.
                    (*La Belle Dame*, 843–4)

On the other hand, to the most noted living poet of his time, Roos is not humble at all. He has obviously read the earlier work of Lydgate, with its more chivalric appeal, *The Troy Book*, written for Prince Hal, and *The Sege of Thebes*; and he borrows phrases. A single stanza in a fortunately dated poem of Lydgate's gives him a pattern for what will become a criterion of his style:

> of wommanheed
> Truwe ensaumple and welle of al goodenesse,
> Benyngne of poorte, roote of goodelyheed,
> Sooþefast myrrour of beaute and fayrnesse.
> I mene of Holand þe goodely fresshe Duchesse.
>
> (*On Gloucester's Marriage*, 64–8)

But he never falls into the broken-backed line; and certain commonplace epithets, such as Lydgate's universally applied 'sugred' (which Miss Hammond notes), he does not condescend to. As Gloucester's man, Roos would later be familiar with *The Fall of Princes*; and as Eleanor Beauchamp's brother-in-law, he would know the poems commissioned from Lydgate by her family: *Guy of Warwick*, written for her sister Margaret, Countess of Shrewsbury; and *The Title of Henry VI*, translated to the order of her father, the Earl of Warwick. One has only to read those two productions to realize the gulf between the poets; and Lydgate can well spare to Roos some of the tumulus of poetic earth (about 150,000 lines) that has been heaped on him. At first it is difficult to know whether Sir Richard is imitating Lydgate or mocking, as in the references to Parnassus, and to the French relics, in *How a Lover*. Later there is no doubt whatever. He not only mocks, he openly reproves Lydgate for his anti-feminism, and gives him a broad hint not to curry favour with the young queen:[1]

> And of women ye say ryght as ye lyst,
> That trouth in hem may but awhile endure . . .
> A fye for schame O thou envyous man . . .
> Knoke on thy brest, repent now and euer . . .
> O thou vnhappy man, go hyde thy face . . .
> The court ys set, thy falshed is tryed,
> Wythdraw, I rede, for now thou art aspyed.
>
> ('How þe louer is set', ll. 50–77)

Lydgate hit back, I believe, in one of his most successful short poems, *A Mydsomer Rose*. Unaware that Roos never used the flower for his name, he challenges the young court favourite, and preaches a sermon on mutability in his most ornate style. The sting is near the end in his attack on the great emprises of chivalry:

> Wher been of Fraunce al the dozepeers,
> Which in Gawle hadde the governaunce?
> Vowes of the Pecok, with al ther proude cheers . . .

---

[1] There is no evidence that Lydgate wrote poems to Margaret of Anjou, other than possibly the poems for her entry into the City. Robbins's attribution of the

Arrogance, with the peacock crest of pride and empty show, and flaunting like a rose of a day, is rebuked by the monk, not without dignity, and with the final sublimation of the theme in the roses of the wounds of Christ, the Rose of Jericho.

The two poets were fundamentally antagonistic, quite apart from the personal jealousies arising from their being apt to cross each other's path; Lydgate's poetry is conceived in his intellect, and is under the direction of his theology and his piety. Very rarely is there any direct impact on his senses; he has some fine descriptions, but they are literary, and stereotyped by repetition. Roos's poetry, at its best, is like Keats's, drawn up by his senses, and felt in his pulses. Lydgate is the relentless moralist; but against moralizing, the young Roos, the poet of *amour courtois*, revolts: 'Counsell cordes not well in ryme' (*Isle of Ladies*, 1252). Against Lydgate's anti-feminism, Roos proclaims the creed of the devout lover:

> To serve trewlye my lyves space
> awaytinge ever the yere of grace
> wiche may fall yet or I sterve
> yf it please her that I serve
> and serued haue and wildo ever
> For thinge is none that me is lever
> then her seruice, whose presence
> myn heuen is hole, and her absence
> an hell full of diuerse paines
> wiche to the deathe full oft me straynes. (*Ib.*, 901–10)

To return to Roos's reading. Under the tuition *in disciplina et grammatica* of the chantry priest at Belvoir, he must have become a reasonable Latin scholar. He had early and direct access to the *Poetria Nova* of 'English Geoffrey', Geoffrey de Vinsauf. He professed himself a reader of romances to while away the time: *Alexander* he knew well in the alliterative form; Mandeville he must have read early. The description of the garden of the old man of the mountains (Chapter 90) is merged with that of the Rose in *How a Lover*, with its fruit trees, and 'herbs of good smel', its conduit under the earth, its music and fair maidens, a place especially meant for the 'solace and disport' of 'any yong bacheler'. 'The Caan and preter John' are here linked together in one line as senders of aromatic herbs; Cathay is for Mandeville the market of spices, 'trees that beareth cloves and nutmigs and canel . . . and vines' (Chapters 66 and 84; cf. ll. 36–8). The Caane in his court has

Christmas poem on the Eagle to 1446 is due to a confusion between Katherine the Queen Mother, and Margaret the Queen Consort. Katherine died in 1437 (Robbins, *Secular Lyrics*, etc., pp. 88, 258).

philosophers of many sciences, including astronomy and nigromancy (Chapter 71; cf. ll. 131–4). Mandeville's Amazony, like the Isle of Ladies, is 'all environed with water' (Chapter 50); and Roos has probably remembered the men of Pitan (Chapter 89), who live with the smell of wild apples, and 'anon as they lose that savour they die'. In *The Flower and the Leaf*, he sees the knights of the Leaf so richly bedecked with jewels that

> the large wones
> Of Pretir John ne al his tresory
> Might not unneth have bought the tenth party.
>
> (201–3)

He is thinking of Prester John's palace at Suse (Chapter 98), with its shining carbuncles, its sapphire bed, and its gold and emerald throne. Perhaps his later reading of *Perceforest* recalled and enhanced this legendary splendour.

The wide field of French poetry offered Roos the freedom of *Le Roman de la Rose*, the lover's secular scripture. He shows knowledge of some of Chaucer's contemporaries, Machault (a little), Eustache Deschamps (several poems), and Froissart. Of the living French poets, he translates from his senior, Alain Chartier, but is unlikely to have met him, as he may have met some of the lesser men of the courts of Anjou and Burgundy, Pierre Chastellain dit Vaillant, Michaut Taillevent, Achille Caulier, Baudet Herenc. With Charles d'Orléans alone can we be pretty sure that he must have had some direct contact, and later with René d'Anjou, the dilettante of all the arts in France, as Humphrey of Gloucester was in England.

A young fighting squire and knight, never wealthy,[1] could not possibly have afforded to possess in youth collections of these poets, and the earlier Roos family, to judge from their wills, do not seem to have been bookish. But we may assume that Sir Richard in youth had some access to the books of the Beauchamps, especially of Richard Beauchamp, Earl of Warwick. Then would come Gloucester's library, which after 1435 had many acquisitions from Bedford's, which in its turn had absorbed that of Charles V; this was the richest realm of gold that young Roos could then have explored, surpassing that which next he would know, the Royal Library, then only in its beginnings. Charles d'Orléans had many books sent over to him into England, and his brother, Jean

---

[1] The Roos family in the fifteenth century is not recorded to have had a private herald, probably a sign of modest means (see G.E.C., *Complete Peerage*, XI, App. C). 'No lord of Helmsley was ever in full possession of all his family inheritance between 1384 and 1487' ('The English Baronage . . . of 1436' in *Bull. of the Inst. of Hist. Research*, XXVI, May 1953, No. 73).

d'Angoulême, acquired several while a prisoner. The books of King René, Roos may have heard of more than seen, since Nancy was where the royal wedding first took place, and there is no proof that Sir Richard was ever at Angers or Blois. A monastic library open to Roos's inspection, if he ever accompanied Gloucester to his favourite abbey, would be Whethamstede's, at St. Albans, of which Belvoir Priory was a cell. It owned a fifteenth-century English version of Mandeville, which Caxton borrowed towards the end of his life (April 6, 1490; now Egerton MS. 1982). Perhaps Roos had told Caxton of it. With little money at first for any but the cheapest possible purchases, Roos nevertheless had opportunities unsurpassed then in England for a young man of poetic tastes.

We can venture further, and assert that certain manuscripts of the period still extant, including some of the most famous, were probably seen and even handled by Roos. To start with a certainty, there is his 'grete booke', his own valued copy of the *Quête del Graal*, a French manuscript of the early fourteenth century (Royal 14.E.iii), not authoritative textually, but a fine volume. Probably also in his possession in youth was MS. Ashmole 44, the alliterative *Alexander*, bearing on the first page 'R R ANON.' The *Vœux du Paon* (MS. Add. 30864) with 'Roos R a moy le mieulx' at the end is a practical certainty as his, and so probably is the rough collection of French fifteenth-century poems, Royal 19.A.iii, which includes the only known copy in England of *La Belle Dame sans Merci*, with an alternative English envoy to Queen Margaret. Of Warwick's books, he would see the fine collection of Froissart's poems with signatures of the Earl and of Duke Humphrey,[1] probably the very copy presented by Froissart to Richard II; also the splendid manuscript, ordered by Warwick, of Trevisa's translation of Higden's *Polychronicon* made for Warwick's father-in-law, Thomas, Lord Berkeley, grandfather of Eleanor, Lady Roos (MS. Add. 24194). To her may have belonged, when she was Duchess of Somerset, the manuscript of *The Canterbury Tales*, now Bodl. Lib., Laud 600.[2] That Roos may have seen; and there are interesting possibilities with another manuscript of Chaucer and Lydgate, MS. Bodley 686. This may have some connexion not only with the Griffin family, but also with Eleanor's sister, Margaret, Countess of Shrewsbury, if the reading of a name on fol. 139 is correct as 'Belchiam' or 'Belthiam'.[3] But it may be 'B(o)uchard', a name found earlier in the Griffin pedigree,[4] and Roos-

[1] Paulin Paris, *Les manuscrits françois de la Bibliothèque du Roi*, VI, 383-4.
[2] Manly and Rickert, *Cant. Tales*, I, 313.   [3] *Ib.*, I, 69-70.
[4] G.E.C., VII, 451, 456.

Griffin transactions with land are documented. The Vere connexion of the Griffins, noted by Manly, reminds us that one of the greatest manuscripts of *The Canterbury Tales* was owned by John Vere, twelfth Earl of Oxford, cousin of the Roos family through the Badlesmere marriages, Sir Richard's almost exact contemporary, and, like the young Roos brothers, ward of the Duke of Exeter. If these connexions justify the possibility of Roos being shown the Ellesmere manuscript as a masterpiece, then it is a minor irony of fate that his prison-poem to Vere was copied into it as 'per Rotheley'. The beautiful codex of Trevisa's translation of *De Proprietatibus Rerum*, made about 1440 for Sir Thomas Chaworth of Wiverton, soon passed into the hands of the Willoughby family of Wollaton, neighbours and kin of the Chaworths.[1] Roos knew of both families.

Among the books of poetry that Charles d'Orléans took back with him to France, some are not specified (Nos. 39, 44), but one was a copy of *Les Cent Balades* (No. 34), which contains early examples of the double acrostic anagram. Of Duke Humphrey's books, now so deplorably lost or scattered, Roos would certainly see, not only Lydgate's *Fall of Princes*, as it came in, but also the splendid volume of the French translation of Livy (Bibl. de Ste. Geneviève, MS. français, 777), which passed from the library of Charles V to Bedford, by gift to his brother, and from him to Alfonso of Aragon (Vickers, p. 438). When Sir Richard came to have access to the royal books, he would find there Lydgate's *Sege of Thebes*, written for Henry V, the splendid presentation copy of the *Life of St. Edmund*, made for Henry VI (MS. Harl. 2278), and the beautiful Bedford Book of Hours (Add 18850), a Christmas present from Duchess Anne to the boy-king in 1430. And it is probable that already among the royal books was that copy of *Le Roman de la Rose* which, bought by Thomas of Woodstock from the executors of Sir Richard Stury, was owned by the Duke for only a few months, and must then have passed into the King's hands (Royal 19.B.xiii(1)). Another Royal manuscript Roos would most certainly see, the great volume of French reading (Royal, 15.E.vi), a library-in-little, prepared for Talbot as a wedding present to Margaret of Anjou. He does not, however, show much familiarity with its contents; the first item on Alexander he possessed in an English form; and his brother Robert had a copy of *De Regimine Principum*; its many romances in prose and verse do not seem to have left echoes in his work.

Exploring still further, though holding on to known clues, we may

---

[1] R. W. Mitchner, in *Library*, Fifth Ser., VI, June 1951; now Plimpton MS. (de Ricci, No. 263), Columbia University.

conjecture that Sir Richard Roos heard of certain poems through talk, without necessarily seeing the manuscript. It seems hardly possible that he had really read through all the Latin poets and rhetoricians whom he invoked.[1] But he had access to *Architrenius*, and the *Poetria Nova* of Geoffrey de Vinsauf; he used Geoffrey twice, if not thrice. Another interesting conjecture concerns *The Chance of the Dice*; two French manuscripts in the library of the Dukes of Milan at Pavia in 1426 were *Scriptum cum tassilis . . . in gallico* beginning 'Cest le plus grant Ruffian', and another, similarly described, beginning, 'Ceste le plus ville homme darmes' and ending 'la plus rude'. In addition there was a Latin *Liber ad sortes taxillorum*, opening with 'Si talis amat talem'.[2] Did Valentine of Milan introduce these *sortes* to her son, Charles d'Orléans, and did he tell Sir Richard Roos of the game? No source for *The Chance of the Dice* is known, though there is a French poem, *Rageman le Bon*, a predecessor of *Ragman Roll*.

We have then some justification for imagining Sir Richard Roos as seeing, being shown, even handling some of the treasured manuscripts which most of us can only gaze at longingly in museum cases. The bookish man attracts books; he also seeks them out. Books which were in the possession of his soldier friends, or his colleagues in the Household, were probably known to him, such as the two books (unnamed) of John Merston, which his widow Rose recovered in 1471 from the 'clerk' who had purloined them;[3] the two were worth £12 13s. 4d. and must therefore have been manuscripts of some value. It would be interesting to know if Roos was aware of the copies of his poems that were being added to the manuscript collections of his associates. It is probable that, when in old age he frequented the court of Edward IV, he saw some of the king's Burgundian manuscripts. And by then he could visit the printing house of Caxton, who, as Roos himself had done, aimed his production at 'the noble gentlemen of this realm of England.' All Caxton's output before Roos's death in early 1482 would have attracted him,[4] unless his taste had changed, especially *The Recuyell of the Historyes of Troye* (1475), *The Game and the Playe of the Chesse* (1475), and the translations made by Anthony, Lord Rivers, whose first cousin, Richard Haute, Roos's niece Eleanor had married, and

---

[1] In *How a Lover*, ll. 216–26, quoted by Robbins, *Secular Lyrics*, p. xxxiii.

[2] See Ant. Thomas in *Romania*, 1911, xl, 576.

[3] *Cal. Pat. Rolls, 1467–77*, p. 253.

[4] Malory's *Morte darthur* was finished in 1470, though not in print till 1485, after Roos's death. I had hoped to find some contact between Roos and Malory, perhaps through the Warwick family, perhaps involving Roos's manuscript of the *Graal* (Roy. 14.E.iii). It may yet be discovered.

whose patronage Roos sought in his last decade: the *Dictes or Sayengs* (1477), the *Moral Proverbes* of Christine de Pisan (1478), and *Cordyale* (1479). Two of Caxton's books Roos may have known already in manuscript: *Polychronicon* (1480) (see above, No. 103), and that translation of Cicero's *De Senectute* which was made by 'the ordenaunce and desyre' of Sir John Fastolf. The revival in Caxton's *Prohemye* to it (1481) of the memory of forty years of warfare and administration in France is such as only a man of an earlier generation could give to Caxton. Could that man have been Roos himself? And could it have been from Roos himself that Caxton obtained the text of *Anelida and Arcite* and of *The Temple of Glas*, to publish them as anonymous poems in 1477–8? Roos may even have thought to experiment with this new art, of course preserving gentlemanly anonymity. Of the three persons chiefly concerned in the two poems, only Maud Stanhope survived. Elisabeth Cobham, then Lady Kynaston, had died 1453–4; Fawcomberg, by then the Yorkist Earl of Kent, had died, 1462/3. After fifteen to twenty years, the poems might be made public.

Roos was placed in a favoured position as a reader and lover of books. He was equally privileged, though in a restricted field, in his access to other forms of art. It was a period notoriously of unity of style in things seen; there was not yet that palimpsest of styles and overlay of impressions, which now dissipate our interest as we pass from Roman Verulam to medieval York or Oxford, to eighteenth-century Bath, or Regency Brighton. Roos, in England and in northern France, lived in one period in line and colour; the illuminator's art, delicate, exact and brilliant, reflected the arts of architecture and decoration, and was own cousin to the skills of the painter, the glazier, and the herald. It is not then surprising that Roos's poetry shows uniformity of tone, though the pulse may beat unevenly, and the speed may vary. References in his poems show his sensitivity to the forms of art of his day. The stained glass window would be part of his early impressions, with the St. William window to his father in York Minster. What Keats was later to call 'twilight saints, and dim emblazonings' were not dim for Sir Richard; they were clear and brilliant in their newness:

> a windowe, richelye painte
> withe lyves of many a dyverse saynte.
> (*Isle of Ladies*, 1847–8)

Another window that he would certainly observe, perhaps at the time of his wedding, would be the fine Crucifixion window, of which even what remains is extraordinarily arresting, put up in 1427 by his wife's parents, Sir Richard and Dame Benedetta Vernon, in the beautiful

JOHN, SIXTH LORD TALBOT, AND HIS WIFE, MARGARET BEAUCHAMP,
AT COMPTON WYNYATES

frescoed chapel at Haddon Hall. Keats's 'thousand heraldries' Roos saw in windows both ecclesiastical and secular, certainly at Plesaunce (see above, No. 70), probably in Sir John Norris's windows at Ockwells,[1] adjuncts there to portraits of his contemporaries. The painter's art Roos alludes to in passing with a suggestion of having watched a painter changing his colours (*Dice*, st. 55). And he has studied the figures in

> a chaumbre painte
> full of storyes old and diverse,
> . . . old portrature
> of horsemen, hawkes and [of] houndes
> and hurte deare full of woundes,
> some lyke bytton, some hurtte with shott.
>
> (*Ib.*, 1324–5; 2170–3)

With portraiture in the modern sense of individual portrayal Roos has a special and interesting relation, which shows him abreast, even ahead of his time, and at one with the trend of art's development, and with the spirit of the coming age. It can be seen abroad in the St. Vincent altarpiece of Nuno Gonçalves, that 'powerful interpreter of individual contemporaries', who saw a crowd as a concourse of sharply differentiated personalities; it appears again in the striking portraits (often in conventional settings) by Jean Fouquet, of Juvénal des Ursins, Etienne Chevalier, or Jacques Cœur.[2] Even in England we find some memorable portraits, such as those now at Compton Wynyates of John Talbot and his wife Margaret Beauchamp in heraldic mantles. Doubtless most English examples would be the work of foreign artists, as of that 'Hans' who went to paint the Gascon princesses for Henry VI, during Sir Robert Roos's embassy; or as of Petrus Christus, who painted at Brussels in 1446 a three-quarter length of Edward Grimston, then on embassy, later third husband of Philippa Roos, *née* Tiptoft. That long thin brown face, with large eyes, underhung lip, and deep lines round the mouth, and with a curiously crumpled ear, must surely give us Edward Grimston as he was in early manhood, set off by his green surcoat over scarlet, his black cloth hat with long liripipe, and with a collar of SS held across his fingers.[3] Roos's sympathy with this impulse, Renaissance rather than medieval, to depict the individual, is seen in his single-stanza portraits, actual people, not type-characters, seen from without ('se youre fysnamye', *Dice*, st. 11), like the awkward

---

[1] See Everard Green in *Archaeologia*, LVI, Pt. 2, pp. 323–36.
[2] Paul Wescher, *Jean Fouquet and his Time*, 1947.
[3] *Archaeologia*, 1866, XL, Plate 26. David Piper, *The English Face*, Pl. 6.

L L

Ayscogh, who blushed, and twinkled with his 'better eye' (*Dice*, st. 37);
or discerned within, like the specious Lilforth:

> Ye make moche folke to wene that wronge be ryght
> No man shal longe knowe yow by youre vysage.
> (*Dice*, st. 15)

We can be pretty sure that Fawcomberg, the black-avised Avaunter,
was, like Lust,

> full large of brede and length,
> His berd as blak as fethers of the crow.
> (*Court of Love*, 1059–60, cf. 1221)

And we may build up the portrait of the 'old mule', Barbelina, from
stinging touches in the many satires on her. This semi-concealment in
literary reference is in keeping with the 'engins' used in the other arts
in the fifteenth to sixteenth centuries, Holbein's 'hollow-bone' disguised by perspective art, or the puzzle-canons and parody-motets of
the church composers,[1] or, for a modern instance, Mr. Laurence
Whistler's 'conceits' in his engraved glass.

Carving and sculpture Roos also has an interest in, and we remember
that he saw put up the tombs of his father and his eldest brother, probably the production of the famous Derbyshire alabaster workers. He
must have seen too in its first glory the Beauchamp Chapel in St.
Mary's, Warwick, where the effigy of Richard Beauchamp, Earl of
Warwick, still strikes awe by its beauty, the 'exquisitely veined' bronze
hands lifted in adoration to the Virgin sculptured in the boss of the roof.
In *How a Lover*, Roos, praising the lady's perfection of form, defies

> gauer Zeusys and pygmalyon
> Hyr to countrefete by proporcion (ll. 336–7).

'Gauer' may be meant for (en)graver as an epithet; or it may be a form
of 'ʒauel', and be a reference to Henry Yevele, the master-mason of
Lord William's generation. For such perfection, God alone offers the
ideal model, and is the master craftsman, the 'parfyt elymnour' (*How
a Lover*, 281):

> the Lord that her wrought
> couthe well entayle in Imagerye
> and shewed had great masterye
> When he in so litle space
> made suche a body and a face,
> so great beawty with suche features
> (*Isle of Ladies*, 10–15).

---

[1] See Milton Steinhardt, *Jacobus Vaet and his Motets*, Michigan, 1953; and
Thurston Dart, 'Cambrian Eupompus' in *The Listener*, Mar. 17, 1955.

Later he substitutes Dame Nature for the deity, perhaps as more befitting to a revel:

> O myghty goddesse, nature y yow mene
> What ye were highly plesed in that oure
> Which ye this creature formed so clene
> That of all beaute is chefe high toure
> (*Chance of the Dice*, st. 28; cf. *Ragman Roll*, st. 4).

The complement of this appreciation of the ideal human form is a sense of the ugly and grotesque, and here again art and poetry meet. The distorted faces and figures that peer out of the wreathings and entwinings of manuscript margins, or lurk under miséricordes, or 'gape and disembogue a spout' on roofs,[1] have their counterpart in the outspoken and gross physical portrayal of the 'Letters of Derision', or *The Hood of Green*, and in the mockery and humorous distortion of the uncomplimentary stanzas in the two game poems, gargoyles in verse:

> Your Babyr lyppys of colour ded and wan . . .
> And yelow tethe not lyk to the swan.
> (Second letter, ll. 29–31)

Nevertheless the biting personal descriptions in the games are applied less to appearance than to characteristics.

Such 'Devises new vncouthely entayled' ('For lac of sighte', st. 2) can be architectural also, and architecture always attracts Roos. His early taste is for the beautiful fantastic; his first dream castle has a pair of birds singing on each glittering vane:

> and of a suite were all the towers,
> sotilly carven after flowers
> of vncothe colours duringe aye
> that never been none sene in may
> withe many a smale turret highe.
> (*Isle of Ladies*, ll. 81–5)

He has felt the almost childish pleasure and sense of security in gripping a spiral rail:

> I a windinge stayer founde
> and helde the vice ay in my hand
> and vpwardes sauftelye so gan crepe.
> (*Ib.*, ll. 1313–5)

He knows with intimate pleasure the towers, the bay-windows, the paved floors and paths, and the sunk fountain of Plesaunce.

---

[1] Two large, grotesque figures adorn the western face of the Buttery at Haddon Hall, popularly called the man with stomach ache, and the man with toothache. A curious little head with long ears is cut on the face of an arch of the Outer Gateway of Helmsley Castle (V.C.H., *Yorks.*, *N. Riding*, I, 488).

The appeal to the eye is strong in this poet of sharp senses; that to the ear is almost as acute, conventional in its objects, yet fresh in expression. 'The chirme of briddys feir and swete' (*How a Lover*, 100) delights him, whether of the birds grieving for their mate,

> that petye was to here the son,
> and the werbelinge of ther throtes,
> and the complainte in ther nottes
>> (*Isle of Ladies*, ll. 1856–8)

or of the happy birds on Love's ship that

> sate and songe, with voice full owt
> ballades and leyes right Joyouslye,
> as they couthe in ther armonye
>> (*Ib.*, ll. 716–13).

Harmony is his delight, whether of instruments:

> I here also the agreable sownes
> Of instrumentis in her armone
> lusty trumpetes and lyght clariouns,
> harpes, lutes make melody,
> ffloytes shille that so loude crye
> Almoste atteynynge to the firmament
>> ('For lac of sighte,' st. 4);

or of voices heard suddenly:

> The most sweetest and most delicious . . .
> Herde in [his] lyf, for the armony
> And sweet accord was in so good musyk
> That the voice to angels most was lyk
>> (*Flower and Leaf*, ll. 129–33).

More intimately moving is a girl's song:

> Ther is no thynge that gladeth so myn hert
> Ne that from thought so gretly dothe me brynge,
> How so I be or in what peyne I smerte
> As yow to here that fresshly kan synge
> With plesant voys that to my thynkynge
> Was neuer wight set in no gretter ioye
> Syn that Troylus wanne first Creseyde in Troye.
>> (*Chance of the Dice*, st. 20; cf. *Ragman Roll*, st. 26)

The harpist's plaintive art moves his admiration:

> Youre habelte ne kan y not endyte
> To euery play gentil and lustynesse
> There ys no wyght that wolde haue in dispite
> Eche other melodye and freshnesse
> Whan in youre harpe ye compleyn your distresse
> So wel ye konne and eke so pitousely
> With goodely notes alle the strynges ply (*Ib.*, st. 48)

APRIL: FROM *LES TRÈS RICHES HEURES*

Roos may not have had much musical knowledge, but enjoyment he
certainly had. Church music appeals to him, as is shown in the dirge
sung for the dead queen of the Isle,

> many orrysonnes and vearses
> witheowt note full softelye.
> (*Isle of Ladies*, ll. 1806–7)

Just as he turns the solemn service of the mass to the purposes of love,
so in 1445 he also in *To My Soverain Lady* introduces as a Hymn to
Venus the antiphon, *Salve Regina*. Only a year earlier, Henry VI,
drawing up the statutes for his new foundation, Eton College, had
ordained that the choir were to sing this antiphon every evening during
Lent. The king often visited Windsor and Eton, and Roos may well
have been in his retinue. Our slow recovery of English fifteenth-
century music has obscured the high place that it held in the middle of
the century, when John Dunstable was in the Duke of Bedford's service,
and when the French were imitating it, thus counterbalancing our
borrowings from their poetry. As Martin Le Franc wrote, the French
adopted the English style:

> Car ils ont nouvelle pratique
> De faire frisque concordance
> En haulte et en basse musique
> En feinte, en pause et en nuance
> Et ont pris de la contenance
> Angloise, et ensuivy Dunstable
> (*Le Champion des Dames*).

Sir Richard then had access to the art of his period, and his work, his
easy-running style, is in tune with it. The free and flowing arabesques
of illuminated manuscripts, and of stained glass, with their graceful
curves, their flowers and birds and animals, closely correspond in appeal
to the conventional poetic description of spring or the May morning.
It moves from the rejoicing sun to the rejuvenated earth, with the
meadows diapered or powdered (as the heraldic robe is 'poudré, semé')
with the bright flowers that 'perwink' on men. Roos caught the gay
spirit of this better than anyone after Chaucer. We cannot assert that
he ever saw the finest volume of the century, *Les Très Riches Heures du
Duc de Berry*; but nothing in our poetry is more like its idyllic 'April'
scene, where knights and ladies walk and talk among the trees and
flowers, than is the setting of *The Assembly of Ladies*, even though it be
in a September garden:

> In a gardyn, about twayn after noon,
> Ther were ladyes walking, as was her wone, . .

> Of gentilwomen fayre ther were also
> Disporting hem, everiche after her gyse,
> In crosse-aleys walking, by two and two,
> And some alone, after her fantasyes . . .
> And yet, in trouthe, we were not al alone;
> Ther were knightes and squyers many one.

Throughout his early poetry, Sir Richard shows his delight in these arts of his time; in his two long poems written later, these pleasures are seen in maturity, ripened by a life's experience, and flowering in the refinements of *The Assembly* and the brilliant displays of *The Flower and the Leaf*. Above all, Roos enjoys the art of living. That seemliness and elegance which France contrived to retain even through her miseries, which the castles of the Loire evince, and which René d'Anjou cultivated and enhanced, were not appreciated by many in England. Sir Richard is a link in this between Humphrey, Duke of Gloucester, and Anthony Wydville, Lord Rivers. One may even wonder whether he might have felt more at his ease with Jean de Berry at the fairy palace of Mehun-sur-Yèvre, or with René at Angers or Tarascon, than with Talbot at Gisors.

A poet so sensitive to artistic beauty is not likely to be blind to natural beauty. *How a Lover* shows Roos rejoicing in the blazing sunshine of a park and garden which bring to life again the conventional landscape, the *locus amœnus*, of the Rose. Henceforth his descriptive poetry will be as clear as its shining streams, 'The gravel gold, the water pure as glas'. In *The Black Knight* he catches the moment of the May dawn just after

> the misty vapour was agoon,
> And clere and faire was the morowning,

while the dew is silvery on the leaves, and before the fiery sun has dried the grass. At the end of the poem, the *allegro* mood changes to pensiveness; the sun has set beneath the ocean-wave, the twilight closes over the last red streaks, and far in the west Hesperus rises, brilliant at eve, 'So glad, so fair, so persaunt eek of chere', Hesperus who is also Venus. His other May morning is no mere repetition; it begins before sunrise at the very 'spring of the day', in the cool shade of young oaks, whose new leaves flashed into colour as the light reached them and

> sprongen out ayein the sonne shene,
> Som very rede, and som a glad light grene.
> (*The Flower and the Leaf*, ll. 34–5)

The narrow, overgrown path leads to an arbour, a 'feuillie', and a thick hedge bordering a cornfield; in the hawthorn tree the goldfinch pecks at the buds and sings, and from the laurel the nightingale answers.

Roos has as keen a sense of fragrance as has Keats, with the advantage of having been a child in the famous pleasant-smelling county, 'Leicestershire full of beans'. He loves the 'hoolsom air' of the earth after showers (*Ib.*, l. 6), and the 'sote baume' of honeysuckle; the scent of eglantine will bring a man from despair,[1] and when the pungent smell of laurel is added as a complement, the poet is ravished as into Paradise. His love of all country sights and sounds and scents is not superficial merely. Just as Henryson rejoiced at the spring sowing (*Fables*, viii, 96–105) with a countryman's practical interest in the wheat-yield, so too Sir Richard looks at the cornfield.

> So rich a field coud not be espyed
> On no cost, as of the quantitee,
> For of al good thing ther was plentee (*Ib.*, 75–8)

When he observes the fruit-trees, he not only enjoys the beauty of the 'blossomes whyte', but also looks forward to their bearing, and rejoices that the 'smothe wind' from the west will not injure the

> smale buddes and rounde blomes lyte . . .
> To yeve us hope that hir fruit shal take,
> Ayens autumpne, redy for to shake.
> (*Black Knight*, 60–3)

Sir Richard has then the sharp sensuous perception that induces the 'state of vivid sensation', and he rejoices more than other men of his time (notably Lydgate) in 'the spirit of life that is in him'. He was fortunate also in having under his eyes particularly rich and unified artistic splendours. He had too for his time and purpose a very fair acquaintance with poetry on both sides of the Channel. His equipment as a poet is therefore more than adequate. He commences versifier under the influence of the native metre, the alliterative, strongly stressed line. Chaucer, and Lydgate up to a point, teach him the ways of regular, accentual, stanzaic verse, itself influenced by French syllabic methods. There is evidence, an unusual survival at this period, of Roos's self-discipline in this; four poems exist in two forms, and show that his rough draft was in that flexible stress-metre which, as a modern poet and translator[2] says, 'allows for great variety of pace and inflexion'. This early, untrammelled style is seen at its gay best in the vigorous and ingenuous (yet pedantic) *How a Lover prayseth hys Lady*, a youthful surge of poetic force, as unregulated as a waterfall, and soon to be directed into the formal channels and watercourses of the walled medieval

---

[1] This passage (*Flower and Leaf*, ll. 78 ff.) of his 'favourite Chaucer' is praised by W. H. Hudson (*A Hind in Richmond Park*, 1929, p. 69).

[2] C. Day Lewis, in *The Listener*, Aug. 2, 1951.

garden. Roos then turns to syllabic precision, the accepted phraseology of 'amour courtois', and the courtly verse forms, rhyme royal, the eight-line stanza, the octosyllabic couplet. *The Flour of Curtesye* and *The Black Knight* are the fine flower of his attainment at this stage. Charles d'Orléans offers him as models lyrics simple, delicate, and musical, and with his prisoner's melancholy tones down Roos's exuberance. Alain Chartier brings him a weightier, closer style, a language grave and noble. Roos is fortunate in the influence of these two poets, and in forming his style early enough to escape the fireworks and cathrinee wheels of the *Rhétoriqueurs* of the later fifteenth century, such as Jean Molinet. He was by nature dangerously open to this kind of super-ficial excitement; the rhetorical antitheses and oxymora of Alain de L'Isle and Guillaume de Lorris have sufficiently impressed him, and when in his maturity he once more, in the *Compleynt* (No. 78), lays the reins on the neck of his poetic steeds, these come galloping forth with the *élan* of circus ponies.

French models also give him varieties of *le débat*, the preliminary forms of the tourney in *Le Cœur et l'Œil*, formality controlling emotion in the arguments of *La Belle Dame*. After the coming of Margaret of Anjou, other forms of debate, chorus, and parody are used, and, aided by the royal badges, Roos re-introduces the theme of the Flower and the Leaf. *The Birds' Praise of Love* and *The Assembly of Ladies* afford variations of chorus and antiphon. Influences of the 'tençon' take another turn in the satiric attacks or the flytings of the two game poems and the letters of derision. French models are modified on occasion by a touch of Spanish, but this is only temporary, in *The Lover's Mass* (No. 69), and his poetry never fully escapes out of the French setting.

As with Roos's great predecessor Chaucer, France's only rival is Italy. The most revolutionary aspect of Roos's work is the new view of the Petrarchan sonnet's place in our literature forced on us by the anagrams of the 'Wyatt' and 'Surrey' sonnets. Already in the third decade of the fifteenth century, under the aegis of the Italian enthusiast, Humphrey of Gloucester, Roos is writing these early translations and imitations which we, misdirected by Tottel, have assigned to a century later. At first he translates as he would French poetry, with feminine double rhymes, and the phraseology of chivalric love. But he learns by rewriting; and we can now lay 'The longe love' beside his own other version, 'Love, that liueth, and reigneth in my thought', the one written for Elisabeth Beaumont, the other for Eleanor Cobham, perhaps a severer critic. The firm control of the 'Surrey' version shows where practice is taking him. He increasingly treats the structure and the rhyme-scheme with freedom, perhaps born of misunderstanding; and so he arrives at forms which Sidney and Shakespeare will adapt or adopt as from 'Wyatt'. He tries original sonnets on personal matters ('Eche man me telleth I chaunge moost my devise'); the poignant sonnet, 'Though I my self be bridilled of my mynde', shows how far he had gone towards thinking and feeling like Petrarch. After Lady Bounte's death, this Italianate writing is kept for the ladies of Plesaunce, for the imprisoned Duchess ('I abide and abide and better abide'), and for Antigone D'Amancier ('Such is the course that natures kinde hath wrought'). There is none for the new queen; her coming revived in Roos the French influence for ceremonial poetry. And we have only one sonnet for his wife, a prison-poem of war-time, 'Surrey's' 'When Windsor walles'; by then Roos is fully skilled in the form and can produce it casually. But we may guess that this more stringent form from Plesaunce days never replaced French models in his affection or practice. Nor does the 'Majestie, Perfection, and Solidity' of *ottava rima*[1] often, except in Epigrams, seduce him from the French eight-line stanza, with its linked quatrains. 'Terza rima' he did attempt, only to have his efforts attributed later to Chaucer, and to Surrey.

As for lyric, Roos's range is almost unlimited, and he steals laurels from Chaucer and from Wyatt. The high virtuosity of *Anelida and Arcite* and *The Lover's Mass* is in sharp contrast to the 'popular' tone of 'I can be wanton and yf I will', or of 'Thayr ys no myrth vnder the sky, Harpyng, lutyng nor no mery dance', where the syncopated beat belies the mournful words. When to the songs of MS. Ff. 1.6 are added those of the 'Wyatt' manuscripts, with the subtle lute-lyrics, the variety of the measures almost defies classification. The rich diversity of the stanza-forms, the sudden artful shifts of weight and emphasis ('*In eternum* I was ons determed'), the loitering or the sudden sally in long or short lines, the permutations and combinations in the placing of rhymes, all these by their sure touch forestall the skill of Campion and the Metaphysicals. It is Roos, not Wyatt, who may 'be argued to be one of the technical fathers of modern poetry'.[2] But as little as 'Wyatt's'—or Herrick's—should his lyrics be read in bulk, or straight on.

Lastly, it is from France (if not from Chaucer) that Roos learnt the trick of the complex anagram, 'a tangled chain, nothing impaired, but all disordered', and used it constantly, much to our present advantage. We may feel at first as one who, lifting up a stone, has let loose a swarm

---

[1] Drayton, *Barons Warres*, 1603, To the Reader.
[2] *Times Lit. Suppl.*, March 16, 1956.

of scurrying insects. Soon we realize that to Roos these are no indis-
tinguishable creatures. They are the people of his environment, whom
he knew as persons to be loved or hated or laughed at. The anagram is
simply a medieval 'engin' for writing 'vers de société'. Three centuries
later, Roos would have written of Chloe and Papillia, of Atticus and
Sporus; for Eleanor Cobham and Margaret of Anjou, he frames
anagrams of the actual names: Antigone of the sweet voice, Elisabeth
Beaumont, the well of goodlihead, Ismania Scales, chaste and faithful,
Anne of Woodstock, ageing and gracious, Maud Stanhope the well-
spoken (perhaps later the blue-stocking of the court, its Dame Philologye), Margaret Stanlow, sensible and well-mannered; and on the
other side of the picture, the hateful Barbelina, gross, vulgar, and disgusting. We see through Roos's eyes the arbiters of the country's
destiny, the gentle, pious Henry, 'Lord of virtue', and Margaret, regal
and gracious in her 'Assembly'; Eleanor Cobham, in her height as
'Auctor of norture', and later as a caged bird beating against prison
walls; the Duke of Buckingham, a pattern of worth and breeding;
Eleanor of Somerset, the model of an agreeable, well-bred woman.
Again we have his judgments on the covetousness of Cardinal Beaufort,
on the avarice and envious ambition of Eleanor Cobham's necromantic
familiars, on Lord Fawcomberg, the Don Juan of the court, and Elisabeth Cobham who knew no rule of measure. Through him, we have for
the first time pungent personal criticism of lesser officials, their sloth
or irresponsibility, the dissembling of John Daunt, the unreliability in
love of Thomas Daniel.

In a sense, it is this sharp criticism that restores our confidence in
Roos's acumen. At first he lets us see little of the darker side. It is
difficult to remember that the great Talbot and his wife, Margaret
Beauchamp, are the pair who, with a ferocity unequalled except in
Lear's daughters, imprisoned the rival claimant to the Berkeley title,
and hounded his unhappy wife to her death; from the Compton Wynyates portraits, one would guess Lady Talbot as the more ruthless.
Or that the Black Knight, the object of Roos's admiration, is the avari-
cious, self-seeking Duke of Somerset, whose unworthy conduct at the
siege of Caen reduced the national strife to a personal feud between
himself and Richard of York, as Holinshed tells us. It is not till later
that Sir Richard Roos sees the court with a sardonic eye. It is to his
honour that even then he does not put darkness for light, but retains a
balanced view. Only one person, the Almain waiting gentlewoman,
reduces him to scurrility and obscenity. In the outrageous *Hood of
Green*, Roos lays aside all the chivalric reticence of *amour courtois* to

invert the catalogue of the lady's beauty. Chaucer had whimsically done the same for a carpenter's wife, but she, for all her wantonness, is in her person as wholesome as a 'hoord of apples leyd in hey'. There is nothing wholesome left to Barbelina when Roos has done with her; she revolts every sense. He might say, like Villon of his Grosse Margot, 'Mon cuer a mort la hait'.

Finally, under the cover of generalized sentiment, we find Roos entering the confessional, passing judgment on his earlier follies and mistakes, when he was deceived by 'merours of fals plesaunce'. The strictly documented life of him (Chapter II) presented a featureless figure; now we can see him in the round. The many minute poems are as so many fleeting expressions on his countenance ('in my visage eche thought depaynted')[1] and all his poetry is the reflection, like entries in a diary, of his life with his associates. Roos is the only English medieval writer who, like Dante, Petrarch, and Boccaccio, has left us a coherent and detailed account of his love-story, and of the emotions that swayed him for some dozen years. We can hardly doubt that in the autumn of 1441 it was of his own impulse, and not under the guidance of Duke Humphrey, that he set out to borrow from the life and death of Laura the expression of feelings to which his own made quick response:

> For in the middes of all the welth
> That brought my hart to happinesse,
> This wicked death he came by stelthe
> And robde me of my ioyfulnesse.
>
> He came when that I little thought
> Of ought that might me vexe so sore:
> And sodenly he brought to nought
> My pleasantnesse for euermore. . . .
>
> For by this cursed deadly stroke
> My blisse is lost, and I forlore:
> And no help may the losse reuoke,
> For lost it is for euermore.

This unpretentious and plaintive poem, commonplace in metre but with the touching sincerity of true grief, proves to be the narrative stem from which all the early love-lyrics hang as flowers and fruit. Again, we know now that Roos's marriage with Margaret Vernon was indeed a love-match. We watch his despairing parting in March at the gate—was it at Haddon Hall? We listen smiling as he insinuates to her the comfortable doctrine that widows should re-marry; or read with sympathy his

[1] Wyatt, *Poems*, ed. Muir, No. 12.

insistence that Elisabeth Beaumont no longer ruled his heart and memory, his oblique confession that he had wasted years in a barren pursuit. But for the reader of poetry he is no dry tree.

With the key so long lost, we can unlock Roos's heart, as we can that of no other Englishman of his age, and not his heart alone. He presents the feelings of others in fictional disguise; the misery of Eleanor Cobham (Cleopatra); the determination of Antigone Powys to marry her Frenchman; the desertion of Alice FitzAlan (Dido), the humiliation of the supplanted Elisabeth Strange (Anelida), the suicide for wounded honour of John Beaufort. And here Roos sheds light on queries left unsolved by historians. A later poem asserted that Beaufort had been gored to death by a bull ('the bull to gronde hym cast cruellye').[1] Roos says suicide, and he had good reason to know. Was Antigone really Eleanor Cobham's daughter? Yes, on the evidence of the prisoner's passionate grief at her departure for France. Did the Lancastrian line assume the style of Plantagenet? No, says Ramsay (II, 83, 134); but Roos applies the name in anagrams to Duke Humphrey and to Henry VI. Was the title of Lord Dunster actually allowed to William Herbert, Earl of Pembroke? Yes, according to an anagram in Fragment C of *The Romaunt of the Rose*. History can find this court poet coming to its aid in a period ill furnished with personal records. Had Roos lived on beyond 1487, he might by an anagram have clarified for us the fate of the two little Princes.

The world of Plesaunce, and still more the world of the last Lancastrian court, are preserved for us by one who daily moved freely and unselfconsciously in them. Nowhere else, not even in the Paston Letters, do we see these people as intimately as by the moving searchlight of Roos's verse. Just as Chaucer depicted the time of Richard II, so does Roos that of Henry VI. Poems apparently fictitious prove to be dark mirrors of the life around. Others which have long seemed casual, vague, and undirected are now seen in sharp focus on a person or event. The reader has also been warned to be chary of reading as mere conventional love-poetry poems of deeper or different import. The gain to the student of literature or history is clear.

It would be regrettable, however, if Sir Richard Roos were labelled Roos the anagrammatist, a mere mechanical versifier. He is much more than that. We are justified in seeing him as an attractive figure, of some significance in the French as well as the English tradition of his century. And not of his century only, since from time to time he attains the beauty that is without epoch. These lines from *The Romaunt* have as little the

---

[1] MS. Rawl. C.813, *Anglia*, XXXI, 326, No. 10, st. 6.

air of translation as has Spenser's 'Rose of love'; they could almost have
been written in the seventeenth century:

> Ah slowe sun, show thine emprise,
> Speed thee to spread thy beames bright,
> And chase the darkness of the night,
> To put away the stoundes strong
> Which in me lasten all too long.
>
> *(The Romaunt, 2636–40)*

From time to time, too, he writes lines of a depth and validity far beyond
their immediate courtly application:

> Pite is ded.
> Allas that day! that ever hyt shulde falle!
> What maner man dar now hold up his hed?
> To whom shal any sorwful herte calle?
> Now Cruelte hath cast to slee us alle,
> In ydel hope, folk redeles of peyne,
> Syth she is ded, to whom shul we compleyne?

It voices the despair of the refugees of every war.

Roos is a poet to whom environment counts for much. It produces in
his work unity, not to say some monotony of tone, though there are
always inner modulations from mood to mood, from the excitement of
How a Lover, to the narrative convolutions of *The Isle of Ladies*, and to
the unsurpassed and rich smoothness of *The Flower and the Leaf*. He
does not write solely from his own passions and instincts; he is subdued
to what he works for, the artificiality of courts, and the social elegance,
the refined sensibilities of women. The economic theorist will get no
help from him; Roos may appreciate the artist-craftsman, but no
labourer crosses his path in the cornfield, no gardener works in the
alleys of Plesaunce. In moments of exasperation the critic may wish
that daydream of civility, *The Assembly of Ladies*, at the bottom of the
Thames; he would be wrong. True, it is the nearest to the merely modish
in the poetry of Sir Richard, and generally his waters flow both fresher
and deeper; but even here the setting is ideal, the autumn garden, with
the plashing fountain and the last of the summer flowers. It may have
been a misfortune for the poet to swing between the brilliant instability
of Duke Humphrey, the weak insipidity of Henry VI, and the proud
wilfulness of Queen Margaret. Under other inspiration, his powers as a
poet and as a man might have ripened greatly and differently. It is
tempting to speculate how this court poet might have blossomed and
fruited if his service had been dedicated like Spenser's to England's
Elizabeth, and not to the foreign queen, also brilliant, also a driving
force, but lacking any conception of queenship other than personal or

dynastic power. If 'poetry is a game', as has been said, it should remain a personal game; with Roos, it too soon turned into a society game. Nevertheless it thereby became representative of a period and of a group. These poems are not to be dispersed across the century and read in isolation; concentrated in its middle years, they reflect, not the taste of this or that commissioning noble, not the efforts of a cleric seeking a patron, but the talent and taste of one man and of his social group, the Lancastrian society. There is a resultant independence. Limited though these poems are, they derive assurance and some power from the writer's status, and from his clear realization of his audience's demands and response. The servility of tone that infuriates the modern class-conscious reader is almost entirely absent from this poetry. *La Belle Dame sans Merci* is, it is true, a command performance, a 'penaunce', but the poet's tone has a faint air of humorous resignation, the equivalent of a whimsical shrug. This amateur status, this aristocratic *nonchaloir*, is almost a criterion for Roos's authorship. It comes natural to him to observe the distinctions; he never falters or makes a false step in the intricacies of the courtly dance. Within his demesne, he can write for his own pleasure, on his own terms, with his natural sweetness and ease. Once only do we hear a sulky tone, as if the Duke's comments had been too sharp:

> Me list no more to sing. . . .
> Men dede my songis mistake.
> My songes ware to defuse (Muir, 138).

He is no conscientious and laborious Lydgate, no worthy and slow-oozing George Ashby, no hard-fisted John St. Amand, but a poet of high skill and proficiency, who takes his place lightly in this circle as of lineal right. What was hard won was the proficiency. Roos was endowed by nature with fluency of expression, acute senses, appreciation of beauty, and an eye for the grotesque. His sense of structure is generally good. The anagram-portraits throw into relief, and may have partly conditioned, the ten, twenty, even thirty-line paragraphing of long poems. The effect is like that of single-figure panels of tapestry, or of the painted figures in *Le Roman de la Rose*. Lengthy Roos often is, but seldom straggling. The rest came with self-training, writing and rewriting. He inherits an epic tradition, as in the alliterative *Alexander*, and a highly developed system and allegory of love. He will add to this last his own little myth of the death and resurrection of Pity; and he begins in our poetry the union of the chivalric and the pastoral with even better right than Sidney, who embraced the chivalric tradition with ardour, and fused the two strains.

The flow of allegory in Roos is continuous, the deepening to symbol only intermittent. Symbolists like Yeats and some of his interpreters would take the spiral stair which comes into two of his dream poems as a symbol of 'the cycle, the gyre of history'. *The Isle of Ladies* is indeed full of suggestions of deeper, more traditional, even more instinctive conceptions, and of feelings 'on the edge of consciousness'—the far isle, the lonely rock, the herb of healing, the magic fruit that defeats time. It has been suggested that medieval thought seems to be 'comparatively untroubled by time',[1] and it is true that the persecution of the 'unforgiving minute' did not much afflict men before the Renaissance invention of the watch as a personal time-gauge. But Guillaume de Lorris muses on it; and Roos, in a century of transition, is in youth haunted as by an extradimensional sense of time. The fruit that holds life static for seven-year periods, the reverie on the bridge in *How a Lover* (eighty years for some, for others no more than an hour by the dial shadow), these are replaced in later life by a sense of 'tyme passed and loste and tyme to come' ('The Prisoner to Vere', 6). Roos's antitheses and balancing of thought may be no more than the common rhetorical trick; yet thought preoccupies him as much as time: 'Think and have, it is na more'. He questions too the mystery of sleep and dreams, as did Chaucer, but in his own ways; he dreamt, yet he slept not; a good spirit carried him off through some 'curious port'. He knows too the dreamer's confusion on returning to the actual world, as he wakes feverish and distressed. He is always conscious of sleep's brother, death; the fatalities in his family had forced it early on his thoughts. 'Youth never hopeth to deye'; and he wishes that the magic fruit had had the power to prevent death. The herb of healing is interposed to snatch youth and beauty and love from the grave.

In this romance, *The Isle of Ladies*, death and mourning are hallowed with orthodox, religious ritual. Elsewhere Roos has recourse to the classical personifications, 'Parcas sustren' who spin a man's destiny (*Black Knight*, l. 488), 'Antropos', who untwines the thread and sets the hour of death, as he says in the interpolation on the Swan in *Reson and Sensuallyte* (ll. 1252–61); and 'Antropos' comes fittingly into his stanzas of classical reference in *The Temple of Glas* (l. 782). In spite of Roos's orthodox training, and his sympathetic treatment of the Church's funeral rites, I do not think that he wrote any formal religious poetry. The aureate 'Commendation of our Lady', though attached by Thynne to *My Soverain Lady*, is not so found in its two manuscripts, and is not, I believe, by either Roos or Lydgate; it might be by the author of *The*

[1] Georges Poulet, *Etudes sur le Temps Humain*, 1951.

Court of Sapience. Roos's devotional poems are dramatic, as addressed by Eleanor Cobham to the large bounty and unfailing succour of the Virgin Mary, and later to the power of the Holy Name; his other reference to the Virgin is in defence of good women (*Reson*, etc., ll. 6546–56; cf. *Horns Away*, stt. 7–9). The ritual parody of the Mass and of Mattins, in *The Lover's Mass* and *The Court of Love*, does not show deliberate irreverence, as it would now, but merely the common fusing of religious forms with the morality of love. In the prison-poem alone, which has broken away from *amour courtois*, and presents reality, though disguised for safety, Roos offers a devout and humble prayer for aid to the blessed Trinity. The terms and bequests of his will show him as an orthodox supporter of the Church; this one would expect in a member of his family.

In the crucial year, 1441, the young poet and lover made the humiliating discovery of the power of the real world, ruthless and inescapable, which broke in upon his world of dreams and delight. The experience is not great enough to turn him at once into contrary paths; he still wanders in a conventional 'Forêt de Longue Attente'. 'I am not happy enough for silken phrases and silver sentences', wrote Keats at the last to Fanny Brawne; Roos, more fortunate, seems to have been granted a second spring of happiness and interest, and a new impulse to personal poetry. Then the political crisis fell like an axe, and almost stopped him from exercising his easy talent. At least we are spared the many dreary complaints such as Eustache Deschamps flowed with, against bad government, malaise, old age, life and death; only one such may be discerned, and with its reflective humour it has already been taken to the heart of the English—'I lothe that I did loue'.

Readers of this study must have often felt that the Lancastrian party were like the 'damned Whigs' of Sir Robert Walpole's imprecation, 'all cousins'. So were the Yorkists; and so were the two factions mutually. It was that very inter-knitting and cohesion which, though bitter at first, in time allowed wounds to close and scars to heal, and in time brought Sir Richard, his nephew, and his niece into the court of Edward of York and Elizabeth Wydville. The great difficulty of this period is that although genealogists and historians have given us many pedigrees, and many facts of events and even of conduct, including some bewildering instances of *volte-face*, we can seldom do more than guess at feeling and motives. In the absence of intimate documents, of self-revelation, we know little or nothing of the inner compulsions, the processes of thought or purpose. The insight of the mature Shakespeare alone could convincingly re-create them; even his youthful historical trilogy often carries the conviction, 'Thus must it have been with them'. It is then clear gain to have a body of poetry, however apparently superficial, which displays the personality of one man in a sequence of circumstances and in known surroundings.

At a time when landmarks are fast perishing, and a sense of historical continuity slipping away from many, it is heartening to trace the chain of poetic and historic succession linked in this knightly poet. The 'liquid history' of the river Thames furnished Roos with the background for many of his poems, as it did Spenser; Pleasaunce, which Spenser knew as Greenwich Palace, has gone from its banks, but another storehouse of national achievement has taken its place, the record of many 'a longe perileuse viage',

> over the waves highe and grene
> wiche were large and depe betwene.

Hamlake lies in ruins, but Belvoir still, in rejuvenated form, dominates its countryside. It is not too farfetched a fancy to imagine Sir Robert and Sir Richard Roos riding in the forest not far from More End, under the boughs of Judith's Tree (Norman Judith, wife of Earl Waltheof) then in its prime of less than four hundred years, now an impressive ruin, known to Cowper as Yardley Oak. The elder brothers at Agincourt must have seen, catching the light on the king's helmet, the Black Prince's ruby which still gleams in the Imperial State Crown. Sir Richard's treasured volume has lain for over four centuries among the royal books, with his signature, and that of his niece whose husband fell a victim to the schemes of Richard III; also with the signatures of two queens, one who took the place of his own mistress, the ill-fated and ambitious Margaret, and one who was sacrificed in youth to the ambitions of others. Now that Sir Richard Roos has been called back from the shades, he comes not only as a poet of courtly love and coterie satire, but also as the Lancastrian poet whose poems were collected by the ladies and knights, the squires and clerks of the Household, as the singer of plesaunce.

This corpus of verse has suffered by being continually presented as spurious Chaucer, or debatable Lydgate; it has been a *corpus vile*, always being dissected, seldom or never being read (even by some of its editors) with interest, much less pleasure, as poetry, as the expression of one man's talent and preoccupations. Under this treatment, its particular and delicate aroma vanishes, except perhaps in *The Flower and the Leaf*, where a more substantial literary form, the French prose romance, has come to its support. As the work of one man whose life ran a very different course from that of either Chaucer or Lydgate, it is seen to

M M

have coherence and unity. It is one and the same man, a knight and not a cleric, who compares the wayward aim of Love to the random shooting of an archer dazzled and blinded:

> Withoute avys he let his arowe go,
> For lakke of sight and also of resoun
> (*Black Knight*, 464–5);

or who depicts Despite as an armourer sharpening swords, grinding arrows (*ib*. 252–3); who sees the strong castles of Refus as 'stuffed with ordinaunce' (*La Belle Dame*, l. 818); and who hardens clerkly generalization into soldierly particularity in the military portions of *The Romaunt of the Rose*. The poems are enlivened by the experience of a man of activity, fighting, hunting, hawking. The correspondences in phrase and vocabulary and theme are not borrowings merely, they are the leaves and flowers of a living organism, of the mind and personality of the writer. The poet repeats himself because he is using the terms natural to his cast of thought, to his individual sensibility. They are the outward and recognizable signs of an inward working of mind and spirit.

The general effect of all this coherence is concentration, rather than dissipation of interest: concentration in time, within the middle years of the fifteenth century; concentration in scope, within the interests and loyalties of the Lancastrian allegiance; and in lieu of anonymity and doubtful attributions, concentration on a single writer, redintegration of a single personality, Richard Roos, chevalier, of Hamlake and Belvoir, Gloucester's man, King's Knight, lover of Elisabeth Beaumont, husband of Margaret Vernon of Haddon Hall, romancer, lyrist, satirist, and poet of plesaunce.

APPENDIX A

SIR RICHARD ROOS'S WILL. MARCH 8, 1481/2

IN THE NAME OF the blissud trynyte fader and sonne and hoolly goost
Amen THE viij[th] daie of marche in the yere of our lord god m¹cccclxxxj
And in the yere of the Reigne of king Edward the iiij[th] aftir the conquest
the xxij I SIR RICHARD Roos knyght hole of mynde and in gode
memory being blessud be almighty god make and ordeyne this my present
testament conteignyng my last wille in this wise FFIRST I BIQUETH
and committe my soule to almighty god my maker and redemer and to our
blissud ladie saint marie his moder and to saint Andrewe and to all the
hole courte of heven and my bodie to be buried in the sewerist wise that
it canne be with the costes and expenses after the discrecioun of myne
executours vnderwritten in the churche of the white ffreres in ffletestrete
in london that is to saie in such a place ther as canne be thought moost
conuenient and according by my saide executours to gider with thassent
of the priour of the saide hows and church AND I BIQUETH to the
saide priour and conuent for my burying therin so to be had, and to
thentente that the same priour and conuent specially pray for my soule
in their suffrages and praiers xl s. ALSO I WOLL afore all oþer thinges
that all and singuler my dettes which canne be founde that I owe to anny
persone of right be truly paied and contented ALSO I GIUE and biqueth
to Dame margett my wife all my mesuage with the gardein therto adioyn-
yng with all and singuler therin apperteining in Estgrenewich in the
countie of Kente which I late purchaced of John Bellacourte To haue and
to hold all the saide mesuage and gardein with all and singuler therin
apperteining to the saide Dame margarete to her heires and her assignes
foreuermor ALSO I BIQUETH to the workes of the bodie of the parish
church of saint petirs the litle in Thamystrete of london where I am
nowe a parishener an Image of our ladie of siluer and gilte to thentente
to haue my soule specially praied for amonges the praiers of the parisshens
of the same parish ALSO I BIQUETH to the saide priour and conuent
of the saide hous of white ffreres my Tablett of the coronacioun of our
ladie made of the moder of perle garnysshed and sett in siluer and gilte
and with a fote therto of siluer and gilte So that the same priour and
conuent haue my soule to god specially recommended ALSO I BIQUETH
to sir henry Roos my nephieu my coller of golde of the kinges lyvery and
my Ring of golde sette with a camahewe that I was wont to wer and my
Sparver of silke that serued me in the kinges courte ALSO I BIQUETH
to Alianore hawte my Nece suster of the saide sir henry Roos my litle
Roos of golde sett and garnysshed with a Ruby and viij perles and my
litle potte of siluer and parcell gilte withoute foote and coueryng and my
grete booke called saint Grall bounde in boordes couerde with rede leder

547

and plated w*ith* plates of laten ALSO I BIQUETH to Elizabeth Roos my Nece dwellyng w*ith* my ladie of Suffolk my flatte cheyne of golde made w*ith* a borage flour and a diamond sett in the myddes of the same chayne ALSO I BIQUETH to the wif of william parker drap*er*er my Nece my litle booke of praiers closed in plat*es* of siluer and eneled w*ith* an Image of the Crucifixe on the oon side and an Image of our ladie on the oþer side of the same ALSO I biqueth to my ladie the countes of Oxford my Tablett of Ivorie wrought w*ith* Imagery ALSO I biqueth to mary Vernon nece vnto the saide dame margerete my wif a Be for her nek sett with ij diamond*es* and a Rubie and a perle and the white bedde complete that the same mary is wonte to lie inne and a furr of beale menyver which lieth in my gowne of blue velwett and my gowne of chamelett lynyng and all to make her a kirtill ALSO I BIQUETH to Elyn han*n*ing my se*r*ua*u*nte a brode harneis for a gurdell of siluer and gilte and the barys that longith therto and the clothe of my blak gowne that was furred w*ith* grey to make her a kirtill and xiijs and iiijd in money ALSO I BIQUETH to sir Roger ap Thomas my chapeleyne xxs in moneye so that he con-tynnewe still in se*r*uice with the saide dame margett my wife after my decesse ALSO I BIQUETH to mawde wadiluf late my se*r*ua*u*nte my crosse of golde shapen like a sonne eu*er*y weie and my bedes of corall gaudied w*ith* calcedonyes and xxs in moneie ALSO I biqueth to mabill lacon my Robe of Scarlett furred w*ith* the hode therto fur*r* and all and xiijs iiijd in moneye ALSO I BIQUETH to Robert Stephenson my long Russett gowne furred w*ith* blak lambe furr and all and my doublett of blak velwett and my trussing spone of siluer w*ith* a knop att the ende and xiijs iiijd in moneye ALSO I biqueth to william dansey my se*r*ua*u*nt vis viijd ALSO I biqueth to Edward miller my se*r*ua*u*nt my shorte blak gowne furred w*ith* blak lambe and xs in moneye ALSO I biqueth to howell vaughan my seruante vis viijd in moneye ALSO I biqueth to Thomas Beall my se*r*ua*u*nte my doublett of chamelett and all my hosen that I was wonte to wer and vis viijd in moneye ALSO I biqueth to Stephen Stonal my se*r*ua*u*nte vjs viijd in moneye Also I biqueth to margarete merysete my se*r*ua*u*nte vis viijd in moneye ALSO I biqueth to Gunnett my se*r*ua*u*nte iijs iiijd in moneye ALSO I biqueth to John Richardeson my se*r*ua*u*nte vis viijd in moneye ALSO I biqueth to George fferby my se*r*ua*u*nte vis viijd in moneye ALSO I biqueth to Thomas ffoxe my se*r*ua*u*nt my long knyfe and vis viijd in moneye ALSO I WILLE that myn executours vnderwritten Immediately aftir my decesse dele and distribute among*es* poue*r* people xxs in moneye by penny mele and ij penny mele if it so be that it be nott doon and p*er*fourmed by me in my life tyme ALSO I BIQUETH to the saide dame margett my wife my standing cuppe coue*r*de *with* a double belly of siluer all gilte and my salte saler made w*ith* colombynes and w*ith* a couering therto of siluer and ouer gilte and my ij Basons of parys siluer and myn Ewer of siluer and ouer gilte and my potte of siluer w*ith* borders gilte Also my salte saler of siluer w*ith* borders gilte w*ith* the coue*r*yng therto of siluer w*ith* a eymyrawd sett on the knopp of the same coue*r*yng Also my bolle pece of siluer of Roone making Also half doseyne of siluer spones w*ith* long steles and gilte knoppes Also half doseyne of siluer spones w*ith* shorte steles and my

bedde of silke made with white hartes that is to seie with celour Testour
Cuyrteins and all thing that longith therto And also all the stuff that
longith to my closett and chapell that is to saie chalice cruettes belle and
paxe the lesse masboke and the portuous with all other ornamentes that
longith to my saide closett and chapell Also my clok and all my Naperey
that longith to the Botrye withall other stuff that longith to that office
Also all my stuff that longith to the kechyn and all my stuff of bedding
such as is nott biquathed ALSO I WILL that Anneys the wife of John
Edward Baker haue that narrowe cors girdull of silke travuersed with
siluer And the paire bedes of corrall gaudied with siluer and gilte which
she laide to me in plegge for xiijs iiijd so that the same Anneys paie to
my saide executours the saide xiijs iiijd ALSO I biqueth to the saide
Robert Stephenson myn own sadill that I was wonte to ride inne and a
bridell So that the same Robert be reddy atte all tymes to ride for the
erandes of the said dame margarett my Wife AND I WILL that all oþer
myn hors harneys be solde by myn executours And that the money
commyng of the saide sale be egally delte and distributed amonges my
seruantes by my saide executours Savyng oonely I will that my saide
executours reward Edward my seruaunt that kepith myn horses mor thann
anny of his feleship aftre their gode discrecioun AND THE RESIDUE
OF ALL my goodes aboue natt biquethed aftir my dettes paied my burying made and this my present testament fulfilled I giue and biqueth holly to
the saide dame margarett my Wife therof to do and dispose her owne fre
wille as with her owne goodes for euer mor And that she of the same
ordeigne and dispose for my soule and for the soules of my fader and
moder and all my gode frendes soules and all christen soules in masses
to be song to poure people moost nedie and in oþer charitable dedes as
she shall seme best for the pleasure of god and the proufite of my soule
Which saide dame margarete my Wife I make and ordeigne principall
executryce of this my present testament And I make and ordeigne the
forsaide sir Roger ap thomas and the saide Robert Stephenson executours
with the saide dame margarete my Wife of my saide testament And I will
that the saide dame margarete my Wife of and with my goodes reward
the saide sir Roger ap thomas and Robert for their labours in the premisses
to be had aftre her gode discrecioun ALSO I BIQUETH to the saide
sir Roger my saulter clasped with siluer and a paire bedes of calcedonyes
of xv IN WITTNESSE whereof to this my present testament I haue sett
my seale YOUEN the daie and yere abouesaide AND BESIDE all other
my biquestes I will that the forsaide priour and conuent of the white
ffreres haue v marc of the xv li due vnto me by the Erle of huntingdon
whanne that it is paied by the saide Erle vpon condicioun that the saide
priour and conuent kepe and obserue an honest obite euery Anniuersarie
yerely for my soule in their propre churche by vj yere next folowyng
aftre my decesse that is to saie with placebo and dirige by note the daie
that it shall happen me to decesse on and with masse of Requiem by note
on the morowe folowyng aftre the custume and vsage of keping of oþer
obites in the saide churche ALSO I BIQUETH to the saide howell
vaughan the clothe of my sayde blak gowne furred with blak lambe being
in the kinges courte ALSO I BIQUETH to John Richardeson that kepith

my stuff in the saide courte my shorte gowne lyned that I was wont to ride inne and the stuff of the bedd that the same John was wonte to lie inne him silf that is in the court ALSO I BIQUETH to the forsaide prio*ur* and conuente of the white ffreres my gowne of blue Veluett

PROBATUM fuit p*rae*dic*tum* testam*entum* apud Lamehith primo die mens*is* Aprilis Anno d*omi*ni etc. lxxxijdo ac app*ro*batum etc. ET COM-MISSA fuit admi*ni*stracio bonorum etc. d*omine* Margarete Relic*tae* eiusdem ac executrici etc. de bene et fideli*ter* admi*ni*strando bona huius Ac de ple*no* Inventario omni*um* bon*orum* etc. citra festum sancti petri quod dicitur ad vincula proxim*um* etc. necnon de plano et vero compoto etc Jura*tur* etc RESERUATA POTESTATE alijs c*um* etc.

these are read up the stanza to produce three names of two persons, DOROTHY, and CVTBERT, HALSALL. Salusbury signs the poem's last line I.S., using the initials of the line's first and last words (p. 49). The succeeding Posie IV (probably by Parry) is extremely complex, running one name in acrostic down the first lines of fourteen stanzas (DOROTHI HALSALL), another down the second lines (FRANSIS WILOWBI), and two more in succession down the remaining five lines of the stanzas. Yet another complication appears in Posie VIII, where the first and second words of each line furnish the acrostic letters, for Dorothy Halsall and I.S. (again backward). It is surely ridiculous to assume that a key was sent to Mistress Halsall with each poem; she must have been aware in general of the possibilities, and was prepared to use her wits.

The seventeenth century played endlessly with acrostics, combining them with pattern poems, with pyramids, pillars, etc., as did Joshua Sylvester in his dedicatory poems. I have quoted in Chapter IV above an American critic on the almost philosophic demands made on the practice by New England poets.

The shifting of an acrostic to the right of anaphora can be exemplified even in the fifteenth century in an English quatrain on LOVE, where it is pointed out by the scribe in a Latin introduction; whereas a Latin acrostic by four epithets on MORS in the same manuscript (evidently a preacher's mnemonic) is missed by the English translator (Furnivall, *Political*, . . . *Poems*, E.E.T.S. 15, pp. 260, 254).

A poet like Eustache Deschamps is so fertile in variation that he is forced to explain to his patron how he works his half word backward device in his COUCY-EUSTACE poem; but if the Sieur de Coucy had tried to unravel all his poet's efforts by this pattern, he would not have got far. Indeed the possibilities for verbal variation are limited only by the poet's inventiveness, not by the critic's rules. This even Dickens knew when he made Mr. Slum offer Mrs. Jarley an advertisement of her waxworks in the form of an acrostic: 'the name at this moment is Warren, but the idea is a convertible one, and a positive inspiration for Jarley' (WARrEn; jARlEy). There is nothing solemn about rules here; but convertibility can hardly appeal to a stickler for Procrustean uniformity.

(3) The anagram falls under displeasure. Again it has a respectable ancestry in English. Cynewulf seems to have obeyed a sudden impulse to further privacy when in one poem only (*The Fates of the Apostles*) he turned his runic acrostic signature backwards into a kind of anagram. Throughout the sixteenth and seventeenth centuries the exactly corresponding anagram is the usual practice, so many letters and no more; but not invariably, e.g. Isabella Lambard turned into 'A bride's all balm' (p. 116 above) leaves one 'a' in the name unused; and the minor French poet, Nicholas Denisot, inventing his pen-name, Comes d'Alcinois, imported two letters (c, m) from the air, and left another two (n, t) as residue: CO–ES DAL–INOIS.

(4) The combination of anagram with acrostic is the 'final, fatal step' of the present solver, and therefore also presumably of any luckless poet to whom it might occur as a device. Here especially we come up against those *a priori* rules (*b*) to (*f*) which the scientific cryptologist lays as chains

upon the free working of the poet's fantasy, or of his immediate purpose. 'There is only ONE valid solution to a cryptogram' (*c*). Why necessarily in poetry? The poet may have even intended more than one (see above, Nos. 44 and 48). 'If two investigators . . . get two different answers, the method has no validity' (*d*). Why necessarily? The one investigator may be more skilled, better informed in the poet's doings and way of thought, than the other. 'The anagrammatical process . . . must be controlled or guided by some key' (*e*). Why controlled? since this implies imposed rules, bridling the invention and imagination. Guided, yes, certainly, but the guidance should come from within the poet's mind and purpose, not from without, and may lead to further complexity. In the present instance, guidance is given by the pattern of the double caesural acrostic.

The scientific cryptologist follows rules; the literary enquirer must try to find the intention and follow the movement, even the impulses of the writer. I am blamed for drawing up a series of 'rules'; at least they are rules not brought from without, or from future systematization, but deduced from the practice of the writer under consideration, his observed irregularities, his *ad hoc* expedients, successes and failures. It must be remembered that the poet's primary aim is verse, if not poetry; the cryptogram is a secondary matter, an added ornament, or an amusement for his immediate readers, or a means of addressing or signing the verse. Whereas for the iron-bound political cipher-maker, the cipher is the thing; and the writer's remaining ingenuity is expended on making the cloak of it (letter, pamphlet, or what not) as drably unrevealing and unremarkable as he can. The necessity of a prisoner to get out a message may entail his using every means he can devise, as is done here in 'The Prisoner to Vere' (No. 100). I am reminded of a letter from an officer, a prisoner after the fall of Kut in World War I, which the Turkish Censorship let through, but in which the British Censors found a long account of a successful escape from the P/W camp, with several names of the escapers. This was done in a long, chatty, familiar letter by every simple means (initial letters, isolated or 'broken' letters, unnecessary capitals, underlining, 'accidental' dots and blots, numbers, inversion) devisable by an ingenious, presumably amateur mind. A heavy charge made against the anagrammatic practice here is that it allows of residue. That is a consequence, almost inevitable, of the medium being verse. The parallelism here is with words or names concealed in a prevailing or half-obliterating material; as with monograms, none too easy to read in the arabesques of filigree; or the insulting remarks in the embroideries of 'Mandarin' coats sold to unsuspecting tourists; or with the name of the rubricator (Lity, Lyty) inserted in the ornament of colophons in 'Astley's manuscript', Bodleian 638 (E. Hammond, *Chaucer*, p. 336).

A few details of the Friedmans' difficulties (p. 198) may be dealt with here.

(i) French acrostics using the second or even the third letter of the word. The poem by Deschamps cited above in Chapter III, section ii, is perhaps an extreme example, using as it does whole words or phrases ('Le,

Appendix C

Non-aym, D'or mont'). More ordinary examples from the fifteenth century will be found in *Le Jardin de Plaisance*:

Vol. II, p. 205, No. 414, JEHANE DE LUS (with two unneeded letters breaking into the acrostic in the twelve-line stanza);
Vol. II, pp. 253–4, No. 599, PIERRE DANCHE (repeated backwards in st. 2);
Vol. II, p. 144, No. 132, MARIE MORELET;
Vol. II, p. 189, No. 330, ME[R for actual E]GVERJTE (E. Droz's reading); or, MA[R]GVERJTE, ECLAT (my reading)—all backwards.

Also in *Fleurs de Rhétorique*, ed. Kathleen Chesney, 1950, pp. 42–3: André de la Vigne, *Majesté Royalle*:

ll. 1–12, CHArLES DE VALOJS;
ll. 13–24, CHARLES DE VALOIS (backwards);
ll. 25–36, CHArLES DE VALOJS (initial); CHARLES DE VALOIS (caesural, backwards);
ll. 37–42, CHARLES (initial); DE VALOJS (caesural).

(ii) Similar anagrams uniting Yolande and Ferry: see No. 67 above.
(iii) 'I confidently take my own conclusions for granted': that is merely to say that I present them with sincere belief, judge them to be valid as a hypothesis, base conclusions on them, and act on them. Yes, that is so.
(iv) 'We know of only three lengthy ciphers based upon unkeyed anagrammatic method'. All three, it should be noted, are by scientists (Roger Bacon is a medieval worker). Why should this preclude the use of unkeyed anagrams by literary writers—or by a poet little more than a century later than Roger Bacon? Is the cruse of discovery to run no more oil, no hitherto unnoticed phenomenon to be discerned.[1] This is the sclerosis of critical apprehension.

If the Friedman statute of limitation is allowed to run in literary and poetic territory, then no poet may frame a cryptogram without the book of rules beside him, and another copy at his lady's elbow. But, in anagrams as in more important matters, there is an appeal open from dead system to creative life.

[1] During this proof-reading, M. Tristan Tzara, artist and poet, has announced his discovery of anagrams in the poems of Villon (forthcoming), with results apparently somewhat similar to mine in *Studies in Villon* (etc.), but probably on a different method (see Jean Couvreur, 'Du Nouveau sur François Villon?' in *Le Monde* 22 déc., 1959, p. 9).

APPENDIX D. A BRIEF 'WHO'S WHO'

ANJOU. Isabel of Lorraine, wife of René, mother of Margaret; d. Feb. 1453.

Margaret (1430–82), dau. of René and Isabel; m. Henry VI, 1445; d. in France, 1482.

René (1409–80), King of Sicily, Duke of Anjou.

Yolande of Aragon; m. Louis II of Anjou, 1400. Mother of René; d. 1442.

Yolande (1428–83), elder sister of Margaret; betrothed (1432) and m. (1445) Ferry de Vaudémont, son of Antoine de V., claimant (1431) to the duchy of Lorraine.

ANTIGONE. Illegit. dau. of Humphrey, Duke of Gloucester, putative dau. of Eleanor Cobham; m. (1) 1435–6, Henry Grey, Lord POWYS; (2) 1450–1, Jean D'AMANCIER who d. 1459.

ARUNDEL. Alice FitzAlan, dau. of Richard FitzAlan, Lord A.

Joan 'FitzAlan', illegit. dau. of Alice and of Henry BEAUFORT (later cardinal). (See STRADLING.)

Sir John A., Lord A. and Mautravers, b. 1408, killed 1435 ('The English Achilles'). His 2nd wife Maud Stafford, née Lovell, was the 'Lady Beauty' of Charles d'Orléans; d. 1436.

Margaret A., dau. of Sir John A. (died at sea, 1379) and of Eleanor Mautravers; m. 1394, William, 6th Lord Roos; mother of the poet; d. Aug. 1438.

Sir William, Lord A. and Mautravers; brother of Sir John; d. 1487; Yorkist; owner of MS. Royal 17 D.vi.

ASHBY, George. Member of the Escort, 1444–5; Clerk of the Signet to Queen Margaret; poet of *Active Policy of a Prince* (for Prince Edward, b. 1453) and of *A Prisoner's Reflections*, 1463.

BABTHORP(E) of B., Yorkshire. Sir Robert B. the elder, d. 1436. Comptroller of the Household and executor to Henry V; Gloucester's nominee as Steward of the Household, 1432; m. (2) Bridget Pilkington of Lancs. (*Test. Ebor.*, II. 121).

Ralph B., son and heir; killed with his heir at 1st St. Albans, 1455 (*Paston Letters*, No. 239).

Robert B. the younger, son of Sir Robert. Keeper of Galtres and of Dartmoor (1444 and 1452); King's Squire, 1452 (*Cal. Pat. Rolls*); d. 1466.

Ralph B., son of Robert the younger; d. 1490.

BARBELINA. See HERBERQUYNE.

BARDOLF. See PHELIP, CHAUCER.

BEAUCHAMP. Richard B., Earl of Warwick (d. Apr. 1439); m. (1) Elizabeth Berkeley; (2) 1423, Isabella Despenser; d. Dec. 1439.

Margaret B., eldest dau. of Richard and Elizabeth; m. John, Lord TALBOT (killed, 1453). Her motto, 'Tyl deth depart' (i.e. divide).

Eleanor B., 2nd dau. of Richard and Elizabeth; m. (1) Thomas, 8th Lord ROOS (d. 1430); (2) c. 1435–6, Edmund BEAUFORT, Count of Mortain. She died 1467/8. Her motto 'Never Newe'.

Elizabeth B., 3rd dau. of Richard and Elizabeth; m. (1) 1436, George Neville, Lord LATIMER who d. insane, 1469; (2) Thomas Wake. She died before 1480. Her motto 'Til my Lyves Ende'.

Henry B., Earl of Warwick, son and heir of Richard, d. 1446.

Anne, sister and heir of Henry;

m. Richard Neville, *jure uxoris* Earl of Warwick (The King-maker).

BEAUCHAMP of Bletsoe. Margaret, dau. of Sir John B. of B. and of Edith Stourton; m. (1) Sir Oliver St. John; (2) c. 1440, John BEAUFORT, 3rd Duke of Somerset; (3) Lionel de Welles, Lord W. She d. 1482/3. Mother of the Lady Margaret BEAUFORT.

BEAUFORT. Legitimated descendants of John of Gaunt and Catherine Swynford.

Edmund, grandson of Gaunt, son of John B., 1st Duke of Somerset; 1430/1, Count of Mortain; 1441, Earl and (1443) Marquess of Dorset; 1444, Earl and (1448) Duke of Somerset; m. c. 1435 Eleanor BEAUCHAMP, widow of Thomas, Lord ROOS; killed at 1st St. Albans, 1455 ('The Black Knight').

Henry B., son of Gaunt; 1398 Bp. of Lincoln; 1404, Bp. of Win-chester; 1426, Cardinal; d. Apr. 1447.

Joan B., dau. of Gaunt; m. (1) Sir Robt Ferrers; (2) as 2nd wife, 1397 Ralph Neville, 1st Earl of Westmoreland (d. 1425); d. 1440.

Joan B., sister of Edmund; m. 1424, James I of Scotland.

John B., 3rd Duke of Somerset, elder brother of Edmund; 1421, captured at Baugé; c. 1440 m. Margaret BEAUCHAMP of Bletsoe; 1443, Lt. General of Aquitaine; May 27, 1444, committed suicide. Children of Edmund and Eleanor B. (See *Flower and Leaf.*)

   i. Henry B., 5th Earl of Somerset; beheaded after Hexham, 1464.

   ii. Edmund B., 'Duke of Somer-set'; beheaded after Tewkesbury, 1471.

   iii. John. B., killed at Tewkes-bury, 1471.

   iv. Anne B., m. (1466–9) William Paston, son of Judge P.

   v. Eleanor B., m. (1) 1458, James Butler Earl of Wiltshire and of Ormond; (2) c. 1470, Sir Robt Spencer of Spencercombe, Devon. She d. 1501.

   vi. Elizabeth B., m. Sir Henry FITZLEWIS. Their dau. Mary m. Anthony WYD-VILLE.

   vii. Joan B., m. 1478, Robert St. Lawrence, 15th Lord Howth.

   viii. Margaret B., m. (1) Hum-phrey STAFFORD, killed at 1st St. Albans 1455 (see *Court of Love*); (2) Sir Richard Darell (see ch. 12) of Littlecote.

BEAUMONT of Folkingham. John, 1st Viscount B. 1441 K.G., 1450, Great Chamberlain; m. (1) Eliza-beth, dau. of Sir William PHELIP, Lord Bardolf, d. 1441; (2) Katharine Neville; 1460, killed at Northampton.

BEDFORD. John of Lancaster, Duke of B., 3rd son of Henry IV, b. 1389. Regent of France, 1422–Sept. 14, 1435; m. (1) Anne of Burgundy, sister of Philip, Duke of Burgundy, d. Nov. 1432; (2) Apr. 1433, Jacquetta de St. Pol of Luxem-burg. She m. (2) by March 1436/7, Richard WYDVILLE, later Lord Rivers.

BOLIN(G)BROK(E). Roger B. or O(o)nly, priest of Oxford, and necro-mancer; accomplice of Eleanor Cobham; executed, 1441.

BOURCHIER. See SCALES, STAFFORD.

BRADBOURN(E). See VERNON.

BUCKINGHAM. See STAFFORD.

CHARLTON. See VERNON.

CHAUCER. Alice, dau. of Thomas C. and Maud Burghersh; m. (1) as 3rd wife Sir John PHELIP (d. 1415), bro. of William P., Lord Bardolf; (2) Nov. 1424, Thomas Montagu, Earl of Salisbury (d. 1428); (3) Nov. 1430, William de la Pole, 3rd Duke of Suffolk (murdered 1450). She d. 1475.

CHAWORTH. Sir Thomas C. of The Park, Wiverton, Notts.; m.

(1) Nicole Braybrooke; (2) before Aug. 1449, Isabella Aylesbury; 'a prudent man' (see No. 37).

Elisabeth or Isabella C., dau. of Thomas and Nicole C., m. by 1418 John Lord Scroop of Masham, Treasurer in 1432, and a grandson of Maud ROOS.

Alice C., younger dau. of Thomas C.

CHICHELE, Henry. 1408–14, Bp. of St. David's; 1414–43, Abp. of Canterbury. Founder of All Souls' College. Presided over the first stages of the enquiry into the Duchess of GLOUCESTER, to Oct. 1441. (See *Complaint against Fortune.*)

CLIFFORD. Thomas C., 6th Lord C. of Skipton, d. 1391; m. Elisabeth Roos, sister of William, 6th Lord ROOS; she d. 1424.

Maud (Matilda) C., dau. of Thomas; m. (1) John, Lord Neville; divorced; (2) as 2nd wife, Richard Plantagenet of Conisbrough, Earl of Cambridge; executed 1415.

Thomas C., 8th Lord C., grandson of Elisabeth ROOS and of Thomas, 6th Lord C. Member of the Escort, 1444–5. Killed at 1st St. Albans, 1455.

CLIFTON. Sir Gervaise C. of Brabourne, Kent. Treasurer to Humphrey, Duke of GLOUCESTER, Aug. 1461; m. (1) Isabella Scott (*née* Herbert) d. 1457; (2) Maud Neville, dowager Lady Willoughby (*née* STANHOPE). Treasurer of Calais after Sir Richard VERNON, 1453–61. Executed after Tewkesbury, 1471.

COBHAM of Stirborough, Surrey. Eleanor C., dau. of Sir Reginald, Lord Cobham and of Eleanor Colepeper; mistress and later wife of Humphrey, Duke of GLOUCESTER; disgraced and divorced, 1441; d. 1454 ('Cleopatra').

Elisabeth C., sister of Eleanor C.; m. (1) 1439, Richard Lord STRANGE of Knokyn (d. 1449); (2) Sir Roger Kynaston. ('Anelida'.)

Sir Reginald C., 3rd Lord C.; son of Reginald, 2nd Lord C. and of Eleanor MAUTRAVERS (grandmother of the poet); father of the Duchess of GLOUCESTER; 1436–8, Keeper of Charles d'ORLÉANS; m. (1) Eleanor Colepeper; (2) c. 1421, Joan Bardolf. (See PHELIP.)

COKAYN. See VERNON.

CURTEYS, William. Abbot of Bury St. Edmunds, 1429–46.

D'AMANCIER (Damancy). Jean D'A. Master of the Horse to Charles VII. By June, 1451, m. ANTIGONE. On missions for Charles VII to Savoy, 1452, 1453; to Burgundy, 1455; to Milan, 1458. Ambassador to Venice, and d. there Oct. 1459.

DUDLEY. See SUTTON.

FAWCOMBERG(E). William Neville, son of Ralph N., Earl of Westmoreland, and of Joan BEAUFORT; m. c. 1422, Joan F., dau. and heiress (*idiota*) of Sir Thomas F. of Skelton; Lord F. *jure uxoris*; 1461, Earl of Kent; Yorkist; d. 1462–3; apparently conducted intrigues with Lady STRANGE, Maud STANHOPE, and B. HERBERQUYNE.

FITZLEWIS or FISLOWYS, of Horndon and Ingrave, Essex (also known as (Fitz)John).

Sir Lewis John, m. (1) Alice de Vere; (2) Anne MONTAGUE; Steward of the Duchy of Cornwall; d. Oct. 27, 1442; see G.E.C. V, 210–11.

Sir Henry (Fitz)Lewis, son of above and Alice; m. (1) Elizabeth BEAUFORT, dau. of Edmund and Eleanor B.; (2) Alianore —. 1460 knighted at Northampton; at Tours later with Queen Margaret. d. May 1480.

Mary F., dau. of Sir Henry F. and Elizabeth B., born c. 1465; m. before Oct. 1480 (as 2nd wife) Anthony WYDVILLE, Lord Rivers.

Elizabeth and Matilda (Fitz)Lewis, probably sisters of Sir Henry; occur in the Queen's Jewels

Accounts. (See *Assembly of Ladies.*)

Jane (Joan) Fitzlowes; probably aunt or elder sister of above. (See *Ragman Roll.*)

GASCOIGNE, Sir William G. (d. 1419), Chief Justice of the King's Bench. Supposed to have sent Prince Hal to prison; sent with William Lord ROOS to the rebel lords in 1405; type of upright judge. (See No. 37.)

GLOUCESTER. Humphrey, Duke of G., youngest son of Henry IV; m. (1) Jacqueline of Hainault; (2) Eleanor COBHAM; uncle and Regent of Henry VI; builder of Plesaunce, Kent; d. 1447. No legitimate issue. (See ANTIGONE.)

GREY. See POWYS and WYDVILLE.

GREY of Heaton, Yks. Elizabeth G. (*née* Fitzhugh), wife of Sir Ralph G. (killed in France before Nov., 1444); member of the Escort, 1444–5, and of the queen's Household till 1453 at least.

Sir Ralph G., son of above.

GREYSTOKE (Greystock). John G., 4th Lord G. d. 1436.

Ralph G., 5th Lord G. (1414–87); member of the Escort 1444–5; m. (1) Elizabeth Fitzhugh; (2) Elizabeth Tyrell.

John G., 6th Lord G., 2nd son of Ralph G. d. 1500/1; owner of MS. Tanner 346, possibly collected by his father.

HAUT(E), Hawt(e). Sir Richard H., son of Sir William H. of Broxbourne, Kent (d. 1462), and of Jane WYDVILLE, aunt of Queen Elizabeth W.; m. by July 1474, Eleanor ROOS, dau. of Sir Robert R. of More End, and widow of (1) Robert Lovell and (2) John Proute. 1482, knighted in Scotland; 1483, comptroller of the Household to Edward V; 1483, executed with Sir Thomas Vaughan at Pontefract by Richard III; had been nominated by Anthony WYDVILLE as overseer of his will, but pre-deceased him.

Sir Richard H. the younger. Probably son of above. Courtier under Henry VII.

Jane H., sister of Sir Richard H. the elder; m. Sir George Darell of Littlecote.

HERBERQUYNE, Barbelina; 'Almain' waiting woman to Queen Margaret. Naturalized, 1449.]

HOLLAND. See MONTAGUE.

HOWTH. See under BEAUFORT.

JOURDAIN. Margery J. or Jourdemain, called The Witch of Eye; one of Eleanor COBHAM's necromantic accomplices; burnt at Smithfield, 1441.

KEMP, John. 1425 Abp. of York; 1439, Cardinal; 1452, Abp. of Canterbury. d. 1454. One of Eleanor COBHAM's judges, 1441. (See *Complaint against Fortune.*)

KYRIEL(LE) or KERIEL(LE) of Bellevue, Kent. Sir Thomas K., victor at Crotoy, 1435; captured at Formigny, 1448; executed as Yorkist after 2nd St. Albans, 1461.

John K., younger brother of Sir Thomas, and owner of MS. Pepys 2006, possibly collected by his brother.

LATIMER. George Neville, Lord L., son of Ralph N., Earl of Westmoreland, and of (2) Joan BEAUFORT; m. 1436, Elizabeth BEAUCHAMP. He became insane in 1451 and d. 1469.

LATIMER of West Wardon, Northants. Sir Thomas L. (B(o)uchard), Lord L.; d. 1402.

Elizabeth L., his sister and heir, m. Sir Thomas Griffin.

Nicholas G., 8th Lord L., greatgrandson of Elizabeth; transferred land to Sir Richard and Henry ROOS in 1451/2.

LEWIS, LOWIS. See FITZLEWIS.

LONGUEVILLE. Sir George L. of Little Billing, Nthants., son of John L. and Joan Hunt; m. (1) Elizabeth, dau. of Thomas Lord

Roche; (2) Margaret, dau. of John SUTTON, Lord Dudley.

Richard L. of Whitacre, Warwicks., son and heir of Sir George. b. before 1423, and still a minor in 1444, when his marriage was granted to Sir Richard VERNON. Husband of Margaret V.; d. ?1448. She m. (2) Sir Richard ROOS.

Richard L., possibly son or grandson of Sir George and of Margaret Sutton. m. Anne —; d. Aug.– Oct. 1458. John Lord Dudley his executor (Will, PCC., Stokton 26).

LOVELL of Titchmarsh. William L., Lord L. and Holland, 1397–1455, m. Alice Deincourt (d. 1473/4). His sons, John L., heir, William L. m. Eleanor MORLEY, Robert L. m. Eleanor ROOS, d. of Sir Robert R. of More End.

John L. Lord L. and Holland, c. 1433–64/5, m. Joan BEAUMONT, dau. of John Viscount B., and of Elisabeth PHELIP.

Francis L., Lord and Viscount L., c. 1456–87 (d. after battle of Stoke), m. Anne FitzHugh; no issue.

Henry L. and Alice L. (See MORLEY.)

LYDGATE, John, 'Monk of Bury' (?1370–1449 or 1450). Religious, didactic and historical poet, but not a writer of poetry of courtly love. Under the patronage of Henry V and VI, Dukes of BEDFORD and GLOUCESTER, Lady Margaret TALBOT, Richard BEAUCHAMP, etc.

MARGARET, Queen. See ANJOU.

MARGARET of Scotland, sister of James III. Projected marriage with Anthony WYDVILLE, Lord Rivers, 1479.

MAUTRAVERS. See ARUNDEL.

MOLINS, MOLEYNS. Adam M., ambassador to René d'ANJOU; Bp. of Chichester; murdered, 1450.

Anne M., dau. of John Whalesborough, m. (1) 1423, William,

Lord M. (killed, 1429 at Orléans); (2) 1442, Edmund Hampden of the Household (killed, 1471 at Tewkesbury). She was the second English lady courted by Charles d'Orléans in his English poems, 1438–40; see Maud ARUNDEL. She d. 1487.

MONTAGUE. Alice M., *née* CHAUCER; m. (2) before Nov. 1424, Thomas, 7th Earl of Salisbury.

Alice M., dau. and heir of this Thomas and of his 1st wife Eleanor Holland; m. 1420/1, Richard Neville, *jure uxoris* Earl of Salisbury. He d. at Wakefield, 1460. She d. 1462.

Anne M., dau. of John M., 6th Earl of Salisbury and of Maud Francis; m. (1) Sir Richard Hankford (d. 1430/1); (2) Sir Lewis John of Horndon (d. 1442); see FITZLEWIS; (3) John Holland, Duke of Exeter (b. 1395); he had m. (1) 1427, Anne STAFFORD, dau. of Anne of Woodstock; she d. 1439; Exeter d. 1447; the duchess d. 1457.

MORLEY. Robert M., Lord M. 1418– Sept. 25, 1442; 1436, wardship and marriage granted to Edmund BEAUFORT; m. before June 1442, Elizabeth ROOS, dau. of William Lord R. (sister of the poet).

Eleanor M. Baroness M. b. Oct. 10, 1442: posthumous dau. and heir of Robert M.; by Jan. 1, 1464/5 m. William LOVELL, second son of William Lord L. by Alice Deincourt, summoned to Parliament as William Lovell de Morley, Chl'r. Both died 1476.

Henry LOVELL, Lord M. (c. 1465– 89), son of William L. and of Eleanor M.; m. Elizabeth de la Pole, dau. of Duke of Suffolk and of Elizabeth Plantagenet, sister to Edward IV. (He is *not* 'Lovel our dogge', for whom see Francis LOVELL.)

Alice LOVELL, sister of Henry L. (c. 1465–1518), Baroness M. after 1489; m. (1) before March 8, 1481/2 Sir William Parker (see will of Sir Richard ROOS); (2) before Jan. 1505/6 Sir Edward Howard, son of Thomas H., Duke of Norfolk and uncle of Surrey the poet.

MORTAYN. See Edmund BEAUFORT.

MOWBRAY. John M., 3rd Duke of Norfolk (1415–Nov. '61); m. (1424), Eleanor Bourchier, dau. of Anne of Woodstock (see STAFFORD); 1460–1, turned Yorkist.

John M.,4th Duke of N.(1444–75/6), son and heir of above; m. before Nov. 1448, Elizabeth, dau. of John TALBOT, Earl of Shrewsbury, and of Margaret BEAUCHAMP. Yorkist.

NEVIL(L)E. See BEAUFORT, FAWCOMBERG, LATIMER, STANHOPE.

PHELIP. Sir John P., m. Alice CHAUCER.

Sir William P., *jure uxoris* Lord Bardolf, of Dennington; b. 1383; fought at Agincourt; executor (1426) of Duke of Exeter; m. before 1407, Anne Bardolf, dau. and co-heiress with Joan B. of Thomas B., Lord B. (killed 1407); d. June 6, 1441.

Elisabeth P., dau. and heir of Sir William P., Lord Bardolf; m. (c. 1433) John Viscount BEAUMONT; d. 1441. (The poet's 'Lady Bounte'.)

PICARD. Possibly a member of the Pichard family of Ocle-Pichard, Herefordshire. Writer of the 'Devynayl' of 'My Lady Dere' (No. 44).

POWYS, Grey of. Henry Grey, Lord P., Count of Tankerville; b. 1419.; m. 1435/6, ANTIGONE; d. Jan. 1449/50.

Richard Grey, Lord P., son and heir of Henry and Antigone; b. Nov. 5, 1436. Yorkist. d. 1466.

Elisabeth Grey, sister of Richard; m. 1464 as 2nd wife, Sir Roger Kynaston. (See STRANGE.)

RIVERS. See SCALES, WYDVILLE.

ROOS of Hamlake and Belvoir. Sir

William R., 6th Lord R. (1368/9–1414); m. 1394, Margaret ARUNDEL; follower of Henry IV.

Sir John R., 7th Lord R., son and heir of above; m. Margery Despenser (who m. (2) Roger Wentworth); killed at Baugé, 1421.

Sir William R., 2nd son of Lord William; killed at Baugé, 1421.

Sir Thomas R., 8th Lord R., 3rd son of Lord William; m. before 1427, Eleanor BEAUCHAMP; drowned in the Marne, 1430.

Sir Thomas R., 9th Lord R. (1427–64), son and heir of above; m. Philippa Tiptoft; executed after Hexham, 1464.

Edmund R., 10th Lord R. (1464–1508), son and heir of above; 1492, found to be insane; died, 1508, without issue.

Sir Robert R. of More End, 4th son of Lord William; ambassador to Guyenne and Anjou; m. Anne Bohun, *née* Halsham; d. 1449.

Sir RICHARD ROOS (c. 1410–82), 5th son of Lord William; member of the Escort, 1444–5; m. 1450–2, Margaret LONGUEVILLE, *née* VERNON; courtier and poet.

Richard R. Esquire, of Norwich, 2nd son of Thomas, 8th Lord R.; prisoner in France, 1449–c. 1464; m. Joan Toppes, *née* Knevitt.

Sir Henry R., son of Sir Robert R.; m. ? Margaret Grey, *née* Tuchet; Maud —, widow of Harbord and Gorges; d. 1504. Follower of Queen Margaret.

Elizabeth R., Lady MORLEY, dau. of Lord William.

Eleanor R., dau. of Sir Robert of More End; m. (1) Robert Lovell; (2) John Proute; (3) 1474, Sir Richard HAUT.

SALISBURY. See MONTAGUE, CHAUCER.

SCALES. Thomas S., 7th Lord S. and Lord Newsells (Neucelles); fighter in France; m. (before Oct. 1437) Ismania Whalesborough of Cornwall; killed July 1460, when escaping from the Tower.

Elizabeth S., dau. and heir of above;

m. (1) Sir Henry Bourchier, 2nd
son of Earl of Essex, who d.
c. 1458; (2) 1460/1, Sir Anthony
WYDVILLE, later Lord Rivers and,
jure uxoris, Lord S. and Newsells.
She d. Sept 2, 1473.

SOMERSET. See BEAUFORT.

SOUTHWELL, Thomas, Canon of St.
Stephen's, Westminster; necro-
mancer and accomplice of Eleanor
COBHAM; d. in prison, 1441.

STAFFORD. Anne of Woodstock, b.
Apr. 1383, d. by Oct. 24, 1438;
dau. of Thomas of Woodstock,
Duke of Gloucester, son of Edward
III; m. (1) Thomas, 3rd Earl of S.;
(2) Edmund, 5th Earl of S., killed
at Shrewsbury, 1403; (3) Sir
William Bourchier, Count of
Eu.

Humphrey S., 6th Earl and 1st
Duke of Buckingham; son and
heir of Edmund and Anne; m.
Anne Neville.

Humphrey S., son and heir of
Humphrey; m. Margaret BEAU-
FORT; killed at 1st St. Albans,
1455.

Henry S., son of Humphrey and
Margaret; Duke of Buckingham;
1466 m. Catherine WYDVILLE.
Supporter of Richard III.

Sir William Bourchier, step-father
of Humphrey S., 6th Earl.

Anne S., dau. of Anne of Woodstock.
(See MONTAGUE.)

Avice S., dau. of Sir Richard S. and
of Maud LOVEL; m. c. 1438, James
Butler, Earl of Ormond and Wiltshire; she d. 1457. (See BEAU-
FORT.)

STANHOPE. Maud, dau. of Sir Richard
S. and of Maud Cromwell. She
m. (1) as 2nd wife, before Jan 9,
1449, Robert Willoughby, 6th
Lord W. d'Eresby and son of
William, 5th Lord W., and Lucy
Strange of Knokin. He d. July
1452; (2) Aug. 1453, Sir Thomas
Neville, son of Richard, Earl of
Salisbury, and nephew of FAW-
COMBERG. He was killed at
Wakefield, 1460; (3) August 1461,
Gervaise CLIFTON, executed after

Tewkesbury, 1471. She d. childless, 1497.

STANLEY. Sir Thomas S., Lord S.
1446, Keeper of Eleanor COBHAM
at Peel Castle. Comptroller of
the Household, 1447; Lord
Chamberlain, 1455. Yorkist. d.
1459. Collector of MS. Fairfax
16.

John S. (See VERNON.)

STANLOW. John S., Treasurer in
France, 1446.

Margaret S. His wife (?*née* Fulpot,
Philpot). Member of the Escort
1444-5, and later of the Household as gentlewoman to Queen
Margaret.

Jacquetta S. ?dau. of above and
gentlewoman to Q. Margaret;
m. 1452-3.

STIWARD (Stewart). Sir John S. of
Calais and Norfolk; of Scottish
descent. One of the Keepers of
Eleanor COBHAM, 1441. 1439,
Knight of the Body and Constable
of Leeds Castle, Kent, m. a dau.
of Sir Thomas Kiriel. d. 1447
(P.C.C. Wills, Luffenham 33).

STRADLING. Sir Edward S. of St.
Donat's, Glamorgan, knighted
1421/2; m. Joan 'FitzAlan' (see
ARUNDEL); d. 1452-3.

STRANGE (Le Strange) of Knokyn.
Richard Le S., Lord S. (1381-
1449); m. (1) Constance —, who
d. March 1438-9; (2) after March
1439, Elizabeth COBHAM, dau. of
Sir Reginald C. of Stirborough
and of Eleanor Colepeper; sister
of the Duchess of Gloucester. She
m. (2) Sir Roger Kynaston of
Middle and d. 1453-4. He m.
(2) 1465, Elizabeth Grey of
Powys, dau. of ANTIGONE.

SUFFOLK. See CHAUCER.

SUTTON (DUDLEY). Sir John S., d.
1406. m. Constance Blunt of
Barton, Derbyshire.

John S., 1st Lord Dudley, son
and heir of above; d. 1487.

Humphrey S. (Dudley), younger
son of Sir John S.; m. 1448-9,
Eleanor ROOS of Hunmanby.

Oliver Dudley, son of Lord D.,

m. Katherine Neville, dau. of Lord LATIMER and of Elizabeth BEAUCHAMP. She d. 1469.

Margaret D., sister of Oliver D., m. as 2nd wife, Sir George LONGUEVILLE (d. 1457), father-in-law of Margaret ROOS, *née* VERNON.

TALBOT. John T. (?1384–1453), 6th Lord T., 1st Earl of Shrewsbury. Count of Clermont (1434); m. (1) by 1407, Maud, Baroness Furnivall; (2) 1425, Margaret BEAUCHAMP, eldest dau. of Richard B., Earl of Warwick. Killed at Châtillon, 1453.

Beatrice, Lady T. *née* Pinto, wife of Gilbert T., 5th Lord T., elder brother of John T. Member of the Escort, 1444–5; m. (2) Thomas Fettiplace; d. 1447.

THYNNE. Sir John T. the elder, son of Thomas T. of Church Stretton; m. Christiana Gresham of Holt; builder of Longleat; d. 1580.

Sir John T. the younger, son and heir of above; d. 1623.

William T., uncle of Sir John the elder; Clerk of the Kitchen to Henry VIII; ed. Chaucer etc. 1532; d. 1546. Possibly collector of MSS. Longleat 256 and 258.

Francis T. (1545–1608), son of William T. Lancaster Herald; commentator on Speght's ed. of Chaucer, 1598.

VAUDÉMONT. See ANJOU.

VERE. John V., 13th Earl of Oxford (1442–1513), 2nd son of John V., 12th Earl, and of Elizabeth Howard. 1462–70, Yorkist; 1470, joined Queen Margaret, and aided Re-adeption of Henry VI; 1474–1485 imprisoned by Edward IV in Hammes Castle; 1485, escaped and joined Richmond; m. (1) Margaret Neville, dau. of Richard N., Earl of Salisbury, and of Alice Montagu. She d. 1506 (mentioned in the poet's will, 1482). The earl owned the Ellesmere MS. of *The Canterbury Tales*, into which is copied the Prison Poem addressed to him.

VERNON of Haddon Hall, Derbyshire. Sir Richard V., 1432 Speaker of Parliament at Leicester, Steward for the Peak; 1450, Treasurer of Calais; m. Benedicta (Bennet) Ludlow.

Sir William V. of Tonge (Shrops.), son and heir of the above; Treasurer of Calais and Knight Constable of England; m. Margaret Pipe of Spernore.

Foulke V., son of Sir Richard; member of the Escort, 1444–5.

Margaret V., dau. of Sir Richard V., m. (1) c. 1444, Richard LONGUEVILLE; (2) 1450–2, Sir Richard ROOS the poet.

Anne V., dau. of Sir Richard; m. John Bradbourne of Hough or Hulland; monument in Ashbourne.

Agnes V., dau. of Sir Richard; m. John Cockayne of Ashbourne.

Benedicta V., dau. of Sir Richard; m. (?Sir) Thomas Charleton.

Elizabeth V., dau. of Sir Richard; m. John Stanley.

Mary V., dau. of Thomas V., brother of Sir Richard V.; m. Reginald Leigh of Egginton, Derbyshire. (See the poet's will.)

WENLO(C)K. Sir John W. of W., Salop; 1446–7, Usher of the Chamber to Q. Margaret; by 1447, knighted; 1449, Chamberlain to the queen; 1455, fought at 1st St. Albans; 1460, fought as Yorkist at Towton, and attainted; under Edward IV, K.G., P.C. and Baron; 1469–70, Lieutenant of Calais; May 4, 1471, killed at Tewkesbury on Lancastrian side; m. Elisabeth, dau. of Sir John Drayton.

WHALESBOROUGH. See MOLEYNS and SCALES.

WHETHAMSTEDE. John W., Abbot of St. Albans; humanistic scholar, and friend of Humphrey of GLOUCESTER; d. 1465.

WHITTINGHAM. Sir Robert the elder; executor (1435) of John of Bedford; d. 1452.

Sir Robert the younger, son of above; King's Serjeant; member of the Escort 1444–5; m. 1448, Katharine Gatevyne, Angevin gentlewoman of Queen Margaret; 1458, Keeper of the Great Wardrobe to the queen; 1461, attainted; 1471, killed at Tewkesbury; effigy with collar of SS now at Aldbury, Herts.

Catherine, ?dau. of Sir Robert the elder; apparently gentlewoman to Elisabeth BEAUMONT.

WILLOUGHBY. See STANHOPE.

WIMBISH (Wimbush, Wymbysshe). Nicholas W., ? of Nocton Park and Lincoln; Sept. 1434–51, Master in Chancery; 1438, an executor of Anne of Woodstock

(STAFFORD); 1443, King's Clerk; 1448, Clerk of the Chancery; ?1441, Canon residentiary, Lincoln Cathedral; ?1459, rector of Olney; d. 1461.

WYDVILLE. Jacquetta W. (See BEDFORD.)

Elizabeth W., eldest dau. of Jacquetta, m. (1) Sir John Grey; (2) Edward IV, 1466.

Anthony W. (1440–83), son and heir of Sir Richard W., Lord Rivers, and of Jacquetta; 1462, Lord Scales, *jure uxoris*; 1469, Lord Rivers; m. (1) 1460/1 as 2nd husband, Elisabeth Bourchier, *née* SCALES; she d. 1473; (2) by 1480, Mary FITZLEWIS. Courtier and patron of letters under Edward IV. Executed at Pontefract, June 1483, by order of Richard III; no issue.

Index of First Lines

A. CHAPTERS V TO XII, i

(The alphabetical order is that of modern spelling. The figures in brackets indicate the poem's number here.)

B. POEMS IN CHAPTER XII, ii

(The figures in brackets refer to Muir's *Wyatt's Poems*. Figures in bold type indicate the main entries.)

General Index

(Figures in bold type indicate the more important references. Figures in italics indicate references to anagrams.)

573

o o